How Do You Say "Epigram" in Arabic?

Brill Studies in Middle Eastern Literatures

FORMERLY STUDIES IN ARABIC LITERATURE

Edited by

Suzanne Pinckney Stetkevych (*Georgetown University*)
Ross Brann (*Cornell University*)
Franklin Lewis (*University of Chicago*)

VOLUME 40

The titles published in this series are listed at *brill.com/bsme*

How Do You Say "Epigram" in Arabic?

Literary History at the Limits of Comparison

By

Adam Talib

BRILL

LEIDEN | BOSTON

Cover illustration: Stereoview of Temple of Seti I Pillars at Abydos, Underwood & Underwood, 1897.
Courtesy of Rare Books and Special Collections Library, American University in Cairo.

The Library of Congress Cataloging-in-Publication Data is available online at http://catalog.loc.gov
LC record available at http://lccn.loc.gov/2017036748

Typeface for the Latin, Greek, and Cyrillic scripts: "Brill". See and download: brill.com/brill-typeface.
This publication has been typeset by A. El-khattali using DecoType Emiri and Naskh for Arabic script.

ISSN 1571-5183
ISBN 978-90-04-34996-4 (hardback)
ISBN 978-90-04-35053-3 (e-book)

This book is printed on acid-free paper.

For Geert Jan and Thomas

The effort to find counterparts must employ some criteria, whether formal, ideological, or functional. And there are certain things about which we should not deceive ourselves. [...]

The most serious deception of all is to think that relativism allows us to privilege western phenomena over others. There is all too little danger that Sanskrit poems or *nō* will be taken as forms that require us to depreciate western equivalents. Quite the opposite. There is instead a hegemonic presumption that western practice provides the norm for which we must dig and dig to find some counterpart in another literature, something that will be certain to differ enough as to prove the point that it is inferior.

(EARL MINER, *Comparative Poetics*, 225)

•••

This incommensurability between what scholars might want to uphold as the ethical as well as theoretical ideal of an inclusive world literature, on the one hand, and the actual events that take place in the name of comparison, on the other, requires us to conceive of a fundamentally different set of terms for comparative literary studies.

(REY CHOW, *The Age of the World Target*, 80)

Contents

Note to Readers IX
Acknowledgments XI
List of Abbreviations XIII

Preamble: Growth and Graft 1

PART 1
On Wholeness

1 A Bounding Line 13
2 The Sum of its Parts 71

PART 2
Arabic Poetry, Greek Terminology

Preliminary Remarks 158
3 Epigrams in the World 162
4 Hegemonic Presumptions and Atomic Fallout 183
5 Epigrams in Parallax 213

Appendix 223
Annotated Bibliography of Unpublished Sources 264
Sources 287
Index 328

Note to Readers

This book is divided into two parts. In the first part, I present the history of a highly popular genre of Arabic poetry, prevalent in the period from 1200–1900 CE. In doing so, I describe and explain the genre's features, its operation as a literary text, and the contexts in which it appeared. I also discuss its main practitioners and give an idea of how the genre was treated in contemporary sources. Throughout Part 1, I use the neutral term *maqāṭīʿ* (sing. *maqṭūʿ*, or occasionally *maqṭūʿah*) when writing about this poetic genre as that is the term that was used by pre-modern Arabic poets and authors. Readers may enjoy perusing the appendix (pp. 223–63) and the annotated bibliography of unpublished sources (pp. 264–287) after—or indeed while—reading Part 1. In the second part of the book, I connect this new literary phenomenon and my analysis of it to broader issues in the study of pre-modern Arabic poetry and comparative literature more generally. Part 2 specifically concerns the relationship between the world-literary category epigram and its potential equivalents in the Arabic tradition, including its nearest equivalent *maqāṭīʿ*.

I have translated into English all citations from languages other than English and have often relegated the original-language quotations to the footnotes to facilitate reading. Arabic citations take precedence, however, for obvious reasons. This book includes many long extracts from Arabic primary sources in part because much of this material is terra incognita even for specialists and in part because I want readers to get a feel for the evidence that is being deployed. Unless otherwise specified, all editions and translations are my own. The transliteration system used for Arabic is, for all intents and purposes, the style set out by *IJMES*, with the exception of (1) I write non-construct *tāʾ marbūṭah* as *-ah* and (2) I represent the assimilation of the definite article before a Sun Letter. Prosody is respected in the transliteration of poetry. The pausal form is used when transliterating prose unless case effects an orthographic change (e.g. accusative *tanwīn*). Out of respect for other sources whose transliteration systems differ from my own, I keep to their system when quoting from them. I write Persian according to the *IJMES* system and Ottoman per the scholarly system, which takes the post-language reform Turkish alphabet as its starting point. For modern names written in non-Roman characters, the most prevalent version is used, especially if it has been possible to determine how that person prefers to spell their own name (e.g., El-Said Badawi rather than as-Saʿīd Badawī). The reader should take note of a common naming convention in Arabic studies: the abbreviations "b." and "bt." stand for "*ibn*" (son of) and "*bint*" (daughter of) respectively. When referencing the Qurʾan, I cite chapters by both name and number.

Where it is not too cumbersome, I give dates in both the Western and Islamic calendars. I write the Hegirae date before the Common (*scil.* Christian) Era date. Reference to other calendrical systems is made explicit.

Acknowledgments

It is a pleasure to thank the people and institutions who supported me materially and emotionally as I wrote this book. The Clarendon Fund enabled me to study with Geert Jan van Gelder at the University of Oxford and the Deutscher Akademischer Austauschdienst awarded me a scholarship so that I could spend a year in Münster working with Thomas Bauer. It is to these two generous, kind, and erudite scholars that I dedicate this book. Many librarians and booksellers across the world provided the essential materials without which this study could not have been written. I would like especially to thank four of them: Mark Muehlhaeusler, Ola Seif, Lidio Ferrando, and Mark Bainbridge. Lidio and Mark also gamely double-checked my translations from the Italian and Latin respectively. Thomas Bauer and Denis McAuley generously shared with me copies of manuscripts in their possession. I would also like to acknowledge those scholars who read and commented on earlier drafts of this work and to thank them for their comments, criticisms, and advice: Marlé Hammond, Nadia Jamil, Wilferd Madelung, Julia Bray, Hilary Kilpatrick, Laurent Mignon, Gregor Schoeler, Dwight Reynolds, Suzanne Pinckney Stetkevych, and of course the anonymous external reviewer. I thank the editors of Brill Studies in Middle Eastern Literatures for accepting this monograph in their series, and Teddi Dols and Kathy van Vliet-Leigh from the Brill staff for their courteous assistance. Harvard, Princeton, Northwestern, and Brandeis universities, as well as the American Oriental Society and the Zukunftsphilologie World Philologies Seminar kindly gave me the opportunity to share parts of this book with thoughtful and engaged audiences to whom I am grateful. I would also like to thank my students who always challenge me to make better sense of the Arabic literary tradition.

I was very fortunate to be trained by attentive and excellent teachers at UCLA, including Michael Cooperson, the late Michael Henry Heim, Hala Halim, Jean-Claude Carron, Patrick Geary, Eleanor Kaufman, Arthur L. Little, Teofilo Ruiz, and Richard A. Yarborough, before traveling to Cairo where I studied with Mahmoud el-Rabie, Mohamed Birairi, Nelly Hanna, and the late El-Said Badawi. I think of them now that I am myself a teacher and hope very much that I will one day live up to their example. I never had the pleasure of studying in a classroom with the late George T. Scanlon, but he was *sprezzatura* incarnate and I shall never forget him. Hugh Griffith and Christina Hardyment opened their homes to me when I moved to Oxford, and my late uncle Bijan did the same when I moved to Germany.

The best part of becoming a scholar is the privilege of joining a community of colleagues around the world, some of whom I have the pleasure of acknowledging here: Manan Ahmed, Muzaffar Alam, Michael Allan, Sinan Antoon, Monica Balda-Tillier, Orit Bashkin, Laura Brueck, Deborah Cameron, Ananya Chakravarti, Elliott Colla, Islam Dayeh, Humphrey Davies, Jonathan Decter, Jean Druel, Amina Elbendary, Samuel England, Khaled Fahmy, Maria-Magdalena Fuchs, Pascale Ghazaleh, Ferial Ghazoul, Camilo Gómez-Rivas, Zoe Griffith, Mark Griffith, Beatrice Gruendler, Li Guo, May Hawas, Syrinx von Hees, Dina Heshmat, Konrad Hirschler, Robert Hoyland, Domenico Ingenito, Matthew Kelly, Ellen Kenney, Hanan Kholoussy, Rajeev Kinra, Frédéric Lagrange, Margaret Larkin, Marcia Lynx Qualey, Dina Makram-Ebeid, Danilo Marino, Alev Masarwa, Samia Mehrez, Christopher Melchert, Matthew Melvin-Koushki, Adam Mestyan, Amy Motlagh, Elias Muhanna, Harry Munt, Muhsin al-Musawi, Daniel Nicolae, Steve Nimis, Avigail Noy, Bilal Orfali, Hakan Özkan, Ivan Panovic, Nefeli Papoutsakis, Carl Petry, Maurice Pomerantz, Wim Raven, Kristina Richardson, Everett Rowson, Hakem Al-Rustom, Emmanuelle Salgues, Samah Selim, Sherene Seikaly, Emily Selove, Lennart Sundelin, Hani Sayed, Yassin Temlali, Mathieu Tillier, Shawkat Toorawa, and Philip Wood.

There is a life beyond the page and the classroom and I know how lucky I am that mine is full of adventure, ideas, and love. It has not been easy these past eleven years to be an ocean away from my parents, grandparents, sister, aunt, uncles, cousins, and old friends, but I am grateful for their patience and understanding. Living in Cairo has been the greatest privilege of my life and I owe it to the most solicitous and spirited friends anyone could hope for. My partner, Katharine Halls, doesn't need to read a book to know how much she means to me.

Oxford–Münster–Cairo, 2008–2017

List of Abbreviations

EAL	*Encyclopedia of Arabic Literature*
EI^2	*Encyclopaedia of Islam, Second Edition*
EI^3	*Encyclopaedia of Islam, Third Edition*
EIRAN	*Encyclopaedia Iranica*
GAL	*Geschichte der arabischen Litteratur*
GAP	*Grundriss der arabischen Philologie*
WKAS	*Wörterbuch der klassischen arabischen Sprache*
AS/EA	*Asiatische Studien/Études Asiatiques*
BEO	*Bulletin d'Études Orientales*
BSOAS	*Bulletin of the School of Oriental and African Studies*
IJMES	*International Journal of Middle East Studies*
JAL	*Journal of Arabic Literature*
JAOS	*Journal of the American Oriental Society*
JNES	*Journal of Near Eastern Studies*
JRAS	*Journal of the Royal Asiatic Society*
JSAI	*Jerusalem Studies in Arabic and Islam*
JSS	*Journal of Semitic Studies*
MEL	*Middle Eastern Literatures*
MSR	*Mamlūk Studies Review*
PMLA	*Publications of the Modern Language Association of America*
QSA	*Quaderni di Studi Arabi*
RSO	*Rivista degli Studi Orientali*
SI	*Studia Islamica*
ZDMG	*Zeitschrift der Deutschen Morgenländischen Gesellschaft*

Preamble: Growth and Graft

> In certain [world] literatures, the short poem (*al-qaṣīdah al-qaṣīrah*) occupies a special place and is considered its own separate genre with distinct attributes. These are not merely the number of verses (or half-verses) it has, or the number of metrical feet [per line], but also the occasions [it is used for] and [the fact that] it has a separate name by which it is known.
>
> This [type of] poem has become noticeable in modern Arabic poetry in such a way that suggests that choosing [to write a poem] in that form (*shakl*) is a deliberate choice (*amr mutaʿammad*). But [this type of poetry] is not known by a specific name, and is perhaps not limited to any [specific] theme. What then is this poem (*qaṣīdah*)?[1]

•••

This is how Iḥsān ʿAbbās, one of the 20th century's most prominent scholars of Arabic literature, chose to begin a series of articles on the short poem in modern Arabic poetry, which he published in *ad-Dustūr* newspaper in the spring of 1993. In his contribution, ʿAbbās briefly discussed Greek and Latin epigram and Japanese Tanka and Haiku—a common move that is also repeated in Part Two of this book—before addressing the history of short poems in Arabic before the modern era. ʿAbbās explained that there was no consensus among premodern critics about what length distinguished a short poem (*maqṭūʿah*) from a long one (*qaṣīdah*), and that the short poem was never associated with any particular genre (*gharaḍ*) or theme (*mawḍūʿ*).[2] What is perhaps most interesting about the way that ʿAbbās framed his study of modern Arabic poetry is that the material being studied—the literary archive—is required to fit itself into the space left by two paradigmatic pillars: the categories of world literature (here represented by Classical epigram and Japanese Tanka and Haiku) and the categories of pre-modern Arabic literary critics. This methodological approach is repeated time and time again in the study of classical Arabic poetry as well. But what if the history of classical Arabic poetry does not fit? What if the premodern systematizers of Arabic literature were indeed unreliable? And what if our world-literary categories—the terms that make up our scholarly argot—prove too ahistorically accommodating and too Eurocentric to be suitable?

1 Iḥsān ʿAbbās, "*al-Qaṣīdah al-qaṣīrah fī sh-shiʿr al-ʿarabī al-ḥadīth*" in ʿAbbās ʿAbd al-Ḥalīm ʿAbbās (ed.), *Iḥsān ʿAbbās. Awrāq mubaʿtharah: buḥūth wa-dirāsāt fī th-thaqāfah wa-t-tārīkh wa-l-adab wa-n-naqd al-adabī* (Irbid: ʿĀlam al-Kutub al-Ḥadīth, 2006), 326–34, at 326 [originally published in *Jarīdat ad-Dustūr*, 12 March 1993].

2 ʿAbbās, "*al-Qaṣīdah al-qaṣīrah*", 331–32.

 | DOI 10.1163/9789004350533_002

These questions are not genuine and the "if" that grounds them is more apotropaic than unknowing. This book argues that the existing paradigm is inadequate, that the pre-modern systematizers (and their modern counterparts) did overlook a highly popular and important genre, and that our literary argot—like all languages—will continue to serve only the interests of its creators and prestige users until and unless we determine to repurpose it. Let us first turn, however, to the genres of pre-modern Arabic poetry and their interrelation.

This brief introductory chapter takes as its theme the semantic field surrounding one of the words for poetic genre in Classical Arabic: *nawʿ*. This word, meaning "type", is related to verbs that describe the movement of a swaying bough (*nāʿa, tanawwaʿa, istināʿa*) and a fifth-form verb (*tanawwaʿa*) that means "to ramify".[3] This should not be understood as an attempt to force an etymological *fait accompli*, however. I could have easily invoked the figure of a spoked wheel, celestial constellation, or menagerie as a metaphorical representation of the interrelation of classical Arabic poetic genres. That being said, it does seem to me valid to speak of classical Arabic poetry as something both firmly rooted but lofty, delicate but solid, tangible but too grand to apprehend in its entirety. And despite its bewildering diversity of shape, theme, style, and content, there is something predictably organic about its construction: the cellulose of its rhythms and rhymes. The tree metaphor is inapt in one rather glaring way, though; unlike our experience of one of nature's leafy giants, we see classical Arabic poetry's crown more clearly than its trunk. In fact, we may have to content ourselves with simply positing that this tree has a trunk, that there is a structure supporting its many branches, that their roots are one.

Classical Arabic poetry is highly formalistic. Each line must conform to prosodic rules and most poetic genres adhere to a system of rigid monorhyme. These two formalistic parameters were the key defining features of poetry in Classical Arabic from Late Antiquity until the 20th century and they also influenced the style of much Arabic dialect poetry. I say that Classical Arabic poetry is highly formalistic, even though one of the most common analyses of Arabic poetic genres is that they are formalistically ambiguous

3 See Ibn Manẓūr, *Lisān al-ʿArab* (Būlāq: al-Maṭbaʿah al-Kubrā al-Miṣriyyah, 1300–08/1882–91), s.r. "*n-w-ʿ*" and J. G. Hava, *al-Farāʾid al-durriyyah: Arabic-English dictionary* (Beirut: Catholic Press, 1915), s.r. "*n-w-ʿ*".

and can only be defined by their theme. Let us isolate this inconsistency as our first aporia.

Aporia no. 1: Arabic poetry is highly formalistic; Arabic poetic genres resist formalistic definition.

It is true that a few genres of Arabic poetry do admit formalistic definition. For example, the *dūbayt* is a two-line poem in a particular meter with one of two possible rhyme schemes.[4] These are a small minority, however. Most genres of Arabic poetry are formalistically promiscuous. That means that in the classical Arabic tradition an elegy can be written in any of the standard poetic meters and can be of any length. The only formal parameter that a poem must conform to is that all of its lines should display the same meter and rhyme. If one were to attempt to classify Arabic poems based only on their meter and rhyme—a peculiar exercise, I admit—the resulting sets would be a hodgepodge including every possible poetic theme and poems ranging from one-liners to poems of more than one hundred lines long.

Beyond the strict requirements of meter and rhyme, classical Arabic poems often respect stylistic conventions, which despite not being obligatory, can be found across a variety of genres. Despite tremendous differences in context such as a poem's theme or its performance context, or the period or region in which it was composed, there is a certain consistency in the Arabic poetic idiom that gives it an air of profound endurance.

Aporia no. 2: Different voices in different places at different times have used a somewhat similar poetic idiom to express both familiar ideas and wildly new ones.

This impression of stylistic consistency is due in large part to the easy mixing of genre conventions and generic cross-pollination that characterizes the tradition.[5] Yet if meter and rhyme are universal, and thus neutral, and stylistic conventions are diffuse and imbricated across genre, how can we distinguish one type of poetry from another?

One hermeneutically tidy way of approaching this question is to examine the native generic classification system that was operative at the time. This is the achievement of Gregor Schoeler's 2012 article "The Genres of Classical Arabic Poetry. Classifications of Poetic Themes and Poems by

4 *EI*^{3}, s.v. "*Dūbayt* a. in Arabic" [Adam Talib].

5 *EAL*, s.v. "genres, poetic" [J. S. Meisami].

Pre-Modern Critics and Redactors of Dīwāns".[6] Schoeler surveys a range of critical material to discern different ways in which Arabic poetry was classified, chiefly in the Umayyad and Abbasid periods. Working diachronically, Schoeler finds

> That the matter of categories arrived at through classification [...] is less one of *genres* than of *poetic themes* is to be inferred from the fact that some of these categories, at least in pre- and early Islamic poetry [...], are found not at all as poems in their own right but only contained within the framework of polythematic *qaṣīdas*. This is the case, e.g., for wine description and, above all, simile.[7]

This insight about thematic predominance is taken from what Schoeler calls the pre-systematic phase of genre classification, and it seems to be borne out in the systematic phase by the chapter division of the earliest *Dīwān* to be organized by genre, the *Dīwān* of Abū Nuwās:[8]

1. Flytings (*naqā'iḍ*)
2. Panegyrics (*madā'iḥ*)
3. Elegies (*marāthī*)
4. Poems of reproach (*'itāb*)
5. Invective poetry (*hijā'*)
6. Poems of renunciation (*zuhdiyyāt*)
7. Hunting poems (*ṭarad* [*ṭardiyyāt*])
8. Wine poems (*khamriyyāt*)
9. Love poems in the feminine (*al-ghazal al-mu'annath*)
10. Love poems in the masculine (*al-ghazal al-mudhakkar*)
11. Obscene poems (*mujūn*)

It is interesting to note that *naqā'iḍ* does not appear as its own chapter in another 10th-century redaction of the *Dīwān*, that of Abū Bakr aṣ-Ṣūlī, ostensibly because it is a special (or one might occasional) form of *hijā'* (invective verse).[9]

6 Gregor Schoeler, "The Genres of Classical Arabic Poetry. Classifications of Poetic Themes and Poems by Pre-Modern Critics and Redactors of Dīwāns", *QSA*. n.s. 5–6 (2010–11); *idem*, "The Genres of Classical Arabic Poetry. Classifications of Poetic Themes and Poems by Pre-Modern Critics and Redactors of Dīwāns. Addenda". *QSA*. n.s. 7 (2012). See also further discussion of this article below (p. 210).

7 Schoeler, "The Genres of Classical Arabic Poetry", 9.

8 The following list is adapted from G. Schoeler's breakdown of Ḥamzah al-Iṣfahānī's chapter division ("The Genres of Classical Arabic Poetry", 26).

9 Schoeler, "The Genres of Classical Arabic Poetry", 26.

And yet for some reason, erotic poetry addressed to a (grammatical) woman and erotic poetry addressed to a (grammatical) man were deemed sufficiently different to merit their own respective chapters. In many cases, according to Schoeler, a poem's thematic (or thematic-generic) identity was a question of degree and remained ambiguous until it had to be classified: "Moreover wine and love poems are sometimes difficult to distinguish and are classified differently because, in the former, descriptions of the (beloved) cupbearer—male or female—take up much space."[10] One wonders what category such thematically ambiguous poems fell into before the emergence of this *Dīwān* classification. If we combine Julie Scott Meisami's insight about the cross-pollination of genre conventions with Gregor Schoeler's analysis of core thematic genres, we are confronted with the question: was polythematic poetry a genre in its own right?[11]

At this point, the astute reader will notice that I have guided the discussion to a perverse and provocative impasse. Nearly every study of classical Arabic poetic genres begins with the polythematic *qaṣīdah* and with good reason. The pre-Islamic *qaṣīdah* is the canonical exemplar, the ur-text of the entire poetic tradition, and the *qaṣīdah* remained "the privileged form in classical literature" in Arabic and the poetic traditions it inspired for more than a millennium.[12] Seen diachronically, it is the *qaṣīdah* that gave birth to most other Arabic poetic genres, if by parthenogenesis. In this analysis, the *qaṣīdah* is the tree trunk from which a number of boughs of Arabic poetic genres sprouted: from the amatory prelude (*nasīb*) came the *ghazal*, out of the travel episode (*raḥīl*) and boasting or panegyric sections (*fakhr* or *madīḥ*) came the hunting poem (*ṭardiyyāt*), from famous pre-Islamic descriptions of wine-drinking came wine poetry (*khamriyyah*), etc.[13] By the same logic, a given *qaṣīdah* is itself only ever a sub-genre of the model *qaṣīdah* according to the theme of its

10 Schoeler, "The Genres of Classical Arabic Poetry", 29.

11 Schoeler, "The Genres of Classical Arabic Poetry", 42: "Among the challenges the redactors saw themselves confronted with was, for one, the question of in which chapters poems dealing with more than one theme should be accommodated."

12 Sunil Sharma, *Persian Poetry at the Indian Frontier: Mas'ûd Sa'd Salmân of Lahore* (Delhi: Permanent Black, 2000), 69.

13 On Arabic hunting poetry and its generic development, see Jaroslav Stetkevych, *The Hunt in Arabic Poetry* (Notre Dame, IN: Univ. of Notre Dame Press, 2016). Inverting this evolutionary model while keeping the *qaṣīdah* at the center of it, James T. Monroe and Mark Pettigrew have argued that it was the staleness of the court *qaṣīdah* that drove innovation in new genres that borrowed heavily from the aesthetics of popular literature beginning in the 10th century See James T. Monroe and Mark F. Pettigrew, "The Decline of Courtly Patronage and the Appearance of New Genres in Arabic Literature: the case of the *zajal*, the *maqāma*, and the shadow play", *JAL* 34:1–2 (2003).

concluding movement: panegyric (*madḥ*), boasting (*fakhr*), invective (*hijāʾ*), elegy (*rithāʾ*), etc. Setting aside the question of whether this reconstruction is historically defensible—or historically true of all the generic developments mentioned above—the case of the *qaṣīdah* calls into question the use of generic names in the Arabic tradition. When a historical trajectory (and thus a generic character) is not presumed, the *qaṣīdah* can be juxtaposed to other poetic forms: the *urjūzah* and the *qiṭʿah*, and in this analysis, it seems that theme is not an operative category.[14] The *urjūzah* is defined by its meter (*rajaz*), so it cannot be mistaken for a *qaṣīdah* or a *qiṭʿah*, but there has never been a historical consensus regarding the distinction between the latter two (i.e., how long is long?). This lack of consensus need not disturb us, however, for as Schoeler explains, there is no evidence that the ambiguous distinction between a *qaṣīdah* and a *qiṭʿah* ever practically hindered the classification or appreciation of a poet's work.[15]

Aporia no. 3: The indeterminacy of a named phenomenon hides behind a recognizable name; the existence of an unnamed phenomenon is hidden by the absence of a recognizable name.

As we can see from the breakdown of chapters in the 10th-century recension of Abū Nuwās' *Dīwān* presented above, Arabic has never lacked for terminology to describe different types of poetry. A rather intimidating example of this proclivity for thematic classification can be seen in the table of contents of Shihāb ad-Dīn Abū l-ʿAbbās Aḥmad b. Muḥammad al-ʿInnābī's (d. 776/1374) poetry anthology, *Nuzhat al-abṣār fī maḥāsin al-ashʿār*. This poetry anthology is divided into seven chapters—a number we will see repeated—and what is most interesting about this chapter division is the extent to which it ignores our conventional understanding of poetic genre division in the classical tradition. Having built our model of poetic genres upward from the poly-thematic *qaṣīdah*'s concluding movements—as though the polythematic *qaṣīdah* were the trunk and its many *aghrāḍ* its thickest boughs—the thematic variety and specificity of al-ʿInnābī's anthology threatens to weigh our notional boughs down so much that the generic system appears rather more like a diffuse shrub than a linear tree:[16]

14 Schoeler, "The Genres of Classical Arabic Poetry", 39–40.

15 Schoeler, "The Genres of Classical Arabic Poetry", 40.

16 al-ʿInnābī, *Nuzhat al-abṣār fī maḥāsin al-ashʿār*, ed. as-Sanūsī and Luṭf Allāh (Kuwait: Dār al-Qalam, 1986), 18–20; al-Maktabah al-Waṭaniyyah (Rabat) MS 269 *qāf*, [pp.] 3–4.

Chapter One: Praise poems, poems about virtuous qualities, poems about intelligence, poems about knowledge, poems about modesty, poems about wisdom, poems about integrity, poems about gratitude, poems about reticence, poems about forbearance, poems about trust in God, poems about asceticism, poems about contentment, poems about piety, poems about fearing God, poems about pardon, poems about forgiveness, poems about paying people compliments, poems about companionship, poems about being slow to do a thing, poems about doing favors, poems about lineage, poems about family-bonds, poems about protecting those in your care [or: being a good neighbor], poems about generosity, poems about munificence, poems about spending liberally, poems about high status, poems about being pleasant, poems about being virtuous, poems about camaraderie, poems about managing one's wealth wisely, poems about thrift, poems about fatalism, poems about intervening in life's affairs, poems about not betraying another's trust, poems about fulfilling one's promises, poems about forming an opinion and seeking the advice of others, poems about resolve, poems about trials [one has faced], poems about battle, poems about hospitality, and poems of self-praise

الباب الأول في المدح ☆ ومكارم الأخلاق ☆ والعقل ☆ والعلم ☆ والحياء ☆ والحكم ☆ والصدق ☆ والشكر ☆ والصمت ☆ والصبر ☆ والتوكّل ☆ والزهد ☆ والقناعة ☆ والتقوى ☆ والورع ☆ والعفوة ☆ والصفح ☆ ومدارا[ة] الناس ☆ والرفق ☆ والتأني ☆ والمعروف ☆ والصيغة ☆ وصلة الرحم ☆ وحسن الجوار ☆ والجود ☆ والسخاء ☆ وبذل المال ☆ والجاه ☆ والبشر ☆ وحسن الخلق ☆ والمرافقة ☆ وإصلاح المال ☆ والاقتصاد ☆ وتقدير العيش ☆ والتوسّط في الأمور ☆ وكتمان السر ☆ والوفاء بالوعد ☆ والرأي والمشورة ☆ والحزم ☆ والتجارب ☆ والحرب ☆ والضيف ☆ والافتخار

Chapter Two: Praise poems between peers, literary correspondence, poems about passion, poems about separation, poems about farewell, poems about messengers [between lovers], poems of chastisement, poems of apology, poems of congratulations, gift-exchange poems, poems about visits, poems begging another's sympathy, poems asking for intercession, poems asking another's permission [or forgiveness], poems about visiting the sick, [poems including] prayers, poems about imprisonment, poems about liberation, poems of mourning, poems of consolation.

الباب الثاني في الاخوانيات ☆ والمكاتبات ☆ والشوق ☆ والفراق ☆ والوداع ☆ والرسول ☆ والعتاب ☆ والاعتذار ☆ والتهاني ☆ والتهادي ☆ والزيارة ☆ والاستعطاف ☆ والشفاعة ☆ والاستماحة ☆ والعيادة ☆ والأدعية ☆ والحبس ☆ والإطلاق ☆ والمراثي ☆ والتعازي

Chapter Three: Wisdom and Comportment

الباب الثالث في الحكم والآداب

Chapter Four: Erotic Verse and Amatory Preludes

الباب الرابع في الغزل والنسيب

Chapter Five: Ekphrastic poems, poetic descriptions of flowers, fruit, clouds, rains, the night, the day, mountains and the desert, rivers, seas, the cooing of birds, raptors, predators and wild animals, beasts of burden, horses, weapons, fire, bathhouses, and houses

الباب الخامس في التشبيهات ☆ وأوصاف الأزهار ☆ والثمار ☆ والغيوم ☆ والأمطار ☆ والليل ☆ والنهار ☆ والجبال والقفار ☆ والأنهار ☆ والبحار ☆ وسجع الأطيار ☆ والجوارح ☆ والسباع والوحوش ☆ والدواب ☆ والخيل ☆ والسلاح ☆ والنار ☆ والحمام ☆ والدار

Chapter Six: [Poems about] the ranks in society, poems about kings, poems about rulers, poems about ministers, poems about secretaries, poems about litterateurs and grammarians, poems about poetry and poets, poems about judges and jurisprudents, poems about preachers, poems about Sufi sermonizers and mendicants, poems about sages, poems about philosophers, poems about physicians and astrologists, poems about heart-stirring singers, poems about party-crashers, poems about merchants, poems about the rabble, poems about peasants, poems about women and marriage

الباب السادس في طبقات الناس ☆ والملوك ☆ والسلاطين ☆ والوزراء ☆ والكتّاب ☆ والأدباء والنحاة ☆ والشعر والشعراء ☆ والقضاة والفقهاء ☆ والخطباء ☆ والوعاظ الصوفية والفقراء ☆ والحكماء ☆ والفلاسفة ☆ والأطباء والمنجمين ☆ والمغاني المطربين ☆ والطفيليين ☆ والتجار ☆ والسوقة ☆ والزراعين ☆ والنساء ☆ والتزويج

Chapter Seven: On poetic peculiarities, types of versification, punning with pointing[18], poetic riddles and enigmas, and poetic puzzles

الباب السابع في غرائب صناعة الشعر ☆ وفنون النظم ☆ والتصاحيف ☆ والمعمّى والألغاز ☆ والأحاجي

There is much to say about the above list, but two insights seem most crucial to our immediate concern with genre: (1) thematic divisions were subjective and descriptive and (2) recognizing poetry types by the names they were given will only get us so far. We must go beyond descriptive categorizations of different poetic types to see how these poetic types circulated, how they were identified (both explicitly and implicitly), how they related to other poetic types, and how they functioned in social moments and the wider literary system. Beyond these highly important vectors of inquiry, however, it seems we must also first establish a given genre's rhetorical structure (what I will also refer to as its operational logic).[18] To complicate questions of genre further, I must also

17 On this, see Pierre Cachia, *The Arch Rhetorician. Or, The Schemer's Skimmer: a handbook of late Arabic* badīʿ *drawn from ʿAbd al-Ghanī an-Nābulsī's* Nafaḥāt al-azhār ʿalā nasamāt al-asḥār (Wiesbaden: Harrassowitz, 1998), no. 36.

18 In the introduction to his study of Arabic hunting poetry and its generic evolution, Jaroslav Stetkevych exhorts us to do just that: "[…] [I]n this new genre-poem of the hunt, the need increases—not just for scholarship but for criticism—to be more alert and

mention that al-ʿInnābī also includes a sub-section of eight *dūbayt* poems at the end of chapter seven, as though the *dūbayt*'s formalistically determined character marked it out—not for exclusion or disaffiliation from the larger body of poetry in the work—but for a measure of demarcation.[19]

The types in the above list are clearly distinguished by theme or subject, but theme was never the only criterion at play. In the case of the poly-thematic *qaṣīdah,* which enjoys a privileged and outsized place in our understanding of what classical Arabic poetry was, theme is not the primary criterion. It is an important secondary criterion, determined exclusively by the poem's concluding movement, but it is not what makes the *qaṣīdah* a *qaṣīdah,* as it were. That is the presence of one or two earlier movements in the poem (the *nasīb* and *raḥīl*) and it is only when these elements are combined in a single poem that it is transformed from a long poem (*qaṣīdah*) into the genre of poly-thematic poem (also *qaṣīdah*) that conjures up such evocative examples in the minds of readers, students, and scholars. A monothematic poem may be called a *qaṣīdah* on account of its length, but no matter how long it is, it cannot pass for a poly-thematic *qaṣīdah.* Some short poems should not properly be considered short or monothematic (e.g. a wine-poem of twelve lines that describes the handsome wine-bearer at length) but we consider them short because they can never be mistaken for a poly-thematic *qaṣīdah.* The poly-thematic *qaṣīdah* is immune to ambiguity in large part because of its ample reception tradition and canonical status. The history of the reception of the *qaṣīdah*'s counterpart, the *qiṭʿah,* will be discussed at length in Chapter Four. It may be a historical fluke that the poly-thematic *qaṣīdah* has become reified as the Arabic poetic form *par excellence* but that process has had profound and irrevocable consequences for both the poly-thematic *qaṣīdah* and all other genres of Arabic poetry. This is a book about one of them.

---

analytically more sharply incisive, in order to arrive at a sense of identification of form through structure […]." (J. Stetkevych, *The Hunt in Arabic Poetry*, 3).

19 al-ʿInnābī, *Nuzhat al-abṣār*, 590–92.

PART 1

On Wholeness

CHAPTER 1

A Bounding Line

Sometime in the 13th century or perhaps slightly earlier, Arab littérateurs started referring to very short poems as *maqāṭīʿ* (sing. *maqṭūʿ*, or *maqṭūʿah*).[1] They did so without comment, however, and at no point in the nearly eight centuries that have followed has anyone thought it necessary to explain the new term.[2] The most plausible reason for this is that the term's meaning is sufficiently clear from its use in context. In his *Dīwān* (Collected Poems), the eminent *ḥadīth*-scholar Ibn Ḥajar al-ʿAsqalānī (d. 852/1449) devoted an entire chapter to *maqāṭīʿ*-poems.[3] The *Dīwān* includes seven chapters in total:

1 See also in Hans Wehr, *Dictionary of Modern Written Arabic* (ed. J. Milton Cowan, 4th ed., Wiesbaden: Harrassowitz, 1979), s.v. "*maqṭūʿ* pl. *maqāṭīʿ*"; but cf. s.v. "*dhahabī*": "*āyah dhahabiyyah* golden word, maxim, epigram". Pre-modern Arabic dictionaries do not provide much insight into the nature of the term *maqāṭīʿ* precisely because the term took on its technical connotation of a brief poem so late. In these lexicons, the word *maqāṭīʿ* (as a term relating to poetry) is defined as "metrical feet in a line of poetry" (see, *inter alia*, Ibn Manẓūr, *Lisān al-ʿArab*, s.r. "*q-ṭ-ʿ* "). In Ibn Rashīq al-Qayrawānī's *al-ʿUmdah fī maḥāsin ash-shiʿr wa-ādābihi wa-naqdih* in a discussion of *al-qiṭaʿ wa-ṭ-ṭiwāl*, the author cites the critic ʿAbd al-Karīm an-Nahshalī (d. 405/1014) who says that al-Mutanabbī was the greatest composer of single lines and short sections of verse ("*aḥsan an-nās maqāṭīʿ* ") (ed. Muḥammad Muḥyī ad-Dīn ʿAbd al-Ḥamīd. 2 vols. Cairo: al-Maktabah at-Tijāriyyah al-Kubrā, 1383/1963, 1:188); a case of the term *maqāṭīʿ* being used to discuss short poetic compositions as a precedent to its later terminological meaning. The word is used as a technical term in other fields as well: music, *sajʿ*, *ḥadīth*, prosody, etc. See also Li Guo, "Reading *Adab* in historical light: factuality and ambiguity in Ibn Dāniyāl's 'occasional verses' on Mamluk society and politics", in *History and Historiography of Post-Mongol Central Asia and the Middle East. Studies in Honor of John E. Woods*, ed. J. Pfeiffer and S. A. Quinn, with E. Tucker (Wiesbaden: Harrassowitz Verlag, 2006), 392. The two grammatical schools of Basra and Kufa disagreed about whether the *yāʾ* is obligatory in the plural with the grammarians of Kufa allowing *maqāṭiʿ* as an alternative plural. Another study could be written about the rise of the term *qaṣāʾid muṭawwalāt* in the same period. We will see a few examples of this new terminology as the juxtaposed terms (*maqāṭīʿ* and *qaṣāʾid muṭawwalāt*) seemed to emerge in tandem.

2 That does not mean of course that scholars have not engaged with this material whether as individual poems or as part of a thematic collection. See, for example, Jurgen W. Weil, *Mädchennamen, verrätselt. Hundert Rätsel-Epigramme aus dem adab-Werk Alf ǧāriya wa-ǧāriya (7./13. Jh.)* (Berlin: Klaus Schwarz Verlag, 1984) and *passim*.

3 See *EI*², s.v. "Ibn Ḥadjar al-Asḳalānī" [F. Rosenthal] for Ibn Ḥajar's biography and scholarly legacy. For full bibliographic information for the *Dīwān*, (See in the annotated bibliography: 15th century, 7. a). On his poetry, see Thomas Bauer, "Ibn Ḥajar and the Arabic *ghazal* of the Mamluk Age" *Ghazal as World Literature. Vol. 1: Transformations of a Literary Genre*,

 | DOI 10.1163/9789004350533_003

Chapter One: Poems for the Prophet (*nabawiyyāt*)
Chapter Two: Poems for kings (*mulūkiyyāt*)
Chapter Three: Poems for peers (*ikhwāniyyāt*)
Chapter Four: Erotic poems (*ghazaliyyāt*)
Chapter Five: Varied themes (*aghrāḍ mukhtalifah*)
Chapter Six: *Muwashshaḥāt*
Chapter Seven: *Maqāṭīʿ*-poems

In keeping with the organizing principle of seven, the first six chapters are each made up of seven long poems (*qaṣāʾid*, sing. *qaṣīdah*), while the last chapter—the *maqāṭīʿ*-chapter—is made up of seventy poems, ten *maqāṭīʿ*-poems counting as one *qaṣīdah* in al-ʿAsqalānī's scheme.[4] The chapters of the *Dīwān* are organized primarily by theme. In the introduction to his *Dīwān*, al-ʿAsqalānī speaks of having composed in "seven genres [of poetry]"—the word he uses is *anwāʿ* (sing. *nawʿ*, "type")—but there is a formalistic dimension to the organization as well.[5] After all, it is the shape of the poetry in the chapters of *muwashshaḥāt* (a form of strophic poetry) and *maqāṭīʿ*-poems that distinguishes them from other chapters and each other as well. Strictly speaking, *dūbayt, mawāliyā,* and two-line *maqāṭīʿ*-poems can appear indistinguishable on the page.[6] The rhyme scheme of the *dūbayt* (AAXA, and rarely AAAA) and

ed. Thomas Bauer and A. Neuwirth (Beirut: Ergon Verlag [Würzburg], 2005) and as-Sakhāwī, *al-Jawāhir wa-d-durar fī tarjamat Shaykh al-Islām Ibn Ḥajar*, ed. Ibrāhīm Bājis ʿAbd al-Majīd (Beirut: Dār Ibn Ḥazm, 1999), esp. 2:849–57. On heptadic division, see aṣ-Ṣafadī's *Ṭard as-sabʿ ʿan sard as-sabʿ* (an exemplar), al-Maktabah al-Waṭaniyyah (Rabat) MS D 1646 (see Yā-Sīn ʿAllūsh and ʿAbd Allāh ar-Rajrājī, *Fihris al-makhṭūṭāt al-ʿArabiyyah al-maḥfūẓah fī l-khizānah bi-r-Ribāṭ. al-Qism ath-thānī (1921–1953)* (Casablanca: Maṭbaʿat an-Najāḥ al-Jadīdah [for al-Khizānah al-ʿĀmmah li-l-Kutub wa-l-Wathāʾiq], 1997), 63–4, no. 1926) and printed edition of the same work, ed. Muḥammad ʿĀyish Mūsā (Jeddah: Dār al-Minhāj, 1439/2017) [unseen]. See also Beatrice Gruendler, "Ibn Abī Ḥajalah" in *Essays in Arabic Literary Biography 1350–1850*, ed. Joseph Lowry and Devin Stewart (Wiesbaden: Harrassowitz, 2009), 120.

4 See Ibn Ḥajar al-ʿAsqalānī, *Dīwān*, Selly Oak Colleges (Birmingham) MS Mingana 1394, f. 33b; ibid., ed. as-Sayyid Abū al-Faḍl (Hyderabad, J. M. Press, 1381/1962), 1; *idem, Dīwān as-Sabʿ as-sayyārah an-nayyirāt*, ed. Muḥammad Yūsuf Ayyūb (Jeddah: Nādī Abhā al-Adabī, 1992), 78; *idem, Uns al-ḥujar fī abyāt Ibn Ḥajar*, ed. Shihāb ad-Dīn Abū ʿAmr (Beirut: Dār ar-Rayyān li-t-Turāth, 1988), 47.

5 Ibn Ḥajar, *Dīwān*, ed. Abū al-Faḍl, 1; *idem, Dīwān as-Sabʿ as-sayyārah an-nayyirāt*, ed. Ayyūb, 78; *idem, Uns al-ḥujar fī abyāt Ibn Ḥajar*, ed. Abū ʿAmr, 47: "*fa-katabtu fī hādhihi al-awrāq sabʿat anwāʿ min kull nawʿ sabʿat ashyāʾ illā al-akhīr minhu*" ["In these pages, I have composed in seven genres and in each genre [I have composed] seven items except in the last of these"]. Elsewhere, al-ʿAsqalānī tells us that he exchanged *maqāṭīʿ*-poems with his peers (see in appendix, no. 29).

6 See *EI*^{2}, s.v. "*Mawāliyā*" [P. Cachia]; EAL, s.v. "*Mawāliyā*" [P. Cachia].

mawāliyā (AAAA) distinguishes them from *maqāṭīʿ*-poems, which are monorhymed (xAxA) and flexible in the matter of *taṣrīʿ* (rhyming the first and second hemistichs).[7] The *dūbayt*, like the more famous Persian *rubāʿī*, is written in its own particular meter, as well.[8] It is—like the *muwashshaḥ*, etc.—one of the few instances of a strictly formalistic poetic genre in the Arabic tradition.[9] We can perceive the native system of generic distinction in a biographical entry on the poet Sharaf ad-Dīn Ibn Rayyān (d. 769 or 770/1367–8 or 1368–9) in aṣ-Ṣafadī's *al-Wāfī bi-l-Wafayāt* (*Consummating «The Passing»*):[10]

> He was an avid and accomplished poet and he composed poetry in all its various forms, including the meters of the Arabs [i.e. the Khalilian meters], *muwashshaḥ*, *zajal*, *bullayq*, *mawāliyā*, and *dūbayt*.

What is perhaps most striking about al-ʿAsqalānī's *maqāṭīʿ* chapter is that each of the seventy poems is two lines long. This may seem exceedingly concise—

---

7 cf. Brockelmann's confusion as discussed in Thomas Bauer, "„Was kann aus dem Jungen noch werden!" Das poetische Erstlingswerk des Historikers Ibn Ḥabīb im Spiegel seiner Zeitgenossen" in *Studien zur Semitistik und Arabistik. Festschrift für Hartmut Bobzin zum 60. Geburtstag*, ed. Otto Jastrow, Shabo Talay, and Herta Hafenrichter (Wiesbaden: Harrassowitz, 2008), 17, § 1.

8 On the *dūbayt*, see *EI*^{2} s.v. "*Rubāʿī* (pl. *Rubāʿiyyāt*). 3. In Arabic" [W. Stoetzer] and *idem*, "Sur les quatrains arabes nommés '*dubāyt*'", QSA 5–6 (1987–88). See also related to this T. Seidensticker, "An Arabic Origin of the Persian *Rubāʿī*", *MEL* 14:2 (2011) and *EI*^{3}, s.v. "*Dūbayt* a. in Arabic" [Adam Talib].

9 Discussing the organization of Ṣafī ad-Dīn al-Ḥillī's (d. 1350) *Dīwān*, Gregor Schoeler comments that "[…] as regards the arrangement of the stanzaic poems and the other, new, formal genres, al-Ḥillī did not set up special chapters for them in his Dīwān, rather, he mixed them with the 'old', non-stanzaic poems. This means that a thematic chapter might include the following formal genres: *qaṣīda*, *qiṭʿa*, *muwaššaḥ*, *musammaṭ* (including its special form, the *muḫammas*), *dūbayt*." (Schoeler, "The Genres of Classical Arabic Poetry", 39).

10 aṣ-Ṣafadī, *al-Wāfī bi-l-Wafayāt*, 30 vols, ed. Helmut Ritter, et al, 2nd ed. (Wiesbaden: Franz Steiner Verlag, 1931–2007), 12:369: "*wa-tawallaʿa bi-n-naẓm ilā an ajāda fīhi wa-naẓama fī sāʾir anwāʿih min awzān al-ʿArab wa-l-muwashshaḥ wa-z-zajal wa-l-bullayq wa-l-mawāliyā wa-d-dūbayt*". See also Ibn Ḥajar al-ʿAsqalānī, *ad-Durar al-kāminah fī aʿyān al-miʾah ath-thāminah*, 6 vols, ed. Fritz Krenkow and Sharaf ad-Dīn Aḥmad (Hyderabad: Maṭbaʿat Majlis Dāʾirat al-Maʿārif, 1929–31), 2:55–6. This poet has not attracted much attention in scholarship, but see Maurice A. Pomerantz, "An Epic Hero in the *Maqāmāt*? popular and elite literature in the 8th/14th century", *Annales Islamologiques* 49 (2015) and Adam Talib, "Caricature and obscenity in *mujūn* poetry and African-American women's hip hop" in *The Rude, the Bad and the Bawdy. Essays in Honour of Professor Geert Jan van Gelder*, ed. Adam Talib, Marlé Hammond, and Arie Schippers (Cambridge: Gibb Memorial Trust, 2014), 280–3.

and relative to other Arabic poetic forms, it is—but the reader should recall that a single line of Arabic verse can be as long as thirty syllables (e. g. in the *Kāmil* meter) or as short as four or eight syllables (e. g. in the *Rajaz* meter). Although al-ʿAsqalānī's *maqāṭīʿ* chapter is one of the most length-restrictive, this level of concision is typical of the genre. For example, Ibn ash-Sharīf Daftarkhʷān (d. 655/1257), who did not use the term *maqāṭīʿ* to describe the poems in his collection *Kitāb Alf ghulām wa-ghulām* (*One Thousand and One Young Men*), did make a point of remarking in the introduction to that work that all the poems included in it are three lines long.[11] Historians of Arabic literature have long been aware of the predominance of short poems in this period and this awareness is reflected even in school textbooks:[12]

وقد كثر الميل إلى المقطوعات القصيرة في هذا العصر، لأن أكثر ما كان يدعو الشعراء إلى القول إنّما هو إبراز لطيفة بديعية، أو نكتة مخترعة، أو تورية رائعة، ومثل هذا يكتفي فيه بقليل من الأبيات. وكان في الشعراء عادة التراسل بالشعر فكانوا يكتفون بإرسال قطع قصيرة تتناول أغراضهم، والمُطَّلِع على ديوان ابن نباتة المصري، وهو خير من يمثّل هذا العصر يرى فيه كثيرًا من الثنائيات والثلاثيات والرباعيات وهلم جرا.

There was an increased tendency toward short poems (*maqṭūāt*) in this period because the major impetus for poets to compose poetry was either a mannerist expression, original witticism, or excellent double entendre,

11 Escorial MS árabe 461, f. 1b, last line (all but illegible): "*wa-qultu fī ṣifat kull [ghulām thalā]thata abyāt*" ("I described each young man in three verses"). See further in the annotated bibliography: 13th century, 2. a.

12 ʿAlī al-Jārim writing in the Egyptian school textbook *al-Mufaṣṣal fī tārīkh al-adab al-ʿArabī*, vol. 2, ed. Aḥmad al-Iskandarī et al. (Cairo: Maṭbaʿat Miṣr, 1934), 203–4; see also repr. in ʿAlī al-Jārim, *Jārimiyyāt: buḥūth wa-maqālāt ash-shāʿir wa-l-adīb al-lughawī ʿAlī al-Jārim*, ed. Aḥmad ʿAlī al-Jārim (Cairo: Dār ash-Shurūq, 1992 [repr. 2001]), 88. See also Muṣṭafā Ṣādiq ar-Rāfiʿī, *Tārīkh ādāb al-ʿArab* (Cairo: Maṭbaʿat al-Akhbār, 1329–1332/1911–14). This feature of the period's poetry was also remarked upon by al-Sayyid Abū al-Faḍl, the editor of Ibn Ḥajar's *Dīwān*, who alleged that Arabic *maqāṭīʿ* were a domestication of the Persian *Rubāʿī*: "*Do Bait*: Taken from the Persian Rubaʿi, the quatrain, they had two couplets in one piece. [...] When the adaptation was complete and they began to treat it as one of their own forms they began to use all kinds of Arabic metres and measures for these and named them al-Maqatiʿ (Sing: al-Maqtuʿah المقطوعة) literally a piece." (Ibn Ḥajar, *Dīwān*, ed. Abū al-Faḍl, 15n; on *maqāṭīʿ*, see also ibid., 41).

> and no more than a few verses were needed for that purpose. Poets were accustomed to exchanging their poems in letters so they were content to send short pieces (*qiṭaʿ qaṣīrah*) on the subjects that concerned them (*tatanāwal aghrāḍahum*). Anyone who takes a look at the *Collected Poems* (*Dīwān*) of Ibn Nubātah al-Miṣrī, the period's best representative, will find many two-line, three-line, four-line poems and so forth.

This study proposes to take these condensed poems seriously as a distinct and new genre in Arabic.

In the 14th century, four poets would publish solo-authored *maqāṭīʿ* collections that represented a turning point in the history of the genre:

> Jamāl al-Dīn Ibn Nubātah (d. 768/1366), *al-Qaṭr an-Nubātī* (*Ibn Nubātah's Sweet Drops*)
> Badr ad-Dīn Ibn Ḥabīb al-Ḥalabī (d. 779/1377), *ash-Shudhūr* (*The Particles of Gold*)
> Ṣafī ad-Dīn al-Ḥillī (d. c. 750/1350), *Dīwān al-Mathālith wa-l-mathānī fī l-maʿālī wa-l-maʿānī* (*The Collection of Two-liners and Three-liners on Virtues and Literary Motifs*)
> Ṣalāḥ ad-Dīn aṣ-Ṣafadī (d. 764/1363), *ar-Rawḍ al-bāsim wa-l-ʿarf an-nāsim* (*Fragrance Wafting in the Smiling Garden*) and *al-Ḥusn aṣ-ṣarīḥ fī miʾat malīḥ* (*Pure Beauty: On One Hundred Handsome Lads*)

I will have much more to say about the significance of these collections later in Chapter Two, but for the moment let us confine our focus to the issue of poem length. Ṣafī ad-Dīn al-Ḥillī, for one, foregrounded the length of the *maqāṭīʿ* in his collection by calling the work *Dīwān al-Mathālith wa-l-mathānī fī l-maʿālī wa-l-maʿānī* (*The Collection of Two-liners and Three-liners on Virtues and Literary Motifs*).[13] Thomas Bauer, who was the first scholar to point to the importance of these collections, has shown that, while not all poet-collectors were as stringent about poem length as al-ʿAsqalānī or Ibn Sharīf Daftarkhʷān, there is a clear proclivity toward brevity:

> Whereas Ibn Ḥabīb and [Ṣafī ad-Dīn] al-Ḥillī strictly limited themselves to two-liners and three-liners only, Ibn Nubāta[h] allowed himself [to include] six four-liners and even one six-liner. Two-liners clearly predominate among all three of them, however: amounting to approximately 80% in al-Ḥillī's [anthology], 85% in Ibn Nubāta[h]'s [anthology] (229

13 For bibliographic information about this text, see in the annotated bibliography: 14th century, 2. a.

two-liners, 35 three-liners, and seven others), and 97% in Ibn Ḥabīb's [anthology] (360 two-liners and ten three-liners).[14]

Consider also the following survey of poem length in a sample of *maqāṭīʿ* collections from the 14th–18th centuries:

Ibn Nubātah, *al-Qaṭr an-Nubātī*:[15]

Two-liners	230 (460 lines)	78% of total
Three-liners	35 (105)	18%
Four-liners	5 (20)	3%
Six-liners	1 (6)	1%

Badr ad-Dīn Ibn Ḥabīb al-Ḥalabī, *ash-Shudhūr*:[16]

One-liners	1 (1 line)	0.1% of total[17]
Two-liners	360 (720)	96%
Three-liners	10 (30)	4%

aṣ-Ṣafadī, *ar-Rawḍ al-bāsim wa-l-ʿarf an-nāsim*:[18]

Two-liners	349 (698 lines)	66% of total
Three-liners	44 (132)	12%
Four-liners	36 (144)	14%
Five-liners	9 (45)	4%
Six-liners	2 (12)	1%
Seven-liners	2 (14)	1%
Eight-liners	1 (8)	0.75%
Ten-liners	1 (10)	0.9%

14 Bauer, "„Was kann aus dem Jungen noch werden!"", 19: "Während sich Ibn Ḥabīb und al-Ḥillī streng an die Zwei- und Dreizeiligkeit halten, erlaubt sich Ibn Nubāta sechs Vierzeiler und gar einen Sechszeiler. Bei allen überweigt jedoch der Zweizeiler deutlich, der bei al-Ḥillī ca. 80%, bei Ibn Nubāta 85% (229 Zweizeiler, 35 Dreizeiler, sieben sonstige), bei Ibn Ḥabīb gar 97% (360 Zweizeiler, zehn Dreizeiler) beträgt."

15 This breakdown is based on Thomas Bauer's edition in progress, not the figures cited in the quotation above (on this work, see in the annotated bibliography: 14th century, 4. a).

16 This breakdown is based on Paris MS 3362, ff. 160b–204a.

17 Due to rounding, some of the totals presented here do not exactly equal 100%.

18 This breakdown is provided by the editor of the work. See aṣ-Ṣafadī, *ar-Rawḍ al-bāsim wa-l-ʿarf an-nāsim*, ed. Muḥammad ʿAbd al-Majīd Lāshīn (Cairo: Dār al-Āfāq al-ʿArabiyyah, 2004), 29.

aṣ-Ṣafadī, *Kashf al-ḥāl fī waṣf al-khāl*:[19]

One-liners	4 (4 lines)	0.5% of total
Two-liners	320 (640)	80%
Three-liners	38 (114)	14.25%
Four-liners	8 (32)	4%
Five-liners	2 (10)	1.25%

aṣ-Ṣafadī, *al-Ḥusn aṣ-ṣarīḥ fī miʾat malīḥ*:[20]

Two-liners	210 (420 lines)	98% of total
Three-liners	1 (3)	0.7%
Four-liners	1 (4)	0.9%

an-Nawājī, *Ṣaḥāʾif al-ḥasanāt fī waṣf al-khāl*:[21]

One-liners	1 (1 line)	0.2% of total
Two-liners	187 (374)	86%
Three-liners	10 (30)	7%
Four-liners	7 (28)	6%

Pseudo-Thaʿālibī, *fī asmāʾ al-ghilmān al-ḥisān*:[22]

Two-liners	59 (118 lines)	84% of total
Three-liners	6 (18)	13%
Four-liners	1 (4)	3%

In order to understand how such economic poetic expression works in practice, let us examine a poem from the *maqāṭīʿ* chapter of Ibn Ḥajar's *Dīwān*. The following poem, a two-line poem in the *Basīṭ* meter, consists of only nineteen words or forty syllables:[23]

---

19 This breakdown is based on the edition by ʿAbd ar-Raḥmān al-ʿUqayl (See further in the annotated bibliography: 14th century, 3. c).

20 This breakdown is based on the edition by Aḥmad Fawzī al-Hayb (See further in the annotated bibliography: 14th century, 3. a).

21 This breakdown is based on the edition by Ḥasan Muḥammad ʿAbd al-Hādī (Amman: Dār al-Yanābīʿ, 2000). See further in the annotated bibliography: 15th century, 3. a.

22 Edited in Adam Talib, "Pseudo-Ṯaʿālibī's *Book of Youths*", *Arabica* 59:6 (2012): 619–49. See further in the annotated bibliography: 17th century, 7. a).

23 Ibn Ḥajar, *Dīwān*, Selly Oak Colleges (Birmingham) MS Mingana 1394, f. 33b; *idem*, ed. Abū al-Faḍl, 129.

[من مخلّع البسيط]

بالله سِرْ يا رَسولَ حُبّي إلَيْـهِ إذ ظلَّ لي مُباعِـدْ*

فإنْ جَرَى عِنْدَهُ حَديثي أَعِنْ وكُنْ لي يـدًا وساعِـدْ

O messenger of my love, go—by God—
to him, for he is keeping his distance.
And if conversation turns to me [in his presence],
Step in: be my hand and help out! [or: forearm].

The reader will already have realized that this poem, like many *maqāṭīʿ*-poems, hinges on the reading of the last word of the last hemistich of the last line. This effect of reading is indeed similar to point in the Martialian epigram tradition or the punchline of a joke.[24] In this case, the poem begins as a plaintive entreaty from the lover to an intermediary. As the lover's speech develops and he specifies what it is he wants the intermediary to do on his behalf, the poet introduces a *tawriyah* (double entendre), punning on an imperative verb and parts of the human body. The word *sāʿid* that ends the poem can be read as the imperative verb "help" (second person, singular) or—with poetic license—the noun "forearm". In the final hemistich of the poem, the lover tells his intermediary to "Be a hand to me" (*kun lī yad^{an}*), or in other words: "help me out", but the anatomical vocabulary in this idiomatic expression primes the reader to misread the double entendre that follows. The reader is inclined to read the phrase *wa-sāʿid* as "and a forearm" as a continuation of the previous construction: "Be a hand to me" but that is of course unlikely for two reasons: (1) the forearm does not belong to the manual idiom and more significantly (2) the semantic context of the hemistich—as well as Arabic's preference for parallelism—rather calls for another imperative verb with the meaning to help. In this way, the poet deploys the concluding *tawriyah* to feint—to interpolate a fanciful, anatomical expansion of the idiom—while satisfying the reader's

*بالله سر] في المخطوطة: «سر بالله» . مباعد] في المخطوطة: «يباعد» .

24 Susanna de Beer makes the important point that "[…] wit and point are not the same, even though they often go together." She stresses that "[…] pointedness is not in itself witty or humorous. […] The *pointe* itself may be perceived as witty only if the pointed closure is surprising […] or if it finishes a poem of which the content is ambiguous." (Susanna de Beer, "The *Pointierung* of Giannantonio Campano's Epigrams: theory and practice" in *The Neo-Latin Epigram. A Learned and Witty Genre*, ed. Susanna de Beer et al. (Leuven: Leuven University Press, 2009), 143–4).

expectation of parallelism. Many *maqāṭīʿ* poems operate in this way and can thus be said to respect a common and coherent rhetorical logic.

Maqāṭīʿ display all the *badīʿ* characteristics familiar from other contemporary forms of poetry in the period, especially *tawriyah*. The following poem, for example, heads a micro-collection of *maqāṭīʿ* within a chapter on beautiful male and female youths from an anonymous Ottoman-era anthology.[25] Several collections of *maqāṭīʿ* on beautiful male youths begin with poems about youths named Muḥammad, followed by the first four caliphs and other important religious personalities from Islamic history (e.g. Ḥasan, Ḥusayn, Ibrāhīm, Mūsā, et al.).[26] This is intended to provoke more than a wicked *frisson*; the entire conceit of the poem depends on homonymy.

مؤلّفه في محمّد: [من الطويل]

نَبِيُّ جَمالٍ لِلمُحِبّينَ مُرسَلٌ وآيتُهُ ذالكَ ٱلعِذارُ ٱلمُزَرَّدُ

يَضِلُّ بِلَيلِ ٱلشَعرِ عُشّاقُ حُسنِهِ ويَهديهِمُ صُبحُ ٱلجَبينِ ويُرشِدُ

وكم مُعجِزٍ أبدى لنا حُسنُ وَجهِهِ ولا عَجَبٌ ذو ٱلمُعجِزاتِ مُحمّدُ*

The author on Muḥammad:[27]

Prophet of beauty, to the adorers heaven-sent;
His sign those chain-links of beard's first growth.
Those enamored of his beauty go astray in his hair's night
But the morning of his brow surely guides them back to right.
So many miracles are revealed in the beauty of that face
It's no wonder that this miracle-worker is called Muḥammad.

*معجز] في الأصل: معجزة.

25 This poem is given anonymously in the anonymous Ottoman-era anthology *Khadīm aẓ-ẓurafāʾ wa-nadīm al-luṭafāʾ*, Bodleian Library (Oxford) MS Huntington 508, f. 63b (See in the annotated bibliography: 17th century, 5. a). It is not entirely clear to which chapter this belongs as there is no demarcation of Chapter Six in the text. It belongs either to "Chapter Five: The Seductive Garden: On Male and Female Slaves or Youths" (*al-qism al-khāmis: ar-Rawḍ al-fattān fī l-jawārī wa-l-ghilmān*) or "Chapter Six: Chamomile Blossoms: Descriptions of Beauties" (*al-qism as-sādis: Anwār al-aqāḥ fī awṣāf al-milāḥ*).

26 See, for example, in Talib, "Pseudo-Ṯaʿālibī's *Book of Youths*".

27 The poem is by the author of the anthology *Khadīm aẓ-ẓurafāʾ wa-nadīm al-luṭafāʾ*, whose identity has not been preserved.

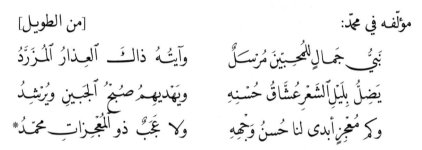

This poem is a unit—that much is clear—and like much of Arabic love poetry it is highly committed to its conceit.[28] The feature that makes the poem's cohesion most apparent and anchors its subject is its very last word; its point, as it were.

Maqāṭīʿ on names, which are normally introduced with the heading "*fī [fulān]*" ("On so-and-so"), were a very popular subgenre and they form the core of a number of *maqāṭīʿ* collections.[29] The mode of the name-*maqṭūʿ* can vary widely: it can be riddling, erotic, descriptive, bawdy, invective, etc. or indeed some combination of modes, but the general structural outline of this kind of poem adheres to a well established formula that can be seen across the thematic spectrum of *maqāṭīʿ*-poetry. The *maqṭūʿ* begins with a proposition—here it is the figure of "the prophet of beauty" (*nabī al-jamāl*). This proposition, which we can also think of as a premise, is further developed using features of the erotic mode and allusion. The prophet of beauty is "sent" (*mursal*) to the "adorers" (*al-muḥibbūn*) in parodic emulation of the Prophet of Islam's own mission to the Muslims (*al-muslimūn*): "You are one of those sent [by God]" (*innaka la-min al-mursalīn*).[30] The prophet of beauty's "sign" (*āyah*, pl. *āyāt*) is his incipient beard, a key erotic topos which the poet elevates to a manifestation of divine will. Signs in the Qurʾan (*āyāt*) include the natural manifestations of God's glory as well as historical parables of disbelief and impiety so the beloved's beard becomes a site of both divine majesty and pious devotion.[31] Rather more germane, however, to the poet's characterization of the youth as a "prophet of beauty" is the role signs (*āyāt*) play in authenticating a prophetic message.[32] The second line of the poem further develops the combination of erotic mode and prophetic theme, and even addresses—subtly and, perhaps, with tongue in cheek—the impious dialectical territory the poet is traversing here. The *maqṭūʿ* acknowledges that those who love the young man are indeed led astray (*yaḍill*) by his tenebrous locks—another touchstone of beauty in erotic poetry—perhaps here alluding to the God of the Qurʾan's own selective dispersal of gnosis:

---

28 See Benedikt Reinert, "Der Concetto-Stil in den islamischen Literatur" in *Orientalisches Mittelalter*, ed. Wolfhart Heinrichs (Wiesbaden: AULA-Verlag, 1990).

29 See Weil, *Mädchennamen, verrätselt* and Talib, "Pseudo-Ṯaʿālibī's *Book of Youths*".

30 Qurʾan *Yā-Sīn* 36:3.

31 See *EI*^{3}, s.v. "Āya" [Andrew Rippin].

32 "An understanding of signs recited in the scripture as that which brings a person to faith, then, becomes centrally tied to the text of the Qurʾān itself, as manifested in the application of the word *āya* to the verses of scripture, which are in themselves 'signs' for people to understand. The 'signs' in this sense stand as proof of the status of Muḥammad as a prophet, by establishing the truth of his message (as compared to the role of miracles, which establish the authority of the prophet)." *EI*^{3}, s.v. "Āya" [Andrew Rippin].

إِنَّ اللَّهَ لَا يَسْتَحْيِي أَن يَضْرِبَ مَثَلاً مَا بَعُوضَةً فَمَا فَوْقَهَا فَأَمَّا الَّذِينَ آمَنُوا
فَيَعْلَمُونَ أَنَّهُ الحَقُّ مِن رَبِّهِمْ وَأَمَّا الَّذِينَ كَفَرُوا فَيَقُولُونَ مَاذَا أَرَادَ اللَّهُ بِهَـذَا
مَثَلاً يُضِلُّ بِهِ كَثِيرًا وَيَهْدِي بِهِ كَثِيرًا وَمَا يُضِلُّ بِهِ إِلَّا الْفَاسِقِينَ

> God is not ashamed to strike a similitude
> even of a gnat, or aught above it.
> As for the believers, they know it is the truth
> from their Lord; but as for unbelievers,
> they say, "What did God desire by this
> for a similitude?" Thereby He leads
> many astray, and thereby He guides
> many; and thereby He leads none astray
> save the ungodly.[33]

Yet—because the tone of the erotic mode rarely ventures beyond gentle condemnation—the second hemistich quickly redeems both the wayward lover and the wicked beauty who led him astray. Though the prophet of beauty may occasionally get his lovers into trouble at nighttime, his splendid brow always leads them back to the true path by morning. In preparation for the pointed ending with which the majority of *maqāṭīʿ* conclude, the poet even shifts from third to first person (*lanā*), concretizing the effect of the prophet of beauty's miraculous presence. Here the concluding point rests on the beloved's name (Muḥammad), which is of course also an adjective meaning "praiseworthy". By this point in the poem, the beloved's name is a foregone conclusion—it has already been presaged, explicitly by the heading and tacitly by the rhyme—but the denouement is essential nonetheless. Most *maqāṭīʿ* follow a structural formula, and although no classical Arabic description of it survives, it is both distinctive and unmistakable. *Maqāṭīʿ* begin with a proposition (or premise), which is then developed and fleshed out, and by the end of the poem, usually at the very end (the point), the premise is resolved, often with a witty turn of phrase (resolution). The point of the point is not to surprise the reader—the ubiquity of headings in *maqāṭīʿ* collections makes this clear—but rather the value of the premise-exposition-resolution formula rests on the reader's ability to observe the author's technique and style as he or she negotiates the stations of the *maqṭūʿ*. Even an attentive listener would likely be able to predict the final destination of a name-*maqṭūʿ* early on in the journey. The pitch of the

33 Qur'an *al-Baqarah* 2:26. Translated in A. J. Arberry, *The Koran Interpreted*, 2 vols, (London: Allen & Unwin, 1955), 1:32.

operation builds steadily and it is the resolution—the concluding point of the *maqṭūʿ*, something rather like a punchline—that explodes the accumulating pressure, resolving the dialectical tension between signifier (a beloved named Muḥammad) and signified (the cultural, religious, historical, and affective nexus surrounding the figure of the Prophet).

This basic operational formula gives the *maqṭūʿ* its general structure—as opposed to a purely formalistic quality like the number of verses—and it is therefore one of the principal hallmarks of the genre. Readers became accustomed to this operational structure and it informed their expectations, tastes, and broader understanding of the genre's place in the tradition. This operational logic (premise-exposition-resolution) is also analogous to other poetic structures in the Arabic poetic tradition, especially among the pithier poetic forms. Thomas Bauer has identified a composite structure in Abū Tammām's (d. 231/846) relatively short erotic (*ghazal*) poems. Bauer argues that "[…] the four liner, already common yet not outstandingly represented in Abū Nuwās, starts to become a distinct formal type of *ġazal* poem with Abū Tammām."[34] He shows that Abū Tammām adopted and refined the compositional structure of "2 + 2"—that is to say two pairs of associated couplets—which was also the "predominant form in the four liners of Abū Nuwās". In Abū Nuwās' (d. c. 198/813) poems, these building blocks were "[o]ften […] semantically only loosely connected, if at all" and "[i]n some of [Abu Nuwās'] four liners, there is no discernable [*sic*] structure whatsoever", but in Abū Tammām's quatrains the poet manages to "[transform] this rather monotonous structure into a pattern which reveals a clear development."[35] In addition to this composite structure, Bauer identifies what he calls a "frame structure" in Abū Tammām's erotic (*ghazal*) quatrains:

> […] [T]he opening line gives a pregnant resumé of the main theme, which is then expressed in more detail in lines 2–3. One can often compare this relation between line 1 on the one hand and lines 2–3 on the other to the musical structure of exposition and development. Line 4 is then consequently the recapitulation, which refers back to the opening theme. […] [H]ere the structure, which one may call the "frame-structure," is clearly discernable [*sic*]: the opening and closing lines form a kind of "frame," into which the two middle lines are embedded. About one third of all

34 Thomas Bauer, "Abū Tammām's Contribution to ʿAbbāsid *Ġazal* Poetry", *JAL* 27:1 (1996): 19. See also the poetry of Khālid b. Yazīd al-Kātib, edited in Albert Arazi, *Amour divin et amour profane dans l'Islam médiéval. À travers le Dīwān de Khālid al-Kātib* (Paris: G.-P. Maisonneuve et Larose, 1990).

35 Bauer, "Abū Tammām's Contribution", 19.

> *ġazal* four liners of Abū Tammām follow this structure, which is comparatively rarely encountered in the *dīwān* of Abū Nuwās, where it often seems to come about purely accidentally.[36]

These model structures: composite (2+2) and frame (exposition-development-recapitulation), are clearly analogous to the basic operational structure of *maqāṭīʿ* as outlined above (premise-exposition-resolution). Nevertheless they are sufficiently dissimilar to demonstrate that something unique—and innovative—is taking place within the *maqāṭīʿ*-genre.

This operational formula is by no means unique to the name-*maqṭūʿ*, though of course the parameters of exposition and resolution inevitably depend on the nature of a poem's premise. Some *maqāṭīʿ*, like the following, are entirely humorous, so the operation depends chiefly on achieving the desired comic effect.[37] This example of a humorous *maqṭūʿ*, a poem on "Nighttime assignations", is especially pithy.

في الزيارة في الليل: [من الكامل]

زارَ ٱلحبيبُ بلَيلةٍ وَوُشاتُهُ لَمْ يَشْعُرُ

فَضَمَمْتُهُ وَلَثَمْتُهُ وَفَعَلْتُ ما لا يُذْكَرُ

On nighttime assignations:

My beloved came to me by night;
 while those who gossip were oblivious,
I took him in my arms and kissed his lips
 and did that thing that cannot be mentioned.

The poem is in the *Kāmil* meter, but a short dimetrical (two-footed) variety of it with a maximum of twenty syllables per line (ten syllables per hemistich),

36 ibid., 20.

37 See also, on a related poetic form, the Persian *rubāʿī*, Michael Craig Hillman, "The Persian Rubāʿī: common sense in analysis", ZDMG 119 (1970): 99–100: "[...] the *rubāʿī* [...] usually, by virtue of its brevity, meter, and rhyme scheme, culminates in a 'punch' line [...], which drives home a point, completes a verbal irony or paradox, or sums up a moral lesson."; L.P. Elwell-Sutton, "The Omar Khayyam Puzzle", *Journal of the Royal Central Asian Society* 55:2 (June 1968): 172: "Being so brief, the *rubāʿī* [*sic*] lends itself particularly to the expression of pithy, epigrammatic thoughts; and indeed one striking characteristic of all of them is the final, 'punch' line summing up the moral of the whole [...]".

and thus roughly equivalent to four lines of iambic pentameter.[38] Indeed in this poem only one of the four hemistichs (hemistich three) is ten syllables long, the others are made up of nine syllables, and it will not have escaped the reader's attention that the third hemistich is where the action is, so to speak. Here I render the poem loosely as a heroic stanza:

> Sweet beloved, come to me by night—
> while resentful gossips snooze in bed—
> that we may kiss, caress, and that we might
> do the thing I better leave unsaid.

This *maqṭūʿ* is clearly intended to be humorous so it can be helpful to think of the premise-exposition-resolution formula operating as a joke. The premise (set-up) is simple and is laid out in the first hemistich, while the second hemistich adds coincidental detail relevant to the setting (color). The beloved comes to the lover at nighttime when the coast is clear, and the two hemistichs of the final line give us the poem's exposition (development) and resolution (punch-line), respectively. When the beloved arrives under cover of night, the lover embraces him and kisses him, as may be expected, so again the humor of the *maqṭūʿ* is not dependent upon a narrative twist, but rather audience voyeurism. The reader or listener knows to expect something in the final hemistich of the final line of the poem so—as with all jokes—the punch-line is anticipated well in advance. What makes the joke funny is not that the couple meet in secret to make love—or even that the calumniators are caught snoozing as it were—but that the narrator becomes so disingenuously coquettish at the precise moment that the story reaches its climax; as though the progression of the narrative ends with a deceptive cadence. The punch-line—here an example of affirmation through denial or apophasis—is a sudden departure from the narrative tone: the rather blunt and straightforward erotic narrative is halted by an instance of arch modesty at what is precisely the most immodest moment in the action.

In ekphrastic, or descriptive, *maqāṭīʿ*-poems, the same operation (premise-exposition-resolution) is transposed on to the structure of an extended simile or metaphor, often ending with a phantasmagoric comparison (the point). Ekphrastic *maqāṭīʿ*-poems were a very popular subgenre and they are related to a long tradition of ekphrastic (*waṣf*) poetry in Arabic, as well as the study of rhetorical features such as topoi, motifs (*maʿānī*), and similes

38 This poem is also taken from *Khadīm aẓ-ẓurafāʾ wa-nadīm al-luṭafāʾ*, Bodleian Library (Oxford) MS Huntington 508, f. 99b, where it is cited anonymously.

(*tashbīhāt*), which spawned a great many volumes.[39] Ekphrastic *maqāṭīʿ* also provided yet another opportunity for poets to integrate the subjects of urban life and luxury into their art. The subject matter may appear somewhat peculiar at first to the contemporary reader, but ekphrastic poetry was once an extremely prominent genre in pre-modern European literature as well.[40] The following *maqṭūʿ*, "On a roast chicken", comes from the same Ottoman-era anthology as the two poems just discussed. This poem is from the chapter devoted to the necessary elements for a successful party: "Chapter Eight. Satisfaction Guaranteed: Everything a party could need" (*al-qism ath-thāmin: bulūgh al-munā fīmā yaḥtājuhu majlis al-hanā*[ʾ]).[41]

في دجاجة مشوية: [من السريع]

دَجاجَةٌ صَفْراءُ مِن شَيِّها حَمْراءُ كالوَرْدِ مِنَ ٱلوَهَجِ
كأنَّها والجَمْرُ مِن تَحْتِها أُتْرُجَّةٌ مِن فوقِ نارَنْجِ

On a roast chicken:

A chicken that's golden from roasting
and red like a rose from the flame.
It appears, as the coals beneath it glow,
like a citron atop a bitter orange.

The structure of this poem is altogether similar to that of the other *maqāṭīʿ*-poems we have considered. The subject of the poem (its premise), a roast chicken, is the first thing mentioned in the poem and additional descriptive elements follow in the first and second hemistichs of the first line. The first hemistich of the second line, which specifies that the coals beneath the chicken are glowing,

39 The most recent work on Arabic ekphrastic poetry is Akiko Motoyoshi Sumi, *Description in classical Arabic poetry: waṣf, ekphrasis, and interarts theory* (Leiden: Brill, 2004). See also Ruth Webb, "*Ekphrasis* ancient and modern: the invention of a genre", *Word & Image* 15:1 (January–March 1999).

40 cf. Giambattista Marino (1569–1625), *La galeria del cavalier Marino: distinta in pitture, & sculture* (Milan: Appresso Gio. Battista Bidelli, 1620); Graham Zanker, "New Light on the Literary Category of 'Ekphrastic Epigram' in Antiquity: the new Posidippus (Col. X 7-XI 19 p. Mil. vogl. VIII 309)", *Zeitschrift für Papyrologie und Epigraphik* 143 (2003); Christopher Chinn, "Statius Silv. 4.6 and the Epigrammatic Origins of Ekphrasis", *The Classical Journal* 100:3 (February–March 2005).

41 *Khadīm aẓ-ẓurafāʾ wa-nadīm al-luṭafāʾ*, Bodleian Library (Oxford) MS Huntington 508, f. 104b.

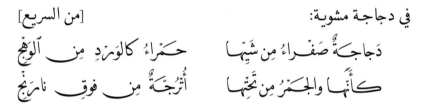

develops the initial premise (exposition), and the punchline is the result of an over-the-top, phantasmagoric comparison of a chicken roasting over coals to a citron stuck on top of an orange. Even the linguistic structure of the poem contributes to the tension of anticipated resolution. The parallel constructions in the first hemistichs of both lines: *min shayyihā* and *min taḥtihā* further augment the caesural tendency of lines of Arabic poetry (sing. *bayt*) to separate into two equal halves (sing. *miṣrāʿ*), giving the poem a structural rhythm that can be represented as:[42]

1. element → 2. complement

3. element' → 4. complement'

This element-complement repetition is, of course, broken in the final pairing by the introduction of a phantasmagoric comparison. This rhetorical device puts one in mind of similar poetic trends in European literature like the Marinistic and metaphysical schools, as well as famous and controversial examples from earlier Arabic poetry.[43] In this poem, the point is the peculiar comparison that completes the simile and its humor lies in throwing the resolution off course. Many Arabic rhetoricians were highly critical of overwrought language (*takalluf*) in poetry, but this did not stigmatize all uses of simile (*tashbīh*) or creative aetiology (*ḥusn at-taʿlīl*). The aversion toward phantasmagoria may have been abandoned in the later period, or perhaps the aversion toward it felt by some critics—always a minority within the literary community—was further marginalized as later authors embraced and elevated various so-called decadent rhetorical features.[44] This ekphrastic *maqṭūʿ*-poem uses the abrupt shift to an absurd image to drive its point home, but—as I have mentioned be-

42 I have benefited from the discussion of parallelism in Chinese poetry in Hans H. Frankel, *The Flowering Plum and the Palace Lady* (New Haven, CT: Yale University Press, 1976), 144–85.

43 See, *inter alia*, Mansour Ajami, *The Neckveins of Winter: the controversy over natural and artificial poetry in medieval Arabic literary criticism* (Leiden: Brill, 1984).

44 On this topic, see Wolfhart Heinrichs, "Literary Theory: the problem of its efficiency" in *Arabic Poetry: theory and development*, ed. G. E. von Grunebaum (Malibu, CA: Undena, 1973); *idem*, "Manierismus in der arabischen Literatur" in *Islamwissenschaftliche Abhandlungen. Fritz Meier zum sechzigsten Geburtstag*, ed. R. Gramlich (Wiesbaden: Franz Steiner Verlag, 1974); Stefan Sperl, *Mannerism in Arabic Poetry: a structural analysis of selected texts (3rd century AH/9th century AD—5th century AH/11th century AD)* (Cambridge: Cambridge University Press, 1989); Beatrice Gruendler, *Medieval Arabic praise poetry: Ibn al-Rūmī and the patron's redemption* (London: RoutledgeCurzon, 2003), ch. 13, 219–26.

fore—the phantasmagoric point of ekphrastic *maqāṭīʿ*-poems like this one is something of an anti-climax. Perhaps the most unambiguous case of a *maqṭūʿ* deriving its pointedness—its total resolution—from the climax of mounting poetic tension can be found in riddle-*maqāṭīʿ*.

Riddles (*alghāz*, sing. *lughz*) in *maqāṭīʿ* form—like their sister-form the chronogram (*taʾrīkh*)—may testify to the circulation of *maqāṭīʿ* collections primarily as written, rather than oral, texts.[45] They also exemplify the genre's crescendo rhythm, although when it comes to riddle-*maqāṭīʿ* and chronograms, the poetic tension can only be resolved after the poem itself has finished. Let us consider the following paronomastic riddle on a youth called Ẓālim (Tyrant).[46]

وقال في غلام اسمه ظالم: [من الخفيف]

وَبديعٍ في حُسْنِهِ   ما لَهُ مِنْ مُماثِلِ
صَبُّهُ لَيْسَ يَرْعَوي   فيهِ مِنْ عَذْلِ عاذِلِ
كيفَ أَرْجو إِنْصافَهُ   وٱسْمُهُ ضِدُّ عادِلِ

On a boy called Tyrant:

A gorgeous one
    who has no match.
His ardent lover won't mend his ways
    despite the blamer's blame.
How can I beg him to be fair,
    When [even] his name is the opposite of "Just"?!

This poem—as the heading itself tells us—describes a beautiful youth called Tyrant (*ẓālim*). Just as with the poem "On Muḥammad" (discussed above, pp. 21–4), the conceit (or premise) of this poem provides an opportunity for the poet to explore a whole semantic field associated with a particular topic; in this case, fairness. This is an erotic poem that uses the riddle device to supplement its affective aim. Indeed the poem's very first line alludes to its

45 Riddling in rhetoric is known as *ilghāz* (See Cachia, *The Arch Rhetorician*, no. 114). See also Ali Asghar Seyed-Gohrab, *Courtly Riddles: enigmatic embellishments in early Persian poetry* (West Lafayette, IN: Purdue University Press, 2008).

46 This poem is cited in Ibn ash-Sharīf Daftarkhʷān's *Kitāb Alf ghulām wa-ghulām*, Escorial MS árabe 461, f. 92a.

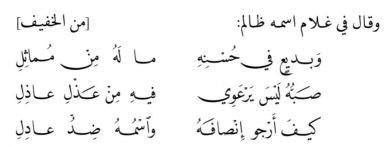

rhetorically complex, paronomastic, and riddling mode. The young man at the center of the poem—who is perhaps meant to be a slave, or an Arab Bedouin, as the name is not altogether common—is said to be "an original beauty" (*badīʿ fī ḥusnihī*); the adjective in this expression (*badīʿ*) is also the term used to describe a wide range of rhetorical devices or "figures of speech".[47] The youth is also—in the second hemistich of the same line—said to be "without peer" (*mā lahū min mumāthil*) and the word for peer (or "match", as in the translation above) is itself also a rhetorical term used to describe a specific type of homographic paronomasia.[48] It will come as no surprise then to the reader or listener that the poem's conclusion should depend on a semantic nexus, in this case a major cultural dichotomy: *ẓulm* and *ʿadl* (injustice and fairness).[49] Most beloveds in Arabic poetry act cruelly—whether or not they are indeed malicious—but in this poem the beloved's cruelty is genuinely intractable. The beloved in this poem is such a caricature of the conventionally hard-hearted beloved that even his name means Tyrant.[50] What distinguishes the resolution of a riddle-*maqṭūʿ* from other *maqāṭīʿ*-poems is that it depends on the reader deducing the point after the poem has been read.

We can see the same process at work in the following riddle-*maqṭūʿ* by Shihāb ad-Dīn Ibn al-Khiyamī that is cited in Shihāb ad-Dīn al-Ḥijāzī al-Khazrajī's collection *Rawḍ al-ādāb* (discussed at length below, pp. 55–57):[51]

شهاب الدين بن الخيمي في الملعقة: [من المتقارب]

ومَهْـدودةٍ كَـيَدِ ٱلمُجْتَـدي بِكَفٍّ عَـلَى ساعـدٍ مُسْعَـدِ

تَـرَى بَعْضَها في فَمِي كالِلسانِ وحَمَّلَتُها في يَـدِي كاليَـدِ

Shihāb ad-Dīn Ibn al-Khiyamī on a spoon:

Feeble like the hand of a beggar,
his palm laid against the arm of a fortunate man.

47 See *EI*[3], s.v. "Badīʿ" [Geert Jan van Gelder].

48 See *EI*[2], s.v. "Tadjnīs" [W. P. Heinrichs].

49 "Frequently [*ẓulm*] is [...] used as the antonym to *ʿadl, inṣāf* and *ḳisṭ* [...]" (*EI*[2], s.v. "Ẓulm" [R. Badry]).

50 The name of the beloved here may also refer to the practice of ironic slave names (Camphor, Tyrant, etc.). There is no evidence in the poem itself to suggest that the beloved depicted here is a slave, but it may be assumed.

51 The poem occurs on f. 117b (scil. 116b; the MS is misnumbered) of British Library MS Add 19489. See further in the annotated bibliography: 15th century, 6. a. II.

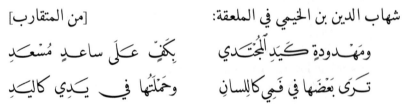

You see part of it in my mouth like a tongue,
    while I hold the handle in my hand like a hand.

Strictly speaking—according to the pre-modern Arabic generic classification—chronogram-poems (*taʾrīkh*) are not the same as *maqāṭīʿ*.[52] In practice, however, many of these poems are structured in the same way and share an analogous operational logic (i.e. premise-exposition-resolution) so considering a chronogram-poem during the course of our discussion of *maqāṭīʿ*-poetry helps to clarify aspects of both genres. Māmayah ar-Rūmī (d. 985/1577) was perhaps the most prolific and celebrated composer of Arabic chronogram-poems and the anthology of his poetry known as *Rawḍat al-mushtāq wa-bahjat al-ʿushshāq* includes poems on a number of significant public occasions including the erection of public buildings (Darwīsh Pasha's *Sabīl*, Suleiman the Magnificent's *Khān*, Murād Pasha's Mosque), deaths, births, the Ottoman conquest of Cyprus, etc. as well as more private matters like the purchase of a house, a wedding, and a reconciliation. The following poem is especially poignant in light of the horror of irreversible climate change:[53]

وله تأريخ[:] مطر هلّ بعد يأس   [من الرجز]

قَـدْ جاءَنا صَوْمٌ جليـلٌ قـدرُهُ   والحقُّ فينا قَـدْ أرانا قُدْرَتَـهْ

وعَمَّنـا ٱلانسـانَ في تأريخِـهِ   وأَنْـزلَ ٱللهُ عَلَيْـنا رَحْمَتَـهْ

[سـنة ٩٧٤]

A chronogram-poem on rainfall after despair set in:

We were visited by a period of abstention of great duration
    The Truth showed us his power.
And then it encompassed every human on that day (*taʾrīkh*)
    that God rained down on us his mercy.

This poem unfolds in much the same way as the *maqāṭīʿ*-poems discussed above except for one crucial difference. In chronogram-poems, the exposition

---

52 Cachia, *The Arch Rhetorician*, no. 63. See further Thomas Bauer, "Vom Sinn der Zeit: aus der Geschichte des arabischen Chronogramms", *Arabica* 50:4 (2003). See, too, Maria Eva Subtelny, "A Taste for the Intricate: the Persian poetry of the late Timurid period", ZDMG 136 (1989): 19.

53 Staatsbibliothek zu Berlin MS Wetzstein II 171, f. 41b (see further in the annotated bibliography: 16th century, 3. a. i).

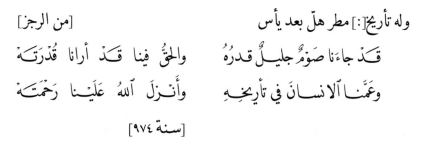

of the initial premise is relatively protracted because of the nature of the resolution in such poems. Thus in this chronogram-poem, the premise (a drought) is presented in the first hemistich of the first line and the following two hemistichs build on the premise (exposition) as in other *maqāṭīʿ*-poems. This poem departs from the pattern at the end of line two, hemistich one, with the code-word *taʾrīkh*, signaling the coming of a chronogram (the poem's resolution). The chronogram-poem is not resolved by poem's end, however; like riddle-*maqāṭīʿ*, chronogram-poems require the reader or hearer to work out the solution in the silent interstice between text and epiphany. For the contemporary Arabist, arriving at the appropriate solution requires consulting a reference work and some basic arithmetic, and while we can assume that pre-modern Arabs were more adept at computing *abjad*-numerals than we are, evidence of scratchwork in manuscript copies of Māmayyah's collection is apparent.[54]

Solution = the year 974/1566

سنة		ه	ت	م	ح	ر	ا	ن	ي	ل	ع	ه	ل	ل	ا	ل	ز	ن	أ	و
974	=	5	400	40	8	200	1	50	10	30	70	5	30	30	1	30	7	50	1	6

Chronograms and riddles depend on the reader or listener's ingenuity. These poems do not divulge their complete meaning simply by being read once over, rather the reader or listener must take a final creative step to deduce the point on which the poem hinges. This process is not altogether different from how a reader or listener deciphers a double entendre. The first-order meaning of a double entendre is apparent upon a first reading, but the poet also wants the reader or listener to be aware of the word's other meanings, and it is often a more recondite, second-order meaning of a word that is integral to understanding the poem. Classical Arabic Poets were great practitioners of double entendre (*tawriyah*) and by the later period this rhetorical device suffused a majority of poems.[55] A favorite 20th-century example are two invective lines by the Egyptian neo-classical poets and rivals Ḥāfiẓ Ibrāhīm (1871–1932) and Aḥmad Shawqī (1868–1932).[56] Ibrāhīm began by punning on his rival's name in the line [*Ṭawīl* meter]:

54 See e.g. Staatsbibliothek zu Berlin MS Wetzstein II 171, ff. 55a–55b.

55 Cachia, *The Arch Rhetorician*, no. 106.

56 On these two poets, see Ṭāhā Ḥusayn, *Ḥāfiẓ wa-Shawqī* (Cairo: Maktabat al-Khānjī wa-Ḥamdān, 1933).

yaqūlūna ʾanna sh-shawqa nārun wa-lawʿatun
fa-mā bālu shawqī aṣbaḥa l-yawma bāridū
They say that passion (*shawq*) blazes and torments
So how is it that I find my passion/**Shawqī** so cold (dull) today?

Shawqī's reply was, if anything, less subtle [*Ṭawīl* meter]:

wa-awdaʿtu ʾinsānan wa-kalban wadīʿatan
fa-ḍayyaʿahā l-insānu wa-l-kalbu ḥāfiẓū
I entrusted a man and a dog with something for safekeeping;
the man betrayed [me], but the dog was reliable/**Ḥāfiẓ**

Istikhdām is a particular variety of *tawriyah* (double entendre) in which both meanings of the word are intended, including often a second-order meaning derived from a specific terminological or technical field, as in the following example by Saʿd ad-Dīn Ibn Muḥyī ad-Dīn Ibn al-ʿArabī (d. 656/1258).[57]

Muḥyī ad-Dīn Ibn al-ʿArabī (d. 638/1240), known to his followers as ash-Shaykh al-Akbar, is—along with Jalal ad-Dīn Rūmī (d. 1273)—the most famous mystic in the Islamic tradition and certainly the most important Sufi thinker in the Arabic tradition. His son Saʿd ad-Dīn is, despite his father's fame, a considerably more obscure figure, forgotten by modern scholarship, although he was well known to his contemporaries as a poet of some renown. Manuscripts of his *Dīwān* (Collected Poems) can be found in several libraries around the world.[58] I have chosen to discuss the following poem—"On a Sufi youth"—not only because it is a *maqṭūʿ* poem and because Saʿd ad-Dīn was himself a scion of Sufi royalty, as it were, but because its rhetorical style reflects wider trends in Mamluk and Ottoman poetry.[59]

وقال ايضًا في غلام صوفي [من السريع]

عَلِقْتُ صوفيًّا كَبَدْرِ ٱلدُّجى لكنّه في وصلِهِ ٱلزَّاهِدُ
يَشْهَدُ دَمْعي بِغَرامي لَهُ فَدَيْتُ صوفيًّا له شاهِدُ

57 Cachia, *The Arch Rhetorician*, no. 107.

58 See Muḥsin Jamāl ad-Dīn, "*Dīwān Saʿd ad-Dīn Ibn ʿArabī al-Andalusī. Shāʿir al-ḥiraf wa-ṣ-ṣināʿāt*", *al-Mawrid* 2:2 (Ḥazīrān [June] 1973).

59 British Library MS 3866, f. 84a (see further in the annotated bibliography: 13th century, 3. a. i).

On a Sufi youth:

> I fell for a Sufi—[with a face] like the full moon—
> but when it came to union, he was ascetic.
> My tears testify to my love for him.
> I'd give my life for a Sufi with a witness/a sign of divine beauty.

Here again the poem revolves around the final word of the final line, its point or punch-line. The poet tells us that he has fallen in love with a handsome Sufi, but that the young man is abstinent when it comes to romantic affection. The poet explicitly contrasts the young man's identification as a Sufi with his behavior, which he associates more with ascetics (*zuhhād*, sing. *zāhid*). In the second line of the poem, the poet sets up the parallelism that will culminate in the double entendre at the heart of the poem.

The second line begins with the poet saying that his tears testify to his love. Here he uses the verb *shahida-yash'hadu* ("to testify, witness"), which will be reprised in the poem's final word—an instance of what is known as *radd al-ʿajz ʿalā aṣ-ṣadr* or *taṣdīr* ("echo").[60] In the final hemistich, the poet says that he would sacrifice his own life for the Sufi youth whom he loves. A handsome young Sufi who—the poet tells us—has a *shāhid*, a word whose first-order meaning is witness. Thus we can read the final hemistich as: "I would sacrifice my life for a Sufi who has a witness [to testify to his beauty or worth, which is me or my tears]", but of course the word *shāhid* also has a specific terminological meaning in Sufism. For the purposes of this discussion, I translate the term *shāhid* as "a sign of divine beauty" and direct readers to the work of Annemarie Schimmel and Cyrus Ali Zargar for a richer discussion of the term and its use as a poetic motif.[61] If we interpret the word *shāhid* along Sufi lines, the final hemistich will mean something like: "I would sacrifice myself for a Sufi, who reflects a sign of divine beauty, which I—as a *connoisseur* of divine beauty—enjoy contemplating in him." This use of the word *shāhid* should also put us in mind of classical Persian poetry and the figure of the *shāhid*, the handsome young beloved. Indeed the word *shāhid-bāzī* meaning "contemplating God's beauty as reflected on the faces of young

60 See Cachia, *The Arch Rhetorician*, no. 56.

61 Annemarie Schimmel, *Mystical Dimensions of Islam* (Chapel Hill, NC: Univ. of North Carolina Press, 1975) and Cyrus Ali Zargar, "The Poetics of *Shuhūd*. Ibn al-ʿArabī's 'Intuitive, Enamored Heart' and the Composition of Erotic Poetry", *Journal of the Muhyiddin Ibn ʿArabi Society* 54 (2013).

men" is a common byword in Persian erotic verse as in the following hemistich by Ḥāfiẓ (d. c. 791/1389):[62]

جهان فانی و باقی فدای شاهد و ساقی

> That handsome young man (*shāhid*) and that cupbearer are worth more than this world and the next

Saʿd ad-Dīn's poem plays on both senses of the term *shāhid*—including as a specialized term from the Sufi tradition—and thus presents an instance of the rhetorical device *istikhdām*, which is distinct from *tawriyah* (double entendre) though they are of course related. The use of *tawriyah* and *istikhdām* —truly ubiquitous in poetry composed in the later period of Arabic literary history, including *maqāṭīʿ* poems—betokens more than a sophisticated poetic register.[63] The breadth of knowledge and readerly aptitude required by the frequent use of double entendre reflect the broad education of readers and listeners in the period, and even if these readers and listeners were not always quite as broadly educated as they needed to be to understand a given poem, poets and anthologists in the Mamluk and Ottoman periods were sufficiently confident that readers and listeners could secure this knowledge from other literary sources being produced at the time, including of course encyclopaedic works.[64]

In addition to studying the text of *maqāṭīʿ*-poems themselves, contemporary paratextual sources and biographies enrich our understanding of the genre, as well as its literary, cultural, and social contexts and its relation to the Zeitgeist. For example, while the copies of Saʿd ad-Dīn's *Dīwān* that I have consulted do not refer to this poem on a Sufi youth as a *maqṭūʿ*-poem—or indeed to any of Saʿd ad-Dīn's short poems as *maqāṭīʿ*—we know that they were thought of as such in the centuries immediately following his death, and perhaps during his lifetime as well. Aṣ-Ṣafadī writes in his biographical

62 Ḥāfiẓ, *Dīvān-i Ḥāfiẓ*. ed. Qāsim Ghanī, Muḥammad Qazvīnī, and Muṣṭafā Khudādādī (Tehran: Kitābkhānah-yi Millī-yi Īrān, SH 1377/1998), 399.

63 See, *inter alia*, Seeger A. Bonebakker, *Some Early Definitions of the Tawriya and Ṣafadī's* Faḍḍ al-Xitām ʿan al-tawriya wa-l-istixdām (The Hague: Mouton, 1966). I have also benefited from Li Guo's presentation on Ibn Ḥijjah al-Ḥamawī and aṣ-Ṣafadī's discussions of *Tawriyah* in May 2012 at the International Conference on Mamluk Literature hosted by the University of Chicago's Middle East Documentation Center (MEDOC) and the Center for Middle Eastern Studies under the auspices of the *Mamlūk Studies Review*.

64 See Elias Muhanna, "Encyclopaedism in the Mamluk Period: the composition of Shihāb al-Dīn al-Nuwayrī's (d. 1333) *Nihāyat al-arab fī funūn al-adab*" (Unpublished doctoral thesis. Harvard University, 2012) and other studies cited there.

dictionary *al-Wāfī bi-l-Wafayāt* that "[Saʿd ad-Dīn] was a talented poet who excelled at *maqāṭīʿ*-poetry, which he composed about young men [...]".[65] Aṣ-Ṣafadī's voluminous biographical dictionary is a key source—albeit an idiosyncratic one—of literary evaluations and information about poets active into the 14th century, as well as about *maqāṭīʿ*-poetry. Poets who, like Saʿd ad-Dīn, appear not to have used the term *maqāṭīʿ* to describe their own work are fitted into the history of the literary development of that genre by aṣ-Ṣafadī and other biographers. Aṣ-Ṣafadī tells us that Mujīr ad-Dīn Ibn Tamīm (d. 684/1285), a contemporary of Saʿd ad-Dīn, was only ever good at writing *maqāṭīʿ*-poems, though the poet was unlikely to have said such a thing about himself and the term *maqāṭīʿ* is not used in the published editions of his *Dīwān*:[66]

> [...] he only ever excelled at *maqāṭīʿ*-poems, for when he carried on and composed long poems, his poetry slumped and didn't rise up [...]

Ṣafī ad-Dīn al-Ḥillī (d. c. 750/1350), on the other hand, "[...] excelled at both long poems and *maqāṭīʿ*-poems [...]".[67] Al-Ḥillī is noteworthy also for having been the only one of the four 14th-century auto-anthologists mentioned above (al-Ḥillī, Ibn Nubātah, aṣ-Ṣafadī, and Ibn Ḥabīb) not to have used the term *maqāṭīʿ* himself. This did not stop others, like aṣ-Ṣafadī, from using it to describe his poems, however.[68] Al-Ḥillī's younger contemporary Ibn Ḥabīb (d. 779/1377) wrote in his annalistic chronicle *Tadhkirat an-nabīh fī ayyām al-Manṣūr wa-banīh* that he "studied [al-Ḥillī's] *al-Mathālith wa-l-mathānī fī l-maʿālī wa-l-maʿānī*, a collection of *maqāṭīʿ* comprising twenty chapters on different subjects, with the author".[69] We will return to al-Ḥillī and subsequent generations of *maqāṭīʿ* poets shortly, but let us now turn to the earliest uses of the term to sketch a tentative chronology of the genre's historical development.

---

65 aṣ-Ṣafadī, *al-Wāfī*, 1:186: "*wa-kāna shāʿir^{an} mujīd^{an} ajāda al-maqāṭīʿ allatī naẓamahā fī l-ghilmān*".

66 aṣ-Ṣafadī, *al-Wāfī*, 5:228: "*illā annahu lā yujīd illā fī l-maqāṭīʿ fa-ammā idhā ṭāla nafasuh wa-naẓama al-qaṣāʾid inḥatta naẓmuh wa-lam yartafiʿ* ". Compare Ibn Abī Ḥajalah at-Tilimsānī's comments on Ibrāhīm al-Miʿmār (see in appendix, no. 11b).

67 aṣ-Ṣafadī, *al-Wāfī*, 18:482: "*ajād al-qaṣāʾid al-muṭawwalah wa-l-maqāṭīʿ*". Further examples of aṣ-Ṣafadī's use of the term *maqāṭīʿ* are to be found in the appendix (see nos 3–8).

68 See aṣ-Ṣafadī, *al-Wāfī*, 18:482 (also in appendix, no. 8c).

69 Ibn Ḥabīb al-Ḥalabī, *Tadhkirat an-nabīh fī ayyām al-Manṣūr wa-banīh*, 3 vols, ed. Muḥammad Muḥammad Amīn and Saʿīd ʿAbd al-Fattāḥ ʿĀshūr (Cairo: al-Hayʾah al-Miṣriyyah al-ʿĀmmah li-l-Kitāb, 1976), 3:139: "*thumma qaraʾtu ʿalayhi jamīʿ «al-Mathālith wa-l-mathānī fī l-maʿālī wa-l-maʿānī» wa-huwa kitāb min maqāṭīʿ shiʿrih yashtamil ʿalā ʿishrīn bāb^{an} fī anwāʿ mukhtalifah*".

The earliest systematic use of the term *maqāṭīʿ* (also *maqṭūʿ* or *maqṭūʿah*) to denote a particular poetic form is to be found in a few thirteenth-century works: ʿAlī b. Ẓāfir al-Azdī's *Badāʾiʿ al-badāʾih* (*Excellent Improvisations*), al-Qurṭubī's *Rawḍat al-azhār wa-bahjat an-nufūs wa-nuzhat al-abṣār* (*The Flower-Garden, the Soul's Delight, and the Vision's Amusement*), Ibn al-ʿAdīm's *Bughyat aṭ-ṭalab fī tārīkh Ḥalab* (*All One could Want: on the history of Aleppo*), and Ibn Khallikān's biographical dictionary *Wafayāt al-aʿyān wa-anbāʾ abnāʾ az-zamān* (*The Passing of the Notables and the Sons of the Age*). While the word *maqāṭīʿ* had already been circulating for centuries, its use in the aforementioned works represents the very earliest stage of the word's new terminological usage. The Andalusian Al-Azdī (d. 613/1216 or 623/1226) wrote in passing, in a report that would later be repeated by al-Maqqarī (d. 1041/1632), that Abū Bakr b. al-Milḥ—vizier to al-Muʿtamid b. ʿAbbād (d. 487/1095) and father of the poet Ibn al-Milḥ—once "improvized several *maqāṭīʿ*-poems".[70] Another Andalusian, Abū ʿAlī al-Ḥasan b. ʿAlī b. Khalaf al-Qurṭubī (d. 602/1205), described the contents of Chapter Twenty-Four in his anthology *Rawḍat al-azhār wa-bahjat an-nufūs wa-nuzhat al-abṣār* (*The Flower-Garden, the Soul's Delight, and the Vision's Amusement*): "*maqṭūʿāt* of precious poetry [displaying] ekphrasis and parallelism".[71] In Ibn ʿAdīm's (d. 660/1262) *Bughyat aṭ-ṭalab fī tārīkh Ḥalab*, the term is used several times, such as in the entry on Sālim b. Saʿādah al-Ḥimṣī (d. 618/1221): "*wa-anshadanā min shiʿrih ʿiddat maqāṭīʿ wa-qaṣāʾid*" ("He recited several of his *maqāṭīʿ*-poems and long poems to us [...]").[72] Many more occurrences of the term come a few decades later in Ibn Khallikān's (d. 681/1282) biographical dictionary, which he wrote in Cairo between 1256–60 and 1271–74 (i. e. shortly before the births of Ṣafī ad-Dīn al-Ḥillī (b. 677/1278 or 678/1279 in Ḥillah) and Ibn Nubātah (b. 686/1287 in Fusṭāṭ).[73] Ibn Khallikān is also an important figure in the history of the genre because he roamed relatively far and wide in his lifetime: from Irbil to Aleppo and Damascus to Mosul then eventually to Cairo, where he began compos-

70 al-Azdī, ʿAlī b. Ẓāfir, *Badāʾiʿ al-badāʾih*, ed. Muḥammad Abū l-Faḍl Ibrāhīm, (Cairo: Maktabat al-Anjlū al-Miṣriyyah, 1970), 373: "*fa-ṣanaʿa al-wazīr fīhimā ʿiddat maqāṭīʿ badīhan*" See also in appendix, no. 56. On Abū Bakr b. al-Milḥ, see *Biblioteca de al-Andalus*, s.v. "Ibn al-Milḥ, Abū Bakr" [Ahmad Damaj and Belén Tamames Holgado-Cristeto] and Shari L. Lowin, *Arabic and Hebrew Love Poems of al-Andalus* (London: Routledge, 2013), 257–60.

71 Chester Beatty Library (Dublin) MS 4601, f. 140a: "*al-bāb ar-rābiʿ wa-l-ʿishrūn fī maqṭūʿāt min ash-shiʿr an-nafīs fī t-tashbīh wa-t-tajnīs*". See further in the annotated bibliography: 13th century, 1. a.

72 Ibn al-ʿAdīm, *Bughyat aṭ-ṭalab fī tārīkh Ḥalab*, ed. Suhayl Zakkar (Beirut: Dār al-Fikr, 1995–98), 4106.

73 *EI*^{2}, s.v. "Ibn Khallikān" [J. W. Fück].

ing his *Wafayāt al-aʿyān*.[74] It is not clear, therefore, where and when he first encountered the term—nor when he began to think of *maqāṭīʿ*-poems as distinct from other short poetry in Arabic. Ibn Khallikān's own poetry is even cited in chapters of *maqāṭīʿ*-verse in later centuries.[75] At the same time, Ibn Khallikān's use of the word *maqāṭīʿ* in his biographical dictionary is variable, which suggests that the specific terminological meaning of *maqāṭīʿ* as a genre identifier was still evolving in the second half of the thirteenth century. He certainly did use the term *maqāṭīʿ* to describe a specific type of short poem, but his use of the term is not exclusive.[76]

In the course of a biographical entry on Abū Bakr b. al-Milḥ's patron al-Muʿtamid b. ʿAbbād, the last of the ʿAbbādid rulers of Seville, Ibn Khallikān remarked that the poet Ibn al-Labbānah (d. 507/1113) wrote several *maqāṭīʿ*-poems and long poems (*qaṣāʾid muṭawwalāt*) on the fall of the dynasty after his patron al-Muʿtamid was deposed in 484/1091:[77]

> He [Ibn Labbānah] composed several *maqāṭīʿ*-poems and long poems (*qaṣāʾid muṭawwalāt*) lamenting their bygone rule and the fall of their dynasty, which he collected in a slim volume entitled *Pearls on Strings: a warning for kings*.[78]

What is perhaps most interesting about this example—besides the use of the term *maqāṭīʿ* in contrast to long poems (*qaṣāʾid muṭawwalāt*)—is that certain manuscript copies of Ibn Khallikān's *Wafayāt* substitute the variant *maqṭūʿāt* for *maqāṭīʿ* in this report.[79] Elsewhere in his *Wafayāt*, it appears that Ibn

---

74 On Ibn Khallikān's innovative work and its legacy, see Jacqueline Sublet and Muriel Rouabah, "Une famille de textes autour d'Ibn Ḫallikān entre VIIe/XIIIe et XIe/XVIIe siècle", *BEO* 58 (2009).

75 See below, p. 152–53.

76 See in appendix, no. 2a–n.

77 Ibn Khallikān, *Wafayāt al-aʿyān wa-anbāʾ abnāʾ az-zamān*, 8 vols, ed. Iḥsān ʿAbbās (Beirut: Dār Ṣādir, 1977), 5:34: "*wa-lahu fī l-bukāʾ ʿalā ayyāmihim wa-ntithār niẓāmihim ʿiddat maqāṭīʿ wa-qaṣāʾid muṭawwalāt yashtamil ʿalayhā juzʾ laṭīf ṣadara ʿanhu fī ṣūrat taʾlīf wa-hayʾat taṣnīf sammāhu «Naẓm as-sulūk wa-waʿẓ al-mulūk»*". See also ibid., 5:23. See also *EI*^{2}, s.vv. "al-Muʿtamid Ibn ʿAbbād" [E. Lévi-Provençal; R. P. Scheindlin] and "Ibn al-Labbāna" [F. de la Granja].

78 This work appears not to have survived.

79 Ibn Khallikān, *Wafayāt al-aʿyān*, 5:34n. These four MSS are not particularly old, nor do they seem to belong to one stemmatic branch. They were copied in 739/1339 (MS *qāf*; on this MS, see ibid., 4:*jīm*), c. 9th–10th/15th–16th century (MS *bāʾ-rāʾ*; on this MS, see ibid., 4:*jīm–dāl*), 1155/1742 (MS *rāʾ*; on this MS, see ibid., 2:7), and 830/1426 (MS *nūn*; on this MS, see ibid., 3:6). The last of these, MS *nūn*—the editor Iḥsān ʿAbbās surmises—may be based on the author's partial draft of 659/1260.

Khallikān occasionally used the term *maqāṭīʿ* to describe something wholly different from short poems. For example in his entry on al-Manāzī al-Kātib (Aḥmad b. Yūsuf, d. 437/1045), Ibn Khallikān wrote that "people have in their possession some portions of his poetry (*maqāṭīʿ*) but [a copy of] his *Collected Poems* (*Dīwān*) is very rare indeed".[80] One could interpret this comment as "people have in their possession *maqāṭīʿ*-poems by him" rather than "portions of his poetry", but I would submit that the second interpretation is more plausible because in this sentence *maqāṭīʿ* is a correlate of *Dīwān* (a poet's collected works). Similarly, Ibn Khallikān noted that the poet Ibn ʿUnayn (d. 630/1233) was not interested in collecting his own poetry and that is why he never compiled a *Dīwān*.[81] It is for this reason, Ibn Khallikān explained, that some people had in their possession "portions" (*maqāṭīʿ*) of his poetry, but not a complete *Dīwān*. He remarked that an abridged *Dīwān* of Ibn ʿUnayn's poetry, which was compiled later by others, is neither complete nor entirely authentic:[82]

> [Ibn ʿUnayn] had no purpose in collecting his poetry so for that reason he did not record it all. Portions (*maqāṭīʿ*) [of it] are scattered among various people and one Damascene did in fact compile a small *Dīwān* [of his poetry], but it contains no more than a tenth of what he wrote and includes works not by him.

Here again it seems likely that the word *maqāṭīʿ* is intended to mean portions of a poet's collected work rather than short poems.[83] It is probable, too, that in Ibn Khallikān's day the strict concision typical of *maqāṭīʿ*-poems in the 14th century and thereafter had likewise not yet become predominant.[84] Nevertheless it bears reiterating that these examples run counter to the meaning

---

80 Ibn Khallikān, *Wafayāt al-aʿyān*, 1:144: "*wa-yūjad lahu bi-aydī n-nās maqāṭīʿ wa-ammā dīwānuh fa-ʿazīz al-wujūd*".

81 Ibn Khallikān, *Wafayāt al-aʿyān*, 5:17.

82 Ibn Khallikān, *Wafayāt al-aʿyān*, 5:17: "*wa-lam yakun lahu gharaḍ fī jamʿ shiʿrih fa-li-dhālika lam yudawwinhu fa-huwa yūjad maqāṭīʿ fī aydī n-nās wa-qad jamaʿa lahu baʿḍ ahl Dimashq dīwān*^{an} *ṣaghīr*^{an} *lā yablugh ʿushr mā lahu min an-naẓm wa-maʿa hādhā fa-fīhi ashyāʾ laysat lahu*". Khalīl Mardam Bek produced a modern edition of Ibn ʿUnayn's *Dīwān* (Damascus: al-Majmaʿ al-ʿIlmī al-ʿArabī, 1946).

83 The term *maqṭūʿ* also appears to have been used in this sense (Ibn Khallikān, *Wafayāt al-aʿyān*, 6:188), but cf. ibid., 6:204 where it seems another meaning is intended.

84 See, e.g. Ibn Khallikān, *Wafayāt al-aʿyān*, 6:206, where a five-line poem is cited as an example of one of the *maqāṭīʿ*-poems. See also ibid., 6:204.

intended in a majority of occurences of the term *maqāṭīʿ* in Ibn Khallikān's biographical dictionary; these are cited below in the appendix.[85]

Moreover, it is significant that Ibn Khallikān used the term *maqāṭīʿ* to describe poems cited in other anthological and biographical texts whose authors would have never thought to use the term. In an entry on Ibrāhīm al-Ghazzī (d. 524/1129), for example, Ibn Khallikān described some of al-Ghazzī's poetry as *maqāṭīʿ* but the term is not used in ʿImād ad-Dīn al-Kātib al-Iṣfahānī's (d. 597/1201) famous biographical dictionary of poets, *Kharīdat al-qaṣr wa-jarīdat al-ʿaṣr* (*The Palace's Unbored Pearl: a catalogue of* [*our*] *age*), nor in ʿImād ad-Dīn's source Ibn ʿAsākir's (d. 571/1176) *Tārīkh madīnat Dimashq*.[86] Similarly in his entry on Ibrāhīm b. Naṣr b. ʿAskar al-Mawṣilī (d. 610/1213), Ibn Khallikān remarks that Sharaf ad-Dīn Abū l-Barakāt Ibn al-Mustawfī (d. 637/1239), the author of a history of Ibn Khallikān's hometown, cited numerous *maqāṭīʿ*-poems by Ibrāhīm b. Naṣr in his history, and yet in the printed edition of Ibn al-Mustawfī's text the term *maqāṭīʿ* is never used in connection with this poet.[87] More examples of Ibn Khallikān's use of the term can be found in the appendix.

It is clear that Ibn Khallikān—even while deferring to the authority of earlier historical sources—chose to characterize this form of poetry in a novel way, such that earlier writers may not have understood his meaning at first. Aṣ-Ṣafadī, a great biographer as well as a *maqāṭīʿ* composer himself, was to do much the same in the following century. Aṣ-Ṣafadī wrote, for example, that Ibn Sharīf Daftarkh^{w}ān "wrote a great deal of poetry, *maqāṭīʿ* and otherwise" though there is no evidence that Ibn Sharīf Daftarkh^{w}ān, who lived a century earlier, ever used the term *maqāṭīʿ* himself.[88] In addition to Saʿd ad-Dīn Ibn al-ʿArabī and Ibn Sharīf Daftarkh^{w}ān, aṣ-Ṣafadī also used the term *maqāṭīʿ* to describe the work of earlier poets including Ibn Qalāqis (d. 567/1172) and Mujīr ad-Dīn Ibn Tamīm, as well as to describe, of course, the work of his contemporaries including Ibn Nubātah, Ṣafī ad-Dīn al-Ḥillī, Ibrāhīm al-Miʿmār (d. 750/1350), and himself.[89]

Already in the 13th century in the work of Ibn Khallikān, we see the emergence of a new terminological meaning of the word *maqāṭīʿ*—a case

85 Certain instances of the term *maqāṭīʿ* in the *Wafayāt* are to all intents and purposes unworkably ambiguous (e.g. on 6:125).

86 See in appendix, no. 2b.

87 Though it is clearly erroneous, I note in passing that de Slane translated the term as "extracts". See Ibn Khallikān, *Ibn Khallikān's Biographical Dictionary*, 4 vols, trans. Baron MacGuckin de Slane, (Paris: Oriental Translation Fund of Great Britain and Ireland, 1842–71), 1:16.

88 aṣ-Ṣafadī, *al-Wāfī*, 21:466 and in appendix, no. 8g.

89 See in appendix, nos 3–8.

of semantic shift—and entries in biographical dictionaries like aṣ-Ṣafadī's *al-Wāfī bi-l-Wafayāt* (*Consummating «The Passing»*) and Muḥammad b. Shākir al-Kutubī's (d. 764/1363) *Fawāt al-Wafayāt* (*What «The Passing» Passed Over*) suggest that this meaning achieved priority in less than a century.[90] This process can also be traced in 14th-century paratexts, both narrative and non-narrative, including the first instances of Arabic poets saying that they themselves composed *maqāṭīʿ*-poems. Paratexts, like biographical and critical accounts, are crucial sources for the history and circumstances of a genre's emergence and development.[91] Ibn Nubātah's *al-Qaṭr an-Nubātī* (*Ibn Nubātah's Sweet Drops*)—a collection of more than two-hundred *maqāṭīʿ*-poems arranged into five thematic chapters—was completed before 729/1328 and is acknowledged to be the first solo-authored *maqāṭīʿ*-collection.[92] It was dedicated to Ibn Nubātah's patron, Abū l-Fidāʾ, al-Malik al-Muʾayyad (r. 1310–1331), the governor of Hama. While the text and its author make no mention of its precedence, its generic classification is highlighted more than once.[93] The title page of the Paris manuscript of *al-Qaṭr an-Nubātī* copied in 732/1332 reads:[94]

كتاب القطر النباتي

من مقاطيع الشيخ الإمام العالم الفاضل جمال الدين

محمد بن محمد بن نباتة

The book *al-Qaṭr an-Nubātī*
maqāṭīʿ-poems by the esteemed scholar Jamāl ad-Dīn
Muḥammad b. Muḥammad b. Nubātah

---

90 See in appendix, nos 8–9.

91 See Andreas Görke and Konrad Hirschler (eds), *Manuscript Notes as Documentary Sources* (Würzburg, Ergon Verlag, 2011).

92 This work has never been published—rumors of an edition by ʿUmar Mūsā Bāshā appear unfounded—but Thomas Bauer is preparing an edition, which he kindly shared with me. I have relied on this edition and four MSS for this study (see in the annotated bibliography: 14th century, 4. a). Bauer has recently published an edition and translation of twenty-one poems from one chapter of the text in Thomas Bauer, "Dignity at Stake: *mujūn* epigrams by Ibn Nubāta (686–768/1287–1366) and his contemporaries" in *The Rude, the Bad and the Bawdy. Essays in Honour of Professor Geert Jan van Gelder*, ed. Adam Talib, Marlé Hammond, and Arie Schippers (Cambridge: Gibb Memorial Trust, 2014).

93 Thomas Bauer, "Ibn Nubātah al-Miṣrī (686–768/1287–1366): Life and Works. Part I: The Life of Ibn Nubātah", *MSR* 12:1 (2008): 4.

94 Ibn Nubātah, *al-Qaṭr an-Nubātī*, Bibliothèque Nationale (Paris) MS 2234, f. 158b.

Manuscript title pages were rarely written by a work's author, but they are of great value as a source of information about how the work was presented to readers and understood by those who disseminated it. Their impulse to classify the work as a *maqāṭīʿ*-collection chimed entirely with Ibn Nubātah's own vision as can be seen from the author's preface. There Ibn Nubātah wrote of his collection that: "I had put out [...] a small selection of my long poems * which I presented to have its protracted ideas tested * and then a selection of my short poems (*maqāṭīʿ*) raised its head * and asked for its turn".[95] In another manuscript, this time a copy of Ibn Nubātah's *Dīwān* written before 1755, we find two more references to *maqāṭīʿ* composition as well as another mention of the poetic form in a manuscript copy of Ibn Nubātah's epistolary anthology *Zahr al-manthūr*.[96] We know from contemporary biographical accounts that Ibn Nubātah's peers also considered his poems to have belonged to the *maqāṭīʿ*-genre. Badr ad-Dīn Ibn Ḥabīb (d. 779/1377) wrote that, "[Ibn Nubātah] made the flutes [*mawāṣīl*, or connected things] silent with his *maqāṭīʿ* [short poems, or disconnected things]" and a century later, Ibn Ḥajar al-ʿAsqalānī—who, as we have seen, used the term *maqāṭīʿ* to describe his own poems—would write of Ibn Nubātah that he "[...] wrote lovely books, including *al-Qaṭr an-Nubātī*, in which he limited himself exclusively to *maqāṭīʿ*-poems".[97] Ibn Nubātah's younger contemporary and occasional rival, aṣ-Ṣafadī recounted that, "[Ibn Nubātah] would petition the judge Shihāb ad-Dīn [Ibn Faḍl Allāh al-ʿUmarī] quite often for [an apostille] with brilliant *maqāṭīʿ* and verses imbued with excellence" after joining the Damascus chancery in 743/1342.[98] Aṣ-Ṣafadī's own epistolary anthology *Alḥān as-sawājiʿ bayn al-bādī wa-l-murājiʿ* (*Tunes of Cooing Doves, between the Initiator and Responder* [*in Literary Correspondence*][99]) is itself an important source of paratextual literary history for the *maqāṭiʿ* genre.

---

95 Ibn Nubātah, *al-Qaṭr an-Nubātī*, Bibliothèque Nationale (Paris) MS 2234, f. 159a. See also in appendix, no. 16 below.

96 See in appendix, no. 17.

97 Ibn Ḥabīb, *Tadhkirat an-nabīh*, 3:305; Ibn Ḥajar, *ad-Durar al-kāminah*, 5:487 (also in appendix, nos 14a and 27a). The pun on flutes (*mawāṣīl*) and *maqāṭīʿ*-poems, or connected things and disconnected things, is very common in discussions of *maqāṭīʿ*-poetry and indeed this semantic pair (*waṣala* and *qaṭaʿa*) is often linked in Arabic rhetoric as in the divine pronouncement (*ḥadīth qudsī*): "*fa-man waṣalaka waṣaltahu wa-man qaṭaʿaka qaṭaʿtahu*" ["Treat kindly anyone who treats you kindly and spurn anyone who spurns you"].

98 aṣ-Ṣafadī, *al-Wāfī*, 1:330. See also in appendix, no. 8b.

99 Title as translated in Everett K. Rowson, "al-Ṣafadī" in *Essays in Arabic Literary Biography 1350–1850*, ed. Joseph Lowry and Devin Stewart (Wiesbaden: Harrassowitz, 2009), 341.

There aṣ-Ṣafadī reproduced the text of a letter he had written in Shaʿbān 729/ May 1329 asking Ibn Nubātah's permission (*ijāzah*) to promulgate his works:[100]

«[...] وإثبات ما يحسن إيراده في هذه الإجازة من المقاطيع الرائقة والأبيات اللائقة [...]»

> and setting down in this certificate (*ijāzah*) which of the fine *maqāṭīʿ*-poems and fitting verses he [i. e. aṣ-Ṣafadī] may transmit

Aṣ-Ṣafadī was also an author and anthologist of *maqāṭīʿ*-poems in his own right of course and he did not hesitate to use that term to describe the poems in his collections.[101] Two of his solo-authored *maqāṭīʿ*-collections survive: *ar-Rawḍ al-bāsim wa-l-ʿarf an-nāsim* (*The Smiling Garden and the Wafting Fragrance*) and *al-Ḥusn aṣ-ṣarīḥ fī miʾat malīḥ* (*Pure Beauty: on one hundred handsome lads*).[102] The latter, written between 1337 and 1338, is a collection of aṣ-Ṣafadī's own *maqāṭīʿ*-poems on a hundred types of male youth described according to their professions, trades, clothing, ethnicities, bodily defects, names, etc.[103] It follows in the tradition of ath-Thaʿālibī's lost *Kitāb al-ghilmān* and two collections by Ibn ash-Sharīf Daftarkhʷān. Other anthologies in this genre were written by Ibn al-Wardī (d. 749/1349), an-Nawājī (d. 859/1455), Taqī ad-Dīn al-Badrī (d. 894/1489), and others, and it has been linked thematically to the *shahr-angīz* or *şehrengiz* tradition in Persian and Turkish literatures.[104] Aṣ-Ṣafadī's much larger and thematically diverse collection *ar-Rawḍ al-bāsim wa-l-ʿarf an-nāsim*

100 Ṣalāḥ ad-Dīn Khalīl b. Aybak aṣ-Ṣafadī, *Alḥān as-sawājiʿ bayn al-bādī wa-l-murājiʿ*, 2 vols, ed. Muḥammad ʿAbd al-Ḥamīd Sālim (Cairo: al-Hayʾah al-Miṣriyyah al-ʿĀmmah li-l-Kitāb, 2005), 2:319; Staatsbibliothek zu Berlin MS Wetzstein II 150, f. 128a. (See further in the annotated bibliography: 14th century, 3. b). See also in appendix, no. 4.

101 See in appendix, nos 5–7. Of the four 14th-century, *maqāṭīʿ* auto-anthologists (Ibn Nubātah, Ibn Ḥabīb, al-Ḥillī, and aṣ-Ṣafadī) aṣ-Ṣafadī is the only one not to have been discussed in Thomas Bauer's foundational article, "„Was kann aus dem Jungen noch werden!"".

102 See e.g. in Ibn Taghrībirdī, *al-Manhal aṣ-ṣāfī wa-l-mustawfī baʿd al-Wāfī*, 8 vols, ed. Muḥammad Muḥammad Amīn (Cairo: al-Hayʾah al-Miṣriyyah al-ʿĀmmah li-l-Kitāb, 1984–99), 5:243; the other *maqāṭīʿ*-collection mentioned there, *al-Mathānī wa-l-mathālith*, has not survived. See also aṣ-Ṣafadī, *Alḥān as-sawājiʿ*, ed. Sālim, 2:170n, and *idem*, *al-Wāfī*, 2:365.

103 Rowson, "al-Ṣafadī", 348; see also the editor's introduction to aṣ-Ṣafadī's *al-Ḥusn aṣ-ṣarīḥ*.

104 See Talib, "Pseudo-Ṯaʿālibī's *Book of Youths*", esp. 605 and 614. Aṣ-Ṣafadī accused Ibn al-Wardī of plagiarizing his collection (see Rowson, "al-Ṣafadī", 351). See also in appendix, no. 27b.

was written at some point before 756/1355.[105] The collection is made up of 444 poems divided over forty-six thematic chapters and while these poems are for the most part quite short, a few of them exceed the usual upper limit of four lines. In addition to these stand-alone collections of his own *maqāṭīʿ* (auto-anthologies), aṣ-Ṣafadī included *maqāṭīʿ* collections as parerga in several of his literary treatises. In literary anthologies on subjects like moles (*Kashf al-ḥāl fī waṣf al-khāl*; or *Revealing the Situation about Describing Beauty Marks*[106]), crescent moons (*Rashf az-zulāl fī waṣf al-hilāl*; or *A Sip of Pure Water: describing the crescent moon*), tears (*Ladhdhat as-samʿ fī waṣf ad-damʿ*[107]; or *Pleasing the Ears by Describing the Tears*) etc., aṣ-Ṣafadī often included collections of *maqāṭīʿ* by a large number of poets.[108]

One of the only extant descriptions we have of what appears to be *maqāṭīʿ*-composition comes from Yūsuf Ibn Taghrībirdī's (d. 874/1470) biographical dictionary *al-Manhal aṣ-ṣāfī wa-l-mustawfī baʿd al-Wāfī* (*The Pure Fount: fulfilling the promise of «The Passing»*) in which he recounts a description by [Muḥammad b. ʿAbd ar-Raḥīm] Ibn al-Furāt (735–807/1334–1405), who had received permission (*ijāzah*) from aṣ-Ṣafadī to transmit the latter's poetry. Ibn al-Furāt explains that he observed aṣ-Ṣafadī taking old poetic themes and composing new couplets (i.e. two-line poems) based on them:[109]

> But I have seen his own poetry, in his own hand, in which he emulates one of his talented poetic predecessors. He takes a motif (*al-maʿnā*) or a pun (*an-nuktah*) and composes two lines on it, which are quite good all things considered, but then he composes another two lines on the exact same topic (*al-maʿnā bi-ʿaynih*), and then another two lines and then another, and he carries on like that on the same topic, saying "And this is what I composed" until the [reader's] eye grows bored, his soul weary,

---

105 See Bauer, "Dignity at Stake", 172–73.

106 Title as translated in Rowson, "al-Ṣafadī", 342.

107 This text is also known as *Kitāb Tashnīf as-samʿ bi-nsikāb ad-damʿ* and it was under this title that it was printed in 1903.

108 See in appendix, nos 5–7.

109 Ibn Taghrībirdī, *al-Manhal aṣ-ṣāfī*, 5:257: "*lākin raʾaytu min naẓmih bi-khaṭṭih ʿindamā yuʿāriḍ baʿḍ man taqqadamahu min mujīdī sh-shuʿarāʾ fī maʿn*^{an} *min al-maʿānī al-laṭīfah fa-yaʾkhudh dhālika l-maʿnā aw an-nuktah fa-yanẓimuhā fī baytayn wa-yujīd fīhimā bi-ḥasab al-ḥāl thumma yanẓim ayḍ*^{an} *fī dhālika l-maʿnā bi-ʿaynih baytayn ukhar thumma baytayn thumma baytayn wa-lā yazāl yanẓim fī dhālika l-maʿnā wa-huwa yaqūl «wa-qultu ana» ilā an yamallahu n-naẓar wa-tasʾamahu n-nafs wa-yamujjahu s-samʿ fa-law taraka dhālika wa-taḥarrā fī qarīḍih la-kāna min ash-shuʿarāʾ al-mujīdīn li-mā yaẓhar lī min quwwat shiʿrih wa-ḥusn ikhtirāʿih*". (Also translated in Rowson, "al-Ṣafadī", 356, where it is attributed to Ibn Taghrībirdī himself).

and his ears repulsed. If only he'd given up that [habit of his] and taken more care in composing poetry, he'd have been one of the great poets for I did detect a strength and inventiveness in his poetry.

Ibn al-Furāt criticized aṣ-Ṣafadī for recycling poetic themes *ad nauseam* in his *maqāṭīʿ*-poetry, but Shams ad-Dīn an-Nawājī (d. 859/1455) went even further by alleging that most of the *maqāṭīʿ*-poems of his contemporary Ibn Ḥijjah al-Ḥamawī (d. 837/1434) had been recycled from the latter's long poems:[110]

[...] غالب مقاطيعه مأخوذة برمّتها من قصائده المطوّلة ولهذا شطّبت على غالبها من ديوانه وكتبت بإزائها تقدّم هذا المقطوع بلفظه في قصيدته الفلانية فلا حاجة إلى تكثير السّواد به

Most of his *maqāṭīʿ*-poems are taken in their entirety from his long poems so I crossed most of them out in [my copy of] his *Dīwān* and wrote beside them: "The exact text of this *maqṭūʿ*-poem has already appeared in poem X by him, so there's no need to spill more ink for its sake"

While we must regard an-Nawājī as a polemical source on account of his rivalry with Ibn Ḥijjah, these two brief extracts give a clear indication that (1) *maqāṭīʿ*-poems were considered a genre of poetry (distinct e.g. from *qaṣāʾid*), (2) that their content was supposed to be original, and (3) that plenty of poets recycled ideas and indeed texts in the composition of new poems, but that this did not go unnoticed by their peers, who were often disparaging in their assessments of this practice.

The term *maqāṭīʿ* long figured in musical discourses (see e.g. in *Kitāb al-Aghānī*) and there is some suggestion that unspecified *maqāṭīʿ*-poems circulated as popular song lyrics. For example Muḥammad Jamāl ad-Dīn al-Qāsimī (d. 1332/1918) records in his anti-*bidʿah* tract *Iṣlāḥ al-masājid min al-bidaʿ wa-l-ʿawāʾid*, that people decried the coming of Ramadan by "taking turns singing *maqāṭīʿ*-poems" (*yatanāwabūn maqāṭīʿ manẓūmah*).[111] The clearest evidence for the place of *maqāṭīʿ*-poetry in the song-lyric tradition comes courtesy of Dwight Reynolds, who kindly shared with me a poem

110 al-Maktabah al-Waṭaniyyah (Rabat) MS 1805 *dāl*, f. 7a; Azhar Library MS 526 - Abāẓah 7122, f. 5b. On this work, see in the annotated bibliography: 15th century, 3. d.

111 Muḥammad Jamāl ad-Dīn al-Qāsimī, *Iṣlāḥ al-masājid min al-bidaʿ wa-l-ʿawāʾid*, 5th ed., ed. Muḥammad Nāṣir ad-Dīn al-Albānī (Damascus; Beirut: al-Maktab al-Islāmī, 1403/1983), 1:146.

identified as a *maqṭūʿah* in a North African songbook that is the subject of a recent article.[112] An-Nawājī also cited a short poem by Kushājim in his collection *ash-Shifāʾ fī badīʿ al-iktifāʾ*, which hints at the connection between the musical meaning of terms like *mathānī* and *mathālith* and their meaning when applied to poetry:[113]

[من الطويل]

يقولونَ تُبْ والكأسُ في كفِّ أغيدٍ   وصوتُ ٱلمَثاني والمثَالِثِ عالي
فقُلتُ لَهُم لوكُنتُ أَضمَرتُ توبةً   وعايَنْتُ هذا في ٱلمَنامِ بَدا لي

They tell me to repent, but a long-necked one is holding the goblet
    and the sounds of the second and third strings of the lute ring out.
So I tell them: "Even if I were to resolve in my heart to repent,
    if this vision were to come to me in a dream, my view on the matter would change."

In a musical context, the words *mathānī* and *mathālith* mean the second and third strings of the lute, respectively and they have been translated thus above. There may be some reason to suspect that Kushājim is also alluding, punningly, to the lyrics of the songs being two and three-line poems, however. Scholars have long associated short Arabic poetry with the burgeoning of sung verse, but while this presumptive co-evolution may seem plausible at first glance, historical evidence does not support the claim.[114] Music is a common motif in *maqāṭīʿ*-poems, just as in other lyrical and erotic poetry in Arabic, but until more work has been done on the development of the Arabic sung-verse

112 See Dwight Reynolds, "Lost Virgins Found: the Arabic songbook genre and an early North African exemplar", *QSA* n.s. 7 (2012): 89–90.

113 Shams ad-Dīn Muḥammad b. Ḥasan an-Nawājī, *ash-Shifāʾ fī badīʿ al-iktifāʾ*, ed. Ḥasan Muḥammad ʿAbd al-Hādī (Amman: Dār al-Yanābīʿ, 2004), 121; see also in Maḥmūd b. al-Ḥusayn Kushājim, *Dīwān Kushājim*, ed. Khayriyyah Muḥammad Maḥfūẓ (Baghdad: Wizārat al-Iʿlām, 1390/1970) 405, no. 395, with variation; and *idem*, *Dīwān Kushājim*, ed. Majīd Ṭarād (Beirut: Dār Ṣādir, 1997), 250, with minor variation.

114 For an example of this assumption, see Mustafa M. Badawi, "ʿAbbasid Poetry and its Antecedents" in *ʿAbbasid Belles-Lettres*, ed. Julia Ashtiany et al. (Cambridge: Cambridge University Press, 1990), 152 and for a rebuttal based on literary-historical evidence, see Owen Wright, "Music and Verse" in *Arabic Literature to the end of the Umayyad Period*, ed. A. F. L. Beeston et al. (Cambridge: Cambridge University Press, 1983), 449. Wright does agree that the exigencies of song may have influenced the trend toward shorter poetic meters for sung verse.

tradition, its connection to the new genre of *maqāṭīʿ*-poetry remains no more than a tantalizing possibility.

The Aleppan wunderkind Badr ad-Dīn Ibn Ḥabīb (d. 779/1377) wrote *ash-Shudhūr*—a collection of nearly four-hundred *maqāṭīʿ* divided into seven thematic chapters—around 1326 when he was only seventeen or eighteen years old.[115] As ambitious as he was precocious, Ibn Ḥabīb then solicited commendations on the work (*taqārīẓ*, sing. *taqrīẓ*) from Ibn Nubātah and Ṣafī ad-Dīn al-Ḥillī, the two most prominent poets of his time and fellow *maqāṭīʿ*-composers.[116] In his commendation on the work, Ibn Nubātah wrote:[117]

«[...] وأطربتْ مقاطيعها المشبّبة فلم أدر أهي مقاطيع أم مواصيل [...]»

> [...] its erotic *maqāṭīʿ*-poems stirred the heart so I didn't know whether they were *maqāṭīʿ*-poems (or disconnected things: *maqāṭīʿ*) or flutes (or connected things: *mawāṣīl*)

And the colophon of the only surviving copy of Ibn Ḥabīb's *maqāṭīʿ*-collection reads:[118]

«تمّت المقاطيع المتهكّمة بالمواصيل ☆ وانتظمت الشذور الجميلة المشتملة

على الجمل والتفصيل [...]»

> the *maqāṭīʿ*-poems (or disconnected things), which mock flutes (or connected things), have come to an end * and the lovely fragments (*ash-shudhūr*) which include the bigger picture and the details have been strung together

The fourth of these pioneering collections, Ṣafī ad-Dīn al-Ḥillī's *Dīwān al-Mathālith wa-l-mathānī fī l-maʿālī wa-l-maʿānī* (*The Collection of Two-liners and*

115 See Bauer, "„Was kann aus dem Jungen noch werden!"". The collection was completed before 730/1329, when Ibn Nubātah visited Aleppo (ibid., 18). Interestingly Ibn Ḥabīb describes his own poems as *muqaṭṭaʿāt* (see Ibn Ḥabīb, *Tadhkirat an-nabīh*, 2:203; 2:216; 2:307; 3:298), but cf. in appendix, nos 13 and 15.

116 These commendations have been edited in Bauer, "„Was kann aus dem Jungen noch werden!""

117 Cited in Bauer, "„Was kann aus dem Jungen noch werden!"", 47, l. 8, edited from Bibliothèque Nationale (Paris) MS 3362, f. 204b–205a; see also in Ibn Ḥabib, *Tadhkirat an-nabīh*, 2:203.

118 Bibliothèque Nationale (Paris) MS 3362, f. 204a; see also Bauer, "„Was kann aus dem Jungen noch werden!"".

Three-liners on Virtues and Literary Motifs) was written sometime between 1331 and 1341.[119] It was dedicated to al-Malik al-Afḍal (r. 1332–41), the patron whom al-Ḥillī and Ibn Nubātah both served at the princely court in Hama. It is, as the title suggests, a collection of two and three-line *maqāṭīʿ*-poems—although there is no evidence that al-Ḥillī ever used the term himself—divided "quite precisely into twenty [thematic] chapters":[120]

الباب الأوّل في الأدبيات ☆ والفوائد الحكميات

Chapter One: On Politeness and Good Sense

الباب الثاني في الحماسة ☆ والفخر والرئاسة

Chapter Two: On Courage, Boasting, and Rule

الباب الثالث في الصفات ☆ ومحاسن التشبيهات

Chapter Three: On Attributes and Excellent Similes

الباب الرابع في الخمريات ☆ ونعت مجالس اللذّات

Chapter Four: Wine-poems and Descriptions of Pleasure-Parties

الباب الخامس في الغزل والنسيب ☆ ومطلق التشبيب

Chapter Five: Poems Erotic and Amatory

الباب السادس في التشبيب بغلمان مخصوصة بالاسماء والسمات ☆ والفنون والصفات

Chapter Six: Love Poems on Young men, specifically their Names and Characteristics and Various Types and Attributes

119 Bauer, "„Was kann aus dem Jungen noch werden!"", 19. The text has been published in a poor and bowdlerized edition by Muḥammad Ṭāhir al-Ḥimṣī (Damascus: Dār Saʿd ad-Dīn, 1998), based on Damascus Ẓāhiriyyah MS 3361. For the purposes of this study, I have relied on Bibliothèque Nationale (Paris) MS 3341. (See in the annotated bibliography: 14th century 2. a).

120 Bauer, "„Was kann aus dem Jungen noch werden!"", 19: "[…] [A]l-Ḥillī seinen Epigrammdīwān sehr minutiös in zwanzig Kapitel einteilt (ähnlich wie seinen „großen" Dīwān) […]". Translation: "[…] al-Ḥillī organized his epigram anthology very precisely into twenty chapters (just like his larger *Dīwān*) […]". The table of contents reproduced here is give on Bibliothèque Nationale (Paris) MS 3341, ff. 2b–3b. See also Bauer, "Dignity at Stake", 170–72. Compare the twelve chapters of al-Ḥillī's *Dīwān* (Ṣafī ad-Dīn ʿAbd al-ʿAzīz b. Sarāyā al-Ḥillī, *Dīwān*, 3 vols, ed. Muḥammad Ḥuwwar (Beirut: al-Muʾassasah al-ʿArabiyyah li-d-Dirāsāt wa-n-nashr, 2000), 1:38–9).

الباب السابع في المدح والثنا[ء] ☆ والشكر والهنا[ء]
Chapter Seven: On Praise and Tribute and Gratitude and Congratulations

الباب الثامن في الاخوانيات ☆ وصدور المراسلات
Chapter Eight: Poems for Peers and Correspondence

الباب التاسع في شكوى قرب الديار ☆ وبعد المزار
Chapter Nine: Complaining that Home isn't Near and that the Goal is Far

الباب العاشر في استنجاز الجواب ☆ عن مكاتبات الأصحاب
Chapter Ten: Asking for a Speedy Answer when Writing to Friends

الباب الحادي عشر في الاستزارة ☆ وشكر الزيارة
Chapter Eleven: Asking [Friends] to Visit and Thanking Guests for Coming

الباب الثاني عشر في الهدايا والاستهدا[ء] ☆ لمؤانسة الاودّا[ء]
Chapter Twelve: On Gifts and Seeking the Right Path to Keep Loved Ones Company

الباب الثالث عشر في استنجاز الوعود ☆ وطلب الموعود
Chapter Thirteen: Asking for the Fulfillment of Promises and for the Things that were Promised

الباب الرابع عشر في العتاب ☆ عن عدّة أسباب
Chapter Fourteen: Reproach for a Number of Reasons

الباب الخامس عشر في الاعتذار ☆ والاستعطاف والاستغفار
Chapter Fifteen: Expressing Regret and Seeking Sympathy and Forgiveness

الباب السادس عشر في الالغاز ☆ بطريق الايجاز
Chapter Sixteen: Riddles Abridged

الباب السابع عشر في التقييد ☆ لعلوم تفيد
Chapter Seventeen: Setting Down Useful Knowledge

الباب الثامن عشر في الاهاجي ☆ بلطيف التناجي
Chapter Eighteen: Invective Poems as Sweet as Whispered Conversation

الباب التاسع عشر في الهزل والإحماض ☆ لعدّة أغراض
Chapter Nineteen: Silly and Light-Hearted Poetry on a Number of Subjects

الباب العشرون في التزهّد ☆ والعفّة والتجرّد
Chapter Twenty: On Asceticism, Chastity, and Unworldliness

Later poets and anthologists were, if anything, more enthusiastic about using the term *maqāṭīʿ* to describe their work and to situate it within an emergent and flourishing genre. Ibn Abī Ḥajalah at-Tilimsānī (d. 776/1375) wrote a work that appears not to have survived with the title *Mawāṣīl al-maqāṭīʿ* (*Connected Disconnections* or *The Flutes of Maqāṭīʿ-poems*) and he devoted chapter twenty-seven of his *Dīwān aṣ-Ṣabābah* to "*maqāṭīʿ* and love lyrics on rosy cheeks, pomegranate breasts, etc."[121] In his anthological preview-cum-call for submissions entitled *Maghnāṭīs ad-durr an-nafīs* (*Attracting Priceless Pearls*), Ibn Abī Ḥajalah solicited contributions from male and female poets and writers of his day for an anthology he was planning along the lines of ath-Thaʿālibī's *Yatīmat ad-dahr* with the provisional title *Mujtabā l-udabā* [*sic*].[122] What is most remarkable about this remarkable text is that Ibn Abī Ḥajalah gave quite precise instructions about what information poets should send to him in Cairo to be included in the anthology-in-progress and among this was a sample of their *maqāṭīʿ*-poems:[123]

فاقول وبالله التوفيق المسئول من الواقف على هذه الرسالة ممّن دخل مغناها وعرف معناها وطالع دروسها ورشف كؤوسها من اهل هذه الصناعة وتجّار هذه البضاعة أن يكتب الى منشئها بالقاهرة المغربية المحروسة باسمه واسم ابيه وجدّه وحسبه ونسبه ومولده وبلده وذكر طرف مختار من شعره وجيد نثره وما يؤثر أن ينقل عنه من حكاية لطيفة ونادرة ظريفة ممّا رآه او رواه او روي عنه من اهل هذا الفنّ الى آخر هذا القرن حسب الطاقة ومن المعلوم أن الأديب لا يخلو من

121 On the lost *Mawāṣīl al-maqāṭīʿ*, see Ḥājjī Khalīfah, *Kitāb Kashf aẓ-ẓunūn ʿan asāmī al-kutub wa-l-funūn*, 2 vols, ed. Şerefettin Yaltkaya and Rifat Bilge (Istanbul: Maarif Matbaası, 1941) 2:1889; on *Dīwān aṣ-Ṣabābah*, see in appendix, no. 12.

122 The inclusion of female poets and writers is explicit (see Yale MS Landberg 69, f. 1b). On this work, see in the annotated bibliography, 14th century, 5. a, as well as a forthcoming article by Nefeli Papoutsakis whose presentation on this work I attended in Münster in April 2015 and from which I benefited greatly.

123 Yale MS Landberg 69, ff. 20b–21a.

[ق ٢١أ] هذه الفصول او بعضها وهي فصل في ذكر تصانيفه وتواليفه من فوائده العلمية ونكته الأدبية فصل في ذكر طرف مختار ممّا له من الفوائد الربّانية والمدائح النبوية فصل في ذكر طرف من ما له من المقاطيع الموصولة بالبديع فصل في ذكر ما له من الغزل ومخالفة من عذل فصل فيما له من المدائح وشكر المنائح[124] فصل في وفائه بحسن رثائه فصل في مجونه ونادر فنونه فصل في رياض منثوره وساجعات طيوره ونحو ذلك فهو إن كتب إليّ بهذه الفصول فصل واحد منها او مقطوع واحد او موشّحة او زجل او بلّيقا اوكان وكان ونحو ذلك كان ممدوحي وعديل روحي لا جَرَمَ إني أنوّه بذكره واجلو من بنات فكره وانظم ترجمته كالدرّ في السلوك [...]

I say—and it is only God who grants success—that the one who has come across this treatise and entered its abode and understood its meaning and examined its lessons and drunk from its cups is asked, if he is one of the masters of this trade and one who trades in this product, to write to its author in the Safeguarded, North African city of Cairo with his name and the names of his father and grandfather, giving his station and lineage, and his birthplace and hometown, as well as a pleasant selection of his poetry and worthy prose, and what he would like cited from the pleasant stories and amusing anecdotes he has experienced, or narrated, or have been said about him by the people of this art until this century comes to an end—if I make it, that is—and it goes without saying that a littérateur does not lack for [material for] these chapters, or some of them at any rate:

A chapter listing his works and what he has composed of scholarly wisdom and literary pleasantries

A chapter with a pleasant selection of his divine wisdom and poems in praise of the Prophet

124 The MS has *al-nāyiḥ* but it is clear from the parallelism and other headings in the text (e.g. f. 10b) that this should be *al-manāʾiḥ*

A chapter with a pleasant selection of his *maqāṭīʿ*-poems [or: disconnected things], which are connected to verbal artistry

A chapter giving his poetry on love and rebuking those who blame [him for loving]

A chapter giving his praise poems and poems of thanks for gifts

A chapter on his loyalty [as seen in] his elegies

A chapter on his obscene poems and more obscure compositions

A chapter on the gardens of his prose (*manthūr*, also gillyflowers) and the cooing (*sājiʿāt*, *sajʿ* = rhymed prose) of his birds, and so forth.

For if he were to write to me with these chapters or a single chapter, or a single *maqṭūʿ*-poem, or a *muwashshaḥah*, or a *zajal*, or a *bullayq*, or a *kān wa-kān*, and so on, he would be the object of my praise and the equal of my spirit, and there is no question that I will make him famous by mentioning him [in my anthology] and burnish the daughters of his mind [i.e. his thoughts] and string his biography onto this necklace like a pearl […]

Ibn Abī Ḥajalah also cited *maqāṭīʿ*-poems by Burhān ad-Dīn al-Qīrāṭī, Ibrāhīm al-Miʿmār, and himself in that work to give an idea of what the planned anthology would contain.[125] Ibn Abī Ḥajalah's contemporary and anthological subject Burhān ad-Dīn al-Qīrāṭī (d. 781/1379), a great admirer of Ibn Nubātah, was known for his *maqāṭīʿ*-poems as prefaces to recensions of his *Dīwān* make clear.[126] One of the collectors of al-Qīrāṭī's *Dīwān*, Ibn Ḥijjah al-Ḥamawī (d. 837/1434) also described some of the poetry included in Ibn aṣ-Ṣāʾigh's (d. 776/1375) response to Ibn Abī Ḥajalah at-Tilimsānī's work *Dīwān aṣ-Ṣabābah* as *maqāṭīʿ*.[127] We have already seen how Ibn Ḥajar al-ʿAsqalānī (d. 852/1449) used the term *maqāṭīʿ* to describe a chapter of poems in his own *Dīwān* as well as Ibn Nubātah's anthology *al-Qaṭr an-Nubātī*, but it also bears mentioning that it was a *maqṭūʿ*-poem that caused his falling out with the prolific anthologist Shams

125 See in appendix, no. 11.

126 See in appendix, nos 20–1. Ibn Ḥajar al-ʿAsqalānī wrote of al-Qīrāṭī that "he followed the path of Ibn Nubātah and was a student of his and a correspondent" (*ad-Durar al-kāminah*, 1:31, no. 77). See also Ibn Abī Ḥajalah at-Tilimsānī's comments on al-Qīrāṭī in his *Maghnāṭīs ad-durr an-nafīs* (see in appendix, no. 11a and further on this work in the annotated bibliography: 14th century, 5. a).

127 See in appendix, no. 24.

ad-Dīn an-Nawājī (d. 859/1455). The biographer as-Sakhāwī (d. 902/1497), who studied with both men, suggested that Ibn Ḥajar became angry with an-Nawājī when the latter included a *maqṭūʿ*-poem by the former in his well known oeno-anthology *Ḥalbat al-kumayt* (*The Racecourse of the Bay*).[128]

In the preface to that anthology, an-Nawājī wrote that he had gathered "a fine and elegant selection of *maqāṭīʿ*-poems on wine" and that was a pattern that he would deploy in many other poetry anthologies during his prolific career.[129] Indeed an-Nawājī may have been the most successful anthologist in the Mamluk period, which—as Thomas Bauer has argued—was a golden age of literary anthologies.[130] In anthologies like *Ḥalbat al-Kumayt*, *Marātiʿ al-ghizlān fī waṣf al-ḥisān min al-ghilmān* (*The Pastures of Gazelles: describing handsome young men*), *Khalʿ al-ʿidhār fī waṣf al-ʿidhār* (*Throwing Off Restraint in Describing Cheek-Down*), *Ṣaḥāʾif al-ḥasanāt fī waṣf al-khāl* (*Surfaces of Beauty Marked with Descriptions of Beauty-Marks*), and other rhetorical works, an-Nawājī perfected the format of the popular, engaging, and entertaining multi-authored *maqāṭīʿ*-collection.[131] His success no doubt encouraged the efforts of his younger contemporaries Shihāb ad-Dīn as-Suʿūdī (d. 870/1466), Shihāb ad-Dīn al-Ḥijāzī al-Khazrajī (d. 875/1471), and Taqī ad-Dīn al-Badrī (d. 894/1489).[132] As-Suyūṭī recorded that as-Suʿūdī and an-Nawājī exchanged riddles in verse and it is clear from the text of these poems that they were *maqāṭīʿ*-poems:[133]

---

128 See in appendix, no. 41b. Ibn Ḥajar was not a puritan, at least when it came to poetry, see, for example, a *mujūn* poem by him below (on p. 146–47) and further in Bauer, "Ibn Ḥajar and the Arabic *ghazal* of the Mamluk Age". The translation of the title of an-Nawājī's anthology is taken from Geert Jan van Gelder, "A Muslim Encomium on Wine: *The Racecourse of the Bay* (*Ḥalbat al-kumayt*) by al-Nawāǧī (d. 859/1455) as a post-classical Arabic work", *Arabica* 42:2 (June 1995).

129 See in appendix, no. 30.

130 There are, for example, at least twenty-four surviving MSS of an-Nawājī's erotic *maqāṭīʿ*-anthology, *Marātiʿ al-ghizlān fī waṣf al-ḥisān min al-ghilmān* (*The Pastures of Gazelles: describing handsome young men*); this betokens an uncommon popularity. (See further in the annotated bibliography: 15th century, 3. c). See also Thomas Bauer, "Literarische Anthologien der Mamlūkenzeit" in *Die Mamlūken: Studien zu ihrer Geschichte und Kultur: zum Gedenken an Ulrich Haarmann, 1942–1999*, ed. S. Conermann and A. Pistor-Hatam (Hamburg, 2003).

131 See in appendix, nos 30–4.

132 See in appendix, nos 36–40.

133 Jalāl ad-Dīn as-Suyūṭī, *Naẓm al-ʿiqyān fī aʿyān al-aʿyān*, ed. Philip Hitti (New York, NY: Syrian-American Press, 1927), 37.

وقال ملغّزًا في بلقينة وكتب به الى الاديب شمس الدين النواجي: [من السريع]

يا بلدةً غرّاءَ في بَعْضِها جاريةٌ تَشْدو بِصَوْتٍ رَطيبْ

والقلبُ منها إنْ تأمّلْتَهُ وصفٌ لِمن باتَ ضَجيعَ ٱلحَبيبْ

فأجابه النواجي: [من السريع]

يا سيّدًا أَهَلَّني لُغْزُهُ في بَلْدَةٍ يأوي الَيْها ٱلغَريبْ

تَصْحيفُها مِنْكَ تَلَقَّيْتُهُ وَهْيَ ٱلتي سادَتْ بِحِبْرٍ نَجيبْ

He sent a riddle-poem on Bulqaynah[134] *to Shams ad-Dīn an-Nawājī:*

O magnificent city, somewhere inside you
    A servant-girl sings softly,
and the heart/reverse of one who [hears] her, if you could spy it
    [would look] just like [the heart] of someone who'd finally climbed into bed with his beloved

And an-Nawājī answered him:

O master whose riddle appeared to me,
    in this city where strangers take refuge.
I received (*talaqqaytuhu*) your jumble
    for it is the one that prevailed [in its] noble ink.

The key to solving the riddle of as-Suʿūdī's poem lies in the first word in the second line: *qalb*. Meaning both "heart" and "reversal (of letters)", *qalb* is a clue in riddle-poems that signals how the conundrum's solution should be deduced.[135] In this case, the solution is "Happy of heart" (*haniyy*^{u} [scil. *hanī*ʾ] *qalb*^{in}), a phrase that is formed by the same letters (scil. the consonants and long vowels) that spell the name of the town Bulqaynah but in reverse order.[136]

134 Presently in Egypt's Gharbiyyah Governorate.

135 See Cachia, *The Arch Rhetorician*, no. 59.

136 The solution could also be "Come to me, heart" (*tinī qalbu*), but I find the other suggested answer more probable. In any case, both suggested solutions should be taken as provisional.

بُلَقَيْنَةَ ↔ هَنِيٌّ قَلْبٍ

An-Nawājī's response includes its own wordplay, signaled by the word in the same position as the signal-word in the original poem. *Taṣḥīf* (l. 2, hemistich 1) is a form of paronomasia in which words of the same shape, but different pointing, are juxtaposed.[137]

تلقّيته → ٮلڡٮٮه ← بلقينة

Shihāb ad-Dīn Aḥmad b. Muḥammad al-Ḥijāzī al-Khazrajī (790/1388–875/1471), one of the literary lights of the 15th century, wrote several important collections of amatory *maqāṭīʿ*-poems, including *Jannat al-wildān fī l-ḥisān min al-ghilmān* (*The Paradise of Youths: on handsome young men*[138]) *Kunnas al-jawārī fī l-ḥisān min al-jawārī* (*The Withdrawing Celestial Bodies: on pretty young women*[139]), *Nadīm al-kaʾīb wa-ḥabīb al-ḥabīb* (*The Sullen one's Companion and the Beloved one's Beloved*), and *al-Lumaʿ ash-Shihābiyyah min al-burūq al-Ḥijāziyyah* (*Flashes of meteor/Shihāb in the Ḥijāzī lightning-storm*) as well as a larger prosimetric anthology, *Rawḍ al-ādāb* (*The Garden of Literary Arts*), completed in 826/1423.[140] The latter anthology is divided, in the first instance, into five parts based on form, and then further sub-divided along formalistic and thematic lines.

Part One: Long poems	الباب الأوّل في المطوّلات
Part Two: Zajal and Muwashshaḥ poetry	الباب الثاني في الازجال والموشّحات
Part Three: *Maqāṭīʿ*-poems	الباب الثالث في المقاطيع

---

137 See Cachia, *The Arch Rhetorician*, no. 36.

138 The first phrase in the title, "*jannat al-wildān*" ("The Paradise of Youths"), is an allusion to Qurʾan *al-Wāqiʿah* 56:17 : «*yaṭūfu ʿalayhim wildānun mukhalladūn*» ("immortal youths going round about them", trans. Arberry, *The Koran Interpreted*, 2:254). See in appendix, no. 36.

139 The first phrase in the title, "*kunnas al-jawārī*" ("The Withdrawing Celestial Bodies"), is an allusion to Qurʾan *at-Takwīr* 81:16: «*al-Jawāri l-kunnas*» ("the runners, the sinkers", trans. Arberry, *The Koran Interpreted*, 2:326).

140 On the author, see as-Suyūṭī, *Naẓm al-ʿiqyān*, 63–77, no. 42; *idem*, *Kitāb Ḥusn al-muḥāḍarah fī akhbār Miṣr wa-l-Qāhirah*, 2 vols (Cairo: Maṭbaʿat al-Mawsūʿāt, 1321/1903), 1:275. On this rich—and still unpublished—anthology, see in the annotated bibliography: 15th century, 6. a.

Part Four: Prose pieces الباب الرابع في النثريات

Part Five: Stories الباب الخامس في الحكايات

The section on *maqāṭīʿ*-poems (Part Three) is further sub-divided into ten chapters, demonstrating the thematic promiscuity of *maqāṭīʿ*-poems and highlighting an ambivalent attitude toward strictly formalistic classification in the tradition. The themes in Part Three are greatly varied and range from the ekphrastic, satiric, erotic, and bacchic-cum-sympotic to the less commonly represented panegyric, riddling, obscene, invective, and elegiac.[141]

Chapter One: Panegyric الفصل الأوّل في المديح

الفصل الثاني في الحسان من الغلمان وهو على قسمين
Chapter Two: On pretty male youths, with two sub-sections

القسم الأوّل في الغزل ووصف المحاسن
Section One: On love and descriptions of beauty

القسم الثاني في الوظائف والصنائع والحرف والأوصاف والاسماء
Section Two: On professions, trades, crafts, features, and names

الفصل الثالث في الحسان من الجواري وهو على قسمين
Chapter Three: On pretty young women, with two sub-sections

القسم الأوّل في النسيب ووصف المحاسن
Section one: On love and descriptions of beauty

القسم الثاني في الوظائف والصنائع والحرف والأوصاف والاسماء
Section two: On professions, trades, crafts, features, and names

الفصل الرابع في الغزل المطلق والدمع والخيال والعبرة وطول الليل وقصره
Chapter Four: On love, tears, specters, weeping, and long and short nights

الفصل الخامس في الخمر والسقاة وما يناسب هذا الباب
Chapter Five: On wine and cup-bearers, and everything related

141 Chapter headings are given, *inter alia*, in British Library MS Add 19489, f. 52b; 54a; 69a; 81b; 88b [scil. 87b]; 92a [scil. 91a]; 100b [scil. 99b]; 107a [scil. 106a]; 116b [scil. 115b]; 118b [scil. 117b]; 122a [scil. 121a]; and 123a [scil. 122a]; also listed in Princeton MS Garrett 145H, ff. 1b–2a.

الفصل السادس في الرياض والمياه والنواعير والزهور والفواكه وما يناسب ذلك
Chapter Six: On gardens, water, water-wheels, flowers, fruit, and everything related

Chapter Seven: Riddles — الفصل السابع في الألغاز

Chapter Eight: Libertine poems — الفصل الثامن في المجون

Chapter Nine: Invective poems — الفصل التاسع في الأهاجي

Chapter Ten: Elegiac poems — الفصل العاشر في المراثي

Here, as in the collected poems of Ibn Ḥajar al-ʿAsqalānī, *maqāṭīʿ*-poems are first singled out based on a loose formalistic criterion: length, which despite being a vague and subjective measure is clearly correlated across the tradition. In Part Three, which is devoted to *maqāṭīʿ*-poems the average poem length is 2.04 lines. Two-line poems make up 96% of the total poems and account for 94% of the total verses in that part of the text.[142]

	Total number of poems	Total number of verses
Part Three (total)	928	1894
Two-Liners	893	1786
Three-Liners	32	96
Four-Liners	3	12

Within this loose grouping, the *maqāṭīʿ*-poems are then sub-divided along thematic lines, with the clear distinction that *maqāṭīʿ* are categorically different from other strict and acknowledged forms like *muwashshaḥ* and *zajal*, etc. A similar sort of classification is applied in al-Ḥijāzī al-Khazrajī's *Dīwān* as well. In the Escorial Library mansucript of his collected poetry and prose entitled *al-Lumaʿ ash-Shihābiyyah min al-burūq al-Ḥijāziyyah*, the contents are presented as follows:[143]

Section One: Verse, in eight types — النوع الأوّل المنظوم وهو ثمانية فنون

142 These statistics and those provided in the table above are based on British Library MS Add 19489.

143 Escorial MS árabe 475, ff. 3a–4b. (See in the annotated bibliography: 15th century, 6. d).

الفنّ الأوّل الشعر وفيه أربعة أبواب
Type One: Poetry, in four categories

الباب الأوّل في القصائد والمراسلات
Category One: Long poems and epistolary poems

الباب الثاني في الاراجيز
Category Two: *Rajaz*-poems

الباب الثالث في المقاصير
Category Three: Constrained poems[144]

الباب الرابع في المقاطيع وفيه خمسة فصول
Category Four: *Maqāṭīʿ*-poems, in five chapters

الفصل الأوّل في الاقتباس وهو مفرد بتصنيف
Chapter One: Poems with Qurʾanic quotations (this chapter is not subdivided) [ff. 156a–164b]

الفصل الثاني في الحسان من الغلمان وهو مفرد بتصنيف
Chapter Two: Poems on handsome male youths (this chapter is not subdivided) [ff. 165a–184b]

الفصل الثالث في الحسان من الجواري وهو مفرد بتصنيف
Chapter Three: Poems on pretty female youths (this chapter is not subdivided) [ff. 184b–193a]

الفصل الرابع في الاهاجي وهو مفرد بتصنيف
Chapter Four: Invective Poems (this chapter is not subdivided) [ff. 193b–198a]

الفصل الخامس في معانٍ شتّى
Chapter Five: Poems on sundry themes [ff. 198b–204b]

الفنّ الثاني الموشّح
Type Two: *Muwashshaḥ* poetry

الفنّ الثالث الزجل
Type Three: *Zajal* poetry

الفنّ الرابع المواليا
Type Four: *Mawāliyā* poetry

144 The poems in this chapter are not short poems but "constrained" poems (compare *luzūmiyyāt*), which achieve various mannerist constraints, i.e. the rhyme letter proceeds in alphabetical order over the course of the poem or a homograph is used in a poem in all its different meanings.

Type Five: *Dūbayt* poetry	الفنّ الخامس الدوبيت
Type Six: *Kān wa-kān* poetry	الفنّ السادس كان وكان
Type Seven: *Qūmā* poetry	الفنّ السابع القوما
Type Eight: *Ḥammāq* poetry	الفنّ الثامن الحماق
Section Two: Prose, in six parts	النوع الثاني في المنثور وفيه ستّة ابواب
Part One: Sermons	الباب الأوّل في الخُطَب
Part Two: Marriage Contracts	الباب الثاني في صدور الأصْدِقَة
Part Three: Correspondence	الباب الثالث في المُراسلات
Part Four: Certificates of Learning	الباب الرابع في الاجائز
Part Five: Riddles	الباب الخامس في الالغاز
Part Six: Miscellaneous	الباب السادس في اشياء شتّى

Shihāb ad-Dīn al-Ḥijāzī al-Khazrajī also wrote a *taqrīẓ* (or commendation) for Taqī ad-Dīn al-Badrī's (d. 894/1489) large, and still unedited, collection of erotic *maqāṭīʿ*-poems, *Ghurrat aṣ-ṣabāḥ fī waṣf al-wujūh aṣ-ṣibāḥ* (*The Flash of Dawn: beautiful faces described*), as did ʿAbd al-Barr b. Shiḥnah (d. 921/1515), who would later become chief Ḥanafī judge in Cairo.[145] This large collection of erotic and ekphrastic poetry on handsome young men and women is divided into seventeen chapters:[146]

الباب الأوّل: في الاسما ☆ والقاب الرشأ الألمى

Chapter One: On names and the epithets of the red-lipped fawn

الباب الثاني: في المتجنّسين ☆ من الملاح المتحسّنين

Chapter Two: On the various types of prettified beauties

145 See in appendix, no. 40a. On this work, see in the annotated bibliography: 15th century, 9. a.

146 British Library MS ADD 23445, ff. 4b–5b.

الباب الثالث: في وصف لباس ☆ غزلان الكناس
Chapter Three: On descriptions of clothing [worn by] the gazelles in the thicket

الباب الرابع: اصحاب الرئاسة ☆ وارباب المناصب والسياسة
Chapter Four: On rulers, post-holders, and officials

الباب الخامس: في اصحاب الردائع ☆ وارباب الوقائع
Chapter Five: On defenders and attackers

الباب السادس: في اصحاب الرماية ☆ وارباب الصيد والدراية
Chapter Six: On archers, hunters, and prudent ones

الباب السابع: في اصحاب الوظائف ☆ وذوي اللطائف
Chapter Seven: On those who work and those who tell charming tales

الباب الثامن: في اصحاب المتاجر ☆ وارباب الجواهر
Chapter Eight: On those who own shops and those who trade in jewels

الباب التاسع: في اصحاب الصنائع ☆ وارباب البضائع
Chapter Nine: On tradespeople and traders

الباب العاشر: في المتسبّبين ☆ من السوقا [هكذا] والمتعيّشين
Chapter Ten: On small traders from the rabble and those who scrape by

الباب الحادي عشر: في اصحاب فواكه الصدور ☆ وارباب اطباق الزهور
Chapter Eleven: On the fruit-breasted and those who bear trays of flowers

الباب الثاني عشر: في سقاة الحَسان ☆ ووصف ذوي الالحان
Chapter Twelve: On handsome wine-pourers and descriptions of songsters

الباب الثالث عشر: في وصف المليح ☆ وما في محاسنه من المديح
Chapter Thirteen: On attractive ones and their praiseworthy qualities

الباب الرابع عشر: في [المبتدأين] الذين تحزّ اليهم الجوارح ☆ وارباب الجرائح
Chapter Fourteen: On [naifs] who are attacked by predators and wounded people

الباب الخامس عشر: في غزلان مختلفة ☆ وملاح محتلفة

Chapter Fifteen: On divided gazelles and allied beauties

الباب السادس عشر: في ما أبداه الحال ☆ من وصف الخال

Chapter Sixteen: What has been revealed about depictions of beauty-marks

الباب السابع عشر: في مدح العارض الهاتن ☆ ووصف العذار الفاتن

Chapter Seventeen: In praise of the gushing rain-cloud: on descriptions of alluring beard-down

This collection, like others on the subject, follows a tradition of erotic *maqāṭīʿ*-collections by others such as ath-Thaʿālibī, Ibn ash-Sharīf Daftarkh-ʷān, aṣ-Ṣafadī, Ibn al-Wardī, and an-Nawājī.

Shams ad-Dīn an-Nawājī also taught two scholars who are well known today for their biographical and historical works, Shams ad-Dīn Muḥammad b. ʿAbd ar-Raḥmān as-Sakhāwī (d. 902/1497) and Yūsuf Ibn Taghrībirdī (d. 874/1470). As-Sakhāwī is notable not only for his connection to both Ibn Ḥajar al-ʿAsqalānī and an-Nawājī mentioned above, but also for having used the term *maqāṭīʿ* repeatedly in his biographical dictionary of 9th-century (AH) notables.[147] In one of these entries, as-Sakhāwī reported that Ibn Taghrībirdī "composed an anthology called *Ḥilyat aṣ-ṣifāt fī l-asmāʾ wa-ṣ-ṣināʿāt* (*An Ornament of Description on Names and Professions*) made up of *maqāṭīʿ*-poems, historical accounts, and literary anecdotes organized alphabetically".[148] This text has never been edited, although it survives in two manuscripts, only one of which I have been allowed to access.[149] The introduction to the work is made available here for the first time:[150]

147 See in appendix, no. 41.

148 Muḥammad b. ʿAbd ar-Raḥmān as-Sakhāwī, *aḍ-Ḍawʾ al-lāmiʿ li-ahl al-qarn at-tāsiʿ*, 12 vols (Cairo: Maktabat al-Qudsī, 1353–55/1934–36), 10:307–8. Original quotation cited in appendix (no. 41f).

149 See in the annotated bibliography: 15th century, 7. a.

150 Ibn Taghrībirdī, *Ḥilyat aṣ-ṣifāt*, Raza Library (Rampur) MS 4373, ff. 3b–4a.

بسم الله الرحمٰن الرحيم ربّ تِمِّمْ بخير

الحمد لله الذي أحسن ابتدا[ء] خلقنا بصنعه ☆ و[أولا نا][151] من جزيل النعم بفضله ومنّه ☆ نشكره شكر مَن عرف بديع صفاته فهامَ في المحبّة ☆ وتحوّط باسمائه فصار سالِمًا من كلّ نقمة ☆ الذي وهب لأولى الالباب محاسن الاداب وملك اهل الأدب زمام البراعة ☆ وأطلعهم على سرّ الصِناعة ☆ فملأت للسامع درّها ☆ فيا لله دَرُّها ☆ وقلّدت الاجياد في نحرها ☆ والصحيح أنّها نافثة من سحرها ☆ وموصول الصلاة والسلام على المقطوع بشرف نبوّته ☆ محمد خير خلق الله وصفوته ☆ وعلى آله واصحابه وشيعته ☆ والمستمسكين بحبل شريعته ☆ وبعد:

فقد ألّفتُ هذا المجموع على حبّ الطاقة على معنىً خَطَرَ لي ☆ لا لشيء عَرَضَ لي ☆ بل الفراغ والشبيبة ☆ تُلجئ المرءَ محلَّ الرِّيبة ☆ وذكرتُ عدّة مقاطيع من ابيات فِصاح ☆ في الصِناعات واسماء الملاح ☆ على أنّي أوردتُ فيه من واهي كلام الشعراء ما لا يُعجبني لامتهانه ☆ وانحطاطه عن كمال رتبة البلاغة ونقصانه ☆ حيث لم أجد في ذلك المقصد من النظم الرائق العالي ☆ ولا ظفرتُ في ذلك المعنى بما أرتجيه من اللفظ الفائق الغالي ☆ ولا بدَّ من ذكر بيتين في كلّ صفةٍ او اسمٍ مشهور ☆ فما وقع لي فيه [انْ لا] أكتبه وانا في ذلك معذور ☆ لقلّة نظم الشعراء في [ق ١٤أ] هذا المعنى ولمقتضاه ☆ وأنسبه لناظمه فقد أعجبه وارتضاه ☆ ولا أبرئ هذا التأليف من زللٍ وإن طاب مورده الزلال ☆ ولا أنزّهه من خللٍ وإن حوى أحسن الخلال ☆ وسميّته حلية الصفات ☆ في الاسماء والصناعات ☆ وما قارب او شابه هذا المعنى ورتّبتُهُ على الحروف ليسهِّل فيه المُطالَعة

151 This reading is provisional because the MS is unclear here.

In the name of God, the most merciful, the most compassionate. Lord bring [this work] to its end without incident.

Praise be to God who excelled at the beginning of our creation with His handiwork * and [brought us] near to His great munificence through His generosity and grace * We thank Him as one who recognizes His unparalleled qualities and has fallen in love with Him * and has been encircled by His names and is thus protected from any evil deed * He who has made a gift of the advantages of the social arts (*ādāb*) to those who perceive and who has entrusted the practitioners of those arts with the reins of skill * And let them in on the secret of the craft * [its pearls have filled the ears of listeners] * and by God, how excellent they are! * [and have decorated the necks of the steeds] * The truth [of the matter] is that they emerge from its magic * Prayers and blessings without end for the one who stands alone, honored by his prophecy * Muḥammad, God's greatest creation and the purest * And [prayers and blessings] for his family and companions, and those who follow him * And those who cling firmly to the laws he handed down * Now to the matter at hand:

I composed this collection because I wanted to work on an idea that occurred to me * not for some other reason that was proposed to me * Spare time and a youthful spirit * cause one to take shelter in perilous territory * I cited several *maqāṭīʿ*-poems of eloquent verse * on the trades and the names of handsome youths * I found some feeble verses by poets on the topic, which didn't please me because they were so shoddy * and because they fell so short of the mark of perfect eloquence * When I failed to find verse on a given topic that was superb and fluent * unable to satisfy my desire for something outstanding and brilliant * and because it was necessary to cite a couplet for every prominent trade or name * I had no choice but to compose one myself and for that I cannot be blamed * because the poets have so rarely composed on this matter and all related * I attribute verses to their authors and [I hope] that pleases them * I do not contend that this work is immune from errors even if sweet water flows from it * and I do not claim that it is free from shortcomings even if it contains the greatest attributes * and I titled it *An Ornament of Description * on Names and Professions* * and anything related or similar to that topic and I organized it alphabetically to facilitate consultation

☆ وتحصيل الغرض منه ولم أذكر فيه من القصائد المطوّلات غير قصيدة بارعة ☆ أذكر ذلك في آخر كلّ حرفٍ يكتب بعد فراغ المقاطيع التي أوردتُها ☆ أختم بها الحرف المذكور وإن كانت في غير ما نحن فيه من الشروط التي ألزمتها ☆ وأذكر ايضًا بعض من يحضرني في مولده ووفاته شاعرًا كان او عالِمًا أديب ☆ عندما أذكر شيئًا من نظمه مرّة واحدة من غير تكرار ولا ترتيب ☆ وإن وقع لي ايضًا مِن شعر مَن مَضَتْ ترجمته ثانيا ☆ أذكره وأنسبه له من غير ترجمة ولم أكن في هذا متوانيا ☆ لأنّ المقصود في هذا المجموع غير تاريخ شعر الزمان ☆ وهو إيراد ما تقدّم ذكره من مقاطيع الشعراء وبالله المستعان

* and achieve its intended goal; I have not cited any long poems except for one outstanding long poem * at the end of every alphabetical chapter after the *maqāṭīʿ*-poems that I cite * to conclude the alphabetical chapter and even though it goes beyond the rubric I followed [in composing this] * I also record the birth and death dates of some of my contemporaries whether poets or littérateurs * when I cite some verses by him, but only once—no more—and in no particular order * and if I cite verses by someone whose biography has already been presented * then I give the attribution but [do not repeat] the biography and not because I'm lazy * but because the point of this collection isn't to write a history of contemporary poetry * rather to present *maqāṭīʿ*-poems by poets, as was previously mentioned; I take refuge in God

The book is for the most part a collection of *maqāṭīʿ*-poetry, as the title suggests, on trades and characteristics of urban people as well as biographical information about the poets cited. The following poems give some idea of the collection's thematic diversity and playfulness, as well as the rich urban tapestry that it sought to represent.

[ا]بن نباتة له في محتسب   [من المتقارب]

تُهَنَّأُ بِها حِسْبَةٌ أُدْرِكَتْ   بأيّامِ فَضْلِكَ ما تُرْتَقَبْ
فإنَّكَ من أُسْرَةٍ تُصْطَفَى   وتُرْزَقُ من حَيْثُ لا تُحْتَسَبْ

Ibn Nubātah on a market inspector:[152]

Be congratulated on this appointment that came
  unexpectedly during blessed days [of repose].
For you are from a chosen family,
  and how you earn your money, no one knows!

[ا]بن الصائغ له في لوطي: [من السريع]

رُبَّ فتًى في عَصْرِنا لا يَطِي   تِجارةَ ٱلعِلْقِ بِهِ لا تَبورْ
مُنْهَتِكٌ يقْصُدُ أنْ يَخْتَفي   مع أنّه ما زالَ يَبْغي ٱلظُّهورْ

Ibn aṣ-Ṣāʾigh on a sodomite:[153]

How many a young man these days fails to hide that—
  as long as he's around—the faggot trade will remain «a constant profit».[154]
A degenerate, he wants so badly to hide it,
  but he still lusts after rears.

152 Ibn Taghrībirdī, *Ḥilyat aṣ-ṣifāt*, Raza Library (Rampur) MS 4373, f. 135a. This poem does not appear in the poet's printed *Dīwān*.

153 Ibn Taghrībirdī, *Ḥilyat aṣ-ṣifāt*, Raza Library (Rampur) MS 4373, f. 132a.

154 The concluding phrase is an allusion to Qur'an *Fāṭir* 35:29 : "*inna -lladhīna yatlūna kitāb Allāh wa-aqāmū ṣ-ṣālah wa-anfaqū mimmā razaqnāhum sirran wa-ʿalāniyatan yarjūna tijāratan lan tabūr*".

[ا]بن الوردي له في امرأة تهوى السحاق: [من السريع]

قولوا لِمَن تَهوى السِّحاقَ ٱلذي   حَرَّمَهُ ٱلشَّرْعُ وما فيهِ خيرْ
أخْطأتِ يا كامِلَةَ ٱلحُسْنِ إذْ   أَقَمْتِ إسحاقَ مقامَ ٱلزُّبَيْرْ

Ibn al-Wardī on a woman who enjoys having sex with other women:[155]

Tell the one who can't get enough of lesbian sex (*siḥāq*), which
divine law forbids and is devoid of all that is good:
"You missed the mark, O perfect beauty, when
you put Isḥāq in the place of az-Zubayr!"

The punchline in the final hemistich of this poem depends on two name-puns: the name Isḥāq sounds like the word for lesbian sex (*siḥāq*) and the name az-Zubayr is a homonym of the word for "tiny penis" (*zubayr*, dimunitive of *zubr*, "penis"). This poem is followed by another poem—this time a *mawāliyā*—on the same topic by an unnamed poet.[156]

غيره في المعنى مواليا: [مواليا]

ستّي ٱلكبيرة لها الخدّام والحِشْمَة   تحلف على النيك بالمُصْحَف وبالخَتْمَة
جاها ٱلطَّواشي لَوْلَها نالَ مِنْ كِلْمَة   راحَتْ يَمينُ ٱلقواقية عَلَى قَرْمَة

Another poet has a mawāliyā on the same topic:

My lady has servants and attendants;[157]
when it comes to fucking, she swears on the Qur'an and her signet.

155 Ibn Taghrībirdī, *Ḥilyat aṣ-ṣifāt*, Raza Library (Rampur) MS 4373, f. 34a. On this topic, see Sahar Amer, "Medieval Arab Lesbians and Lesbian-Like Women", *Journal of the History of Sexuality* 18:2 (May 2009).

156 Ibn Taghrībirdī, *Ḥilyat aṣ-ṣifāt*, Raza Library (Rampur) MS 4373, f. 34a. Also recorded in 'Alā' ad-Dīn 'Alī b. 'Abd Allāh al-Ghuzūlī, *Maṭāli' al-budūr fī manāzil as-surūr*, 2 vols (Cairo: Maṭba'at Idārat al-Waṭan, 1299–1300/1882–83), 1:34 (with the variant in l. 2, hemistich 1: *'afḥashat law nāla* instead of *law lahā nāla*) and Ibn Ḥijjah al-Ḥamawī, *Khizānat al-adab wa-ghāyat al-arab*, 5 vols, ed. Kawkab Diyāb (Beirut: Dār Ṣādir, 2001), 3:532 (with similar variant *'afshakhat*, as well as *al-ḥurmah* for *al-ḥishmah* in l. 1, hemistich 1). The *mawāliyā* form is written in a modified *Basīṭ* meter (see EI^2, s.v. "*Mawāliyā*" [P. Cachia]).

157 The word *ḥishmah* can mean both "decorum, modesty" or "retinue" (viz. *ḥasham*). The second seems the likelier meaning in this case.

When the eunuchs go to her, if any of them should say a word to her [about it],
then lurch's right hand goes on the chopping block!

لبعضهم على لسان الاطفال [مواليا]

يا مَنْ وَصا لولا طْفالُ ٱلمحَبّةْ بَحّ قَتَلْتِني بالتَّحامي آهْ أو آهْ احْ

صَيَّرْتَ في ٱلقلبِ وَاْوَاْ والتَّصَبّرْ بَحّ كلُّ ٱلْوَرى بِعّ في عيني وشَخْصَكْ دحْ

A poet [using] baby talk[158]

You told me if it weren't for kids, love would be all gone! (*baḥḥ*)
You shunned me to death with your ow and arghs (*āh-aw-āh*), hot ouch! (*aḥḥ*)
And you made a boo-boo (*wāwā*) in my heart and my wits are now all gone! (*baḥḥ*).
Everyone else is uh-oh (*biʿʿ*) to me, but you I wuv (*daḥḥ*)!

غيره في المعنى: [مواليا]

ربّيتُكُمْ كِخّ سِوائِي بَقيتُواْ دَحّ أَحُذُكُمْ البِعّ مِنّي واصطباري بَحّ

فاه اواه ان زرتمْ وزال الوح طيفتكم بُفّ وَبِما وحت النح

Another poet [using] the same technique:[159]

I raised you icky (*kikhkh*), but despite me you turned out all right (*daḥḥ*).
I warned you, "step over this line, and you'll get a boo-boo (*biʿʿ*)." My patience had gone bye-bye (*baḥḥ*).

---

158 Ibn Taghrībirdī, *Ḥilyat aṣ-ṣifāt*, Raza Library (Rampur) MS 4373, f. 132a. On Arabic baby talk, see Charles A. Ferguson, "Arabic Baby Talk" in *Structuralist Studies in Arabic Linguistics. Charles A. Ferguson's Papers, 1954–1994*, ed. R. Kirk Belknap and Niloofar Haeri (Leiden: Brill, 1997) and several entries in Martin Hinds and El-Said Badawi, *A Dictionary of Egyptian Arabic: Arabic-English* (Beirut: Librairie du Liban, 1986). Many of the baby-talk words in this poem and those that follow are still used in Cairo today. That being said, we know very little about baby talk in the period and these translations should be taken as highly provisional.

159 Ibn Taghrībirdī, *Ḥilyat aṣ-ṣifāt*, Raza Library (Rampur) MS 4373, f. 132a.

> So boo hoo (*āh-aw-āh*) if, by the time you'd arrived, the meal [?] (*waḥḥ*)[160] was all finished.
> Your visiting specters are din-din (*buff*) and the message they brought was yum (*naḥḥ*).

This specifc style of poetry, *mawāliyā*-poems using baby talk and rhyming in -*aḥḥ*, seem to have been a trend, as can be seen from the inclusion of another such poem—this time a five-line *mawāliyā aʿraj* by Ibn Ḥajar al-ʿAsqalānī—in the margin of a manuscript of ʿAbd ar-Raḥmān aṣ-Ṣaftī's (d. 1264/1848) *Talāqī l-arab fī marāqī l-adab* (*Meeting One's Desire while Scaling the Literary Heights*):[161]

وللحافظ ابن حجر[:] [مواليا]

يَـا مَنْ سَكَنْ فِي ٱلحَشَـا والقَـلْبُ وَاوَا أَحّْ
غَـيْرِي تَوَاصَـلْ ونَـالِي مِنْ وِصَـالكْ بَحّْ
البُـفّْ أُطْعِـمْكَ والنَّنَـمْ وقُولَتْ نَحّْ
يَـا لِلعَجَـبْ مَنْ بِخَـتِي عَـلِّمَ ٱلأَطْفَـالْ
بُعْبُـعْ أَنَـا كِخّْ يَـا فَـتَى وغَـيْرِي دَحّْ

> You're holed up inside of me, while my heart has a boo-boo (*wāwā*), hot ouch! (*aḥḥ*)
> Others have had union with you, but my share of union went bye-bye (*baḥḥ*).
> I feed you snackies (*buff*) and food (*namnam*) and how to say yummie (*naḥḥ*)!
> What a sight! Someone as fortunate as me [reduced to] teaching children.
> Am I the bogeyman (*buʿbuʿ*)—eww (*kikhkh*!)—boy? And all the others swell (*daḥḥ*)?

We have seen that by the 8th/14th century, *maqāṭīʿ*-poetry had become established as a genre in its own right and by the 9th/15th century, the new terminological meaning of the word had become unmistakable. The term

---

160 Compare the word *ʾuḥḥ* ("something hot") included by Charles A. Ferguson in his list of baby talk terms (see Ferguson, "Arabic Baby Talk", 181; 184).

161 Riyadh University Library MS 152, f. 21b. See further in the annotated bibliography: 19th century, 2. a.

maqāṭīʿ would continue to be used in subsequent centuries by poets and anthologists including Ibn al-Jiʿān (d. 882/1477), Jalāl ad-Dīn as-Suyūṭī (d. 911/1505), al-Maqqarī (d. 1041/1632), Najm ad-Dīn al-Ghazzī (d. 1061/1651), Ḥājjī Khalīfah (d. 1068/1657), al-Murādī (d. 1206/1791), ash-Shawkānī (d. 1250/1834), Aḥmad Taymūr Bāshā (1871–1930), and many others.[162] While paratextual evidence and the analysis of individual *maqāṭīʿ*-poems themselves is an important plank in the argument for the recognition of this new genre, the next chapter will demonstrate that it was in the anthology that *maqāṭīʿ*-poems truly came into their own.

162 Examples of these usages are cited in the appendix.

CHAPTER 2

The Sum of its Parts

As early as the 14th-century, *Maqāṭīʿ*-poems were brought together in large poetry collections or anthologies, which remain the main context in which we encounter them today.[1] Indeed, one could say that before *maqāṭīʿ*-poems were anthologized—before context singled them out as a distinct form of short poetry in Arabic—they could not be recognized, could not be identified as a new and distinct genre. Scholars of Arabic literature have long been interested in Arabic poetry anthologies, especially the early canonical exemplars al-Mufaḍḍal's (d. c. 164/780) *al-Mufaḍḍaliyyāt* and Abū Tammām's (d. 231/846) *Dīwān al-Ḥamāsah* (*Valor*), but the study of anthologies as literary works themselves is still nascent across literary studies.[2] Yet for all that the study of

1 There is an argument to be made that such collections are indeed much older, as old as any collection of short Arabic poems, thus dating back to the beginning of the anthological tradition itself. I am sympathetic to that argument but I have chosen not to promote that view in this monograph. In a recent article, I put forward some evidence I hope will contribute to building a case for that view. See Adam Talib, "Woven Together as Though Randomly Strung: variation in collections of naevi poetry compiled by al-Nuwayrī and al-Sarī al-Raffāʾ" *MSR* 17 (2013).

2 There are many important studies in this nascent field from which I have benefited, chief among them Anne Ferry, *Tradition and the Individual Poem: an inquiry into anthologies* (Stanford, CA: Stanford University Press, 2001). See also Neil Fraistat, *The Poem and the Book: interpreting collections of Romantic poetry* (Chapel Hill, NC: University of North Carolina Press, 1985) and *idem* (ed.), *Poems in their Place: the intertextuality and order of poetic collections* (Chapel Hill, NC: University of North Carolina Press, 1986); Richard D. Altick, *The English Common Reader: a social history of the mass reading public, 1800–1900*, 2nd ed. (Columbus, OH: Ohio State University Press, 1998); Barbara M. Benedict, *Making the Modern Reader: cultural mediation in early modern literary anthologies* (Princeton, NJ: Princeton University Press, 1996); Seth Lerer, "Medieval English Literature and the Idea of the Anthology" *PMLA* 118:5 (October 2003). See also, in connection to this, Alastair Fowler, "The Formation of Genres in the Renaissance and After", *New Literary History* 34:2 (Spring 2003). I owe a great intellectual debt to two studies from the Classics: Kathryn J. Gutzwiller, *Poetic Garlands: Hellenistic epigrams in context* (Berkeley, CA: University of California Press, 1998) and Peter Bing, *The Scroll and the Marble: studies in reading and reception in Hellenistic poetry* (Ann Arbor, MI: University of Michigan Press, 2009). In the study of pre-modern Islamicate literatures, Bilal Orfali, *The Anthologist's Art: Abū Manṣūr al-Thaʿālibī and his* Yatīmat al-dahr (Leiden: Brill, 2016); Hilary Kilpatrick, *Making the Great Book of Songs: compilation and the author's craft in Abū l-Faraj al-Iṣbahānī's* Kitāb al-Aghānī (London: RoutledgeCurzon, 2003); and Suzanne Pinckney Stetkevych, *Abū Tammām and the poetics of the ʿAbbāsid Age* (Leiden: Brill, 1991), Part Three are the pre-eminent studies.

 | DOI 10.1163/9789004350533_004

this important genre is retarded, pre-modern Arabic critics were not at all coy about the anthologist's authorial prerogatives. In his anthology *al-Kashf wa-t-tanbīh ʿalā l-waṣf wa-t-tashbīh*, a large collection centred around ekphrasis and similes, aṣ-Ṣafadī explains why and how he compiled the work and how it is connected to the well known genre of *tashbīhāt* collections (this genre is discussed at length below):[3]

وقد أحببت أن أجمع من التشبيه ما وقع لمن علمته من الشعراء و تبيّن له أنه تبوّأ غرف البلاغة ولم ينبذ بالعراء فإنّه ما خلا شاعرٌ ولا كاتبٌ من تشبيه ولكن أين من نقول فيه بلسان المغاربة «آش بيه» وكلّ ديوان ففيه منه حاصل ساقه القلم باقيًا [...]

فاخترتُ من التشبيهات التي جمعها ابن أبي عون والحاتمي وابن ظافر والثعالبي في شعار الندماء والوطواط الكتبي في مباهج الفكر وما في رَوْح الروح وما في مجاميع الفضلاء [...] هذا إلى ما أثبتّه من الزيادات التي لم يذكروها والتشبيهات التي لو عرفوا مظانّها لم ينكروها والتقطتها من الدواوين والمجاميع

I wanted to make a collection of similes by poets of my acquaintance who—it is plain to see—have entered the chambers of eloquence and not cast [their verses] into a wasteland. There is not a poet or a writer who hasn't tried his hand at crafting similes; but where's the one about whom we can say, like they do in Maghribī Arabic, "Check him out!"[4] for in every *Dīwān*, [one finds] a product (*ḥāṣil*), which the pen has caused to remain[5] (*bāqī*) [] [...]

3 aṣ-Ṣafadī, *al-Kashf wa-t-tanbīh ʿalā l-waṣf wa-t-tashbīh*, ed. Hilāl Nājī (Leeds: Majallat al-Ḥikmah, 1999), 52–3.

4 *āsh bīh*: (literally) "what about him/it?".

5 In mathematics, *bāqī* can mean "remainder" and *ḥāṣil* "product".

> So I chose from the similes that had been collected by Ibn Abī ʿAwn,[6] al-Ḥātimī,[7] Ibn Ẓāfir,[8] ath-Thaʿālibī in *Shiʿār an-nudamāʾ*,[9] and al-Waṭwāṭ in *Mabāhij al-fikar*[10] and from *Rawḥ ar-rūḥ*[11] and the content of the collections of the esteemed [...] And to this I added further examples, which they did not include and which they—had they seen their signs of quality—would not have left out. I picked these out from *dawāwīn* [sing. *dīwān*] and anthologies [*majāmiʿ*, sing. *majmūʿah*].

This explanation gives us some idea of aṣ-Ṣafadī's working method as well as the range of earlier texts available to him. An author's sources tell us a great deal about the present state of knowledge when a work was being written, and indeed Quellenforschungen have become a familar model in Arabic literary scholarship, but beyond this, when an author enumerates his influences and predecessors, he is in a way writing himself into a generic tradition; *taqārīẓ* (commendations, sing. *taqrīẓ*) and *ijāzāt* (diplomas, sing. *ijāzah*) operate in much the same way.

In addition to grounding the genre in a canon, collections of *maqāṭīʿ*-poetry were also fundamental for the genre's profile. The strong contextual and thematic links forged in *maqāṭīʿ*-collections allowed the *maqāṭīʿ*-genre to remain recognizable as a genre because while *maqāṭīʿ*-poems may be thematically promiscuous and can be found themselves in a huge variety of written and spoken contexts, they hew to a particular generic profile that was first established in the *maqāṭīʿ*-collections that brought them prominence. It is for

---

6 Ibn Abī ʿAwn (d. 322/933). Aṣ-Ṣafadī is presumably referring to his *Kitāb at-Tashbīhāt*. Published as *The Kitāb al-Tashbīhāt of Ibn Abī ʿAun*, ed. M. ʿAbdul Muʿīd Khān (London: Luzac, 1950).

7 Muḥammad b. al-Ḥasan al-Ḥātimī (d. 388/998). Aṣ-Ṣafadī may be referring to al-Ḥātimī's anthology *Ḥilyat al-muḥāḍarah*, ed. Hilāl Nājī, (Beirut: Dār Maktabat al-Ḥayāh, 1978). Al-Ḥātimī also wrote a famous takedown of al-Mutanabbī called *ar-Risālah al-mūḍiḥah*, ed. Muḥammad Yūsuf Najm (Beirut: Dār Ṣādir; Dār Beirut, 1965); see also Seeger A. Bonebakker, *Materials for the History of Arabic Rhetoric* (Naples: Istituto orientale, 1975), though this is a less likely candidate.

8 ʿAlī b. Ẓāfir al-Azdī (d. 613/1216 or 623/1226), author of *Gharāʾib at-tanbīhāt ʿalā ʿajāʾib at-tashbīhāt*, ed. Muḥammad Zaghlūl Sallām and Muṣṭafā aṣ-Ṣāwī al-Juwaynī (Cairo: Dār al-Maʿārif, 1971).

9 No information about this text survives. It is not mentioned, for example, in Bilal Orfali, "The Works of Abū Manṣūr al-Thaʿālibī (350–429/961–1039)", *JAL* 40:3 (2009).

10 This text is known both as *Manāhij al-fikar wa-mabāhij al-ʿibar* and *Mabāhij al-fikar wa-manāhij al-ʿibar*: see Jamāl ad-Dīn Muḥammad b. Ibrāhīm al-Waṭwāṭ al-Kutubī, *Manāhij al-fikar wa-mabāhij al-ʿibar*, 2 vols, ed. Fuat Sezgin and Mazin Amawi (Frankfurt: Institut für Geschichte der arabisch-islamischen Wissenschaften, 1990) [fascimile edition].

11 See in Orfali, "The Works of Abū Manṣūr al-Thaʿālibī", 306, no. 57.

this reason that the formal organization, rhetorical structures, poetics, and thematic content of *maqāṭīʿ*-collections are so important for the genre as a whole. This chapter will treat the "macropoetics" or "contextural [*sic*] poetics" of Arabic *maqāṭīʿ*-collections.[12]

جَمْع

Curating

Ibn Ḥabīb (d. 779/1377), author of the *maqāṭīʿ*-collection *ash-Shudhūr*, was also the author of a very popular anthology entitled *Kitāb Nasīm aṣ-ṣabā* (*The Breeze of the East Wind*), a collection of poetry and wisdom literature arranged over thirty thematic chapters. In Chapter Two (*fī sh-shams wa-l-qamar*: "On the Sun and the Moon"), Ibn Ḥabīb presents a litany of lunar attributes in rhymed prose (*sajʿ*) and then quotes an unattributed poem that includes many of these same comparisons. This poem—and especially its concluding line—may give us some insight into the attitude of later littérateurs toward a process I describe as curating (i.e. composing by collecting):[13]

[من الكامل]

وتَرَى ٱلهِلالَ يَلوحُ في أُفُقِ ٱلسَّما   يَبدو كَقَوسٍ بالمُنَى يَرمِيني
أو شَبهِ فَخٍّ أو كَدُملُجِ غادةٍ   وكَجانِبِ ٱلمِرآةِ والعُرجونِ
وجَبينِ حِبٍّ بالعِمامَةِ قَدْ زَها   وكَوَجهِ خَودٍ بالنِقابِ مَصونِ
وَكَنابِ فيلٍ أو قُلامةِ أَنمُلٍ   وكَزَورَقٍ وكَحاجِبٍ مَقرونِ

12 These two terms are borrowed from the work of Joseph R. Allen, "Macropoetic Structures: the Chinese solution", *Comparative Literature* 45:4 (Autumn 1993) and Neil Fraistat, *Poems in their Place*, respectively.

13 Ibn Ḥabīb al-Ḥalabī, *Nasīm aṣ-ṣabā fī funūn min al-adab al-qadīm wa-l-maqāmāt al-adabiyyah*, ed. Maḥmūd Fākhūrī (Aleppo: Dār al-Qalam al-ʿArabī, 1993), 24. Many of these comparisons have precedents in the history of Arabic literature: *qaws* (see in al-Azdī, *Gharāʾib at-tanbīhāt*, 14); *shibh fakhkh* (ibid., 12); *dumluj* (Ibn Abī ʿAwn, *Kitāb at-Tashbīhāt*, 12); *mirʾāh* (al-Azdī, *Gharāʾib at-tanbīhāt*, 12); *al-ʿurjūn* (ibid., 15); *jabīn* (ibid., 14); *nāb al-fīl* (Ibn Abī ʿAwn, *Kitāb at-Tashbīhāt*, 12); *qulāmah* (ibid., 12; 13); *zawraq* (ibid., 12); *ḥājib maqrūn* (al-Azdī, *Gharāʾib at-tanbīhāt*, 14); *siwār* (ibid., 13); *nūn* (Ibn Abī ʿAwn, *Kitāb at-Tashbīhāt*, 13; al-Azdī, *Gharāʾib at-tanbīhāt*, 15); *ka-shāfat al-kaʾs* (ibid., 16); *minjal* (ibid., 14); *jām* (ibid., 16).

[٥] أوكالسّوارِ أُزيلَ مِنهُ ٱلبعضُ أو   قَربوسِ سَرجٍ مُذهَبٍ أو نونِ
[٦] وكَشافةِ ٱلكأسِ ٱلمُخبّأ بَعضُهُ   ضِمنَ ٱلشِّفاهِ ومِنجَلٍ مَسنونِ
[٧] هو مِنجَلُ ٱلأعمارِ للحَصدِ ٱلّذي   يُفني أُولي ٱلتَّزيينِ والتَّحسينِ
[٨] وإذا مَضَى سَبعٌ تَراهُ كأنَّهُ   نِصفٌ لِتَعويذٍ بَدا لِعُيونِ
[٩] وإذا تَكامَلَ صارَ جاماً صافيًا   وكَأنَّهُ مِنْ لؤلؤٍ مَكنونِ
[٠١] أو غادةٌ قَدْ أسفَرَتْ عَنْ وَجهِها   غَنِيَتْ عَنِ ٱلتَّحسينِ والتَّزيينِ
[١١] هٰذا هو ٱلمَشهورُ في تَشبيهِهِ   قِدمًا وذٰلِكَ جَمعُهُ يَكفيني

You see how the crescent moon appears on the horizon
like an archer's bow targeting me with desire;
Or rather like half of a net or a young maid's bracelet
or better yet like a mirror-sliver or a palm-tree bough;
or else like a be-turbaned beloved's gleaming brow,
or a girl's face protected behind a veil;
or like an elephant's tusk or the paring of a fingernail,
or else it's like a boat or a pair of joined eyebrows;
Or like a bracelet that's missing [a few links],
or like a saddle's pommel or like the letter *nūn* [ن];
Or like the rim of a goblet, partly hidden[14]
behind drinking lips, or like a sharpened sickle—
That life-lopping sickle that's used in the harvest to
obliterate the prettied and the pretty.
And seven days later, [the moon] looks to you like
half of a lucky charm that you can clearly see.
Then when it is full, it becomes a pure silver cup
made as if from a well hidden pearl;
Or else a maid who's drawn back her veil,
one who needs no embellishment, no making up.
These are the famous similes that were crafted
in times gone by and just to collect them is enough for me.

14 The printed edition reads: *ka-sha'fat al-ka's*, but *shāfah* (or *shāffah*: "rim, edge") is a better reading (see also Dozy, *Supplément aux dictionnaires arabes*, 2 vols (Leiden: Brill, 1881. [repr. Beirut: Librairie du Liban, 1991]), s.v. "*shāffah*").

The last line of this poem is ambiguous, but it may nevertheless reflect a conscious embrace of the anthological method. It is clear that the poet is summarizing the previous litany by acknowledging that these comparisons have perhaps become shop-worn by now and that they may strike the pre-modern reader (to say nothing of the jaded post-romantic reader) as hackneyed. Yet saying something is not the same as meaning it. One would not expect a poet or an anthologist who recycles clichés to draw attention to this fact, so by doing just that Ibn Ḥabīb impels us to rethink our first impression of the litany.

Ibn Ḥabīb's audience did not groan when they heard the moon compared to a girl's face—or else, one naturally assumes, the poets would have given up that habit back in the 8th century. Rather the audience must have appreciated the poet's skill in innovating and recasting comparisons, or inventing a new and surprising image, or expressing the familiar more eloquently, or linking a comparison and its complements in a larger thematic structure, etc.[15] How then should we interpret the second half of this last verse: is it that the poet is emphasizing the longevity of these tropes and that this is what merits approval, or is he claiming that these tropes are the most well known and that he is not motivated to pursue ever more recherché and far-fetched comparisons? These interpetations are somewhat unlikely for there is a certain ambiguity in the word *jamʿ* here.[16] The question is whether the poet means to say that he finds all these comparisons sufficient when taken together (scil. *jamʿ* for *jamīʿan*) or is instead alluding to the legitimate value of curating as a creative act? If we embrace this second possibility, what we have is a recognition of the place of anthologizing in the literary sphere. Assembling tropes in a single poem in one's own wording is, of course, different from assembling verses and poems by others, but the anthological method is not exclusively limited to this latter model. A poet can achieve through eloquent rephrasing, but they add value by being able to collect and

15 See also Daniel Javitch's comments on the alien aesthetics of pre-19th-century literary composition: "Given that inventiveness in this system of composition stemmed from the capacity to modify the already told, it becomes understandable why an author's ability to vary would be highly valued. But even if we can understand the need for such skill at *variatio*, our predilection for Romantic originality prevents us from enjoying rhetorical variation as early modern readers did. In particular, we do not share their fondness for repetition of the same action, varied in what may seem to us too subtle, because largely stylistic, ways." (Daniel Javitch, "The Poetics of *Variatio* in *Orlando Furioso*", *Modern Language Quarterly* 66:1 (March 2005): 1).

16 Ambiguity is no cause for alarm and in fact it is a hallmark of pre-modern Islamicate culture: see Thomas Bauer, *Die Kultur der Ambiguität. Eine andere Geschichte des Islams* (Berlin: Verlag der Weltreligionen im Insel Verlag, 2011) and forthcoming English translation (Columbia Univ. Press).

curate these eloquent rephrasings in order to create a new whole.[17] I expect many Arabic anthologists felt the same as al-Ḥuṣrī (d. 413/1022) who—in the introduction to his anthology *Zahr al-ādāb wa-thimār al-albāb* (*The Flower of Literary Arts and the Fruit of Hearts* [lit. *Minds*])—wrote that the thing he was most proud of in his book was his excellent selection because a man's discernment is a reflection of his intellect.[18]

Although it may strike us as strange—or at least counterintuitive—there is ample reason to believe that pre-modern poets, readers, anthologists, and critics validated what some people deride as the hackneyed tropes common to classical Arabic poetry: the stock comparisons, modes, totems, etc. Poets, critics, and anthologists documented, parodied, celebrated, repurposed, and recast these tropes constantly over more than a millennium and every literary sophisticate was expected to have a comprehensive knowledge of these tropes, as well as their trajectory in literary history. With this paramount contextual circumstance in mind, Ibn Ḥabīb's perspective can be read as combining his interest in literary history with his regard for the anthological method of composition. Likewise other such collections operate on both anthological and literary-historical planes. In his treatise-cum-poetry-anthology on moles, aṣ-Ṣafadī (d. 764/1363) presents a great deal of pseudo-scientific, historical, and theological information in two introductory sections (sing. *muqaddimah*).[19] In the first of these introductory sections (*al-muqaddimah al-ūlā*, "the first premise"), he presents a lexicographical discussion of *khāl* and *shāmah* (both "mole") with attestations from poetry, Qur'an,

17 Geert Jan van Gelder has spoken of the notion of *insijām* in similar terms. See G. J. van Gelder, "Poetry for Easy Listening: *insijām* and related concepts in Ibn Ḥijjah's *Khizānat al-Adab*", MSR 7:1 (2003). See also in a *taqrīẓ* on al-Badrī's *Ghurrat aṣ-ṣabāḥ*, British Library MS ADD 23445, f. 4a, l. 1: "*ḥusn insijāmih*".

18 "[…] *wa-laysa lī fī ta'līfih min al-iftikhār akthar min ḥusn al-ikhtiyār wa-khtiyār al-mar' qiṭ'ah min 'aqlih tadull 'alā takhallufih aw faḍlih* […]" ["The thing I am most proud of in writing this is the quality of my curation (*ikhtiyār*), for a man's curation (*ikhtiyār*) is part of his intellect and it indicates whether he is inadequate or excellent."] (al-Ḥuṣrī, *Zahr al-ādāb wa-thimār al-albāb*, 2 vols, ed. Zakī Mubārak (Cairo: al-Maṭba'ah ar-Raḥmāniyyah, 1925), 1:3). See also a similar sentiment expressed in *idem*, *Nūr aṭ-ṭarf wa-nawr aẓ-ẓarf: Kitāb an-nūrayn*, ed. Līnah 'Abd al-Quddūs Abū Ṣāliḥ (Beirut: Mu'assasat ar-Risālah, 1996), 101–5. This motto first appears in al-Jāḥiẓ's *al-Bayān wa-t-tabyīn* where it is attributed to Yūnus b. Ḥabīb (al-Jāḥiẓ, *al-Bayān wa-t-tabyīn*, 4 vols, ed. 'Abd as-Salām Muḥammad Hārūn (Cairo: Lajnat at-Ta'līf wa-t-Tarjamah wa-n-Nashr, 1948–50), 1:77). See also ar-Rāghib al-Iṣfahānī, *Muḥāḍarāt al-udabā'*, 2 vols (Būlāq: Jamī'at al-Ma'ārif, 1287/1870), 1:55: "*ikhtiyār ar-rajul ash-shi'r qiṭ'ah min 'aqlih*" ["Curating (*ikhtiyār*) poetry is part of one's intellect"].

19 On the (syllogistic) structure of aṣ-Ṣafadī's anthologies, see Ibn Nubātah's brief comment recorded in aṣ-Ṣafadī, *Alḥān as-sawāji'*, ed. Sālim, 2:322.

prophetic sayings, and other literary sources. In the second introductory section (*al-muqaddimah ath-thāniyah*, "the second premise"), he discusses medical opinions about the nature of naevi, the reasons for their appearance, and interpretations of their position on the body, in line with divinatory techniques (*ʿilm al-firāsah*).[20] Aṣ-Ṣafadī even includes a list of famous personalities who were known to have had moles. What is most interesting for our present discussion is that in the second introductory section, aṣ-Ṣafadī gives the reader a précis of common poetic comparisons for naevi:[21]

وقد اختلف الشعراء في تشبيه الخال وانا أذكر الآن ما يجوز من التشبيه الواقع في ذلك بحسب الإمكان فأقول يجوز أن يُشبّه بنقطةٍ لنون الحاجب وفيه تسامح وبنقطةٍ لخاء الخدّ وبنقطةٍ سَقَطَتْ من قلمٍ كَتَبَ نون الحاجب وبنقطةِ غاليةٍ على تفّاحةٍ وبنقطةٍ انحدَرَتْ من كحل الجفون وبكوكبٍ كَسَفَ وبقطعةِ عنبر في مجمرٍ أو ندٍّ أو مسكٍ أو بأثرِ شرارة وَقَعَتْ في ثوبِ أطلسَ أحمرَ وبفحمةٍ من نارٍ وبجنانٍ يَحْرُسُ حديقةَ وردٍ وبنكتةِ الشقيق وبملكٍ من الزنج في حلّةٍ حمراءَ وبراهبٍ يتعبّد وببلبلٍ في سياج العذار وبحَبّةٍ لفخّ العذار وبحَبّةِ القلب وقد وَقَعَتْ بنارِ الخدّ وبالحجر الأسود في كعبةِ الوجه الحسن وببلالٍ يؤذّن في صبحِ الغُرّة وبكرةٍ تلقّفها صَوْلجانُ العذار وبختامِ مسكٍ لمدام الريق وبذبابةٍ وَقَعَتْ على شهدِ الريق وبمجرمٍ في النار وبهنديٍّ تعبّد بإلقاء نفسه في النار.

Poets have compared beauty marks in various ways, and here I will mention what types of comparisons are appropriate to the extent possible. I say that it can be compared to:

1. the dot of the *nūn* [ن] of the eyebrows (poetic licence here);
2. the dot of the *khāʾ* [خ] of the cheek (*khadd*);
3. a drop [of ink] that has fallen from a pen writing the *nūn* [ن] of the eyebrows;
4. a spot of *ghāliyah* perfume on an apple;

20 See *EI*2, s.v. "Firāsa" [T. Fahd].

21 aṣ-Ṣafadī, *Kashf al-ḥāl*, ed. al-ʿUqayl, 171–73.

5. a drop that has fallen from eyeliner [drawn] on the eyelids;
6. an eclipsed planet;
7. a piece of ambergris in a censer;
8. or [a piece of] *nadd* incense;
9. or [a piece of] musk;
10. a spot burnt by a spark on a red satin garment;
11. a burning coal;
12. a gardener protecting a rose garden;
13. the spot of an anemone;
14. a king of the blacks (*zanj*) dressed in red;
15. a monk in prayer;
16. a nightingale in the snares of [the beloved's] incipient beard;
17. bait in the trap of [the beloved's] incipient beard;
18. the kernel of the heart (*ḥabbat al-qalb*) fallen into the fire of [the beloved's] cheek;
19. the black stone of the *Kaʿbah* of a beautiful face;
20. Bilāl reciting the call to prayer at dawn;[22]
21. a ball caught in the polo stick of [the beloved's] incipient beard;
22. a seal of musk on the wine of [the beloved's] saliva;
23. a fly alighting on the nectar of [the beloved's] saliva;
24. a transgressor in the fire;
25. a Hindu being pious by throwing himself into the fire.

These similes are well represented in the poetry anthology that makes up the latter half of aṣ-Ṣafadī's text. Aṣ-Ṣafadī refers to this collection of *maqāṭīʿ*-poems as *an-natījah* (the conclusion) and there presents 372 poems arranged alphabetically by rhyme letter. Notably, aṣ-Ṣafadī tends to include poems of his own at the end of many of the rhyme-letter sections.[23] While aṣ-Ṣafadī chose to organise his collection of naevi-poems by rhyme letter and not theme, his list of similes testifies to the fact that the repeated use of specific metaphors and figures was regarded as a matter of course and that both poets and anthologists recognized that there was a further stage of composition beyond the crafting of comparisons. For poets, this meant that—in addition to attempting to create new comparisons—they were also concerned with re-casting well known comparisons in innovative ways. For anthologists, this meant that they

---

22 The Prophet's *muʾadhdhin*, see *EI*², s.v. "Bilāl b. Rabāḥ" [W. ʿArafat]. That Bilāl was a black slave from Ethiopia is relevant for the imagery here.

23 See in ʿAbd ar-Raḥmān al-ʿUqayl's introduction: "*wa-qad iltazama aṣ-Ṣafadī an yakhtim ākhir akthar al-qawāfī bi-shayʾ min naẓmih* [...]" ["aṣ-Ṣafadī made sure to conclude most of the chapters organized by rhyme-letter with compositions of his own [...]"] (aṣ-Ṣafadī, *Kashf al-ḥāl*, ed. al-ʿUqayl, 69).

could also create new works of literary compilation by curating these poetic comparisons in anthologies. In much the same way, *maqāṭīʿ*-poems could be collected together into thematically linked volumes and in their proximity and association transcend the sum of their parts.

In his examination of the genesis of Hellenistic epigram anthologies, Lorenzo Argentieri has distinguished three phases of collection: "To come up with a general formula, we can say that epigram collections are divisible into three types: the sylloge, in which [there is] compilation without creation; the booklet (*libellus*), in which [there is] creation without compilation; and the anthology, in which there is creation through compilation."[24] While we cannot adopt this model wholesale for collections of Arabic short poetry, this division can be a useful guide to permutations of the larger genre. From very early on (i.e. the 9th century), short poems (including single verses) were presented as parerga in rhetorical works, e.g. Ibn Abī ʿAwn's (d. 322/933) *Kitāb at-Tashbīhāt* (*The Book of Comparisons*), Ibn al-Muʿtazz's (d. 296/908) *Kitāb al-Badīʿ* (*The Book of Innovative* [*Style*]), the Brothers Khālidiyyān's *Kitāb al-Ashbāh wa-n-naẓāʾir* (*The Like and the Analogous*), etc. as well as in biographical collections, e.g. Ibn al-Muʿtazz's *Ṭabaqāt ash-shuʿarāʾ* (*Biographical Dictionary of Poets*) and of course ath-Thaʿālibī's *Yatīmat ad-dahr wa-maḥāsin ahl al-ʿaṣr* and the many works it inspired, etc. These parerga were sylloges—according to Argenteri's scheme—included within a larger work. In the history of Arabic poetry anthologies, however, it was multi-authored anthologies (*anthologia*) that preceded the solo "booklet" (*libellus*). *Dawāwīn* (sing. *Dīwān*), the collected poems of a single poet, are obviously single-authored and indeed quite ancient, but they are not collections of short poems. Early Abbasid anthologies including those compiled by al-Mufaḍḍal (d. c. 164/780), al-Aṣmaʿī (d. c. 216/831), Abū Tammām (d. 231/846), Ibn Dāwūd al-Iṣbahānī (d. 297/909), and others are collections of poetry by a large number of poets, and compilers did in some cases include some of their own poems; a habit that continued throughout the pre-modern period. These anthologies became arenas for literary exchange masterminded by erudite and creative anthologists, who often downplayed their paramount curatorial role.

---

24 Lorenzo Argentieri, "Epigramma e Libro. Morfologia delle raccolte epigrammatiche premeleagree", *Zeitschrift für Papyrologie und Epigraphik* 121 (1998): 2: "Sintetizzando con una formula generale, possiamo dire che le raccolte epigrammatiche si dividono in tre tipi: la *silloge*, in cui si compila senza creare; il *libellus*, in cui si crea senza compilare; l'*anthologia*, in cui si compila per creare." On the composition of Hellenistic poetry books, see—in addition to the sources mentioned above—Peter Bing, *The Scroll and the Marble* and Kathryn J. Gutzwiller, "Anyte's Epigram Book", *Syllecta Classica* 4 (1993).

Works like *Kitāb al-Muḥibb wa-l-maḥbūb wa-l-mashmūm wa-l-mashrūb* (*Who Loves, Who is Loved, What is Smelled, and What is Drunk*) by as-Sarī ar-Raffāʾ (d. c. 362/972), *ash-Shihāb fī sh-shayb wa-sh-shabāb* (*The Shooting Star: on gray hair and youth*) by ash-Sharīf al-Murtaḍā (d. 466/1044), *Aḥsan mā samiʿtu* (*The Best I Ever Heard*) by ath-Thaʿālibī, and many others present short poems as well as extracts from longer poems by a great many poets. These collections were frequently, though not always, polythematic. Yet while these anthologies were collections of short poems—almost always eschewing the presentation of *qaṣāʾid* (sing. *qaṣīdah*), they certainly predate the recognition of a separate genre of *maqāṭīʿ*-poems at some point in the 13th century. For example, as-Sarī ar-Raffāʾ uses the term "*muqaṭṭaʿāt*" in his anthology, but even in the 14th century, Badr ad-Dīn Ibn Ḥabīb would continue to use the same term, although he and his contemporaries had already identified a new genre they called *maqāṭīʿ*.[25] These all belong on a spectrum of different genres of short poetry in Arabic. Nevertheless *maqāṭīʿ*-poems can be distinguished as a separate and emergent genre on account of their form and its operational logic, their modal and thematic ambit, and especially the anthological context that most clearly signals a nascent genre-consciousness; this in addition of course to the distinction signaled by the new terminological descriptor devised by pre-modern Arabs.

To say that collecting and naming *maqāṭīʿ*-poems reflects genre-consciousness and is materially determinant of their generic status is an insight gained from close attention to literary-historical development. Indeed it is analogous to the emergence of opera's genre-consciousness in 17th-century Venice as described by Ellen Rosand:[26]

---

25 Ibn Ḥabīb—in his history *Tadhkirat an-nabīh*—records that when Ibn Nubātah came to Aleppo in the year 730/1329–30, Ibn Ḥabīb shared with him his *muqaṭṭaʿāt* (presumably his *maqāṭīʿ*-collection, *ash-Shudhūr*) and then he gives the text of Ibn Nubātah's reaction (i.e. *taqrīẓ*, commendation), in which Ibn Nubātah uses the term *maqāṭīʿ* (Ibn Ḥabīb, *Tadhkirat an-nabīh*, 2:203–4. See also ibid., 3:139; Bauer, "„Was kann aus dem Jungen noch werden!"'"; and in appendix, no. 15). Elsewhere in his obituary for Ibn Nubātah, Ibn Ḥabīb writes, "*wa-akhrasa al-mawāṣīl bi-maqāṭīʿih*" ["He made the flutes (also connected things) (*mawāṣīl*) silent with his disconnected things (*maqāṭīʿ*-poems"] (*Tadhkirat an-nabīh*, 3:305; in appendix, no. 14a). He also uses this term in his obituary for Ṣafī ad-Dīn al-Ḥillī (see in appendix, no. 14b). See also, *inter alia*, Muḥammad b. Shākir al-Kutubī, *Fawāt al-Wafayāt wa-dh-dhayl ʿalayhā*, 5 vols, ed. Iḥsān ʿAbbās (Beirut: Dār Ṣādir, 1973–74), 1:206.

26 We can also understand the generic trajectory of *maqāṭīʿ*-poetry as mirroring somewhat the history of *ḥadīth*-texts. *Ḥadīth*-texts had been collected before the 9th century, but it was not until then that a "discursive shift" took place, which "canonized" (that is, reified) the proto-genre of *ḥadīth* as a category of legal text, which would then allow for the appearance of canonical collections. See Ahmed El Shamsy, *The Canonization of Islamic Law: a social and intellectual history* (Cambridge: Cambridge Univ. Press, 2013).

> It was not until the middle of the seventeenth century, then, after more than a decade of vigorous operatic activity—more than thirty operas by some twenty librettists and ten composers, in five theaters—that Venetian librettists began to designate their works *dramma per musica* with any consistency [...]. Although it may seem like a matter of mere semantics, the terminological consensus thus reflected on the title pages of printed librettos actually represented a significant step in the history of the art. It was one of many indications that opera had aesthetically come of age, that it had achieved the status of a genre in its own right.[27]

In the 14th century, four influential Arab *maqāṭīʿ*-poets did something similar and while they should not be understood as having invented the *maqāṭīʿ*-genre, it is in their solo-authored collections that the genre came of age:

> Jamāl al-Dīn Ibn Nubātah (d. 768/1366), *al-Qaṭr an-Nubātī* (*Ibn Nubātah's Sweet Drops*)
>
> Badr ad-Dīn Ibn Ḥabīb al-Ḥalabī (d. 779/1377), *ash-Shudhūr* (*The Particles of Gold*)
>
> Ṣafī ad-Dīn al-Ḥillī (d. c. 750/1350), *Dīwān al-Mathālith wa-l-mathānī fī l-maʿālī wa-l-maʿānī* (*The Collection of Two-liners and Three-liners on Virtues and Literary Motifs*)
>
> Ṣalāḥ ad-Dīn aṣ-Ṣafadī (d. 764/1363), *ar-Rawḍ al-bāsim wa-l-ʿarf an-nāsim* (*Fragrance Wafting in the Smiling Garden*) and *al-Ḥusn aṣ-ṣarīḥ fī miʾat malīḥ* (*Pure Beauty: on one hundred handsome lads*)

Neither short poems nor poetry collections were new phenomena in Arabic literary history by the 14th century—not by a long shot—but the long lineages of this new genre do not negate the potential for innovation or evolution. *Maqāṭīʿ*-poems can exist outside of anthologies, of course, and it would be reductive to assert that *maqāṭīʿ*-poems outside of *maqāṭīʿ*-collections are somehow out of place.[28] Nevertheless, that does not mean that the primary context

27 Ellen Rosand, *Opera in seventeenth-century Venice. The Creation of a Genre* (Berkeley and Los Angeles, CA: University of California Press, 1991 [repr. 2007]), 35–6.

28 It is not certain, but it is likely that the "couplet" found among the trove of documents recovered from Quseir in Egypt is akin to the type of poem examined here, though without a contextual analysis there is very little we can conclude. (See Li Guo, *Commerce, Culture, and Community in a Red Sea Port in the thirteenth century: the Arabic documents from Quseir* (Leiden: Brill, 2004), 314, Text No. 84).

of a genre is a trivial parameter when it comes to its mode of being and literary expression. *Maqāṭīʿ*-poems are mobile and malleable and Arab authors deployed them in a dizzying variety of contexts, but the literary-historical record shows that their primary habitat was the *maqāṭīʿ*-collection. There is no need to be overly prescriptive on this point, but it is nonetheless crucial to understand that *maqāṭīʿ*-poems owe much of their success and popularity—to say nothing of their generic consciousness and the ability to be identified—to their primary context.

As even the most cursory examination demonstrates, pithy poetry was an extremely popular and prevalent literary art form in Arabic throughout the pre-modern period. This is not reflected in the paucity of attention it receives in scholarship today. We struggle to appreciate pithy poetry because we struggle to understand it in its context. Most scholarly discussions of pre-modern Arabic poetry focus on individual poems, or individual poets, etc. and they rarely address the substantive question of a poem's textual context, although ample attention is now being given to a poem's historical context (e.g. the context of a panegyric poem's composition and performance).[29] All the same, it would be unwise to attempt to understand the meaning of a short poem only two, three, or four lines long without appreciating the context in which it is presented—whether anthological, epistolary, etc.—and no less unwise to attempt to identify its generic qualities in the same way. This crucial factor—which has so far been lacking in previous discussions of short poetry in Arabic—is the poem's *Sitz im Leben* and it is this point to which we now turn our attention.

Let us consider, for example, a small anthology of short poems by one the most famous anthologists in the Arabic tradition, Abū Manṣūr ath-Thaʿālibī (d. 429/1038).[30] His anthology, *Aḥsan mā samiʿtu* (*The Best I Ever Heard*), is an apparent abridgement of a larger collection entitled *Aḥāsin al-maḥāsin* (*The*

29 See e.g. Beatrice Gruendler, "*Qaṣīda*. Its Reconstruction in Performance" in *Classical Arabic Humanities in their Own Terms: Festschrift for Wolfhart Heinrichs on his 65th birthday presented by his students and colleagues*, ed. Beatrice Gruendler (with Michael Cooperson) (Leiden: Brill, 2008), 353–55; 371–73, and *idem, Medieval Arabic Praise Poetry*; Suzanne Pinckney Stetkevych, *The Poetics of Islamic Legitimacy: myth, gender, and ceremony in the classical Arabic ode* (Bloomington, IN: Indiana University Press, 2002); Samer M. Ali, *Arabic Literary Salons in the Islamic Middle Ages: poetry, public performance, and the presentation of the past* (Notre Dame, IN: University of Notre Dame Press, 2010); Robert C. McKinney, *The Case of Rhyme versus Reason: Ibn al-Rūmī and his poetics in context* (Leiden: Brill, 2004), and others.

30 The latest work on ath-Thaʿālibī's literary output is Bilal Orfali, *The Anthologist's Art.*

Best of the Best), which is a compilation of prose and poetry.[31] The poems in the anthology *Aḥsan mā samiʿtu* are divided into twenty-two thematic chapters:

1. On God (*fī l-ilāhiyyāt*)
2. On the Prophet (*fī n-nabawiyyāt*)
3. On rulers (*fī l-mulūkiyyāt*)
4. On friends (*fī l-ikhwāniyyāt*)
5. On good comportment (*fī l-adabiyyāt*)
6. On wine (*fī l-khamriyyāt*)
7. On spring and its signs (*fī r-rabīʿ wa-āthārih*)
8. On summer, autumn, and winter (*fī ṣ-ṣayf wa-l-kharīf wa-sh-shitāʾ*)
9. On celestial figures (*fī l-āthār al-ʿulwiyyah*)
10. On this world and fate (*fī d-dunyā wa-d-dahr*)
11. On places and buildings (*fī l-amkinah wa-l-abniyah*)
12. On food (*fī ṭ-ṭaʿāmiyyāt*)
13. On women and courting (*fī n-nisāʾ wa-t-tashbīb*)
14. On love poetry for [male] youths (*fī l-ghazal* [*al-mudhakkar*][32])
15. On youth and going gray (*fī sh-shabāb wa-sh-shayb*)
16. Poems on virtues and panegyrics (*fī makārim al-akhlāq wa-fī l-madāʾiḥ*)
17. Poems of thanks, apology, supplication, asking for permission, etc. (*fī sh-shukr wa-l-ʿudhr wa-l-istimāḥah wa-l-istibāḥah wa-mā yajrī majrāhā*)
18. Poems on character faults and invective poems (*fī masāwiʾ al-akhlāq wa-l-ahājī*)
19. On illness, visiting the sick, and affiliated concerns (*fī l-amrāḍ wa-l-ʿiyādāt wa-mā yanḍāf ilayhā*)
20. On offering congratulations and exchanging gifts (*fī t-tahānī wa-t-tahādī*)
21. Poems of mourning and consolation (*fī l-marāthī wa-t-taʿāzī*)
22. Varied pieces in varied order (*fī funūn min al-aḥāsin mukhtalifat at-tartīb*)

The following breakdown shows that the anthology is essentially a collection of short poems:

31 ath-Thaʿālibī, *Aḥsan mā samiʿtu*, ed. Muḥammad Ṣādiq ʿAnbar (Cairo: al-Maktabah al-Maḥmūdiyyah, n.d. [1925]). On the supposed abridgment, see Orfali, "The Works of Abū Manṣūr al-Thaʿālibī", 281–82; 305.

32 The modifier "*al-mudhakkar*" is missing from the list of chapters in the introduction to the work, but is there in the chapter heading. It is unclear whether this reflects the state of the MS (or *editio princeps*) or is an oversight by the editor.

		As a percentage of the total
Total number of poems	535	
Total number of lines	1208	
Average length	2.26	
One-line poems	50	9.35%
Two line poems	373	69.72%
Three-line poems	75	14.02%
Four-line poems	27	5.05%
Poems of five or more lines	10	1.87%
Poems of four lines or fewer	525	98.13%

Of course, ath-Thaʿālibī never used the term *maqāṭīʿ* in any of his collections of short poems, but his anthological style—like that of his near contemporary as-Sarī ar-Raffāʾ (d. c. 362/972)—was an influential predecessor of the *maqāṭīʿ*-genre that developed in the 13th–14th centuries.[33]

The 14th-century solo-authored collections of *maqāṭīʿ*-poems that we have discussed were—like Argentieri's "booklets" (*libelli*)—arranged according to theme.[34] This initial sally of self-authored *maqāṭīʿ*-collections was followed by a flood of multi-authored anthologies, which were both mono- and poly-thematically arranged. Here again, the pattern Argentieri established for Hellenistic epigram collections mirrors the development of Arabic *maqāṭīʿ*-collections: "The anthology [represents] a major step forward due to the inclusion of many authors, but it is still [made up] exclusively of epigrams".[35] Setting aside forerunners like the anthologies by ath-Thaʿālibī and as-Sarī ar-Raffāʾ mentioned above, following the solo-authored *maqāṭīʿ*-collections by Ibn Nubātah, Ṣafī ad-Dīn al-Ḥillī, Ibn Ḥabīb, and aṣ-Ṣafadī, the Arabic literary landscape was soon inundated with multi-authored, monothematic or polythematic *maqāṭīʿ*-collections. These occasionally appeared as part of a variety of longer texts (e.g. in al-Ibshīhī's *al-Mustaṭraf fī kull fann mustaẓraf* (*The Most Exquisite of Every Elegant Art*), as-Suyūṭī's *Ḥusn al-muḥāḍarah* (*Excellent Conversation*), an-Nuwayrī's *Nihāyat al-arab* (*The*

33 See Talib, "Pseudo-Ṯaʿālibī's *Book of Youths*".

34 Argentieri, "Epigramma e Libro", 17: "Come già detto per i *libelli*, l'organizzazione avveniva per *temi* e non per *generi*." ["As has already been said about booklets (*libelli*), the arrangement was made on the basis of themes, not genres."]

35 ibid., 19: "Con l'*anthologia* si compie un significativo passo in avanti con l'inclusione di molti autori; ma si tratta pur sempre di epigrammi."

Ultimate Ambition in the Arts of Erudition[36]), al-Ghuzulī's *Maṭāliʿ al-budūr* (*The Rising-Places of the Full Moons*), Ibn Iyās' *Badāʾiʿ az-zuhūr* (*The Marvelous Blossoms*[37]), etc.). They were presented just as often in stand-alone anthologies in a variety of typical poetic modes: erotic, ekphrastic, satiric, riddling, etc. These collections—and, of course, the thematic and modal diversity of the *maqāṭīʿ*-genre—allowed anthologists to demonstrate their curatorial skills in designing entertaining and edifying poetic collections. Alan Cameron has explained the logic of Hellenistic epigram collections in a similar way: "Fifty or even a hundred epigrams will have made a very slim book, and too many by the same writer on the same sort of themes, however excellent in themselves, might become monotonous. The epigram was in fact destined by its very nature to be anthologized."[38] These collections also provided an apposite forum for the projection of a wide and contemporary literary community in the period during which—for the first time in the history of Arabic literature—the court was no longer the center of poetic performance and production.

This preference for contemporary poetry is so strong that the poetry of earlier generations was crowded out of these *maqāṭīʿ*-collections. Consider, for example, the distribution of poets cited in a few exemplary anthologies: (1) aṣ-Ṣafadī's *Kashf al-ḥāl fī waṣf al-khāl*, (2) Ibn Abī Ḥajalah's *Dīwān aṣ-Ṣabābah* (chs 10 and 12), and (3) the anonymous 16th–17th-century collection of *maqāṭīʿ*-poems on male youths erroneously thought to be ath-Thaʿālibī's lost *Kitāb al-Ghilmān*.

aṣ-Ṣafadī (d. 764/1363), *Kashf al-ḥāl fī waṣf al-khāl*[39]

death date	number of poets cited
1st/7th century	1
2nd/8th century	0
3rd/9th century	1
4th/10th century	2
5th/11th century	7

36 This is Elias Muhanna's translation of the title of this work (see his recent abridged translation of this work in the Penguin Classics series). On an embedded micro-anthology in this most voluminous work, see Talib, "Woven together as though randomly strung".

37 See e.g. in vol. 1, pt. 1.

38 Alan Cameron, *The Greek Anthology: from Meleager to Planudes* (Oxford: Clarendon Press, 1993), 4.

39 Based on aṣ-Ṣafadī, *Kashf al-ḥāl*, ed. al-ʿUqayl.

6th/12th century	21
7th/13th century	58
8th/14th century	18

Ibn Abī Ḥajalah (d. 776/1375), *Dīwān aṣ-Ṣabābah*, chapters 10 and 12:[40]

death date	percent of total verses
pre-Islamic	2%
1st/7th century	1%
2nd/8th century	1%
3rd/9th century	10%
4th/10th century	3%
5th/11th century	5%
6th/12th century	4%
7th/13th century	24%
8th/14th century	32%

Pseudo-Thaʿālibī, *Kitāb al-Ghilmān* (late 16th–17th c.)[41]

death date	percent of total verses
3rd/9th century	3%
4th/10th century	8%
5th/11th century	0%
6th/12th century	4%
7th/13th century	18%
8th/14th century	28%
9th/15th century	12.5%
10th/16th century	18%
11th/17th century	2%

40 Based on Ibn Abī Ḥajalah at-Tilimsānī, *Dīwān aṣ-Ṣabābah*, ed. Muḥammad Zaghlūl Sallām, (Alexandria: Munsha'at al-Maʿārif, n.d.).

41 Based on Talib, "Pseudo-Ṯaʿālibī's *Book of Youths*", 610.

These anthologies demonstrate a marked emphasis on the poetry of later poets, especially those contemporary to the anthologists. This tendency is a key feature of collections of short poems, including *maqāṭīʿ*, and it evinces not only a preference for contemporary poetry, but the instrumental role of anthologies in disseminating new poetry across a wide geographical area and between elite and non-elite classes. It was inevitable that they would gain traction as the centrality of courts to poetic production diminished.

The *maqāṭīʿ*-genre did not develop in a vacuum and its perpetuation in Arabic literary culture for several centuries depended on a social network that produced and consumed collections of this *maqāṭīʿ*-poetry with gusto. The identities of most of these consumers, as well as many of the minor producers (poets, copyists, et al.), have been lost to us, so it is all the more critical that we establish a solid understanding of who the anthologists who composed and contributed to these collections were. This is essential not only for the empirical aims of literary history; it is an indivisible component of the context of these works. Scholars who have worked on Hellenistic epigram collections have been able to situate these texts within a specific cultural frame that may suggest a pattern also present in Mamluk- and Ottoman-era Arabic culture:

> In the Hellenistic age great libraries sprang up accompanied by an unprecedented spread of poetry books, and a new literary culture emerged in the great *metropoleis* of the Hellenistic kingdoms, generating new products, attitudes and approaches, though always with reference to the Greek past. The intensive study of contemporary and past authors was a typical feature of the age, and every serious author was conscious of having to face a public as well read as himself—or at least he supposed it to be. In addition to the specialized audience of the royal courts, there was a larger public of studious readers who influenced the character of literary production, as papyri have shown.
>
> The *G*[*reek*] *A*[*nthology*] itself is an example of the dynamics which grew from the diffusion of a culture of reading. The interaction of authors and readers evolved into a "communication" across the times, a dialogue in which authors and readers played different parts: poets enact themselves as readers and let their own reading experiences be reflected by their epigrams; collectors arrange epigrams for other readers; moreover, the genre

> of literary commentary develops, reflecting an interest in, and work on, the literary *oeuvre* of other authors.[42]

A similar climate of literary activity existed in Arabic culture from at least as early as the *tadwīn* movement, but the Mamluk period (and perhaps the Ottoman period, though this remains to be explored) saw an energetic renewal of such activity that greatly overshadows earlier efforts.[43] Nita Krevans sees Hellenistic anthologies as a manifestation of a specific form of non-hierarchical, experimental, and archivally minded literary culture, which accords with much of what we suppose was happening in Arabo-Islamic literary culture in the Mamluk and Ottoman periods.[44]

The anthologists who composed—that is to say, curated—these works did so by stitching together dozens, and often hundreds, of *maqāṭīʿ*-poems in an aesthetically sophisticated arrangement designed to engage and edify readers. These anthologists occasionally auto-anthologized, but multi-authored anthologies are more common. Arabic *maqāṭīʿ*-poetry is markedly ecumenical and encompasses the entire pantheon of poetic subjects and modes, though erotic, lyric, and ekphrastic themes predominate. Thematic and stylistic proclivities thus helped to shape the anthologists' selection biases, as it were, but this alone does not account for their conspicuous partiality toward contemporary and near-contemporary poets at the expense of their pre-Islamic, Umayyad, and Abbasid counterparts. This bias for contemporary literature was especially expedient as courts, the erstwhile poles of Arabic literary conglomerates, diminished in importance to the point of irrelevance during the Mamluk period. Literary salons (*majālis*, sing. *majlis*)

---

42 Doris Meyer, "The Act of Reading and the Act of Writing in Hellenistic Epigram" in *Brill's Companion to Hellenistic Epigram: down to Philip*, ed. Peter Bing and Jon Steffen Bruss (Leiden: Brill, 2007), 187.

43 See Bauer, "Literarische Anthologien der Mamlūkenzeit".

44 Nita Krevans, "The Arrangement of Epigrams in Collections" in *Brill's Companion to Hellenistic Epigram: down to Philip*, ed. Peter Bing and Jon Steffen Bruss (Leiden: Brill, 2007), 131–32: "The anthology is [...] a quintessentially Hellenistic form, a textual analogy to the ultimate Hellenistic collection—the great library at Alexandria. While there are earlier precedents for these works, the dominance of the anthology in Hellenistic culture is new and significant.[...] [P]apryus finds bear witness to a wide range of literary and sub-literary anthologies—excerpts from drama, gnomic treasuries, themed collections of verse. Many of these compilations appear to be the work of ordinary readers assembling a group of favorite selections; they offer compelling evidence for a general fascination with collecting and excerpting far beyond the precincts of the Museum in Alexandria." On Mamluk literary culture, see Muhsin J. al-Musawi, *The Medieval Islamic Republic of Letters. Arabic Knowledge Construction* (South Bend, IN: Univ. of Notre Dame Press, 2015).

were undoubtedly important, but the history of their role in literary culture is only beginning to be written.[45]

Within the leaves of Mamluk and Ottoman era *maqāṭīʿ*-collections, there exists a discernible cluster of poets. Alongside Ibn Nubātah (d. 1366), aṣ-Ṣafadī (d. 1363), Ibrāhīm al-Miʿmār (d. 750/1350), and others, we find a whole range of poets whose literary output has been almost completely obscured by time and scholarly neglect. The recurrence of the same names over a range of epigram anthologies—and the stylistic, thematic, and modal resemblances in their poetry, to whatever extent these were engendered by the nature of the anthological process itself—give the impression of a poetic school. Many of these epigrammatists knew one another and had collegial relationships (e.g. ash-Shihāb al-Ḥijāzī and Taqī ad-Dīn al-Badrī)—while others had more hostile relationships (e.g. an-Nawājī and Ibn Ḥijjah)—and some were not linked in any way except *ex post facto* through neighboring citations in poetry collections. In his *taqrīẓ* (commendation) on Shams ad-Dīn an-Nawājī's (d. 1455) bacchic anthology *Ḥalbat al-kumayt*, Ibn Ḥijjah al-Ḥamawī (d. 1434) lists nearly forty poets who are cited in the anthology and says that were it not for fear of testing the reader's patience, he would have listed them all.[46] Evidence of these literary relationships can be seen clearly in the exchange of *maqāṭīʿ*-poems between authors and in the interaction of *maqāṭīʿ*-poems within anthologies themselves.

In *Khulāṣat al-athar fī aʿyān al-qarn al-ḥādī ʿashar* (*The Choicest Traces: the great ones of the eleventh century*), a biographical dictionary of 11th/17th-century notables, the author Muḥammad al-Amīn b. Faḍl Allāh al-Muḥibbī (1061–1111/1651–1699) relates the story—narrated by Shaykh al-Islām Ismāʿīl an-Nābulusī—of a handsome boy of Aleppo and the *maqāṭīʿ*-poems he inspired.[47] These poems all end in the phrase "Beauty lies beneath the turban of the *Anṣārī*" (*wa-l-ḥusnu taḥta ʿimāmati l-anṣārī*), a humorous allusion (imperfect *taḍmīn*) to a line by the poet al-Akhṭal (d. c. 92/710). Al-Akhṭal, a Christian Arab and a favorite of the Umayyad court, composed two famous invective (*hijāʾ*) poems against the supporters of the Prophet (the *Anṣār*) at

45 The most recent contribution to the history of the literary *majlis* is Ali, *Arabic Literary Salons*.

46 Ibn Ḥijjah al-Ḥamawī, *Qahwat al-inshāʾ*, ed. Rudolf Veselý (Beirut [Berlin]: Klaus Schwarz Verlag, 2005), 411. This was obviously written before the two fell out.

47 See *EI*^{2}, s.v. "al-Muḥibbī. 3. Muḥammad al-Amīn" [C. Brockelmann]. al-Muḥibbī also uses the term *maqāṭīʿ* in another of his works: *Nafḥat ar-rayḥānah wa-rashḥat ṭilāʾ al-ḥānah*, 5 vols, ed. ʿAbd al-Fattāḥ Muḥammad al-Ḥilw (Cairo: Dār Iḥyāʾ 1389/1969). See also a similar *maqāṭīʿ*-poetry fad inspired by a turban reported in Ibn Ḥajar, *Inbāʾ al-ghumar bi-anbāʾ al-ʿumar*, ed. Ḥasan Ḥabashī, 3 vols (Cairo: al-Majlis al-Aʿlā li-sh-Shuʾūn al-Islāmiyyah, 1392/1972) 1:10–11.

the behest of the Umayyad Caliph Yazīd b. Muʿāwiyah (r. 60–4/680–83).[48] One of these poems ends in a cutting line that includes the hemistich these *maqāṭīʿ*-poems would allude to some nine centuries hence:[49]

dhahabat Qurayshu bi-l-makārimi wa-l-ʿulā
wa-l-luʾmu taḥta ʿamāʾimi l-anṣārī

Quraysh have gone and taken with them [all] virtue and distinction.
Now only baseness [remains], beneath the turbans of the *Anṣār*.

There is a slight difference, however, in the way the quotation is used in these later poems. In al-Akhṭal's poem, the turbans are plural as are the Supporters of the Prophet, but in the later poems it is the turban of the descendant himself. The slight morphological modification would not be heard in recitation, however, as at the end of the line of verse the *-iyyi* ending must be pronounced *-ī*. Here is al-Muḥibbī's account of the exchange, followed by a translation:[50]

48 See *EI*³, s.v. "al-Akhṭal" [Tilman Seidensticker].

49 See, *inter alia*, in Abū l-Faraj al-Iṣbahānī, *Kitāb al-Aghānī*, 16 vols, ed. Muṣṭafā as-Saqqā (Cairo: Dār al-Kutub, 1927–61), 16:36. See also Ibn Sallām al-Jumaḥī, *Ṭabaqāt fuḥūl ash-shuʿarāʾ*, 2 vols, ed. Maḥmūd Muḥammad Shākir (Cairo: Maṭbaʿat al-Madanī, 1974), 397; Ibn Qutaybah, *ash-Shiʿr wa-sh-shuʿarāʾ*, 2 vols, ed. Aḥmad Muḥammad Shākir (Cairo: Dār al-Maʿārif, 1966–67), 1:484.

50 al-Muḥibbī, *Khulāṣat al-athar fī aʿyān al-qarn al-ḥādī ʿashar*, 4 vols (Cairo: 1248/1867–8 [repr. Beirut: Dār Ṣādir, n.d.]), 1:105, in the entry on Abū Bakr b. Manṣūr al-ʿUmarī ad-Dimashqī (d. 1048/1638).

نشأ بحلب غلام بديع الجمال من أقارب شيخ الاسلام المرحوم الشيخ زين الدين عمر العرضي والغلام شريف أنصاري فنظم فيه أدباء حلب مقاطيع كثيرة في آخر كل مقطوع منها «والحسن تحت عمامة الانصاري» ثمّ أرسلوا الى دمشق يطلبون من أدبائها مقاطيع على نمط ما نظموه فنظم أدباء الشام مقاطيع كثيرة وأرسلوها اليهم منها

[من الكامل]

سألوا عَنِ ٱلحُسنِ ٱلبديعِ تجاهُلاً … والحقُّ لا يخفَى عَلَى ٱلابصارِ
فأجبتُ ما هذا ٱلتّجاهُلُ والعَمَى … والحسنُ تحتَ عِمامةِ ٱلانصاري

ومن ذلك قولي فيه [من الكامل]

قالواهَلِ ٱجْتَمَعَتْ صِفاتُ ٱلحسنِ في … أحدٍ ولم تُحْجَبْ عَنِ ٱلابصارِ
قُلْتُ ٱلملاحةُ والجمالُ بأسْرِهِ … والحسنُ تحتَ عِمامةِ ٱلانصاري

ومن ذلك قولي فيه أيضاً [من الكامل]

ما حُلْتُ عَنْ حَلَبٍ وكُنْتُ مُهاجِراً … للحُسنِ حيثُ ٱلسَّعدُ مِنْ أنصاري
فالسَّعدُ لاحَ بِوجهِ أنصارِها … والحُسنُ تحتَ عِمامةِ ٱلانصاري

There was a very handsome adolescent boy in Aleppo who was a relative of the late Shaykh al-Islām Zayn ad-Dīn ʿUmar al-ʿUrḍī and was himself a descendant (*sharīf*) of both the Prophet and one of the Prophet's early supporters (*Anṣārī*).[51] The literati of Aleppo composed many *maqāṭīʿ*-poems, all ending [in the phrase] "Beauty lies beneath the turban of the *Anṣārī*" (*wa-l-ḥusnu taḥta ʿimāmati l-anṣārī*).[52] They then wrote to the literati of Damascus asking them to compose *maqāṭīʿ*-poems in the style of what they had composed so the literati of Damascus composed many *maqāṭīʿ*-poems as well and sent them to them.

[Poem 1] One of these was:
They asked about wondrous beauty, feigning ignorance,
although the truth hides not from any who would see,
So I replied: "What's all this feigned ignorance and blindness
for «beauty lies beneath the turban of the *Anṣārī*»?"

[Poem 2] and in this vein, I wrote:
They asked: "Is it true that all the signs of beauty could be
present in a single person and they not be hidden from view?"
and I answered: "Delicacy and beauty, the whole lot,
for «beauty lies beneath the turban of the *Anṣārī*»."

[Poem 3] and in this vein, I also wrote:
I never had to leave Aleppo during my migration (*muhājir*) in search of beauty
because good luck (*saʿd*) is on my side (*anṣārī*).[53]
There, good omen (*saʿd*) shines in the face of the descendants of the *Anṣār* in the city
for «beauty lies beneath the turban of the *Anṣārī*».

---

51 See, *EI*², s.v. "al-Anṣār" [W. Montgomery Watt].

52 cf. Adriana Valencia and Shamma Boyarin, "*'Ke adame filiolo alieno'*: three *muwaššaḥāt* with the same *Kharja*" in *Wine, Women and Death: medieval Hebrew poems on the good life*, ed. Raymond P. Scheindlin (Philadelphia, PA: Jewish Publication Society, 1986).

53 The use of the word *muhājir* has particular resonance here as the Prophet's migration to Medinah from Mecca (the *Hijrah*) is a key event in the formation of the earliest Muslim religious community.

This story provides further evidence for the *maqāṭīʿ*-genre, but what is more crucial is its depiction of the broad literary public's awareness of that genre, its role in social life, and its strong—though by no means exclusive—association with lyric themes. A similar example comes from another Ottoman-era biographical collection and reinforces the importance of *maqāṭīʿ*-poems in exchange. In this case, as in the following example from al-Muḥibbī's biographical dictionary, we see that *maqāṭīʿ*-poems were an important venue for literary competition, co-production, and interaction across a wide geographical area.

In the course of an entry on his paternal uncle, the Damascene Ibrāhīm b. Muḥammad al-Murādī (d. 1142/1730), the author of the biographical dictionary *Silk ad-durar fī aʿyān al-qarn ath-thānī ʿashar*, Muḥammad Khalīl al-Murādī (d. 1206/1791) presents a micro-anthology of *maqāṭīʿ*-poems on a single subject: the juice of myrtle berries (*māʾ ḥabb al-ās*).[54] Al-Murādī begins this micro-anthology by citing three poems by his paternal uncle, which end with the same concluding phrase present in the other poems, and then he transitions into presenting a literary history of this motif and the fad it inspired among the poets of Damascus.[55] The micro-anthology ends with a brief prose description of the myrtle plant and its medicinal properties and uses. It is at that point in the micro-anthology that al-Murādī chooses to elaborate further on the motif in literature and cites a further three *maqāṭīʿ*-poems on the subject. The micro-anthology comprises a total of twenty-nine poems (a total of 82 verses):[56]

54 On myrtle, see David Waines (ed.), *Food Culture and Health in Pre-Modern Islamic Societies* (Leiden: Brill, 2011), 181. See also *Wikipedia*, s.v. (Arabic) "*ās*" <https://ar.wikipedia.org/wiki/آس>. On a recent trip to Sardinia, my partner and I enjoyed sampling homemade mirto, a local liqueur produced by macerating myrtle berries and leaves.

55 Muḥammad Khalīl b. ʿAlī al-Murādī, *Kitāb Silk ad-durar fī aʿyān al-qarn ath-thānī ʿashar*, 4 vols, ed. Muḥammad ʿAbd al-Qādir Shāhīn (Beirut: Dār al-Kutub al-ʿIlmiyyah, 1997), 1:31–6.

56 The section on myrtle extends beyond the boundaries of the micro-anthology—as I have determined it—but this boundary is only notional and could indeed be said to encompass the additional myrtle-related material, which I cite and translate here.

[وللعّم المذكور في ماء حبّ الآس قوله: [من الخفيف]

إنَّ مَن يُذكِرُ الحَبيبَ بِوَصلٍ   عِندَ مُضناهُ زائدُ الوَسواسِ
ذاكَ عَذبٌ يُرى ولو بِمَلامٍ   هوَ أحلى مِن ماءِ حَبِّ الآسِ

[وقوله في ذلك: [من الخفيف]

بِأبي أغيدٌ يَصولُ عَلى الصَبِّ   بِلَحظٍ مُفَوَّقٍ نَعّاسِ
وحَلا مِنهُ للمُتَيَّمِ نُطقٌ   هوَ أحلى مِن ماءِ حَبِّ الآسِ

[وقوله في ذلك: [من الخفيف]

يا فَريداً في الحُسنِ أرفِق بِصَبٍّ   داؤهُ مُعجِزٌ لِحَبِّ الآسِ
ثُمَّ جُد سَيّدي بِرَشفِ رُضابٍ   هوَ أحلى مِن ماءِ حَبِّ الآسِ

وفي ذلك مقاطيع شعرية صدرتْ من أدباء دمشق لأمرٍ اقتضاه ذلك فممّن أنشد فيه وأبدع في التشبيه الشيخ محمد بن احمد الكنجي الذي هو المبتدع لتضمينه والمبتكر لإيجاده واقتراع أبكاره وعونه

[فقال: [من الخفيف]

ظَبيُ إنسٍ بَدا بِرَونَقِ حُسنٍ   يَتَهادى بِقَدِّهِ المَيّاسِ
وحَباني مِن ثَغرِهِ بِرُضابٍ   هوَ أحلى مِن ماءِ حَبِّ الآسِ

[Poem 1] [My] uncle, mentioned above, wrote this poem on the juice of myrtle berries:

One who would remind his beloved that he's been promised a visit,
even as [love] causes him to waste away, simply gives fodder to his misgivings.
That water is sweet, even if it's issued in rebuke;
Sweeter even than the juice of myrtle berries.

[Poem 2] Also by him on that topic:

[I'd sacrifice] my father for that delicate boy who leaps to love
with his sleep-stirred, drowsy glances.
To the love-enraptured his every word is sweet;
Sweeter even than the juice of myrtle berries.

[Poem 3] Also by him on that topic:

O uniquely beautiful one, be merciful with your love,
his illness has proved impossible for myrtle berries.[58]
Rather give generously, my lord, of your saliva, which is
Sweeter even than the juice of myrtle berries.

There are other *maqāṭīʿ*-poems on this topic by the littérateurs of Damascus, which were written for some exigency or other. Among those who composed poetry (*ʾanshada*) on this topic and who excelled at similes [related to it] was ash-Shaykh Muḥammad b. Aḥmad al-Kanjī [a.k.a. Ibn Abī ʿAṣrūn, d. 1153/1740]. He was the one who pioneered this allusion (*taḍmīn*) [i.e. including the concluding phrase or refrain: *huwa aḥlā min māʾi ḥabbi l-āsī*] and came up with the idea (*mubtakir*) of including it and deflowering its virgins (*abkār*) and married women (*ʿūn*).

[Poem 4] This is by him:

A gazelle in human form, who appeared in beauty's splendor,
his hips swing as he walks past.
He granted me the saliva of his mouth, which was
sweeter even than the juice of myrtle berries.

58 A common medicament in the period. See Leigh Chipman, *The World of Pharmacy and Pharmacists in Mamlūk Cairo* (Leiden: Brill, 2010).

وله:[57] [من الخفيف]

يا رَسولَ ٱلرِّضا و[يا] خَيْرَ هادٍ   للبَرايا ورَحْمَةً للنَّاسِ
طيبُ ذِكراكَ في فَمي كُلَّ حِينٍ   هو أَحْلَى مِنْ ماءِ حَبِّ ٱلآسِ

ومن ذلك قول الشيخ سعدي العمري [من الخفيف]

يا مُثيرَ ٱلغَرامِ في كُلِّ قَلْبٍ   ما لِجُرْحِ ٱللِحاظِ غيرَكَ آسِ
داوِ مَرْضَى ٱلهَوَى بِرَشْفِ رُضابٍ   هو أَحْلَى مِنْ ماءِ حَبِّ ٱلآسِ

ومن ذلك قول أخيه الشيخ مصطفى العمري [من الخفيف]

بَدْرُ تِمٍّ حُلْوُ ٱلشَّمائِلِ غَضٌّ   وافِرُ ٱلظَّرْفِ بالمَحاسِنِ كاسِي
يَحْتَسِي ٱلسَّمْعُ مِنهُ طيبَ حَديثٍ   هو أَحْلَى مِنْ ماءِ حَبِّ ٱلآسِ

ومن ذلك قول المولى حامد العمادي المفتي [من الخفيف]

يا حَبيبي إذا سأَلْتَ سؤالاً   عَزَّ نَقْلاً وفيهِ نَفْعُ ٱلنَّاسِ
أَنْشُرِ ٱلكُتْبَ كالجَداوِلِ لَيْلاً   ونَهاراً مَعَ ٱجْتِماعِ حَواسِّي
فَسُروري بِنَقْلِ قَوْلٍ صَحيحٍ   هو أَحْلَى مِنْ ماءِ حَبِّ ٱلآسِ

وله مُداعباً رجل طلب منه ذلك: [من الخفيف]

قالَ شَخْصٌ طَبْخُ ٱلكُنافَةِ لَيْلاً   وٱقْتِناصي لِنَقْلِها وٱخْتِلاسي
وٱقْتِطافي قَطْرَ ٱلقَطائفِ مَعْها   هو أَحْلَى مِنْ ماءِ حَبِّ ٱلآسِ

57 I have suggested an emendation in l. 1a to fit the meter.

[Poem 5] Also by him:

O prophet of delight, most excellent guide
of men, and their greatest mercy,
The sweet mention of your name in my mouth from time to time is
sweeter even than the juice of myrtle berries.

[Poem 6] There is another poem on this subject by ash-Shaykh Saʿdī al-ʿUmarī [d. 1147/1734]:

O stoker of passion in every heart,
no one but you can cure (*āsī*) the wounds of [sharp] glances,
Cure the lovesick with a dose of your saliva, which is
sweeter even than the juice of myrtle berries.

[Poem 7] His brother ash-Shaykh Muṣṭafā al-ʿUmarī [d. 1143/1730] composed a poem on this subject as well:

[One with a face] like a full moon, his features are sweet and he is ripe.
His charm is abundant and he's bedecked in beautiful qualities.
People's ears drink delicious conversation from him, that's
sweeter even than the juice of myrtle berries.

[Poem 8] Our friend Ḥāmid al-ʿImādī, the Mufti, composed a poem on this subject as well:[59]

My darling, if you ask a question
that's difficult to transmit but that's of benefit to the people,
disseminate it in a steady stream of writing night
and day with all [your] senses.
The pleasure I feel when true words are disseminated is
sweeter even than the juice of myrtle berries.

[Poem 9] Another poem by him, here teasing a man who'd asked to be teased:

Someone who once said: baking *kunāfah* at nighttime,
and hunting it as it's transported and trickery,
and snatching ([*i*]*qtiṭāfī*) the sugar syrup of the *qaṭāʾif* along with it are
sweeter even than the juice of myrtle berries.[60]

---

59 Ḥāmid al-ʿImādī served as Muftī of Damascus for 34 (lunar) years. He was born in that city on 10 Jumādā al-Ākhirah 1103 / 28 February 1692 and died there on 6 Shawwāl 1171 / 13 June 1758 (see al-Murādī, *Silk ad-durar,* 2:15–24).

60 *Kunāfah* and *qaṭāʾif* are pastries sweetened with *qaṭr* (flavored sugar syrup).

[ومن ذلك قول المولى سعيد السعسعاني: [من الخفيف]

بيَ ريمٌ يَسْبي بِمِسْكِهِ خالٌ يتلألأ في جيدِهِ ٱلألماسي*

عَلَّني من رَحيقِ ثَغْرٍ بكأسٍ هو أحْلَى مِنْ ماءِ حَبِّ ٱلآسِ

[ومن ذلك قول الشيخ أحمد [بن] علي المنيني: [من الخفيف]

قُلْتُ للأهْيَفِ ٱلمُمَنَّعِ لَمَّا صَعَّدَتْ ماءُ خَدِّهِ أنْفاسي

ماءُ وَرْدٍ بِوَجْنَتَيْكَ لِصادٍ هو أحْلَى مِنْ ماءِ حَبِّ ٱلآسِ

[وتَفَنَّنَ في ذلك فنقله إلى لغة الألثغ فقال: [من الخفيف]

لَسْتُ أنْساهُ أغْيَدًا قَدْ أثارَتْ لُثْغَةٌ مِنْهُ لَوْعَتي بانبِعاثِ

قامَ يجْلو مِنَ ٱلمُدامِ كُؤوسًا بَيْنَ مَثْنَى يُرِيدُها وثَلاثِ

قائلاً هاكَ من رُضابي كأثًا هو أحْلَى مِنْ ماءِ حَبِّ ٱلآثِ

---

*بمسكه خال] في الأصل المطبوع: «بمسكي خال»

[Poem 10] There is another poem on this subject by our friend Saʿīd as-Saʿsaʿānī:[61]

I'm in love with a white antelope whose beauty-mark takes prisoners with its musk;[62]
it shines on his diamond-bright neck.
Give me a second cup of the wine of his mouth to drink, for it is
sweeter even than the juice of myrtle berries.

[Poem 11] There is another poem on this subject by ash-Shaykh Aḥmad b. ʿAlī al-Manīnī:[63]

I told the slender, unapproachable one,
when the moisture (*māʾ*) of his cheeks caused me to pant
To a thirsty man the rose-water (*māʾ ward*) of your cheeks is
sweeter even than the juice of myrtle berries.

[Poem 12] He tried different things with the subject, including recasting [the phrase] in a lisp as in the following poem:

I'll never forget that handsome one whose
lisp stoked my passion and revived it.
He stood up [and began] to hand out wine in cups,
as the second and third [strings of the lute] played [songs he selected]
and said, "Here's a glath of my thaliva
"thweeter even than the juith of myrtle berrieth."[64]

61 Saʿīd as-Saʿsaʿānī, b. Damascus c. 1070/1659, d. Damascus 23 Dhū l-Qaʿdah 1144 / 18 May 1732 (see al-Murādī, *Silk ad-durar,* 2:146–52).

62 The beauty mark (*khāl*) was often compared to a grain of musk. Musk is taken from a gland in antelopes.

63 Aḥmad b. ʿAlī al-Manīnī, b. Manīn 12 Muḥarram 1089 / 6 March 1678, d. 19 Jumādā al-Ākhirah 1172 / 17 February 1759 (see al-Murādī, *Silk ad-durar*, 1:153–66).

64 The beloved's lisp is a common motif in Arabic erotic poetry (see, *inter alia*, the poem by aṣ-Ṣāḥib b. ʿAbbād (d. 385/995) translated in Kristina Richardson, *Difference and Disability in the Medieval Islamic World: Blighted Bodies* (Edinburgh: Edinburgh University Press, 2012), 12).

[٧ ومن ذلك قول الشيخ صادق الخَرّاط: [من الخفيف]

يا بِروحي مَنْ جاءَ يُخطِرُ عُجْبًا   في حِلا ٱلمُلْكِ كالقَنا ٱلمَيّاسِ
ناظِرٌ للوَرى بِطَرْفٍ غضوبٍ   بينَ قَومي وَلَمْ يَخَفْ من باسِ
قُلْتُ لا تَغْضَبَنَّ شَتْمُكَ عِنْدي   هو أَحْلَى مِنْ ماءِ حَبِّ ٱلآسِ*

[٧ ومن ذلك قول الشيخ محمّد المحمودي وفيه التورية: [من الخفيف]

قَدْ حَباني آسًا بِحَبٍّ عَجيبٍ   قالَ هذا مُفَرِّحُ ٱلأَكْياسِ*
قَدْ عَجَنّا أجزاءَ هذا بماءٍ   ذيبَ مِنْ سُكَّرٍ كَما الأَلماسِ
فَرَآهُ ٱلحَبيبُ فاشْتاطَ غَيْظًا   قُلْتُ دَعْهُ ولا تَخَفْ من باسِ
وتَعَوَّضْ عَنْهُ بِرَشْفِ رُضابٍ   هو أَحْلَى مِنْ ماءِ حَبِّ ٱلآسِ

[٧ ومن ذلك قول الفاضل محمّد بن رحمة الله الأيّوبي مُخاطِبًا محمّد الكنجي:

[من الخفيف]

يا هُمامًا حازَ ٱلكَمالاتِ طُرًّا   بابْتِكارِ ٱلتَّخْييلِ والاحْتِراسِ
دُمْتَ في حَلْبَةِ ٱلفَضائِلِ فَرْدًا   حائِزَ ٱلسَّبْقِ زائِدَ ٱلإِيناسِ
كَمْ لَكُمْ مِنْ بَديعِ دُرِّ نِظامٍ   هو أَحْلَى مِنْ ماءِ حَبِّ ٱلآسِ

* شتمك] في الأصل المطبوع: «فشتمك»
* حباني آسًا] في الأصل المطبوع: «حباني الآس». قلت] في الأصل المطبوع: «قال».

[Poem 13] There is another poem on this subject by ash-Shaykh Ṣādiq al-Kharrāṭ:[65]

I'd give my life for the one who's like a wonder
[dressed] in the finery of kings, his body like a spear, strutting.
He espies people with an irritable eye;
[but] among my tribe he fears no harm.
"No need to be angry," I said. "To me an insult from you would be
"sweeter even than the juice of myrtle berries."

[Poem 14] There is another poem on this subject by ash-Shaykh Muḥammad al-Maḥmūdī (including a double entendre):

He gave me a gift of myrtle with strange berries [or: wondrous affection]
and said, "This brings joy to elegant people."
We made a dough with parts of it mixed with water,
in which we'd melted sugar resembling diamonds.
And when the beloved saw it, he flew off the handle,
but I said, "Let it go. Don't be so upset.
"Take restitution with a drink of this saliva that's
"sweeter even than the juice of myrtle berries."

[Poem 15] There is another poem on this subject by the great Muḥammad b. Raḥmat Allāh al-Ayyūbī, addressing Muḥammad al-Kanjī:[66]

O hero who's acquired all perfection, all,
with his creative imagination and close watch,
Long may you remain a solitaire in the arena of noble qualities,
champion of the race, amplifier of companionship.
How many brilliant/eloquent pearls you've strung on necklaces/poems that are
sweeter even than the juice of myrtle berries.

65 Ṣādiq b. Muḥammad, known as al-Kharrāṭ, was ʿAbd al-Ghanī an-Nābulusī's son-in-law. He died in Damascus on 5 Shaʿbān 1143 / 13 February 1731 (see al-Murādī, *Silk ad-durar*, 2:219–27).

66 Muḥammad b. Raḥmat Allāh al-Ayyūbī was born in Damascus in 1081/1670 and died in Istanbul on 7 Shaʿbān 1150 / 30 November 1737 (see al-Murādī, *Silk ad-durar*, 4:59–61).

[٢ ومن ذلك قول الشيخ صالح بن المزوِّر: [من الخفيف]

أَسَرَ ٱلقَلْبَ حُبُّ ظَبْيٍ غَرِيرٍ ثَوبُ حُسْنٍ لَهُ ٱلمُصَوِّرُ كاسي
أَخَذَ ٱلهَجْرَ والصُّدودَ دَلالاً بفؤادٍ عَلَى ٱلمُتَيَّمِ قاسي
قُلْتُ جُدْ لي بِنَظْرَةٍ مِنْ مُحَيّا كَ حَبيبي فَقَدْ عَدِمْتُ حواسي
فَحَباني مِنْهُ بِساعَةِ وَصْلٍ هي أَحْلَى مِنْ ماءِ حَبِّ ٱلآسِ

[٢ ومن ذلك قول الشيخ موسى المحاسني: [من الخفيف]

بَدْرُ تَمٍّ بَدا بِحُسْنِ ٱللِّباسِ يَتَباهَى بِقَدِّهِ ٱلمَيّاسِ
يَزْدَري بالغُصونِ لِيناً وقَدّاً والظِّبا لفتةً مَعَ ٱسْتيناسِ
أَسْكَرَتْني أَلفاظُهُ بِحَديثٍ هوأَحْلَى مِنْ ماءِ حَبِّ ٱلآسِ

[٢ ومن ذلك قول الشيخ سعيد الكاني: [من الخفيف]

يا سُروري بَعْدَ طولِ ٱلتَّنائي باللقا وٱعْتِناقِ ظَبْيٍ كَناسِ
فَبِروحي وما حَوَيْتُ بَشيراً رَدَّ إذ جاءَ ناظِري وحَواسي
عِنْدَما دارَ لي مِنَ ٱلبُشْرِ كأساً هوأَحْلَى مِنْ ماءِ حَبِّ ٱلآسِ

[Poem 16] There is another poem on this subject by ash-Shaykh Ṣāliḥ b. al-Muzawwir:[67]

The heart is prisoner to the love of an inexperienced gazelle
The Former of All Things (*al-muṣawwir*) has dressed him in the robes of beauty.
He has learned [to practice] separation and rejection as a form of coquetry
with that heart of his so cruel to lovers in his thrall.
"Grant me," I said, "a glance from that face
"of yours, my dear, for I have lost my senses."
So he gave me the gift of time spent in union with him and it was
sweeter even than the juice of myrtle berries.

[Poem 17] There is another poem on this subject by ash-Shaykh Mūsā l-Maḥāsinī:[68]

[One with a face like] the full moon appeared in beautiful clothes,
showing off his strutting gait.
He puts the branches to shame with his supple, slender figure
and with his sidelong glance and docility [mocks] gazelles.
He intoxicated me with his words in conversation that was
sweeter even than the juice of myrtle berries.

[Poem 18] There is another poem on this subject by Saʿīd al-Kinānī:[69]

How happy I was—after a long and distant separation—
to meet and embrace that gazelle of the thicket.
My soul and all the hope I'd held
were returned to me when he appeared before my eyes and senses
and handed me a cup of glad tidings
sweeter even than the juice of myrtle berries.

---

67 Ṣāliḥ b. al-Muzawwir was born in Damascus c. 1090/1679 and died there during Rabīʿ ath-Thānī 1152/1739 (see al-Murādī, *Silk ad-durar,* 2:231–38).

68 Mūsā l-Maḥāsinī was born in Damascus and died there in Muḥarram 1173/1759 (see al-Murādī, *Silk ad-durar,* 4:255–59).

69 Saʿīd al-Kinānī died in Istanbul at the end of 1155/1743 (see al-Murādī, *Silk ad-durar,* 2:141–46).

[ومن ذلك قول الماهر مصطفى بن بيري الحلبي [من الخفيف]

بأبي مُشْرِقُ ٱلجيُوبِ بِوَجْهٍ   هوكالبدرِ في دُجَى ٱلأغلاسِ
قَدْ جلَتْهُ يَدُ ٱلتَّلاقي علَينا   مُسْفِرًا في مَلابِسِ ٱلايناسِ
وأمالَ ٱلعِناقَ نحْوِي عَطْفًا   يَزْدَهي مِنْ قَوامِهِ ٱلمَيَّاسِ
فتجارَتْ سَوابِقي مِنْ دُموعي   قَطَّرَتْها صَواعِدُ ٱلأنفاسِ*
فتَلَقَّى بِفاضِلِ ٱلرُّدْنِ دَمْعي   مُذْرأى فَيْضَ عِبْرَتي ذاٱنْبِجاسِ
فتأوَّهْتُ حينَ أنْكَرَحالي   قائلاً وَهْوَ بانْعِطافي مُواسي
إنَّ دَمْعَ ٱلسُّرورِغِبَّ ٱلتَّلاقي   هوأحلى مِنْ ماءِ حَبِّ ٱلآسِ

[ومن ذلك قول البارع حسين ابن مصلي: [من الخفيف]

زادَ مِنْها زَبَرْجَدُ ٱلوَشْمِ ثَغْرًا   سُكَّرِيًّا مُعَطَّرَ ٱلأنفاسِ
أرْشَفَتْني رُضابَهُ ثُمَّ قالَتْ   هوأحلى مِنْ ماءِ حَبِّ ٱلآسِ

[ومن ذلك قول الكامل محمّد بن عبد الله كتخدا اوجاق اليرلية:

[من الخفيف]

ما عَلى مَنْ قَضَى مَمَرَّ ٱللَّيالي   صارِفًا نَقْدَ عُمْرِهِ لِلكاسِ
يَتَعاطَى مَشْمولةً بِمِزاجٍ   هوأحلى مِنْ ماءِ حَبِّ ٱلآسِ

* فتجارت] في الأصل المطبوع: «فتجاورت».

[Poem 19] There is another poem on this subject by the skilled Muṣṭafā b. Bīrī al-Ḥalabī:[70]

[I'd sacrifice] my father for this one who shines in hearts with his face
like the full moon at night's end.
The hand of meeting revealed him to us
unveiled in the garments of companionship.
And then he inclined his neck toward me,
showing off his haughty figure.
They vied with one another, the racers of my tears,
which were dripped there by the [condensing] vapor of my sighs.[71]
He received my tears in the ample fabric of his sleeve
after he saw the flood of weeping gushing out.
I sighed when he pretended not to know what a [sorry] state I was in,
and said—as if to console me out of sympathy—
"Tears of joy drunk at the occasion of meeting [the beloved] are
"sweeter even than the juice of myrtle berries."

[Poem 20] There is another poem on this subject by the the talented Ḥusayn ibn Muṣallī:[72]

The green gems of her tattoo were joined by a mouth
as sweet as sugar her breath like perfum.
She gave me a drink of [her] saliva, then said, "It's
sweeter even than the juice of myrtle berries."

[Poem 21] There is another poem on this subject by the excellent Muḥammad b. ʿAbd Allāh, colonel-commandant of the local janissary corps in Damascus (*ōcāq al-yerliyya*, scil. *Yerlü Čeri*):[73]

Someone who spends his nights,
wasting the coin of his life on drink
can never appreciate a cooled, mixed wine that is
sweeter even than the juice of myrtle berries?

70 Muṣṭafā b. Muḥammad, known as Ibn Bīrī, died in Istanbul in 1148/1735 (see al-Murādī, *Silk ad-durar,* 4:231–41).

71 The same verb used for "to drip" (*qaṭṭara*) can also mean "to tie riding animals in a line", which the word *sawābiq* (race horses) in the previous hemistich would lead readers to expect. This is another example of *tawhīm*.

72 Ḥusayn b. Aḥmad, known as Ibn Muṣallī, was a student of ʿAbd al-Ghanī an-Nābulusī. He died in Damascus c. 1152/1739 (see al-Murādī, *Silk ad-durar,* 2:48–53).

73 See *EI*^{2}, s.v. "Yerliyya" [Abdul-Karim Rafeq].

ومن ذلك قوله أيضًا: [من الخفيف]

هاتِ حَدِّثْ عَنْها ولا تَخْشَ لَوْمًا   وَٱسْقِنيها بالجامِ أو بالكاسِ
بِنْتُ كَرْمٍ مِزاجُها وَصَفاها   هو أحلى مِنْ ماءِ حَبِّ ٱلآسِ

ومن ذلك قول الشيخ الخليل بن محمّد الفتّال: [من الخفيف]

جَسَّ نَبْضي ٱلطَّبيبُ قالَ عليلٌ   في هَوَى أغْيَدٍ شَديدِ ٱلباسِ
قُلْتُ خَلِّ ٱلهوى وعُدْ جَسَّ نَبْضي   إنَّ هذا يَزيدُ في ٱلوَسْواسِ
قالَ إنّي لَناصِحٌ بِكَلامي   لَيْسَ إلّا مِنْ أعْيُنٍ نُعّاسِ
قُلْتُ صِفْ لي مُفَرِّحًا يَجْلُ هَمّي   ويُزِلْ حَرَّ مُهْجَتي وحواسي
قالَ فارْشُفْ مِنْ ريقِهِ رَشَفاتٍ   هي أحلى مِنْ ماءِ حَبِّ ٱلآسِ

ومن ذلك قول الكامل إبراهيم بن مصطفى الأسطواني مُخاطِبًا الكنجي:

[من الخفيف]

يا فَريدًا في عَصْرِهِ والمَزايا   مَنْ حَوَى ٱلعِلْمَ والحِجَى باقْتِباسِ
هو خِلِّي ٱلكَنْجي بَحْرُ نِظامٍ   مَعْدَنُ ٱلجُودِ عاطِرُ ٱلأنْفاسِ
لَمْ يَدَعْ لِلْمَقالِ مَعْنًى بَديعًا   يَجْتَني مِنْهُ حارَ فيهِ حواسي
أوْدَعَ ٱلسَّمْعَ مِنْ حَلاهُ حَديثًا   هو أحلى مِنْ ماءِ حَبِّ ٱلآسِ

[Poem 22] Another poem by him:

Come and tell me about her! Do not fear reproach.
Pour her out to me in cups, silver and glass.
The daughter of the vine, whether diluted or pure, she's
sweeter even than the juice of myrtle berries.

[Poem 23] There is another poem on this subject by ash-Shaykh al-Khalīl b. Muḥammad al-Fattāl:[74]

The physician took my pulse and said, "He's afflicted
with the love of a bold young beauty."
"Don't mind about love," I said, "and take my pulse again.
"All this talk just disturbs one's thoughts even more."
"I'm giving true advice," he said.
"The only thing causing this is those languid eyes."
"So prescribe me something pleasant that will dispel my worry", I said.
"Something that will break the fever of my heart and senses."
And so he said, "Drink many gulps of his saliva, which is
"sweeter even than the juice of myrtle berries."[75]

[Poem 24] There is another poem on this subject by the excellent Ibrāhīm b. Muṣṭafā al-Usṭuwānī in which he addresses [Muḥammad] al-Kanjī:

O solitaire of his age and of all qualities,
the one who collected knowledge and intelligence on his firebrand
[or: with Qur'anic quotations in poetry]
He is my close friend al-Kanjī, the sea of poetry,
the mine of generosity, the perfume of breath.
He never leaves a single eloquent motif,
but harvests them all. He bewilders all my senses.
In our ears, the pleasantness of his conversation is
sweeter even than the juice of myrtle berries.

74 Khalīl b. Muḥammad, known as al-Fattāl (the roper), was a student of Aḥmad b. ʿAlī al-Manīnī. He was born in Damascus in 1117/1705 and died in Dhū l-Ḥijjah 1186/1773 (see al-Murādī, *Silk ad-durar*, 2:112–15).

75 This poem best represents the frequent use of the rhetorical device *al-murājaʿah* ("repartee") in *maqāṭīʿ*-poems. See Cachia, *The Arch Rhetorician*, no. 146.

وقوله وتَعَرَّضَ لذكر وصف رجلٍ يُعْرَفُ بابن الفُستُقي من أهالي الصالحية على طريق المُداعِبة: [من الخفيف]

قُلْتُ يومًا للفُستُقيِّ تأدَّبْ   واشْهَدِ ٱلحَقَّ مُعلِنًا في ٱلنَّاسِ
قالَ دَعْني ولا تَكُنْ لي نَصوحًا   فاقَتي أَزْعَجَتْ جَميعَ حَواسي
دِرْهَمٌ في شِهادَةِ ٱلزُّورِ عِنْدي   هوأحلى مِنْ ماءِ حَبِّ ٱلآسِ

ومن ذلك ما أنشد فيه الأستاذ الشيخ عبد الغني النابلسي بقوله:

[من الخفيف]

نَزَلَ ٱلغَيْثُ بَعْدَ طولَ رَجاءٍ   فَهَنيئًا بِهِ لِكُلِّ ٱلنَّاسِ
وَحلا عِنْدَهُمْ وطابَ كَثيرًا   فهوأحلى مِنْ ماءِ حَبِّ ٱلآسِ

ومن ذلك قول الشيخ مصطفى اللقيمي الدمياطي نزيل دمشق:

[من الخفيف]

رَوْضُ حُسْنٍ فيه ٱلحَبيبُ تَجَلَّى   بِدَلالٍ تِيهًا عَلى ٱلجُلَّاسِ
قَدْ سَقاني مِنَ ٱلعِبادِ بِوَصْلٍ   هوأحلى مِنْ ماءِ حَبِّ ٱلآسِ

ومن ذلك قول الشيخ محمّد بن عُبَيْد العطّار: [من الخفيف]

صادَ قلبي بِلَحْظِهِ مُذْ تَبَدَّى   يَتَثَنَّى بِعِطْفِهِ ٱلمَيَّاسِ
رشأٌ كامِلُ ٱلمَحاسِنِ فَرْدٌ   في بَهاءٍ مُعَطَّرِ ٱلأنفاسِ
وَصْلُهُ بُغْيَتي وَرَشْفُ لِماءٍ   هوأحلى مِنْ ماءِ حَبِّ ٱلآسِ

[Poem 25] Another poem he wrote after he was asked to describe teasingly a man known as Ibn al-Fustuqī from the Ṣāliḥiyyah neighborhood [of Damascus]:

I said to the pistachio-seller (*al-fustuqī*) one day, "Behave yourself,
"And let people hear you testify to the truth."
"Leave me alone," he said, "and spare me your advice.
"My poverty disturbs all of my senses.
"To me a silver coin for a false testimony is
sweeter even than the juice of myrtle berries."

[Poem 26] There is another poem on this subject composed by the master ash-Shaykh ʿAbd al-Ghanī an-Nābulusī [d. 1143/1731]:

Showers of rain have fallen after much prayer.
Congratulations to all the people
for they are pleased by it and it has done them good
for it's sweeter even than the juice of myrtle berries.

[Poem 27] There is another poem on this subject by ash-Shaykh Muṣṭafā l-Luqaymī, a Damiettan who moved to Damascus:[76]

In a garden of beauty, there the beloved was revealed,
coquettish and haughty toward those who were seated.
He gave me—out of everyone—union to drink and it was
sweeter even than the juice of myrtle berries.

[Poem 28] There is another poem on this subject by ash-Shaykh Muḥammad b. ʿUbayd al-ʿAṭṭār:[77]

He hunted my heart with that glance of his as soon as he arrived on the scene,
swaying about, with that inclining, proud gait of his.
A stumbling fawn; every attribute of beauty is his; he has no peer
in splendor; and his breath is sweet.
It is union with him that I wish for, a gulp of water
sweeter even than the juice of myrtle berries.

---

76 Muṣṭafā b. Asʿad was born in Damietta in Rabīʿ al-Awwal 1105/1693 and died in Damascus on 27 Dhū l-Ḥijjah 1178 / 17 June 1765 (see al-Murādī, *Silk ad-durar*, 4:180–92, esp. the chronogram-*maqṭūʿ* on 192.)

77 Muḥammad b. ʿUbayd al-ʿAṭṭār (the herbalist) was born in Damascus in 1130/1717 and died there on the first of Rabīʿ al-Awwal 1157 / 14 April 1744 (see al-Murādī, *Silk ad-durar*, 4:74–6).

[ومما وُجِدَ على هامش هذا الكتاب فألحقناه وهو للمولى السيّد حسين المرادي المفتي بدمشق الشام بيتين في هذا المعنى ومشطّرهم السيّد محمّد أمين الأيّوبي في سبك المعنى طَعمًا ورائحة: [من الكامل]

شاماتُ حَبِّ ٱلآسِ لمّاَ أنْ بَدتْ في خَدِّهِ أسبَتْ عُقولَ ٱلنّاسِ
وتَكامَلَتْ أوْصافُهُ لمّاَ غَدتْ مِنْ صُدْغِهِ في وَجْنَةِ ٱلألْماسِ
فانْظُرْ إلى ريقٍ حلا في ثَغْرِهِ أشْهَى وأزْهَى مِنْ سُلافِ ٱلكاسِ*
والثِمْ لَمَى ذاكَ ٱلثُّغَيْرِ لأنَّهُ أزْكَى شَذاً مِنْ ماءِ حَبِّ ٱلآسِ

وفي ذلك غيرُ ما ذكَرْنا من المقاطيع وأمّا الآس ففضائله عظيمة حتّى ذُكِرَ أنّ عصا موسى عليه السلام كانت منه وخضرته دائمة وله زهرة بيضاء طيّبة الرائحة وثمرته سوداء ومنها ما هو أبيض كاللؤلؤ بين ورق الزبرجد وعصارة ثمرته رطبًا تفعل فعل الثمرة في المنفعة وهي جيّدة للمعدة وله خصائص غير ذلك وطبعه بارد يابس مُجَفِّف يولّد سهرًا ودفع مضرّته بالبنفسج ويُصلح الأمزجة الباردة بالخاصيّة

*حَلا] في الأصل المطبوع: «خلا» .

[Poem 29] Another poem, which was found in the margin of this book and which I include here was written by our friend, as-Sayyid Ḥusayn al-Murādī, the Mufti of Damascus.[78] That poem on the same subject was two lines long and the person who amplified it by halving the lines and inserting new hemistichs (*mushaṭṭiruhum*) was as-Sayyid Muḥammad Amīn al-Ayyūbī, who recast the [existing] figure with taste and fragrance:[79]

When the beautymarks of myrtle berries appeared
 on his cheek, they captured the people's hearts (lit. minds).
And his appearance was perfected when they [arose]
 on his temple against his diamond cheeks.
So look to that saliva so sweet in his mouth
 tastier and more proud than must in a glass,
And kiss the red lips of that tiny mouth for its
 bouquet is more aromatic than even the juice of myrtle berries.

There are more *maqāṭī*ʿ-poems on this subject than those we have cited here. As for myrtle, its benefits are legion. It is even said that Moses' staff was made of myrtle wood. It is evergreen and it has white, sweet-smelling flowers. Its fruit [berries] is black but there is a variety with white fruit, which looks like pearls on leaves of green gemstone. The juice of its fruit is moist and has the same benefit as the fruit itself. It is good for digestion and for other uses as well. Its nature is cold and dry. It has dehydrating and stimulant properties and it can be counteracted with violets. It is particularly suited to those of a cold humor.

---

78 The book that al-Murādī is referring to here is almost certainly Muḥammad al-Kanjī's treatise (*risālah*) *Riḍwān al-maḥbūb wa-mufarriḥ al-qulūb* (*Pleasing the Beloved and Delighting Hearts*), in which he collected the poems that quote the line "Sweeter even than the juice of myrtle berries". See further in appendix, no. 70. The poet cited here, Ḥusayn al-Murādī, was the biographer's paternal uncle. He was born in Damascus in 1138/1725 and he succeeded his brother, the biographer's father, as Muftī of that city upon his death in Shawwāl 1184/1771. He served in this position until his own death on 15 Ramaḍān 1188 / 19 November 1774 in Damascus (see al-Murādī, *Silk ad-durar*, 2:79–81).

79 Muḥammad Amīn b. Ibrāhīm al-Ayyūbī was born in Damascus and was nearly one-hundred (lunar) years old when he died in 1177/1763 (See al-Murādī, *Silk ad-durar*, 4:32).

[٧ وأنشد في تشبيهه سليمان بن محمّد الطرابلوسي [هكذا] قوله: [من المجتث]

أَحْبِبْ بِقُضْبانِ آسٍ ... في سائِرِ ٱلدَّهْرِ تُوجَدْ

كأنّها حينَ تَبْدو ... سَلاسِلٌ مِنْ زَبَرْجَدْ

[٧ وقال الأستاذ عبد الغني النابلسي: [من الكامل]

ولَقَدْ أَتَيْنا لِلحَدائِقِ بُكْرَةً ... والطَّلُّ يَقْطُرُ فَوْقَ أرضٍ أَتْفَرَ

وكَأنَّ حَبَّ ٱلآسِ فَوْقَ غُصونِهِ ... عِقْدُ ٱللآلي ضِمْنَ سِلْكٍ أَخْضَرَ*

[٧ وقد قال ابن حِجَّة تتبعّتُ ما قيلَ في الآس فما أرماني إلّا قولُ القائل:

[من الطويل]

خَليلَيَّ ما للآسِ يَعْبُقُ نَشْرُهُ ... إذا ٱشْتَمَّ أنفاسَ ٱلرِّياحِ ٱلبَواكِرِ

حَكَى لَوْنُهُ أصداغَ ريمٍ مُعَذَّرٍ ... وصورَتُهُ آذانَ خيلٍ نوافِرِ

*غصونه] في الأصل المطبوع: «غضونه» ورغمًا عن قاعدة أعراف تحقيق النصوص المسّمى «أندر القراءات المحتملة أقواها» فالمعنى هنا يُفضل على قراءة «غصونه».

[Poem 30] Sulaymān b. Muḥammad aṭ-Ṭarābulūsī wrote the following poem that includes a simile on it:

[Make sure you] like myrtle stems,
they'll be there for the rest of time.
And when they appear it's as though
they're chains of green gemstone.

[Poem 31] There is another poem by the master ʿAbd al-Ghanī an-Nābulusī:

We arrived at the garden early in the morning,
as the dew was still dripping on budding ground.
And the myrtle berries on their stems appear like
so many pearls strung on a chain of green.

[Poem 32] Ibn Ḥijjah said, "I have followed what has been written about myrtle and the only poem that struck me was this one":

My two companions, why should myrtle exude the fragrance of its foliage,
when it can smell the early morning breezes in the air?
The color [of its leaves] mimics the temples of a white antelope with a sprouting beard,
and their shape the ears of timid horses.

The coherence of this *maqāṭīʿ*-collection is made clear by the recurring concluding phrase present in twenty-eight of the *maqāṭīʿ*-poems, and the fact that every one of the thirty-two poems in this micro-anthology treats the myrtle plant and its fruit in one way or other. Poem 29 does not end on the phrase "even sweeter than the juice of myrtle berries" with which the previous twenty-eight poems conclude, but the slightly different expression with which it ends: "more aromatic than even the juice of myrtle berries" links it implicitly to those poems that preceded it. Poems 30–32 can be said to fall outside of the bounds of the micro-anthology, but many *maqāṭīʿ*-collections are paired with presentations of edifying and anecdotal information so while we may think of those poems as being of general interest or being present solely for the purposes of rhetorical or literary history, we should be aware that in the history of classical Arabic literature it is generic intermixing and adjacency that is the norm, not strict division. Within the micro-anthology of twenty-nine poems, coherence is also demonstrated through the use of what I have called variation, a process of linking poems in sequence through thematic, lexical, metrical, or figurative junctions. Poems 1 and 2 share the theme of speech, while Poems 2 and 3 are linked by the word *ṣabb* ("love"); it is the word *ruḍāb* ("saliva") that in turn links Poems 3 and 4. Lexical links such as these—which can be orthographic as well as radical—connect many of the poems in the micro-anthology:

Poems 4 and 5: *h-d-y*

Poems 5 and 6: the vocative construction yā X of Y; *riḍā* ("delight") and *marḍā* ("those laid low")

Poems 8 and 9: *naql* (relating speech/moving an object)

Poems 13 and 14:[80] *ʿ-j-b*

Poems 21 and 22: *mazāj* (mixing wine and water)

Poems 23 and 24: *khalli* ("leave off") and *khillī* ("my friend")

The reader should note that none of these lexical junctions are based on words rhyming in *-āsī*, which of course recur repeatedly in many of the poems owing

80 These poems also share the construction: negation + *khāfa* (jussive, sing.) + *min bāsī* but such syntactic parallels are common in poems that share the same meter and rhyme-word.

in part to the requirement of monoryhme. Thematic links in Arabic erotic poetry are a far more ambiguous case to make because classical Arabic love poetry does tenaciously enjoy certain associations of imagery, activity, setting, and metaphor specific to the genre. That these feature prominently in the junctions between poems does not mean that the technique of variation is not in operation, simply that thematic variation is a process that emerges from within the tradition itself and takes advantage of its generic proclivities:

Poems 7 and 8: speech

Poems 9 and 10: stealing/capturing

Poems 16, 17, and 19: clothing

Many of the other poems share the theme of drinking (usually wine) and being given to drink, as would be expected based on the hemistich that they all quote in conclusion. Other poems are related for literary-historical reasons (in some cases, in addition to the process of variation): Poems 6 and 7 were written by brothers, while Poems 1–3, 4–5, 8–9, 11–12, 21–22, and 24–25 respectively were written by the same poet.

This long exchange, which Muḥammad b. Aḥmad al-Kanjī initiated and later collected in a treatise (*risālah*), demonstrates the extent to which *maqāṭīʿ*-poems brought the littérateurs of 12th/17th-century Damascus together. Earlier biographical accounts also emphasize the importance of literary correspondence among members of the educated urban population and the prominent role played by *maqāṭīʿ*-poems in this correspondence. Consider the following example from aṣ-Ṣafadī's (d. 764/1363) epistolary collection *Alḥān as-sawājiʿ bayn al-bādī wa-l-murājiʿ*.[81] Here aṣ-Ṣafadī relates a *maqāṭīʿ*-exchange he had with Ibn Nubātah (d. 768/1366) over doves, which

81 The edition presented here is based on two previous editions of the text (aṣ-Ṣafadī, *Alḥān as-sawājiʿ*, ed. Sālim, 2:441–46; ed. Ṣāliḥ, 2:261–64) as well as the autograph manuscript of the text (Staatsbibliothek zu Berlin MS Wetzstein II 150, ff. 180b–82a. For full bibliographical information, see in the annotated bibliography: 14th century, 3. b. Compare other reports of *maqāṭīʿ*-correspondence such as in al-Murādī, *Silk ad-durar*, 1:31–6 (discussed on pp. 94–117), as well as non-epistolary circulation such as in Ibn Ḥajar, *Inbāʾ al-ghumar*, 3:145.

was probably inspired by a poem by Ṣafī ad-Dīn al-Ḥillī (d. c. 750/1350) that ends with the verses:[82]

[من المديد]

وشَدَتْ في الدّوْحِ صادِحةٌ   بِضُروبِ ٱلسَّجْعِ والمُلَحِ
كُلّما ناحَتْ عَلَى شَجَنٍ   خِلْتُها غَنّتْ عَلَى قَدَحِ

wa-shadat fī d-dawḥi ṣādiḥatun
bi-ḍurūbi l-saj'i wa-l-mulaḥī
kullamā nāḥat 'alā shajanin
khiltuhā ghannat 'alā qadaḥī

From within the great big tree, she sang a high note
on the last foot of a line of verse, cooing [or: rhymed prose] *bon mots*
Whenever she cooed [or: wailed], her emotion swelling up,
I had the feeling she was singing for my cup.

Here I have reproduced and translated their *maqāṭī'*-exchange:

82 See in aṣ-Ṣafadī, *al-Wāfī*, 18:486. See also in al-Murādī, *Silk ad-durar*, 2:143–44 where in an entry on Sa'īd al-Kinānī (d. 1155/1743) the author presents several *"maqāṭī'*-poems" on doves by past and present poets (*mutaqaddimūn wa-muta'akhkhirūn*) including poem no. 1, which he attributes to as-Sarrāj (d. 500/1106), author of the collection *Maṣāri' al-'ushshāq* (*Lovers' Deaths*).

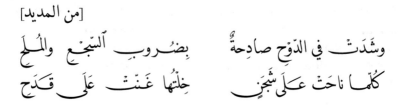

[ق١٨٠ب]

ولمّا وقف على مقاطيع لي نظمتها في الحمامة وهي

قولي: [من الخفيف]

ربّ ورقاءَ في ٱلدياجي تُناجي … إلفها في غُصونها ٱلميّادهْ*
فتُثيرُ ٱلهوى بلحنٍ عجيبٍ … يشهدُ ٱلسمعُ أنّها عوّادهْ
كُلّما رَجّعَتْ تَوَجّعْتُ حزنًا … وكأنّا في وَجْدِنا نتَبادهْ

وقولي أيضا: [من الوافر]

ورُبَّ حمامةٍ في ٱلدّوحِ باتَتْ … تُجيدُ ٱلنّوحَ فنًّا بَعْدَ فَنِّ
أُقاسِمُها ٱلهوى مهما ٱجتَمَعْنا … فَمِنْها ٱلنّوحُ والعَبَراتُ مِنّي

وقولي أيضًا: [من الوافر]

ولَيلَةَ نادَمَتْني ذاتُ طَوْقٍ … تَميلُ بِها ٱلأراكَةُ في ٱلتَّثَنّي
فَتَصدَحُ كُلّما أمْسَكْتُ كأسي … لَقَدْ باتَتْ عَلَى قَدَحي تُغَنّي

وقولي أيضًا: [من الوافر]

مُطَوّقَةٌ عَلَى غُصُنٍ … مُخَضّبَةٌ مِنَ ٱلفَرَحِ
لَها سَجْعٌ تُكَرّرُهُ … غَدا في ٱللّهْوِ مُقتَرِحي
إذا أمْسَكْتُ كأسي [في] … يَدي غَنّتْ عَلَى قَدَحي

[ق١٨١أ]

*تناجي] في «صالح»: تنادي. وكأنا] في «سالم»: فكأنما (وهذا يكسر الوزن) وفي «صالح»: فكأنّا.

When he [Ibn Nubātah] came across [some] *maqāṭīʿ*-poems I'd composed on a dove, including:

[Poem 1]
In the dark of night, a dove whispers a secret
to her close friend on the swaying boughs.
Stirring feelings of love with a wondrous song,
and all ears swear she must be a lutist.
Every time she makes a trilling sound, I feel the pain of sadness;
it's as though—in our love—we vie in extemporization.

and also:

[Poem 2]
How many doves in a great, big tree excel
in cooing in one style, then another.
I share love with her whenever we meet;
hers is the wailing and mine are the tears.

and also:

[Poem 3]
A night when I was kept company by a collared dove,
the branches of the toothbrush-tree bent and brought her near
Everytime I reached for my wine glass she cried out,
and spent [the evening] singing for my cup.[83]

and also:

[Poem 4]
A collared dove on a branch,
henna'd for a wedding feast.[84]
She has a coo she repeats again and again,
which I improvise upon in our amusements.
And whenever I take my goblet in hand,
she begins to sing for my cup.

83 The tense used in this poem (four hemistichs) may confuse some readers. The first hemistich is in the past tense. Hemistichs two and three should be read as a *ḥāl*-clause and hemistich four resumes the initial past tense.

84 The henna in this case is likely a reference to the dove's reddish-brown coloration.

] وقولي أيضًا: [من الخفيف]

لا تَقيسوا إلى ٱلحمامةِ حزنًا   إنّ فضلي تدري بِهِ ٱلعُشّاقُ

أنا أُمْلي ٱلغرامَ عن ظَهرِ قلبٍ   وَهْيَ تُملي وحَوْلَها ٱلأوراقُ

] وقولي أيضًا: [من الكامل]

لا تحسَبي يا وُرْقُ أنّكِ في ٱلهوى   مِثلي فلَيسَ يفوزُ إلّا مَنْ صَدَقْ

أمليتُ مِنْ قلبي ٱلغرامَ وأنتِ ما   تُملينَ حرفًا إنْ خَرَجْتِ عَنِ ٱلوَرَقْ

] وقولي أيضًا: [من الوافر]

مُطوَّقةٌ عَلى غُصْنٍ نَضيرٍ   تَهيجُ لِيَ ٱلصَّبابةَ والهُياما

إذا ناحَتْ بَكَيْتُ وإنْ تَغَنَّتْ   طَرِبْتُ لَقَدْ تَقارَضْنا ٱلغَراما

] وقولي أيضًا: [من الوافر]

أرَى وَرْقاءَ ذاتَ شَجًا وشَجْوٍ   لَها هَتْفٌ غدا سَبَبًا لِهَتْكي

تقولُ أما خُلقنا يا مُعَنَّى   سِوى أنّي أنوحُ وأنتَ تَبْكي

] وقولي أيضًا: [من الطويل]

أقولُ لِورْقاءِ ٱلحِمَى لا تُشَبِّهي   بِوَجْدي فإنَّ ٱلفَرْقَ للنّاسِ قدْ بانا

[ق١٨١ب]

تَغَنَّيْتِ بينَ ٱلبانِ في ٱلدَّوحِ فَرِحَةً   ونُحْتُ أنا حَزنًا عَلى غُصُنٍ بانا

and also:

[Poem 5]
Don't compare [my] sadness to the dove;
all the lovers know I'm pre-eminent.
I dictate (*umlī*) love from mere memory, while the dove
dictates, surrounded by leaves [or: folios].

and also:

[Poem 6]
O grey doves, don't think you're like me
when it comes to love, for only the honest shall prosper.
I write about love from the heart, but you wouldn't
be able to fill a page [lit. write a letter of the alphabet] if you ever left the foliage.

and also:

[Poem 7]
A collared dove on a blossoming branch
she makes me swoon and incites me.
When she cries, I weep, and when she sings,
I'm impassioned. In love, we improvise poems for each other.[85]

and also:

[Poem 8]
I spy a dove who grieves and who mourns,
and her call has become the reason for my disgrace.
She says, "Have we not been created,[86] O tormented one,
for me to wail and for you to weep?"

and also:

[Poem 9]
"Don't make similes out of my ardour", I tell the dove
of the sanctuary (*al-ḥimā*) 'for the difference is clear to all (*bānā*).
"You sing euphorically from the lofty Ben-tree (*al-bān*) while
I wail for one [slender like] a branch who has left me (*bānā*)."

---

85 For the game of literary improvisation "*taqāruḍ*", see Albert de Biberstein Kazimirski, *Dictionnaire arabe-français*, Nouvelle edition, 2 vols (Paris: G.-P. Maisonneuve, 1960), s.r. "*q-r-ḍ*".

86 This could also be read as *khaluqnā* ("we are suited for").

كتب هو [اي ابن نباتة] إليّ مقاطيع نظمها نظير ذلك

وهي قوله:[87] [من البسيط]

مالي نَديمٌ سِوَى وَرْقاءَ ساجِعَةٍ مِنْ بَعْدِ مُغْتَبَقي فيكُمْ ومُصْطَبَحي
إذا أدارَ ٱدِّكارُ ٱلوَصْلِ لي قَدَحاً مِنَ ٱلْمَدامِعِ غَنَّتْني عَلَى قَدَحي*

وقوله: [من المنسرح]

مـا لي نديمٌ سِوَى ٱلحَمائـمِ مِنْ بَعْدِكُمْ والبُكـا مِنَ ٱلتَّرَحِ
إذا أدارَ ٱدِّكارُكُمْ قَدحـاً مِنْ دَمْعِ عَيْنِيَ غَنَّتْ عَلَى قَدَحي

وقوله:[88] [من الكامل]

وحَديقـةٍ واصَـلْتُ جِلْوَتَهـا مـا بيـنَ مُغْتَبَقٍ ومُصْطَبَحِ
فـإذا أَخَـذْتُ بِظِلِّها قَدَحـاً غَنَّتْ حَمائِمُـها عَلَى قَدَحي

وقوله:[89] [من الرمل]

رُبَّ دَوْحٍ باكَـرَتْهُ عَزْمَـتي ونَـديمي بَعْـدَ أحْبـابي ٱدِّكارُ
فـإذا أعْـمَلْتُ فيـهِ قَدَحـاً شَبَّبَ ٱلوَصْـفُ وغَنَّاني ٱلهَزارُ

*من المدامع] في «سالم» و«صالح»: من أحمر الدمع.

87 Also recorded (with variants) in Ibn Nubātah, *Dīwān*, ed. Muḥammad al-Qalqīlī (Cairo: Maṭbaʿat at-Tamaddun, 1323/1905), 119 (see further in the annotated bibliography: 14th century, 4. b) and al-Ghuzūlī, *Maṭāliʿ albudūr*, 1:71.

88 Also recorded in Ibn Nubātah, *Dīwān*, 119 (with variants).

89 Also recorded in Ibn Nubātah, *Dīwān*, 253.

He [Ibn Nubātah] sent me some *maqāṭīʿ*-poems he'd written in response and among them were:

[Poem 1]
I have no boon-companion but for a cooing dove when, thinking of you,
I take a nightcap and a morning draught.
If the recollection of unison were to pass me a glass
of tears, the doves would sing [perched] on my cup.

and also:

[Poem 2]
My only companions are the doves
now that you've left, and tears I spill from sorrow.
If the memory of you were to pass me a glass,
of my eyes' tears, the doves would sing [perched] on my cup.

and also:

[Poem 3]
A garden which I persisted in until it was unveiled [to me],
between my evening and my morning draught.
And when I took refreshment under its shade,
the doves all sang [perched] on my cup.

and also:

[Poem 4]
How many a branching tree did I greet steadfastly early in the morning
after my boon-companion and my loved ones had become a memory.
Then if I stopped for [under it] for a drink, ekphrasis flirted [or: composed love poetry for me], and the nightingales sang for me.

[ق ١٨٢أ]

وقوله:[90] [من الكامل]

أَحْسِنْ بِوادِي ٱلجَنكِ تَشْدُو وُرْقُهُ في دَفِّ أَشْجارٍ تَمِيلُ بِعِطْفِها
فإذا تَناوَلَ كَأْسَهُ مُتَنَزِّهٌ غَنَّتْ عليه بِجَنْكِها وبِدُفِّها*

وقوله: [من البسيط]

وُرْقُ ٱلحَمامِ عَلَى أقداحِ قَهْوَتِنا قَدْ صُوِّرَتْ فاسْتَفَزَّتْنا مِنَ ٱلفَرَحِ
إذا سَرَتْ أَرْيَحِيّاتُ ٱلْمُدامِ بِنا كادَتْ حَقِيقًا تُغَنِّينا عَلَى ٱلقَدَحِ

*متنزّه | في «سالم»: منتزّه.

90 Also recorded—though with such significant variation it can hardly be called the same poem—in Ibn Nubātah, *Dīwān*, 333. See also Ibn Nubātah, *Dīwān*, 335, ll. 9–10.

and also:

[Poem 5]
How excellent that valley of harps: its doves sing sweetly
on the sides (*daff*) of trees, which lean to the side (*ʿiṭf*).[91]
And if a relaxed one should take his cup in hand
they sing for him with their cymbals and tambourines.

and also:

[Poem 6]
The doves on our wine goblets were
pictured [on our cups] and they provoked in us exultation.
As the joys of the wine swept us away,
the doves nearly became [real] and sang![92]

91 Compare the poem by Ibn Nubātah recorded in al-Ghuzūlī, *Maṭāliʿ al-budūr*, 1:71–2. The instruments *jank* and *daff* are often mentioned together (compare, Ibn Ḥijjah al-Ḥamawī, *Qahwat al-inshāʾ*, ed. Veselý, 333, l. 4).

92 The Arabic reads *ḥaqīqan* (meaning, "worthy, deserving"; "fit, competent, entitled to" always with *bi-*). I have chosen to translate this as "real", however, as the context seems to necessitate such a reading. The word *ḥaqīq* here may be read as analogous to the common words *ḥaqīqah*, *ḥaqq*, or *ḥaqqan*.

Another *maqṭūʿ*-poem by Ibn Nubātah—this time from his *Dīwān*, not from his exchange with aṣ-Ṣafadī, reinforces the image of ornamental figures along the rim of a glass or metal goblet and may have been an allusion to this long epistolary exchange of *maqāṭīʿ*-poetry:[93]

[من المنسرح]

سَقياً لأيّامي ٱلَّتي سَلَفَتْ ما بينَ ذاكَ ٱلنَّعيمِ والمَرَحِ

لا يُنْزِلُ ٱلدَّهْرُ عن يدي قَدَماً كأنّني صورةٌ على قَدَحِ

Blessed be my past days,
  Spent among riches and delights.
Fate never stripped high rank [also: a foot] from my hand[94]
  as though I were a figure on the rim of a cup.

These poetic exchanges demonstrate the ways in which the scholarly class interacted culturally in the post-court era and the place of poetry and belles-lettres in their social relationships. It also provides evidence for the acknowledged status of *maqāṭīʿ*-poetry as a distinct literary form with its own operational logic—its own grammar, as it were—and an awareness of the specific contexts in which it was most commonly found. Thus while the *maqṭūʿ* in isolation or in literary correspondence is clearly identifiable as a specific type of poetry, it is only in concert with others of its kind that the *maqṭūʿ* emerges as an architext—a larger, malleable literary category—that can be identified in different contexts outside the anthological context in which it first emerged as a genre. The apposition of *maqāṭīʿ*-poems in a specific anthological context was vital for the development of the genre's genre-consciousness and it was this—firmly rooting *maqāṭīʿ*-poems in the anthology as part of an aggregate—that, paradoxically, gave the individual *maqṭūʿ*, or the *maqāṭīʿ* micro-set, the freedom to roam widely and infiltrate every conceivable form of Arabic literary writing.

One very popular sub-genre of *maqāṭīʿ*-poetry was *mujūn* (obscene) verse; or, to put it another way, *maqāṭīʿ*-poetry became a successful and popular vehicle for *mujūn* poetry in the later period, especially in literary antholo-

93 Ibn Nubātah, *Dīwān*, 116.

94 The double entendre here (*qadam* means high rank and foot) is made nearly triple on account of the parallelism between fate (*dahr*, also time) and *qidam* (antiquity).

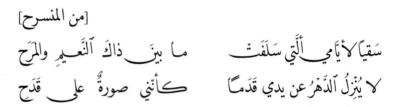

gies.[95] This was partly because *maqāṭīʿ*-poetry was exceedingly mobile as is made apparent by the following anecdote. In this literary report taken from Ibn Abī Ḥajalah's *Maghnāṭīs ad-durr an-nafīs* (*Attracting Priceless Pearls*), the author recounted a quarrel between the subject of the biographical entry, Burhān ad-Dīn al-Qīrāṭī (d. 781/1379), and Ibn aṣ-Ṣāʾigh (d. 776/1375) in which both he and *maqāṭīʿ*-poetry played pivotal roles.[96]

فصل في مجونه ونادر فنونه

قال: [من الكامل]

أَصْبَحْتَ يا ٱبْنَ ٱلصَّائِغِ ٱلحَنَفِيَّ في كُلِّ ٱلقَبائِحِ أَوْحَدَ ٱلأَزْمانِ
في مِصْرَ رأْيَ أَبي حَنيفَةِ تَدَّعي جَهْلاً وانتَ مَعَرَّةُ ٱلنُّعْمانِ

هذا المقطوع سارت به الرقاق وطبقت الآفاق ودخل الحجاز من البُوَيْب ووقع ببغداد من باب الطاق أخبرني برهان الدين المذكور أنّ ابن الصائغ قال له إنني نظمت ثمانين مقطوعًا في جواب هذا المقطوع قلت وقد أنشدني منها ما ينيف من عشرة مقاطيع وليس فيها ما بفي بوزنه ولا يدخل في ددنه لا جرم أنّه وقع في الأمر المشطّ ودفنها عن الناس كالقط وكان قد سألني أن أنظم شيئًا معه في مساعدته فقلت هذا بلديّك وانا رجل غريب بينكما وليس لي عادة بهذا ولا يحفظ عنّي إلى يومنا هذا أحد شيئًا من الهجو فقال لا بدّ من ذلك فقلت:

95 The latest and most comprehensive treatment of the topic of *mujūn* is Zoltán Szombathy, *Mujūn: libertinism in mediaeval Muslim society and literature* (Cambridge: Gibb Memorial Trust, 2013). See also Sinan Antoon, *The Poetics of the Obscene in Premodern Arabic Poetry: Ibn al-Ḥajjāj and sukhf* (New York, NY: Palgrave Macmillan, 2014) and Adam Talib, Marlé Hammond, and Arie Schippers (eds), *The Rude, The Bad and the Bawdy* (Cambridge: Gibb Memorial Trust, 2014), esp. chs 6 and 9 by Nefeli Papoutsakis and Thomas Bauer respectively.

96 I have edited the relevant portion of the entry on al-Qīrāṭī from Yale MS Landberg 69 (f. 11b) and translated it.

[من الكامل]

أَهَجَوْتَ شَمْسَ ٱلدِّينِ هَجْوًا فاحِشًا   وزَعَمْتُ أَنْحاءَ ٱلْكَلامِ أَواطي*
هَيْهاتَ شِعْرُكَ لا يُساوي حَبَّةً   مُذْ صارَ مُنْتَسِبًا إلى ٱلقيراطي

فرضي بقولي هذا فلمّا بلغ برهان الدين عتبني فقلت ما أردت به إلّا التفوّق بقولك فإن كلّ من سمع قولي «أهجوت شمس الدين هجوًا فاحشًا» قال يا ترى ما هذا الهجو[97] الفاحش فيحرص على سماعه والوقوف عليه فرضي بذلك فلمّا بلغ شمس الدين أنّ هذا مقصودي تأذّى منه أكثر من الأوّل فبقيت بينهما في حيرة

Chapter of his [i.e. Burhān ad-Dīn al-Qīrāṭī's] obscene verse and less common poems

He wrote this poem:

O Ibn aṣ-Ṣā'igh you've become a *ḥanafī* in
 every disgraceful deed, the solitaire of your age!
In Egypt, you pretend to follow the judgment of Abū Ḥanīfah
 in ignorance. Meanwhile you're the crime of Nuʿmān! (i.e. sodomy)
 [or: in Maʿarrat an-Nuʿmān][98]

This *maqṭūʿ*-poem got the camels moving and folded up [i.e. traversed] the horizons. It entered the Hijaz from al-Buwayb [i.e. the little door] and it came upon Baghdad through The Gate of the Arch. The aforementioned Burhān ad-Dīn informed me that Ibn aṣ-Ṣā'igh had told him, "I composed eighty *maqāṭīʿ*-poems in response to that *maqṭūʿ*-poem [of yours]." I myself heard Ibn aṣ-Ṣā'igh recite more than ten of these *maqāṭīʿ*-poems. None of them adhered to their meter or entered the [spirit] of the joke [so] there's no question that having gone overboard in this matter, he

*أنحاء الكلام] في الأصل المخطوط: «أنحا في الكلام».

97 The MS has *al-hajr* for *al-hajw* here; it is an obvious misreading.

98 In order to understand this poem, one must know that the Ḥanafī *madh'hab* held that cases of sex between men should not be treated *prima facie* as equivalent to fornication (*zinā*). See Khaled El-Rouayheb, *Before Homosexuality in the Arab-Islamic World, 1500–1800* (Chicago, IL: University of Chicago Press, 2005). *Maʿarrat an-Nuʿmān* is a city, but it can also be interpreted as "the crime (*maʿarrah*) of Nuʿmān [Abū Ḥanīfah's first name]."

buried them like a cat so that people wouldn't find them. [At one point] he asked me to compose a poem alongside his own, by way of coming to his aid, but I said "You and he hail from the same city and I am nothing but a stranger between you two. [Plus] this isn't the sort of thing I usually do. To this very day, no one can recall any invective verse by me for you." "You must," he said. So I wrote this:

Did you insult Shams ad-Dīn in in verse vile and vulgar?
And so I decided to compose [a response]with the same rhyme?
Look now! Your poetry is worth less than a *ḥabbah*
ever since it got attributed to al-Qīrāṭī [or: the carat].[99]

It pleased him, but then when Burhān ad-Dīn heard about it, he reproached me. I explained to him, "All I wanted to do was to put people in mind of the poem you wrote. Now everyone who hears my verse "Did you insult Shams ad-Dīn in verse vile and vulgar" will say to himself, 'Ooh, I wonder what this "verse vile and vulgar" is' and will be dying to hear it and look it out." This pleased him, but then when Shams ad-Dīn [Ibn aṣ-Ṣā'igh] learned that this had been my intention he was hurt even more than he'd been at the beginning. So there I was stuck between the two of them with no idea what to do.

The easy mnemonic portability and circulation of *maqāṭīʿ*-poems is essential to the type of interaction described above, just as it essential to Ibn Abī Ḥajalah's own genius response. His response depends entirely on his, no doubt, sound assumption that al-Qīrāṭī's *maqṭūʿ*-poem, with which Ibn Abī Ḥajalah's linked his poem intertextually with onomastic puns, would be accessible to the interested reader or listener in one form or other.

The vitality, sophistication and sheer diversity of the *mujūn-maqṭūʿ* subgenre can be seen equally well in the following micro-collection of *mujūn maqāṭīʿ*-poems from Shihāb ad-Dīn al-Ḥijāzī al-Khazrajī's (d. 875/1471) *Rawḍ al-ādāb* (part three, chapter eight), an important literary anthology discussed in the previous chapter:[100]

99 There is a pun here on the poet's name al-Qīrāṭī and two measures: *ḥabbah* (the weight of a grain in the avoirdupois system) and *qīrāṭ* (a carat, equivalent to 4 grains). See *EI*², s.v. "Makāyil. 1. In the Arabic, Persian and Turkish lands" [E. Ashtor].

100 See further on this work in the annotated bibliography: 15th century, 6. a. I have edited this chapter from British Library (BL) MS Add 19489, ff. 118b–122a (scil. 117b–121a) and BL MS Add 9562, ff. 140a–143a. The chapter is missing from the other British Library MS (Or. 3843) of the text. The order and number of poems in this section of the text in BL MS Add 9562 is different from those in BL MS Add 19489. Poems 9, 15, 33, and 34 do not

الفصل الثامن في المجون

[ابن يغمور: [من الخفيف]

وملِيحٍ تَعَلَّمَ ٱلنَّحْوَ يُلْقي   مُشْكِلاتٍ منه بِلَفْظٍ وَجيزِ
ما تَمَيَّزْتُ وَجْهَهُ قطُّ إلّا   قامَ أيْري نَصْبًا عَلَى ٱلتَّمييزِ

[القيراطي: [من السريع]

أيْرِيَّ نَحْوِيٌّ وأفْعالُهُ   في حَرَكاتٍ ذاتَ إعْرابِ
قامَ يُريدُ ٱلجَرَّ لَمّا غَدا   مُنْتَصِبًا يَرْفَعُ أثوابي

[المعمار: [من الرجز]

أيْري إذا نَدَبْتُهُ   لِحاجَةٍ تَخْتَصُّ بي
قامَ لَها بِنَفْسِهِ   ما هو إلّا عَصَبي

[غيره: [من الرمل]

لِيَ أيْرٌ فيهِ كِبْرٌ وَجَفا   لا يَرَى لي وَهْوَ مِنّي وإلَيَّ
كُلَّما أغْضَبَني أرْضَيْتُهُ   وإذا أرْضَيْتُهُ قامَ عَلَيَّ

appear in BL MS Add 9562; Poem 9 is given along with Poems 10 and 11 in BL MS Add 19489 in the margin of f. 117b. I have brought these into the main body of the edition here following Poem 8 because they treat the same subject. The order of BL MS Add 9562 is also somewhat different to that presented here: Poems 10 and 11 are interposed between Poems 6 and 7 and Poem 8 is followed immediately by Poem 12. This entire chapter is missing from BL MS Or. 3843.

[Poem 1] Ibn Yaghmūr:

A handsome one who's learned his grammar; he throws out
problems of his own making in the fewest possible words.
I would never have been able to single out his face were it not for
my cock standing up (*naṣb*) as I sorted through [them] (*at-tamyīz*)[101]

[Poem 2] al-Qīrāṭī:

My cock's a grammarian and it does things (*afʿāluhū*)[102]
with movements (*ḥarakāt*) whose meaning is plain (*iʿrāb*).[103]
It stands up asking to be pulled (*jarr*) when it's
erect (*muntaṣib*), causing my clothes to tent (*yarfaʿu ʾathwābī*)[104]

[Poem 3] Ibrāhīm al-Miʿmār:

Whenever I assign my cock
a task that concerns me,
it sees to the matter itself.
That's how loyal a companion it is![105]

[Poem 4] Another poet:

My cock's a haughty one and churlish.
it never thinks about my interest even though it's part of me and on my side.
Whenever it gets angry, I please it
and whenever I please it, it rises up against me!

---

101 The final hemistich of this poem contains a double entendre (*tawriyah*)—fittingly—on grammar. The word *nasḅ* means the accusative case as well as erection and the act of sorting through (or *tamyīz*) is also the name of a form of specification in Arabic syntax that takes the accusative case.

102 The word *afʿāl* means verbs as well as actions.

103 The words *ḥarakāt* and *iʿrāb* are also grammatical double entendres: *ḥarakāt* means short vowels and *iʿrāb* is the name for the terminal vowels that give Arabic its desinential inflection.

104 This verse alludes to all three Arabic grammatical cases in a series of double entendre (*tawriyah*): the word here meaning to pull (i.e. to wank) *jarr* refers to the genitive case (*al-majrūr*), the word meaning erection refers to the the accusative case (*al-manṣūb*), and the word meaning to raise (here the speaker's clothes) refers to the nominative case (*al-marfūʿ*).

105 The word for a loyal companion who is zealous in fighting for his company (*ʿaṣabī*) also means "sinewy" so this may also be a double entendre (*tawriyah*).

آخر: [من المتقارب]

وَلِي أَيْرُ سُوءٍ كَثِيرُ الْخَنَى يُقَابِلُ بِاللُّؤْمِ مَنْ يُكْرِمُهْ

إِذَا نِمْتُ قَامَ وَإِنْ قُمْتُ نَامَ فَلَا رَحِمَ اللهُ مَنْ يَرْحَمُهْ

خليل بن ايبك [الصفدي]: [من الكامل]

عَهْدِي بِأَيْرِي وَهْوَ فِيهِ تَيَقُّظٌ كَمْ قَامَ مُنْتَصِبًا إِذَا نَبَّهْتُهُ

وَالْآنَ كَالطِّفْلِ ٱلَّذِي فِي مَهْدِهِ يَزْدَادُ نَوْمًا كُلَّمَا حَرَّكْتُهُ

غيره: [من السريع]

قَالَتْ وَقَدْ قُلْتُ ٱلْعَبِي لِيْ بِهِ مِنْ بَعْدِمَا قَامَتْ وَقَدْ نَامَا

لَوْكَانَ إِسْرَافِيلُ فِي رَاحَتِي يَنْفَخُ فِي أَيْرِكَ مَا قَامَا

ابن نباتة مضمّنًا:[106] [من الطويل]

دَنَوْتُ إِلَيْهَا وَهْوَ كَالْفَرْخِ رَاقِدٌ فَيَا خَجَلِي لَمَّا دَنَوْتُ وَأَدْلَالِي

فَقُلْتُ ٱمْعَكِيهِ بِالْأَنَامِلِ فَالْتَقَى «لَدَى وَكْرِهَا ٱلْعُنَّابُ وَالْحَشَفُ ٱلْبَالِي»

106 The final hemistich of this poem quotes (*taḍmīn*) a hemistich from a well known poem rhyming in L (*lāmiyyah*) by the pre-Islamic poet Imru' al-Qays (see ibid., *Dīwān*, ed. Muḥammad Abū l-Faḍl Ibrāhīm (Cairo: Dār al-Maʿārif, 1964), 38, l. 4). As if to exemplify the gender-indifference of the normative literary paradigm of classical Arabic sexuality, BL MS Add 9562 substitutes *ilayhi* for *ilayhā* in the first hemistich of the first line of this poem. Both are plausible metrically, but the second-person feminine addressee in line two suggests that *ilayhā* is the correct reading. Poem found in Ibn Nubātah, *Dīwān*, 424–25. It does not occur in Thomas Bauer's edition of twenty-one *mujūn* poems by Ibn Nubātah (Bauer, "Dignity at Stake", 174–85) or in the Bibliothèque Nationale (Paris) MS of Ibn Nubātah's *al-Qaṭr an-Nubātī*.

[Poem 5] Another poet:

I've got a wicked cock that's always so lewd.
It rebukes those who pay it a kindness.
When I sleep, it gets up, but when I get up, it lies [limp].
May God never have mercy (*raḥima*) on someone who takes pity on it (*yarḥamuhū*)!

[Poem 6] Khalīl b. Aybak [aṣ-Ṣafadī]:

I've long known my cock to be awake,
whenever I'd rouse it, it would rise.
And now it [lies] like a baby in its crib:
the more I shake it, the deeper it sleeps.

[Poem 7] Another poet:

She said—after I'd told her to "Play with it a bit"
since once she'd risen, it had gone to sleep—
"Even if I were holding Isrāfīl in my hand,
and he was blowing into your cock, it still wouldn't rise/be resurrected (*qāma*)"[107]

[Poem 8] Ibn Nubātah (including an allusion):

I approached her—while it lay [limp] like a young bird—
so imagine how ashamed I was when I approached [her]! How humiliated!
So I said to her, "Rub it with your fingertips" and then
« at her nest jujube and withered dates» came together.

107 Isrāfīl is the angel who Muslims believe will blow the trumpet to announce the Day of Resurrection (*yawm al-qiyāmah*).

[وغيره:[108] [من البسيط]

تَقولُ لِيَ وَهيَ غَضبى مِن تَدَ[لُّلِها] وقَدْ دَعَتْني إلَى شَيْءٍ فَما كانا*

إنْ لَمْ تَنكْني بِنَيكِ ٱلْمَرءِ زَوجتَهُ فَلا تَلُمْني إذا أَصْبَحْتَ قَرنانا

كأنَّ أيرَكَ مِنْ شَمعٍ رَخاوَتُهُ فكُلَّما عَرَكَتْهُ راحَتي لانا

[السراج الورّاق: [من المجتثّ]

اِنْحَلَّ أيرِيَ مِنّي كأنَّهُمْ عَقَدُوهُ

وَصارَ يَحْضُنُ بَيْضي كأنّهم رَقَدُوهُ

[وله ايضاً:[109] [من الرمل]

كانَ أيرًا صارَ سَيرًا يَلْطِمُ ٱلاكْساسَ سُخْرَهْ

كيفَ لا يَنفِرْنَ عَنّي ومَعِي شَيْبٌ ودِرَّهْ*

* من تدلّلها] في الأصل المخطوط (وهو مخطوطة ٩٨٤٩١): هذه العبارة مبتورة نتيجة بري الورقة. إذا أصبحت] في الأصل المخطوط: «اذ اصبحت».

* ينفرن] في الأصل المخطوط: «يناون».

108 This poem is by Ibn al-Ḥajjāj (d. 391/1001) as attested by other sources. See, *inter alia*, aṣ-Ṣafadī, *al-Wāfī*, 12:334–35.

109 This poem is also recorded in Ibn Ḥijjah al-Ḥamawī, *Khizānat al-adab*, ed. Kawkab Diyāb, 3:205 (with variant).

[Poem 9] Another poet:

She said to me—and she was pissed off about being coddled
    [because] she'd invited me to something that didn't take place—
"If you don't fuck me like a man fucks his wife,
    "Then don't blame me if you end up a cuckold!
"It's as if your cock is made of wax, it's so flaccid.
    "Whenever I rub it in my palm, it droops."

[Poem 10] as-Sarrāj al-Warrāq:

My cock has become slack/untied (*inḥalla*)
    as though they'd had it tied in a knot.
And now it's hugging my balls/eggs (*bayḍ*)
    as though they made it brood!

[Poem 11] And also by him:

I had a cock, it's now a belt,
    it slaps pussies in jest.
How come they don't run away from me
    since I've gone grey and carry a whip?

وله [اي: ابن نباتة] غفر الله له:[110] [من الكامل] [

يا رُبَّ لَيْلٍ بِتُّهُ مُتَنَعِّماً بِرَشِيقَةٍ تَعْيَى بِرِدْفٍ مُثْقِلِ*

أَيْرِي بِجانِبِ كُسِّها في جُحْرِها «عَرَفَ ٱلمَحَلَّ فَباتَ دونَ ٱلمَنْزِلِ»

القيراطي عفا الله عنه:[111] [من الطويل] [

هَجَمْتُ عَلَيْها في ٱلدُّجَى بَعْدَ رَقْدَةٍ وِمِثْلي عَلَى ٱلأَمْرِ ٱلعَظيمِ هَجُومُ*

فَما مَكَّنَتْني حِينَ جِئْتُ لِمانِعٍ أَلَمَّ ولكِنْ ذالِكَ لَيْسَ يَدومُ

وعاتَبَني أَيْري فَقُلْتُ لَهُ ٱتَّئِدْ «لَعَلَّ لَها عُذْراً وانتَ تَلومُ»

*تعيى] في الأصل المخطوط: «تغني»

*الأمر] في مخطوطة ١٩٤٨٩: «الأير» .

110 Poem found (with variants) in Bauer, "Dignity at Stake", 176, no. 4; Ibn Nubātah, *al-Qaṭr an-Nubātī*, Bibliothèque Nationale (Paris) MS 2234, f. 187b; *idem*, *Dīwān*, 421. The final hemistich is a quotation (*taḍmīn*) from a poem by Muslim b. al-Walīd (d. 208/823). See *idem*, *Dīwān Ṣarīʿ al-Ghawānī*, ed. Sāmī ad-Dahhān (Cairo: Dār al-Maʿārif, 1958), 338. Another *mujūn-maqṭūʿ* that includes this hemistich (*taḍmīn*) is given by Ibn Abī Ḥajalah in his *Maghnāṭīs ad-durr an-nafīs* (f. 14b). He claims to have heard Ibn Rayyān recite it himself in Damascus in 752/1351:

wa-la-qad nazaltu bi-rāḥatī fī ẓahr-i man / amsā yadullu siyāḥatan mutanaḥḥalī
kaffī bi-jānibi ʿunqihī fī ẓahrihī / ʿarafa l-maḥalla fa-bāta dūna l-manzilī

My palm alighted on the back of one, who
began to guide me on a journey, bluffing proudly.
On his back, my palm lay beside his neck;
«It knew that halting-place [well] and so spent the night outside the inn.»

111 The final hemistich is a quotation (*taḍmīn*) from a poem by Muslim b. al-Walīd (d. 208/823). See *idem*, *Dīwān Ṣarīʿ al-Ghawānī*, 340.

[Poem 12] And by him [that is, Ibn Nubātah], may God pardon his sins:
How many nights have I spent in the blessed
company of a slender girl, afflicted with an ample rear?
My cock just beside her cunt in her buttocks (*juḥr*);[112]
«It knew that halting-place [well] and so spent the night outside the inn.»

[Poem 13] al-Qīrāṭī, may God excuse his sins:
I attacked her late at night after a brief sleep;
people like me are aggressive where that great matter is concerned.
Yet when I came to her, she prevented me because an obstacle
was paying her a short visit. [No matter] it doesn't last long.
My cock blamed me for it, but I said, "Be patient.
"«Perhaps her excuse is valid and you're simply being unfair to her.»"

112 In his translation of this poem, Thomas Bauer suggests that there is a pun on the word *juḥr* ("burrow", also "buttocks"). I concur that there is a pun, but I would suggest that Ibn Nubātah is actually punning on the word *ḥijr* ("lap"). This part of the body is beside the vagina and therefore the reader would expect to read that word, which in Arabic differs from the word *juḥr* only in its pointing. This rhetorical device is known as *tawhīm* ("false clue") (see Cachia, *The Arch Rhetorician*, no. 108).

[ابن خطيب داريا:[113] [من البسيط]

وغادةٍ غـارَ مِنّي زَوْجُها فَسَعى … يُريـدُ قَتْلي وفي أحْشائهِ ضَـرِمُ*

يا زَوْجَها كُفَّ عَنْ قَتْلي مُسامَحَةً … بَيْني وبَيْنَكَ لَوْ أنْصَفْتَـني رَحِـمُ

[جامعه أحمد بن الحجازي: [من الكامل]

[الآدَمِيّـانِ ٱللَّذانِ] تَزاحَمـا … في عِشْقِ أغْيَدَ عَنْ هَوىً مُتَزايِـدِ*

مُتَواقِفـانِ ولا عَجيبٌ إذْ هُمـا … مُتَوارِدانِ عَلَى مَحَلٍّ واحِـدِ

[ابن نباتة:[114] [من الرمل]

قـالَ لي خِلّي تَزَوَّجْ تَسْـتَرِحْ … مِنْ أذَى ٱلفَقْرِ وتَسْتَغْني يَقيـنا

قُـلْتُ دَعْ نَصْحَكَ وٱعْـلَمْ أنّني … لَمْ أضَعْ بَيْنَ ظُهورِ ٱلمُسْلِمينا

*يريد] في مخطوطة رباط: «يروم» . قتلي (البيت الثاني)] في مخطوطة رباط: «حزني» . بيني] في مخطوطة ٩٨٤٩١: «منك بيني» .

*الآدميين] في الأصل المخطوط (وهو مخطوطة ٩٨٤٩١): «إن الآدميين» . اللذان] في الأصل المخطوط: «الذين» . أغيد] في الأصل المخطوط: «غيداء»

113 Poem found in Ibn Khaṭīb Dāriyā, *Dīwān*, al-Maktabah al-Waṭaniyyah (Rabat) MS 225 *qāf*, f. 89a [p. 177]. See further in the annotated bibliography: 15th century, 1. a.

114 Poem found in Ibn Nubātah, *al-Qaṭr an-Nubātī*, Bibliothèque Nationale (Paris) MS 2234, f. 183a; *idem*, *Dīwān*, 535. It is not one of those edited in Bauer, "Dignity at Stake".

[Poem 14] Ibn Khaṭīb Dāriyā [(d. 810/1407)]:

A young woman. Her husband is jealous of me so he
decided he wants to kill me; passion burns inside him.
O husband of hers, drop your plan to kill me out of forgiveness,
for—if you're fair to me, [you'll admit]—that you and I share a womb/are family (*raḥim*).

[Poem 15] The man who made this collection, Aḥmad b. al-Ḥijāzī:

The two men who are competing for the
ardor of a young beauty—each one trying to outbid the other in love—
Are in dispute, but that should come as no surprise because
they're both heading (*mutawāridān*) for the exact same place.[115]

[Poem 16] Ibn Nubātah:

My friend told me, "Get married and be relieved
of poverty's suffering and become wealthy in certain knowledge [that you won't commit sin]."
"Drop the advice", I said, "and just know
that I'm not one who goes around putting it in Muslims' backs[ides]!"

115 This final hemistich plays on the notion of *tawārud* (coincidental composition of the same figure in a line of poetry), except the two rivals are here said to be heading toward the same halting-place (i.e. beloved) to drink.

ابن الصائغ مضمّنًا:[116] [من المنسرح]

للهِ ظَبيٌ مُهفهفٌ غَنِجٌ ... لاطَفتُهُ بالكلامِ إذْ زارا

وقلتُ دُرْ يا لَبيبُ يا فَطِنًا ... فَدارَ لي «واللبيبُ من دارا»

آخر: [من السريع]

لَمّا جفا ٱلمحبوبُ ناديتُهُ ... قابَلْتَ حُبّي فيكَ بالبُغْضِ

فعِندَها نامَ علَى وَجْهِهِ ... وقالَ وَجْهي مِنكَ في ٱلأرضِ

غيره: [من الكامل]

سُلطانُ حُسنٍ كَمُلَتْ أوصافُهُ ... فاقَتْ مَكارِمُهُ مَكارِمَ حاتِمِ

يُعطي ٱلأمانَ لعاشقيهِ مِنَ ٱلجفا ... ويَجودُ بالمَنديلِ بَعْدَ ٱلخاتَمِ

النور الأسعردي: [من الطويل]

لَقَدْ غَرَّني أيْري بِرِقَّةِ قَلْبِهِ ... عَلَى أنَّهُ جافٍ يَجورُ ويَعْدِلُ

بَكَى رَحْمَةً مِنْ عَيْنِهِ عِنْدَما رأى ... ٱلخُصَى بَعْدَهُ مِسْكينَةً لَيْسَ تَدْخُلُ*

---

* بعده] في مخطوطة ١٩٤٨٩: «مِن بعد».

116 The final hemistisch of this poem quotes (*taḍmīn*) a line of verse in the same *Munsariḥ* meter from al-Ḥarīrī's *al-Maqāmah as-Samarqandiyyah* (ash-Sharīshī, *Sharḥ Maqāmāt al-Ḥarīrī*, 5 vols, ed. Muḥammad Abū l-Faḍl Ibrāhīm, (Cairo: al-Muʾassasah al-ʿArabiyyah al-Ḥadīthah li-ṭ-Ṭabʿ wa-n-Nashr wa-t-Tawzīʿ, 1970–76), 3:357):

wa-ṣbir ʿalā khulqi man tuʿāshiruhū / wa-dārihī fa-l-labību man dārā

Be patient when it comes to the personality of one with whom you keep company
and flatter him (*dārihī*) for the clever one is the one who flatters (*dārā*).

[Poem 17] Ibn aṣ-Ṣāʾigh (including an allusion):
By God, [he's] a slender, coquettish gazelle,
to whom I speak sweetly when he comes to see me.
"Turn around (*dur*), clever one", I told him,
so he turned around for me, and «the clever one is the one who flatters (*dārā*)» / turns around (*dārā*).

[Poem 18] Another poet:
When my beloved was cruel to me, I called to him,
"You've repaid my love for you with cruelty."
So then he lay face-down,
and said, "My face is in the dirt for your sake!"

[Poem 19] Another poet:
The Sultan of beauty, his every facet is perfect,
and his noble qualities surpass even those of Ḥātim [aṭ-Ṭāʾī][117]
He protects those who love him from mistreatment,
and he generously gives a handkerchief after [he gives] a ring / [his] anus (*khātim*).[118]

[Poem 20] Nūr ad-Dīn al-Asʿardī
My cock beguiled me with its sensitive heart
although it's uncouth, tyrannical at times and at other times fair.
It cried from its eye when it saw
that the poor testicles wouldn't follow in after it.

117 Ḥātim aṭ-Ṭāʾī: a pre-Islamic poet legendary for his generosity.

118 This is another case of *tawriyah*: the word *khātim* may mean both "ring" and "anus" and while the beloved's generosity leads the reader to believe that the gift of a handkerchief simply follows the gift of a ring, it is clear from context that the beloved's generosity is being discussed ironically in line with other attributes common to idealized sultans in Arabic poetry.

شهاب الدين الحاجبي: [من السريع]

رُبَّ صَغيرٍ حينَ وَلَّفتُهُ أيقَنتُ لا يَدخُلُ إلّا ٱليَسيرْ

أَلفَيتُهُ كالبِيرِ في وُسعِهِ حتّى عَجِبنا مِنْ صَغيرٍ كَبيرْ

ابو الحسن الجزّار: [من الطويل]

وَلَمْ أَنسَ عِلقًا نكتُهُ وَهوَ واسِعٌ طويلٌ عريضُ ٱلمَنكِبَينِ نَتيفُ

يَقولُ ٱلخُصَى لِلزِّبِ نَقعُدُ هاهُنا فَقالَ ٱدْخُلا ضَيفُ ٱلكِرامِ يُضيفُ*

صدر الدين بن عبد الحقّ: [من الكامل]

أيري كَبيرٌ والصَّغيرُ يقولُ لي أُطعُنْ حَشايَ بِهِ وكُنْ صِنديدا

فأجَبتُ هذا لا يجوزُ فقالَ لي عِندي يَجوزُ فِنكتُهُ تَقليدا

ابن مظفّر الذهبي:[119] [من المنسرح]

وأَمرَدٌ ضاقَ عَنْ مُعامَلَتي أَوْدَعتُ فاهُ خَفيفَ دينارِ

فَقالَ بَهرَجتَ ذا ٱلخَفيفِ لَنا فَقُلتُ والضَّربُ خارِجَ ٱلدّارِ*

*الكرام] في مخطوطة ٩٥٦٢: «الكريم» .

* بهرجت] في مخطوطة ٩٥٦٢: «هرجت» .

119 In al-Kutubī's *Fawāt al-Wafayāt*, this poem is attributed to Tāj ad-Dīn Muẓaffar b. Maḥāsin adh-Dhahabī (b. Damascus 607/1211, d. 686/1288 (4:150–56 at 152), not—presumably—his son as it is given here.

[Poem 21] Shihāb ad-Dīn al-Ḥājibī:
How many a young/small one (*ṣaghīr*) have I packed
knowing full well that I'd only get the tip in.
I found him as wide as a well [*bīr*, viz. *bi'r*]
and I was surprised by this small one like a well/who was big.[120]

[Poem 22] Abū l-Ḥasan al-Jazzār:
I'll never forget that loose bottom (*ʿilq*) I once fucked;
he was tall, and broad, and plucked.
My balls told my cock, "Let's sit right here"
and he said, "Come right in! The guest of a generous host may bring his own guests."[121]

[Poem 23] Ṣadr ad-Dīn Ibn ʿAbd al-Ḥaqq:
I've got a big (*kabīr*) cock. So when the young boy (*ṣaghīr*) said,[122]
"Stab my insides and be valiant!"
I said, "It's not permitted." But he replied,
"I say it is" so I fucked him on his own authority (*taqlīd*).[123]

[Poem 24] Ibn Muẓaffar adh-Dhahabī
A beardless young man who was annoyed by the way I was treating him.
I deposited a light gold coin (*khafīfa dīnārī*) in his mouth.[124]
"You've adorned this trivial thing for me", he said.
"But shouldn't the striking take place inside the mint/the house?", I replied.[125]

120 The joke in the final hemistich revolves around the paronomasia in the expression "like a well (i.e. loose)" *ka-bīr* (viz. *ka-bi'r*) and the word *kabīr* meaning "big", which is of course the antonym of small/young (*ṣaghīr*).

121 This is a proverbial expression.

122 The words *kabīr* (big) and *ṣaghīr* (young but also small) form an antithesis (See Cachia, *The Arch Rhetorician*, no. 79).

123 The word *taqlīd* is a term of art in Islamic jurisprudence meaning the adoption of a legal opinion authored by another jurisprudent without a concomitant determination of one's own ruling on the matter.

124 *Dīnār khafīf* mean a gold coin of light weight. See also the one-line poem by Ibn ar-Rūmī (*idem*, *Dīwān*, 6 vols, ed. Ḥusayn Naṣṣār et al. (Cairo: Maṭbaʿat Dār al-Kutub, 1973–81), 3:1241, no. 1018) mentioned in Robert McKinney, *The Case of Rhyme versus Reason*, 154.

125 The last hemistich of this poem contains a pun on the word for "mint" (*dār aḍ-ḍarb*). The notion of striking (*ḍarb*) outside the house (*dār*) may refer to the impropriety of disciplining members of one's household in public.

[٢ المعمار مضمّنًا:[126] [من الكامل]

كَلَّفْتُهُ مـا ليسَ يَحْمِلُ بَعْضَهُ … فرأيْتُـهُ تَحْـتي يَروغُ ويَلْعَبُ*

وبَكَى ومَصَّصَني ٱللّسانَ وقالَ لي … رِفقًا سأَحْمِلُ قالَ أيْري يَكْذِبُ

«يُعْطيكَ مِنْ طَرَفِ ٱللِّسانِ حَلاوةً … ويَروغُ عَنْكَ كَما يَروغُ ٱلثَّعْلَبُ»

[٢ فخر الدين بن مكانس: [من السريع]

شَكَى إلَيَّ ٱليُتْمَ إذ نِكْتُهُ … مُراهِقٌ فيهِ حَلا هَتْكي*

بِتُّ أُسَلِّيهِ عَلَى يُتْمِهِ … وكُلَّما سَلَّيْتُهُ يَبْكي

[٢ قاضي القضاة شهاب الدين بن حجر:[127] [من الرجز]

وعاشِقٍ لَيْسَ لَهُ … إلَى ٱلحيا أدْنَى سَبَبْ

دَبَّ عَلَى مَعْشوقِهِ … فَما رأى مِنْهُ أَدَبْ

[٢ نور الدين الأسعردي:[128] [من المتقارب]

ولي صاحِبٌ قالَ نِلْتُ ٱلْمُنَى … بِمَنْ هو دونَ ٱلوَرَى مُنْيَتي

فَقُلْتُ أَتَى زائِرًا قالَ لا … ولٰكِنْ جَلُدْتُ ولي نِيَّتي*

---

* يروغ (البيت الأوّل)] في مخطوطة ١٩٤٨٩: «يغور». من طرف] في مخطوطة ٩٨٤٩١: «من طرف من طرف» (إعادة كتابة)

* شكى اليّ اليتم] في مخطوطة ٩٨٤٩١: «شكى اليتم اليّ»

* جلدت] في مخطوطة ٩٥٦٢: «جلوت».

---

126 The final line of this poem is a quotation (*taḍmīn*) of a famous verse that is attributed to ʿAlī b. Abī Ṭālib as well as others.

127 A bowdlerized version of this poem is recorded in the appendix (*dhayl*) of Ibn Ḥajar's *Dīwān* (ed. Abū al-Faḍl, 170).

128 This poem is also recorded in al-Kutubī, *Fawāt al-Wafayāt*, 3:276.

[Poem 25] al-Miʿmār (including an allusion):
I gave him a burden that he couldn't even bear part of,
and watched him beneath me, trying to dodge it and play a trick.
Then he cried and sucked on my tongue and said,
"Be gentle. I'll bear it." "He lies" was my cock's reply.
"«He'll give you sweetness from the tip of his tongue,
and then he'll run away just like a fox»."

[Poem 26] Fakhr ad-Dīn Ibn Makānis:
He'd whine and tell me he was an orphan when I fucked him,
this pubescent boy in whom lies the sweetness of my disgrace.
So I started to distract him from [thoughts of] orphanhood,
but whenever I distracted him, he'd start to cry.

[Poem 27] Chief Justice (*qāḍī l-quḍāh*) Shihāb ad-Dīn Ibn Ḥajar [al-ʿAsqalānī]:
A lover without any
reason to be proper.
He crawled up to his beloved [as he slept],
and showed [the poor lad] zero decorum.

[Poem 28] Nūr ad-Dīn al-Asʿardī:
I have a friend who said, "I've attained my [greatest] desire
with one who was the one I wanted out of all the people."
"Has he come to visit you?" I asked. "No," he said,
"But I'm unbowed [or: I masturbated] and my intention is steadfast."[129]

129 The verb *jaluda* means "to be resolute" but it also puts the reader in mind of the phrase *jald ʿumayrah*, a euphemism for male masturbation.

آخر:[130] [من الطويل]

تَرَكْتُ هِجا إبليسَ ثُمَّ مَدَحْتُهُ وذاكَ لأمرٍ عزَّ عِنْدي سُلوكُهُ

يُمَيِّلُ مَنْ أهواهُ حِيناً فإنْ أَبَى حكاهُ خيالاً في ٱلكَرَى فأَنِيكُهُ

الصفدي مُضَمِّنًا:[131] [من البسيط]

رأيتُهُ تَحتَ عَبْدٍ باتَ يَرْهَزُهُ فقُلْتُ تَرْضَى بِذا قُبِّحْتَ مِنْ رَجُلِ

وكَيْفَ يَعلوكَ عَبْدُ ٱلسُّوءِ قالَ نَعَمْ «لي أُسْوَةٌ بِٱنْحِطاطِ ٱلشَّمْسِ عَنْ زُحَلِ»

سيدي ابو الفضل بن وفا:[132] [من البسيط]

عاتَبْتُ أَبْيَضَ لَوْنٍ تَحْتَ أَسْوَدِهِ فقالَ حَسْبُكَ ما قالوهُ في ٱلمَثَلِ

«وإنْ عَلاني مِنْ دوني فلا عَجَبٌ لي أُسْوَةٌ بِٱنْحِطاطِ ٱلشَّمْسِ عَنْ زُحَلِ»

ابن دانيال: [من السريع]

ما عايَنَتْ عَيْنايَ في عُطْلَتي أَقَلَّ مِنْ حَظّي ولا بَخْتي

قَدْ بِعْتُ عَبْدي وحِماري وقَدْ أَصْبَحْتُ لا فَوْقي ولا تَحْتي

130 This poem is also recorded in Ibn Abī Ḥajalah, *Dīwān aṣ-Ṣabābah*, 150; aṣ-Ṣafadī, *al-Ghayth al-musajjam fī sharḥ Lāmiyyat al-ʿAjam*, 2 vols, ed. Ṣalāḥ ad-Dīn al-Hawwārī (Sidon; Beirut: al-Maktabah al-ʿAṣriyyah, 1430/2009), 1:265 (both with a variant first hemistich in l. 1).

131 This poem is also recorded in aṣ-Ṣafadī, *al-Ghayth al-musajjam*, 2:269. The hemistich cited here is from aṭ-Ṭughrāʾī's poem known as "*Lāmiyyat al-ʿAjam*" (see ibid., 2:228).

132 The line cited here is from aṭ-Ṭughrāʾī's poem known as "*Lāmiyyat al-ʿAjam*" (see ibid., 2:228).

[Poem 29] Another poet:

I used to insult Satan, but now I praise him
on account of a matter in which his behavior impresses me.
He makes the one I fancy incline toward me for a time, but if the guy refuses,
Satan tells him a [riveting] dream and I fuck him as he sleeps!

[Poem 30] aṣ-Ṣafadī (including an allusion):

I saw him beneath a male slave who'd begun to move him about
so I said, "You're OK with this? You're being debased by a man!
"How can you let a wretched slave get on top of you?" "Yes," he answered,
"«I mimic the Sun as it sinks beneath Saturn»"

[Poem 31] My lord Abū l-Faḍl b. Wafā:

I rebuked a fair-skinned man who was beneath his own black man
and he replied, "It's enough just to [remind you] how the saying goes:
«If he manages to get on top of me, then it's no surprise,
for I mimic the Sun as it sinks beneath Saturn.»"

[Poem 32] Ibn Dāniyāl:

My eyes have never seen—since I've fallen on hard times—
worse than my luck, than my misfortune.[133]
I [had to] sell my male slave and my donkey so now
I've got nothing to ride and no one to ride me!

---

133 In order to appreciate the pun in l. 1, it is relevant to know that Ibn Dāniyāl was a *kaḥḥāl* (opthalmologist).

ابن ريّان:[134] [من المجتثّ]

رَأَيْتُ تَحْتَ فُلانٍ عِلْقًا عَلَى ظَهْرِ تَخْتِ

وفي ٱسْتِهِ أيْرُ عَبْدٍ كَأَنَّهُ زَنْدُ بَخْتِ

فَلُمْتُهُ قالَ دَعْني لَذِذْتُ أيْري واسْتي

عَلَيَّ لِلهِ فَضْلٌ ألْخَيْرُ فَوْقي وتَحْتي

جامعه أحمد بن الحجازي:[135] [من المجتثّ]

قَدْ قالَ أيْري لِحِبّي انا ٱلْمُشَوَّقْ لِنَيْكَكْ

وبِالْمَدامِعِ بالِكْ وداخِلٌ تَحْتَ ذَيْلَكْ

وله عفا الله عنه: [من مخلّع البسيط]

خاصَمْتُ حِبّي فَقالَ دَعْني إذْ لَمْ تَزَلْ ناحِيًا وَرائي*

جَعَلْتُ فِي ٱلأَرْضِ مِنْكَ وَجْهي قَلَبْتُ ذَيْلي عَلَى قَفائي

* إذ] في مخطوطة ١٩٤٨٩: «اذا»

134 In British Library MS Add 19489, this poem is not attributed to a particular poet. The attribution to Ibn Rayyān comes from British Library MS Add 9562, f. 142b.

135 The language of this poem does not respect all the grammatical rules of classical Arabic.

[Poem 33] Ibn Rayyān:[136]

I saw so-and-so topping
    a bottom, who lay supine on the bed,
while in his own ass he had a slave's cock,
    the size of a lucky fire-stick![137]
So I rebuked him for this behavior but he said, "Leave me be.
    "I've pleased both my cock and my ass!
"By God, I'm blessed.
    "For I'm granted benefits from above and from beneath."

[Poem 34] The man who made this collection, Aḥmad b. Ḥijāzī:

My cock said to the one I love,
    "I'm the one who longs to fuck you.
"And the one who sheds tears,
    and slips in beneath your clothes."

[Poem 35] And also by him, may God excuse his sins:

When I quarreled with my beloved, he said to me, "Come on, let me.
    "After all you're still following after me.
"And I'm lying facedown in the dirt for you,
    with my clothes pulled all the way up over my neck."

---

136 In British Library MS Add 19489, this poem is not attributed to a particular poet.

137 The phrase *zandu bakhtī* is difficult for me to interpret. I am inclined to read it as *zandu bukhtī,* meaning a stone wrapped in rags and placed into a Bactrian camel-mare's vagina to make her feel that she has given birth in order to induce her to nurse another camel-mare's foal (see Lane, *An Arabic-English Lexicon*, s.r. "*z-n-d*") but above I have translated it to mean "fire-brand (*zand*) of luck (*bakht*)." I admit that I do not know what such a thing is other than a stick of some sort, which is sufficient to give the image required by the meaning of the verse. It may serve as a synonym for *ʿaṣā bakht*, the word *ʿaṣā* being connected to magic, though again I am not sure what such a thing would be.

[٧ قاضي القُضاة شمس الدين بن خلّكان: [من المنسرح]

تَحامَقَتْ بَغْلَتي فأَشْبَهَتِ ٱلبَرْقِ فَلَمّا وَنَتْ مِنَ ٱلتَّعَبِ
تَشَبَّهَتْ بالبُراقِ جاهِلةً أما تَراها في ٱلسَّيْرِ تَعْرجُ بِي*

[٧ وفيه لبرهان الدين القيراطي: [من السريع]

لي بَغْلَةٌ قَدْ أَتْعَبَتْ راحَتي والرِّجْلُ مِنْ فَخْذي إلَى كَعْبي
طَباعُها خارِجَةٌ كُلُّها وقَطُّ ما تَمْشي عَلَى ٱلضَّرْبِ*

[٧ آخر: [من الكامل]

رَقَصَتْ بَراغيثُ ٱلشِّتافأَجابَها ٱلناموس منه بالغِنا[ءِ] ٱلمُعْلَمِ
وتَواجَدَ ٱلبَقُّ ٱلكَثيفُ بِطَبْعِهِ طَرَبًا عَلَى شُرْبِ ٱلمُدامَةِ مِنْ دَمي*

*بالبراق] في مخطوطة ٩٨٤٩١: «بالبرق»
*تمشي] في مخطوطة ٩٨٤٩١: «يمشي».
*دمي] في مخطوطة ٩٥٦٢: «دم»

[Poem 36] Chief Justice (*qāḍī l-quḍāh*) Shams ad-Dīn Ibn Khallikān:[138]

My she-mule was acting a fool one day and began to resemble
lightning, [her color had drained] because she suffered exhaustion.
The she-mule imitated the mythical Burāq in her stupidity.
Can't you see how she hobbles/ascends (*taʿrajū/taʿrujū*) with me as she walks?[139]

[Poem 37] Burhān ad-Dīn al-Qīrāṭī has a poem on the same topic:

I've got a she-mule that's worn out my palm,[140]
and my leg from my thigh right down to my heel.
Her entire nature is beyond [acceptable limits]
and she never walks when hit (*ʿalā ḍ-ḍarbī*).[141]

[Poem 38] Another poet:[142]

The winter fleas danced and were answered
by mosquitoes singing what they'd been taught.
And the gnats, a numerous [swarm] by their very nature, made a show
of passion as they drank the wine of my blood.

---

138 The mule is a stock character in the *mujūn* genre. See e.g. Bauer, "Dignity at Stake", 177. The word for she-mule (*baghlah*) may also mean female slave but that valence does not seem to be at play in this poem.

139 There is another pun in this line in addition to the pun on hobbling (*ʿarija*) and ascending (*ʿaraja*) that calls to mind the night-journey (*miʿrāj*) on which the mythical Burāq-creature took the Prophet Muḥammad. The word for walking (*sayr*) also calls to mind the *Sīrah* (the prophetic biography of Muḥammad) in which the night-journey receives substantial attention.

140 This first hemistich can be read as an example of *tawhīm* (or false clue) in which the word "palm" (*rāḥah*), common in the vocabulary of sexually obscene poetry, deceives the reader into believing that the intended meaning of *baghlah* is not she-mule, but female slave. The second hemistich makes it clear that the word "palm" is merely a synonym for hand in this poem (see Cachia, *The Arch Rhetorician*, no. 108).

141 The phrase "walks when hit" (*tamshī ʿalā ḍ-ḍarbī*) also calls to mind the phonetically proximate phrase "walks along the path" (*tamshī ʿalā d-darbī*). The word *ḍarb* (viz. English: "beat off") may also allude to masturbation, which was already hinted at by the use of the word for "palm" in l. 1, hemistich 1.

142 Fleas and other pesky insects are stock characters in the *mujūn* genre. See e.g. Bauer, "Dignity at Stake", 166–67.

[٣ آخر: [من الطويل]

بَعوضٌ وبَرْغوثٌ وبَقٌّ لَزِمْنَني   حَسَبْنَ دَمي خَمْرًا فَلَذَّ لَها ٱلخَمْرُ*
فَيَرْقُصُ بَرْغوثٌ لِزَمْرِ بَعوضَةٍ   وبَقُّهُمُ سَكْتٌ لِيُسْتَمَعَ ٱلزَّمْرُ

[٤ غيره: [من البسيط]

لَيْلُ ٱلبَراغِيثِ لَيْلٌ لا نَفاذَ لَهُ   لا بارَكَ ٱللهُ في لَيْلِ ٱلبَراغِيثِ
كأَنَّهُنَّ بِجِسْمي مُذْ حَلَلْنَ به   يَدُ ٱلشُّهودِ عَلَى مالِ ٱلمَوارِيثِ*

[٤ المعمار: [من السريع]

ومازِحٍ أَنْزَلَ بِي صَفْعَةً   فاغْتَظْتُ إذْ ضَيَّعَ مِنْ حُرْمَتي*
وقالَ في كِتْفِكَ جاءَتْ يَدي   فَقُلْتُ لا والعَهْدُ مِنْ رِقْبَتي

[٤ وله عفا الله عنه: [من الكامل]

ومُماجِنٍ يَهْوَى ٱلصَّفا   عِ وَلَمْ يَكُنْ إذْ ذاكَ فَنّي*
ناولته عُنُقي ٱلرَّقِيـ   قَ فَراحَ يَنْخُلُهُ بِغَبْنِ
ما إنْ سَمَحْتُ لَهُ رِضًى   لكِنَّهُ مِنْ خَلْفِ أُذْني
لَوْ لا يَدٌ سَبَقَتْ لَهُ   لأَمَرْتُهُ بالكَفِّ عَنّي

---

*لزمنني] في مخطوطة ٢٦٥٩: «لزممن».
*مذ حللن] في مخطوطة ٢٦٥٩: مدخلان
*بي] في مخطوطة ٩٨٤٩١: «به». صفعة] في مخطوطة ٢٦٥٩: «صبغة».
*ذاك] في مخطوطة ١٩٤٨٩: «ذلك». بغبن] في مخطوطة ١٩٤٨٩: «بغبني».

[Poem 39] Another poet:

The mosquitoes, fleas, and gnats, they cling to me.
They take my blood for wine, and that wine tastes great to them!
A flea dances to a mosquito's clarinet (*zamr*)[143]
and the gnats (*baqq*) are quiet so the music (*az-zamr*) can be heard.[144]

[Poem 40] Another poet:

A night of fleas never ends (*lā nafādha lahū*).[145]
May God never bless the night of fleas!
It's as if—ever since they landed on my body—they [hold fast]
like the hands of witness on the wealth of the probate administration!

[Poem 41] al-Miʿmār:

A jester slapped me
and I got so mad on account of the shame he caused me.
"My hand fell on your shoulder," he said to me [in protest]
"No, it didn't" I said, "and I'm true to my word/I'm used to it on the back of my neck."[146]

[Poem 42] And also by him, may God excuse his sins:

A jester who liked to play the slapping-game;
that wasn't my thing at all.[147]
But I gave him my slender neck
and he proceeded to rain down [blows] on it, the sneak!
As soon as I gave him consent,
there he was behind my ear.
If it weren't for his hand that beat me to the mark,
I'd have told him to get the hell away from me![148]

143 The buzzing of a mosquito sounds somewhat like the buzzing of a double clarinet (viz. *zamr, mizmār*) and fleas are known to hop around as though they are dancing.

144 The word for gnats (*baqq*) puts the listener in mind of the word for a loquacious person (*baqqāq*, see also *baqbāq*) thus creating a proximate pun as they are "being silent".

145 The word *nafādh* also means "execution of a legal ruling", which is a technical meaning that is only signaled by the mention of probate in the final hemistich.

146 The phrase *al-ʿahd min riqbatī* means "I keep my promise" but the word *riqbah* puts the listener in mind of the word *raqabah* ("the neck", here "back of the neck"), which is where the offending slap would have fallen.

147 The word *aṣ-ṣafāʿ* (here translated as "slapping") is not attested in any dictionaries that I checked but its meaning is clear. The attested word *aṣ-ṣaffāʿ* ("buffoon who slaps") does not fit the meter, nor indeed does the regular verbal noun for slapping, *aṣ-ṣafʿ*.

148 The final expression in the last hemistich (*la-ʾamartuhū bi-l-kaffi ʿannī*) includes the word *kaff*, a homonym of the word for "palm" (also *kaff*), hence the pun.

This collection of 42 *maqāṭīʿ*-poems (91 verses in total) treats many common *mujūn* subjects including humiliation at the hands of a jester, pesky bugs, stubborn animals, and above all sexual matters that were considered shameful at the time: impotence, infidelity and cuckoldry, and what we now call bottoming (in male-male anal sex).[149] The use of variation, as in previous examples, is also clear: e.g. Poems 1–7 all use the verb *qāma* ("to rise; to occupy"), not uncommon when making light of penises, of course, with Poems 1–2 playing specifically on the verb's use as a technical grammatical term; Poems 5–10 are about impotence, with poems 5–7 straddling the two groups by including the verb *qāma*. I confess it is not clear to me whether Poem 11 is also about impotence, but in any case this poem and those that follow (Poems 11–35) form what we might think of as the kinky core of the *mujūn-maqāṭīʿ* chapter. Here we have poems on whipping vulvas (Poem 11), eschewing a vagina for an anus (Poem 12), menstruation preventing intercourse (Poem 13), sexual competition (Poems 14–15), male-male anal sex (Poems 16–23; 25–27; 29–35), and masturbation (Poem 28). There may also be an allusion to anal sex in Poem 24 that is not entirely clear to me and Poem 33 actually ridicules someone topping and bottoming in anal sex at the same time in the only depiction of a threesome in classical Arabic verse known to me. Poem 32, in its lament of the loss of a donkey and a slave who is compelled to perform anal sex on the poet-persona, foreshadows the poems on stubborn animals that follow the kinky core of the micro-anthology. These *maqāṭīʿ*-poems (Poems 36–37) are followed by poems about pesky bugs (Poems 38–40), which are followed themselves by the two concluding poems (Poems 41–42) on a particular type of pesky human, the jester. The poems obviously speak to one another in the order in which al-Ḥijāzī placed them, but in addition to that, several of them (Poems 8; 12–13; 25; 30–31) cite famous lines of verse and so they—as well as the deep thematic associations of *mujūn* verse more broadly—help link these poems to the wider classical Arabic poetic tradition, in which *maqāṭīʿ*-poetry had become one of the most innovative, dynamic, productive, and popular genres of all time. Seen individually or in conjunction with others of their type—or in references to them in paratextual and biographical sources—*maqāṭīʿ*-poems appear quite manifestly as a genre of their own with their own unique history. The next part of this study asks why it should have taken scholarship so long to recognize the emergence, development, and overwhelming popularity of *maqāṭīʿ*-poetry and ventures an answer that has ramifications for the study of pre-modern Arabic literature as well as the discipline of comparative literature itself.

149 The preponderance of these 42 *maqāṭīʿ*-poems is poems of two lines (37 in total, or 88%). The remainder are three lines long (3) or four lines long (2). See also Bauer, "Dignity at Stake" in which he proposes three thematic categories of *mujūn-maqāṭīʿ*.

PART 2

Arabic Poetry, Greek Terminology

Preliminary Remarks

> Japanese, Chinese, and Af[rican] trad[ition]s exhibit their own versions of e[pigram], though the term is hard to translate into any non-Western lang[uage].[1]

•••

> The universalism that is inherent in the task of rethinking the concept of world literature thus has to be confronted with linguistic heterogeneity and the concept itself uncoupled from the effects of standardization and homogenization both within and across languages and cultures that come masked as diversity.[2]

The second part of this study traces the origins and permutations of the term epigram in world literature to understand better how and why it has been applied to pre-modern Arabic poetry. In doing so, I demonstrate that while the Arabic *maqāṭīʿ*-genre has much in common with the world-literary category of epigram, scholars of comparative literature must take the issue of commensurability—especially in the case of transcultural and transhistorical comparisons—more seriously than they have in the past.[3] The seemingly simple question that serves as this book's title can be answered *per se*—though any answer would inevitably be arbitrary—but in Part Two, I argue that the question itself contains epistemological, historical, and ultimately political subtexts that deserve to be unpacked in the course of giving even an arbitrary answer. The question, as I have asked it, presupposes a range of values that

---

1 A. Preminger and T. V. F. Brogan (eds), *The New Princeton Encyclopedia of Poetry and Poetics*, s.v. "Epigram" [Frederic Will] (Princeton, NJ: Princeton University Press, 1993). It is clear from the entry that epigram as a literary category is used to mean pithy and satiric, not necessarily verse, forms. It is interesting to note that the entry on "epigram" in the latest edition of this reference work (4th ed., 2012) omits any reference to epigram traditions outside Europe and North America. The title of this part of the study is modified from the title of Wolfhart Heinrichs' masterful *Arabische Dichtung und griechische Poetik: Ḥāzim al-Qartağannīs Grundlegung der Poetic mit Hilfe aristotelischer Begriff* (Beirut: [In Kommission bei Franz Steiner Verlag, Wiesbaden], 1969) in homage.

2 Aamir R. Mufti, *Forget English! Orientalisms and World Literatures* (Cambridge, MA: Harvard Univ. Press, 2016), 250.

3 I draw inspiration from recent work by Rey Chow and Natalie Melas, to whose 2007 book *All the Difference in the World: postcoloniality and the ends of comparison* (Stanford, CA: Stanford Univ. Press, 2007) the subtitle of this monograph alludes.

 | DOI 10.1163/9789004350533_005

constrain the nature of all potential responses just as it reflects the historical conditions that frame it. The question is, for example, asked in English, the reigning hegemonic language of the current world-system and the globalized academy in which you and I work or study. Note, too, that the question in the book's title asks a question about Arabic as a monolith and thus presumes a lack of dialectal and regional specificity set against an undifferentiated, ahistorical backdrop. This question and questions like it also presuppose the ineluctable existence of a direct transcultural equivalent, which would not—one presumes—have been posited if the unequal linguistic dyad were reversed; how many scholars of Middle English literature have ever wondered to themselves, "What's the English for *maqāmah*?" As Rey Chow argues, "The grid of intelligibility here is that of literature as understood in Europe, and historical variations are often conceived of in terms of other cultures' welcome entries into or becoming synthesized with the European tradition."[4] Similarly we cannot overlook the fact that the question highlights a term that is a Greek importation into modern European languages and thus evokes the much mythologized legacy of Athens and Rome that is integral to a teleological vision of political history that continues to influence transnational bodies like the EU and NATO.[5]

The question is hardly remarkable in the flow of quotidian academic speech, and yet many readers would reject the question categorically: they would assert that it is meaningless either because it presumes a dubious commensurability or because the term epigram has itself become so nebulous that it has nothing to do with its classical antecedent, or else because—as some maintain—literary genres and forms may not be juxtaposed except in cases in which the borrowing by one culture or the influence of another can be demonstrated explicitly. In line with scholarly consensus at present, it can be assumed for the purposes of this study that the pre-modern Arabic poetic tradition was not at all influenced by actual Greek poetry despite the impact of the Greco-Arabic translation movement and the importance

---

4 Rey Chow, *The Age of the World Target: self-referentiality in war, theory, and comparative work* (Durham, NC: Duke University Press, 2006), 76.

5 Consider Richard Serrano's snappy summation: "[...] according to the dominant Hellenophile paradigm, Greek culture is absorbed by Rome a couple of centuries before Christ and Athens promptly, magically and retrospectively (especially in eighteenth-century Germany) becomes the source of all Western culture [...]" (Richard Serrano, *Neither a Borrower: forging traditions in French, Chinese and Arabic poetry* (Oxford: Legenda, 2002), 103). On this key constituent of modernity, see Suzanne L. Marchand, *Down from Olympus: archaeology and philhellenism in Germany, 1750-1970* (Princeton, NJ: Princeton University Press, 1996). NB: it was this same cultural environment that gave rise to "the modern debate on genre" (David Duff (ed.), *Modern Genre Theory* (Harlow: Longman, 2000), 3).

of texts like Aristotle's *Poetics* to Arabic rhetoric.[6] The reader therefore has every right to wonder why the term epigram is even being uttered. After all, I am sympathetic to the view that considers it inappropriate and unsatisfactory to employ terminology derived from specific cultural milieux without examining these terms and their applicability to other—alien—cultural contexts. And yet despite this methodological pose, I believe it is legitimate to use imperfect, alien terms such as epigram and anthology to describe a wide range of phenomena in world literature in part because these terms can always be modified to suit specific cultural contexts and in so doing provide both specialists and non-specialists a common ground for their discussions. It should also be said that for those of us charged with representing non-Western, pre-modern literary traditions in the Western academy such terms play a key role in domesticating the exotic literatures one is obliged to present to an academic audience and wider public, who are more comfortable with the predominant Western tradition.[7] But, as the following survey of uses of the term epigram will show, it is not merely in the cross-cultural instance that the literary terms we so frequently use need to be defined and scrutinized. The truth of the matter is that epigram—like its handmaiden, the anthology—is a

6 To complicate matters further, note, too, that the paramount intermediary in the transmission from Greek into Arabic, Syriac, boasts almost no tradition of secular poetry to speak of. (See Jack B. V. Tannous, "Syria Between Byzantium and Islam: making incommensurables speak", 2 vols (unpublished doctoral thesis. Princeton University, 2010), 1:209: "[...] the Syrians held on to some secular Greek genres—most notably philosophy and medicine, but they also continued to write history, had an interest in science, and even dabbled in Homer and studied rhetoric—but they did not hold on to other genres—say, epigrams, imperial panegyric and certain kinds of literature.") The best resource on the subject of Hellenistic influence is still Iḥsān ʿAbbās, *Malāmiḥ Yūnāniyyah fī l-adab al-ʿArabī*, 2nd ed. (Beirut: al-Muʾassasah al-ʿArabiyyah li-d-Dirāsāt wa-n-Nashr, 1993); see also, *inter alia*, Garth Fowden, *Quṣayr ʿAmra: art and the Umayyad elite in late antique Syria* (Berkeley, CA: University of California Press, 2004); Dimitri Gutas, *Greek Thought, Arabic Culture: the Graeco-Arabic translation movement in Baghdad and early ʿAbbāsid society (2nd–4th/8th–10th centuries)* (London: Routledge, 1998); Franz Rosenthal, *The Classical Heritage in Islam*, trans. Emile and Jenny Marmorstein (London: Routledge and Kegan Paul, 1975) and *idem*, *Das Fortleben der Antike im Islam* (Zürich: Artemis Verlag, 1965); *EAL*, s.v. "Greek Literature" [O. Leaman]; the introduction to Jaroslaus Tkatsch, *Die arabische Übersetzung der Poetik des Aristoteles und die Grundlage der Kritik des griechischen Texts*, 2 vols (Vienna and Leipzig: Akademie der Wissenschaften in Wien, 1928), 1:3–219; and Uwe Vagelpohl, *Aristotle's* Rhetoric *in the East: the Syriac and Arabic translation and commentary tradition* (Leiden: Brill, 2008).

7 As Rey Chow laments, "On these scholars [that is, scholars of Asian languages and literatures], the pressure is that of an imperative to acquire global breadth—to be cosmopolitan in their knowledge—even if they choose to specialize in esoteric languages and subject matters." (Rey Chow, *The Age of the World Target*, 13).

flexible literary category, which over its long history has stretched to contain a multitude of characteristics only some of which are applicable to analogous forms in the Arabic poetic tradition. It is for this reason that this empirical exercise is predicated on parallax—or the ability to contain two disparate and perspectives—and that the reader is being asked not to forget the dialectical process that has framed the question being posed and the historical and political contexts of the inquiry.

CHAPTER 3

Epigrams in the World

> EPIGRAM, properly speaking, anything that is inscribed. Nothing could be more hopeless, however, than an attempt to discover or devise a definition wide enough to include the vast multitude of little poems which at one time or other have been honoured with the title of epigram, and precise enough to exclude all others. Without taking account of its evident misapplications, we find that the name has been given—first, in strict accordance with its Greek etymology, to any actual inscription on monument, statue or building; secondly, to verses never intended for such a purpose, but assuming for artistic reasons the epigraphical form; thirdly, to verses expressing with something of the terseness of an inscription a striking or beautiful thought; and fourthly, by unwarrantable restriction, to a little poem ending in a "point," especially of the satirical kind.[1]

The term epigram can mean anything from "[...] a short verse inscription or label on vases, cups, votive gifts, funeral steles, herms, etc." to "[a] form of writing which makes a satiric or aphoristic observation with wit, extreme condensation, and, above all, brevity."[2] Of course, the term is used in this study

1 *Encyclopaedia Britannica*, 11th ed., 1911, s.v. "epigram".

2 The first of these definitions is taken from *Brill's New Pauly*, s.v. "Epigram. I. Greek. A. Beginnings" [Enzo Degani]. Compare Peter Bing and Jon Steffen Bruss, "Introduction to the Study of Hellenistic Epigram": "This term [sc. epigram], in its most basic sense, signifies no more than 'inscription', a text engraved upon an object. But already from its earliest attestations (in Herodotus and Thucydides), the word was used preeminently of one epigraphic subset, the verse-inscription—short poems, most often engraved on tombstones, religious offerings, or honorific monuments." (in *Brill's Companion to Hellenistic Epigram: down to Philip*,ed. Peter Bing and Jon Steffen Bruss (Leiden: Brill, 2007), 1.
cf. Marco Schöller's comments: "Especially in the realm of Arabic poetry, whose material is scattered over a wide range of the most diverse literary sources, there is a huge number of verses which were composed to be written upon lamps, tiles and carpets, saddles, swords and arches, cups, rings and seals, sticks and even nosebags. As said before, those verses need not actually be inscribed on objects—although this could be done, in particular on swords, seals or signet rings—, but the actual practice of engraving something on objects of the sorts mentioned also offered a seductive pretext for poetic creativity. There are no formal criteria to differentiate between 'common' or 'regular' verses and such rhymed 'inscriptions', but their status is chiefly determined by the accompanying paratext, e.g. when verses were preceded by a line saying 'The following was written on a lamp', or 'He composed the following inscrip-

 | DOI 10.1163/9789004350533_006

to describe a form of poetry, which is generally how scholars of pre-modern literary traditions use the term, but the second definition given above (taken from *The New Princeton Encyclopedia of Poetry and Poetics*) is illustrative. It is a clear example of the term epigram's transformation from its etymologically formalistic origins to something based rather more on a generic foundation; as this same definition goes on to say: "tone defines it [i.e., epigram] better than form."[3] What is most interesting for a comparative study of the pre-modern epigram is that this genre anxiety—that is to say the encroachment of generic features onto an ostensibly neutral pattern—is present already in the ancient Greek tradition that gave rise to the term.

The relevance of a word's etymology to its meaning is debatable and I generally consider it unproductive to focus on the etymological dimension of a literary term when there are plenty of examples of the genre in action, so to speak. These examples will no doubt be more illustrative of a genre's characteristics than abstracted conjecture based on etymology or theoretical discussions, but etymology can be informative when it is contrasted with such examples as it may provide an insight into why a culture adopted a specific term to describe a literary form or genre. In the case of Ancient Greece, where the term epigram is said to have been used originally for a literary form that was wholly congruent with the etymon, it is worth noting that the culture chose to preserve the etymon by transforming it into a newly abstracted—that is, metaphoric—terminological description. The term epigram, which derives from the Classical Greek tradition, is thus itself a kind of calque made up of historical accommodations and borrowings. It bears reiterating that the goal of this study is not to identify an Arabic equivalent of a literary universal, but (1) to acknowledge the undeniable weight of Greek, Latin, and other western European literary heritages upon the study of other world-literary traditions, including Arabic, (2) to determine the ways in which this disciplinary background has influenced scholarly judgments, and (3) to model a

tion on a sword'." (Werner Diem and Marco Schöller, *The Living and the Dead in Islam: studies in Arabic epitaphs*, 3 vols (Wiesbaden: Harrassowitz, 2004), 2:315–16.)

The second definition comes from A. Preminger and T. V. F. Brogan (eds), *The New Princeton Encyclopedia of Poetry and Poetics*, s.v. "Epigram" [Frederic Will]. The latest edition of this encyclopedia echoes this sentiment: "Epigrams encompass an almost infinite variety of tone and subject, but they are defined by concision (relatively speaking: while many epigrams are two to four lines long, others are considerably longer.)" (Roland Greene et al. (eds), *The Princeton Encyclopedia of Poetry and Poetics*, 4th ed. (Princeton, NJ: Princeton Univ. Press, 2012), s.v. "Epigram" [Ann Baynes Coiro]).

3 A. Preminger and T. V. F. Brogan (eds), *The New Princeton Encyclopedia of Poetry and Poetics*, s.v. "Epigram" [F. Will].

more critical engagement with the literary and scholarly legacies of European and non-European literary traditions.

The study of comparative literature has depended upon a Eurocentric conception of certain literary genres for which more and more remote parallels from outside the North Atlantic homeland of the field have been adduced over the course of the discipline's history. In cases where a clear and relatively unambiguous chain—or spectrum—of influence can be traced (e.g. the novel, genre fiction, the sonnet, etc.), the delimiting of a given genre is less fraught. In fact, non-European antecedents, like the 11th-century Japanese masterpiece *The Tale of Genji*, are welcomed for while they may predate a genre's canonical European examplars, they inhabit a marginal space outside the mainstream of the genre's historical development and serve only as a footnote in accounts of a genre's gestation.[4] For most world-literary categories, however, there is no evidence of influence, nor is there any expectation of it. In this case, a form of literary syncretism is practised, in which traits are taken from one culture and another to form a composite definition that is intended to account for the features of a wide variety of literary traditions, but which ultimately fails to provide a satisfying distillation of any.[5] In the case of the epigram, what literary syncretism exists is a contemporary phenomenon that has regrettably overlooked features of pre-modern, non-European literary traditions in order to accommodate a dominant, Eurocentric system of literary classification. In his very useful trilingual dictionary of literary terms prepared to help Arab students learn Western literary theory, the Egyptian scholar of English literature Magdi Wahba (1925–91) suggested the following Arabic equivalents for the concept of epigram:[6]

a). *al-ʿibārah al-manqūshah* [inscribed phrase];
b.) *al-maqṭūʿ al-lādhiʿ* [cutting excerpt];
c.) *al-ḥikmah as-sākhirah* [sarcastic aphorism]; and
d.) *al-mulḥah adh-dhakiyyah* [clever witticism]

---

4 One need look only at the *Wikipedia* entry "Novel" <http://en.wikipedia.org/wiki/Novel> [last accessed July 2015], which includes a section entitled "Early forerunners", listing a variety of Sanskrit, Japanese, Arabic (!), and Chinese "works of extended fictional prose". My debt to Earl Miner's *Comparative Poetics: an intercultural essay on theories of literature* (Princeton, NJ: Princeton University Press, 1990) will be clear to anyone who has read that work.

5 David Fishelov distinguishes between what he calls historical and metaphysical genres. See David Fishelov, *Metaphors of Genre: the role of analogies in genre theory* (University Park, PA: Pennsylvania State University Press, 1993).

6 Magdi Wahba, *A Dictionary of Literary Terms* (*English-French-Arabic*) (Beirut: Librairie du Liban, 1974), s.v. "Epigram".

Let us grant that these equivalents are accurate insofar as they describe the contemporary Western conceptualization of the genre. What is more interesting and more relevant than the definition's accuracy, to my mind, is the absolute lack of any conceptual space for extra-European contributions. While Wahba cites a few verses of Arabic invective poetry (*hijāʾ*), he does not attempt to connect the epigram to anything in the Arabic tradition. It is safe to assume that for Wahba—educated at Cairo University, the Sorbonne, and Oxford and a specialist of English literature—the epigram is exclusively a Western genre, that its origins and development are to be sought in classical and vernacular European literary traditions, and that the absence of a pre-modern Arabic equivalent can be assumed as a matter of course. This is not to say that Wahba was unaware of non-European epigram parallels; one cannot know. Rather Wahba's definition exemplifies a tendency to disregard the original contributions of non-European literary traditions like Arabic in the formation of a world-literary canon in which European literature is cast as the standard against which all other literary traditions, past and present, are to be calibrated. The point is not that Arabic cannot have enriched the pantheon of world-literary genres, rather that any contribution was—according to the teleological paradigm—trivial at best.

Definitions of the term epigram given in contemporary reference works like *The Princeton Encyclopedia of Poetry and Poetics*, *Oxford English Dictionary*, *The Oxford Dictionary of Literary Terms*, *Wikipedia*, *Encyclopædia Britannica*, and others reflect a common process in terminology by which a once narrow and specific description is extrapolated and widened until its particular characteristics dissolve into a billow of adjectives that can be applied to a wide variety of cases.[7] This process is natural, common, and of

7 The definition begins "1. An inscription, usually in verse." but is soon fleshed out: "2. a. A short poem ending in a witty or ingenious turn of thought, to which the rest of the composition is intended to lead up. b. loosely used for a laudatory poem. 3. a. A pointed or antithetical saying. b. Epigrammatic expression." (*Oxford English Dictionary*, 2nd ed., s.v. "epigram, *n.*"). "A short poem with a witty turn of thought; or a witty condensed expression in prose." (Chris Baldick, *The Oxford Dictionary of Literary Terms*, 3rd ed. (Oxford University Press, 2008), s.v. "epigram"). "An epigram is a brief, interesting, memorable, and sometimes surprising or satirical statement." (*Wikipedia.org*, s.v. "Epigram" <https://en.wikipedia.org/wiki/Epigram>, last accessed July 2015). "epigram, originally an inscription suitable for carving on a monument, but since the time of the Greek Anthology applied to any brief and pithy verse, particulary if astringent and purporting to point a moral. By extension the term is also applied to any striking sentence in a novel, play, poem, or conversation that appears to express a succinct truth, usually in the form of a generalization." (*Encyclopædia Britannica. Encyclopædia Britannica Online Academic Edition*, s.v. "epigram"). "[A] short poem with a witty ending" (Frank Abate (ed.), *The Oxford American Dictionary of Current English* (Oxford: Oxford University Press, 1999), s.v. "epigram, *n.*"); "1: a concise poem dealing pointedly and often satirically with

course entirely harmless, but it does impact the terms used for analysis.[8] The term epigram in English derives from the Greek term *epigramma* (*ἐπίγραμμα*), by way of Latin (*epigramma*) and its Romance legatees (i.e., the French *épigramme*).[9] Its etymological meaning is rooted in the preposition-verb combination, "upon" + "to write" (*epi+graphein* or *ἐπί* + *γράφειν*), hence its first-order meaning: "A verse inscription".[10] "The epigram", Enzo Dagani tells us, "was a part of Greek literature throughout its entire history (the oldest documents coincide with the first examples of alphabetic script)."[11] And the physical meaning epitomized by the word's etymology was not simply one aspect of the form among others: it was the dominant reflected meaning of the term in the Hellenistic period and played a key role in its development and its place in the literary pantheon.[12] The epigram form would eventually transform in

---

a single thought or event and often ending with an ingenious turn of thought[.] 2: a terse, sage, or witty and often paradoxical saying [...]" (*Webster's Third New International Dictionary, Unabridged*, s.v. "epigram").

8 T. K. Whipple tackled exactly the same issue in his study of English epigrams published nearly a century ago now: "The very word *epigram* is unfortunately not free from ambiguity. At the present time, it is most often used to indicate a *bon mot*, a pointed saying which pleases by some ingenious turn of thought or expression [...]. This usage, however, in spite of its popularity, is of very recent origin [...]." Whipple explained that this ambiguity is as old as the term itself—"The source of this obscurity is to be found in the early history of the *genre*"—and he preferred in his study to use the term as it was understood in the English tradition, that is a poem with point. (T. K. Whipple, *Martial and the English Epigram. From Sir Thomas Wyatt to Ben Jonson* (Berkeley, CA: University of California Press, 1925), 281–82).

9 See *Oxford English Dictionary*, s.v. "epigram, *n.*"

10 M. C. Howatson (ed.), *The Oxford Companion to Classical Literature*, 3rd ed. (Oxford: Oxford University Press, 2011), s.v. "epigram".

11 *Brill's New Pauly*, s.v. "Epigram I. Greek" [Enzo Degani]. On Ancient Greek epigram, see Manuel Baumbach et al. (eds), *Archaic and Classical Greek Epigram* (Cambridge: Cambridge University Press, 2010), esp. the editors' introduction (1–20).

12 On the magnitude of this key cultural resonance, see, for example, Peter Bing, "The Un-Read Muse? Inscribed Epigram and its Readers in Antiquity" in *Hellenistic Epigrams*, ed. M. A. Harder et al. (Leuven: Peeters, 2002), which incidentally highlights another—wholly separate—point of commonality between Greek and Arabic poetry: scenes of readers confronting poetic inscriptions (e.g. the story of the caliph Hārūn ar-Rashīd's visit to *Dayr Hind* discussed in Adam Talib "Topoi and Topography in the histories of al-Ḥīra" in *History and Identity in the Late Antique Near East*, ed. Philip Wood (New York, NY: Oxford University Press, 2013), 141–42).

the Hellenistic period into the epigram genre, but awareness of its etymological and historical origins persisted, especially in the genre's semantic field:[13]

> What originally began as an inscription now becomes essentially literary: the occasion increasingly becomes fictitious as is obvious, above all, in the epitymbia (funeral inscriptions) to personalities who had died centuries earlier.[14]

Kathryn J. Gutzwiller, whose *Poetic Garlands: Hellenistic epigrams in context* is a ground-breaking analysis of the Hellenistic epigram to which I am indebted, has discussed the epigram's transformation from a minor (inscribed) form to an engine of poetic creativity in the Hellenistic period.[15] As she explains, "It was the writtenness of the epigram, as its essential feature, that for centuries confined it to the ranks of the minor arts, to the category of the decorative and the trivial".[16] This prejudice against a written knowledge-culture in favor of oral transmission will be familiar to students of early Islamic culture familiar with the work of Gregor Schoeler and others.[17] The epigram had to break free of its instrumental, epigraphic function in order to enter the realm of culture proper: "As long as the epigram was confined to its monument, it was excluded from the arena of oral discourse where poetry could obtain rank and status by performance, and reperformance, before a collective audience."[18] Greek

---

13 Calling the epigram a form is not over-determining it: "The metre of the epigram was the epic hexameter, sporadically in combination with a dactylic pentameter, an iambic trimeter, or in rare exceptions appearing in yet other combinations." (*Brill's New Pauly*, s.v. "Epigram I. Greek" [E. Degani]).

14 *Brill's New Pauly*, s.v. "Epigram I. Greek" [E. Degani].

15 "Only at the beginning of the Hellenistic age did epigrams emerge as fully literary forms; in fact, they became a favorite of those on the cutting edge of literary development." (Gutzwiller, *Poetic Garlands*, 3).

16 Gutzwiller, *Poetic Garlands*, 2.

17 "During this period literary works of higher rank obtained written form only for mnemonic purposes, to be preserved for the oral performance" (Gutzwiller, *Poetic Garlands*, 2). Compare Gregor Schoeler, *The Genesis of Literature in Islam: from the aural to the read*, trans. and ed. Shawkat M. Toorawa (Edinburgh: Edinburgh University Press, 2009), an English edition of Schoeler's *Écrire et transmettre dans les débuts de l'islam* (Paris: Presses universitaires de France, 2002), and other articles; see also Gregor Schoeler, *The Oral and the Written in Early Islam*, trans. Uwe Vagelpohl, ed. James E. Montgomery (Abdingdon and New York, NY: Routledge, 2006), a collection of several of his most seminal articles translated into English.

18 Gutzwiller, *Poetic Garlands*, 3. One of the most interesting aspects of the inscription to codex transition in the history of the epigram genre is the rise of female epigrammatists in the Hellenistic period. Inscribed epigrams were, as Gutzwiller puts it, "unmarked

epigram—like all good memes—survived parasitically, according to Gutzwiller; its leap off the monument and onto the respectability of the page was facilitated by simultaneous developments in elegiac and sympotic poetry, as well as by the spread of books, specifically poetry collections.[19] This contextual transformation was key for the epigram's generic development, as Gutzwiller explains:[20]

> When an author or editor transfers an epigram from its site of inscription to a papyrus roll, it is signaled by a cultural convention that a more literary form of interpretation is now expected of the reader. The poem is no longer an "epigram" in the original sense of an inscription but a representation of such an "epigram." The monument adorned by the epigram is no longer visually present, but like the banqueting hall as the site of the sympotic epigram, must now be reconstructed in the reader's imagination.

According to Gutzwiller, "[t]he illusion of inscription maintained in many literary epigrams may also have boosted the genre's appeal to this bookish age, concerned with the visual as well as the more strictly literary aspects of the written word."[21] What was once denotation became connotation, thus beginning the process by which the term lost its generic specificity over time. Already in the Greek tradition by the Hellenistic period (4th century BC), when we speak of epigram, we are in fact speaking of a literary form, which exists already at one remove: epigram' or $\text{epigram}_{\text{book}}$ and not an undifferentiated, persistent phenomenon.[22] This fact may be historically extraneous, but it is in generic interstices like these that scholars of non-European literatures can find the audacity to repurpose world-literary categories and enhance them.

---

and so gendered male" but "[b]y publishing epigrams under their own names and often with content that reflected the interests of their gender, women epigrammatists made an important contribution to the new literary character of epigram [...]." (Kathryn J. Gutzwiller, "Gender and Inscribed Epigram: Herennia Procula and the Thespian Eros", *Transactions of the American Philological Association* 134 (2004), 383).

19 Gutzwiller, *Poetic Garlands*, 4–5.

20 Gutzwiller, *Poetic Garlands*, 7.

21 Gutzwiller, *Poetic Garlands*, 4.

22 See Peter Bing, "Between Literature and the Monuments" in *Hellenistic Epigrams*, ed. M. A. Harder et al. (Leuven: Peeters, 2002), esp. 29–40. NB: I use subscript notation to highlight the distinction between the contexts in which epigrams appear: either as epigraphs ($\text{epigram}_{\text{inscription}}$) or in codices ($\text{epigram}_{\text{book}}$). The prime symbol (Epigram') is used in mathematics to signify a derivative function and is thus apt.

The epigraphic pre-history of the epigram is simultaneously irrelevant to and immanent in the eventual fate of the epigram genre in literary history.[23] The epigraphic phase of Greek epigram, though brief, lived on implicitly in Hellenistic poetry and transculturally in the etymon, where it has often overshadowed more germane literary features (see e.g. Wahba's first-order definition above). Nevertheless, the reason that the term epigram entered the common parlance of literary scholarship and exercised such a profound influence on Greek, Latin, and vernacular European literatures is precisely because it was rescued from the ignominy of monumental adornment and brought into the literary mainstream in the Hellenistic period.[24] It cannot be put any more concisely than in Alan Cameron's formulation: "The epigram was in fact destined by its very nature to be *anthologized*."[25] Kathryn Gutzwiller has argued that even when epigrams were not immediately composed as written texts, they were always composed with written preservation in mind: "Even if Hellenistic poets sometimes composed for the stone and sometimes recited their epigrams to friends at social gatherings, they were nevertheless self-consciously aware that their epigrams would ultimately reside with other poetry in a written context."[26] Scholars of Islamicate literary traditions have often promoted the attitude that short poems hold more interest for their role in social interactions than their aesthetic value.[27] Peter Bing and Jon Steffen Bruss have remarked that this attitude toward

23 Cf. Simon Hornblower et al. (eds), *The Oxford Classical Dictionary*, 4th ed. (Oxford: Oxford University Press, 2012), s.v. "Epigram" [G. A. Highet and J. W. Duff]: "Throughout 1,000 years of development the poetic epigram never wholly lost its original meaning".

24 Peter Bing and Jon Steffen Bruss note, too, that "Collections of short elegy, such as that attributed to Theognis, containing poems that were often abbreviated or excerpted, likely became available at about the same time as collections of inscribed epigram, by the fourth century B.C." (Bing and Bruss, "Introduction to the Study of the Hellenistic Epigram", 11). This, they explain, had a great influence on the epigram genre and eventually "The confluence of sympotic and erotic elegy and traditional types of verse-inscription enlarged the thematic scope of literary epigram. Thus by the third century B.C. the meaning of the term itself expanded so as to comprise any brief, mainly elegiac poem, whether of the conventional epigraphic kind, or erotic-sympotic." (12). I mention here briefly that Gutzwiller (*Poetic Garlands*, 4n) and Alan Cameron, following Richard Reitzenstein, disagree about the primacy of writing vs. performance as concerns the early Hellenistic epigram. Cameron argues that "The principal forum for the epigram in the early third century [...] was the symposium." (Alan Cameron, *Callimachus and his Critics* (Princeton, NJ: Princeton University Press, 1995), 78).

25 Cameron, *The Greek Anthology*, 4.

26 Gutzwiller, *Poetic Garlands*, 5–6.

27 e.g. "[...] many of the short poems of Anvari and Sa'di translated here read like off-the-cuff occasional pieces which were then thought witty enough to preserve." (Dick

epigram composition can be reductive and uncritical, and their note of caution is equally good advice for scholars of Islamicate literatures:

> No doubt, some epigrams were recited at symposia; some may even have been composed and performed over wine in the course of the party. Yet it is striking that, of the many sources that describe poetic performance at Hellenistic symposia, not one ever mentions the recital of epigram—apart, that is, from the scenes envisioned in the epigrams themselves. We must therefore take care not to confuse a poem's description of an occasion with the actual circumstances of its composition/reception.[28]

For Kathryn Gutzwiller, "[t]he literariness of the Hellenistic epigram depends, then, not upon some 'bookish' element in form, style, or theme (though some poems do seem unlikely candidates for inscription), but upon the context in which the poem is found."[29]

The canon of the Western epigram is composed of two strands: the Hellenistic epigram tradition studied by Gutzwiller and others, and the Latin epigram tradition, whose most famous practitioners were Martial and Catullus.[30] The tradition of the Greek epigram was adopted in Rome, where many Greek epigrammatists actually lived and worked, and it is interesting that this transfer was also linked to the form's epigraphic origins.[31] It is not clear whether Catullus (1st century BC), thought of his own short poems as epigrams, but the tradition did use that term to describe them.[32] Yet despite

Davis, *Borrowed Ware: medieval Persian epigrams* (London: Anvil Press, 1996; rev. ed. Washington, DC: Mage Publishers, 2004), 23).

28 Bing and Bruss, "Introduction to the Study of the Hellenistic Epigram", 13–4. Ewen Bowie treated this proposed generic evolution at length in an article in the same volume. See Ewen Bowie, "From Archaic Elegy to Hellenistic Sympotic Epigram?" in *Brill's Companion to Hellenistic Epigrams: down to Philip*, ed. Peter Bing and Jon Steffen Bruss (Leiden: Brill, 2007). For Kathryn Gutzwiller, "[t]he advent of literary epigrams [...] seems directly tied to the invention of the poetry book as a literary form." (Kathryn J. Gutzwiller, "The Literariness of the Milan Papyrus or 'What Difference a Book?'" in *The New Posidippus: a Hellenistic poetry book*, ed. Kathryn J. Gutzwiller (Oxford University Press, 2005), 287.)

29 Gutzwiller, *Poetic Garlands*, 7.

30 A recent work on Martial is William Fitzgerald, *Martial: the world of epigram* (Chicago, IL: Univ. of Chicago Press, 2007). cf. Hornblower et al. (eds), *The Oxford Classical Dictionary*, s.v. "Epigram. (3) Graeco-Roman" [G. A. Highet and J. W. Duff] and James Hutton, *The Greek Anthology in Italy to the year 1800* (Ithaca, NY: Cornell University Press, 1935), 10.

31 *Brill's New Pauly*, s.v. "Epigram. II. Latin. B. History" [M. Lausberg]: "Since the 2nd half of the 3rd cent[ury] BC, the custom of inscriptional funeral epigrams [was] adopted from Greece first by upper class families like the Scipio clan [...]".

32 *Brill's New Pauly*, s.v. "Epigram. II. Latin. B. History" [M. Lausberg].

Catullus' important influence, it was Martial who developed the style of satiric epigram that would define the Latin art and overtake the Hellenistic epigram in historical influence.[33] Martial cultivated the epigram as a high verbal art and established the satiric, pointed epigram format that typifies the genre to this day.[34] In the words of James Hutton, "The practice of Martial established the form for the Western Middle Ages. Brevity and point were everything."[35]

1 Modern Epigram

> The modern epigram bears the stamp of Martial and Catullus, and has become a brief, pointed, witty remark, instead of the vaguer but richer form which the Greeks filled with such manifold and delicate emotion.[36]

Epigrams, like Arabic *maqāṭīʿ*-poems, depend—not only generically, but ontologically—on their anthological contexts. The ambiguous generic status of the epigram is often blamed on a literary-critical gap and it is clear that as a minor verse form, the epigram has often been ignored: "The ancients have left no extended theory of the epigram. [...] If all periods are taken together, the Greek epigram does not admit of definition, in the sense in which tragedy and the epic poem do. Its only *differentia* is brevity."[37] Of course, the fate of the epigram genre once it was adopted into the canon of European literature—during the climax of that canon's formative period—diverged from its more generically ambiguous classical past. The modern European epigram genre was inspired by *The Greek Anthology*, a didactic collection of Hellenistic epigrams, as well as the distilled style of Martial's epigrams, and was fuelled by a fervent project to reclaim

33 "Catullus' work differs from Hellenistic epigram poetry [...] in its serious presentation of love." (*Brill's New Pauly*, s.v. "Epigram. II. Latin. B. History" [M. Lausberg]).

34 "Martial aims at elevating the literary status of the genre by imposing high demands on quality, in contrast to the common perception that regarded the epigram as a playful side activity for amateurs. Aside from the mocking epigrams most often noticed in literary reception, most other types of epigrams (except for love epigrams) are represented as well. In his supreme utilization of the Latin and Greek traditions, Martial led epigram poetry to a high point in which keen pointedness is connected to a rich and lively description of detail." (*Brill's New Pauly*, s.v. "Epigram. II. Latin. B. History" [M. Lausberg]).

35 Hutton, *The Greek Anthology in Italy*, 55. Compare the definition given in David Mikics, *A New Handbook of Literary Terms* (New Haven, CT: Yale University Press, 2007), 106: "The epigram is, by definition, compact, pungent, and insightful [...]."

36 Hornblower et al. (eds), *The Oxford Classical Dictionary*, s.v. "Epigram" [G. A. Highet and J. W. Duff].

37 Hutton, *The Greek Anthology in Italy*, 55.

the classical past. The modern European epigram was filtered—re-filtered, in fact—through the Latin legacy of Italy, first in the Roman period and then again in the mediaeval Latin tradition. While the history of the Latin epigram in Italy begins as early as the 3rd century BC and continued under influence of the Hellenistic model until the 4th century AD, by the 15th century, "the general run of Latin epigrams then written savor more of Martial than of the Anthology."[38] It was in the 15th century that the recension of Hellenistic Greek epigrams compiled by Maximus Planudes in 1301 was brought to Italy by Byzantine immigrants. This text was subsequently printed for the first time in 1494 in Florence by Janus Lascaris (d. 1535). The arrival of this text, which we now know as the *Greek Anthology*, came at a propitious time for the development of the vernacular epigram in Italian and French.[39] Once again the process of generic development is not simply the story of inheritance and application, but a multifaceted process of accommodation, inspiration, and approximation:

> The Italians and French had several small verse-forms, more or less "lyrical" in character, well-accepted in the vernacular tradition—*strambotti, rispetti, dizains, madrigali, ballati,* and above all the sonnet. These were often in many respects the equivalents of the Greek epigram. Writers of these forms in the Renaissance became conscious of the similarity, and their consciousness led to formal modification as well as to substantial borrowing.[40]

This project was itself analogous to the Hellenistic-era project in which scholars went through the record of archaic poetry to discover epigrams that had—up until that point—only been epigrammatic.[41]

In 1538 in France, Clément Marot (1496–1544) "undertook to modify the old *dizains* [*ten-liners*] and the like by importing into them the substance and movement of Martial and the neo-Latin epigram" going so far as to call his collection *Épigrammes.*[42] This development in nomenclature is important,

38 Hutton, *The Greek Anthology in Italy*, 43.

39 Hutton, *The Greek Anthology in Italy*, 35; 42. On the tradition of neo-Latin epigrams, see Susanna de Beer et al. (eds), *The Neo-Latin Epigram. A Learned and Witty Genre* (Leuven: Leuven University Press, 2009).

40 Hutton, *The Greek Anthology in Italy*, 56. See also *idem*, "Ronsard and the Greek Anthology", *Studies in Philology* 40:2 (April 1943); and Daniel Russell, "The Genres of Epigram and Emblem" in *The Cambridge History of Literary Criticism. Vol. 3: The Renaissance*, ed. Glyn P. Norton (Cambridge: Cambridge Univ. Press, 1999).

41 Hornblower et al. (eds), *The Oxford Classical Dictionary*, s.v. "Epigram. (2) Hellenistic" [G. A. Highet and J. W. Duff]

42 Hutton, *The Greek Anthology in Italy*, 58.

but common generic characteristics of the Western epigram can be found in earlier French poetry as well:

> Je suis François, dont ce me poise,
> Né en Paris emprès Ponthoise.
> Or, d'une corde d'une toise,
> Saura mon col, que mon cul poise.
> (*François Villon, 1431–c. 1463*)[43]

In Italy, on the other hand, the break with vernacular tradition for the sake of idealized tradition was more radical:

> In Italy the vernacular epigram came into existence just following the bloom of the Latin epigram under Leo X [aka Giovanni de Medici, r. 1513–1521], and found its models preferably among the Latin epigrammatists of that age. It appears not to have grown out of a modification of the *strambotti* or *rispetti*, but was an immediate imitation of Latin and Greek form.[44]

Luigi Alamanni (1495–1556), whose epigrams—"completed before 1546"—were "the first [...] in Italian to be widely known, and influential" also "modeled himself directly on the Greek and Latin writers without reference to mediaeval forms."[45] Crucially, these collections were written against the backdrop of a stream of theoretical activity diagnosing and reifying the epigram genre, the first such attempt in literary history. It should come as no surprise perhaps that Marot's *Épigrammes* were mostly modified *dizains* in light of the proposed equivalence between sonnet and epigram that prevailed in this period.[46] This

43 François Villon, *The Complete Works of François Villon*, trans. Anthony Bonner (New York, NY: Bantam, 1960): "I am Françoys, which is no pleasure, / Born in Paris near Pontoise; / And soon my neck, by a rope measure, / Will learn how much my bottom weighs." Quoted with the original in Raymond Oliver, *Poems Without Names: the English lyric, 1200–1500* (Berkeley and Los Angeles, CA: University of California Press, 1970), 130.

44 Hutton, *The Greek Anthology in Italy*, 58. Interestingly, Thomas Wyatt (1503–42) attempted his own brand of syncretism in this respect, "[adapting] [...] Italian lyrics in the form of English epigrams" but Whipple suggests that "[i]t is not improbable that Wyatt himself had no conscious intention of writing epigrams as such; he may have purposed merely to introduce the *strambotto* into English verse." (Whipple, *Martial and the English Epigram*, 312).

45 Hutton, *The Greek Anthology in Italy*, 59.

46 Interestingly, this same equivalence did not carry over into the English tradition: "In England, however, the sonnet and the epigram came to be regarded as antithetical by the last decade of the sixteenth century [...]". (A. C. Hamilton (ed.), *The Spenser Encyclopedia*

assertion is first voiced in Sebillet's *Art Poétique*, published in 1548: "'Sonnet n'est autre chose que le parfait épigramme de l'italien comme le dizain du françois.'"[47] This is an early modern form of the same tendency toward literary syncretism we continue to practice in comparative literary studies today.

The most influential theoretician of the modern European epigram was Julius Caesar Scaliger (1484–1558), who was almost exclusively interested in the pointed Latin epigrams of Martial and Catullus.[48] According to Alastair Fowler, Scaliger's analysis "reflects remarkable progress towards useful genre criticism, giving detailed descriptions of kinds, based on rhetorical *dispositio*."[49] In his *Poetics* (*Poetices*, published posthumously in 1561), he defines the epigram as: "'Epigramma igitur est poema breve cum simplici cuiuspiam rei, vel personae, vel facti indicatione, aut ex propositis aliquid deducens.'"[50] That is to say: "Epigram is, therefore, a short poem that indicates some simple matter, person, or deed, or [else] deduces something from an [earlier] proposition". Scaliger is also well known for his division of the epigram into "tastes".[51] What is key in Scaliger, beyond the emphasis placed on point, is the idea of composite epigrams that expand on the proposition as it is first presented.[52] This same idea is taken up by later theorists, including Gotthold

(London: Routledge, 1990), s.v. "epigram" [Robert V. Young]). Rosalie Colie has proposed to call the epigram and sonnet "countergenres", that is they are "twinned and yet opposite" (Rosalie L. Colie, *The Resources of Kind: genre-theory in the Renaissance* (Berkeley and Los Angeles, CA: University of California Press, 1973), 67).

47 Translation: "[The] Sonnet is nothing other than the perfect Italian epigram [and is thus] like the French *dizain*". French original quoted in Hutton, *The Greek Anthology in Italy*, 56. According to Hutton, "The first elaborate theory of the epigram was the work of Robortello (1548) [who] [s]o far as possible [treated] the epigram [genre] on principles drawn from the *Poetics* of Aristotle." (ibid., 60–61). The first theory of the vernacular epigram was propounded by Thomas Sebillet (1512–89) in 1548 (ibid., 62).

48 "[Scaliger's] interest, however, is almost wholly Latin, and, while he pays his respects to the Greek epigrams, he is mainly thinking of only two styles—that of Catullus and that of Martial." (Hutton, *The Greek Anthology in Italy*, 64–5).

49 Fowler, "The Formation of Genres in the Renaissance and After", 186.

50 Quoted in Hutton, *The Greek Anthology in Italy*, 64.

51 "Scaliger, in the third book of his *Poetics*, gives a fivefold division, which displays a certain ingenuity in the nomenclature but is very superficial: the first class takes its name from *mel*, or honey, and consists of adulatory specimens; the second from *fel*, or gall; the third from *acetum*, or vinegar; and the fourth from *sal*, or salt; while the fifth is styled the condensed, or multiplex." (*Encyclopædia Britannica*, 11th ed., 1911, s.v. "epigram"). For more genre metaphors at the time, see Colie, *The Resources of Kind* and the list given in Fowler, "The Formation of Genres in the Renaissance and After", 191.

52 Hutton, *The Greek Anthology in Italy*, 64.

Lessing, and it is especially relevant for the structure of Arabic *maqāṭīʿ*-poetry discussed above.[53]

Antonio Possevino (1533–1611), a Jesuit pedagogue, provided a lucid analysis of epigrammatic discourse in his *Tractatio de Poësi et Pictura* (published in 1595 in Lyons), "[…] [recognizing] two main parts in an epigram—*expositio* and *clausula* or *conclusio* […]."[54] This idea of the composite epigram—nascent in Scaliger, and mature in Possevino—is conceptualized in the analysis proposed by Gotthold Lessing (1729–81) with reference, crucially, to the pre-history of the epigram, or $\text{epigram}_{\text{inscription}}$. In the modern period, as the epigram was re-introduced to Latin Europe, combining twin strands from the neo-Latin tradition drawing on Martial and the erotic-sympotic Hellenistic epigrams collected in the Byzantine *Greek Anthology*, "[…] it encountered a goodly number of small forms already established, which satisfied the desire of brevity and neatness and took up many of the impulses that were expressed in Greek and Latin through the epigrammatic form."[55] These native vernacular traditions were not displaced, but rather were incorporated into the modern epigram.[56] This process of adoption caused an element of genre anxiety and necessitated a renewed attempt at reification and legitimization. Lessing, recounting the mythic history of the epigram, developed an ingenious analysis of the epigram that linked its modern style to its ancient origins:

> Lessing's idea, in order to solve the problem of the definition of epigram […] was to force on the epigram form a bipartite structure. The epigram is a poem which, as though it were a genuine inscription, excites and holds

---

53 Scaliger's analysis—according to Hutton—"caught the attention of the world north of the Alps, and the attention of the Jesuit schoolmasters"—and this was instrumental in spreading the gospel of the neo-classical epigram throughout western Europe (ibid., 64–5). Alastair Fowler has discussed how "humanistic education" led to a "new grasp of genre" (Fowler, "The Formation of Genres in the Renaissance and After", 186). "The epigram", he explains, "[…] was of course a common medieval form, but it now came to be practiced with a distinctive precision." (ibid., 186). For a discussion of the development of epigram in Martial's native Spain, see J. P. Sullivan, *Martial, the Unexpected Classic: a literary and historical study* (Cambridge: Cambridge University Press, 2005), 273–79. See also Živilė Nedzinskaitė, "'Finis epigrammatis est anima eius': Transformations of the Content of the Latin Epigram in the Epoch of the Baroque", *Interlitteraria* 19:2 (2014).

54 Hutton, *The Greek Anthology in Italy*, 66.

55 Hutton, *The Greek Anthology in Italy*, 64–5.

56 Hutton, *The Greek Anthology in Italy*, 64–5.

our attention and curiosity about a particular subject (*Vorwurf, Erwartung*) and then proceeds to satisfy that curiosity (*Aufschluss*)[57]

Johann Gottfried von Herder (1744–1803) disagreed with this diagnosis, "[arguing] that the basic epigram was simply exposition",[58] but Lessing had "isolated [...] the one predominant element that Martial had made his own [...], the element of the pointed and witty conclusion".[59]

Lessing was not the first critic to apply anachronistic syncretism, but his was perhaps the most ingenious deployment of it. The modern European epigram is not merely a calque, but a highly anxious calque at that. Early modern Europeans would not contemplate conceding incommensurability with Classical modes so they repurposed, accommodated, and grafted features of Greek and Latin epigram to vernacular epigrammatic forms to produce a literary hybrid that satisfied the ambitions of their renaissance project.[60]

---

57 Sullivan, *Martial, the Unexpected Classic*, 298. See Gotthold Ephraim Lessing, "Zerstreute Anmerkungen über das Epigramm" in *Gotthold Ephraim Lessings Sammtliche Schriften, 1. Theil* (Berlin: In der Vossischen Buchhandlung, 1771).

58 Sullivan, *Martial, the Unexpected Classic*, 298. See Johann Gottfried Herder, "Anmerkungen über die Anthologie der Griechen, besonders über das griechische Epigramm" in J. G. Herder, *Zerstreute Blätter*, 2. Ausgabe (Gotha: bei Carl William Ettinfer, 1791–98). James Hutton notes that "The amatory epigrams [...] are not part of the Anthology most often translated or directly imitated, at any rate down to the beginning of the nineteenth century. One observes that Meleager of Gadara, who to-day in the minds of many stands as the typical amatory epigrammatist, was hardly distinguished as a personality before the end of the eighteenth century." (Hutton, *The Greek Anthology in Italy*, 75).

59 Sullivan, *Martial, the Unexpected Classic*, 298. On Martial's influence, see Whipple, *Martial and the English Epigram* and de Beer, "The *Pointierung* of Giannantonio Campano's Epigrams", 143–47.

60 This was not simply the concern of romance languages either. The German poet Martin Opitz (1597–1639), who was "[b]y common consent [...] the spokesman of orthodox literary opinion of his time and country [...] made it his life work to show that Germany could have all the literary genres possible in other languages." (Lawrence Marsden Price, *English Literature in Germany* (Berkeley and Los Angeles, CA: University of California Press, 1953), 7–8). See also Geoffrey H. Hartman, "Beyond Formalism", *MLN* 81:5 (December 1966); repr. in Geoffrey H. Hartman, *Beyond Formalism: literary essays, 1958–1970* (New Haven, CT: Yale University Press, 1970).

2 Epigram Goes Global

On 4 June 1902, Basil Hall Chamberlain (1850–1935)—the British-born Professor of Japanese at Tokyo Imperial University—presented a paper entitled "Bashō and the Japanese Poetic Epigram" to the Asiatic Society of Japan.[61] Chamberlain began his article by explaining that "All Japanese poems are short, as measured by European standards. But there exists an ultra-short variety consisting of only seventeen syllables all told." The form Chamberlain was talking about, the *haiku*, is well known in the West today; It is a poem of three lines of five, seven, and five syllables respectively.[62] The issue of brevity and normative poem length weighed heavily on Chamberlain as he sought to explain the particular nature of Japanese poetry to a non-Japanese audience; this much is clear from his language and manner of argument. Chamberlain explained that the *haiku*'s extreme concision had not hindered it in any way, rather that "[t]he poets of Japan [...] produced thousands of these microscopic compositions, which enjoy a great popularity, have been printed, reprinted, commentated, quoted, copied, in fact have had a remarkable literary success."[63] All the same, the brevity inherent in the *haiku* form means, Chamberlain suggested, that these poems "[...] must evidently differ considerably from our ordinary notions of poetry, there being no room in so narrow a space for most of what we commonly look for in verse."[64] In order to make the *haiku* more familiar to his English-speaking audience, Chamberlain adopted a domesticating strategy by which he associated it with the familiar poetic type of the epigram:[65]

---

61 See in Hiroaki Sato (trans.), *Japanese Women Poets: an anthology* (Armonk NY; London: M. E. Sharpe, 2008), XXXVIII.

62 Basil Hall Chamberlain, "Bashō and the Japanese Poetical Epigram" in Basil Hall Chamberlain, *Japanese Poetry* (London: John Murray, 1911). The article first appeared in *Transactions of the Asiatic Society of Japan* 30, pt. 2 (1902).

63 Chamberlain, "Bashō and the Japanese Poetical Epigram", 145.

64 ibid., 145–46. The advent of Twitter and micro-blogging has brought the issue of relative orthographic concision to the fore once again. See, *inter alia*, "Twtr. Which tongues work best for microblogs?" *The Economist* (31 March 2012).

65 We find the exact same tendency in scholarship on other non-European literary traditions in the period during which Chamberlain was writing (i.e. Paul Elmer More, *A Century of Indian Epigrams. Chiefly from the Sanskrit of Bhartrihari* (London and New York, NY: Harper and Brothers, 1899), 8: "Under [Bhartrihari's] name we have a little book of epigrams called the Çataka-trayam, or Century-triad, in which he unfolds in somewhat broken sequence his experience of life." and A. Berriedale Keith, *A History of Sanskrit Literature* (Oxford: The Clarendon Press, 1928), 208; 348). On short poetry in Sanskrit, see S. N. Dasgupta et al. (eds), *A History of Sanskrit Literature, Classical Period* (Calcutta: University of Calcutta [Press], 1947–), 364–418. See also similar issues discussed in Ming

> Their native name is *Hokku* (also *Haiku* and *Haikai*), which in default of a better equivalent, I venture to translate by "Epigram," using that term, not in the modern sense of a pointed saying,—*un bon mot de deux rimes orné*, as Boileau has it,—but in its earlier acceptation, as denoting any little piece of verse that expresses a delicate or ingenious thought.[66]

For Chamberlain, it was primarily the succinctness and delicacy of *haiku* that made his job as cultural go-between so discomfiting. The *haiku*, he struggled to explain,

> [...] is the tiniest of vignettes, a sketch in barest outline, the suggestion, not the description, of a scene or circumstance. It is a little dab of colour thrown upon a canvas one inch square where the spectator is left to guess at the picture as best he may. Often it reminds us less of an actual picture than of the title or legend attached to a picture.[67]

Elsewhere he averred that the *haiku* presents "[n]o assertion [...] for the logical intellect [...]".[68] Chamberlain also succumbed to the pull of etymological denotation in his analysis.[69]

Chamberlain identified what were, for him, the "permanently distinctive characteristics" of the *haiku*, or Japanese epigram:

1. "[...] it is quite free in its choice whether of subject or of diction"[70]
2. "[...] it is essentially fragmentary, the fact that it is part only of a complete

Xie, *Ezra Pound and the Appropriation of Chinese Poetry* (New York, NY: Garland, 1999), esp. 6–13; 60–2 on the epigram-paradigm as applied to pre-modern Chinese poetry.

66 Chamberlain, "Bashō and the Japanese Poetical Epigram", 145. The term *Hokku* refers to the first part (a unit of seventeen syllables) of the *tanka*, a 31-syllable poem. *Haikai* refers to the concise independent poems that make up *Renga* anthologies, and *Haiku* is a combination of the two. (See ibid., 158; 164). The Boileau here is Nicolas Boileau-Despréaux (1636–1711), who in his didactic poem *L'Art poétique*, defined the epigram as: "L'Épigramme, plus libre en son tour plus borné, / N'est souvent qu'un bon mot de deux rimes orné." Elsewhere, Chamberlain does concede, however, that the term *haikai* cannot always be translated as epigram and that meaning depends on context (Chamberlain, "Bashō and the Japanese Poetical Epigram", 178).

67 ibid., 149–50.

68 ibid., 148. We also find him calling them "Lilliputian versicles, or semi-versicles" (202) and "not pearls, but only tiny beads" (206).

69 On *haiku* and inscribed verse, see ibid., 153; 190.

70 ibid., 164. Elsewhere he remarked that "[t]he washing, the yearly house-cleaning, Christmas (or rather December) bills, even chilblains (!), come under the epigrammatist's ken. In fact, nothing is too trivial or too vulgar for him." (ibid., 152).

> stanza, and that it is consequently not expected to do more than adumbrate the thought in the writer's mind, having never been lost sight of."[71]

This second point of his analysis—that the *haiku* is inevitably "fragmentary"—is linked to the same Eurocentric discomfort toward short poetry that Chamberlain himself acknowledged at the beginning of his paper. It should come as no surprise to Arabists that this discomfort is given a veneer of empirical legitimacy by means of an origin story, not unlike the constant references to epigram's etymological meaning. In the Japanese literary tradition, the *tanka*, "[…] a poetic form of 31 syllables in 5 lines: 5, 7, 5, 7, 7" was "[t]he première form of Japanese court poetry."[72] The *tanka* can itself be divided into two "semi-independent" hemistichs—one of seventeen, the other of fourteen syllables—of which the first, the "upper" or "initial" hemistich, eventually became the *haiku* form.[73] Chamberlain concluded based on this pre-history and the *haiku*'s unfamiliar discursive style that it must essentially be fragmentary.[74] One might argue that Chamberlain's analysis of the *haiku* as fragmentary and sub-rational had nothing to do with his views on Japanese society and culture—that it was simply a good-faith analysis of condensed, lyric-affective, epigrammatic poetry—but I hardly think it a coincidence.[75]

In his analysis, Chamberlain drew an explicit connection between the *haiku* as a defective and fragmentary poetic form and basic patterns of Japanese thought. He states that the Japanese language is, compared to English, "[…] incomparably inferior as a vehicle for poetry […]" and moreover that the East is fundamentally orientated in such a way as to preclude "genius":[76]

---

71 ibid., 164.

72 Robert H. Brower and Earl Miner, *Japanese Court Poetry* (Stanford, CA: Stanford University Press, 1961), 511.

73 Chamberlain, "Bashō and the Japanese Poetical Epigram", 158.

74 He also criticises the *Renga* "linked-verse" anthologies for the same sin (ibid., 162).

75 After all, this is the same person who wrote that "[t]he current impression that the Japanese are a nation of imitators is in the main correct. As they copy us to-day, so did they copy the Chinese and Coreans a millennium and a half ago. […] [The] one original product of the Japanese mind is the native poetry." (Basil Hall Chamberlain, *The Classical Poetry of the Japanese* (London: Trübner & co., 1880; repr. London: Routledge, 2000), 1–2). See also his opinions on Ancient Japanese poetry (*idem*, "Bashō and the Japanese Poetical Epigram", 153–54) and Japanese cultural progress under Chinese and Indian influences (ibid., 154–55).

76 ibid., 192.

> Our Western saying that *Poeta nascitur, non fit* [Poets are born, not made] springs from an entirely different mental soil. In China and Japan it is held that every one can become a painter, every one can become a poet, just as every one can learn to read and write and to behave himself. To a certain extent this is true. What renders it doubly true in the Far-East is the absence of real genius,—as we Westerns understand genius,—so that the interval between different degrees of merit is less than with us. In this manner, racial disposition, strengthened by a congenial doctrine and its attendant practice, accounts for the enormous number of persons in these Eastern countries who can paint, poetise, and so on, after a quite respectable fashion. Mediocrity does not displease here, which is fortunate, seeing that the highest excellence is wanting.[77]

The *haiku*—which Chamberlain chose to call the Japanese epigram—is, for him, perfectly suited to a culture of mediocrity. A Japanese preference for compact poems is, therefore, in his analysis a function of their natural cognitive limitations and aesthetic philosophy:

> [...] [T]he classical or semi-classical poets of Japan, for over a thousand years past, have confined themselves to pieces of 31 syllables [the *tanka*] or of 17 [the *haiku*], whereas even our sonnet, which we look on as a trifle, has 140, and our system of stanzas strung together enables us to continue indefinitely till the whole of a complex train of thought has been brought before the mind. But it may well be that, even had Europe been available as a model, no such sustained style would have had much chance of permanently establishing itself in Japan. When an artist—when whole generations of artists have produced one sort of thing, it must always remain extremely doubtful whether, after all, they could have produced another. The tendency to ultra-brevity is too persistent a characteristic of Japanese esthetics to be accidental in any given case.[78]

Chamberlain chose to describe this form of Japanese poetry as epigram not only to make it more familiar to his audience, but to deride it as well. Short poems are, for Chamberlain, an attested, but marginal, phenomenon in the Western literary tradition, and while the term epigram serves its comparative function in introducing the reader to the Japanese *haiku*—by no means as familiar to the average educated English-speaker then as it is today—there is no doubt that Chamberlain also wanted to signal that the *haiku* was sub-po-

77 ibid., 194.

78 ibid., 206.

etic: not quite yet poetry, embryonic, mediocre, defective. The prominence of condensed poetry in the Japanese literary canon was a question in need of an urgent answer and the stakes were not simply literary, but civilizational:

> The interest of such an enquiry as that here undertaken lies in the fact that [...] the epigram is the most thoroughly popular, therefore national, characteristic. By the investigator of the Japanese mind it can be studied almost as the subject-matter of a natural science can be studied, and it yields as its result a picture of the national character. We see this character at work while it is, so to say, at play:—we see it ingenious, witty, good-natured, much addicted to punning and to tomfoolery; we see it fanciful but not imaginative, clever but not profound; we see it joking on the gravest subjects; we see it taking life easily and trifles seriously; we see its minute observation of detail, its endless patience in accumulating materials, together with its incapacity for building with them; we see its knack for hinting rather than describing,—a knack which, when it becomes self-conscious, degenerates into a trick and is often carried past the limit of obscurity, not to say absurdity [...]. We see that comparative weakness of the feeling for colour which characterizes Japanese art reappearing here as a want of feeling for rhyme and rhythm and stanzaic arrangement, for all, in fact, that goes to make up the colour of verse.[79]

Chamberlain's views on literature and Japanese culture did not go unchallenged. As early as 1934, Harold Gould Henderson opposed the translation of *haiku* as epigram in the introduction to his anthology of Japanese poetry in translation. *Haiku*, Henderson argued, is "[...] intended to express and to evoke emotion" so to translate it as epigram "[...] is quite misleading."[80] Henderson's objection was based on a thematic reservation: the idea of epigam as fundamentally satiric.[81] Asatarō Miyamori objects to this translation on similar grounds:

> Some British and American writers call the *haiku* "the Japanese epigram," on the ground that in length it resembles the shortest European poems—the Greek, the Roman and modern epigrams. But this epithet is quite inappropriate, inasmuch as, on the average, the *haiku* is much shorter than

79 Chamberlain, "Bashō and the Japanese Poetical Epigram", 208.

80 Harold Gould Henderson, *The Bamboo Broom: an introduction to Japanese haiku* (London: Kegan Paul, Trench, Trübner, 1934), 5–6.

81 cf. the dissenting review, however: "[...] despite Mr. Henderson's objections the term 'epigram' [...] seems really as good an English equivalent for *haiku* as any [...]" (H. Parlett, review of H. G. Henderson, *The Bamboo Broom*, *JRAS* 2 (1935), 416).

> the epigrams, which sometimes run to twenty or thirty lines, and are quite different in content, in subject matter, from the other. The epigrams, for the most part, treat of human affairs and aim chiefly at humour, cynicism and satire. On the other hand, the *haiku* treat principally of Nature—natural beauties and natural phenomena and always make some reference to the season; and humour is considered bad taste in *haiku*.[82]

Most Japanologists since Chamberlain have been more interested in the structure and meaning of short poetic forms than in their commensurability with Western poetic categories. Kōji Kawamoto has inverted Chamberlain's logic and taken the popularity and prevalence of *haiku* as evidence of its literary efficiency.[83] Robert Brower and Earl Miner, writing about the 31-syllable *tanka*, take the form's succinctness as a given and emphasize the form's achievement in context.[84] They also emphasize aspects of Japanese poetry that Western poetic traditions may be seen to lack:

> The Tanka also has quasi-poetic dimensions unknown to Western poetry by virtue of its social and conventional contexts. A Japanese reader who learns from a headnote that such-and-such a poem was composed when a certain person bade farewell to a friend who took a trip in the autumn immediately sees in this image or that phrase a far greater wealth of situation, circumstance, and tone than any Westerner does in his poetry.[85]

Developments in scholarship on Japanese poetry since Chamberlain have not resulted merely from later generations of scholars' more enlightened attitudes toward race. They are born out of a more accurate historical understanding, sensitive and hermeneutic reading, respect for non-European literary traditions, and an appreciation for context. Chamberlain's attitudes toward Japanese poetry—his views on its fragmentation, deficiency, and molecularity—serve as a salutary example of the perils of seeking out and arbitrarily designating iterations (or paratypes) of Western literary categories in world literature. We will see echoes of Chamberlain's approach in the survey of scholarship on Arabic poetry that follows.

82 Asatarō Miyamori (trans.), *Classic Haiku: an anthology of poems by Basho and his followers* (Tokyo: Maruzen Company, 1932; repr. Mineola, NY: Dover Publications, 2002), 12. See also Kōji Kawamoto, *The Poetics of Japanese Verse: imagery, structure, meter*, trans. Stephen Collington, Kevin Collings, and Gustav Heldt (Tokyo: University of Tokyo Press, 2000), 46.

83 Kawamoto, *The Poetics of Japanese Verse*, 45; 48–9.

84 Brower and Miner, *Japanese Court Poetry*, 436–37.

85 ibid., 437.

CHAPTER 4

Hegemonic Presumptions and Atomic Fallout

> As it often happens in theoretical discourse, a valid point tends to develop till it turns into its opposite by going to the invalid and unhelpful extreme.[1]

Having surveyed various permutations of the epigram in world literature, let us return to the pre-modern Arabic poetic tradition that is the subject of this study. This study attempts to make two points—one heuristically, the other analytically—about the emergence of a new poetic genre in Arabic and its relation to a broad category in world literature known as epigram. This chapter illustrates how previous applications of the term epigram to pre-modern Arabic poetic production tell an important, and somewhat discouraging, story about how Arabic poetry has been treated in modern and contemporary scholarship.[2] Two factors in Western scholarship on Arabic poetry—one foundational and the other incidental—lie at the heart of this inquiry, and by explicating these complex epistemic phenomena, light is shed on attitudes toward the term epigram as well as the broader agenda of scholarship on pre-modern Arabic literature.

The study of Arabic literature in the modern era—in the West as well as in the regions whence this literature came—is altogether inseparable from the study of the Classics and their place in the post-Renaissance university.[3]

---

1 Zhang Longxi, "The Complexity of Difference: individual, cultural, and cross-cultural", *Interdisciplinary Science Reviews* 35:3–4 (2010): 345.

2 Much of the controversial fervor surrounding Said's thesis of Orientalism from supporters as well as detractors has played itself out on a wide, and generalist, stage. Among these, see especially e.g. Bryan S. Turner, *Orientalism, Postmodernism and Globalism* (London: Routledge, 1994). No proper "archaeology of knowledge", with the necessary focus, restraint, and specialization expected of archaeological work, has been produced to date. The Warburg Institute's new Centre for the History of Arabic Studies in Europe is a source for optimism. See also Suzanne L. Marchand, *German Orientalism in the Age of Empire: religion, race, and scholarship* (Cambridge: Cambridge University Press, 2009).

3 e.g. "Die arabischen Fachausdrücke werden oft recht willkürlich (z.B. *qaṣīda idyllium*) mit solchen der antiken Poetik gleichgesetzt. Die antiken Rhetoren werden reichlich zitiert, Parallelen aus der griechischen und lateinischen Dichtung in großer Zahl beigebracht […]" ["The terminology of Arabic studies was often arbitrarily and directly juxtaposed (e.g. *qaṣīda idyllium*) to the terminology of Classical poetry. Ancient rhetoricians were cited amply,

 DOI 10.1163/9789004350533_007

Beyond the walls of academe, scholars have shown that early modern and modern Europe's self-conception depends on Arabo-Islamic civilization's role as an unimportant, but essential, intermediary between the Classical Greek (and to a lesser extent, Roman) tradition and what Europe calls its renaissance and enlightenment.[4] As Thomas Bauer has argued, the dismissal of Islamicate civilizational achievements after the renaissance (whether it begins in the 12th or 14th centuries) is precisely—and merely—the reflection of Europe's instrumentalist view of Islamic civilization.[5] So much of today's Islamophobia is itself based on an atavistic caricature of axiomatically ante- and anti-enlightenment Islamic societies.[6] Similarly in western Europe and North America, Arabic literature was studied—up until two generations ago—mainly by scholars who had been steeped in the study of the Classics. The tendency to see Islamic civilization through the lens of Ancient Greece is not simply the result of a few individuals' pedagogical background, however, and the barbarian makeup of the last three generations of scholars in the post-colonial era (that is, post-World War II) has not done much to undermine that paradigm.

Earlier uses of the term epigram in scholarship on Arabic literature have been systematic, but uncritical. In most cases, scholars have simply neglected to explain what it is they understand epigram to be—in most cases assuming that a consensus definition exists—or they have canonized a series of thematic assumptions (invective, epideictic, ekphrastic, etc.), or—and by no means is it infrequent—they have simply tried to avoid calling

---

[and] numerous parallels from Greek and Latin poetry were presented."] (Johann Fück, *Die arabischen Studien in Europa bis in den Anfang des 20. Jahrhunderts* (Leipzig: Otto Harrassowitz, 1955), 132. See also the discussion in Jaroslav Stetkevych, "Arabic Poetry and Assorted Poetics" in *Islamic Studies: a tradition and its problems*, ed. Malcolm H. Kerr (Malibu, CA: Undena Publications, 1980), 108).

4 Consider what Simon Ockley (1678–1720), the fifth Sir Thomas Adams's Professor of Arabic in Cambridge University and of course also a divine, gave as the merits of studying Arabic: "(1) throwing light on problems of Hebrew lexicography, (2) assisting the study of Jewish philosophy, (3) affording access to the Qurʾān […], (4) aiding geographical and historical studies, and (5) bringing new materials, through the translations, for the critical study of Greek texts" (Arthur J. Arberry, *The Cambridge School of Arabic* (Cambridge: Cambridge Univ. Press, 1948), 14–5).

5 Thomas Bauer, "In Search of 'Post-Classical Literature': a review article", *MSR* 11:2 (2007): 141–42: "Terms like 'Islamic Middle Ages' and 'Arabic postclassical literature' are not as harmless as they seem, but inevitably carry a strong political connotation. According to the Hegelian teleological worldview that is behind them, Islamic culture has to fulfil one single important task, that is, to bring classical thinking (here: science and philosophy of antiquity) to the West during the 'dark' Middle Ages."

6 See e.g. David Pryce-Jones, *The Closed Circle: an interpretation of the Arabs* (London: Harper & Row, 1989) and (regrettably) *passim*.

poems "short".[7] Interestingly, the term epigram (scil. epigram$_{\text{inscription}}$) has not generally been used to describe Arabic verse inscriptions.[8] Mainstream

---

7 e.g. "These [i.e. *qiṭaʿ*] are often short compositions on lighter themes, mostly wine, or love, or epigrams." (Huda J. Fakhreddine, "Defining Metapoesis in the ʿAbbāsid Age", *JAL* 42:2–3 (2011): 225). See also Nefeli Papoutsakis, "Ibn al-Muʿtazz, the Epigrammatist", *Oriens* 40:1 (2012).

8 There has not been much work done on Arabic verse inscriptions, but Werner Diem and Marco Schöller's *The Living and the Dead in Islam: studies in Arabic epitaphs* is a superlative achievement. Diem and Schöller present both the epigraphic and literary evidence for Arabic epitaphs and it is here that the gap between practice and theory viz. verse inscriptions seems quite large. Diem reproduces the verses found as actual epitaphs from Kairouan and other towns in modern Tunisia, but notes that verse-epitaphs are generally quite rare (Diem and Schöller, *The Living and the Dead in Islam*, 1:559–74). Meanwhile, Schöller demonstrates that among the wide variety of epitaphs culled from literary sources there are many in verse (Schöller lists some 237 in his catalogue, 2:338–573). "The statistical evaluation of the catalogue yields another fact of great importance, namely that roughly two thirds of epitaphs quoted in literary sources only report the poetry." (Diem and Schöller, *The Living and the Dead in Islam*, 2:323). Throughout his discussion of epitaphs in verse, Marco Schöller avoids the term epigram preferring the term "epitaph-poetry" (Diem and Schöller, *The Living and the Dead in Islam*, 2:326–27). See also Werner Diem, "The Role of Poetry in Arabic Funerary Inscriptions" in *Poetry and History. The Value of Poetry in Reconstructing Arab History*, ed. Ramzi Baalbaki et al. (Beirut: American University of Beirut Press, 2011); Moshe Sharon, *Corpus Inscriptionum Arabicarum Palaestinae*, 5 vols (Leiden: Brill 1997–), 1:10–3, 2:92 (where it is said that "[…] epitaphs in a poetic form […] became very popular in the second half of the Ottoman period […]"), and 3: XXXIX–XLI; Carmen Barceló, *La escritura árabe en el país valenciano. Inscripciones monumentales*, 2 vols (Valencia: Area de Estudios Árabes e Islámicos, Universidad de Valencia, 1998), 201–04, and other such studies cited in Geert Jan van Gelder, "Pointed and Well-Rounded. Arabic Encomiastic and Elegiac Epigrams", *Orientalia Lovaniensia Periodica* 26 (1995), 106n). A search for *shiʿr* in the Online version of Ludvik Kalus and Frédérique Soudan (eds), *Thesaurus d'Épigraphie Islamique*, 10th edition, October 2011 gives sixty-seven hits, but some of these are false matches and many do not give the text of the poems. Prof. Bernard O'Kane, who led a project to document and preserve monumental inscriptions in Cairo, informed me that the presence of poetry in his digital database of some 3,250 inscriptions is meager. This is runs counter to the impression one gets from pre-modern literary sources, e.g. al-Iṣbahānī (or Pseudo-Iṣbahānī), *Adab al-ghurabāʾ*, ed. Ṣalāḥ ad-Dīn al-Munajjid (Beirut: Dār al-Kitāb al-Jadīd, 1972); translated into English by Patricia Crone and Shmuel Moreh as *The Book of Strangers: mediaeval Arabic graffiti on the theme of nostalgia* (Princeton, NJ: Markus Weiner, 2000). Poetry featured frequently in ornamental inscriptions, see e.g. the famous decscriptions in al-Washshāʾ's (d. 936) *Muwashshā* (or *aẓ-Ẓarf wa-ẓ-ẓurafāʾ*; several eds). Jewish funerary epigrams abound in Graeco-Roman Egypt, see William Horbury and David Noy, *Jewish Inscriptions of Graeco-Roman Egypt* (Cambridge: Cambridge University Press, 1992), XX–XXIV; cf. also Arie Schippers, *Arabic Tradition & Hebrew Innovation: Arabic themes in Hebrew Andalusian poetry*, 2nd rev. ed. (Amsterdam: Institute for Modern Near Eastern Studies, 1988), 297. On the nature and artistry of Arabic inscriptions contemporary with the texts discussed here,

conceptions of the epigram among Arabists over the past century have been—in line with the early modern and modern European cultural perspectives discussed above—decidedly more Latinate. For example, in the *EI*^{2}—generally regarded as the standard reference work for students of pre-modern Islamicate civilizations—the entry "Epigram" (first published in 1963) redirects the reader to the entry "*Hidjā*ʾ" [invective], clearly channeling the paradigm of satiric epigram pioneered by Martial.[9] This is true elsewhere in scholarship on pre-modern Arabic literature, as well, where the term epigram is most often used to describe satiric or invective poetry (*hijā*ʾ).[10] In other cases, the term epigram has been applied to pre-modern Islamicate literatures including Arabic, Hebrew, Persian, Turkish, and Urdu to describe

---

more generally, see Yasser Tabbaa, *The Transformation of Islamic Art during the Sunni Revival* (Seattle, WA: University of Washington Press, 2001). See also Bernard O'Kane, "Persian Poetry on Ilkhanid Art and Architecture" in *Beyond the Legacy of Genghis Khan*, ed. Linda Komaroff (Leiden: Brill, 2006).

9 *EI*^{2}, s.v. "Epigram". The entry to which "Epigram" redirects is "Hidjāʾ", which Charles Pellat defined as an "Arabic term often translated by 'satire', but more precisely denoting a curse, an invective diatribe or insult in verse, an insulting poem, then an epigram, and finally a satire in prose or verse." (*EI*^{2}, s.v. "Hidjāʾ") In the first edition of the *Encyclopaedia* (1913–36), the entry on "Hidjāʾ" begins: "(A[rabic]), satire, epigram [...]" (*Encyclopaedia of Islam*, 1st ed., s.v. "Hidjāʾ").

10 Satiric epigram: see in *EI*^{2}, s.vv. "Hidjāʾ [scil. i. in Arabic]" [Ch. Pellat]; "Bashshār b. Burd" [R. Blachère]; "Ibn al-Rūmī" [S. Boustany]; "al-Ḥamdawī" [A. Arazi]; "Muḥammad b. Yasīr al-Riyāshī" [Ch. Pellat]; "al-Farazdaḳ" [R. Blachère]; "Abū 'l-Asad al-Ḥimmānī"; "Abū Saʿd al-Makhzūmī"; "Abū Nukhayla" [Ch. Pellat]; "Ibn Muʿadhdhal" [Ch. Pellat]; "Abū Shurāʿa" [Ch. Pellat]; "Mūsā Shahawātin" [Ch. Pellat]; "Ibn Lankak" [Ch. Pellat]; "ʿAmr b. Kulthūm" [R. Blachère]; "Dīk al-Djinn" [A. Schaade & Ch. Pellat]; "al-Ḥakam b. Muḥammad b. Ḳandar al-Māzinī" [Ch. Pellat]; "Ibn Bassām" [Ch. Pellat]; "Ibn Thawāba" [S. Boustany]; "Ḥammād ʿAdjrad" [Ch. Pellat]; "Ibn Sharaf al-Ḳayrawānī" [Ch. Pellat]; "al-Uḳayshir" [A. Arazi]; "Ḳayna" [Ch. Pellat]; "Midrār (Banū) or Midrārids" [Ch. Pellat]; "Ibn Rushd" [R. Arnaldez]; "Isḥāḳ b. Ḥunayn b. Isḥāḳ al-ʿIbādī" [G. Strohmaier]; "Sukayna bt. al-Ḥusayn" [A. Arazi].

See also P. A. Mackay, "Patronage and Power in 6th/12th century Baghdad. The Life of the Vizier ʿAḍud al-Dīn Ibn al-Muẓaffar", *SI* 34 (1971): 53; Régis Blachère, "Un jardin secret: la poésie arabe", *SI* 9 (1958): 11; D. S. Margoliouth, "On Ibn al-Muʿallim, the Poet of Wāsiṭ", *Zeitschrift für Assyriologie und verwandte Gebiete* 26 (1912): 335, 338; Ignaz Goldziher, "Der Dîwân des Ġarwal b. Aus Al-Ḥuṭejʾa", *ZDMG* 46 (1892): 520; Gustave Rat's translation of al-Ibshīhī's *al-Mustaṭraf fī kull fann mustaẓraf*: "De l'epigramme et de ses assauts [mordants]" (*Al-Mostaṭraf : recueil de morceaux choisis çà et là dans toutes les branches de connaissances réputées attrayantes par Śihâb-ad-Dîn Âḥmad al-Âbśîhî*, trans. Gustave Rat (Paris: E. Leroux, 1899–1902), vol. 1, ch. 43).

what is called the *qiṭʿah* in Arabic.[11] Again this is done with little, if any, consideration for the anthological context of Hellenistic epigram. This brings us to the other, "incidental" factor that has had a profound impact on the study of pre-modern Arabic poetry and continues to influence how scholars view shorter genres like *maqāṭīʿ*-poetry, the subject of this study.

1 *Atomic Fallout*

> […] the concept of "organic unity" that has long haunted discussions of Arabic poetics—[is] a concept born in a certain historical and literary context (the Romantic confrontation with neo-classical aesthetics) […] and should be consigned to the rubbish-heap of terms which once served a polemic purpose but are of little practical use.[12]

Orientalist ideas about the incoherence of classical Islamicate poetry are as old as the discipline itself.[13] Walter Leaf, writing in 1898, opined that: "We have

11 See e.g., in the case of Hebrew, Peter Cole, *The Dream of the Poem: Hebrew poetry from Muslim and Christian Spain, 950–1492* (Princeton, NJ: Princeton University Press, 2007), 532–33:

> Epigrams are extremely common in both Arabic and Hebrew medieval literature, and they need to be distinguished within the more general category of the *qiṭʿa*, or short poem. As in classical Greek, Latin, and English literature, the Hebrew epigram is characterized by brevity, wit, and its point, or strong sense of closure. In the Arabic tradition, longer qasidas were often "ransacked" by anthologists for epigrammatic lines that could stand on their own, and this anthology contains several of these "detached" epigrams […]. Epigrams ranged widely in theme, but gnomic, satirical, elegiac, and erotic epigrams abound.

See also Norman Roth, "'Deal Gently with the Young Man': love of boys in medieval Hebrew poetry of Spain", *Speculum* 57:1 (January 1982): 44; Arie Schippers, "Arabic Influence in the Poetry of Todros Abulafia" in *Proceedings of the Eleventh World Congress of Jewish Studies,* 9 vols (Jerusalem: World Union of Jewish Studies 1994), 3:18; Wout Jac van Bekkum, *The Secular Poetry of Elʿazar ben Yaʿaqov ha-Bavli. Baghdad, Thirteenth Century on the basis of manuscript Firkovicz Heb. IIA, 210.1 St. Petersburg* (Leiden: Brill, 2007), 17. In the case of Persian, see *EIran*, s.v. "Epigram" [J. T. P. de Bruijn]: "Generally speaking, the atomized structure characteristic of Persian classical poetry fostered the use of an epigrammatic style." See also Davis, *Borrowed Ware.*

12 Julie Scott Meisami, "Arabic Poetics Revisited", *JAOS* 112:2 (1992): 256. See also James E. Montgomery, "On the Unity and Disunity of the *Qaṣīdah*", *JAL* 24:3 (November 1993): 272.

13 A J. Arberry found an example of this sentiment already in the mid-18th century among Willam Jones' circle (Arthur. J. Arberry, "'Orient Pearls at Random Strung'", *BSOAS* 11:4

learnt from our Greek masters to seek the unity of a poem in the thought or mood developed in it. [...] [U]nity is internal and essential. To a Persian poet this is not so [...]".[14] Here again the Classical heritage is, for Leaf, the natural *locus comparationis* for Eastern art. Similarly in 1934 in the first edition of the *Encyclopaedia of Islam*, A. S. Tritton, as if channeling Basil Hall Chamberlain, asserted that:

> Arab poetry is essentially atomic; a string of isolated statements which might be accumulated but could not be combined. Sustained narrative and speculation are both alien to it. It is descriptive but the description is a thumbnail sketch; it is thoughtful but the result is aphoristic. The poet looks on the world through a microscope. Minute peculiarities of places and animals catch his attention and makes his poetry versified geology and anatomy; untranslatable and dull. Forceful speech is his aim and the result is—to Western minds—often grotesque or even repulsive.[15]

The view that Islamicate poems were not artistic wholes, but fragmentary collections of individual verses came to be known as atomism or molecularity.[16] This is an outdated view, which has been thoroughly discredited, so one could argue that it is at best quaint and irrelevant for us today. Nevertheless, I believe it should command our attention for two crucial reasons. First, this controversy—over the perceived incoherence of pre-modern Arabic and Islamicate poetries—is what gave rise to the modern discipline as we practice it today,

---

(February 1946): 703). The atomic paradigm was also applied to other Islamicate poetries (e.g. Ottoman, Urdu, etc.); see Frances W. Pritchett, "Orient Pearls Unsung: the quest for unity in the Ghazal", *Edebiyât* n. s. 4 (1993).

14 Walter Leaf, *Versions from Hafiz. An essay in Persian metre* (London: Grant Richards, 1898), 5 (quoted in Arberry, "'Orient Pearls at Random Strung'", 703–4).

15 *Encyclopaedia of Islam*, 1st ed., s.v. "Shiʿr" [A. S. Tritton]; quoted in Michael Sells, "The *Qaṣīda* and the West: self-reflective stereotype and critical encounter", *al-ʿArabiyya* 20:1–2 (1987): 308.

16 On the first uses of the epithets "atomic" and "molecular" in connection with Arabic poetry, see Geert Jan van Gelder, *Beyond the Line: classical Arabic literary critics on the coherence and unity of the poem* (Leiden: Brill, 1982), 14n. Basil Hall Chamberlain also referred to Japanese *haiku* as "[...] molecules of description, fancy or morality [...]" (Chamberlain, "Bashō and the Japanese Poetical Epigram", 207). The motif of atomism was in the 19th-century air, of course: John Dalton (1766–1844) proposed his atomic theory of the elements at the beginning of the century and the notion is prominent throughout intellectual thought in the era (e.g. in Marx's economic model, see *Das Kapital*, chs 1 and 2). Jaroslav Stetkevych has also pointed out that the same charge of atomism was used to describe aspects of the composition of the Hebrew Bible (J. Stetkevych, "Arabic Poetry and Assorted Poetics", 113n).

and its echoes continue to reverberate through putatively unrelated debates in the field. Second, and more perniciously, the purported fragmentation of Islamicate poetry was deployed as a metonym for the "eastern mind":[17]

> […] The lyric poetry of Persia is indeed a reflexion of the minds of those who sang it—sensual, mystic, recalling the voluptuous dreams of Hashish, the flashes of intuition wherein the Godhead reveals himself in momentary blinding visions to the ecstatic drunk with wine, be it of Heaven or of Earth.[18]

"[H]ighflown nonsense" indeed, to quote A. J. Arberry.[19] Nevertheless, this variety of highflown nonsense was resilient and plagued the discipline for decades, as Jaroslav Stetkevych has explained:

> For more than a century of European scholarly commerce with Arabic poetry, the *Leitmotiv* of that commerce had never really changed: the nature of Arabic poetry was deterministically and dogmatically assumed to exhaust itself in its brick and mortar, in its most basic morphology. It remained quite within the philological mentality of the "perfect text" to search for the nature of something as fragile as the structure of the Arabic poem in its smallest morphological components—in *das Einzelne*. What had once been the Euphrates-like fluidity and the openness of form of Goethe's "*etwas Quodlibetartiges*" is now about to be harnessed into a theory of the nature of Arabic poetry which, together with a more com-

17 Jaroslav Stetkevych has traced the process by which the perspective of singularity proposed by Wilhelm Ahlwardt becomes a site of civilizational bifurcation: "Only a few years later, Theodor Nöldeke will repeat Ahlwardt's critical dictum [i.e. "[…] the Arabs have understanding for the singular [*das Einzelne*] only, by reason of which their poetry is, according to our conception, never a self-contained whole"] almost literally, for by that time the issue had become apparently quite dogmatic. It was up to Nöldeke, however, to give the notion of the *Einzelne* the significant comparativist slant of 'otherness': 'The Oriental has always but the single verse in sight, the single image rendered complete whereas we look always at the whole' (T. Nöldeke, *Beiträge zur Kenntnis der Poesie der alten Araber* [Hannover, 1864], p. 5)." (J. Stetkevych, "Arabic Poetry and Assorted Poetics", 112, 112n; the quotation from Ahlwardt translated by Stetkevych is from Wilhelm Ahlwardt, *Über Poesie und Poetik der Araber* (Gotha: Friedrich Andreas Perthes, 1856), 68–9). See also the discussion in Raymond P. Scheindlin, *Form and Structure in the poetry of al-Muʿtamid Ibn ʿAbbād* (Leiden: Brill, 1974), 1–7.

18 Leaf, *Versions from Hafiz*, 5–6 (quoted in Arberry, "'Orient Pearls at Random Strung'", 704).

19 Arberry, "'Orient Pearls at Random Strung'", 704.

> prehensive anthropological theory of the Arab mind, will result in the seductive and conveniently scientific formulation of "atomism".[20]

For decades, scholars of Islamicate poetry accepted the view that Arabic poetry was inherently atomistic and occasionally even attempted to inure readers to it:

> The reader unaccustomed to this kind of poetry will have noted a rather disconcerting feature it displays. Each verse forms a closed unit, only slightly interconnected with the others. [...] external incongruity would seem to be a real rule in classic Persian poetry. We are in the presence of a bunch of motifs only lightly tied together.
>
> Now, is this lyrical style so monotonous and invariable, as many have said? We think it is not [...].[21]

It should come as no surprise perhaps that this view only fell out of fashion in the post-colonial period when the civilizational dichotomy underpinning atomism began to be challenged. As Julie Scott Meisami has explained, the dichotomies that atomism supposed—like the one upon which European colonialism rested—were entirely specious:

> The molecular theory is less an aesthetic than a value judgment behind which lies the assumption of the innate superiority of Western culture and literature, defined through a process of selecting certain features as primary or fundamental, hence normative, and applying these as criteria for all literature. The result is the creation of two mutually opposed literary entities, one "Western", one "Oriental", an opposition

20 J. Stetkevych, "Arabic Poetry and Assorted Poetics", 113.

21 Alessandro Bausani, "The development of form in Persian lyrics", *East and West* n.s. 9:3 (September 1958): 149. cf. "An Arabic (or Persian) *ḳaṣīda* is a very artificial composition; the same rhyme has to run through the whole of the verses, however long the poem may be. [...] The result is that we cannot expect much beautiful poetry [...] the description of the desert and its animals and terrors may have a certain charm at first, but when the description recur in endless poems expressed in the same manner, only with different words, the monotony becomes nauseous." (*Encyclopaedia of Islam*, 1st edition, s.v. "Ḳasīda" [F. Krenkow]). Decades later in the *EI*², Gérard Lecomte (1926–97), who had taken on the responsibility of revising and updating Krenkow's entry, echoed many of these—by then, outdated—prejudices: "The Arabic ḳaṣīda is a very conventional piece of verse, with one rhyme, whatever its length, and in a uniform metre. Consequently, the charm and originality of certain of the themes employed cannot prevent boredom and monotony from reigning over these never-ending poems." (*EI*², s.v. "Ḳaṣīda" [G. Lecomte]).

> which constitutes an important part of the paradigm of cultural identity produced by Orientalist scholarship.[22]

Nevertheless, despite the clear shift in scholarly opinion against the hegemonic presumption at the root of atomism following the Second World War essentialism continued to influence literary analysis well into the 20th century.[23] The debate over atomism fixated on the form and nature of the *qaṣīdah*, its compositional logic, and the way in which it ought to be read. Proponents of the atomic position found pre-modern Arabic (and other Islamicate) poetry disjointed, staccato, and incoherent, where their opponents exposed underlying semantic, formalistic, ritual, etc. patterns in these putatively molecular poems, thereby demonstrating unmistakable artistic and organic unities.

After World War II, as European colonialism gave way to American hegemony and the discipline of Oriental Studies was reborn as Near Eastern (or Middle Eastern) Studies, atomism became discredited as one element in a larger Orientalist *Weltanschauung*.[24] This same period was also the heyday of structuralism, which—it will come as no surprise—offered revisionist scholars in the post-colonial era a means of disproving the bigoted dogma of atomism and making pre-modern Islamicate poetic traditions whole again.[25]

In the 1980s two scholars associated with the University of Chicago, Jaroslav Stetkevych and his student Michael Sells, traced the history of this

---

22 Julie Scott Meisami, *Structure and Meaning in medieval Arabic and Persian poetry: Orient Pearls* (London: RoutledgeCurzon, 2003), 2.

23 See e.g. Gustave von Grunebaum, *Medieval Islam*, 2nd ed. (Chicago, IL: University of Chicago Press, 1954), 266: "Convention backed by what might be called the atomizing outlook of the Arab on people and things prevented for the most part the drawing of fully individualized portraits in poetical form." NB: Arberry's article was published in 1943.

24 e.g. "For a century the dominant image of the *qaṣīda* has oscillated between the barbarism hypothesis [...] and the atomism and objective description hypotheses, the Arabs as imaginationless, versifying geologists, endlessly enumerating, to no apparent purpose, monotonous strings of unrelated descriptive data. This double-image reaffirms in the field of Arabic poetry a mechanism of Orientalism as presented by Edward Said, but not explicitly applied by him to Western studies of Arabic literature: the splitting of the subject culture into passionate savages on the one hand and strings of data and dead facts on the other." (Sells, "The *Qaṣīda* and the West", 323). See also Suzanne Pinckney Stetkevych's discussion of trends in Arabic literary scholarship in her introduction to *Early Islamic Poetry and Poetics*, ed. Suzanne Pinckney Stetkevych (Farnham: Ashgate, 2009).

25 e.g. "Evidently a correct appreciation of the Arabic poetic experience has implications for a general evaluation of the Arab mentality, and revision of the established opinion about poetry might necessitate a rethinking of the general cultural problem." (From the introduction to Scheindlin, *Form and Structure*, 6).

important evolution in scholarship with great erudition and lucidity.[26] Sells' description of Orientalist misconceptions of the *qaṣīdah* and their uncritical acceptance and application in scholarship gives some idea of the impatience—if not disbelief—of his generation:

> A stereotype was created of the *qaṣīda* and the *qaṣīda* was labeled stereotyped. Literary judgments were made without criteria and the *qaṣīda* was labeled arbitrary. Themes like the wine song were taken out of poetic context and trivialized, and the *qaṣīda* ethos was labeled trivial. Despite a mass of data, no coherent understanding of the *qaṣīda* was achieved and the *qaṣīda* was labeled atomistic.[27]

In the seven years that followed Jaroslav Stetkevych's article (published in 1980), his plea for a re-evaluation of the *qaṣīda* on its own terms had been answered ably—by scholars including himself and Suzanne Stetkevych—so by the time Michael Sells published his own article in 1987, the unitarians had clearly won the argument.[28]

The past forty years has seen the publication of many structuralist studies of Islamicate poetry, which have greatly improved our understanding of the nature and function of poetry in pre-modern Islamicate cultures.[29] I do not

---

26 The articles are: J. Stetkevych, "Arabic Poetry and Assorted Poetics" and Sells, "The *Qaṣīda* and the West: self-reflective stereotype and critical encounter".

27 Sells, "The *Qaṣīda* and the West", 323.

28 Sells could identify four "interconnected" groups of scholars "who [had] taken the classical Arabic poetic tradition seriously": "(A) the structuralist interpretations of Bateson, Haydar, and Abu Deeb; (B) the work of J[aroslav] Stetkevych and several of his students and former students, what may be called the 'Chicago school'; (C) studies of the oral-performative nature of early Arabic poetry, notably those of James T. Monroe and Michael Zwettler; and (D) the work of Suzanne Pinckney Stetkevych, related to the Chicago school, but now developed into a comprehensive understanding that deserves separate treatment." (Sells, "The *Qaṣīda* and the West", 324).

29 e.g. Kamal Abu Deeb, "Towards a Structural Analysis of Pre-Islamic Poetry", *IJMES* 6 (1975); *idem*, "Towards a Structural Analysis of Pre-Islamic Poetry (II), the Eros vision", *Edebiyât* 1 (1976); and *idem*, "Studies in Arabic Literary Criticism: the concept of organic unity", *Edebiyât* 2 (1977); Andras Hamori, *On the Art of Medieval Arabic Literature* (Princeton, NJ: Princeton University Press, 1974), esp. ch. 4; *idem*, *The Composition of Mutanabbī's Panegyrics to Sayf al-Dawla* (Leiden: Brill, 1992); Scheindlin, *Form and Structure*; James E. Montgomery, "Dichotomy in *Jāhilī* Poetry", *JAL* 17 (1986); Sperl, *Mannerism in Arabic Poetry*; Thomas Bauer, *Altarabische Dichtkunst: eine Untersuchung ihrer Struktur und Entwicklung am Beispiel der Onagerepisode*, 2 vols (Wiesbaden: Harrassowitz, 1992); Suzanne Pinckney Stetkevych, *The Mute Immortals Speak: pre-Islamic poetry and the poetics of ritual* (Ithaca, NY: Cornell University Press, 1993); Dagmar Riedel, "The sum

mean to suggest that these structuralist studies are perforce concerned with the issue of poetic unity, or that structuralism as a method would not have come to dominate the study of Islamicate literatures in the second half of the 20th century were it not for the atomism controversy. Rather I believe that there is a discernible link between the introduction of structuralist methods for the study of Islamicate poetries and the older issue of atomism; it is axiomatic that all new methodological developments must conform and confront underlying dynamics in a given discipline as they are adopted into scholarly practice. Nor has atomism or the anti-atomic backlash gone completely dormant even as the field moves away from structuralism, like the wider discipline of literature, toward a more historicist orientation.[30] In 2004, for example, a scholar of classical Arabic poetry saw fit to describe the overarching contribution of her research in light of the atomic controversy: "I believe that my major contribution to the scholarly study of the *qaṣīdah* is to strengthen this sense of artistic integrity."[31] The view that pre-modern Arabic poetry lacks artistic integrity—and the decades-long campaign to discredit it—forms an active and determinant disciplinary legacy for all scholars of pre-modern Arabic poetry. Even superficially innocent remarks must be qualified and the extent to which such remarks are indeed innocent is a question of some urgency in our field. When, for example, Geert Jan van Gelder noted that "[...] longer poems are often composed, as it were, of a series of

---

of the parts: a pre-Islamic *qaṣīda* by Bišr b. Abī Ḫāzim al-Asadī", *Der Islam* 79 (2002); Meisami, *Structure and Meaning*. See also Raymond Farrin, *Abundance from the Desert: classical Arabic poetry* (Syracuse, NY: Syracuse University Press, 2011), XIII–XVIII, 3–4, 222–23; and James T. Monroe, *Structural Coherence and Organic Unity in the Poetry of Ibn Quzman* (Leiden: Brill, forthcoming [unseen]).

But cf. Mary C. Bateson, *Structural Continuity in Poetry: a linguistic study of five Pre-Islamic Arabic odes* (The Hague: Mouton, 1970), one of the first structuralist studies, which was panned by Suzanne Pinckney Stetkevych: "[Bateson's] 'impressionistic thematic analyses' are nothing more than a summary of the poem at the most superficial level; there is nothing analytical about them. In brief, Bateson's work cannot be considered a scholarly contribution to the understanding of pre-Islamic poetry." (Suzanne Pinckney Stetkevych, "Structuralist Interpretations of Pre-Islamic Poetry: critique and new directions", *JNES* 42:2 (April 1983): 86).

30 A few examples of this historicist trend in scholarship are: Susanne Enderwitz, *Liebe als Beruf. Al-ʿAbbās ibn al-Aḥnaf und das Ġazal* (Beirut [Stuttgart]: Franz Steiner Verlag, 1995); Gruendler, *Medieval Arabic Praise Poetry*; Ali, *Arabic Literary Salons*; Marlé Hammond, *Beyond Elegy: classical Arabic women's poetry in context* (Oxford: Oxford University Press [for the British Academy], 2010); Jocelyn Sharlet, *Patronage and Poetry in the Islamic World: social mobility and status in the medieval Middle East and Central Asia* (London: I.B. Tauris, 2010).

31 Sumi, *Description in classical Arabic poetry*, 2.

epigrams, be they single lines or short passages. Most Arabic poems are either epigrams or epigrammatic",[32] he hastened to add—albeit in a footnote—that the above statement "[…] does not necessarily imply a lack of unity or coherence […]", as if prophylactically, in order to stave off the inevitable charge of atomism. Here in one sentence of analysis and a single footnote we see how, for students and scholars of pre-modern Arabic poetry, the term epigram has been dragged into a heated, centuries-old, and often absurd, debate, as though exemplifying Wilhelm Stekel's dictum that "[i]f a taboo exists concerning certain objects, everything associated to the object also becomes taboo."[33] The taboo of atomism in Arabic literary studies is legitimate and it has a history, but it is nonetheless a taboo that may have contaminated analysis and may continue to do so.

The earliest Arabic poetry excluding *rajaz* (i.e. *qarīḍ* poetry) is said to be divided either into the *qaṣīdah* or the *qiṭʿah form*. The *qaṣīdah* does not display very strict formal requirements beyond rhyme and meter, but in modern scholarship it is fundamentally reckoned to be a polythematic poem.[34] This definition is not the same as that used by pre-modern littérateurs themselves.[35] Its counterpart—in both pre-modern Arab and contemporary Western definitions—is the *qiṭʿah*. This form, while equally as ancient and prevalent as the *qaṣīdah*, has been treated—by scholars and theorists, if not by poets—for more than a millennium as the *qaṣīdah*'s lesser antithesis.[36] As the *qiṭʿah* is conceived of as nothing more than a poem that fails to be a *qaṣīdah*, it is usually defined as

32 van Gelder, "Pointed and Well-Rounded", 101.

33 Wilhelm Stekel, "Criminal Impulses" in Wilhelm Stekel, *Compulsion and Doubt*, trans. Emil Gutheil (London: Peter Nevill, 1950), 157 (as cited in Henry Bond, *Lacan at the Scene* (Cambridge, MA: MIT Press, 2009), 135n (scil. 220n14).

34 By "very strict formal requirements", I mean to contrast the loose formal restrictions of the *qaṣīdah* with more regimented forms like the sonnet, rondeau, etc. See Renate Jacobi, "The Origins of the Qaṣīda Form" in *Qasida Poetry in Islamic Asia and Africa*, ed. Stefan Sperl and Christopher Shackle, 2 vols (Leiden: Brill, 1996).

35 "The term *qaṣīda* is used in indigenous Arabic literature theory and critique differently, namely, in a broader sense than in Arabic literature studies in the West. […] Western Arabists […] normally designate as *qaṣīda* only the polythematic long poem generally beginning with *nasīb* and having the same meter and rhyme [….]." (Schoeler, "The Genres of Classical Arabic Poetry", 39–40); on this point, see ibid., 39–43. See also Ali Hussein, "Classical and Modern Approaches in Dividing the Old Arabic Poem", *JAL* 35:3 (2004).

36 See e.g. aṣ-Ṣafadī's comments on Mujīr ad-Dīn Ibn Tamīm and Ibn Abī Ḥajalah's comments on Ibrāhīm al-Miʿmār (in appendix, nos 8d and 11b) and also van Gelder, "Pointed and Well-Rounded", 106.

short or monothematic or both.[37] Like the *qaṣīdah*, the *qiṭʿah* is given much formalistic license.[38] Geert Jan van Gelder explains that:

> The word *qiṭʿa*, literally "piece, fragment", became the customary term for any shortish poem that was not properly a *qaṣīda*, which was unfortunate, firstly since it suggests that a *qiṭʿa* is always a piece of an originally larger entity, and secondly because it yokes together a term that often—at least in modern studies—refers to a definite structure (*qaṣīda*) and a term that merely denotes the absence of this same structure, as if a *qiṭʿa* could not have a structure of its own. The term *qiṭʿa* is used for both "a short poem" and "a poem with only one theme", even though some *qiṭʿas* have more than one theme and some long poems have only one.[39]

Jaroslav Stetkevych has shrewdly argued that many of our scholarly misconceptions are the result of mishandled evidence taken from the tradition itself: "[...] it rather appears that every misconception and every static compartmentalization of literary-critical theoretical formulations and ideas were precisely due to an excessively naïve receptivity to whatever Arabic literary theory was then available and accessible."[40] It will come as no surprise that this methodological failing is not exclusive to the study of classical Arabic literature.[41] Naïve

---

37 e.g. "a short monothematic poem or fragment of a poem, in contrast to the long (often polythematic) poem, the *ḳaṣīda*" (*EI*², s.v. "Ḳiṭʿa" [G. Schoeler]).

38 "[...] [T]he Arabs, aware of the fact that not every poem could be called a *qaṣīda*, distinguished the *qiṭʿa* from the *qaṣīda* purely in terms of length. The result was a number of opinions as to the minimal *qaṣīda*, rather arbitrarily given as twenty, sixteen or fifteen, ten or seven, or even three lines. Nowhere is an explanation or a justification of the number given." (Geert Jan van Gelder, "Brevity: The long and the short of it in classical Arabic literary theory" in *Proceedings of the Ninth Congress of the Union européenne des arabisants et islamisants: Amsterdam, 1st to 7th September 1978*, ed. Rudolph Peters (Leiden: Brill, 1981), 79).

39 *idem*, "Pointed and Well-Rounded", 105.

40 J. Stetkevych, "Arabic Poetry and Assorted Poetics", 117.

41 "What this rapid survey shows is that the gap between theory and practice in the Greek and Roman discourse on genre is pronounced. In particular, it shows that the 'implied theory' instantiated in ancient poetry is far more sophisticated than the explicit theory developed by philosophers and literary critics [...] It is, however, the explicitly theoretical tradition, exclusively I would say, that has played a role in our modern histories of genre theory. There is no point in deploring this situation, which is now a historical fact. [...] The most important point I can make in closing is to urge that the implicit theory of genre embedded within Greek and Roman literature come to play a significant role in any future attempt to assess the history of discourse about genre." (Joseph Farrell, "Classical Genre in Theory and Practice", *New Literary History* 34:3 (Summer 2003): 402–3).

receptivity gave rise to the *qaṣīdah-qiṭʿah* dichotomy, a static compartmentalization that scholars have claimed is the fundamental bifurcation of forms in pre-modern Arabic poetry.

Before going any further, let us pause briefly to dismiss the sly whisper of etymology that surrounds the term *qiṭʿah*.[42] The term *qiṭʿah* is derived from the root *q-ṭ-ʿ* (cutting, breaking, cutting across; the same root as in the term *maqāṭīʿ*) and this etymological association has affected, indeed obscured, attempts to investgate the literary phenomenon empirically and contextually.[43] Just as the etymological association of inscription affected the mood of Hellenistic epigram, so the cutting, extraction, and fragmentation implicit in the term *qiṭʿah* has loomed large in analyses of Arabic poetry, especially as they concern the ontological status of these *qiṭaʿ*-poems. An over-reliance on one theoretical paradigm—drawn primarily from the famous theoretical discussion of the *qaṣīdah* in Ibn Qutaybah's (d. 276/889) *Kitāb ash-Shiʿr wa-sh-shuʿarāʾ* (*The Book of Poetry and Poets*)—has led to a dynamic in which, according to literary scholarship, the *qaṣīdah* was always the Arabic poetic archetype, and every other type of poetry should be classified either as subsidiary or post-classical.[44] A particularly egregious

42 On the danger of etymology as explanation, See Walid A. Saleh, "The etymological fallacy and Qurʾānic studies: Muḥammad, paradise, and Late Antiquity" in *The Qurʾān in Context: historical and literary investigations into the Qurʾānic milieu*, ed. A. Neuwirth et al. (Leiden: Brill, 2007) and *idem*, "A piecemeal Qurʾān: *furqān* and its meaning in classical Islam and modern Qurʾānic studies", JSAI 42 (2015); as well as Andrzej Zaborski, "Etymology, Etymological Fallacy, and the Pitfalls of Literal Translation of some Arabic and Islamic Terms" in *Words, Texts and Concepts Cruising the Mediterranean Sea. Studies on the sources, contents and influences of Islamic civilization and Arabic philosophy and science. Dedicated to Gerhard Endress on his sixty-fifth birthday*, ed. R. Arnzen and J. Thielmann (Leuven: Peeters, 2004). The etymological fallacy is a manifestation of what Alison Gopnik has called "the drive for causal understanding". See Alison Gopnik, "Explanation as orgasm and the drive for causal understanding: the evolution, function and phenomenology of the theory-formation system" in *Explanation and Cognition*, ed. F. Keil and R. Wilson (Cambridge, MA: MIT Press, 2000).

43 Even when the form is recognized as wholly independent of the *qaṣīdah*, the spectre of fragmentation continues to stalk it, e.g.: "[…] *qiṭʿah*s, which are poetry fragments without direct links to the *qaṣīdah* […]" (Schippers, *Arabic Tradition & Hebrew Innovation*, 214). Geert Jan van Gelder has suggested that "[t]he negative connotations of the term *qiṭʿa* may be partly responsible for the neglect of the early Arabic shorter poem and epigram in Arabic studies, in which the *qaṣīda* is, understandably but excessively, favoured to the point of ignoring the *qiṭʿa*." (van Gelder, "Pointed and Well-Rounded", 106). Compare the Chinese genre of concise poetry, the *Chüeh-chü*, meaning "broken-off lines" (Frankel, *The Flowering Plum and the Palace Lady*, 212).

44 See Ibn Qutaybah, *ash-Shiʿr wa-sh-shuʿarāʾ*, ed. Aḥmad Muḥammad Shākir, 1:74–7. In her review of Geert Jan van Gelder's *Beyond the Line*, Suzanne Pinckney Stetkevych

example of this sort of deracinated theorizing is found in an important handbook on Arabic literature:

> All pre-Islamic *rajaz* belonged to the class of the *qiṭʿah*, the short piece, consisting of seven or ten lines at most. Some short pieces, written in the non-*rajaz* metres, occurring for example in such celebrated anthologies as the *Ḥamāsah*, are in fact selected from longer poems. We do not really possess true examples of short pieces originally composed as such, for selection can always be assumed in these cases.[45]

This passage is made up of a series of errors and misconceptions that illustrate why the study of non-*qaṣīdah* Arabic poetry is retarded.[46] Firstly *rajaz* and *qarīḍ* poetry form two distinct traditions and the application of the term *qiṭʿah* to non-*qarīḍ* poetry is inapt.[47] Secondly, as Alan Jones has explained, "[...] it is

---

wrote: "The Peroration offers some interesting remarks on the 'mode of existence' of the Arabic poem that lead in turn to the question of the 'integrity' of the poem that appears once as a full *qaṣīda* in the poet's *dīwān*, again as a fragment in an anthology such as the *Ḥamāsa*, and whose individual verses appear scattered among literary critical works. I think that the author has perhaps underestimated the power and pervasiveness of the *qaṣīda*-form in determining Arabic poetic perception and sensibility: it is precisely the 'given' framework of the *qaṣīda* that allows for the multiformity and dismemberment of the poem." (Suzanne Pinckney Stetkevych, Review of G. J. van Gelder, *Beyond the Line*, *JNES* 47:1 (January 1988): 64).

While Jaroslav Stetkevych has criticized Theodor Nöldeke for not having appreciated Ibn Qutaybah's model of the tri-partite *qaṣīdah* (J. Stetkevych, "Arabic Poetry and Assorted Poetics", 118), the systematic division of the *qaṣīdah* form into three sections (*nasīb*, *raḥīl*, and concluding movement) is not supported by the bulk of literary evidence; see e.g. Renate Jacobi, *Studien zur Poetik der altarabischen Qaṣīde* (Wiesbaden: Franz Steiner Verlag, 1971); Julie Scott Meisami, "The Uses of the *Qaṣīda*: thematic and structural patterns in a poem of Bashshār", *JAL* 16 (1985); James E. Montgomery, "Of models and amanuenses: the remarks on the *Qaṣīda* in Ibn Qutayba's *Kitāb al-Shiʿr wa-l-shuʿarā*" in *Islamic Reflections, Arabic Musings: studies in honour of Professor Alan Jones*, ed. Robert Hoyland and Philip Kennedy (Cambridge: E. J. W. Gibb Memorial Trust, 2004); Nefeli Papoutsakis, *Desert Travel as Form of Boasting: a study of Ḏū r-Rumma's poetry* (Wiesbaden: Harrassowitz, 2009). Cf. Renate Jacobi, "2.2 Die altarabische Dichtung (6.–7. Jahrhundert) 2.2.2.1 Gattungen und Formen" in *GAP*, 2:23–6.

45 Abdulla El Tayib, "Pre-Islamic Poetry" in *Arabic Literature to the end of the Umayyad Period*, ed. A. F. L. Beeston et al. (Cambridge: Cambridge University Press, 1983), 37–8.

46 These misconceptions are debunked resolutely by Alan Jones in his *Early Arabic Poetry, Vol. 1: Marāthī and ṣuʿlūk poems* (Reading: Ithaca Press, 1992), 7.

47 "Schon früh war man sich der Sonderstellung des Rağaz bewußt. Man betrachtet ihn nicht als „Poesie" im vollen Sinne. Nur das, was in den großen Metren Ṭawīl, Basīṭ, Kāmil, Wāfir usw. gedichtet ist, gilt als eigentliche Poesie, als *šiʿr, qarīḍ, qaṣīd.*" ["The special status of

nonsense to deny the existence of the *qiṭʿa* as a class"; Jones went so far as to include examples of such poems in the first volume of his anthology of *Early Arabic Poetry* to drive the point home.[48] Geert Jan van Gelder has shown that there is good reason to believe that many of the poems in Abū Tammām's anthology *al-Ḥamāsah* (*Valor*) are indeed whole poems.[49] Moreover, even if many early *qiṭaʿ* (sing. *qiṭʿah*) were in fact excerpted from longer poems—and here again we must be sensitive to the reflex of determinant etymology—it is highly peculiar that we should consider these independent excerpts as sub-poetic; that is, unless we are prepared to concede that such a view fetishizes the *qaṣīdah*. If in a given context—often anthological—a poem is whole both in its mien and its meaning, what—other than a kind of partitive, or originalist, fetishism—would possess someone to deny its independence and integrity? And if this fetishistic attitude is validated in scholarship, how can we imagine it not to affect adversely the study of short poetic genres?[50]

Renate Jacobi in her definition of the *qiṭʿah* also attempts to link it to the issue of monothematic structure and characterizes the form as being equivalent to the last segment of a *qaṣīdah*.[51] Alan Jones, on the other hand, sees the *qaṣīdah* as a composite of *qiṭaʿ*: "It seems likely that the *qiṭʿa* was the original form of composition and that the *qaṣīda* was developed from it, perhaps

---

Rajaz was known from very early on. It was not considered to be 'poetry' in the full sense of the word. Only [verse] composed in the major metres (*ṭawīl, basīṭ, kāmil, wāfir*, etc.) was counted as poetry, as *shiʿr, qarīḍ, qaṣīd*."] (Manfred Ullmann, *Untersuchungen zur Rağazpoesie. Ein Beitrag zur arabischen Sprach- und Literaturwissenschaft* (Wiesbaden: Otto Harrassowitz, 1966), 1), *pace* Alfred Bloch's schematization. See Alfred Bloch, "Qaṣīda", *AS/EA* 2 (1948): 116, and further Gregor Schoeler, "Alfred Blochs Studie über die Gattungen der altarabischen Dichtung", *AS/EA* 56 (2002).

48 Jones, *Early Arabic Poetry*, 1:7.

49 33 of 134 poems in the *Ṭawīl* meter in the first chapter of the *Ḥamāsah* display *kharm*, i.e. the first syllable is dropped, a phenomenon that occurs virtually always in the first line of a poem. This, van Gelder concludes, "[…] strongly suggest[s] that a large proportion of the 'fragments' collected by Abū Tammām were in fact complete short poems and not excerpted from longer ones […]" (van Gelder, "Pointed and Well-Rounded", 108–9; see also *idem, Sound and Sense in Classical Arabic Poetry* (Wiesbaden: Harrassowitz, 2012), 41n62).

50 Compare Geert Jan van Gelder, "Al-Mutanabbī's Encumbering Trifles", *Arabic & Middle Eastern Literatures* 2:1 (1999), and Schoeler, "Alfred Blochs Studie", 738f.

51 R. Jacobi, "2.2 Die altarabische Dichtung (6.–7. Jahrhundert) 2.2.2.1 Gattungen und Formen" in *GAP*, 2:24: "[…] *qiṭʿa* (Bruchstück), einem kurzen Gedicht mit einheitlicher Thematik, das nach seinem Inhalt und den Einleitungs- und Schlußformeln dem letzten Teil der Qaṣīde gleicht" ["[…] *qiṭʿah* (fragment), a short monothematic poem that resembles the last section of a polythematic ode (*qaṣīdah*) with respect to its content and opening and concluding formulas"].

by putting together in one poem two or three *qiṭʿas* of differing thematic content or by developing the thematic treatment so that a poem had at least two quite distinct sections."[52] It is to his credit that he acknowledges that "evidence to support these suggestions is slim".[53] He, too, bases his definition on the modern structural axis though he chooses to emphasize its indeterminacy:

> Perhaps the furthest we can go is to define a *qiṭʿa* as an "occasional piece" of not more than twenty lines and without the *qaṣīda*'s distinctive thematic development. We cannot be more precise than that. It is a relatively amorphous form, and its definition must accordingly remain loose and vague.[54]

The reader would be right in thinking that—when compared to the *maqāṭīʿ*-genre discussed above—the history of the *qiṭʿah* and its place in the Arabic literary system is indeed far murkier. I do not believe this is owed entirely to generic ambiguity, though that of course plays a significant role. Another crucial factor that has led to this situation is—as Jaroslav Stetkevych signalled—an overreliance on literary-critical, that is theoretical, discussions of a phenomenon at the expense of poetic evidence. In this regard, the present study is radically different. It eschews this approach—in part because theoretical discussions of the *maqāṭīʿ*-genre do not exist—and instead delineates the contours and conventions of the *maqāṭīʿ*-genre by putting poetic evidence front and center.[55]

---

52 Jones, *Early Arabic Poetry*, 1:7. This is not unlike what Alastair Fowler calls "Aggregation", one of eight processes by which genres are transformed. See Alastair Fowler, *Kinds of Literature: an introduction to the theory of genres and modes* (Oxford: Oxford University Press, 1982).

53 Jones, *Early Arabic Poetry*, 1:7. See also in van Gelder, "Pointed and Well-Rounded", 105n12.

54 Jones, *Early Arabic Poetry*, 1:7.

55 It is no coincidence that later generic developments in Arabic poetry have been analyzed not on formalistic criteria but on their thematic orientation, by both pre-modern Arabic literary critics as well as modern scholars. Indeed Alfred Bloch's schematic division of forms is itself organized chiefly by theme although formal criteria do play a part. An unhappy externality of this debate has been its impact on scholarship on related literary traditions. Are Arabists not responsible in large part for the erroneous conclusions drawn by Edward Granville Browne (1862–1926), the most influential Persianist outside Iran (E. G. Browne, *A Literary History of Persia,* 4 vols (Cambridge: Cambridge University Press, 1920–25), 2:23):

> The *fard* ("unit" or hemistich) and the *qiṭʿa* ("fragment"), as well as the *bayt* (or couplet, consisting of two hemistichs), have also no right to be reckoned as separate verse-forms, since the first and last are the elements of which every poem consists, and the

If further corroboration were needed to prove that the foundational controversies surrounding atomism and fragmentation have influenced, and continue to influence, research on pre-modern Arabic poetry, Geert Jan van Gelder's 1982 monograph *Beyond the Line: classical Arabic literary critics on the coherence and unity of the poem* is an ideal test case. Van Gelder clearly had his sights set on the new dogma of poetic unity.[56] He was keen to show that the unitarian fad was unfarily discounting, misinterpreting, or sacrificing pre-modern Arabic literary critics for the sake of organic unity, which he did not take as a *sine qua non* of literary quality like so many others.[57] Accepting

---

> "fragment" is merely a piece of a *qaṣída*, though it may be that no more of the *qaṣída* was ever written [...].

Note, too, the adoption of this conventional paradigm into Turkish scholarship: "Eski Arap şairlerinden intikal eden bazı kısa manzumeler arasında uzun şiirlerden kalmış parçalar kadar kıta şeklinde söylenmiş kısa şiirler de vardır. Daha sonraki dönemlerde aşka dair konularla dinî, felsefî konuların işlendiği kıtaların çıkış noktası bu şiirler olmuştur" ["Among some shorter poems (*manzumeler*) transmitted from the ancient Arab poets, there are fragments of longer poems as well as short poems composed in the form of the *kıta* [*qiṭʿah*]. These poems are the origins of the later *qiṭaʿ* that treated themes related to love as well as religious and philosophical themes."] (*Türkiye Diyanet Vakfı İslâm Ansiklopedisi* (Istanbul, 1988–), s.v. "Kıta"), but cf. *İslam Ansiklopedisi* (Istanbul: Millî Eğitim Basımevi, 1943–), s.v. "Kıt'a" and Atilla Özkırımlı, *Türk Edebiyati Ansiklopedisi* (Istanbul: Cem Yayınevi, 1982–87), s.v. "kıta". I thank Laurent Mignon for his help with this translation.

56 Andras Hamori called *Beyond the Line* "[...] a vigorously polemical work [...]" in his review of the book, while acknowledging that "[o]n the matter of unity, van Gelder's evaluation of the evidence is scrupulous and his distinctions are just." (Andras Hamori, review of G. J. van Gelder, *Beyond the Line*, *JAOS* 104:2 (April–June 1984): 385). James Montgomery writes that "[van Gelder's] cautious, and rather negative, appraisal of the 'cult' of 'organic unity' in modern research, especially Western [...] can now, with hindsight, be understood as a protest against the excessive application to Arabic verse of what might be termed 'trendy' theories of literary appreciation, were it not for the fact that by the time they had been imported into the field of Middle Eastern Studies they had been discarded as obsolete elsewhere. Indeed [*Beyond the Line*] is, in its entirety, such a protest." (Montgomery, "On the Unity and Disunity of the *Qaṣīdah*", 271).

57 See in van Gelder, *Beyond the Line*, 203. It is not difficult to see how van Gelder's analysis would be read against the background of atomist Orientalist scholarship as described by J. Stetkevych some years prior:

> [...] Ahlwardt's *das Einzelne* had its origin in the Arabic critical notion of the "sufficient poetic statement" (*al-maʿnā al-mufīd*) and the equally traditionally Arabic formal insistence on a stratification of the poem into clearly distinguishable thematic and structural layers. From these morphological working elements Orientalist criticism proceeded to derive its cultural-anthropological generalisation of the paratactic, compartmentalized, atomistic nature of Arabic poetry. (J. Stetkevych, "Arabic Poetry and Assorted Poetics", 116).

the unitarian conclusions of structuralist studies, van Gelder preferred to turn his attention to literary-critical sources to see what attention was paid to poetic unity.[58] Neither his method nor his conclusions did much to sway unitarians, however.[59] Writing in the *JNES*, Suzanne Stetkevych commented that "[v]an Gelder's well-researched volume strikes the student of classical Arabic literary criticism as somewhat strange, in that it takes as its main issue what was for that particular tradition a non-issue: the coherence and unity of the poem."[60] It took the *JAL* eleven years to review what James Montgomery eventually called, in a review published in that journal in 1993, "so significant, and in many ways so seminal, a work as *Beyond the Line* [...]".[61] Montgomery is full of praise for the work and it is clear that in the intervening years, as he puts it, "[...] the wider enthusiasms of the Seventies have largely [...] been tempered and it is to be hoped that the study of Classical Arabic Poetry is leaving its adolescence behind."[62] The only aspect of van Gelder's argument that Montgomery takes issue with is his "[...] equation of creation and reception, the blurring of poet and critic [...];" or in other words, an overreliance on critical, rather than poetic, evidence.[63] This again is a recurring theme in

58 van Gelder, *Beyond the Line*, 194.

59 See, e.g. J. Stetkevych, "Arabic Poetry and Assorted Poetics", 116. Another argument employed by some unitarians against the reference to pre-modern Arab literary critics is that their criticism is not wholly applicable to literary evidence itself: "Without taking the fundamental distinction between pre-Modern and Modern literary «criticism» into account, it is the case that some students of Arabic poetry have attempted to apply the principles of Medieval rhetoric and poetics (which were never designed to highlight the differences between one poem and another in the first place), to individual Arabic poems. As a result, they have come up with some bizarre theories." (James T. Monroe, "«Its *Maṭlaʿ* and *Ḫarja* are Twofold in Function»: form and content in Ibn Quzmān's «*Zajal* 59» and «138»", *Boletín de Literatura Oral* 1 (2011): 16). Compare also Julie Scott Meisami, "Unsquaring the Circle: rereading a poem by al-Muʿtamid ibn ʿAbbād", *Arabica* 35:3 (November 1988): 294n and Earl Miner, "On the Genesis and Development of Literary Systems", Part I, *Critical Inquiry* 5:2 (Winter 1978) and Part II, *Critical Inquiry* 5:3 (Spring 1979).

60 S. P. Stetkevych, review of G. J. van Gelder, *Beyond the Line*, 63. See also Ewald's Wagner review in *ZDMG* 135 (1985) and Roger Allen's in *Edebiyât* n.s. 1:2 (1989). See also J. C. Bürgel, review of S. Sperl, *Mannerism in Arabic Poetry*, *JSS* 39:2 (Autumn 1994): 367.

61 Montgomery, "On the Unity and Disunity of the *Qaṣīdah*", 271. Many of the articles in Sasson Somekh (ed.), *Studies in Medieval Arabic and Hebrew Poetics* (Leiden: Brill, 1991) reflect on van Gelder's monograph.

62 Montgomery, "On the Unity and Disunity of the *Qaṣīdah*", 273.

63 ibid., 274.

Arabic literary scholarship, which seems immune to important conceptual breakthroughs like Hans Robert Jauß' Reception Theory.[64]

The latest salvo in the atomic wars came in the form of a censorious response to van Gelder's monograph more than twenty years after it was published. Raymond Farrin—first in a doctoral thesis written at Berkeley and eventually in the book that thesis would become—casts van Gelder as an atomist irredentist:[65]

> [...] van Gelder would have us refrain from rigorously demanding unity in classical Arabic poetry. [...] [H]e sets out to demonstrate that classical Arabic critics were not at all concerned with structural cohesion in poems. On the basis of many passages from treatises, commentaries, and so on, cited to support his fundamental contention that, almost to a man, critics of poetry restricted their focus to the individual line and did not bother with what lay beyond it, he draws a conclusion that poets themselves were not aware of the desirability of overall unity and so did not think to compose poems that cohere (that throwing lines together might be a slapdash way of composition, we are left to deduce, never occurred to the composers).[66]

Van Gelder responded to this characterization by stating that he had, "[...] argued [...] no such thing, but [that he had] apparently angered a number of Arabists by merely providing a counterweight against the excesses of seeking unity at all costs, and by arguing that Arabic poems can also be (and are) enjoyed without paying much attention to the overall structure."[67] This scholarly spat is merely the latest episode in a nearly three hundred year-old controversy as old as the discipline itself. The debate over atomism (or molecularity) has—for almost all concerned—been settled, but it continues to stalk the field of pre-modern Arabic literature. It has amplified the ambiguity of the *qiṭʿah* form and championed the etymological connotation of fragmentation. It set the

64 See, e.g. Hans Robert Jauß, "Literary History as a Challenge to Literary Theory", *New Literary History* 2:1 (Autumn 1970): 19.

65 Farrin, *Abundance from the Desert*, xiv. Raymond Farrin's doctoral thesis, written in 2006, was titled "Reading Beyond the Line: Organic Unity in Classical Arabic Poetry" (unpublished doctoral thesis, University of California, Berkeley, 2006). His book *Abundance from the Desert: classical Arabic poetry*, which his supervisor James T. Monroe has called a "groundbreaking study" (Monroe, "«Its *Maṭlaʿ* and *Ḫarja* are Twofold in Function»", 17) was published in 2011.

66 Farrin, *Abundance from the Desert*, xv.

67 Geert Jan van Gelder, review of R. Farrin, *Abundance from the Desert, Speculum* 87:4 (2012): 1190.

agenda for literary scholarship for much of the 20th century and it has made the study of short poems suspect or—at best—fringe. The *qiṭʿah* is not itself the subject of this study, but the history of its reception points to weaknesses in our grasp of Arabic literary history, especially as it concerns genre.[68] The case of the *qaṣīdah-qiṭʿah* dichotomy raises a number of issues—e.g. scholars' preference for paradigmatic theoretical discussions at the expense of contextual literary evidence, highly nebulous formalistic criteria taken from the Arabic tradition itself, the emphasis on theme in establishing generic patterns, etc.—that will no doubt affect how scholars make sense of the *maqāṭīʿ*-genre being detailed and analyzed here for the first time. That is why a survey of how the term epigram has been used to describe pre-modern Arabic poetry is both salutary and informative.

By and large, scholars who have used the term epigram to describe Islamicate poetry have paid little attention to the context in which poems are found.[69] Some scholars have tried to limit the use of the term epigram based on theme, along with fairly nebulous formalistic restrictions.[70] One of the

68 More than three decades ago, Jaroslav Stetkevych wrote that, "[...] [T]he *qaṣīda*-versus-the *qiṭʿa* theory imposed itself as being the easiest answer available to a complex question, hindering the development of any further genre—or thematic—criticism." (J. Stetkevych, "Arabic Poetry and Assorted Poetics", 116).

69 e.g. "[...] from numerous anthologies and *dīwāns* one may cull an enormous quantity of pieces of *madīḥ* or *rithāʾ* that answer to the description of the epigram." (van Gelder, "Pointed and Well-Rounded", 101).

70 Van Gelder's article "Pointed and Well-Rounded" was a response to precisely this trend. Huda Fakhreddine uses the term *maqṭūʿah* interchangeably with *qiṭʿah* when referring to poetry from the Abbasid period (See Fakhreddine, "Defining Metapoesis in the ʿAbbāsid Age", 225; *idem*, "From Modernists to *Muḥdathūn*: metapoesis in Arabic" (unpublished doctoral thesis. Indiana University, 2011), 80). The same is true of Khalid Sindawi (See K. Sindawi, "Visit to the Tomb of Al-Husayn b. ʿAlī in Shiite Poetry: first to fifth centuries AH (8th–11th centuries CE)", *JAL* 37:2 (2006): 257n). See also Sabry Hafez, "The Transformation of the Qasida Form in Modern Arabic Poetry" in *Qasida Poetry in Islamic Asia and Africa*, ed. Stefan Sperl and Christopher Shackle, 2 vols (Leiden: Brill, 1996), 1:104; Yosef Tobi, *Proximity and Distance: medieval Hebrew and Arabic poetry* (Leiden: Brill, 2004), 37; 123; 210; 213. Likewise in *idem*, *Between Hebrew and Arabic Poetry: studies in Spanish medieval Hebrew poetry* (Leiden: Brill, 2010), 5: "Also the *maqṭūʿāt*, short poems without multiplicity of divisions but with a single theme, describe the hedonistic social and cultural reality in the patron's court, a state of "eat, drink and be merry, for tomorrow we die"—*carpe diem*: (a) The wine poems (*khamriyyāt*) describe the banquet held in the palace, inside or in the surrounding garden; (b) the poems of passion (*ghazaliyyāt*) sing the praises of the desired young girl (the 'gazelle'), lovely in her outward physical qualities, and details her deception and her disregard for and evasion of those who desire her; this is the servant girl, who performs as singer and dancer, and is an object for illicit sex (*qayna*, pl.: *qiyan*); sometimes the character of the girl is replaced by the character

most pronounced trends in scholarship—after the use of epigram to describe invective poetry (*hijāʾ*)—is the description of ekphrastic poetry (*waṣf*) as epigram.[71] Both Gustave von Grunebaum and Gregor Schoeler use the term epigram in connection with the poetry of Ibn ar-Rūmī (d. 283/896); in the case of Gregor Schoeler, this is one of the few self-aware usages of that term in Arabic literary scholarship.[72] Schoeler even mentions the Greek "literary book epigram", juxtaposing it with the oft-mentioned etymon: $\text{epigram}_{\text{inscription}}$, but prefers not to engage the contextual parameters of the poems he analyzes.[73] Schoeler sets great store by the organizational parameters of poetry

of a desired handsome young man (the "fawn"), the wine-server; (c) poems of nature (*waṣf*, or more precisely *rawḍiyyāt*, *nawriyyāt*, or *wardiyyāt*)." Muḥammad ʿAbd al-Majīd Lāshīn, the editor of aṣ-Ṣafadī's *ar-Rawḍ al-bāsim* also uses the term *maqṭūʿāt* rather than the more common *maqāṭīʿ* (aṣ-Ṣafadī, *ar-Rawḍ al-bāsim*, 28). Generally speaking, it is the term *muqaṭṭaʿah* that is reckoned to be synonymous with *qiṭʿah* (See e.g. in Schoeler, "The Genres of Classical Arabic Poetry", 4; 39. Interestingly, the word *maqṭūʿah* is used commonly in this sense in Andalusian literature (see, e.g. Ibn Hāniʾ al-Andalusī, *Dīwān*, ed. Muḥammad al-Yaʿlāwī (Beirut: Dār al-Gharb al-Islāmī, 1994), 7). In al-Muḥibbī's *Khulāṣat al-athar*, the term is used at one point to denote the stanzas of a *zajal* poem (1:108, penultimate line). On an arbitary, but interesting, use of the term epigram for an Arabic poem with Hebrew translation from al-Andalus, see Luis M. Girón Negrón, "Fortune ibéro-médiévale d'une epigramme arabe", *Horizons Maghrebins* 61 (2009).

71 Gustave E. von Grunebaum, "The Response to Nature in Arabic Poetry", *JNES* 4:3 (July 1945): 148. Von Grunebaum's articles were also translated into German and Arabic and have had a profound impact on scholarship worldwide (e.g. in the work of J. Christoph Bürgel—see below). The Arabic translation of a selection of von Grunebaum's articles: *Dirāsāt fī l-adab al-ʿArabī*, trans. Iḥsān ʿAbbās et al. (Beirut: Dār Maktabat al-Ḥayāh, 1959) has been highly influential in 20th century Arab scholarship. Von Grunebaum himself translated a selection of his articles into German (see Gustave E. von Grunebaum, *Kritik und Dichtkunst. Studien zur arabischen Literaturgeschichte* (Wiesbaden: Otto Harrassowitz, 1955), 28–51). See also in Gregor Schoeler, "Die Einteilung der Dichtung bei den Arabern", *ZDMG* 123 (1973): 23. On Arabic nature poetry more generally, see Gregor Schoeler, *Arabische Naturdichtung: die Zahrīyāt, Rabīʿīyāt und Rauḍīyāt von ihren Anfängen bis aṣ-Ṣanaubarī: eine gattungs-, motiv- und stilgeschichtliche Untersuchung* (Beirut: Orient-Institut der Deutschen Morgenländischen Gesellschaft [Wiesbaden: Franz Steiner], 1974), in which the author traces the history of nature poetry in Arabic and argues that nature poetry properly acquires its genre-consciousness in the work of aṣ-Ṣanawbarī (d. 334/945). cf. Jaroslav Stetkevych's comments about the tendency to characterize Arabic poetry as primarily descriptive (J. Stetkevych, "Arabic Poetry and Assorted Poetics". 114–15).

72 Gregor Schoeler, "On Ibn ar-Rūmī's Reflective Poetry", *JAL* 27:1 (1996) :31. See also Robert McKinney, "Ibn al-Rūmī's Contribution to the "Nautical *Raḥīl*" Tradition", *JAL* 29:3–4 (1998): 96n; and Geert Jan van Gelder, "The Terrified Traveller. Ibn al-Rūmī's Anti-*Raḥīl*", *JAL* 27 (1996): 47.

73 Schoeler, "On Ibn ar-Rūmī's Reflective Poetry", 30.

collections, but he rarely takes the "radical of presentation" (to borrow a term from Northrop Frye's *Anatomy of Criticism*) into account.[74]

A few scholars have sought to explain the emergence of shorter poetic genres in the early Abbasid period in terms of social utility.[75] Beatrice Gruendler has linked the rise of epigrammatic collections of poetic motifs (sing. *maʿnā*) like Abū Hilāl al-ʿAskarī's (d. after 400/1010) *Dīwān al-Maʿānī* (*Book of Literary Motifs*) to the attested deployment of these poetic motifs—and their versatility—in conversation, especially in the context of elite literary salons (*majālis*, sing. *majlis*).[76] There is also good historical evidence for the social—and not exclusively literary—exchange of epigrammatic poetry. Thomas Bauer and Jocelyn Sharlet, alongside Beatrice Gruendler, have emphasized the interactive quality of short poetry: its efficacy in social exchange.[77] One might argue that authors who title their anthologies with punning reference to "companionship" (*uns*), "gatherings" (*majālis*), "sessions" (*muḥāḍarāt*), etc. are in principle embedding a conversational conceit in their works, and while that may be the case, it appears that the dominant method of conveyance for these collections was private, individual, and readerly. The role of poetic motifs (*maʿānī*) in conversation—as well as the conversational conceit inherent in poetic anthologies themselves—is attested and observable, yet one should be careful not to collapse this historical phenomenon into a sterile functional or sociological explanation that may reinforce disciplinary prejudices against these types of poems.[78]

74 See e.g. Schoeler, "The Genres of Classical Arabic Poetry".

75 e.g. Beatrice Gruendler, "Motif vs. Genre: reflections on the *Dīwān al-Maʿānī* of Abū Hilāl al-ʿAskarī" in *Ghazal as World Literature. Vol. 1: Transformations of a Literary Genre*, ed. Thomas Bauer and Angelika Neuwirth (Beirut: Ergon Verlag [Würzburg], 2005); Jocelyn Sharlet, "The Thought that Counts: gift exchange poetry by Kushājim, al-Ṣanawbarī and al-Sarī al-Raffāʾ" *MEL* 14:3 (December 2011): 238–40; Alma Giese, *Waṣf bei Kušāǧim: Eine Studie zur beschreibenden Dichtkunst der Abbasidenzeit* (Berlin: Klaus Schwarz Verlag, 1981), 122–26.

76 Gruendler, "Motif vs. Genre", 76–83. On literary salons more generally, see Ali, *Arabic Literary Salons*. On *maʿānī*-collections, see Joseph Sadan, "Maidens' Hair and Starry Skies. Imagery system and *maʿānī* guides; the practical side of Arabic poetics as demonstrated in two manuscripts" in *Studies in Medieval Arabic and Hebrew Poetics*, ed. Sasson Somekh (Leiden: Brill, 1991).

77 See Thomas Bauer, "'*Ayna hādhā min al-Mutanabbī!*' – Towards an Aesthetics of Mamluk Literature", *MSR* 17 (2013) and Sharlet, "The Thought that Counts", esp. 239–40 where she discusses Habermas.

78 We are not, or are not yet, able to say of Arabic poetry what is commonly accepted in the history of classical Chinese poetry, for example, though certain parallels are evident: "As a rule, the development of a Chinese poetic genre consisted of a long process of imitating, assimilating, and eventually transforming an oral tradition into a purely

Several scholars have applied the term epigram to poems combining concision and "light" themes as a kind of shorthand.[79] J. Christoph Bürgel, drawing on von Grunebaum's description of Arabic nature poetry, links Abū Ṭālib al-Ma'mūnī's (d. 383/993) ekphrastic epigrams explicitly to the Hellenistic archetype: "Something very similar can be found in post-classical Arabic poetry. Here, too, one finds laudatory and defamatory epigrams about poets, scribes, etc. Dedicatory poems [...] as well as the opposite of these: supplicatory poems, poetic reminders of promises, poems of thanks, epigrams of well wishes, among other things."[80] It is perfectly legitimate to describe al-Ma'mūnī's poetic output—or even that of Khālid b. Yazīd al-Kātib (d. c. 269/883) and others—as epigram, but I would argue that in the absence of a comparative generic rubric such a description would be capricious.[81] It goes without saying that such a description also privileges trite and inexact world-literary categories, derived ultimately from the Western literary pantheon, and ignores explicit or implicit generic identifications in the Arabic tradition itself.

Few Arabists have privileged formalistic dimensions of short poetic genres over thematic ones.[82] Jamel Eddine Bencheikh's *Poétique arabe: essai sur les voies d'une création* is a rare example. Bencheikh makes the crucial point that the Arabic tradition eschewed strict formal requirements, beyond monorhyme and meter, except for a few specific verse forms (the *muwashshaḥ*,

---

literary one by the literati. This steady movement from orality to literacy was marked by the gradual disappearance of oral performance, the allegorical appropriation of folk themes, the abandonment of simple language or elegant diction, and the excessive use of allusion. [...] Interestingly, an obsessive pursuit of textuality (diction) and intertextuality (allusions) often marks the last great glory of a thoroughly 'literatified' (*wenren hua*) genre and heralds the rapid ascendancy of a new genre of oral folk origin." (Zong-Qi Cai (ed.), *How to Read Chinese Poetry: a guided anthology* (New York, NY: Columbia University Press, 2008), 6).

79 See e.g. Julia Bray, "Third and fourth-century bleeding Poetry", *Arabic & Middle Eastern Literatures* 2:1 (1999): 82.

80 J. Christoph Bürgel, *Die ekphrastischen Epigramme des Abū Ṭālib al-Ma'mūnī* (Göttingen: Vandenhoeck and Ruprecht, 1966), 223n (original German): "Ganz ähnliches findet sich in der nachklassischen arabischen Poesie. Auch hier gibt es lobende und schmähende Epigramme auf Dichter, Sekretäre usw., Widmungen [...], und das Gegenstück dazu: Bittgesuche, Erinnerungen an gegebene Versprechen und Dank, Glückwunschepigramme u. a. [...]"] Significantly, aṣ-Ṣafadī does not mention *maqāṭīʿ* in connection with al-Ma'mūnī (aṣ-Ṣafadī, *al-Wāfī*, 18:420–22).

81 See Arazi, *Amour divin et amour profane dans l'Islam médiéval.*

82 See e.g. J. Stetkevych, *The Hunt in Arabic Poetry*; *idem*, "The Discreet Pleasures of the Courtly Hunt. Abū Nuwās and the 'Abbāsid *Ṭardiyyah*", *JAL* 39 (2008): 152, 152n; and *idem*, "The *Ṭardiyyahs* of Ibn al-Muʿtazz: breakthrough into lyricism", *JAL* 41 (2010): 220.

dūbayt, etc.[83]) and that it is therefore unlikely that we will find evidence for a generic system in theoretical texts.[84] Instead Bencheikh analyzes poetic evidence, distinguishing among themes, and is able to synthesize important information about the formal dimensions of Arabic poetry in the Abbasid period. Bencheikh demonstrates that among three exemplary practitioners of three key poetic thematic genres—ʿAbbās b. al-Aḥnaf (d. c. 188/803) composing love poetry, Abū Nuwās (d. c. 198/813) composing bacchic poetry, and Abū ʿAtāhiyah (d. 210/825 or 211/826) composing ascetic poetry—the average length of *muḥdath* poetic production is far shorter than a *qaṣīdah*-centered view of pre-modern Arabic poetry would predict.[85] Only thirty of the 589 love poems attributed to ʿAbbās b. al-Aḥnaf exceed fifteen lines.[86] Likewise only approximately a seventh of Abū Nuwās' and Abū ʿAtāhiyah's production in their core genres of bacchic and ascetic poetry, respectively, exceeds fourteen or fifteen lines in length.[87] This observable development in literary history is in itself highly significant, and of great interest for the pre-history of the

---

83 See *inter alia* Martin Hartmann, *Das arabische Strophengedicht. I*[:] *das Muwaššaḥ* (Weimar: Emil Felber, 1897). Hartmann insists that these "forms" ("Versarten") are in fact genres ("Gedichtgattungen") (209).

84 "[…] [I]l n'existe pas de compositions dites à forme fixe ou limitée : pas de règles fixant le nombre de vers ou des strophes, codifiant l'agencement des rimes ; pas de dessin précis dont la géométrie contraignante enserrerait impérativement le discours. Les éléments de théorie sont ici rares, imprécis et de toutes façons tardifs" (Jamal Eddine Bencheikh, *Poétique arabe: essai sur les voies d'une création* (Paris: Éditions Anthropos, 1975), 97–8). ["There are no set [poetic] forms; no rules to specify the number of verses or strophes, or determine the rhyme scheme. There is no specific pattern within whose restrictive architecture the discussion must necessarily be contained. Issues of theory are generally infrequent, ambiguous, and moreover belated."]

85 ibid., 98–109.

86 ibid., 99: "Sur 589 pièces attribuées à Ibn al-Aḥnaf, 30 seulement, soit à peu près le vingtième, ont plus de 15 vers […]."

87 "Il apparaît que [chez Abū Nuwās] le poème bachique (*ḫamriyya*) exige aussi la brièveté: 41 pièces seulement sur 299, soit un peu moins du septième, ont plus de 14 vers […]" ["It seems that [Abu Nuwas'] Bacchic poetry (*khamriyyah*) also calls for brevity: only forty-one poems out of two-hundred and ninety-nine, a little less than one-seventh, are more than fourteen verses long"] (ibid., 100). "Sur 454 *zuhdiyya*-s, qui sont l'essentiel de sa production [c'est-à-dire, la production de Abū ʿAtāhiyah], 63, soit le septième, dépassent 15 vers […]." ["Out of four-hundred and fifty-four poems on asceticism, which is the core of his [i.e. Abū ʿAtāhiyah's] oeuvre, sixty-three, that is a seventh, are more than fifteen lines long"] (ibid., 103). NB: "[…] soit 52 pièces, sur 63, comptant moins de 30 vers." ["Of [the] sixty-three, fifty-two of the poems are less than thirty lines long"] (ibid., 103). The so-called neoclassicist poets Abū Tammām and al-Buḥturī of the following generation do not match this pattern, but Abū Tammām's *ghazal* output is markedly concise (see ibid., 108, and Bauer, "Abū Tammām's Contribution to ʿAbbāsid *Ġazal* Poetry").

maqāṭīʿ-genre, but so is Bencheikh's larger point: "The dimensions of a poem are determined by the choice of genre and register particular to it".[88]

In a seminal article published in 1995, Geert Jan van Gelder set out to correct scholarly misconceptions about the thematic limitations of shorter poetic genres in Arabic.[89] Van Gelder demonstrates that short poems were being written in Arabic in the pre-Islamic period—the earliest period of poetic production—and that these poems included panegyrics and elegies.[90] Elegiac *maqāṭīʿ*-poems are not common in later centuries, but they certainly did exist.[91] Van Gelder also makes the point that "[t]he epigram is characteristic of the *muḥdath* poets."[92] Van Gelder spends a portion of the article discussing the ontology of the epigram—once again defending his thesis that "[Arabic poems] [live] on, in different shapes, in quotations through the ages [...] and become poems in their own right"—but his radical decentering of the hypotext and his agnosticism about poetic ontology are done a disservice by his rather perfunctory use of the term epigram.[93]

Van Gelder begins the article by saying, oracularly, that "There is no Arabic word for 'epigram'. The reason for this lack is perhaps, rather than the absence of epigrams in Arabic literature, their ubiquity."[94] He eventually explains that what he has in mind by epigram is the *qiṭʿah*, broadly speaking,

88 Bencheikh, *Poétique arabe*, 103: "[...] l'espace-poème est determiné par le choix d'un genre et du langage qui lui est spécifique."

89 Van Gelder was responding chiefly to Renate Jacobi, who in her entry on "Abbasidische Dichtung" in the *GAP* wrote—under the heading "Die kurzen Gattungen"—"Neben preisqaṣīde [i.e. *madāʾiḥ*] und Trauerlied [i.e. *rithāʾ*], den zeremoniellen Formen der Hofdichtung, bildet sich in der experimentellen Phase ein System von Gattungen heraus [...]." ["In addition to praise poems [i.e. *madāʾiḥ*] and elegies [i.e. *rithāʾ*], a system of poetic forms (*Gattungen*) was created from the ceremonial forms of court poetry in the experimental phase [...]"] (2:46). See in van Gelder, "Pointed and Well-Rounded", 103 and 103n.

90 Van Gelder, "Pointed and Well-Rounded", 105.

91 See Adam Talib, "The Many Lives of Arabic Verse: Ibn Nubātah al-Miṣrī mourns more than once", *JAL* 44:3 (2013).

92 Van Gelder, "Pointed and Well-Rounded", 105. See also editor's introduction to aṣ-Ṣafadī's *ar-Rawḍ al-bāsim*, ed. Muḥammad ʿAbd al-Majīd Lāshīn, 29–30.

93 Van Gelder, "Pointed and Well-Rounded", 102. See also *idem*, "Al-Mutanabbī's Encumbering Trifles"; and *idem*, "Some Brave Attempts at Generic Classification in Premodern Arabic Literature" in *Aspects of Genre and Type in Pre-modern Literary Cultures*, ed. Bert Roest and Herman Vanstiphout (Groningen, Styx, 1999), 19, § 3.2.

94 *idem*, "Pointed and Well-Rounded", 101. Van Gelder seems to be channeling Lacan here (cf. "Il n'y a pas *La* femme"). See also in *EAL*, s.v. "epigram" [G. J. van Gelder]: "There is no Arabic term for 'epigram', even though the epigram is ubiquitous in classical Arabic poetry, and much Arabic poetry may be said to be profoundly epigrammatic in character."

though he draws the upper limit of length at ten lines; this is, by his own admission, "rather [arbitrary]."[95] Van Gelder's article succeeds in detailing the history and thematic promiscuity of short Arabic poems and rescuing it from ahistorical pigeon-holing, but his presumption that literary categories are homologous—decontextualized universals whose archetype is inevitably Western—and that terminology can be expected to correspond conclusively across literary traditions, typifies the uncritical and incongruous application of literary paradigms, devised *a priori*, to pre-modern Arabic poetry. I worry that a similar tendency reveals itself in the new system of English headwords for abstract nouns conceived for the latest edition of the *Encyclopaedia of Islam* (EI^3).[96] The change is a sensible one—and my objection is neither priggish nor nostalgic—but it does bring to the fore a fascinating epistemological problem that is at the heart of this study: commensurability. Now, in the most canonical repository of Orientalist knowledge, *nadīm* has become "Boon companion",[97] *naskh* "Abrogation",[98] *wakālah* "Attorney",[99] and entries like "'Agnosticism"[100] and "didactic poetry"[101] subsume relevant pre-modern phenomena and modes of thought while simultaneously acknowledging the anachronism inherent in such a classification.[102]

In a series of studies over the past few decades scholars such as Wolfhart Heinrichs, Bo Utas, Stefan Sperl, Geert Jan van Gelder, and—*primus inter pares*—Gregor Schoeler have set out to taxonomize Islamicate poetic production, based primarily on indigenous literary-critical models.[103] In a series of

---

95 ibid., 106n. Cf. Geert Jan van Gelder, "Poetry in Historiography: some observations" in *Problems in Arabic Literature*, ed. M. Maróth (Piliscsaba, The Avicenna Institute of Middle Eastern Studies, 2004), 12–3.

96 See in EI^3, "Preface" where the change is described and discussed briefly.

97 EI^2, s.v. "Nadīm" [J. Sadan]; EI^3, s.v. "Boon companion" [S. Ali].

98 EI^2, s.v. "Naskh" [J. Burton]; EI^3, s.v. "Abrogation" [A. Rippin].

99 EI^2, s.v. "Wakāla" [M. Y. Izzi Dien]; EI^3, s.v. "Attorney" [C. W. Mallat].

100 EI^3, s.v. "Agnosticism" [F. Griffel]: "Within the Islamic tradition there is almost no evidence of thinkers who upheld even the moderate form of agnosticism."

101 EI^3, s.v. "Didactic poetry, Arabic" [G. J. H. van Gelder]: "Arabic didactic poetry, taken in a broad sense, intends to instil morals or impart information. By this definition much of Arabic poetry is didactic [...]. In the terminology of the traditional Arabic classification of poetic genres or modes, this kind of verse was called *ḥikma* ('wisdom'). [...] There is no clear boundary between *ḥikma* and *zuhd* (asceticism, renunciation) [...]."

102 cf. Paul de Man's contention that "[r]hetoric radically suspends logic and opens up vertiginous possibilities of referential aberration". (P. de Man, "Semiology and Rhetoric", *Diacritics* 3:3 (Autumn 1973): 30). NB: de Man was an obscure fascist before becoming a giant of 20th-century literary theory.

103 e.g. Heinrichs, *Arabische Dichtung und griechische Poetik*; *idem*, "„Manierismus" in der arabischen Literatur"; *idem*, "Literary Theory: the problem of its efficiency"; Bo

studies on the topic of poetic genre—culminating in 2012 with the publication of a revised, English version of his first scholarly article, "Die Einteilung der Dichtung bei den Arabern"—Gregor Schoeler has attempted to adapt the category of genre to the case of Arabic poetry by distinguishing between formal and thematic genres.[104] Schoeler argues that while theoreticians generally sought to typify poetry thematically—rather than classify it—the editors of poets' collected works (*Dīwān*, pl. *Dawāwīn*) found themselves, for reasons of pragmatism, organizing the collected poetry generically.[105] Nevertheless, even this generic organization is orientated primarily around theme, especially as there is very little rigidity in the division of forms. In the most recent version of his article published in 2012, Schoeler does mention Thomas Bauer's article on the *maqāṭī*ʿ-collection of Badr ad-Dīn Ibn Ḥabīb al-Ḥalabī (d. 779/1377) in a footnote, even using the term epigram in connection with it, but he does not include that text in his corpus, which is limited almost exclusively to evidence from the pre-Mongol period with the notable exception of Ṣafī ad-Dīn al-Ḥillī's *Dīwān*.[106]

If we understand that the *qaṣīdah-qiṭʿah* dichotomy is fairly crude and that it fails to capture a series of developments in Arabic literary history, and that the indigenous tradition never provided much by way of formalistic demarcations, it will come as no surprise that both Schoeler and van Gelder have continued to tweak, refine, and re-adjust their ideas on poetic genres and

---

Utas, "'Genres' in Persian Literature, 900–1900", in *Literary History: towards a global perspective. Vol. 2: Literary Genres: an intercultural approach*, ed. G. Lindberg-Wada (Berlin: de Gruyter, 2006); Sperl, *Mannerism in Arabic Poetry*; van Gelder, "Some Brave Attempts at Generic Classification"; *idem*, "Dubious Genres: on some poems of Abū Nuwās", *Arabica* 44 (1997); *idem*, "Genres in Collision: *nasīb* and *hijāʾ*", *JAL* 21:1 (1990); Schoeler, "Die Einteilung der Dichtung bei den Arabern" (1972); *idem*, "Die Einteilung der Dichtung bei den Arabern", (1973); *idem*, *arabische Naturdichtung*, esp. 1–9; *idem*, *Einige Grundprobleme der autochthonen und aristotelischen arabischen Literaturtheorie. Ḥāzim al-Qarṭağannīs Kapitel über die Zielsetzungen der Dichtung und der Vorgeschichte der ihm dargelegten Gedanken* (Wiesbaden: Franz Steiner Verlag [in Kommission bei Deutsche Morgenlandische Gesellschaft], 1975); and—most recently—*idem*, "The Genres of Classical Arabic Poetry" (with addenda in second part). See also *idem*, "Alfred Blochs Studie".

104 e.g. Schoeler, "The Genres of Classical Arabic Poetry", 9. See also—vitally on this issue—František W. Galan, "Literary System and Systemic Change: the Prague School of literary history, 1928–48", *PMLA* 94:2 (March 1979): esp. 279.

105 Schoeler, "The Genres of Classical Arabic Poetry", 26–7. Yet it is worth noting that one theoretician, Ibn Wahb, did in fact outline such a generic classification (ibid., 16).

106 See Bauer, "„Was kann aus dem Jungen noch werden!"". Schoeler, "The Genres of Classical Arabic Poetry", 25n; on Ṣafī ad-Dīn al-Ḥillī's *Dīwān*, see ibid., 36–9.

epigram respectively in a variety of formats for decades.[107] Their views have been enriched with further examples as more texts have become available, but their models have not changed much since they were first proposed. For example in a new article on "Epigram 1. Classical Arabic" in the *EI*^{3}, van Gelder begins the entry with the sentence: "The nearest Arabic equivalent of 'epigram,' a short poem with a witty turn of thought, is *maqṭūʿ* or *maqṭūʿa* (lit. 'fragment,' pl. *maqāṭīʿ*) [...]."[108] There is no doubt that van Gelder's thinking on the subject of the Arabic epigram has evolved considerably, under the influence of Thomas Bauer's research—and I flatter myself to think—my own, but other aspects of the entry signal that van Gelder has not so much rethought his position as updated it. Once again, van Gelder emphasizes the witty epigram over other modes, while at the same time reducing the issue to a mere question of length.[109] For van Gelder, epigram continues to hinge

107 Van Gelder is a great fan of the word "epigram" (and "epigrammatical") and has probably used it more than any other Arabist in history. See e.g. van Gelder, "Dubious Genres" 269–70; *idem*, "Mirror for princes or vizor for viziers: the twelfth-century Arabic popular encyclopedia *Mufīd al-ʿulūm* and its relationship with the anonymous Persian *Baḥr al-fawāʾid*", *BSOAS* 64:3 (2001): 327; *idem*, "Mixtures of Jest and Earnest in classical Arabic literature: Part I", *JAL* 23:2 (1992): 101; *idem*, "Mixtures of Jest and Earnest in classical Arabic literature: Part II" *JAL* 23:3 (1992): 179; *idem*, "The Terrified Traveller. Ibn al-Rūmī's Anti-*Raḥīl*", 47; *idem*, "Poetry in Historiography: the case of *al-Fakhrī* by Ibn al-Ṭiqṭaqā" in *Poetry and History. The Value of Poetry in Reconstructing Arab History*, ed. Ramzi Baalbaki et al. (Beirut: American University of Beirut Press, 2011), 65; 68–70; *idem*, review of an-Nawājī, *Kitāb ash-Shifāʾ fī badīʿ al-iktifāʾ*, ed. Ḥasan Muḥammad ʿAbd al-Hādī, *MSR* 11:1 (2007): 234. See also *EI*^{3}, s.vv. "Apology", "Canon and Canonisation, in classical Arabic literature" [Geert Jan van Gelder] and also *EAL*, s.v. "Epigram" [G. J. H. van Gelder]. Cf. however, *EI*^{2}, s.vv. "Muḥdathūn" [G. J. H. van Gelder]; "Shamʿa" [G. J. H. van Gelder]; "al-Maʾmūnī" [J. C. Bürgel]; "al-Ṣanawbarī" [G. Schoeler]; "Zahriyyāt 1. in Arabic" [G. Schoeler]; "Tashbīh" [G. J. H. van Gelder]; "Ḳiṭʿa 1. in Arabic poetry" [G. Schoeler]. cf. also *EI*^{2}, s.v. "ʿArabiyya. Arabic Language and Literature. (III) Third to Fifth Centuries (II) Poetry" [H. A. R. Gibb]; it is not exactly clear to me what Gibb means here by "epigram". cf. also *EI*^{2}, s.vv. "al-Ṣafadī" [F. Rosenthal] (Franz Rosenthal, incidentally, was the very model of a classically trained Arabist and perhaps it was this training that influenced him in his use of the term "epigram"); "al-Warrāḳ" [G. J. H. van Gelder]; "Musāwir b. Sawwār al-Warrāḳ" [G. J. H. van Gelder].

108 *EI*^{3}, s.v. "Epigram 1. Classical Arabic" [Geert Jan van Gelder]. See also *EI*^{3}, s.v. "al-Bilbaysī" [Joseph Sadan]. ʿAbd al-Ḥamīd b. Yaḥyā al-Kātib was said to be "a master of pithy epigram" in the *EI*^{2}, but there is no mention of his poetry in the new entry in the *EI*^{3} (see *EI*^{2}, s.v. "ʿAbd al-Ḥamīd b. Yaḥyā b. Saʿd" [H. A. R. Gibb];, *EI*^{3}, s.v. "ʿAbd al-Ḥamīd b. Yaḥyā al-Kātib" [Wadād al-Qāḍī]).

109 *EI*^{3}, s.v. "Epigram 1. Classical Arabic" [Geert Jan van Gelder].

on Martialian point.[110] This is partly a question of personal preference—after all, to quote Ludwig Wittgenstein, "the meaning of a word is its use in the language"—but this study differs explicitly by focusing on the historical lineage and anthological context of Arabic *maqāṭīʿ*-poetry and by insisting that genre is something more than a name.[111]

When one claims that the pre-modern Arabic tradition did, in fact, possess an epigram genre, one does not intend to suggest that pre-modern Arabs developed a term to describe Hellenistic or Latin epigrams or that they were even aware of these phenomena. Rather this study puts forward two parallel literary-historical arguments. The first line of argument holds that it can be demonstrated, with a certain amount of contextualization, that a cognate epigram form existed in the pre-modern Arabic tradition, that it was a distinct genre with coherent formal and thematic foundations, and that it is almost entirely unknown in the scholarly record.[112] The second argument suggests that any use of the term epigram in this context is qualified owing to specific historical and cultural factors discussed previously. It goes without saying, therefore, that this use of the term epigram is contingent on a nuanced and specific understanding of the generic term—as outlined above—and that it highlights contextual parallels so as to argue for an allomorphic genre of Arabic epigram. These narrow and specific allomorphic parallels fall under the auspices of the wider generic definition of epigram, with critical and historical sensitivity to the context of pre-modern Islamicate literatures. Earlier attempts subscribed uncritically to a historically particular understanding of the genre and overlooked key features of context—specifically the anthological—that give the Arabic epigram its ontological frame. They also ignored innovations within the classical Arabic poetic system itself. Any attempt to answer the question 'How do you say "epigram" in Arabic?' must depend on the ability to understand and make sense of these epistemological concerns and a body of literary-historical evidence.

---

110 "[t]erms such as *qiṭʿa* are also used regularly for any short poem, including those that have no 'point,' punch-line, clever conceit, or witty turn and thus cannot be called epigrams in the strictest sense." (*EI*^{3}, s.v. "Epigram 1. Classical Arabic" [Geert Jan van Gelder]).

111 Ludwig Wittgenstein, *Philosophische Untersuchungen. Philosophical Investigations,* trans. G. E. M. Anscombe, P. M. S. Hacker, and J. Schulte, rev. 4th ed. (Oxford: Wiley-Blackwell, 2009), 25e: "Die Bedeutung eines Wortes ist sein Gebrauch in der Sprache." (25).

112 *Maqāṭīʿ*-poetry is not discussed in, for example, Roger Allen and D. S. Richards (eds), *Arabic Literature in the Post-Classical Period* (Cambridge: Cambridge University Press, 2006).

CHAPTER 5

Epigrams in Parallax

Stephen pointed to a basket which a butcher's boy had slung inverted on his head.

—Look at that basket, he said.

[...]

In order to see that basket, said Stephen, your mind first of all separates the basket from the rest of the visible universe which is not the basket. The first phase of apprehension is a bounding line drawn about the object to be appprehended. [...] You see it as one whole. You apprehend its wholeness.

[...]

Then, said Stephen, you pass from point to point, led by its formal lines; you apprehend it as balanced part against part within its limits; you feel the rhythm of its structure. In other words, the synthesis of immediate perception is followed by the analysis of apprehension. Having first felt that it is *one* thing you feel now that it is a *thing*. You apprehend it as complex, multiple, divisible, separable, made up of its parts, the result of its parts and their sum, harmonious.

[...]

When you have apprehended that basket as one thing and have then analysed it according to its form and apprehended it as a thing you make the only synthesis which is logically and esthetically permissible. You see that it is that thing which it is and no other thing.[1]

•••

---

1 James Joyce, *A Portrait of the Artist as a Young Man*, ed. J. P. Riquelme (New York, NY; London: W. W. Norton & co., 2007), 186–87.

 | DOI 10.1163/9789004350533_008

> Genres are thus entities that can be described from two different viewpoints, that of empirical observation and that of abstract analysis.[2]

•••

> Parallax. I never exactly understood. There's a priest. Could ask him. Par it's Greek: parallel, parallax. Met him pikehoses she called it till I told her about the transmigration. O rocks!
>
> Mr Bloom smiled [...] She's right after all. Only big words for ordinary things on account of the sound.[3]

This is the first study of Arabic *maqāṭīʿ*-poetry, its structure, operational logic, and the contexts of its production and presentation. It argues that *maqāṭīʿ*-poetry emerged as a new genre in the 13th and 14th centuries in large part by being anthologized and that it has obvious yet obscure roots in a long tradition of thematically diverse *qiṭʿah* poetry in Arabic. It is also the first study to treat the notion of an Arabic epigram genre via a historicist examination of literary evidence, using a combination of hermeneutic, contextual, and reception analyses. This study is a work of philology and literary history that owes a great deal to analytical approaches and theoretical orientations in comparative literature.[4] This hybrid perspective may ultimately fail to satisfy both specialists and comparatists, but I have pursued it in the naive hope that it can shed light on methodological problems in both disciplines.

Almost all studies of classical Arabic poetry have confined themselves to evidence from the first half of Arabic literary history (500–1100), and when, on rare occasions, they have ventured into later periods, they have subsumed that literary evidence to a historically undifferentiated and uncritical paradigm. This focus is less pronounced in 20th-century Arabic-language scholarship, primarily because of the drive to create nationalist literary canons led by scholars like Amīn al-Khūlī (1895–1966), but even there the bias against literature written after the year 1100—to say nothing of minor poetic forms—is irrepressible. Nonetheless, these biases cannot distract from the fact that so many *maqāṭīʿ*-collections have survived and thus the contours

2 Tzvetan Todorov, *Genres in Discourse*, trans. Catherine Porter (Cambridge: Cambridge University Press, 1990), 17; French original: *idem*, *Les genres du discours* (Paris: Éditions du Seuil, 1978), 49: "Les genres sont donc des unités qu'on peut décrire de deux points de vue différents, celui de l'observation empirique et celui de l'analyse abstraite."

3 James Joyce, *Ulysses*, [1960 reset ed.] (London: Penguin Classics, 2000), 194.

4 My understanding of the mission of philology is informed by Sheldon Pollock, "Future Philology? The fate of a soft science in a hard world", *Critical Inquiry* 35 (Summer 2009).

of a specific and widespread genre are obvious to anyone who would look. Arabists do not need to try to piece together their original composition; a project that is, in contrast, one of Kathryn Gutzwiller's chief goals in writing the history of Hellenistic epigram collections. *Maqāṭīʿ*-poems may not have attracted much comment—after all we have yet to uncover any didactic or explicit definition of the genre's formal or thematic dimensions—but these poems were transformed from among formalistically similar peers by processes of curation, contextualization in anthologies, and generic identification. It is the anthology or *maqāṭīʿ*-collection—often but not always taxonomically identified—that recasts *maqāṭīʿ*-poetry as epigram. This further step in the genre process is a symptom of deixis. Context is a requisite condition of genre for there can be no identification and recognition without it. Attempts to recover the archaeological legacy of a genre depend on its context—on the genre *in situ,* as it were—and Arabic, unlike the Hellenistic tradition, is fortunate in that most epigram material survives in a recognizable state.[5]

Nonetheless students of the Arabic tradition are not immune to problems of etymology, conceit, and context. For Classicists, the term epigram confuses with its air of inscription, while for the Arabist it is the implied fragmentation and extraction associated with the term *maqāṭīʿ* (and no less *qiṭʿah*) that induces a profound uncertainty regarding a poem's integrity and ontological status. Etymology inheres within the term itself, yes, but etymological valence—like other extra-literary information—must not be privileged over a discernible pattern of being. Analytical literary history requires a conscious vigilance—balancing instance (text) against paradigm (be it derived schema or etymology)—which is akin to the idea of parallax as put forward by Slavoj Žižek, and others.[6]

> The standard definition of parallax is: the apparent displacement of an object (the shift of its position against a background), caused by a change in observational position that provides a new line of sight. The philosophical twist to be added, of course, is that the observed difference is not simply "subjective," due to the fact that the same object which exists "out there" is seen from two different stances, or points of view. It is

---

5 Wen-Chin Ouyang's important intervention on the relevance of ideology to genre is linked fundamentally to an analysis of narrative forms so it is not immediately relevant to the discussion here (See Wen-Chin Ouyang, "Genres, Ideologies, Genre Ideologies and Narrative Transformation", *MEL* 7:2 (July 2004), as well as the other articles in that issue).

6 Žižek draws the concept of parallax from Kojin Karatani, *Transcritique: on Kant and Marx,* trans. Sabu Kohso (Cambridge, MA: MIT Press, 2003). See his review of that work in *New Left Review* 25 (January–February 2004).

> rather that, as Hegel would have put it, subject and object are inherently "mediated," so that an "epistemological" shift in the subject's point of view always reflects an "ontological" shift in the object itself.[7]

Perception is never constant, rather it is constantly displaced and this requires us to reason discursively. It is equally true that an epigram is not an epigram until it is named, or recognized, as such in the epiphanic moment. This is not simply because this study has adopted an originally Greek term to discuss pre-modern Arabic poetry: one need only think of Gutzwiller's insight that $\text{epigram}_{\text{book}}$ served at first metalinguistically as a representation of its putative antecedent, $\text{epigram}_{\text{inscription}}$. This study did not begin by positing *a priori* the existence of a world-literary category known as epigram with the intention of trawling the archive of pre-modern Arabic poetry to find an equivalent. Rather in this case—as in Julia Kristeva's model of intertextuality—one semiotic system (e.g. epigram, anthology, etc.) is transposed on to another, "demand[ing] a new articulation of the thetic—of enunciative and denotative positionality." To treat world-literary categories in comparative literature in this way compels us to recognize that "[i]f one grants that every signifying practice is a field of transpositions of various signifying systems (an inter-textuality), then one understands that its 'place' of enunciation and its denoted 'object' are never single, complete, and identical to themselves, but always plural, shattered, capable of being tabulated."[8]

Arabic *maqāṭīʿ*-poems are epigrams only insofar as they are presented as such, for epigram as a general category can only exist through epistemological observation.[9] As a historical genre, not a metaphysical one (like drama, epic, lyric, etc.), epigram accords with the provisional definition set out by David Fishelov, who defines genre as

---

7 Slavoj Žižek, *The Parallax View* (Cambridge, MA: *MIT* Press, 2006), 17.

8 Julia Kristeva, *Revolution in Poetic Language*, trans. Margaret Waller (New York, NY: Columbia University Press, 1984), 59–60. In the original: "Le terme d'*inter-textualité* désigne cette transposition d'un (ou de plusieurs) système(s) de signes en un autre; mais puisque ce terme a été souvent entendu dans le sens banal de «critique des sources» d'un texte, nous lui préférons celui de *transposition*, qui a l'avantage de préciser que le passage d'un système signifiant à un autre exige une nouvelle articulation du thétique—de la positionnalité énonciative et dénotative. Si on admet que toute pratique signifiante est un champ de transpositions de divers systèmes signifiants (une inter-textualité), on comprend que son «lieu» d'énonciation et son «objet» dénoté ne sont jamais uniques, pleins et identiques à eux-mêmes, mais toujours pluriels, éclatés, susceptibles de modèles tabulaires." (Julia Kristeva, *La Révolution du langage poétique. L'Avant-garde à la fin du XIXe siècle: Lautréamont et Mallarmé* (Paris: Éditions du Seuil, 1974), 59–60).

9 See Thomas O. Beebee, *The Ideology of Genre: a comparative study of generic instability* (University Park, PA: The Pennsylvania State University Press, 1994).

> [...] *a combination of prototypical, representative members, and a flexible set of constitutive rules that apply to some levels of literary texts, to some individual writers, usually to more than one literary period, and to more than one language and culture.*[10]

Genre identification—whether as part of hermeneutic, literary-historical, or comparative analyses—requires us to impose a subjective, epistemological logic, legitimized partly by its efficiency. Thomas Pavel has argued trenchantly that this efficiency serves authors even before it serves readers:

> Genre is a crucial interpretive tool because it is a crucial artistic tool in the first place. Literary texts are neither natural phenomena subject to scientific dissection, nor miracles performed by gods and thus worthy of worship, but fruits of human talent and labor. To understand them, we need to appreciate the efforts that went into their production. Genre helps us figure out the nature of a literary work because the person who wrote it and the culture for which that person labored used genre as a guideline for literary creation.[11]

One should nevertheless be aware of Rosalie Colie's caveat that the pre-modern generic system was fuzzier than we might suppose or are indeed able to represent in retrospective scholarly models.[12] This perhaps explains why *mawāliyā* and *dūbayt* poems occasionally appear in collections of *maqāṭīʿ*-poems.[13] In his theory of the "historicization of genre poetics", Hans Robert Jauß stresses that genre must be understood as a non-static identification so that we can "[seek] a path between the Scylla of nominalist skepticism that allows for only *a posteriori* classifications, and the Charybdis of regression into timeless typologies, a path along which the historicization of genre poetics and of the concept of form are upheld."[14]

---

10 Fishelov, *Metaphors of Genre*, 8 [italics original].

11 Thomas Pavel, "Literary Genres as Norms and Good Habits", *New Literary History* 34:2 (Spring 2003): 202. See also Gary M. Olson, Robert L. Mack, and Susan A. Duffy, "Cognitive Aspects of Genre", *Poetics* 10 (1981).

12 Colie, *The Resources of Kind*, 114–16.

13 I do not agree with the analysis of al-Sayyid Abū al-Faḍl, who, in the introduction to his edition of Ibn Ḥajar al-ʿAsqalānī's *Dīwān*, argues that the *maqṭūʿah* represents the final stage of the integration of the Persian *rubāʿī* genre into Arabic, the Arabic *dūbayt* being, in his analysis, a mid-point in its development (see Ibn Ḥajar, *Dīwān*, ed. Abū al-Faḍl, 15n).

14 Hans Robert Jauß, "Theory of Genres in Medieval Literature" in Hans Robert Jauß, *Toward an Aesthetic of Reception*, trans. Timothy Bahti (Minneapolis, MN: University of Minnesota Press, 1994), 78; *idem*, "Theorie der Gattungen und Literatur des Mittelalters"

Jauß—drawing on Kant—argued that "[...] the category of the exemplary does away with the schema of rule-and-instance and makes possible a processlike determination of the concept of genre in the aesthetic realm."[15] For Jauß, this "processlike determination" is the only way to avoid the twin perils of "nominalist skepticism" and "timeless typologies": "Such a determination no longer applies the generality of literary genres normatively (*ante rem*) or in a classificatory manner (*post rem*), but rather historically (*in re*), that is, in a 'continuity in which each earlier event furthers and supplements itself through the later one' [...]."[16] Jauß' perceptive argument is especially useful for understanding the relationship between *maqāṭīʿ*-poetry and the wider, and older, category of the *qiṭʿah*. If we follow Jauß's reasoning, it becomes clear that the history of the *maqāṭīʿ*-genre will be of major consequence for the still ambiguous history of the *qiṭʿah*-genre:[17]

> [...] the basic principle of a historicization of the concept of form demands not only that one relinquish the substantialist notion of a constant number of unchangeable essential characteristics for the individual

---

in *Grundriss der romanischen Literaturen des Mittelalters, Volume I: Généralités*, ed. H. U. Gumbrecht (Heidelberg: Carl Winter Universitätsverlag, 1972), 109. Jauß goes beyond most other scholars of genre in stressing the fundamental and constitutive role of a work's reception:

> The historical life of a literary work is unthinkable without the active participation of its addressees. For it is only through the process of its mediation that the work enters into the changing horizon-of-experience of a continuity in which the perpetual inversion occurs from simple reception to critical understanding, from passive to active reception, from recognized aesthetic norms to a new production that surpasses them. ("Literature History as a Challenge", 19; German original: "Literaturgeschichte als Provokation der Literaturwissenschaft", 169).

15 H. R. Jauß, "Theory of Genres", 80; *idem*, "Theorie der Gattungen", 111. Žižek draws his idea of parallax from Karatani who is drawing on Kant (Žižek, *The Parallax View*, 4):

> [...] [P]utting two incompatible phenomena on the same level, is strictly analogous to what Kant called "transcendental illusion," the illusion of being able to use the same language for phenomena which are mutually untranslatable and can be grasped only in a kind of parallax view, constantly shifting perspective between two points between which no synthesis or mediation is possible.

16 H. R. Jauß, "Theory of Genres", 80; *idem*, "Theorie der Gattungen", 111.

17 H. R. Jauß, "Theory of Genres", 105; H. R. Jauß, "Theorie der Gattungen", 134: "Der Grundsatz einer Historisierung des Formbegriffs erfordert aber nicht allein, für die einzelne Gattung des substantialistische Vorstellung einer konstanten Zahl unveränderlicher Wesensmerkmale aufzugeben. Er erfordert auch, die korrelate Vorstellung eines Nebeneinanders von in sich abgeschlossenen und gegeneinander abgekapselten literarischen Gattungen abzubauen und nach wechselseitigen Beziehungen zu fragen, die das System der Literatur im gegebenen historischen Augenblick ausmachen."

> genres. It also demands that one dismantle the correlative notion of a sequence of literary genres closed within themselves, encapsulated from one another, and inquire into the reciprocal relations that make up the literary system of a given historical moment.

This same process has been described by Yury Tynyanov as being the trigger for the new genre's genre-consciousness:[18]

> It is impossible to conceive of genre as a static system for the reason that genre-consciousness itself arises as a result of a confrontation with a traditonal genre (i.e. as a result of a sense that the traditional genre has been supplanted, even partially, by a "new" one occupying its place). The point is that the new phenomenon *supplants* the old one, occupies its place, and, without being a "development" of the old, is at the same time its substitute.

Epigram is therefore—to keep with the Kantian idiom—a phenomenon, not a noumenon. Not even the Greek ur-epigram was a noumenon: it was always epigram$_{\text{book}}$, an acknowledged derivative of epigram$_{\text{inscription}}$. Peter Bing and Jon Steffen Bruss explain that:

> Even today the aesthetic experience of aficionados, students, and scholars of Greek epigram, literary and inscribed alike, bears striking resemblance to that of the earliest readers of epigram-collections in all but the rarest situations: whether originally designed for the book or not, epigrams come to us prearranged in published collections. The physical context of both literary and inscribed epigram is divorced from its "original" setting (fictive or real), and readers are automatically implicated in an elaborate *Ergänzungsspiel*, aided by the technical, archeological, epigraphical, and text-critical tools supplied by editors.[19]

We understand intuitively that context bears an extreme influence on our experience of the text, and there is no doubt in my mind that even contextual influences at a substantial remove such as a monograph like this may impact future readings of a text. I have not taken that responsibility lightly.

---

18 Yury Tynyanov, "The Literary Fact", trans. Ann Shukman in *Modern Genre Theory*, ed. David Duff (Harlow: Longman, 2000), 32. David Fishelov has discussed how what he terms literary "family resemblance" can impact generic recognition (see Fishelov, *Metaphors of Genre*, 53–83).

19 Bing and Bruss, "Introduction to the Study of the Hellenistic Epigram", 17.

Many scholars get quite exercised about whether a particular short poem in Arabic is derived or extracted from a longer poem. For them it is the first instantiation of a poem that deserves special ontic status, while all other manifestations can be no more than derivatives of the original.[20] It would be trite to say that this attitude distorts the reality of the literary-historical picture; in truth, it does far worse: it renders context irrelevant. Epigram, like all world-literary genres, has never been an independent, autonomous entity (a "Ding an sich"); it is a phenomenon only visible to us by parallactic examination. Poems that look and sound quite similar to soi-disant *maqāṭīʿ*-poems had existed for centuries before the emergence of this new genre and some of these older poems were reborn as *maqāṭīʿ*-poems simply by inhabiting a new generic context. The anthologists who transformed older poems into *maqāṭīʿ*-poems by placing them alongside the new genre in *maqāṭīʿ*-collections did not have to alter the text of these poems to change their genre; all they had to do was assign them to a different generic context. *Maqāṭīʿ*-poetry became a genre designation and thus a tool, like Heidegger's hammer, ready-to-hand (*zuhanden*); perhaps this is why pre-modern Arabs felt a theoretical discussion of the genre would be superfluous.[21]

This study has presented evidence of a self-classified *maqāṭīʿ*-genre in the pre-modern Arabic tradition and detailed its formalistic, contextual, and literary contours *a posteriori*. This is its foremost contribution, although it has also attempted to survey scholarly understandings of the world-literary genre known as epigram, to ascertain the determinants of this genre, to link its ontological orientation to the context of poetry anthologies, and to demonstrate the parallels between its original Hellenistic paradigm and a hitherto neglected phenomenon in Arabic literary history.[22] My interpretation of

20 On this topic, see James E. Montgomery, *The Vagaries of the Qasidah: the tradition and practice of early Arabic poetry* (Cambridge: Gibb Memorial Trust, 1997) and Talib, "The Many Lives of Arabic Verse".

21 Abdelfattah Kilito has engaged the problem of genre and generic association in the Arabic literary tradition quite profitably and while I am convinced by his argument, I would argue that Kilito generally elides the distinction between *genre* and *mode*. That mode is a highly relevant factor in the production and reception of genres in pre-modern Arabic literature is clear—and Kilito's work is highly effectual in bringing this out—but it is separate from the generic argument being explored here (See, for example, Abdelfattah Kilito, *The Author and His Doubles: essays on classical Arabic culture*, trans. Michael Cooperson (Syracuse, NY: Syracuse University Press, 2001), esp. 60–66). cf. the approach to mode and genre in Claudio Guillén's *Literature as System: essays toward the theory of literary history* (Princeton, NJ: Princeton University Press, 1971).

22 This resemblance I find particularly cheering in light of the long history of disreputable commentary on the divergence of Hellenistic and Semitic so-called races or cultures. See, for example, the discussion in Geoffrey H. Hartman, "Toward Literary History", *Daedalus*

*maqāṭī*ʿ-poetry as epigram is a synthetic proposition that could be described as relativist in contrast to positivist scholarly values of narrow historical specificity and manufactured empiricism. I concede that readily, and would go so far as to say that I subscribe to the values of relativist (or synthetic) literary history put forward by John Frow, who has argued that:[23]

> [...] [E]pistemological relativism [...] is the very opposite of that "scientific" detachment which results from the certainties of discursive mastery; on the contrary, it should make possible a process of political judgment of the knowledge effects produced, and therefore an avoidance of both a sterile historical cataloguing and an obliteration of the dynamics of textual activity in a sociologistic reduction.

This, the first history of the *maqāṭī*ʿ-genre, could have been a "sterile historical cataloguing" and because I know that some may have preferred that, I have tried to inoculate the first half of this study from the "political judgment of knowledge effects produced" that permeates the second half.

Quite apart from my interest in the ways in which Arabic literary history is subsumed in the agenda of world-literary and comparative literary histories, I have framed this history of a previously unrecognized genre in this contrapuntal fashion expressly to avoid the effect of what Jacques Derrida called the Law of Genre:[24]

> As soon as the word "genre" is sounded, as soon as it is heard, as soon as one attempts to conceive it, a limit is drawn. And when a limit is established, norms and interdictions are not far behind [...] If a genre is what it is, or if it is supposed to be what it is destined to be by virtue of its *telos*, then "genres are not to be mixed"; one should not mix genres, one owes it to oneself not to get mixed up in mixing genres. Or more rigorously: genres should not intermix. And if it should happen that they do intermix, by accident or through transgression, by mistake or through a lapse, then this should confirm, since, after all, we are speaking of "mixing," the essential purity of their identity.

99:2 (Spring 1970); repr. in Geoffrey. H. Hartman, *Beyond Formalism: literary essays, 1958–1970* (New Haven, CT: Yale University Press, 1970).

23 John Frow, *Marxism and Literary History* (Oxford: Basil Blackwell, 1986), 124.

24 Jacques Derrida, "The Law of Genre", trans. Avital Ronell, *Critical Inquiry* 7:1 (Autumn 1980), 56–7. On orientalism in the disciplinary history of world literature, see Aamir R. Mufti, "Orientalism and the Institution of World Literatures", *Critical Inquiry* 36 (Spring 2010).

Just as the tortured history of the atomism controversy and inherited misconceptions about the difference between a *qaṣīdah* and a *qiṭʿah* have impacted the study of Arabic poetry, so the pressure of conforming to the world-literary category of epigram will inevitably affect our understanding of Arabic *maqāṭīʿ*-poetry. By telling the story of this new genre in this way, by reflecting on historical methodologies in the study of Arabic poetry, by paying close attention to the circumstances in which this inquiry was conceived, pursued, and framed, and by making as much primary textual evidence of the genre available to readers as is possible in a scholarly monograph of this length, I hope that the law of genre and its strictures do not too greatly distort the picture of *maqāṭīʿ*-poetry drawn here.

Appendix

Corpus of Maqāṭīʿ-Material

This is not a comprehensive corpus, but it is a representative sample of a previously unrecognized genre term in action. All translations are mine unless otherwise indicated.

1. anon. editor of Ibn al-Qaysarānī (d. 548/1153), *Dīwān*:[1]

    وهذه مقاطيع عملها عند قفوله من العراق إلى الشَّام يتشوَّق فيها السَّكن والوطن وذلك سنة سبع وعشرين وخمس مائة

    The [following are] *maqāṭīʿ*-poems that he composed during his journey back to the Levant from Iraq. In these poems, he expresses his yearning for his homeland. This was in the year 527 [1132]

2. Ibn Khallikān (d. 681/1282), *Wafayāt al-aʿyān wa-anbāʾ abnāʾ az-zamān* (*The Passing of the Notables and the Sons of the Age*) (composed between 1256–60 and 1271–74):

    a. biographical notice on Ibrāhīm b. Naṣr b. ʿAskar al-Mawṣilī (d. 610/1213) whose son Ibn Khallikān met in Aleppo:[2]

        ذكره ابو البركات ابن المستوفي [...] وأورد له مقاطيع عديدة[3]

        Abū l-Barakāt ibn al-Mustawfī mentioned him [...] and cited numerous *maqāṭīʿ*-poems by him

    b. biographical notice on Ibrāhīm al-Ghazzī (d. 524/1129), citing Ibn ʿAsākir (d. 571/1176) from his *Tārīkh madīnat Dimashq*:[4]

---

1   Dār al-Kutub (Cairo) MS 1484 *Adab*, f. 27a.
2   Ibn Khallikān, *Wafayāt al-aʿyān*, 1:38.
3   NB: In the edition of Ibn al-Mustawfī's *Tārīkh Irbil*, ed. aṣ-Ṣaqqār (Baghdad, 1980), Ibrāhīm b. Naṣr is not given an entry of his own, but is mentioned in the entry on his son Ismāʿīl; the word *maqāṭīʿ* is not used there.
4   Ibn Khallikān, *Wafayāt al-aʿyān*, 1:58. NB: Ibn ʿAsākir does not use the term *maqāṭīʿ* in his entry on Ibrāhīm [b. ʿUthmān b. Muḥammad] al-Ghazzī in the printed edition of *Tārīkh madīnat Dimashq*, ed. ʿUmar b. Gharāmah al-ʿAmrāwī et al. (Beirut: Dār al-Fikr, 1415/1995),

[...] وانتشر شعره هناك وذكر له عدّة مقاطيع من الشعر

"[...] his poetry spread throughout that area and several *maqāṭīʿ*-poems by him were recorded"

c. biographical notice on Ibn Ṭabāṭabā (d. 345/956 [or 315/927[5]]):[6]

وذكره أبو منصور الثعالبي في كتاب «اليتيمة» وذكر له مقاطيع

Abū Manṣūr ath-Thaʿālibī mentioned him and *maqāṭīʿ*-poems by him in his book *Yatīmat ad-dahr*

d. biographical notice on Usāmah b. Munqidh (d. 584/1188):[7]

وأورد له مقاطيع من شعره

and he cited some *maqāṭīʿ*-poems by him

e. biographical notice on al-Asʿad b. Mammātī (d. 606/1209):

وله ديوان شعر رأيته بخطّ ولده ونقلت منه مقاطيع[8]

He has a collection (*dīwān*) of poetry, which I saw in his son's handwriting, and I copied out some *maqāṭīʿ*-poems from it

وذكره العماد الاصبهاني في كتاب «الخريدة» وأورد له عدّة مقاطيع[9]

[ʿImād ad-Dīn] al-Iṣbahānī mentioned him in his book *Kharīdat al-qaṣr* and cited several *maqāṭīʿ*-poems by him

f. biographical notice on aṭ-Ṭughrāʾī (d. c. 515/1121):[10]

7:51–4, however Ibn al-ʿImād (d. 1089/1679), in his *Shadharāt adh-dhahab* (Cairo: Maktabat al-Qudsī, 1350–51/1931–32), cites Ibn ʿAsākir as having used the term (4:67–8).

5 See in aṣ-Ṣafadī, *al-Wāfī*, 2:211.

6 Ibn Khallikān, *Wafayāt al-aʿyān*, 1:129. See also in the work of Ibn Khallikān's contemporary Ibn ʿUthmān (d. 615/1218), *Murshid az-zuwwār ilā qubūr al-abrār*, ed. Muḥammad Fatḥī Abū Bakr (Cairo: ad-Dār al-Miṣriyyah al-Lubnāniyyah, 1415/1995), 236.

7 ibid., 1:196.

8 ibid., 1:210.

9 ibid., 1:211.

10 ibid., 1:189.

وذكره ابو المعالي الحظيري في كتاب «زينة الدهر» وذكر له مقاطيع

Abū l-Maʿālī al-Ḥaẓīrī mentioned him in his book *Zīnat ad-dahr* and cited *maqāṭīʿ*-poems by him

g. biographical notice on Abū l-Maʿālī al-Ḥaẓīrī (d. 568/1172):[11]

وقد ذكره العماد الكاتب في «الخريدة» وأنشد له عدّة مقاطيع

[ʿImād ad-Dīn al-Iṣbahānī] mentioned him in his book *Kharīdat al-qaṣr* and cited several *maqāṭīʿ*-poems by him

h. biographical notice on an-Nāshiʾ al-Akbar [Ibn Shirshīr] (d. 293/906):[12]

وقد استشهد كشاجم بشعره في كتاب «المصايد والمطارد» في مواضع منها
قصائد ومنها طرديات على أسلوب أبي نواس ومنها مقاطيع

His poetry (including long poems, hunting poems in the style of Abū Nuwās, and *maqāṭīʿ*-poems) is cited in Kushājim's collection *al-Maṣāyid wa-l-maṭārid*

i. biographical notice on Fityān ash-Shāghūrī (d. 615/1218):[13]

وله ديوان شعر فيه مقاطيع حسان

He has a collection of poetry (*dīwān shiʿr*), which includes lovely *maqāṭīʿ*-poems

j. biographical notice on Ibn al-Khall (d. 552–3/1157–1159):[14]

ذكره العماد الاصبهاني في كتاب «الخريدة» وأثنى عليه وأورد له مقاطيع شعر
ودوبيت

11 ibid., 2:366; see also no. 2f above, and ibid., 4:450.

12 ibid., 3:91.

13 ibid., 4:24; see also in the same entry (ibid., 4:26): "He also has another small *Dīwān*, which I saw in Damascus, that only includes *dūbayt* […]".

14 ibid., 4:228.

ʿImād ad-Dīn al-Iṣbahānī mentioned him in his book *Kharīdat al-qaṣr*, where he praises him and cites *maqāṭīʿ* and *dūbayt* poems by him

k. in the biographical notice on al-Mubarrad (d. 286/900), an invective poem by Yaḥyā b. al-Mubārak al-Yazīdī (d. 202/817–18) is cited:[15]

فهجاه في عدّة مقاطيع هذا المقطوع من جملتها

He ridiculed him in several *maqāṭīʿ*-poems, and the [following] *maqṭūʿ*-poem is one of them

l. upon mention of the poet Ibn an-Nābulusī (d. 619/1222):[16]

ولابن عنين فيه عدّة مقاطيع هجو[17]

Ibn ʿUnayn wrote several invective *maqāṭīʿ*-poems about him

m. biographical notice on al-Mihyār ad-Daylamī (d. 428/1037):[18]

وذكره ابو الحسن الباخرزي – المقدّم ذكره – في كتاب «دمية القصر» فقال في حقّه [...] ثمّ عقب هذا الكلام بذكر مقاطيع من شعره وأبيات من جملة قصائده

Abū l-Ḥasan al-Bākharzī (discussed above) mentioned him in his book *Dumyat al-qaṣr* and said about him [...]. He followed this by citing *maqāṭīʿ*-poems by him and verses from his long poems

n. in the biographical notice on Ibn Shaddād (d. 632/1235), story about Ismāʿīl b. Ḥamdawayhi al-Ḥamdawī (3rd/9th c.) and the proverbial *ṭaylasān Ibn Ḥarb*:[19]

---

15 ibid., 4:322.

16 ibid., 5:266.

17 On Ibn ʿUnayn (d. 630/1233), see ibid., 5:14–9, no. 684.

18 ibid., 5:360.

19 ibid., 7:95. See further Josef van Ess, *Der Ṭailasan des Ibn Ḥarb: 'Mantelgedichte' in arabischer Sprache* (Heidelberg: Winter, 1979).

وهو أن أحمد بن حرب ابن أخي يزيد المهلّبي أعطى أبا علي إسماعيل بن إبراهيم بن حمدويه البصري الحمدوي الشاعر الأديب طيلسانًا خليعًا فعمل في الحمدوي مقاطيع عديدة ظريفة سارت عنه وتناقلتها الرواة

"[The story is] that Aḥmad b. Ḥarb, the nephew of Yazīd al-Muhallabī made Abū ʿAlī Ismāʿīl b. Ḥamdawayhi al-Baṣrī al-Ḥamdawī, the poet and littérateur, the gift of an old shawl for which the latter composed pleasant *maqāṭīʿ*-poems, which became well known and passed between narrators"

and *passim*[20]

3. aṣ-Ṣafadī (d. 764/1363), from a letter to Ibn Nubātah (d. 768/1366) asking him to grant an *ijāzah* to relate his works:[21]

[...]وإثبات ما يحسن إيراده في هذه الإجازة من المقاطيع الرائقة والأبيات اللائقة [...]

and setting down in this certificate (*ijāzah*) which of the fine *maqāṭīʿ*-poems and fitting verses he may cite

4. aṣ-Ṣafadī (d. 764/1363), exchange with Ibn Nubātah (discussed above, pp. 117–28):[22]

ولما وقف[اي ابن نباتة]على مقاطيع لي[...]

20 ibid., 1:142; 2:112; 2:131n; 3:279 [on ʿAlī b. ʿAbd al-ʿAzīz al-Jurjānī, author of *al-Wasāṭah*]; 3:291; 3:314 [on ash-Sharīf al-Murtaḍā]; 3:339; 4:376; 4:397 on [Ibn Ẓafar, who died in Hama c. 565/1170]; 4:414 [on Ibn Sukkarah (d. 514/1120)]; 4:430 [on Ibn aṣ-Ṣāʾigh (645–c. 722/1247–c. 1322)]; 4:450; 5:13; 5:41; 5:94; 5:97 [on aṣ-Ṣūlī]; 5:111; 5:248; 5:283; 5:348; 5:376 [on al-Khubzʾarruzī]; 6:51 [on al-Badīʿ al-Asṭurlābī]; 6:70; 6:79 (and see also 3:373); 6:155; 66:249 (see also 7:235); 7:219, 7:226.

21 aṣ-Ṣafadī, *Alḥān as-sawājiʿ*, ed. Sālim, 2:319; also in the autograph manuscript Staatsbibliothek zu Berlin MS Wetzstein II 150, f. 128a. Aṣ-Ṣafadī tells us that the letter was written at the beginning of Shaʿbān 729 (i.e. at the end of May 1329). See also in Ibn Taghrībirdī, *al-Manhal aṣ-ṣāfī*, 5:246; and Ibn Ḥijjah al-Ḥamawī, *Khizānat al-adab*, ed. Diyāb, 3:326.

22 aṣ-Ṣafadī, *Alḥān as-sawājiʿ*, ed. Sālim, 2:441; 443; also in the autograph manuscript Staatsbibliothek zu Berlin MS Wetzstein II 150, ff. 180b, 181b.

When he came across [some] *maqāṭīʿ*-poems I'd composed [...]

كتب هو [اي ابن نباتة] إليّ مقاطيع نظمها نظير ذلك

He [Ibn Nubātah] sent me some *maqāṭīʿ*-poems he'd written in response

5. aṣ-Ṣafadī (d. 764/1363), *al-Ḥusn aṣ-ṣarīḥ fī miʾat malīḥ*:[23]

فأحيت أن أجمع ممّا اتّفق لي نظمه في وصف مائة غلام [...] بشرط أنني لم أقنع في كلّ مقطوع من ذلك بالوزن والقافية

I wanted to collect poems I'd composed describing one hundred young males [...] except that I wasn't content with using the same meter and rhyme for every *maqṭūʿ*-poem

6. aṣ-Ṣafadī (d. 764/1363), *Kashf al-ḥāl fī waṣf al-khāl* (*Revealing the Situation about Describing Beauty Marks*[24]):

من كلّ مقطوع ألذّ من نغمة[25]

[...] from every *maqṭūʿ*-poem, which is more pleasing than a melody (*naghmah*) [...]

النتيجة [:] وهي تشتمل على ما جاء في ذلك للشعراء من المقاطيع العجيبة [...][26]

The collection comprises interesting *maqāṭīʿ*-poems, which poets wrote on the topic

7. aṣ-Ṣafadī (d. 764/1363), *al-Hawl al-muʿjib fī l-qawl bi-l-mūjib* (*An Admirable Shock: on affirmative responses*):[27]

---

23 aṣ-Ṣafadī, *al-Ḥusn aṣ-ṣarīḥ fī miʾat malīḥ*, ed. al-Hayb, 31; also in Princeton MS Garrett Yahuda 935, f. 62b.

24 Title as translated in Rowson, "al-Ṣafadī", 342.

25 aṣ-Ṣafadī, *Kashf al-ḥāl*, ed. al-ʿUqayl, 119; see also the editor's footnote suggesting—erroneously—that aṣ-Ṣafadī compiled a collection of *muqaṭṭaʿāt* (sic), which, he asserts, are poetic pieces of seven verses or fewer.

26 ibid., 195.

27 aṣ-Ṣafadī, *al-Hawl al-muʿjib fī l-qawl bi-l-mūjib*, ed. Muḥammad ʿAbd al-Majīd Lāshīn (Cairo: Dār al-Āfāq al-ʿArabiyyah, 2005), 60.

وقد أحببت أن أضع فيه [...] من الأشعار الرائقة والمقاطيع اللائقة

I wanted to include in it [...] excellent poems and fitting *maqāṭīʿ*-poems

8. aṣ-Ṣafadī (d. 764/1363), *al-Wāfī bi-l-Wafayāt* (*Consummating «The Passing»*):

   a. biographical notice on Badr ad-Dīn Muḥammad b. Aḥmad b. ʿAbd Allāh:[28]

وقد أوردتُ في هذه المادة ولغيري من المتقدمين والمتأخرين عدّة مقاطيع في شرح لاميّة العجم وسوف أوردها إن شاء الله تعالى في ترجمة الحسن بن رشيق القيرواني او في ترجمة الصاحب جمال الدين يحيى بن عيسى بن مطروح

[Elsewhere] I previously reproduced several *maqāṭīʿ*-poems by myself and other contemporary and ancient poets, which comment on [aṭ-Ṭughrāʾī's poem] *Lāmiyyat al-ʿajam*, and I will reproduce these [here] either in the entry on al-Ḥasan b. Rashīq al-Qayrawānī [(d. 456/1065 or 463/1071)] or in the entry on the [Sultan's] companion Jamāl ad-Dīn Yaḥyā b. Maṭrūḥ [(d. 649/1251)]

   b. biographical notice on Ibn Nubātah (d. 768/1366):[29]

وكان القاضي شهاب الدين ابن فضل الله [العمري] قد دخل به الى الديوان بدمشق في اوايل سنة ثلث واربعين وسبع ماية وكان اقام مدّةً يتردد الى الديوان ويَكتب ولم يُكتب له توقيعٌ فكان يتقاضى القاضي شهاب الدين في ذلك كل قليلٍ بمقاطيع مطبوعة وابيات فيها المحاسن مجموعة من ذلك قوله [...]

The judge Shihāb ad-Dīn Ibn Faḍl Allāh [al-ʿUmarī] brought Ibn Nubātah into the chancery (*dīwān*) of Damascus in early 743 [1342] and Ibn Nubātah spent some time going back and forth to the chancery to write,

28 aṣ-Ṣafadī, *al-Wāfī*, 2:77–8.

29 aṣ-Ṣafadī, *al-Wāfī*, 1:330.

but he was not given an apostille.[30] He would petition the judge Shihāb ad-Dīn for this quite often with brilliant *maqāṭīʿ*-poems and verses imbued with excellence, including the following [...]

c. biographical notice on Ṣafī ad-Dīn al-Ḥillī (d. c. 750/1350):[31]

وأجاد القصائد المطوّلة والمقاطيع

he excelled at long poems and *maqāṭīʿ*-poems

d. biographical notice on Mujīr ad-Dīn Ibn Tamīm (d. 684/1285):[32]

إلّا أنّه لا يجيد إلّا في المقاطيع فأمّا إذا طال نفسه ونظم القصائد انحطّ نظمه ولم يرتفع

But he only ever excelled at *maqāṭīʿ*-poems for when he carried on and composed long poems, his poetry slumped and didn't rise up

e. biographical notice on Abū Manṣūr ath-Thaʿālibī (d. 429/1038):[33]

وهي [اي يتيمة الدهر] أحسن تصانيفه. وقد اشتهرت كثيرًا، ولابن قلاقس فيها عدّة مقاطيع

It [i.e. *Yatīmat ad-dahr*] is his best book. It became very famous and Ibn Qalāqis [(d. 567/1172)] wrote several *maqāṭīʿ*-poems about it

f. biographical notice on Saʿd ad-Dīn Muḥammad b. Muḥyī ad-Dīn Ibn al-ʿArabī (d. 656/1258):[34]

وكان شاعرًا مجيدًا أجاد المقاطيع التي نظمها في الغلمان وأوصافهم

30 See Beatrice Gruendler, "Tawqīʿ (Apostille): verbal economy in verdicts of tort redress" in *The Weaving of Words: approaches to classical Arabic literature*, ed. Laleh Behzadi and Vahid Behmardi (Beirut-Wiesbaden: Ergon, 2009).

31 aṣ-Ṣafadī, *al-Wāfī*, 18:482. See also in al-Kutubī, *Fawāt al-Wafayāt*, 2:335: "*ajāda al-qaṣā'id al-muṭawwalah wa-l-maqāṭīʿ* " ["He excelled in composing long poems and *maqāṭīʿ*-poems"].

32 aṣ-Ṣafadī, *al-Wāfī*, 5:228.

33 ibid., 19:194.

34 ibid., 1:186.

He was a talented poet who excelled at *maqāṭīʿ*-poems, which he composed on young men and their attributes

g. biographical notice on Ibn ash-Sharīf Daftarkhʷān (d. 655/1257):[35]

وله شعر كثير مقاطيع وغيرها

He wrote a great deal of poetry, *maqāṭīʿ*-poems and otherwise

h. biographical notice on Ibrāhīm al-Miʿmār (d. 750/1350):

أمّا في المقاطيع الشعرية فإنّه يقعد به / عنها مراعاة الإعراب وتصريف الأفعال ولكنّه قليل الخطأ [...][36]

"Yet when it comes to his *maqāṭīʿ*-poems, he ignores case endings and the morphology of verbs, although he [normally] rarely makes errors"

«فمن مقاطيعه اللائقة قوله [...]»[37]

"The following is one of his apt *maqāṭīʿ*-poems [...]"

i. biographical notice on Jamāl ad-Dīn aṣ-Ṣūfī (b. 693/1293 in Nābulus, d. 18 Rabīʿ II 750/1349 in Damascus of plague):[38]

وهو شاعر مجيد في المقاطيع يجيد نظمها ومعناها

He is a poet who excelled at *maqāṭīʿ*-poems, in both their composition and their imagery

---

35 ibid., 21:466.

36 ibid., 6:173–74. Al-Miʿmār merits an entry in aṣ-Ṣafadī's *Aʿyān al-ʿaṣr wa-aʿwān an-naṣr*, but his *maqāṭīʿ* are not mentioned there. (cf. aṣ-Ṣafadī, *Aʿyān al-ʿaṣr wa-aʿwān an-naṣr*, 3 vols, ed. Fuat Sezgin with Mazen Amawi (Frankfurt am Main: Institut für Geschichte der Arabisch-Islamischen Wissenschaften, 1990), 1:38). Compare what Ibn Abī Ḥajalah at-Tilimsānī writes of al-Miʿmār's language in his *Maghnāṭīs ad-durr an-nafīs* (no. 11b).

37 aṣ-Ṣafadī, *al-Wāfī*, 6:174.

38 aṣ-Ṣafadī, *al-Wāfī*, 29:208.

9. Muḥammad b. Shākir al-Kutubī (d. 764/1363), biographical notice on Nāṣir ad-Dīn al-Ḥasan b. Shāwir b. an-Naqīb (d. 687/1288):[39]

وله ديوان مقاطيع في مجلّدين وشعره جيد عذب منسجم فيه التورية الرائقة اللائقة المتمكّنة [...] ومقاطيعه جيِّدة إلى الغاية

He has a collection of *maqāṭīʿ*-poems in two volumes. His poetry is good, sweet, and harmonious, and it displays lovely, apt, and masterful double entendres [...] His *maqāṭīʿ*-poems are most excellent

10. Lisān ad-Dīn Ibn al-Khaṭīb (d. 776/1374), *Khaṭrat aṭ-ṭayf fī riḥlat ash-shitāʾ wa-ṣ-ṣayf* (*The Phantom's Strut: a journey through winter and summer*):[40]

وقلت نظمت مقطوعتين إحداهما مدح والأخرى قدح

I have composed two *maqṭūʿah*-poems; one is laudatory, the other disparaging

11. Ibn Abī Ḥajalah at-Tilimsānī (d. 776/1375), *Maghnāṭīs ad-durr an-nafīs* (*Attracting Priceless Pearls*):[41]

a. in an entry on the poet Burhān ad-Dīn al-Qīrāṭī (d. 781/1379):

[هو] كامل المقاصد جيّد القصائد موصول المقاطيع بالبديع[42]

[His] meanings are entire, his poems (*qaṣāʾid*) are good, his *Maqāṭīʿ*-poems [or: disconnected things] are connected with verbal artistry

فصل ممّا له من المقاطيع الموصولة بالبديع منها [...][43]

39 al-Kutubī, *Fawāt al-Wafayāt*, 1:324. On this poet, see Ibn an-Naqīb, *Shiʿr Ibn an-Naqīb al-Fuqaysī al-Ḥasan b. Shāwir*, ed. ʿAbbās Hānī al-Chirākh (Baghdad: Dār al-Furāt, 2008). On invective *maqṭūʿ*-poems, see al-Kutubī, *Fawāt al-Wafayāt*, 2:334 (compare aṣ-Ṣafadī, *al-Wāfī*, 18:476).

40 Ibn al-Khaṭīb, *Khaṭrat aṭ-ṭayf: riḥalāt fī l-Maghrib wa-l-Andalus*, ed. Aḥmad Mukhtār al-ʿAbbādī (Beirut: al-Muʾassasah al-ʿArabiyyah li-d-Dirāsāt wa-n-Nashr, 2003), 41.

41 See discussion of this work above pp. 50–2.

42 Yale MS Landberg 69, f. 8a.

43 Yale MS Landberg 69, f. 8b.

> Chapter: some of his *Maqāṭīʿ*-poems [or: disconnected things] that are connected with verbal artistry [...]

(See also the exchange between al-Qīrāṭī and Ibn aṣ-Ṣāʾigh (d. 776/1375) discussed on pp. 129–31 above.)[44]

b. in an entry on the poet Ibrāhīm al-Miʿmār (d. 750/1350):

ولم أعلم في علما[ء] هذا القرن الثامن من جوّد المقاطيع مثله فيما شهد به نقدي وقال فيه حاكم اختياري ثبت عندي وذلك أنّه يسمع المثل السائر وهو سائر من الجمّال والحمّال فينظّمه فيه على البديه ويُفرغه في قالب عجيب واسلوب غريب وهو في الزجل [ا]بن قزمان الزمان وكذلك في البُلَّيْق والمواليا وكان والغالب على شعره استعمال الامثال واستباحة السحر الحلال وليس له حظّ في القصائد المطوّلة فمتى تجاوز البيتين او الثلاثة في الغالب خربت داره وارتفع غباره وبدا عواره ووقف لعدم العربية حماره فربّما في المقطوع المطبوع وقع له فيه اللحن الفاحش والسهم الطائش أخبرني غير واحد من المصريين أنّه قيل له يا شيخ ابراهيم ربّما وقع لك اللحن في شعرك فلو قرأتَ شيئاً[45] من العربية أصلحتَ به لسانك فقال يا مولانا ومن اين يدرك الحمار العربية[46]

> Of all the learned people (*ʿulamāʾ*) of the 8th [14th] century, I know no one who composed *maqāṭīʿ*-poems as well as him, and to this my criticism testifies as does my anthologist's eye and I am certain of it. For he would hear the most current sayings (*al-mathal as-sāʾir*) as he circulated (*sāʾir*) among camel-drivers and porters and would weave it into verse on the spot, pouring it out into a wondrous mold in his peculiar style. In *zajal*, he was the Ibn Quzmān of his day just as he was in *bullayq*, *mawāli-*

44 This is not the well known Ibn aṣ-Ṣāʾigh (d. c. 722/1322) (*EI*², s.v. "Ibn al-Ṣāʾigh") who died around the time of al-Qīrāṭī's birth but Muḥammad b. ʿAbd ar-Raḥmān Ibn aṣ-Ṣāʾigh (d. 776/1375), a chancery secretary and author of a response to Ibn Abī Ḥajalah's *Dīwān aṣ-Ṣabābah* (see no. 24) (on him, see Ibn Ḥajar, *ad-Durar al-kāminah*, 3:499–500).

45 This is emended from the MS: شيا

46 Yale MS Landberg 69, f. 12a.

yā, and *kān wa-kān*. His poetry is dominated by the use of proverbs and the condoning of licit magic [i.e. double entendre, *as-siḥr al-ḥalāl*]. He didn't have much luck with long poems for as soon as he exceeded two or three verses, his abode would crumble, the dust would rise, his blemishes would come to light, and his donkey would halt for lack of a cart/Classical Arabic (*al-ʿarabiyyah*). And also perhaps in his inspired *maqāṭīʿ*-poems, he would fall victim to a vulgar solecism or a stray arrow. More than one Egyptian told me that he was told: 'Shaykh Ibrāhīm, your poetry suffers sometimes from grammatical errors so if you read some Classical Arabic (*al-ʿarabiyyah*), you can set your language straight.' But he would reply, 'Since when do jackasses find their own cart (*al-ʿarabiyyah*), kind sir?'

فصل ممّا له من المقاطيع الموصولة بالبديع [...][47]

Chapter: some of his *Maqāṭīʿ*-poems [or: disconnected things] that are connected with verbal artistry [...]

c. in an entry on himself:

وجوّد القصيدة والمقطوع

He excelled at [composing] *qaṣāʾid* and *maqāṭīʿ*-poems

12. Ibn Abī Ḥajalah at-Tilimsānī (d. 776/1375), *Dīwān aṣ-Ṣabābah* (*The Collection of Passionate Love*):

a. from the introduction:[48]

«أما بعد فإنّ كتابنا هذا كما قيل:

[من الطويل]

كتابٌ حوى أخبار من قتل الهوى وسارَ بهم بالحبّ في كلّ مذهبِ

مقاطيعه مثل المواصيل لم تزلْ يُشَبِّبُ فيه بالرَّبابِ وزينبِ»

47 Yale MS Landberg 69, f. 12b.

48 Ibn Abī Ḥajalah at-Tilimsānī, *Dīwān aṣ-Ṣabābah*, 13–14; idem, *Dīwān Ibn Abī Ḥajalah*, ed. Aḥmad Ḥilmī Ḥilwah (Cairo: Dār al-Kutub wa-l-Wathāʾiq al-Qawmiyyah, 2014), 34. The author composed a work entitled *Mawāṣīl al-maqāṭīʿ*, but it has not survived. See Ḥājjī Khalīfah, *Kashf*, 2:1889.

This book of ours is as it is said:

A Book that includes tales of those killed by passion
and takes them in every direction with love.
Its *maqāṭīʿ*-poems [or: disconnected things] like flutes [or: connected things] never cease
to court Rabāb[49] and Zaynab"

b. chapter (*bāb*) twenty-seven is titled:[50]

الباب السابع والعشرون[:] في ذكر طرف يسير من المقاطيع الفائقة والأغزال الرائقة ممّا اشتمل على ورد الخدود ورمان النهود وغير ذلك ممّا هنالك

Chapter Twenty-Seven: A pleasant selection of superior *maqāṭīʿ*-poems and lovely love-poems, which comprise the roses of the cheeks, the pomegranates of the chest, and other [topics] included there

13. In the colophon of the only extant copy of Badr ad-Dīn Ibn Ḥabīb's (d. 779/1377) *maqāṭīʿ*-collection:[51]

تمّت المقاطيع المتهكّمة بالمواصيل ☆ وانتظمت الشذور الجميلة المشتملة على الجمل والتفصيل

The *maqāṭīʿ*-poems [or: disconnected things], which mock flutes [or: connected things], are now complete * and the lovely fragments which include the bigger picture and the details have been strung together

14. Badr ad-Dīn Ibn Ḥabīb (d. 779/1377), *Tadhkirat an-nabīh fī ayyām al-Manṣūr wa-banīh* (*Informing the Observant: the reign of al-Manṣūr and his sons*):

49 Rabāb is the name of a woman, but also punningly the name of an instrument, the rebec.

50 ibid., 21; 267. cf. Umberto Rizzitano translates this chapter heading: "*Capitolo XXVII* […]. Citazione di un piccolo gruppo di frammenti poetici stupendi, e di squisti componimenti erotici contenenti (descrizioni) su guance di rose e seni di melagrano e simili." (Umberto Rizzitano, "Il *Dīwān aṣ-ṣabābah* dello scrittore magrebino Ibn Abī Ḥaǵalah", RSO. 28 (1953): 70).

51 Bibliothèque Nationale (Paris) MS 3362, f. 204a; see also Bauer, "„Was kann aus dem Jungen noch werden!"".

a. obituary for Ibn Nubātah (d. 768/1366):[52]

وأخرس المواصيل بمقاطيعه

He made the flutes [*mawāṣīl* or: connected things] silent with his *maqāṭīʿ*-poems [or: disconnected things]

b. obituary for Ṣafī ad-Dīn al-Ḥillī (d. c. 750/1350):[53]

[...] ثمّ قرأت عليه جميع المثالث والمثاني في المعالي والمعاني وهو كتاب من مقاطيع شعره يشتمل على عشرين بابًا في أنواع مختلفة

[...] then I read all of his *al-Mathālith wa-l-mathānī fī l-maʿālī wa-l-maʿānī*, a *maqāṭīʿ*-collection comprising twenty chapters on different subjects

15. Ibn Nubātah (d. 768/1366), commendation (*taqrīẓ*) for Badr ad-Dīn Ibn Ḥabīb's (d. 779/1377) *maqāṭīʿ*-collection:[54]

[...] وأطربتْ مقاطيعها المشبّبة فلم أدر أهي مقاطيع أم مواصيل [...]

[...] its erotic *maqāṭīʿ*-poems stirred the heart so I didn't know whether they were *maqāṭīʿ*-poems [or: disconnected things] or flutes [*mawāṣīl*: also connected things]

16. Ibn Nubātah (d. 768/1366), preface to *al-Qaṭr an-Nubātī* (*Ibn Nubātah's Sweet Drops*):[55]

فإنّي كنتُ قدّمتُ [...] نبذةً من قصائد شعري المطوّلة ☆ وعَرَضتُها على نقد خواطره المتطوّلة ☆ فقامَتْ نبذةٌ من المقاطيع تمدّ لحظها ☆ وتطلُب حظّها

52 Ibn Ḥabīb, *Tadhkirat an-nabīh*, 3:305.

53 Ibn Ḥabīb, *Tadhkirat an-nabīh*, 3:139.

54 Cited in Bauer, "„Was kann aus dem Jungen noch werden!"", 47, l. 8, edited from Bibliothèque Nationale (Paris) MS 3362, f. 204b–205a; see also in Ibn Ḥabib, *Tadhkirat an-nabīh*, 2:203.

55 Thomas Bauer edition in progress, 1; Staatsbibliothek zu Berlin MS Sprenger 1196, f. 29b; Bibliothèque Nationale (Paris) MS 2234, f. 159a. In addition, on the title page of Bibliothèque Nationale (Paris) MS 2234 [copied in 732/1332] it reads: "*Kitāb al-Qaṭr an-Nubātī min maqāṭīʿ ash-shaykh al-imām al-ʿālim al-fāḍil Jamāl ad-Dīn Muḥammad b. Muḥammad b. Nubātah* [...]" (f. 158b).

I had put out [...] a small selection of my long poems * which I presented to have its protracted ideas tested * and then a selection of my *maqāṭīʿ*-poems raised its head * and asked for its turn

17. Ibn Nubātah (d. 768/1366), *Zahr al-manthūr* (*The Gillyflower's Blossoms = The Blossoms of Prose*[56]):[57]

وقد نظم المملوك هذه المقاطع [هكذا] التي هي عن الفايد كاسمها والابيات التي ما تساوي الوقوف على رسمها

The slave composed these *maqāṭīʿ*-poems, which are like the title of a benefit in name [?] and like verses, the traces [of the campsite, but also lit. writing] of which aren't worth stopping to look at

18. Ibn Nubātah (d. 768/1366), *Dīwān* (*Collected Poems*):

[...] المقاطيع والموشّحات والأزجال [...][58]

[...] *maqāṭīʿ*-poems, *muwashshaḥāt*, *zajal* poems [...]

وقال في المقاطيع [...][59]

And from his *maqāṭīʿ*-poems [:]

19. al-Yāfiʿī (d. 768/1366), *Mirʾāt al-janān wa-ʿabrat al-yaqẓān* (*The Heart's Reflection and the Observant One's Tears*), obituary of al-Badīʿ al-Asṭurlābī (d. 534/1139–40):[60]

---

56 Title as translated in Thomas Bauer, "Jamāl al-Dīn Ibn Nubātah" in *Essays in Arabic Literary Biography 1350–1850*, ed. Joseph Lowry and Devin Stewart (Wiesbaden: Harrassowitz, 2009), 184.

57 Chester Beatty Library (Dublin) MS 5161, f. 9a.

58 Nuruosmaniye Library (Istanbul) MS 3802, f. 322a, from a verse of *zajal*: The MS is rather damaged here and fairly illegible but these three forms can be read and are clearly listed together in a set.

59 Nuruosmaniye Library (Istanbul) MS 3802, f. 89b.

60 al-Yāfiʿī, *Mirʾāt al-janān wa-ʿabrat al-yaqẓān*, 4 vols, ed. Khalīl al-Manṣūr (Beirut: Dār al-Kutub al-ʿIlmiyyah, 1417/1997), 3:200.

[...] الشاعر المشهور أحد الأدباء الفضلاء [...] وأثنى عليه غير واحد من المؤرّخين وذكروا له عدّة مقاطيع [...]

[...] The famous poet, one of the excellent litterateurs [...] he was praised by more than one biographer and they cited a number of *maqāṭīʿ*-poems by him [...]

20. Burhān ad-Dīn al-Qīrāṭī (d. 781/1379), *Dīwān* (*Collected Poems*):

[...] اذا أنشد قصايده ☆ ومقاطيعه الباردة[61]

When he recited his long poems * and his banal *maqāṭīʿ*-poems

ولم أقتصر على هذه المطوّلات إلّا أنّه لم يظهر لي عند غيرها طائل فلذلك خرجت من بيوتها إلى كلّ مقطوع داخل[62]

I didn't confine myself to these long [poems] but they didn't appear to me to be long compared to others and then I went from their verses to all the transpiercing *maqāṭīʿ*-poems

تمّ ما انتخبته من ديوان الشيخ برهان الدين القيراطي بحمد الله وعفوه ولم أترك شيئًا من الغزل بل استوعبت مقاطيع وبعض المنثور[63]

This is the end of what I selected from the oeuvre (*Dīwān*) of ash-Shaykh Burhān ad-Dīn al-Qīrāṭī, I praise God and ask his forgiveness[.] I didn't neglect to include any of his love poetry, rather I included the *maqāṭīʿ*-poems and even some prose

21. Ibn Ḥijjah al-Ḥamawī (d. 837/1434), Preface (*khuṭbah*) to his collection of Burhān ad-Dīn al-Qīrāṭī's poetry, *Taḥrīr al-Qīrāṭī* (*The Redaction of al-Qīrāṭī's* [*Dīwān*]):[64]

واخترت من المقاطيع المطربة ما يغني عن المواصيل

61 Fatih Kütüphanesi (Istanbul) MS 3861, f. 3a.

62 Staatsbibliothek zu Berlin MS Wetzstein I 45, f. 20a.

63 Staatsbibliothek zu Berlin MS Wetzstein II 196, f. 79b.

64 Ibn Ḥijjah al-Ḥamawī, *Qahwat al-inshāʾ*, ed. Veselý, 493.

I selected out of his moving *maqāṭīʿ*-poems [or: disconnected things] those which obviate the need for any flutes [*mawāṣīl* or: connected things]

22. ʿAlāʾ ad-Dīn al-Ghuzūlī (d. 815/1412), *Maṭāliʿ al-budūr fī manāzil as-surūr* (*The Rising-Places of Full Moons in the Setting-Places of Joy*), writing about Badr ad-Dīn ad-Damāmīnī (d. 827/1424):[65]

فأخبرنا أنّه في زمن الصبا جمع مقاطيع من الخمريات وسماها مقاطع [هكذا] الشرب

We are told that when he was a young man, he collected his *maqāṭīʿ*-poems on wine and named them *The Drinkers' Portions*

23. Ibn Ḥijjah al-Ḥamawī (d. 837/1434), *Kitāb Kashf al-lithām ʿan wajh at-tawriyah wa-l-istikhdām* (*Removing the Veil From the Face of the Rhetorical Figures* Tawriyah *and* Istikhdām[66]):[67]

[...] وأورد فيه [اي صلاح الدين الصفدي في كتابه فضّ الختام عن التورية والاستخدام] نبذة من مقاطيعه ليس لها بالمراد وصله فإنّه ذكر انواع التورية ☆ وما جسر أنْ يلحق مفردًا من المقاطيع بتلك الجملة

[...] in [his book *Faḍḍ al-khitām ʿan at-tawriyah wa-l-istikhdām*] [Ṣalāḥ ad-Dīn aṣ-Ṣafadī] cited a small selection of his *maqāṭīʿ*-poems [or: disconnected things], which were never intended to be continued [?] because he cited the types of double entendre (*tawriyah*) * so it wouldn't do to cite only one of these *maqāṭīʿ*-poems in this collection

24. Ibn Ḥijjah al-Ḥamawī (d. 837/1434), *Taqrīẓ* (commendation) on Ibn aṣ-Ṣāʾigh's (d. 776/1375) *al-Labābah fī muʿāraḍat «Dīwān aṣ-Ṣabābah»* (*The Keen Mind in imitation of «The Collection of Passionate Love»*):[68]

65 ʿAlāʾ ad-Dīn al-Ghuzūlī, *Maṭāliʿ al-budūr*, 1:185. This is one of many instances of the terms *maqāṭīʿ* and *maqṭūʿ* in that work.

66 Title as translated in Devin Stewart, "Ibn Ḥijjah al-Ḥamawī" in *Essays in Arabic Literary Biography 1350–1850*, ed. Joseph Lowry and Devin Stewart (Wiesbaden: Harrassowitz, 2009), 138.

67 Leiden MS 237, f. 2b. See also ff. 2b; 3a.

68 Ibn Ḥijjah al-Ḥamawī, *Qahwat al-inshāʾ*, ed. Veselý, 407. On the author, see fn. p. 233n44.

وأوصل الشبل بمقاطيع لو أدركها ابن سناء الملك [المتوفَّى سنة ٦٠٨ه‍/١٢١١م]
رجع عن [«]مقطّعات النيل[»] [...]

[A]nd he completed the collection with *maqāṭīʿ*-poems, which if Ibn Sanāʾ al-Mulk [d. 608/1211] had known about them, he would have retracted his «*Nile Coves*»

25. Ibn Ḥijjah al-Ḥamawī (d. 837/1434), chapter heading from *Thamarāt shahiyyah min al-fawākih al-Ḥamawiyyah* (*The Tasty Produce from the Fruits of Hama*):[69]

وقال ايضًا رحمه الله فاطرب بمواصيل مقاطيعه

Also by him—may God have mercy on him—*maqāṭīʿ*-poems whose flutes stir [the soul]

26. Ibn Ḥijjah al-Ḥamawī (d. 837/1434), *Khizānat al-adab wa-ghāyat al-arab* (*The Storehouse of Literature and the Utmost in Erudition*):[70]

ومن محاسن الشيخ زين الدين بن الوردي في باب التورية قوله من مقاطيعه التي هي أحسن من [«]مقطعات النيل[»] وأحلى في الأسماع من نغمات المواصيل وهو

[من المجتث]

إِنْ قُلْتُ قَدُّكِ غُصْنٌ   قَالَتْ لِيَ ٱلْغُصْنُ سَاجِدْ
أَوْ قُلْتُ رِيقُكِ ثَلْجٌ   قَالَتْ تَشَبُّهُ بَارِدْ»

Among our master Zayn ad-Dīn Ibn al-Wardī's wonderful poems including *double entendre* are his *maqāṭīʿ*-poems, which are more excellent than the «*Nile Coves*» and which sound sweeter to the ear than the melodies of flutes. This is one of them:

---

69   Bayerische Staatsbibliothek (Munich), MS cod. arab. 531, f. 30b.
70   Ibn Ḥijjah al-Ḥamawī, *Khizānat al-adab*, ed. Kawkab Diyāb, 3:387.

If I were to say, 'Your body is like the bough of a tree';
She'd say, 'The bough prostrates in prayer.'
If I were to say, 'The taste of your mouth (lit. your saliva) is like ice';
She'd say, 'What a chilly/dull simile!'"

27. Ibn Ḥajar al-ʿAsqalānī (d. 852/1449), *ad-Durar al-kāminah fī aʿyān al-miʾah ath-thāminah* (*The Hidden Pearls: on the notables of the eighth century*):

a. biographical notice on Ibn Nubātah (d. 768/1366):[71]

وله تصانيف رائقة منها القطر النباتي اقتصر فيه على مقاطيع شعره

He wrote lovely books, including *al-Qaṭr an-Nubātī*, in which he limited himself exclusively to his *maqāṭīʿ*-poems

b. biographical notice on Ibn al-Wardī (d. 749/1349):[72]

وله الكلام على مائة غلام مائة مقطوع لطيفة والدراري السارية في مائة جارية مائة مقطوع كذلك

He wrote *Let's Talk Lads* (one hundred delightful *maqāṭīʿ*-poems) and *Brilliant Orbs: one hundred female youths* (also one hundred *maqāṭīʿ*-poems)

c. biographical notice on Badr ad-Dīn Ibn aṣ-Ṣāḥib (d. 788/1386):[73]

ونظم القصائد النبوية وأجاد في المقاطيع

He wrote poems in praise of the Prophet and excelled at *maqāṭīʿ*-poems

71 Ibn Ḥajar, *ad-Durar al-kāminah*, 5:487. Ibn Ḥajar mentions Ibn Nubātah's *Dīwān* in his bibliography (*al-Muʿjam al-mufahras aw tajrīd asānīd al-kutub al-mash'hūrah wa-l-ajzāʾ al-manthūrah*, ed. Muḥammad Shakkūr Amrīr al-Mayādīnī (Beirut: Muʾassasat ar-Risālah, 1418/1998), 418, no. 1942), but he does not mention Ibn Nubātah's epigram anthology, nor that of any other poet, among the few poetry books he lists. Reprised in ash-Shawkānī (d. 1250/1834), *al-Badr aṭ-ṭāliʿ bi-maḥāsin man baʿd al-qarn as-sābiʿ*, ed. Ḥusayn b. ʿAbd Allāh al-ʿAmrī (Damascus: Dār al-Fikr, 1998), 770.

72 Ibn Ḥajar, *ad-Durar al-kāminah*, 3:195. Reprised in ash-Shawkānī, *al-Badr aṭ-ṭāliʿ*, 515.

73 Ibn Ḥajar, *ad-Durar al-kāminah*, 1:248.

28. Ibn Ḥajar al-ʿAsqalānī (d. 852/1449), *Dīwān* (*Collected Poems*) (See discussion above pp. 13–16):[74]

فقد سُئِلْتُ غير مرة أن أجرّد من منظومي طرفًا مهذّبًا وأن أُفْرِدَ من مقاطيعي

التي تُلهي عن المواصيل ماكان منها مُرقِصًا أو مُطرِبًا[75]

More than once, I've been asked to make a refined selection of my poetry and single out my *maqāṭīʿ*-poems, which divert [one's attention] from the flutes (*mawāṣīl*), whether they tremble the heart or enrapture it.

[القسم السابع:] المقاطيع

Chapter Seven: *Maqāṭīʿ*-poems

29. Ibn Ḥajar al-ʿAsqalānī (d. 852/1449), *Inbāʾ al-ghumar bi-anbāʾ al-ʿumar* (*Informing the Uninformed about the Sons of Today*), biographical notice on Khalīl b. Muḥammad al-Aqfahsī (d. 820/1417):[76]

ونظم الشعر الوسط ثمّ جاد شعره في الغربة وطارحني مرارًا بعدّة مقاطيع

He was a mediocre poet, but the poems [he wrote] about being away from home were of a high quality. He and I exchanged a number of *maqāṭīʿ*-poems on several occasions

30. Shams ad-Dīn Muḥammad b. Ḥasan an-Nawājī (d. 859/1455), *Ḥalbat al-kumayt* (*The Racecourse of the Bay*[77]):[78]

74 Ibn Ḥajar, *Dīwān*, Selly Oak Colleges (Birmingham) MS Mingana 1394, f. 1b ; ed. Abū al-Faḍl, 1; idem, *Dīwān as-Sabʿ as-sayyārah an-nayyirāt*, ed. Ayyūb, 78; idem, *Uns al-ḥujar fī abyāt Ibn Ḥajar*, ed. Abū ʿAmr, 333. See also the notes of the copyist of the Dār al-Kutub (Cairo) MS 811 *shiʿr Taymūr* cited in the editor's introduction to *Dīwān as-Sabʿ as-sayyārah an-nayyirāt*, 59–60.

75 Selly Oak Colleges (Birmingham) MS Mingana 1394 gives *muntakhab*^{an} instead of *ṭarf*^{an} *muhadhdhab*^{an} presented above.

76 Ibn Ḥajar, *Inbāʾ al-ghumar*, 3:179–80. Compare also no. 41a below.

77 Title as translated in van Gelder, "A Muslim Encomium on Wine".

78 al-Nawājī, *Ḥalbat al-kumayt*, Leiden MS Or. 89, f. 1b; ibid. (Būlāq: Maṭbaʿat al-Mīriyyah al-ʿĀmirah. 1276/1859), 8; ed. in Fahmy Muḥammad Yousuf Ḥarb, "A Critical Edition of Chapters 1–16 of al-Nawājī's Ḥalbat al-Kumait, with a Critical Introduction" (unpublished doctoral thesis. University of Lancaster, 1976), 1 (which has *maqāṭiʿ*).

[...]أن أجمع له من مقاطيع الشرب نبذة رفيعة البزّ رقيقة الحاشية

[...] to collect for him a fine and elegant selection of *maqāṭīʿ*-poems on wine

31. an-Nawājī (d. 859/1455), *Marātiʿ al-ghizlān fī waṣf al-ḥisān min al-ghilmān* (*The Pastures of Gazelles: describing handsome young men*):[79]

فقد سألني بعض الاخوان أن أجمع له نبذة في الحسان من الغلمان تزهو بجواهر لفظها الفريد على درر النحور وتُزْري عقائد معانيها البديعة بربات الخدور فامتثلت أمره العالي وانتقيت له من عقود اللآلي مقاطيع أطيب في السماع من المواصيل وأعذب في رياض الأدب إذا سالت من [«]مقطّعات النيل[»]

I was asked by one of our friends to put together a selection on handsome young men, the gems of whose matchless language would outshine the pearls of the décolletage and the chains of whose inventive meanings would shame the elegant ladies in their apartments[.] So I obeyed his lofty wish and selected, from the pearl necklaces, *maqāṭīʿ*-poems [or: disconnected things] that are sweeter (*aṭyab*) to the ear than flutes [*mawāṣīl* or: connected things] and sweeter (*aʿdhab*) in the course of literature than the *Nile Coves* if they were to flow

32. From the title page of Escorial MS árabe 340, a copy of an-Nawājī's (d. 859/1455) anthology *Ṣaḥā'if al-ḥasanāt fī waṣf al-khāl* (*Surfaces of Beauty Marked with Descriptions of Beauty-Marks*):[80]

صحائف الحسنات للعلّامة النواجي غفر الله له ما سلف ومحا عنه ما اقترف وهو الذي أبدع في تحصيله أحسن إبداع وأودع صفحاته من محاسن المقاطيع أحسن إيداع [...]

79 Princeton Library MS Garrett Yahuda 4249, f. 1b; Princeton MS Garrett Yahuda 615, f. 2b; Dār al-Kutub (Cairo) MS 583 *Adab*, f. 1b; Dār al-Kutub (Cairo) MS 343 *adab Taymūr*, f. 2b; Topkapi MS 722, f. 1b.

80 an-Nawājī, *Ṣaḥā'if al-ḥasanāt*, ed. ʿAbd al-Hādī, 49; see also reproduction in plate on 46.

Surfaces of Beauty by the great scholar an-Nawājī, may God forgive him for all that has come before and wipe out any [sin] he has committed. He [i.e. an-Nawājī] excelled in making the excellent collection and ordered the pages of outstanding *maqāṭīʿ*-poems in an outstanding order

33. an-Nawājī (d. 859/1455), *Kitāb ash-Shifāʾ fī badīʿ al-iktifāʾ* (*The Cure: excellence in truncation*):

ثمّ خرجت من عنده ونظمت في ذلك اليوم عدّة مقاطيع من هذا النوع[81]

Then I left him and that very day I wrote several *maqāṭīʿ*-poems in that style

ورأيت مقطوعًا للشهاب الحجازي قريبًا من ذلك[82]

I once saw a *maqṭūʿ*-poem by ash-Shihāb al-Ḥijāzī that was similar to this one[83]

34. an-Nawājī (d. 859/1455), *al-Ḥujjah fī sariqāt Ibn Ḥijjah* [*al-Ḥamawī* (d. 837/1434)] (*Proof of Plagiarism: the case of Ibn Ḥijjah al-Ḥamawī*):[84]

[...] غالب مقاطيعه مأخوذة برمّتها من قصائده المطوّلة ولهذا شطّبت على غالبها من ديوانه وكتبت بإزائها تقدّم هذا المقطوع بلفظه في قصيدته الفلانية فلا حاجة إلى تكثير السّواد به

Most of his *maqāṭīʿ*-poems are taken in their entirety from his long poems so I crossed most of them out in [my copy of] his *Dīwān* and wrote beside them: 'The exact text of this *maqṭūʿ*-poem has already appeared in poem X by him, so there's no need to spill more ink for its sake'

and *passim.*

81 an-Nawājī, *Kitāb ash-Shifāʾ fī badīʿ al-iktifāʾ*, ed. ʿAbd al-Hādī, 182.

82 ibid., 183.

83 See further nos 36–9 below.

84 al-Maktabah al-Waṭaniyyah (Rabat) MS 1805 *dāl*, f. 7a; Azhar Library MS 526 - Abāẓah 7122, f. 5b.

35. Burhān ad-Dīn Ibrāhīm b. Aḥmad al-Bāʿūnī, (d. 870/1465), *al-Ghayth al-hātin fī l-ʿidhār al-fātin* (*The Copious Downpour: on alluring beard-down*):[85]

وبعد فقد سألني بعض النجباء ☆ من ظرفاء الادباء ☆ أن املي عليه شيئًا في العذار من حفظي ☆ وأنشده ذلك من لفظي ☆ فلم أستحضر فيه من شيئًا أرتضيه ☆ على ما يوجبه الاختيار ويقتضيه ☆ فسألني أن أنظم فيه ما تسمح به البديهة ☆ وتجود به الفكرة النبيهة ☆ فأنشدته هذه المقاطيع عجلا ☆ ونظمت غالبها مرتجلا

I was asked by one highborn * cultured and refined * to dictate something on the incipient beard to him from memory * and to recite for him my own work * but I couldn't find anything that I found suitable * something [so good] it had to be included * so he asked me to compose something that improvisation would allow * and to which distinguished thought would give generously * so I hurriedly recited these *maqāṭīʿ*-poems to him * most of which I improvised

36. Shihāb ad-Dīn Aḥmad b. Muḥammad al-Ḥijāzī al-Khazrajī (d. 875/1471), *Jannat al-wildān fī l-ḥisān min al-ghilmān* (*The Paradise of Youths: on handsome young men*[86]):[87]

فقد سألني بعض الأصحاب اللطفاء والأصدقاء الظرفاء أن أجمع شيئًا من الأشعار [...] مقيّدًا في ذلك أن تكون من المقاطيع في الحسان من الغلمان حسبما يطلبه أبناء الزمان [...]

85 Staatsbibliothek zu Berlin MS Wetzstein II 177, f. 1b. Compare ch. 17 of al-Badrī's *Ghurrat aṣ-ṣabāḥ*.

86 The first phrase in the title, "*jannat al-wildān*" ("The Paradise of Youths"), is an allusion to Qur'an *al-Wāqiʿah* 56:17 : "*yaṭūfu ʿalayhim wildānun mukhalladūn*" ("immortal youths going round about them", trans. Arberry, *The Koran Interpreted*, 2:254).

87 al-Ḥijāzī al-Khazrajī, *Jannat al-wildān*, ed. Riḥāb ʿAkkāwī (Beirut: Dār al-Ḥarf al-ʿArabī, 1998), 49–50; see also 50n1 for the editor's specious gloss on the use of the term *maqṭūʿ* here. This portion of the text is missing from the Copenhagen MS. On this work, see further in the annotated bibliography: 15th century, 6. b.

One of my kind and refined friends asked me to put together a collection of poetry […] with the condition that the poems be *maqāṭīʿ*-poems on handsome young men, which is what people today are demanding

37. Shihāb ad-Dīn Aḥmad b. Muḥammad al-Ḥijāzī al-Khazrajī (d. 875/1471), *Rawḍ al-ādāb* (*The Garden of Literary Arts*):[88]

الباب الثالث في المقاطيع وفيه عشرة فصول

Part Three: *Maqāṭīʿ*-poems, in ten chapters

38. Shihāb ad-Dīn Aḥmad b. Muḥammad al-Ḥijāzī al-Khazrajī (d. 875/1471), *Nadīm al-ka'īb wa-ḥabīb al-ḥabīb* (*The Sullen one's Companion and the Beloved one's Beloved*):[89]

وبعد فقد أثار من لا أستطيع مخالفة أمره ☆ ولا بقدر لساني على استيفا[ء] شكره ☆ أن أجمع شيئًا من المقاطيع المنتخبة ☆ والأشعار المستعذبة ☆ التي يتشاغل بها المحبّ عن حبيبه

It was mooted by one whom I cannot disobey * and my gratitude to whom my tongue cannot even convey * that I gather together some choice *maqāṭīʿ*-poems * and pleasant verses * that are able to distract a lover from thoughts of his beloved

39. Shihāb ad-Dīn Aḥmad b. Muḥammad al-Ḥijāzī al-Khazrajī (d. 875/1471), *al-Lumaʿ ash-Shihābiyyah min al-burūq al-Ḥijāziyyah* (*Flashes of meteor/ Shihāb in the Ḥijāzī lightning-storm*):[90]

الباب الرابع في المقاطيع وفيه خمسة فصول

Category Four: *Maqāṭīʿ*-poems, in five chapters

---

88 British Library MS Add 19489, f. 52b; Princeton MS Garrett 145H, 91b. See also British Library MS Or. 3843 and MS Add 9562. See further Ḥājjī Khalīfah, *Kashf*, 1:916.

89 Staatsbibliothek zu Berlin MS Or. Oct. 3839, f. 2a.

90 Escorial MS árabe 475, f. 3b.

40. *Taqārīẓ* (commendations) on *Ghurrat aṣ-ṣabāḥ fī waṣf al-wujūh aṣ-ṣibāḥ* (*The Flash of Dawn: beautiful faces described*) by Taqī ad-Dīn ʿAbd Allāh b. ʿAbd Allāh ad-Dimashqī al-Badrī (d. 894/1489):

a. *Taqrīẓ* (commendation) of Sarī ad-Dīn Abū l-Barakāt ʿAbd al-Barr b. Shiḥnah (d. 921/1515), chief Ḥanafī judge of Cairo:[91]

أودعه من المقاطيع ما لوسمعه زاهد [. .] لطرب [وأنشده]

He included therein *maqāṭīʿ*-poems, which if a pious ascetic heard them, his heart would be moved and he'd recite them out loud

b. *Taqrīẓ* (commendation) of Shihāb ad-Dīn Aḥmad b. Muḥammad al-Ḥijāzī al-Khazrajī (d. 875/1471):[92]

فلقد أطربت هذه المقاطيع ما لا تطربه المواصيل

These *maqāṭīʿ*-poems [or: disconnected things] moved [me in ways] that flutes [*mawāṣīl* or: connected things] have not

41. as-Sakhāwī (d. 902/1497), *aḍ-Ḍawʾ al-lāmiʿ li-ahl al-qarn at-tāsiʿ* (*The Shining Light: the people of the ninth century*):

a. biographical notice on Khalīl b. Muḥammad al-Aqfahsī (d. 820/1417):[93]

جاد شعره في الغربة وطارح شيخنا [اي: ابن حجر العسقلاني] مرارًا بعدّة مقاطيع [...]

The poems [he wrote] about being away from home were of a high quality and he exchanged a number of *maqāṭīʿ*-poems with our teacher [i.e. Ibn Ḥajar al-ʿAsqalānī] on several occasions

91 British Library MS ADD 23445, f. 2b.

92 ibid., f. 5a. See also Franz Rosenthal, "Male and Female: described and compared" in *Homoeroticism in Classical Arabic Literature*, ed. J. W. Wright, Jr. and E. K. Rowson (New York, NY: Columbia University Press, 1997).

93 as-Sakhāwī, *aḍ-Ḍawʾ al-lāmiʿ*, 3:203. This entry is part-quotation, part-paraphrase of no. 29 above.

b. biographical notice on Shams ad-Dīn an-Nawājī (see nos 30–4 above):[94]

وامتنع شيخنا [اي: ابن حجر العسقلاني] من الجواب قيل لكون المصنّف [اي: النواجي] أورد له فيه [اي: في كتابه «حلبة الكميت»] مقطوعًا

Our teacher [i.e. Ibn Ḥajar al-ʿAsqalānī] did not respond and people say it is because the author [i.e. an-Nawājī] included a *maqṭūʿ*-poem by the former in his book *Ḥalbat al-kumayt*

c. biographical notice on ʿAlī b. Muḥammad b. Ismāʿīl az-Zamzamī (d. 885/1481):[95]

ومن تآليفه في الأدب [...] ديوان يشتمل على مقاطيع جيدة

His literary works include [...] a collection (*Dīwān*) of first-rate *maqāṭīʿ*-poems

d. biographical notice on Muḥammad b. Ibrāhīm b. Barakah az-Zabīdī (d. c. 811/1408):[96]

[...] ثمّ تعانى بالنظم فمهر فيه وله في ذلك مقاطيع مخترعة

[...] then he took up poetry and excelled in it, and he has some brilliant *maqāṭīʿ*-poems to that effect

e. biographical notice on Yaḥyā b. Muḥammad b. ʿAbd al-Qawī (d. 859/1455):[97]

ولقيته بمكّة فكتبت عنه من نظمه عدّة مقاطيع [...]

I found it in Mecca so I copied out from it several *maqāṭīʿ*-poems by him

94 ibid., 7:230.

95 ibid., 5:291.

96 ibid., 6:251.

97 ibid., 10:250.

f. biographical notice on Yūsuf Ibn Taghrībirdī (d. 874/1470) (see also next item below):[98]

وقد صنّف [...] حلية الصفات في الأسماء والصناعات مشتمل على مقاطيع وتاريخ وادبيات رتّبه على حروف المعجم[99]

He composed [...] *Ḥilyat aṣ-ṣifāt fī l-asmāʾ wa-ṣ-ṣināʿāt*, which is made up of *maqāṭīʿ*-poems, biographical notices, literary materials, and is organized alphabetically

and *passim*.[100]

42. Yūsuf Ibn Taghrībirdī (d. 874/1470), *Ḥilyat aṣ-ṣifāt fī l-asmāʾ wa-ṣ-ṣināʿāt* (*An Ornament of Description on Names and Professions*):

وذكرتُ عدّة مقاطيع من أبيات فصاح[101]

I cited several *maqāṭīʿ*-poems of eloquent verse.

ولم أذكر فيه من القصايد المطوّلات غير قصيدة بارعة ☆ أذكر ذلك في آخر كلّ حرف يكتب بعد فراغ المقاطيع التي أوردتها[102]

I have not cited any long poems except for one outstanding long poem at the end of every alphabetical chapter after the *maqāṭīʿ*-poems I cite.

98 ibid., 10:307–8.

99 This text has been preserved in at least two manuscript copies. One in St. Petersburg (Musée Asiatique (St. Petersburg) MS C 37, 167 ff., copied in 860/1456), where the library declined my request for a copy of the manuscript (Personal communication, 15 May 2013). See A. B. Khalidov, *Arabskie rukopisi instituta vostokovedeniīa : kratkiĭ katalog*, 2 vols (Moscow, 1986), 1:396, no. 8962; see also GAL S II, 40. For this study, I had access to a copy of another MS of the text: Raza Library (Rampur) MS 4373. I finally got a copy of the St. Petersburg MS in June 2017, but this book had already gone to proofs.

100 as-Sakhāwī, *aḍ-Ḍawʾ al-lāmiʿ*, 7:189; 11:40.

101 Ibn Taghrībirdī, *Ḥilyat aṣ-ṣifāt*, Raza Library (Rampur) MS 4373, f. 3b.

102 ibid., f. 4a. See also f. 34a.

43. Yūsuf Ibn Taghrībirdī (d. 874/1470), *an-Nujūm az-zāhirah fī mulūk Miṣr wa-l-Qāhirah* (*The Shining Stars: on the rulers of Egypt and Cairo*):[103]

ووقع في هذا المعنى عدّة مقاطيع جيِّدة في كتابي المسمّى بحلية الصِّفات في الأسماء والصِّناعات [...]

There are a number of good *maqāṭīʿ*-poems on this [literary] figure in my book *Ḥilyat aṣ-ṣifāt fī l-asmāʾ wa-ṣ-ṣināʿāt* (*An Ornament of Description on Names and Professions*) [...]

44. Yūsuf Ibn Taghrībirdī (d. 874/1470), *al-Manhal aṣ-ṣāfī wa-l-mustawfī baʿd al-Wāfī* (*The Pure Fount: fulfilling the promise of «The Passing»*):

a. biographical notice on Shihāb ad-Dīn Ibn Faḍl Allāh al-ʿUmarī (d. 749/1349):[104]

ونظم كثيرًا من القصائد والأراجيز والمقاطيع ودوبيت، وأنشأ كثيرًا من التقاليد والمناشير والتواقيع [...]

"He composed a great many long poems, *rajaz* poems, *maqāṭīʿ*-poems, and *dūbayt* poems, and he wrote a great many apostilles, proclamations, and appointments"

b. biographical notice on aṣ-Ṣafadī (d. 1363):[105]

وله [...] الروض الباسم والعرف الناسم، مقاطيع ونظم؛ والمثاني والمثالث، مقاطيع ونظم ايضًا

He also wrote [...] *ar-Rawḍ al-bāsim wa-l-ʿarf an-nāsim*, *maqāṭīʿ*-poems and verse, and *al-Mathānī wa-l-mathālith*, [which is also] *maqāṭīʿ*-poems and verse

103 Ibn Taghrībirdī, *an-Nujūm az-zāhirah fī mulūk Miṣr wa-l-Qāhirah*, 16 vols (Cairo: al-Muʾassasah al-Miṣriyyah al-ʿĀmmah li-t-Taʾlīf wa-ṭ-Ṭibāʿah wa-n-Nashr, 1963–71), 8:195.

104 Ibn Taghrībirdī, *al-Manhal aṣ-ṣāfī*, 2:264.

105 ibid., 5:243.

45. Ibn al-Jiʿān (d. 882/1477), *Masāyil ad-dumūʿ ʿalā mā tafarraqa min al-majmūʿ* (*The Tracks of Tears: once gathered, now separated*):[106]

الباب الثاني[:] في المقاطيع التي تفيض الدموع فيضًا [...]

Chapter Two: *Maqāṭīʿ*-poems which cause tears to pour out copiously

46. Jalāl ad-Dīn as-Suyūṭī (d. 911/1505), *Raṣf al-laʾāl fī waṣf al-hilāl* (*Inlaid Pearl: descriptions of the crescent moon*):[107]

فإنّي عند مطالعتي لتذكرة الإمام صلاح الدين خليل بن ايبك الصفدي رأيته أورد فيها عدّة مقاطيع من نظمه في وصف الهلال فجردتها في هذا الجزء وضممت اليه عدّة مقاطيع

When I took a look at Ṣalāḥ ad-Dīn Khalīl b. Aybak aṣ-Ṣafadī's *Tadhkirah* [Commonplace Book], I saw that he'd included in it several of his own *maqāṭīʿ*-poems describing the crescent moon so I excerpted these in this portion and added several other *maqāṭīʿ*-poems to them

47. Muḥammad b. Qānṣūh [or: Qānṣawh] b. Ṣādiq (d. 911/1505), *Marātiʿ al-albāb fī marābiʿ al-ādāb* (*The Pastures of Hearts in The Meadows of Literary Arts*):[108]

فهذا مجموع جمعته وانا شابّ مشتغل بعلوم الآداب [...] وسميّته مراتع الالباب في مرابع الآداب وقد رتّبته على اشعار مطوّلات على حروف الهجا ومقاطيع مثلها ومخمّسات وموشّحات وازجال ونثريات من مقامات ومفاخرات وحكايات ووقائع ونوادر ورحلة الإمام الشافعي

106 British Library MS 7591 [=Rieu 638], ff. 21b–22a; unfortunately the chapter itself is missing from the MS.

107 Jalāl al-Dīn as-Suyūṭī, *Raṣf al-laʾāl fī waṣf al-hilāl* in *at-Tuḥfah al-badīʿah wa-ṭ-ṭurfah ash-shahiyyah* (Constantinople: Maṭbaʿat al-Jawāʾib 1302/1884), 66.

108 British Library MS ADD 9677 [=Rieu 770]; quoted in Charles Rieu, *Catalogus codicum manuscriptorum orientalium qui in museo britannico asservantur. Pars secunda, codices Arabicos amplectens* (London: Impensis Curatorum Musei Britannici, 1846), 346.

This is a collection that I put together when I was a young man, busy with my literary training [...] and I named it *The Pastures of Hearts in the Meadows of Literary Arts* and I arranged it into long poems ordered alphabetically, then *maqāṭīʿ*-poems, then *mukhammasāt*, then *muwashshaḥāt*, then *zajal* poems, then prose pieces, including *maqāmāt*, boastings, stories, events, funny anecdotes, and the journey of al-Imām ash-Shāfiʿī

48. Muḥammad b. Qānṣūh [or: Qānṣawh] b. Ṣādiq (d. 911/1505), *ar-Rawḍ al-bahīj fī l-ghazal wa-n-nasīj* (*The Cheerful Garden: on spinning* [*love poems*] *and weaving* [*words*]):[109]

[الباب العشرون] في المقاطيع

Chapter Twenty: *Maqāṭīʿ*-poems

49. ʿUways al-Ḥamawī (d. c. 1516), *Sukkardān al-ʿushshāq wa-manārat al-asmāʿ wa-l-āmāq* (*The Sugar-Pot of Lovers and the Lighthouse for Eyes and Ears*):[110]

من هنا ذكر ما قيل وما ورد من المقاطيع والأشعار فيما يذكر في وصف الكتب واقتنائها

now mention will be made of what *maqāṭīʿ*-poems and poems have been composed describing books and the purchasing of them

50. Māmayah ar-Rūmī, Muḥammad b. Aḥmad b. ʿAbd Allāh (d. 985/1577), *Rawḍat al-mushtāq wa-bahjat al-ʿushshāq* (*The Garden of the Yearner and the Joy of Lovers*):[111]

هذا ديوان قيّم الشام وفارس الميدان في النظام ماميه الرومي [...] وهو يشتمل على قصايد واشعار وموال ودوبيت ومقاطيع وجزل ومدايح وهجا الخ

109 Cited in Gudrun Schubert and Renate Würsch, *Die Handschriften der Universitätsbibliothek Basel. Arabische Handschriften* (Basel: Schwabe & Co., 2001), 69.

110 Bibliothèque Nationale (Paris) MS Arabe 3405, f. 97b.

111 John Rylands Library (Manchester) MS 478 [468], f. 1a; quoted in A. Mingana, *Catalogue of the Arabic Manuscripts in the John Rylands Library, Manchester* (Manchester: The Manchester University Press, 1934), 800. The term *maqṭūʿ* is also used in other MSS of the text (e.g. Staatsbibliothek zu Berlin MS Wetzstein II 163, f. 286a).

This collection of poetry (*Dīwān*) is by the governor of the Levant and the knight of the battlefield in poetry, Māmiyah ar-Rūmī [...] and it is made up of long poems, poems, *mawāliyā*, *dūbayt* poems, *maqāṭīʿ*-poems, *jazal* [scil. *zajal*], praise poems, invective poems, etc.

51. Dāwūd al-Anṭākī (d. 1008/1599), *Tazyīn al-aswāq bi-tafṣīl ashwāq al-ʿushshāq* (*Decorating the Markets: the longing of lovers in great detail/ cut to order*):[112]

تتمّة تشتمل على ذكر مقاطيع فائقة وأبيات رائقة يشير مجموعها إلى جميع الأصول السابقة وتترجم عندهم بالغزل والنسيب لإعراب مضمونها عن نحو محاسن الحبيب [...]

Finale, comprising excellent *maqāṭīʿ*-poems and outstanding verses, all of which allude to the preceding subjects and display them in the form of erotic poems and amatory preludes to give voice to their content that concerns the charms of the beloved [...]

52. anon., untitled 16th-century anthology:[113]

مجموع مبارك يشتمل على أوراد شريفة وأدعية لطيفة وقصائد فائقة ومقاطيع رائقة

A blessed collection comprising venerable Qurʾanic extracts [for recitation] and limpid prayers and outstanding poems and delightful *maqāṭīʿ*-poems

53. Ibn Maʿtūq al-Mūsawī (d. 1087/1676), *Dīwān*:[114]

فكم أتى فيها بأشياء عجيبة ☆ من قصائد كالخرائد في بهائها ☆ ومقاطيع كالفرائد في صفائها

112 Dāwūd al-Anṭākī, *Tazyīn al-aswāq bi-tafṣīl ashwāq al-ʿushshāq* (Cairo: al-Maṭbaʿah al-Azhariyyah, 1319/1901), 220. Compare also no. 76 below.

113 Princeton MS Garrett 168H, f. 5a.

114 Bayerische Staatsbibliothek (Munich), MS cod. arab. 1086, f. 2b.

How many a wondrous idea did he present * long poems as majestic as unbored pearls * and *maqāṭīʿ*-poems as flawless as the most precious pearls

و[الباب] الثالث في أشياء متفرقة من مقاطيع ودوبيت وبنود ومواليات[115]

Chapter Three: Various and sundry *maqāṭīʿ*, *dūbayt*, *band*, and *mawāliyā* poems[116]

54. anon., *Khadīm aẓ-ẓurafāʾ wa-nadīm al-luṭafāʾ* (*The Servant of The Refined and The Companion of The Graceful*) (c. 16th/17th century):[117]

ومقاطيع أحسن من «مقطّعات النيل»[118]

[…] *maqāṭīʿ*-poems better than the «*Nile Coves*»

55. ʿAlāʾ ad-Dīn aṣ-Ṣāliḥī al-Ḥarīrī, *ad-Durr al-maṣūn fī niẓām as-sabʿ funūn* (*The Well Guarded Pearl: composing the Seven* [*Poetic*] *Forms*):[119]

الباب الرابع من المقاطيع في الطيّ والنشر[120]

Chapter Four: *Maqāṭīʿ*-poems [exhibiting] *versus rapportati* (*aṭ-ṭayy wa-n-nashr*)

56. al-Maqqarī (d. 1041/1632), *Nafḥ aṭ-ṭīb min ghuṣn al-Andalus ar-raṭīb* (*The Sweet Scent of Andalusia's Supple Bough*):

---

115 Bayerische Staatsbibliothek (Munich), MS cod. arab. 1086, f. 4a. This chapter runs from ff. 98a–108a of the MS, with the *maqāṭīʿ*-poems appearing on ff. 98a–99b.

116 On the *band*-genre, which Ibn Maʿtūq is said to have invented, see ʿAbdullah Ibrahim, "The Role of the Pre-Modern: the generic characteristics of the *band*" in *Arabic Literature in the Post-Classical Period*, ed. Roger Allen and D. S. Richards (Cambridge: Cambridge University Press, 2006) and Adnan Abbas, *The Band as a New Form of Poetry in Iraq, 17th century* (Poznań: Wydawnictwo Naukowe, 1994).

117 Bodleian Library (Oxford) MS Huntington 508, f. 3a.

118 cf. similar language in the preface to Ibn Ḥabīb's epigram anthology (Bauer, "„Was kann aus dem Jungen noch werden!"", 17).

119 Bodleian Library (Oxford) MS Marsh 73.

120 Bodleian Library (Oxford) MS Marsh 73, f. 61b; this folio is nearly illegible.

[...]فجعلت في ذلك عدّة مقاطيع[121]

[...] so I wrote several *maqāṭīʿ*-poems on that

فجلس المعتمد يومًا على تلك البركة والماء يجري من ذلك الفيل وقد أُوقدت شمعتان من جانبيه والوزير أبو بكر ابن الملح عنده فصنع الوزير فيهما عدّة مقاطيع بديهًا [...][122]

al-Muʿtamid sat beside this pond one day as the water ran out of that elephant and two candles had been lit on either side of it. The chancellor Abū Bakr b. al-Milḥ was there and he improvized several *maqāṭīʿ*-poems

57. Aḥmad b. Aḥmad al-Ānisī (d. c. 1030/1640), *Dīwān* (*Collected Poems*):[123]

وممّا قاله الأديب العلّامة أحمد بن أحمد الآنسي رحمه الله في المقاطيع [...]

Among those *maqāṭīʿ*-poems composed by the excellent litterateur Aḥmad b. Aḥmad al-Ānisī—may God have mercy on him—are [...]

58. Najm ad-Dīn al-Ghazzī (d. 1061/1651), *al-Kawākib as-sāʾirah bi-ʾayʿān al-miʾah al-ʿāshirah* (*The Moving Planets: on the notables of the tenth century*), biographical notice on Muḥammad Abū l-Fatḥ al-Mālikī (d. 975/1567):[124]

وكان مغاليًا في نصرة القهوة المتّخذة من البنّ غير منكر له وله فيها مقاطيع مشهورة [...]

121 al-Maqqarī, *Nafḥ aṭ-ṭīb min ghuṣn al-Andalus ar-raṭīb*, 8 vols, ed. Iḥsān ʿAbbās (Beirut: Dār Ṣādir, 1988), 2:467.

122 ibid., 4:263. See also in al-Azdī, *Badāʾiʿ*, 373 (see also above p. 51).

123 Princeton MS Garrett Yahuda 805, f. 60b. The *maqāṭīʿ*-section runs from ff. 60b–64b in the MS.

124 al-Ghazzī, *al-Kawākib as-sāʾirah bi-ʾayʿān al-miʾah al-ʿāshirah*, 3 vols, ed. Khalīl al-Manṣūr (Beirut: Dār al-Kutub al-ʿIlmiyyah, 1418/1997), 3:20. It seems from al-Ghazzī's report that Muḥammad Abū l-Fatḥ was quite a character. In addition to coffee, he was fond of opium—occasionally falling asleep in lessons because he was high—and he "did not shy away from the company of handsome young novices" (ibid., 3:19–20).

He was extreme in his defense of the strong drink (*qahwah*) that is made from coffee beans (i.e. coffee), and was in no way reproachful of it. He [even] wrote some *maqāṭīʿ*-poems about it, which became famous […]

and *passim*.

59. Ḥājjī Khalīfah (Kâtib Çelebi) (d. 1068/1657), *Kitāb Kashf aẓ-ẓunūn ʿan asāmī al-kutub wa-l-funūn* (*Unveiling Surmises: on the names of books*):

منتهى الطلب من أشعار العرب – لابن ميمون «هو علي بن ميمون بن الحسين المالكي الفاسي المتوفى سنة ٩١٧» وهو كتاب يشتمل على أكثر من ألف قصيدة خلا المقاطيع وعدّة ما فيه أربعون ألف بيت

Muntahā ṭ-ṭalab min ashʿār al-ʿArab [(*The Ultimate Wish: on the poetry of the Arabs*)] by Ibn Maymūn [editors: that is ʿAlī b. Maymūn b. al-Ḥusayn al-Mālikī al-Fāsī, who died in 917/1511]. This book comprises more than one thousand long-poems—not counting the *maqāṭīʿ*-poems in it—and a total of 40,000 lines of verse

and *passim*.

60. anon., untitled 17th-century poetry collection:[125]

فصل في المقاطيع

A Chapter of *Maqāṭīʿ*-poems

61. ʿAbd al-Qādir b. ʿUmar al-Baghdādī (d. 1093/1682), *Khizānat al-adab wa-lubb lubāb «Lisān al-ʿArab»* (*The Storehouse of Literature and the Core of the «Arabic Language»*):[126]

وعندي في هذا المعنى مقاطيع جيّدة لولا خشية السأم لسردتها

I wrote [some] good *maqāṭīʿ*-poems on this motif and were it not for the fear of boring you, I would have related them here

125 Staatsbibliothek zu Berlin MS Sprenger 1239, f. 174a.

126 al-Baghdādī, *Khizānat al-Adab wa-lubb lubāb «Lisān al-ʿArab»*, 13 vols, ed. ʿAbd as-Salām Muḥammad Hārūn (Cairo: Dār al-Kātib al-ʿArabī li-ṭ-Ṭibāʿah wa-n-Nashr, 1967–), 5:256.

62. ʿAlī b. Muḥammad al-Makkī (fl. c. 1100/1688), *Nadīm al-mustahām wa-rawḍat ahl al-ʿishq wa-l-gharām* (*The Companion of the Love-crazed and the Garden of the People of Passion and Romance*):[127]

[…] وأحببت أن أعمل مجموعًا مفردًا فيه ما رقّ وراق ☆ من المطوّلات الفائقة ☆ والمقاطيع الرائقة […]

I desired to make a singular collection of the delicate and exquisite * out of splendid long poems * and fine *maqāṭīʿ*-poems

63. Anonymous editor of Ibn Maṭrūḥ's (d. 649/1251) *Dīwān* (*Collected Poems*), Staatsbibliothek zu Berlin MS Sprenger 1127–3:[128]

قصائد كالخرائد في بهائها ومقاطيع كالفرائد في صفائها

Poems as brilliant as unbored pearls and *maqāṭīʿ*-poems as pure as precious pearls/gems

64. ʿUthmān aṭ-Ṭāʾifī ash-Shāfiʿī (17th century), *Kitāb Maḥāsin al-laṭāʾif wa-raqāʾiq aẓ-ẓarāʾif* (*The Book of Pleasant Pleasantries and Delicate Delicacies*):[129]

الباب الثاني في المقاطيع والمواليات ودوبيت

Chapter Two: *Maqāṭīʿ*, *Mawāliyā*, and *Dūbayt* poems

65. Ibn Maʿṣūm (d. 1130/1707), *Sulāfat al-ʿaṣr fī maḥāsin ash-shuʿarāʾ bi-kull maṣr*[130] (*The First Pressing of The Age/Press: on the achievements of poets in every land*), in an entry on al-Mawlā Aḥmad b. Shāhīn ash-Shāmī:[131]

---

127 Staatsbibliothek zu Berlin MS Petermann II 654, f. 2a.

128 Edited in Ibn Maṭrūḥ, *Dīwān*, ed. Jawdah Amīn (Cairo: Dār ath-Thaqāfah al-ʿArabiyyah, 1989), 63–4. On the MS, see Wilhelm Ahlwardt, *Die Handschriften-Verzeichnisse der königliche Bibliotheken zu Berlin. Verzeichniss der arabischen Handschriften* (Berlin, 1887–99), 7:30–1, no. 7755.

129 Staatsbibliothek zu Berlin MS Or. Oct. 3355, f. 51b.

130 I have modified the conventional vocalization of the word *miṣr* (garrison; country; Cairo; Egypt) for the sake of the rhyming pair.

131 Ibn Maʿṣūm, *Sulāfat al-ʿaṣr fī maḥāsin ash-shuʿarāʾ bi-kull maṣr*, Berlin MS Petermann I 630, f. 319a; [printed ed. (Cairo: Aḥmad Nājī al-Jamālī wa-Muḥammad Amīn al-Khānjī,

ولقد انقطع الثلج أيّام الخريف وكانت الحاجة اليه شديدة بعد غيبة سيّدي عن دمشق فتذكّرت شغف شيخي به فزاد على فقده غرامي ☆ فاض عليه تعطّشي وأوامي ☆ فجعلت في ذلك عدّة مقاطيع وأحببت عرضها على سيّدي

[...]

At one point in the autumn, all the ice melted [or: it stopped snowing] and there was a considerable need for it [at the time] after my master had departed Damascus. I recalled my teacher's longing for it [i.e. ice] and this added the feeling of passionate longing to my feelings of loss * My thirst, my burning thirst, for him was too much for me * so I wrote a few *maqāṭīʿ*-poems about that [incident] as I had hoped to show them to my master [...]

66. Shihāb ad-Dīn Aḥmad b. Muḥammad al-Ḥaymī al-Kawkabānī (1073–c. 1151 / 1663–c. 1738), *Ḥadāʾiq an-nammām fī l-kalām ʿalā mā yataʿallaq bi-l-ḥammām* (*Gardens of Wild Thyme: everything there is to know about the bathhouse*):[132]

وقد نظمت أنا في ذلك مقطوعًا بناء على هذا الأصل فقلت

[من السريع]

يا صاحِ خَلِّ ٱلرَّاحَ في مَعْزِلِ أَفْلَحَ مَنْ عَنْ سُكْرِهِ قد صَحا
إِنْ كُنْتَ مِمَّنْ يَشْتَهي نَعْمَةً فبادِرِ ٱلحَمَّامَ وَقْتَ ٱلضُّحَى »

I myself composed a *maqṭūʿ*-poem, riffing on this original, and this is it:

Listen, my friend, leave the wine alone.
He who recovers from his drunkenness is blessed.
If you're someone who desires prosperity,
then get yourself to the bathhouse early in the day!

1324/1906)], 378. On this work, see further in the annotated bibliography: 18th century, 1. a.

132 al-Ḥaymī al-Kawkabānī, *Ḥadāʾiq al-nammām fī l-kalām ʿalā mā yataʿallaq bi-l-ḥammām*, ed. ʿAbd Allāh Muḥammad al-Ḥibshī (Beirut: Dār at-Tanwīr, 1986), 79.

67. anon., Title of an untitled poetry collection:[133]

هذا مجموع لطيف حاوي [هكذا] لكل معنى ظريف يشتمل على قصائد ومقاطيع ودوبيت ومواليات وموشحات من كلام البلغا[ء] المتقدمين وحكايات لطيفة ونكت ظريفة

This is a pleasant collection containing all charming literary figures, which includes long poems, as well as *maqāṭīʿ*, *dūbayt*, *mawāliyā*, and *muwashshaḥāt* poems by the rhetoricians of old, as well as pleasant stories and charming witticisms.

68. *Taqrīẓ* (commendation) by Aḥmad b. ʿAlī al-Manīnī (d. 1172/1759) for a *risālah* on the relative merits of beardless and bearded boys by Saʿīd b. Muḥammad b. Aḥmad ash-Shāfiʿī ad-Dimashqī, known as Ibn as-Sammān (d. 1178/1759):[134]

وحوت من ابكار المعاني كل معنى مبتكر ☆ ومن بنات الافكار ما عقمت عن مثله الفكر ☆ ومن غرر المقاطيع ما تتزين به لبات المحاضر ☆ ويترنم به كل باد وحاضر

It contains rhetorical figures unspoilt, like virgins * and other thoughts are barren when compared to the daughters of its thoughts [i.e. its ideas] * its exquisite *maqāṭīʿ*-poems adorn the chests of the assembled * and all who can be seen and are present sing along

69. Muḥammad Khalīl al-Murādī (d. 1206/1791), *Silk ad-durar fī aʿyān al-qarn ath-thānī ʿashar* (*Stringing Pearls: on the notables of the twelfth century*):

---

133 Gotha MS Orient A 2211, f. 1a.

134 Staatsbibliothek zu Berlin MS Wetzstein II 140, f. 150a. On the MS, see Ahlwardt, *Die Handschriften-Verzeichnisse der königliche Bibliotheken zu Berlin. Verzeichniss der arabischen Handschriften*, 6:506–7, no. 7428. This work by Saʿīd b. as-Sammān was known to al-Murādī and is oft mentioned in his *Silk ad-durar*. On the author of the *taqrīẓ*, see al-Murādī, *Silk ad-durar*, 1:153–66.

a. biographical notice on Abū l-Futūḥ ad-Dabbāgh al-Mīqātī (d. 1174/1760):[135]

وكان شعره رائقًا نضيرًا وله مقاطيع وموشّحات وغير ذلك

His poetry was excellent and fresh, and he wrote *maqāṭīʿ*-poems and *muwashshaḥāt* among other things

b. biographical notice on Ibrāhīm al-Murādī (d. 1142/1730):

وفي ذلك مقاطيع شعرية صدرت من أدباء [...][136]

There are *maqāṭīʿ*-poems by littérateurs on this topic [...]

وفي ذلك غير ما ذكرنا من المقاطيع [...][137]

On this topic there are *maqāṭīʿ*-poems that we have not mentioned

70. Muḥammad Kamāl ad-Dīn al-Ghazzī (d. 1214/1799), biographical notice on Muḥammad b. Aḥmad Imām ad-Dīn al-Kanjī (d. 1153/1740) in the biography of his teacher ʿAbd al-Ghanī an-Nābulusī (d. 1143/1731):[138]

وله [اي: الكنجي] مؤلّفات كثيرة معظمها في الأدب فمنها رسالة سمّاها برضوان المحبوب ومفرّح القلوب جمع فيها تضامين لأفاضل ذلك العصر في ماء حبّ الآس وعرضها على الاستاذ [اي: النابلسي] فكتب له بخطّه جملة من المقاطيع الشعرية [...]

He [i.e. al-Kanjī] [wrote] many books, most of which fall under [the category of] literature. Among these are an epistle by the title *Pleasing*

135 al-Murādī, *Silk ad-durar*, 3:248.

136 ibid., 1:32.

137 ibid., 1:36.

138 *al-Wird al-unsī wa-l-wārid al-qudsī fī tarjamat al-ʿārif ʿAbd al-Ghanī an-Nābulusī*, ed. Samer Akkach in Samer Akkach, *Intimate Invocations. Al-Ghazzī's Biography of ʿAbd al-Ghanī al-Nābulusī (1641–1731)* (Leiden: Brill, 2012), 163 (Arabic). See also al-Murādī, *Silk ad-durar*, 1:31. [NB: Strictly speaking, one would expect "*qudusī*" for the *sajʿ* rhyme with the final element "*al-Nābulusī*" but just as today one would more likely have pronounced the name "*al-Nābulsī*"].

the Beloved and Delighting Hearts in which he collected the quotations (*taḍāmīn*) of his contemporaries on the juice of myrtle berries.[139] When he showed this to the Teacher [i.e. al-Nābulusī], he then wrote a set of *maqāṭīʿ*-poems in his own hand for him

71. anon., *ad-Durar al-fāʾiqah fī l-maqāṭīʿ ar-rāʾiqah* (*The Excellent Pearls: on marvelous* Maqāṭīʿ*-poems*):[140]

وسمّيته الدُّرر الفائقة في المقاطيع الرائقة فحكى الدُّرّ اليتيم والعقد النَّظيم

I gave [my work] the title *The Outstanding Pearls of Delightful* Maqāṭīʿ*-poems*, and it resembles the rarest of pearls and a well-strung necklace[141]

72. Aḥmad b. Muḥammad al-Anṣārī al-Yamanī ash-Shirwānī (d. 1253/1837), *Nafḥat al-Yaman fīmā yazūl bi-dhikrih ash-shajan* (*The Yemeni Breeze that Removes all Grief*):[142]

الباب الثالث يشتمل على مقاطيع جيّدة وقصائد رائقة انتخبتها من الدّواوين التي عثرت عليها [...]

Chapter Three: comprising high-quality *maqāṭīʿ*-poems and wonderful long poems, which I selected from the volumes of *Collected Poems* that I have come across

73. Shihāb ad-Dīn Muḥammad b. Ismāʿīl b. ʿUmar (d. 1274/1857), *Safīnat al-mulk wa-nafīsat al-fulk* (*The Ship/Safīnah of Sovereignty and the Gem of the Ark*), a song collection:[143]

---

139 See pp. 94–117 above.

140 Princeton MS Garrett Yahuda 5902, f. 79b.

141 There is a collection of poetry with the title *ad-Durr al-yatīm wa-l-ʿiqd an-naẓīm* (*The Rarest of Pearls and a Well-Strung Necklace*) by the anthologist Ḥaydar b. Sulaymān al-Ḥillī (d. 1304/1886) (see no. 75), but it seems to have been written after the anonymous anthology cited here. Yet because the anonymous anthology is undated and its author unknown, we cannot be certain of this.

142 ash-Shirwānī, *Nafḥat al-Yaman fīmā yazūl bi-dhikrih ash-shajan* (Cairo: Maṭbaʿat at-Taqaddum, 1324/1906), 79.

143 Shihāb ad-Dīn Ibn ʿUmar, *Safīnat al-mulk wa-nafīsat al-fulk* (Cairo: Maṭbaʿat al-Jāmiʿah, 1309/1891 [repr. Ser. *adh-Dhakhāʾir*, Cairo: al-Hayʾah al-ʿĀmmah li-Quṣūr ath-Thaqāfah, 2010]), 4; 363. See further in Reynolds, "Lost Virgins Found", 75n.

المجداف الثاني فيما يعذب إيراده من المقاطيع الرائقة

Chapter (lit. oar, *mijdāf*) Two: Excellent *maqāṭīʿ*-poems that are easily cited

74. Aḥmad b. ʿAbd ar-Raḥīm al-ʿAṭṭārī (fl. 13th/19th c.), untitled poetry collection:[144]

أذكر نبذةً من مستسهل كلامي ☆ مشتملة على قصار قصائد ☆ ومقاطيع متواصلة الفوائد

I present a selection of my most readable verse * in the form of short poems * and edifying *maqāṭīʿ*-poems

75. Ḥaydar b. Sulaymān al-Ḥillī (d. 1304/1886), Title Page of *Dīwān ad-Durr al-yatīm wa-l-ʿiqd an-naẓīm* (*The Rarest of Pearls and a Well-Strung Necklace*):[145]

هذا هو الدِّيوان الشَّريف والجمع المنيف المسمَّى بالدرّ اليتيم والعقد النَّظيم المشتمل على القصائد والمراثي والمقاطيع والمكاتبات [...]

This is the honorable poetic collection and exalted compilation known as *The Rarest of Pearls and a Well-Strung Necklace*, which includes long poems, dirges, *maqāṭīʿ*-poems, and literary correspondence [...]

76. Muḥammad Ṣiddīq Ḥasan Khān (Nawab of Bhopal, d. 1890) *Nashwat as-sakrān min ṣahbāʾ tadhkār al-ghizlān* (*The Intoxication of the One Inebriated by the Red Wine of the Remembrance of Gazelles*):[146]

للشُّعراء [«]مقاطيع فائقة وأبيات رائقة يشير مجموعها إلى جميع

144 Dār al-Kutub (Cairo) MS 4028 *adab*, f. 1b; Dār al-Kutub (Cairo) MS 4029 *adab*, f. 1b.

145 Ḥaydar al-Ḥillī, *Dīwān ad-Durr al-yatīm wa-l-ʿiqd an-naẓīm* (Bombay: al-Ḥājj Shaykh ʿAlī al-Maḥallātī, 1312/1894), title page.

146 Muḥammad Ṣiddīq Ḥasan Khān, *Nashwat as-sakrān min ṣahbāʾ tadhkār al-ghizlān* (Bhopal: al-Maṭbaʿah ash-Shāh-Jahānī, 1294/1877 [repr. al-Khurunfish, Cairo: al-Maṭbaʿah ar-Raḥmāniyyah, 1338/1920]), 108. The author is quoting directly from Dāwūd al-Anṭākī's *Tazyīn al-aswāq* here (compare no. 51 above). See also ibid., 123.

الأصول السابقة وتترجم عندهم بالغزل والنَّسيب لإعراب مضمونها عن
نحو محاسن الحبيب[»] [...]

The poets have written "excellent *maqāṭīʿ*-poems and outstanding verses, all of which allude to the preceding subjects and display them in the form of erotic poems and amatory preludes to give voice to their content that concerns the charms of the beloved" [...]

77. Aḥmad Taymūr Bāshā (1871–1930), *al-Ḥubb wa-l-jamāl ʿind al-ʿArab* (*Love and Beauty among the Arabs*), collected notes published posthumously, from the introduction:[147]

فهذا مجموع يشتمل على فصول تحوي مقاطيع رائقة وقصائد فائقة من كلّ لفظ
بديع ومعانٍ كأنّها زهر الربيع

This collection [is organized into] chapters and includes excellent *maqāṭīʿ*-poems and superior long poems, [which display] innovative expressions and literary motifs that resemble spring flowers

78. anon., early 19th-century untitled anthology:[148]

الباب الثالث في المقاطيع

Chapter Three: *Maqāṭīʿ*-poems

147 Aḥmad Taymūr Bāshā, *al-Ḥubb wa-l-jamāl ʿind al-ʿArab* (Cairo: ʿĪsā al-Bābī al-Ḥalabī wa-shurakāhu, 1391/1971), 3.

148 Gotha MS Orient A 2175, f. 4a. Chapter Three takes up ff. 50a–59b in the MS.

Annotated Bibliography of Unpublished Sources

The following is a detailed overview of the unpublished sources used to prepare this study (including texts for which no critical edition exists). This is not an exhaustive list of all relevant texts, rather only those cited in the present study. Here they are presented chronologically, but they can also be found in the list of sources below organized alphabetically by author.

12th century

1. Ibn al-Qaysarānī (478–548/1085–1153)

   a. *Dīwān* (*Collected Poems*)
      i. Dār al-Kutub (Cairo) MS 1484 *Adab*, 41 ff., n.d.

13th century

1. Abū ʿAlī al-Ḥasan b. ʿAlī b. Khalaf al-Qurṭubī (d. 602/1205)

   See *GAL* S I 596.

   a. *Rawḍat al-azhār wa-bahjat an-nufūs wa-nuzhat al-abṣār* (*The Flower-Garden, the Soul's Delight, and the Vision's Amusement*)
      i. Chester Beatty Library (Dublin) MS 4601, 212 ff., n.d. (8th/14th century copy).

      See Arthur J. Arberry, *The Chester Beatty Library. A Handlist of the Arabic Manuscripts,* 8 vols (Dublin: Hodges, Figgis & co., ltd., 1964), 6:31, no. 4601.

2. Ibn ash-Sharīf Daftarkh^{w}ān al-Ḥusaynī al-Mūsawī aṭ-Ṭūsī, ʿAlī b. Muḥammad (4 Ṣafar 579–655/1183–1257)

   See *GAL* I 352; (the remarks on *GAL* I 286 are erroneous; see Talib, "Pseudo-Ṯaʿālibī's *Book of Youths*", 604–5); aṣ-Ṣafadī, *al-Wāfī*, 21:466–70.

   a. *Kitāb Alf ghulām wa-ghulām* (*One Thousand and One Young Men*)

      This text has not yet been published and survives uniquely in an Escorial MS, which I have used for the purposes of this study.

      i. Escorial MS árabe 461, 126 ff., n.d.

See Hartwig Derenbourg, *Les manuscrits arabes de l'Escurial* (Paris, 1884 [repr. Hildesheim: Georg Olms Verlag, 1976]), 303–4.

b. *Kitāb Alf jāriyah wa-jāriyah* (*One Thousand and One Young Women*), written before 654/1256.

This text has not yet been published and survives uniquely in a Vienna MS, which I have used for the purposes of this study.

i. Vienna MS 387, 255 ff. This MS includes a *samāʿah* certificate for one Ibrāhīm b. ʿUmar b. ʿAbd al-ʿAzīz al-Qurashī, who heard the book from the author himself; the series of lectures ended on 2 Muḥarram 654 (January 1256).

See Gustav Flügel, *Die arabischen, persischen und türkischen Handschriften der kaiserlich-königlichen Hofbibliothek zu Wien*, 3 vols (Vienna: kaiserliche-königliche Hof- und Staatsdruckerei, 1865), 1:362–62, no. 387. See also Weil, *Mädchennamen, verrätselt* and also Jürgen W. Weil, "Girls from Morocco and Spain: selected poems from an *adab* collection of poetry", *Archív Orientální* 52 (1984).

3. Saʿd ad-Dīn Muḥammad b. Muḥammad b. ʿAlī Ibn al-ʿArabī (618–656 /1221 1258)

See Muḥsin Jamāl ad-Dīn, "*Dīwān Saʿd ad-Dīn Ibn ʿArabī al-Andalusī*".

a. *Dīwān* (*Collected Poems*)

i. British Library MS 3866, 102ff., n.d.

ii. Princeton Library MS Garrett 40H, 73 ff., n.d.

See Philip K. Hitti et al., *Descriptive Catalog of the Garrett collection of Arabic manuscripts in the Princeton University Library* (Princeton, NJ: Princeton University Press, 1938), 21, no. 54.

iii. Princeton Library MS Garrett 41H, 50 ff., n.d.

See Hitti et al., *Descriptive Catalog*, 21, no. 55.

iv. Dār al-Kutub (Cairo) MS 11156 *zāʾ*, 59 ff., n.d.

14th century

1. Hindūshāh b. Sanjar al-Jayrānī (c. 1308).

See *GAL* II 192, S II 256.

a. *Mawārid al-ādāb* (*The Wellsprings of the Literary Arts*), written c. 707/1308

This anthology of poetry (divided into ten chapters, *mawārid*) has not yet been published. For the purposes of this study, I have relied on an autograph MS kept in the British Library.

i. British Library MS ADD 23978, 153 ff., autograph, copied in 707/1308 in Tabriz.

See C. Rieu, *Catalogus* (1846), 653–54, no. 1420. See also *GAL* II 192, S II 256.

2. Ṣafī ad-Dīn ʿAbd al-ʿAzīz b. Sarāyā al-Ḥillī (5 Rabīʿ al-Ākhir 677–c. 750/1278–1350)

See *GAL* II 159–60, S II 199–200; aṣ-Ṣafadī, *al-Wāfī*, 18:481–512; al-Kutubī, *Fawāt*, 2:335. Ibn Ḥabīb, *Tadkhirat an-nabīh*, 2:216; 3:138; Ibn Taghrībirdī, *an-Nujūm az-zāhirah*, 10:238–39; Ibn Iyās, *Badāʾiʿ az-zuhūr fī waqāʾiʿ ad-Duhūr*, 6 vols, ed. Paul Kahle, Muḥammad Muṣṭafā, and Moritz Sobernheim (Wiesbaden: in Kommission bei Franz Steiner Verlag, 1931–32), vol. 1, pt. 1, 526–27.

a. *Dīwān al-Mathālith wa-l-mathānī fī l-maʿālī wa-l-maʿānī* (*The Collection of Two-liners and Three-liners on Virtues and Literary Motifs*), written between 1331–1341.[1]

---

1 On the dating of this work's composition, see Bauer, "„Was kann aus dem Jungen noch werden!"", 19. On numerical descriptive terms for poem length: *mathānī, mathālith* (see also an-Nawājī, *Marātiʿ al-ghizlān fī waṣf al-ḥisān min al-ghilmān*, MS Topkapı (Istanbul) MS 722, f. 2a, l.5; Dār al-Kutub (Cairo) MS 343 *adab Taymūr*, f. 2b, l. 10); Ibn Ḥijjah al-Ḥamawī, *Qahwat al-inshāʾ*, 332, l. 13; *muʿashsharāt* (see e. g. al-Murādī, *Silk ad-durar*, 1:73; Ibn Ḥabīb, *Tadhkirat an-nabīh*, 2:270), as well as Ibn Nubātah's collection (subsumed in his *Dīwān*) *as-Sabʿ as-sayyārah*. See also the anthology *al-Muqtaṭaf min azāhir al-ṭuraf* by Ibn Saʿīd al-Andalusī, ed. Sayyid Ḥanafī Ḥasanayn (Cairo: al-Hayʾah al-Miṣriyyah al-ʿĀmmah li-l-Kitāb, 1983) with chapters on single lines (*al-abyāt al-mufradah*), two-liners (*al-abyāt al-muzdawajah*), three-liners (*al-abyāt al-muthallathah*) and on up to twelve-liners (*al-abyāt al-ithnā ʿashariyyah*) and the 12th/18th-century anthology of ten-line poems called *al-Muʿashsharāt* by ʿAbd al-Ghanī an-Nābulusī (Ẓāhiriyyah Library (Damascus) MS 4393 described in ʿAzzah Ḥasan, *Fihris Makhṭūṭāt Dār al-Kutub aẓ-Ẓāhiriyyah. ash-Shiʿr* (Damascus: al-Majmaʿ al-ʿIlmī al-ʿArabī, 1384/1964), 378–79) and Abū Zayd ʿAbd ar-Raḥmān al-Ghazzāzī al-Andalusī's collection titled *al-Qaṣāʾid al-ʿishrīniyyah fī n-naṣāʾiḥ ad-dīniyyah wa-l-ḥikam adh-dhahabiyyah* (University of Ibadan (Nigeria) MS [unseen]; see entry in aṭ-Ṭayyib ʿAbd ar-Raḥīm Muḥammad, *al-Makhṭūṭāt al-ʿarabiyyah fī Nījīriyā al-Ittiḥādiyyah*, edited and abridged by Khālid ʿAbd al-Karīm Jumʿah (Kuwait: Manshūrāt Maʿhad al-Makhṭūṭāt al-ʿArabiyyah, 1406/1985), 68). NB: *mukhammas* does not mean a five-line poem, rather it is a form of emulation in which a poet adds a fifth line to a pre-existing poem divided into quatrains. I have also seen numerical terms used in Ottoman Turkish poetry: in the *Dīvān* of Muṣṭafā Kamāl Ummī [Bodleian Library (Oxford) MS Turk. d. 51, ff. 115b–116b] there is a series of a few epigrammatic poems at the end of the *dīvān*. These are presented under headings like

No critical edition of this anthology exists. A poor (and expurgated) edition of the text was published in Damascus in 1998. For the purposes of this study, I have relied on a significant Paris MS written during the poet's lifetime, which the editor of the Damascus edition did not consult. The anthology was dedicated to al-Ḥillī's patron in Hama, al-Malik al-Afḍal (r. 1332–41), and this informs the conjectured dating of the work.

i. Paris MS 3341, ff. 1a–52b. The MS includes an *ijāzah* for one of the author's students in the author's own hand and is dated 743/1342.

See baron de Slane, *Catalogue des manuscrits arabes* (Paris: Imprimerie nationale, 1893–95), 584, no. 3341.

ii. Edition by Muḥammad Ṭāhir al-Ḥimṣī, Damascus: Dār Saʿd ad-Dīn, 1419/1998. Al-Ḥimṣī based his edition on Ẓāhiriyyah Library (Damascus) MS 3361, 43 ff., copied in 1002/1593.

3. aṣ-Ṣafadī, Ṣalāḥ ad-Dīn Khalīl b. Aybak (696–764/1297–1363)

See, *inter alia*, Rowson, "al-Ṣafadī"; Muḥammad ʿAbd al-Majīd Lāshīn, *aṣ-Ṣafadī wa-āthāruh fī l-adab wa-n-naqd* (Cairo: Dār al-Āfāq al-ʿArabiyyah, 2004).

a. *al-Ḥusn aṣ-ṣarīḥ fī miʾat malīḥ* (*Pure Beauty: on one hundred handsome lads*), written c. 1337.

A collection of 205 *maqāṭīʿ*-poems on one-hundred male youths (with two MSS including an addendum of seven *maqāṭīʿ*-poems). The text was published for the first time by Aḥmad Fawzī al-Hayb in 2003.

i. Edition by Aḥmad Fawzī al-Hayb (Damascus: Dār Saʿd ad-Dīn, 1424/2003). Al-Hayb based his edition on four MSS: (1) Dār al-Kutub (Cairo) MS 5120 *ādāb*, 35 ff., copied in 738/1337, autograph; (2) Ẓāhiriyyah Library (Damascus) MS 5657, copied in 1321/1903 (the editor believes this MS was copied from an autograph MS); (3) Aya Sofya (Istanbul) MS 3177, n.d.; and (4) British Library MS Or. 3776_1 (see also no. iii below).

See also Fuʾād Sayyid, *Fihrist al-makhṭūṭāt al-muṣawwarah* (Cairo: Dār al-Riyāḍ li-ṭ-Ṭabʿ wa-n-Nashr, 1954), 1:444.

ii. Princeton MS Garrett Yahuda 935, ff. 59b–83b, copied in 773/1371 in Malatya. Al-Hayb did not use this MS to prepare his edition.

See Rudolf Mach, *Catalogue of Arabic Manuscripts (Yahuda section) in the Garrett Collection, Princeton University Library* (Princeton, NJ: Princeton University Press, 1977), 363, no. 4245.

---

murabbaʿ, *musaddas*, and *muthamman*, with the poems being four, six, and eight hemistichs long respectively. These poems are written two hemistichs to a line in the MS (as *dūbayt* and *rubāʿī* poems usually are).

iii. British Library MS Or. 3776_1, ff. 1a–25b, copied in 1079/1668.

See Charles Rieu, *Supplement to the catalogue of the Arabic manuscripts in the British Museum* (London, 1894), 702, no. 1112.

b. *Alḥān as-sawājiʿ bayn al-bādī wa-l-murājiʿ* (*Tunes of Cooing Doves, between the Initiator and Responder* [*in Literary Correspondence*][2]) [collection of correspondence], written c. 1353.

"[…] collection of a lifetime of [aṣ-Ṣafadī's] literary correspondence […]".[3] There are two printed editions of this work. I have relied on these as well as an autograph MS of volume three preserved in the Staatsbibliothek zu Berlin (no. ii below).

i. Edition by Muḥammad ʿAbd al-Ḥamīd Sālim, 2 vols (Cairo: al-Hayʾah al-Miṣriyyah al-ʿĀmmah li-l-Kitāb, 2005). Sālim based his edition on five MSS, and while he does describe a great many MSS copies of the text in his introduction he only uses one of the four oldest MSS he was able to identify: Aḥmad ath-Thālith (Istanbul) MS 2501, copied in 8th century a.h.

ii. Edition by Ibrāhīm Ṣāliḥ, 2 vols (Damascus: Dār al-Bashāʾir, 2004). Ṣāliḥ's edition is based on the following four MSS: (a) Reïsu 'l-kuttab (Istanbul) MS 626, copied in Muḥarram 993/January 1585 by Muḥammad b. Aḥmad ar-Rujayḥī al-Ḥanbalī ash-Shaybānī; (b) Kılıç Ali (Istanbul) MS 794, 229 ff., n.d. but before 1013/1604, an incomplete and faulty text, which includes entries and lines of poetry not present in other copies; (c) Escorial MS árabe 326, 178 ff., originally belonged to the library of the Moroccan King Mawlāy Zīdān (d. 1627); (d) Aḥqāf Library (Tarīm, Yemen) MS no number, 244 ff., n.d.

iii. Staatsbibliothek zu Berlin MS Wetzstein II 150, 244 ff., autograph, c. 1363.

See Ahlwardt, *Die Handschriften-Verzeichnisse der königliche Bibliotheken zu Berlin. Verzeichniss der arabischen Handschriften*, 7:572, no. 8631.

c. *Kashf al-ḥāl fī waṣf al-khāl* (*Revealing the Situation about Describing Beauty Marks*[4])

Three editions of this text have been published since 1999, though only one is critical and of requisite quality. I have relied on this edition (ed. ʿAbd ar-Raḥmān al-ʿUqayl) and Copenhagen MS Cod. Arab. 294, which the editor did not use to prepare his edition. In early 2011, an older manuscript—the oldest known to me (dated to 847/1444)—turned up at a Christie's auction. Although we made inquiries to the auction house, neither Kristina Richardson, who

2 Title as translated in Rowson, "al-Ṣafadī", 341.

3 ibid., 355.

4 Title as translated in Rowson, "al-Ṣafadī", 342.

brought the sale to my attention, nor I have been able to ascertain where it ended up.

i. Royal Library (Copenhagen) MS Cod. Arab. 294, 58 ff., n.d., purchased in Cairo by Frederik Christian von Haven in 1763, available online at <http://www.kb.dk/permalink/2006/manus/254/>.

See Irmeli Perho, *Catalogue of Arabic Manuscripts: codices Arabici and codices Arabici additamenta, book three* (Copenhagen, 2007), 1142–43.

ii. Edited by ʿAbd ar-Raḥman b. Muḥammad b. ʿUmar al-ʿUqayl (Beirut: ad-Dār al-ʿArabiyyah li-l-Mawsūʿāt, 1426/2005). The editor based his edition on Royal Library (Copenhagen) MS Cod. Arab. 293 [copied in 996/1587; unseen], as well as three other MSS [Dār al-Kutub (Cairo), MS 221 *adab Taymūr*; Ẓāhiriyyah Library (Damascus), MS 6927, 25 ff., n. d.; and Bibliothèque Nationale (Paris), MS 3973. All unseen].

See my review of this (and two other editions) in *MSR* 16 (2012).

4. Ibn Nubātah, Abū Bakr Jamāl ad-Dīn Muḥammad b. Muḥammad b. al-Ḥasan (Rabīʿ al-Awwal 686–8 Ṣafar 768/1287–1366)

See Bauer, "Ibn Nubātah al-Miṣrī (686–768/1287–1366): Life and Works. Part I"; Thomas Bauer, "Ibn Nubātah al-Miṣrī (686–768/1287–1366): Life and Works. Part II: The *Dīwān* of Ibn Nubātah", *MSR* 12:2 (2008); *idem,* "Jamāl al-Dīn Ibn Nubātah".

a. *al-Qaṭr an-Nubātī* (*Ibn Nubātah's Sweet Drops*), completed before 729/1328, dedicated to Abū l-Fidāʾ, al-Malik al-Muʾayyad (r. 1310–1331).

Thomas Bauer is currently preparing an edition of this text based on the surviving MSS. For this study, I have relied primarily on Bauer's edition-in-progress as well as on the Berlin, Paris, Florence, and Alexandria MSS upon which his edition is based.

See aṣ-Ṣafadī, *Alḥān as-sawājiʿ*, ed. Sālim, 2:325–26; Ḥājjī Khalīfah, *Kashf*, 2:1351; see also Bauer, "Dignity at Stake" and Talib, "The Many Lives of Arabic Verse".

i. Bibliothèque Nationale (Paris) MS 2234, ff. 159a–200b, copied in 732/1332.

See baron de Slane, *Catalogue des manuscrits arabes*, 392, no. 2234.

ii. Alexandria MS *Adab* 131, 37 ff., copied on 25 Jumādā al-Ākhir[ah] 764/1363.

iii. Staatsbibliothek zu Berlin MS Sprenger 1196, ff. 29b–41b, copied c. 1100/1688. This MS is contained in what Thomas Bauer has ascertained is actually a volume of aṣ-Ṣafadī's massive *Tadhkirah* (Commonplace Book).[5] The attribution on the title page (*Tadkhirat an-Nawājī*) is erroneous.

See Ahlwardt, *Die Handschriften-Verzeichnisse der königliche Bibliotheken zu Berlin. Verzeichniss der arabischen Handschriften*, 7:383, no. 8400.

iv. Biblioteca Medicea Laurenziana (Florence) MS Orientali 286, 108 ff.

b. *Dīwān* (*Collected Poems*)

On the history of Ibn Nubātah's *Dīwān* (and its various recensions), see Bauer, "Ibn Nubātah al-Miṣrī (686–768/1287–1366): Life and Works. Part II".

i. Nuruosmaniye Library (Istanbul) MS 3802, 322 ff., date illegible, but before c. 1755.

See *Defter-i Kütüphane-i Nur-i Osmaniye* (Istanbul: Mahmut Bey Matbaası, 1303/1886), 216, no. 3802.

ii. Edition by Muḥammad al-Qalqīlī (Cairo: Maṭbaʿat at-Tamaddun, 1323/1905).

See Bauer, "Ibn Nubātah al-Miṣrī (686–768/1287–1366): Life and Works. Part II"; and Talib, "The Many Lives of Arabic Verse".

c. *Zahr al-manthūr* (*The Gillyflower's Blossoms* = *The Blossoms of Prose*[6]) [epistolary collection], written in 730/1330

"[...] [A]n ample collection of excerpts—of 224 letters, all together—ranging from two or three lines to several pages in length."[7]

See Ḥājjī Khalīfah, *Kashf*, 2:961.

i. Chester Beatty Library (Dublin) MS 5161, 105 ff., n.d. (c. 8th/14th century).

See Arberry, *The Chester Beatty Library. A Handlist of the Arabic Manuscripts*, 7:53, no. 5161.

d. *Sūq ar-raqīq* (*The Slave Market* = *The Market of Elegance*[8]) [poetry anthology], written c. 1350s

In this anthology, Ibn Nubātah presented a collection of amatory preludes (sing. *nasīb*) from his polythematic poems (sing. *qaṣīdah*) alongside epigrammatic erotic poems (sing. *ghazal*).[9] It has not yet been published, but

5 See Thomas Bauer, "The Dawādār's Hunting Party: a Mamluk *muzdawija ṭardiyya*, probably by Shihāb al-Dīn Ibn Faḍl Allāh" in *O Ye Gentlemen: Arabic studies on science and literary culture in honour of Remke Kruk*, ed. A. Vrolijk and J. P. Hogendijk (Leiden: Brill, 2007). I have also benefited from Frédéric Bauden's presentation of his research on aṣ-Ṣafadī's voluminous *Tadhkirah* in May 2012 at the International Conference on Mamluk Literature hosted by the University of Chicago's Middle East Documentation Center (MEDOC) and the Center for Middle Eastern Studies under the auspices of the *Mamlūk Studies Review*.

6 Title as translated in Bauer, "Jamāl al-Dīn Ibn Nubātah", 184.

7 Bauer, "Jamāl al-Dīn Ibn Nubātah", 194.

8 Title as translated in Bauer, "Jamāl al-Dīn Ibn Nubātah", 184.

9 Bauer, "Jamāl al-Dīn Ibn Nubātah", 199–200.

an autograph MS of the text survives in the Escorial Library, which I was able to use for the purposes of this study.

See Ḥājjī Khalīfah, *Kashf*, 2:1009.

i. Escorial MS árabe 449, 114 ff., autograph., n.d. (14th century).

See Derenbourg, *Les manuscrits arabes de l'Escurial*, 297.

5. Ibn Abī Ḥajalah at-Tilimsānī, (725–776/1325–1375)

See, *inter alia*, Beatrice Gruendler, "Ibn Abī Ḥajalah".

a. *Maghnāṭīs ad-durr an-nafīs* (*Attracting Priceless Pearls*)

A call for submissions to male and female poets for a planned anthology entitled *Mujtabā l-udabā* [*sic*] and an outline of that work. The work was apparently printed in Cairo in 1305/1887 and there is also another MS in the al-Malik as-Suʿūd library but I have not had access to either of these.

See forthcoming study by Nefeli Papoutsakis; Ḥājjī Khalīfah, *Kashf*, 2:1592.

i. Yale MS Landberg 69, 21 ff., copied 1302/1885.

See Leon Nemoy, *Arabic Manuscripts in the Yale University Library* (New Haven, CT: Connecticut Academy of Arts and Sciences, 1956), 54, no. 388.

6. Ibn Ḥabīb al-Ḥalabī, Badr ad-Dīn al-Ḥasan b. ʿUmar (Shaʿbān 710–11 Rabīʿ al-Ākhir 779/1311–1377)

See *GAL* II 36–7, S II 35; aṣ-Ṣafadī, *al-Wāfī*, 12:195–98; Ibn Ḥajar, *Inbāʾ al-ghumar*, 1:162–63; *idem*, *ad-Durar al-kāminah*, 2:29–30; Ibn al-ʿImād, *Shadharāt adh-dhahab*, 6:262.

a. *ash-Shudhūr* (*The Particles of Gold*), written c. 1326

This text has not yet been published and survives in only one MS: Bibliothèque Nationale (Paris) MS 3362.

See Bauer, "„Was kann aus dem Jungen noch werden!"". See also Ḥājjī Khalīfah, *Kashf*, 2:1030.

i. Bibliothèque Nationale (Paris) MS 3362. The text of the anthology is preserved in ff. 160b–204a. The MS contains a copy of Ibn Ḥabīb's *Nasīm aṣ-ṣabā* (published numerous times, but no critical edition exists), *taqārīẓ* (commendations) on this work, and poems by Ibn Nubātah in praise of al-Malik al-Muʾayyad (perhaps *Muntakhab al-hadiyyah fī l-madāʾiḥ al-Muʾayyadiyyah*) in addition to Ibn Ḥabīb's *maqāṭīʿ*-collection and two commendations on this work by Ibn Nubātah and Ṣafī ad-Dīn al-Ḥillī. The MS was copied in 805/1403.

See baron de Slane, *Catalogue des manuscrits arabes*, 587, no. 3362.

7. al-Qīrāṭī, Burhān ad-Dīn Ibrāhīm b. ʿAbd Allāh b. Muḥammad (Ṣafar 726–Rabīʿ al-Ākhir 781/1326–1379)

See GAL II 14, S II 7; Ibn Ḥajar, *ad-Durar al-kāminah*, 1:31, no. 77; Ibn al-ʿImād, *Shadharāt adh-dhahab*, 6:269–70; Ibn Abī Ḥajalah, *Maghnāṭīs ad-durr an-nafīs*, ff. 8a–12a.

a. *Dīwān* (*Collected Poems*)
   i. Bibliothèque Nationale (Paris) MS 3209, 101 ff., copied c. 18th century.
      See baron de Slane, *Catalogue des manuscrits arabes*, 564, no. 3209.

b. *Kitāb Maṭlaʿ an-nayyirayn* (*The Rising-Place of the Sun and Moon*) [*Dīwān* recension]
   i. Fatih Kütüphanesi (Istanbul) MS 3861, 211 ff., copied in 6 Jumādā al-Ākhirah 772/1371.
      See *Defter-i Fatih Kütüphanesi* (Istanbul: Mahmut Bey Matbaası, n. d.), 221, no. 3861.
   ii. Staatsbibliothek zu Berlin MS Wetzstein II 196, 85 ff., copied in 868/1464.
      See Ahlwardt, *Die Handschriften-Verzeichnisse der königliche Bibliotheken zu Berlin. Verzeichniss der arabischen Handschriften*, 7:81, no. 7868.

c. *Taḥrīr al-Qīrāṭī* (*The Redaction of al-Qīrāṭī's* [*Dīwān*]), compiled by Ibn Ḥijjah al-Ḥamawī (see below) in c. 1409.
   See Stewart, "Ibn Ḥijjah al-Ḥamawī", 140.
   i. Staatsbibliothek zu Berlin MS Wetzstein I 45, 56 ff., copied c. 1100/1688.
      See Ahlwardt, *Die Handschriften-Verzeichnisse der königliche Bibliotheken zu Berlin. Verzeichniss der arabischen Handschriften*, 7:81–2, no. 7869.

15th century

1. Ibn Khaṭīb Dāriyā, Jalāl ad-Dīn Muḥammad b. Aḥmad (d. 810/1407)

a. *Dīwān* (*Collected Poems*)
   i. al-Maktabah al-Waṭaniyyah (Rabat) MS 225 *qāf*, 131 ff., n.d.
      See Saʿīd al-Marābiṭī, *Fihris al-makhṭūṭāt al-ʿArabiyyah. Vol 7: Khizānat al-Awqāf* (*ḥarf al-qāf*), 273–74, no. 277.

2. Ibn Ḥijjah al-Ḥamawī, Abū Bakr Taqī ad-Dīn Ibn ʿAlī (767–Shaʿbān 837/1366–1434)

See, *inter alia*, Stewart, "Ibn Ḥijjah al-Ḥamawī".

a. *Kitāb Kashf al-lithām ʿan at-tawriyah wa-l-istikhdām* (*Removing the Veil From the Face of the Rhetorical Figures* Tawriyah *and* Istikhdām[10])

Rhetorical treatise-cum-anthology. This text was printed in Beirut in 1894–95, *editio princeps*), but I have relied on a Leiden MS of the text (see below) for the purposes of this study.

i. Leiden MS Or. 442 (2), ff. 68–160, copied in 1035/1625.

See M. J. de Goeje, *Catalogus codicum orientalium bibliothecae academiae Lugduno-Batavae, volumen quintum* (Leiden: E. J. Brill, 1873), 155–56, no. 2542; M. J. de Goeje and M. Th. Houtsma, *Catalogus codicum arabicorum bibliothecae academiae Lugduno-Batavae, editio secunda, volumen primum* (Leiden: E. J. Brill, 1888), 176, no. 327; P. Voorhoeve, *Handlist of Arabic Manuscripts in the library of the University of Leiden and other collections in the Netherlands* (Leiden: University Library, 1957), 153.

b. *Thamarāt shahiyyah min al-fawākih al-Ḥamawiyyah* (*The Tasty Produce from the Fruits of Hama*)

i. Bayerische Staatsbibliothek (Munich), MS cod. arab. 531, 61 ff., copied in Cairo on 6 Shawwāl 841/2 April 1438.

See Joseph Aumer, *Die arabischen Handschriften der K. Hof- und Staatsbibliothek in Muenchen* (Munich: In Commission der Palm'schen Hofbuchhandlung, 1866), 225, no. 531.

3. an-Nawājī, Shams ad-Dīn Muḥammad b. Ḥasan (788–859/1386–1455)

See, *inter alia*, Thomas Bauer, "al-Nawājī" in *Essays in Arabic Literary Biography 1350–1850*, ed. Joseph Lowry and Devin Stewart (Wiesbaden: Harrassowitz, 2009) and anon., *Muʾallafāt Shams ad-Dīn Muḥammad b. Ḥasan an-Nawājī ash-Shāfiʿī*, ed. Ḥasan Muḥammad ʿAbd al-Hādī (Amman: Dār al-Yanābīʿ, 2001).

a. *Ṣaḥāʾif al-ḥasanāt fī waṣf al-khāl* (*Surfaces of Beauty Marked with Descriptions of Beauty-Marks*).

This anthology based around the figure of moles (naevi), a traditional hallmark of beauty, has been published in a critical edition by Ḥasan Muḥammad ʿAbd al-Hādī.

10 Title as translated in Stewart, "Ibn Ḥijjah al-Ḥamawī", 138.

i. Edition by Ḥasan Muḥammad ʿAbd al-Hādī (Amman: Dār al-Yanābīʿ, 2000).

See also anon., *Muʾallafāt Shams ad-Dīn Muḥammad b. Ḥasan an-Nawājī ash-Shāfiʿī*, ed. ʿAbd al-Hādī, 89–91; Bauer, "al-Nawājī", 328.

b. *Khalʿ al-ʿidhār fī waṣf al-ʿidhār* (*Throwing Off Restraint in Describing Cheek-Down*)

This anthology has recently been edited by Ḥusayn ʿAbd al-ʿĀlī al-Lahībī in *Majallat Kulliyat al-Fiqh* (*Jāmiʿat al-Kūfah*) 10 (1431/2010), 207–64).[11] Al-Lahībī based his edition on Escorial MS árabe 340 (copied in 987/1579 by ʿAlī b. Ḥusayn b. Qizil) and compared it to two additional MSS of the text: Dār al-Kutub (Cairo) MS 646 *adab Taymūr* (see no. iv below) and Azhar MS 7100 *adab* (copied in 1273/1856 [or 1272/1855 according to ʿAbd al-Hādī] by ʿAbd al-Ḥamīd Nāfiʿ). For this study, I relied on the following four MSS. This once highly popular anthology survives in at least eleven manuscripts.

See anon., *Muʾallafāt Shams ad-Dīn Muḥammad b. Ḥasan an-Nawājī ash-Shāfiʿī*, ed. ʿAbd al-Hādī, 78–80; Bauer, "al-Nawājī", 328–29; Ḥājjī Khalīfah, *Kashf*, 1:721–22.

i. Bibliothèque Nationale (Paris) MS 3401, ff. 1b–47a, 16th c. This MS also contains two other anthologies by an-Nawājī, as well as an anthology by ath-Thaʿālibī.

See baron de Slane, *Catalogue des manuscrits arabes*, 592, no. 3401.

ii. Bayerische Staatsbibliothek (Munich) MS Cod. arab. 598, 40 ff., n. d.

See Aumer, *Die arabischen Handschriften der K. Hof- und Staatsbibliothek in Muenchen*, 259–60, no. 598 (where—following Ḥājjī Khalīfah—the text is erroneously attributed to aṣ-Ṣafadī).

iii. Dār al-Kutub (Cairo) MS 226 *adab Taymūr*, Microfilm 27991, 36 ff., copied in 1303/1886.

iv. Dār al-Kutub (Cairo) MS 646 *adab Taymūr*, Microfilm 27906, 49 ff., copied in 1305/1888.

c. *Marātiʿ al-ghizlān fī waṣf al-ghilmān al-ḥisān* (*The Pastures of Gazelles: describing handsome young men*)

This anthology, written in 828/1425, was once hugely popular, but has not yet been published. It survives in at least twenty-four manuscripts. For this study, I have relied on the following five MSS (listed in order of importance).

11 According to the editor's faculty webpage, this edition was also published by the Ḥawḍ al-Furāt publishing house in Najaf in 2014. I regret I have not been able to consult that version.

See anon., *Mu'allafāt Shams ad-Dīn Muḥammad b. Ḥasan an-Nawājī ash-Shāfi'ī*, ed. 'Abd al-Hādī, 97–100; Bauer, "al-Nawājī", 329; See Ḥājjī Khalīfah, *Kashf*, 2:1650–51.

i. Princeton MS Garrett 14L, 190 ff., copied in 889/1484.
Digital reproduction available online through Princeton Digital Library of Islamic Manuscripts. See also Hitti et al., *Descriptive Catalog*, 39–40, no. 101.

ii. Princeton MS Garrett Yahuda 615, 165 ff., copied c. 9th/15th century.
See Mach, *Catalogue of Arabic Manuscripts*, 363, no. 4249_1.

iii. Topkapı (Istanbul) MS 722, 135 ff., copied in 1114/1703.
See Fehmi Edhem Karatay, *Topkapı Sarayı Müzesi Kütüphanesi Arapça Yazmalar Kataloğu*, 4 vols, (Istanbul: Milli Eğitim Basımevi, 1969), 4:337, no. 8598.

iv. Dār al-Kutub (Cairo) MS 583 *adab*, Microfilm 18287, 54 ff., n.d.

v. Dār al-Kutub (Cairo) MS 343 *adab Taymūr*, Microfilm 27904, n.d.

d. *al-Ḥujjah fī sariqāt Ibn Ḥijjah* [*al-Ḥamawī* (d. 837/1434)] (*Proof of Plagiarism: the case of Ibn Ḥijjah al-Ḥamawī*)
See Ḥājjī Khalīfah, *Kashf*, 1:419. There is an edition by Samīḥah Ḥusayn Maḥmūd al-Maḥārimah (unpublished MA thesis, al-Jāmi'ah al-Urdunniyyah, 1988), but I was not able to access it.

i. al-Maktabah al-Waṭaniyyah (Rabat) MS 1805 *dāl*, 183 ff., copied in 1276/1860 by Muṣṭafā Maḥmūd, Microfilm 089_4.
See Muḥammad Ibrāhīm al-Kattānī and Ṣāliḥ at-Tādlī, *Fihris al-makhṭūṭāt al-'Arabiyyah al-maḥfūẓah fī l-khizānah bi-r-Ribāṭ*, vol. 5 (Casablanca: Maṭba'at an-Najāḥ al-Jadīdah (for al-Khizānah al-'Āmmah li-l-Kutub wa-l-Wathā'iq), 1997), 75, no. 3916.

ii. Azhar Library MS 526 - Abāẓah 7122, 151 ff., copied in 1270/1853.

4. Burhān ad-Dīn Ibrāhīm b. Aḥmad al-Bā'ūnī (776–870/1374–1465)

See Bilal Orfali, "*Ghazal* and Grammar: al-Bā'ūnī's *taḍmīn Alfiyyat Ibn Mālik fī l-ghazal*" in *In the Shadow of Arabic: the centrality of language to Arabic culture. Studies presented to Ramzi Baalbaki on the occasion of his sixtieth birthday*, ed. Bilal Orfali (Leiden: Brill, 2011); as-Sakhāwī, *aḍ-Ḍaw' al-lāmi'*, 1:26–9; ash-Shawkānī, *al-Badr aṭ-ṭāli'*, 1:12; as-Suyūṭī, *Naẓm al-'iqyān*, 13–4.

a. *al-Ghayth al-hātin fī l-'idhār al-fātin* (*The Copious Downpour: on alluring beard-down*)
An anthology of poetry on beard-down.

i. Staatsbibliothek zu Berlin MS Wetzstein II 177, 96 ff., copied in 879/1475 by Ibrāhīm b. 'Abd ar-Raḥmān, a scribe from Tripoli.

See Ahlwardt, *Die Handschriften-Verzeichnisse der königliche Bibliotheken zu Berlin. Verzeichniss der arabischen Handschriften*, 7:101–2, no. 7911.

5. Badr ad-Dīn Muḥammad al-Minhājī (no biographical information available)

a. *Basṭ al-aʿdhār ʿan ḥubb al-ʿidhār* (*Explaining Excuses for Adoring Cheek-Down*)

See Ismāʿīl Pāshā, *Īḍāḥ al-maknūn fī dh-dhayl ʿalā «Kashf aẓ-ẓunūn ʿan asāmī al-kutub wa-l-funūn»*, 2 vols, ed. Şerefettin Yaltkaya and Rifat Bilge (Istanbul: Mıllî Eğitim Basımevi, 1945–47), 1:182.

This anthology of verses on beard-down has not yet been published. It survives uniquely in an Escorial MS.

i. Escorial MS árabe 448, 122 ff., copied in 850/1446, apparent autograph.

See Derenbourg, *Les manuscrits arabes de l'Escurial*, 296–97.

6. Shihāb ad-Dīn al-Ḥijāzī al-Anṣārī al-Khazrajī, Aḥmad b. Muḥammad (Shaʿbān 790–Ramaḍān 875/1388–1471)

See *GAL* II 171, S II 11–2; as-Suyūṭī, *Naẓm al-ʿiqyān*, 63–77, no. 42.

a. *Rawḍ al-ādāb* (*The Garden of Literary Arts*) [anthology], written 826/1422–3.

See Ḥājjī Khalīfah, *Kashf*, 1:916; Flügel, *Die arabischen, persischen und türkischen Handschriften*, 1:380–81, no. 400; Voorhoeve, *Handlist*, 286; M. Th. Houtsma, *Catalogue d'une collection de manuscrits arabes et turcs appartenant à la maison E. J. Brill à Leide* (Leiden: E. J. Brill, 1886), 15–16, no. 81; Otto Rescher, "Arabische Handschriften des Top Kapú Seraj [Privatbibliothek S. M. des Sultans]", *RSO* 4 (1911–12), 696 [on Topkapı MS 2293]. Yūsuf Sarkīs mentions an edition printed in Bombay in 1898, but I have not been able to locate this (*Muʿjam al-maṭbūʿāt al-ʿArabiyyah wa-l-muʿarrabah* (Cairo: Maṭbaʿat Sarkīs, 1928), 1151).

i. British Library MS Add 9562, 247 ff., copied in Shawwāl 986/1578.

See Charles Rieu, *Catalogus codicum manuscriptorum orientalium qui in museo britannico asservantur. Pars secunda, codices Arabicos amplectens. Supplementum* (London: Impensis Curatorum Musei Britannici 1871), 505–7, no. 1104

ii. British Library MS Add 19489, 184 ff., copied c. 15th–16th century.

See Rieu, *Catalogus. Supplementum* (1871), 507, no. 1105

iii. British Library MS Or. 3843, 206 ff., c. 15th-century copy.

See Rieu, *Supplement to the Catalogue*, 704–5, no. 1119.

iv. Princeton MS Garrett 145H, 208 ff., c. 1265/1848 in Mecca by Ismāʿīl b. ʿAbd Allāh al-Khālidī.

See Hitti et al., *Descriptive Catalog*, 85, no. 213.

b. *Jannat al-wildān fī l-ḥisān min al-ghilmān* (*The Paradise of Youths: on handsome young men*[12])

This is an anthology of *maqāṭīʿ*-poems on male youths by the poet-anthologist himself. The text has been printed twice, but neither edition is critical. For this study, I have relied primarily on the Copenhagen MS. (See also Rosenthal, "Male and Female"; Richardson, *Difference and Disability*, ch. 3).

i. Royal Library (Copenhagen) MS Cod. Arab. 220_3, ff. 26a–36b, n. d. [purchased in Cairo in 1762].
See Perho, *Catalogue of Arabic Manuscripts*, 840.

ii. *Editio princeps*: printed in ash-Shihāb al-Ḥijāzī, *Thalāth rasāʾil. al-Ūlā «Jannat al-wildān fī l-ḥisān min al-ghilmān», ath-thāniyah «al-Kunnas al-jawārī fī l-ḥisān min al-jawārī», ath-thālithah «Qalāʾid an-nuḥūr min jawāhir al-buḥūr»* (Cairo: Maṭbaʿat as-Saʿādah, 1326/1908). Edited by Muḥammad Amīn al-Kutubī based on an unidentified Dār al-Kutub (Cairo) MS. [unseen].

iii. Edition by Riḥāb ʿAkkāwī, printed as: *al-Kunnas al-jawārī fī l-ḥisān min al-jawārī (wa bi-dhaylihi «Jannat al-wildān fī l-ḥisān min al-ghilmān»)* (Beirut: Dār al-Ḥarf al-ʿArabī, 1998). This edition was not based on any MS, but rather on the 1908 Cairo *editio princeps* (see no. ii above).

c. *al-Kunnas al-jawārī fī l-ḥisān min al-jawārī* (*The Withdrawing Celestial Bodies: on pretty young women*[13])

This is an anthology of *maqāṭīʿ*-poems on female youths by the poet-anthologist himself. The text has been printed twice, but neither edition is critical. For this study, I have relied primarily on the Copenhagen MS. (For further information on this text and its editions, see directly above).

See Ḥājjī Khalīfah, *Kashf*, 2:1520.

i. Royal Library (Copenhagen) MS Cod. Arab. 220_4, ff. 36b–42b, n. d., [purchased in Cairo in 1762].
See Perho, *Catalogue of Arabic Manuscripts*, 840–41.

ii. *Editio princeps*: printed in ash-Shihāb al-Ḥijāzī, *Thalāth rasāʾil* (Cairo, 1908) [see no. b. ii above for further information].

---

12 The first phrase in the title, "*jannat al-wildān*" ("The Paradise of Youths"), is an allusion to Qurʾan *al-Wāqiʿah* 56:17 : «*yaṭūfu ʿalayhim wildānun mukhalladūn*» ("immortal youths going round about them", trans. Arberry, *The Koran Interpreted*, 2:254).

13 The first phrase in the title, "*Kunnas al-jawārī*" ("The Withdrawing Celestial Bodies"), is an allusion to Qurʾan *at-Takwīr* 81:16: «*al-Jawāri l-kunnas*» ("the runners, the sinkers", trans. Arberry, *The Koran Interpreted*, 2:326).

iii. Edition by Riḥāb ʿAkkāwī, printed as: *al-Kunnas al-jawārī* [...]. This edition was not based on any MS, but rather on the 1908 Cairo *editio princeps*. (see also no. b. ii and iii above for further information).

d. *al-Lumaʿ ash-Shihābiyyah min al-burūq al-Ḥijāziyyah* (*Flashes of meteor/ Shihāb in the Ḥijāzī lightning-storm*)

An anthology of poetry and prose.

i. Escorial MS árabe 475, 276 ff., n.d.

See Hartwig Derenbourg, *Les manuscrits arabes de l'Escurial*, 319.

e. *Nadīm al-Kaʾīb wa-ḥabīb al-ḥabīb* (*The Sullen one's Companion and the Beloved one's Beloved*)

A poetry anthology.

See Ḥājjī Khalīfah, *Kashf*, 2:1937.

i. Staatsbibliothek zu Berlin MS Or. Oct. 3839, 155 ff., n.d. [perhaps 11th/17th c.]

See Rudolf Sellheim, *Materialen zur arabischen Literaturgeschichte*. Teil 1 (Wiesbaden: Franz Steiner Verlag, 1976), no. 88.

7. Ibn Ḥajar al-ʿAsqalānī (Shaʿbān 773–Dhū l-Ḥijjah 852/1372–1449)

a. *Dīwān* [incl. *maqāṭīʿ*-chapter] (*Collected Poems*)

Ibn Ḥajar included a chapter of *maqāṭīʿ*-poems in his *Dīwān*. I have consulted a few printed editions of the *Dīwān* and one MS copied from the author's autograph, which none of the editors used to prepare their editions. Ibn Ḥajar himself made a selection of his poems titled *as-Sabʿ as-sayyārah an-nayyirāt*.[14]

i. Selly Oak Colleges (Birmingham) MS Mingana 1394, copied c. 19th century from autograph MS dated 838/1434.

See H. L. Gottschalk, *Islamic Arabic Manuscripts*, Vol. 4 of *Catalogue of the Mingana Collection of Manuscripts* (Birmingham: Selly Oak Colleges Library, 1948), 34, no. 160.

ii. *Dīwān*, edited by as-Sayyid Abū al-Faḍl (Hyderabad: J. M. Press, 1381/1962). [Based on four MSS, incl. Dār al-Kutub (Cairo) MS 811 *shiʿr Taymūr*, Osmania University (Hyderabad) MS, n.d., and an unidentifed Berlin MS].[15]

See ʿIṣām Muḥammad ash-Shanīṭī, *al-Makhṭūṭāt al-ʿArabiyyah fī l-Hind. Taqrīr ʿan al-makhṭūṭāt al-ʿArabiyyah fī khams mudun*

14 cf. The collection Ibn Nubātah made of his own seven-line poems late in life titled *as-Sabʿah as-sayyārah* (Bauer, "Jamāl al-Dīn Ibn Nubātah", 199).

15 The Staatsbibliothek in Berlin possesses more than one MS (incl. fragments) of Ibn Ḥajar's *Dīwān* (see Ahlwardt, *Die Handschriften-Verzeichnisse der königliche Bibliotheken zu Berlin. Verzeichniss der arabischen Handschriften*, 7:96–7, nos 7901–3).

Hindiyyah tammat ziyāratuhā fī shahr Ibrīl / Māyū 1984 (Kuwait: Manshūrāt Maʿhad al-Makhṭūṭāt al-ʿArabiyyah, 1405/1985), 22.

iii. *Dīwān as-Sabʿ as-sayyārah an-nayyirāt* [*The Collection of the Seven Shooting Stars*], edited by Muḥammad Yūsuf Ayyūb (Jeddah: Nādī Abhā al-Adabī, 1992). [Based on seven MSS of *as-Sabʿ as-sayyārah an-nayyirāt*, and two MSS of the *Dīwān* (Escorial MS árabe 444 and a Berlin MS—presumably the same as that used by Abū al-Faḍl). The seven *as-Sabʿ as-sayyārah* MSS are (1 and 2) Dār al-Kutub (Cairo) MS 811 *shiʿr Taymūr* and MS 121 *ādāb*; (3 and 4) Ẓāhiriyyah (Damascus) MS 5796 and MS 3974; (5) Bibliothèque Nationale (Paris) MS 3219; (6) unidentified Berlin MS; and (7) Köprülü (Istanbul) MS 1282.]

iv. *Uns al-ḥujar fī abyāt Ibn Ḥajar* [*A Sitting-Room Companion: poems by Ibn Ḥajar*], edited with commentary by Shihāb ad-Dīn Abū ʿAmr (Beirut: Dār ar-Rayyān li-t-Turāth, 1988). [Based on three MSS: (1) Dār al-Kutub (Cairo) MS 811 *shiʿr Taymūr*; (2) Köprülü (Istanbul) MS 1282; and (3) Escorial MS árabe 444].

8. Ibn Taghrībirdī, Abū l-Maḥāsin Jamāl ad-Dīn Yūsuf (c. 821–5 Dhū l-Ḥijjah 874 / c.1409–5 June 1470)

See *inter alia* EI², s.v. "Abū 'l-Maḥāsin Djamāl al-Dīn Yūsuf b. Taghrībirdī" [W. Popper].

a. *Ḥilyat aṣ-ṣifāt fī l-asmāʾ wa-ṣ-ṣināʿāt* (*An Ornament of Description on Names and Professions*)

See GAL S II, 40; as-Sakhāwī, *aḍ-Ḍawʾ al-lāmiʿ*, 10:307–8.

i. Raza Library (Rampur) MS 4373, 165 ff., copied on 13 Shawwāl 851 / 22 December 1447.

A photograph copy of this MS was made by ALESCO on 4 February 1952 and deposited at the Arab League Manuscript Institute. Not listed in Imtiyaz Ali Khan ʿArshi, *Catalogue of the Arabic Manuscripts in Raza Library, Rampur*, vol. 6.

ii. Musée Asiatique (St. Petersburg) MS C 37, 167 ff., copied in 860/1456 [unseen]

See Khalidov, *Arabskie rukopisi instituta vostokovedenii͡a : kratkiĭ katalog*, 1:396, no. 8962.

9. Al-Badrī, Abū t-Tuqā Taqī ad-Dīn Abū Bakr b. ʿAbd Allāh (Rabīʿ al-Awwal 847–Jumādā [I or II] 894/1443–1489)

See *GAL* II 132, S II 163; as-Sakhāwī, *aḍ-Ḍaw' al-lāmi'*, 11:41; Franz Rosenthal, *The Herb: hashish versus medieval Muslim society* (Leiden: Brill, 1971), 13–15.

a. *Ghurrat aṣ-ṣabāḥ fī waṣf al-wujūh aṣ-ṣibāḥ* (*The Flash of Dawn: beautiful faces described*), written 865/1460

This anthology has not yet been published. It survives uniquely in a British Library MS, which I have used for the purposes of this study.

See Rosenthal, "Male and Female"; Ḥājjī Khalīfah, *Kashf*, 2:1198.

i. British Library MS ADD 23445, 212 ff., copied in 875/1471.

See Rieu, *Catalogus* (1846), 654–55, no. 1423.

10. Ibn al-Ji'ān al-Batlūnī, 'Alam ad-Dīn Shākir b. 'Abd al-Ghanī (790–14 Rabī' al-Ākhir 882/1388–1477)

See *GAL* II 19, S II 13; as-Suyūṭī, *Naẓm al-'iqyān*, 118, no. 89.

a. *Masāyil ad-dumū' 'alā mā tafarraqa min al-majmū'* (*The Tracks of Tears: once gathered, now separated*)

Poetry anthology.

i. British Library MS Add. 7591 *Rich.*, 187 ff., the anthology begins on f. 20, copied before 1124/1712.

See Rieu, *Catalogus* (1846), 301, no. 638.

16th century

1. Muḥammad b. Qānṣūh [or: Qānṣawh] b. Ṣādiq (d. 911/1505)

See *GAL* II 271, S II 381–82.

a. *Marāti' al-albāb fī marābi' al-ādāb* (*The Pastures of Hearts in The Meadows of Literary Arts*), written in 898/1492.

An anthology of poetry and prose.

i. British Library MS ADD 9677, 204 ff., copied in 1162/1749.

See Rieu, *Catalogus* (1846), 346–47, no. 770.

b. *ar-Rawḍ al-bahīj fī l-ghazal wa-n-nasīj* (*The Cheerful Garden: on spinning [love poems] and weaving [words]*), written in 917/1511.

An expanded anthology of poetry and prose.

i. Universitätsbibliothek Basel MS II 43, 501 ff. , autograph MS copied in 917/1511 [unseen].

See Schubert and Würsch, *Die Handschriften der Universitätsbibliothek Basel*, 66–86, no. 31.

2. ʿUways al-Ḥamawī (1451–c. 1516)

See GAL II 56, S II 58.

a. *Sukkardān al-ʿushshāq wa-manārat al-asmāʿ wa-l-āmāq* (*The Sugar-Pot of Lovers and the Lighthouse for Eyes and Ears*),

This anthology has never been published.

i. Bibliothèque Nationale, Paris, MS Arabe 3405, 250 ff., 18th c.

See baron de Slane, *Catalogue des manuscrits arabes*, 593, no. 3405.

3. Māmayah ar-Rūmī, Muḥammad b. Aḥmad b. ʿAbd Allāh (d. 985/1577)

See C. E. Bosworth, "A Janissary Poet of Sixteenth-Century Damascus: Māmayya al-Rūmī" in *The Islamic World: from classical to modern times. Essays in Honor of Bernard Lewis*, ed. C. E. Bosworth et al. (Princeton, NJ: The Darwin Press, 1989).

a. *Rawḍat al-mushtāq wa-bahjat al-ʿushshāq* (*The Garden of the Yearner and the Joy of Lovers*), composed in 971/1563 [according to remark in Staatsbibliothek zu Berlin MS Wetzstein II 171, f. 1b]

i. Staatsbibliothek zu Berlin MS Wetzstein II 171, 63 ff., 19th-century copy

ii. Staatsbibliothek zu Berlin MS Wetzstein II 163, 288 ff., copied on 20 Dhū l-Ḥijjah 1054 / 17 February 1645

iii. Staatsbibliothek zu Berlin MS Wetzstein II 243, 327 ff., 18th-century copy

iv. Staatsbibliothek zu Berlin MS Petermann I 645, 125 ff., 17th-century copy

v. John Rylands Library (Manchester) MS 478 [468]

See Mingana, *Catalogue*, 800.

4. ʿAbd al-Bāqī al-Khaṭīb (d. 1005/1596)

See *GAL* II 378, S II 509.

a. *ʿIqd al-farāʾid fī-mā nuẓima min al-fawāʾid* (*The Necklace of Precious Pearls: versified pearls of wisdom* [*lit. versified useful lessons*]), written in 1005/1596

This anthology of didactic *maqāṭīʿ*-poems and proverbs (similar to a commonplace book or almanac) has not yet been published. For the purposes of this study, I have relied on the Berlin MS (see no. i below), though I have also examined an additional MS of the text in Cambridge:

Cambridge MS Or. 57, 74 ff., copied in 1009/1600. See in Edward G. Browne, *A Supplementary Hand-List of the Muḥammadan Manuscripts in the libraries of the University and Colleges of Cambridge* (Cambridge: Cambridge University Press, 1922), 142–43, no. 869.

i. Staatsbibliothek zu Berlin MS Or. Petermann II 73, copied in 1082/1671.

See Ahlwardt, *Die Handschriften-Verzeichnisse der königliche Bibliotheken zu Berlin. Verzeichniss der arabischen Handschriften*, 7:404, no. 8423. See also *GAL* II, 378, S II 509.

5. ʿAlāʾ ad-Dīn aṣ-Ṣāliḥī al-Ḥarīrī (unknown)

a. *ad-Durr al-maṣūn fī niẓām as-sabʿ funūn* (*The Well Guarded Pearl: composing the Seven* [*Poetic*] *Forms*) (probably 16th century)

Anthology of *sabʿ funūn* poems.

This manuscript is not dated. It was a *khizānah* manuscript and many Mamluk-era poets are cited in it. In addition, the title of the work puts one in mind of the better known anthology by Muḥammad b. Iyās al-Ḥanafī, *ad-Durr al-maknūn fī sabʿat funūn*, which was written—according to Ḥājjī Khalīfah (*Kashf*, 1:732)—in 912/1506. On this latter text, see Hermann Gies, *Ein Beitrag zur Kenntnis sieben neuerer arabischer Versarten* (Leipzig: W. Drugulin, 1879), and *GAL* II 303, S II 414.

i. Bodleian Library (Oxford) MS Marsh 73, 91 ff., n.d.

See Joh. Uri, *Bibliothecae Bodleianae codicum manuscriptorum orientalium catalogi partis secundæ volumen secundum Arabicos* (Oxford: Clarendon Press, 1787), no. 1295; and also Alexander Nicoll, *Bibliothecae Bodleianae codicum manuscriptorum orientalium catalogi partis secundae volumen primum Arabicos complectens* (Oxford: Clarendon Press, 1821), 618, no. 1294.

6. anon.

a. Untitled anthology (*Majmūʿ mubārak yashtamil ʿalā* […])

This anthology was copied by Muḥammad al-Adyīkhī and bears his autograph dated 1006/1597.

i. Princeton MS Garrett 168H, 244 ff., copied 1006/1597.

See Hitti et al., *Descriptive Catalog*, 95, no. 236.

17th century

1. Muḥammad b. Abī l-Wafāʾ al-Maʿrūfī al-Khalwatī al-Ḥamawī (d. 1016/1607)

See *GAL* II 302; 341.

a. Untitled poetry collection: "*Hādhā muntakhab min kalām Abī l-Faḍl wa-ghayrih ḥarrarahu li-nafsih al-faqīr Muḥammad b. Abī l-Wafā'* […]" (f. 33a) ["This is a selection of the writings of Abū l-Faḍl and others chosen by poor Muḥammad b. Abī l-Wafā' for his own use"].

Little is known about the circumstances behind the composition of this short anthology of didactic (or mnemonic) *maqāṭī'*-poems. It has never been published, but an autograph MS survives in Berlin and it is upon this that I have relied for the purposes of this study.

i. Staatsbibliothek Berlin MS Petermann I 600, ff. 33a–41b, autograph written in 992/1584.

See Ahlwardt, *Die Handschriften-Verzeichnisse der königliche Bibliotheken zu Berlin. Verzeichniss der arabischen Handschriften*, 7:242, no. 8205.

2. Aḥmad b. Aḥmad al-Ānisī al-Yamanī (d. c. 1030/1640)

See *GAL* II 524; S II 544. See also Ahlwardt, *Die Handschriften-Verzeichnisse der königliche Bibliotheken zu Berlin. Verzeichniss der arabischen Handschriften*, 7:128, no. 7972_3.

a. *Dīwān* (*Collected Poems*)

i. Princeton MS Garrett Yahuda 805, ff. 59b–104a, n.d.

See Mach, *Catalogue of Arabic Manuscripts*, 358, no. 4188.

3. Ibn Ma'tūq al-Mūsawī (d. 1087/1676),

a. *Dīwān* (*Collected Poems*)

i. Bayerische Staatsbibliothek (Munich), MS cod. arab. 1086, 108 ff., copied on 20 Dhū l-Ḥijjah 1268 [1852].

See Florian Sobieroj and Kathrin Müller, *Arabische Handschriften der Bayerischen Staatsbibliothek zu München unter Einschluss einiger türkischer und persischer Handschriften, Band 1* (Stuttgart: Franz Steiner Verlag, 2007), no. 1086.

4. 'Alī b. Muḥammad al-Makkī (fl. c. 1100/1688)

a. *Nadīm al-mustahām wa-rawḍat ahl al-'ishq wa-l-gharām* (*The Companion of the Love-crazed and the Garden of the People of Passion and Romance*)

i. Staatsbibliothek zu Berlin MS Petermann II 654, ff. 1–100, copied c. 1200/1785.

See Ahlwardt, *Die Handschriften-Verzeichnisse der königliche Bibliotheken zu Berlin. Verzeichniss der arabischen Handschriften*, 7:409–10, no. 8432.

5. anon.

a. *Khadīm aẓ-ẓurafāʾ wa-nadīm al-luṭafāʾ* (*The Servant of The Refined and The Companion of The Graceful*), written before 1028/1618.

This anthology has not yet been edited and survives uniquely in a Bodleian Library (Oxford) MS; a similarly titled Berlin MS appears to be a different text altogether.

Ḥājjī Khalīfah, *Kashf*, 2:1198.

i. Bodleian Library (Oxford) MS Huntington 508

The MS is not dated, but I have concluded that this anthology was written toward the end of the 16th century. There is an MS by the same name in the Staatsbibliothek zu Berlin: MS Wetzstein II 8 [= Ahlwardt 8448], but it is not the same text. There are interesting similarities (e.g. verbatim passages in the introductions to both works), but the Oxford MS is a poetry anthology and the Berlin MS is, as Ahlwardt says, a collection of entertaining stories. See Uri, *Bibliothecae Bodleianae codicum*, no. 1262; and also Nicoll, *Bibliothecae Bodleianae codicum*, 616, no. 1262.

6. anon.

a. Untitled poetry collection

i. Staatsbibliothek zu Berlin MS Sprenger 1239, 216 ff., composed c. 1090/1679, available online at <http://resolver.staatsbibliothek-berlin.de/SBB000146A900000000>.

Ahlwardt, *Die Handschriften-Verzeichnisse der königliche Bibliotheken zu Berlin. Verzeichniss der arabischen Handschriften*, 7:251–52, no. 8224.

7. anon. ["Pseudo-Thaʿālibī"]

a. "*fī asmāʾ al-ghilmān al-ḥisān*" ["On the names of handsome young men"], late 16th–17th century

For nearly a century, this text was mistakenly believed to be ath-Thaʿālibī's lost *Kitāb al-Ghilmān* although the majority of the poems contained within it were written in the 13th–16th centuries. I have published the text of the brief anthology in a critical edition based on the sole surviving MS, along with a discussion of its contents and attribution and it is this edition upon which I have relied here.

i. Edited in Talib, "Pseudo-Ṯaʿālibī's *Book of Youths*", 619–49. The edition is based on the sole surviving MS: Staatsbibliothek zu Berlin MS Wetzstein II 1786, ff. 63b–67b.

See Talib, "Pseudo-Ṯaʿālibī's *Book of Youths*"; Ahlwardt, *Die Handschriften-Verzeichnisse der königliche Bibliotheken zu Berlin. Verzeichniss der arabischen Handschriften*, 7:321–22, no. 8334.

8. ʿUthmān aṭ-Ṭāʾifī ash-Shāfiʿī

Details about the biography of the author of this anthology are unknown. We can assume that he lived in the 17th century or earlier based on the date of his anthology.

a. *Kitāb Maḥāsin al-laṭāʾif wa-raqāʾiq aẓ-ẓarāʾif* (*The Book of Pleasant Pleasantries and Delicate Delicacies*)
   i. Staatsbibliothek zu Berlin MS Or. Oct. 3355, 219 ff., n.d.
      See Ewald Wagner, *Arabische Handschriften. Reihe B. Teil 1* (Wiesbaden: Franz Steiner Verlag, 1976), 1:337–8, no. 407.

9. anon.

a. *ad-Durar al-fāʾiqah fī l-maqāṭīʿ ar-rāʾiqah* (*The Excellent Pearls: on marvelous* Maqāṭīʿ-*poems*)
   i. Princeton MS Garrett Yahuda 5902, ff. 78b–105b [incomplete], n.d.
      See Mach, *Catalogue of Arabic Manuscripts*, 364, no. 4259.

10. anon.

a. Untitled poetry collection
   i. Gotha MS Orient A 2211, 34 ff., n.d. purchased in Aleppo by Ulrich Jasper Seetzen (1767–1811).
      See Wilhelm Pertsch, *Die orientalischen Handschriften der Herzoglichen Bibliothek zu Gotha. Dritter Theil: die arabischen Handschriften* (Vienna: Kaiserlich-königliche Hof- und Staatsdruckerei, 1859–93), 4:230–31.

18th century

1. Ibn Maʿṣūm (d. 1130/1707)

a. *Sulāfat al-ʿaṣr fī maḥāsin ash-shuʿarāʾ bi-kull maṣr*[16] (*The First Pressing of The*

16 I have modified the conventional vocalization of *Miṣr* (Egypt) for the sake of the rhyming pair.

Age/Press: on the achievements of poets in every land)

Biographical dictionary. For this study, I used the Berlin MS and the Cairo ed. of 1906.

i. Berlin MS Petermann I 630, 518 ff., copied in 1112/1701, available online at <http://resolver.staatsbibliothek-berlin.de/SBB0000F5E700000000>.

19th century

1. anon.

a. Untitled anthology

i. Gotha MS Orient A 2175 (arab. 537, Stz. Kah. 1202), 129 ff., n.d. purchased in Cairo in 1808 by Ulrich Jasper Seetzen (1767–1811).

See Pertsch, *Die orientalischen Handschriften. Dritter Theil*, 4:197.

2. ʿAbd ar-Raḥmān aṣ-Ṣaftī ash-Sharqāwī (d. 1264/1848)

See *GAL* S II 721.

a. *Talāqī l-arab fī marāqī l-adab* (*Meeting One's Desire while Scaling the Literary Heights*)

i. Riyadh University Library MS 152, 90 ff., n.d.

3. Aḥmad b. ʿAbd ar-Raḥīm al-ʿAṭṭārī

Details about the biography of the author of this anthology are unknown. A chronogram at the end of his poetry collection allows us to date that work's completion to 1280/1863.

a. Untitled poetry collection

i. Dār al-Kutub (Cairo) MS 4028 *adab*, 11 ff., n.d.

ii. Dār al-Kutub (Cairo) MS 4029 *adab*, 10 ff., n.d.

Sources

Abate, Frank (ed). *The Oxford American Dictionary of Current English.* Oxford: Oxford University Press, 1999.

Abbas, Adnan. *The Band as a New Form of Poetry in Iraq, 17th century*. Poznań: Wydawnictwo Naukowe, 1994.

ʿAbbās, Iḥsān. *Malāmiḥ Yūnāniyyah fī l-adab al-ʿArabī.* 2nd ed. Beirut: al-Muʾassasah al-ʿArabiyyah li-d-Dirāsāt wa-n-Nashr, 1993.

———. "*al-Qaṣīdah al-qaṣīrah fī sh-shiʿr al-ʿArabī al-ḥadīth*". Repr. in *Iḥsān ʿAbbās. Awrāq mubaʿtharah: buḥūth wa-dirāsāt fī th-thaqāfah wa-t-tarīkh wa-l-adab wa-n-naqd al-adabī,* edited by ʿAbbās ʿAbd al-Ḥalīm ʿAbbās, 326–34. Irbid: ʿĀlam al-Kutub al-Ḥadīth, 2006. Originally published in *Jarīdat ad-Dustūr* (12 March 1993).

Abu Deeb, Kamal. "Studies in Arabic Literary Criticism: the concept of organic unity". *Edebiyât* 2 (1977): 57–89.

———. "Towards a Structural Analysis of Pre-Islamic Poetry". *IJMES* 6 (1975): 148–84.

———. "Towards a Structural Analysis of Pre-Islamic Poetry (II), the Eros vision". *Edebiyât* 1 (1976): 3–69.

Ahlwardt, Wilhelm. *Die Handschriften-Verzeichnisse der königliche Bibliotheken zu Berlin. Verzeichniss der arabischen Handschriften.* Berlin, 1887–99.

———. *Über Poesie und Poetik der Araber*. Gotha: Friedrich Andreas Perthes, 1856.

Ajami, Mansour. *The Neckveins of Winter: the controversy over natural and artificial poetry in medieval Arabic literary criticism.* Leiden: Brill, 1984.

Akkach, Samer. *Intimate Invocations. Al-Ghazzī's Biography of ʿAbd al-Ghanī al-Nābulusī (1641–1731).* Leiden: Brill, 2012.

Ali, Samer M. *Arabic Literary Salons in the Islamic Middle Ages: poetry, public performance, and the presentation of the past.* Notre Dame, IN: University of Notre Dame Press, 2010.

Allan, Michael. *In the Shadow of World Literature: sites of reading in colonial Egypt.* Princeton, NJ: Princeton University Press, 2016.

Allen, Joseph R. "Macropoetic Structures: the Chinese solution". *Comparative Literature* 45:4 (Autumn 1993): 305-329.

Allen, Roger. Review of G. J. van Gelder, *Beyond the Line. Edebiyât* n.s. 1:2 (1989): 155–56.

Allen, Roger and D. S. Richards (eds). *Arabic Literature in the Post-Classical Period.* Ser. Cambridge History of Arabic Literature. Cambridge: Cambridge University Press, 2006.

Altick, Richard D. *The English Common Reader: a social history of the mass reading public, 1800–1900.* 2nd ed. Columbus, OH: Ohio State University Press, 1998.

ʿAllūsh, Yā-Sīn and ʿAbd Allāh ar-Rajrājī. *Fihris al-makhṭūṭāt al-ʿArabiyyah al-maḥfūẓah fī l-khizānah bi-r-Ribāṭ. al-Qism ath-thānī (1921–1953). Vol. 2.* Casablanca: Maṭbaʿat an-Najāḥ al-Jadīdah [for al-Khizānah al-ʿĀmmah li-l-Kutub wa-l-Wathāʾiq], 1997.

Amer, Sahar. "Medieval Arab Lesbians and Lesbian-Like Women". *Journal of the History of Sexuality* 18:2 (May 2009): 215–36.

Amīn, Bakrī Shaykh. *Muṭālaʿāt fī sh-shiʿr al-Mamlūkī wa-l-ʿUthmānī.* Beirut: Dār ash-Shurūq, 1972.

al-Ānisī, Aḥmad b. Aḥmad. *Dīwān.* (See in the annotated bibliography: 17th century, 2. a).

anon. *ad-Durar al-fāʾiqah fī l-maqāṭīʿ ar-rāʾiqah.* (See in the annotated bibliography: 17th century, 9. a).

anon. *Khadīm aẓ-ẓurafāʾ wa-nadīm al-luṭafāʾ.* (See in the annotated bibliography: 17th century, 5. a).

anon. *Muʾallafāt Shams ad-Dīn Muḥammad b. Ḥasan an-Nawājī ash-Shāfiʿī.* ed. Ḥasan Muḥammad ʿAbd al-Hādī. Amman: Dār al-Yanābīʿ, 2001.

anon. Untitled anthology. Princeton MS Garrett 168H. (See in the annotated bibliography: 16th century, 6. a).

anon. Untitled poetry collection. Staatsbibliothek zu Berlin MS Sprenger 1239. (See in the annotated bibliography: 17th century, 6. a).

anon. Untitled poetry collection. Gotha MS Orient A 2211. (See in the annotated bibliography: 17th century, 10. a).

anon. Untitled anthology. Gotha MS Orient A 2175 (See in the annotated bibliography: 19th century, 1. a)

al-Anṭākī, Dāwūd. *Tazyīn al-aswāq bi-tafṣīl ashwāq al-ʿushshāq.* Cairo: al-Maṭbaʿah al-Azhariyyah, 1319/1901.

Antoon, Sinan. *The Poetics of the Obscene in Premodern Arabic Poetry: Ibn al-Ḥajjāj and sukhf.* New York, NY: Palgrave Macmillan, 2014.

Apter, Emily. *Against World Literature: on the politics of untranslatability.* London: Verso, 2013.

Arazi, Albert. *Amour divin et amour profane dans l'Islam médiéval. À travers le Dīwān de Khālid al-Kātib.* Paris: G.-P. Maisonneuve et Larose, 1990.

———. "De la voix au calame et la naissance du classicisme en poésie". *Arabica* 44:3 (Juillet 1997): 377–406.

Arberry, Arthur J. *The Chester Beatty Library. A Handlist of the Arabic Manuscripts.* 8 vols. Dublin: Hodges, Figgis & co., ltd., 1964.

———. *The Koran Interpreted.* 2 vols. London: Allen & Unwin, 1955.

———. "Orient Pearls at Random Strung". *BSOAS* 11:4 (February 1946): 699–712.

———. *The Cambridge School of Arabic.* Cambridge: Cambridge University Press, 1948.

Argentieri, Lorenzo. "Epigramma e Libro. Morfologia delle raccolte epigrammatiche premeleagree". *Zeitschrift für Papyrologie und Epigraphik* 121 (1998): 1–20.

———. "Meleager and Philip as Epigram Collectors" in *Brill's Companion to Hellenistic Epigram: down to Philip*, edited by Peter Bing and Jon Steffen Bruss, 147–64. Leiden: Brill, 2007.

ʿArshi, Imtiyaz Ali Khan. *Catalogue of the Arabic Manuscripts in Raza Library, Rampur*. 6 vols. Rampur, U. P.: Raza Library Trust, 1963–68.

Ashtiany, Julia, T. M. Johnstone, J. D. Latham, R. B. Serjeant, and G. Rex Smiths (eds). *ʿAbbasid Belles-Lettres*. Ser. Cambridge History of Arabic Literature. Cambridge: Cambridge University Press, 1990.

Ashtiany, Julia. See further under Bray, Julia Ashtiany.

al-ʿAskarī, Abū Hilāl. *Dīwān al-Maʿānī*. 2 vols in 1. Cairo: Maktabat al-Qudsī, 1352/1933.

———. *Dīwān al-Maʿānī*. ed. Aḥmad Ḥasan Basaj. Beirut: Dār al-Kutub al-ʿIlmiyyah, 1994.

———. *Dīwān al-Maʿānī*. ed. Aḥmad Salīm Ghānim. Beirut: Dār al-Gharb al-Islāmī, 2003.

al-Aṣmaʿī. *al-Aṣmaʿiyyāt*. ed. Aḥmad Muḥammad Shākir and ʿAbd as-Salām Hārūn. Cairo: Dār al-Maʿārif, 1979.

al-ʿAsqalānī, Ibn Ḥajar. *See* Ibn Ḥajar al-ʿAsqalānī.

al-ʿAṭṭārī, Aḥmad b. ʿAbd ar-Raḥīm. Untitled poetry collection. (See in the annotated bibliography: 19th century, 3. a).

Aumer, Joseph. *Die arabischen Handschriften der K. Hof- und Staatsbibliothek in Muenchen*. Munich: In Commission der Palm'schen Hofbuchhandlung, 1866.

al-Azdī, ʿAlī b. Ẓāfir. *Badāʾiʿ al-badāʾih*. ed. Muḥammad Abū l-Faḍl Ibrāhīm. Cairo: Maktabat al-Anjlū al-Miṣriyyah, 1970.

———. *Gharāʾib at-tanbīhāt ʿalā ʿajāʾib at-tashbīhāt*. ed. Muḥammad Zaghlūl Sallām and Muṣṭafā aṣ-Ṣāwī al-Juwaynī. Cairo: Dār al-Maʿārif, 1971.

al-Bāʿūnī, Burhān ad-Dīn Ibrāhīm b. Aḥmad. *al-Ghayth al-hātin fī l-ʿidhār al-fātin*. (See in the annotated bibliography: 15th century, 4. a).

Badawi, Mustafa M. "ʿAbbasid Poetry and its Antecedents" in *ʿAbbasid Belles-Lettres*, edited by Julia Ashtiany et al., 146–66. Ser. Cambridge History of Arabic Literature. Cambridge: Cambridge University Press, 1990.

al-Badrī, Abū t-Tuqā Taqī ad-Dīn Abū Bakr b. ʿAbd Allāh. *Ghurrat aṣ-ṣabāḥ fī waṣf al-wujūh aṣ-ṣibāḥ*. (See in the annotated bibliography: 15th century, 9. a).

al-Baghdādī, ʿAbd al-Qādir ibn ʿUmar. *Khizānat al-Adab wa-lubb lubāb «Lisān al-ʿArab»*. ed. ʿAbd as-Salām Hārūn. 13 vols. Cairo: Dār al-Kātib al-ʿArabī li-ṭ-Ṭibāʿah wa-n-Nashr, 1967–.

Baldick, Chris. *The Oxford Dictionary of Literary Terms*. 3rd Edition. Oxford University Press, 2008.

Barceló, Carmen. *La escritura árabe en el país valenciano. Inscripciones monumentales.* 2 vols. Valencia: Area de Estudios Árabes e Islámicos, Universidad de Valencia, 1998.

Bāshā, ʿUmar Mūsā. *Al-Adab al-ʿArabī fī l-ʿaṣr al-Mamlūkī wa-l-ʿaṣr al-ʿUthmānī.* 2 vols. Damascus: Maṭbaʿat Dār al-Kitāb, 1990.

Bateson, Mary Catherine. *Structural Continuity in Poetry: a linguistic study of five Pre-Islamic Arabic odes.* The Hague: Mouton, 1970.

Bauer, Thomas. "Abū Tammām's Contribution to ʿAbbāsid *Ġazal* Poetry". *JAL* 27:1 (1996): 13–21.

———. *Altarabische Dichtkunst: eine Untersuchung ihrer Struktur und Entwicklung am Beispiel der Onagerepisode.* 2 vols. Wiesbaden: Harrassowitz, 1992.

———. "'*Ayna hādhā min al-Mutanabbī!*' – Towards an Aesthetics of Mamluk Literature". *MSR* 17 (2013): 5–22.

———. "Communication and Emotion: the case of Ibn Nubātah's *Kindertotenlieder*". *MSR* 7:1 (2003): 49–95.

———. "Das Nīlzaǧal des Ibrāhīm al-Miʿmār: Ein Lied zur Feier des Nilschwellenfestes" in *Alltagsleben und materielle Kultur in der arabischen Sprache und Literatur. Festschrift für Heinz Grotzfeld zum 70. Geburtstag*, edited by Th. Bauer and U. Stehli-Werbeck, 69–88. Wiesbaden: Harrassowitz, 2005.

———. "The Dawādār's Hunting Party: a Mamluk *muzdawija ṭardiyya*, probably by Shihāb al-Dīn Ibn Faḍl Allāh" in *O Ye Gentlemen: Arabic studies on science and literary culture in honour of Remke Kruk*, edited by A. Vrolijk and J. P. Hogendijk, 291–312. Leiden: Brill, 2007.

———. "Dignity at Stake: *mujūn* epigrams by Ibn Nubāta (686–768/1287–1366) and his contemporaries" in *The Rude, the Bad and the Bawdy. Essays in Honour of Professor Geert Jan van Gelder*, edited by A. Talib, M. Hammond, and A. Schippers, 164–92. Cambridge: Gibb Memorial Trust, 2014.

———. "Ibn Ḥajar and the Arabic *ghazal* of the Mamluk Age" in *Ghazal as World Literature. Vol. 1: Transformations of a Literary Genre*, edited by Th. Bauer and A. Neuwirth, 35–55. Beirut: Ergon Verlag [Würzburg], 2005.

———. "Ibn Nubātah al-Miṣrī (686–768/1287–1366): Life and Works. Part I: The Life of Ibn Nubātah". *MSR* 12:1 (2008): 1–35.

———. "Ibn Nubātah al-Miṣrī (686–768/1287–1366): Life and Works. Part II: The *Dīwān* of Ibn Nubātah". *MSR* 12:2 (2008): 25–69.

———. "Ibrāhīm al-Miʿmār: ein dichtender Handwerker aus Ägyptens Mamlukenzeit". *ZDMG* 152:1 (2002): 63–93.

———. "In Search of 'Post-Classical Literature': a review article". *MSR* 11:2 (2007): 137–67.

———. "Jamāl al-Dīn Ibn Nubātah" in *Essays in Arabic Literary Biography 1350–1850*, edited by J. Lowry and D. Stewart, 184–202. Wiesbaden: Harrassowitz, 2009.

Bauer, Thomas. *Die Kultur der Ambiguität. Eine andere Geschichte des Islams*. Berlin: Verlag der Weltreligionen im Insel Verlag, 2011.

———. *Liebe und Liebesdichtung in der arabischen Welt des 9. und 10. Jahrhunderts: eine literatur- und mentalitätsgeschichtliche Studie des arabischen Ġazal*. Wiesbaden: Harrassowitz, 1998.

———. "Literarische Anthologien der Mamlūkenzeit" in *Die Mamlūken: Studien zu ihrer Geschichte und Kultur: zum Gedenken an Ulrich Haarmann, 1942–1999*, edited by S. Conermann and A. Pistor-Hatam, 71–122. Hamburg, 2003.

———. "Mamluk Literature as a Means of Communication" in *Ubi Sumus? Quo Vademus? Mamluk Studies—State of the Art*, edited by S. Conermann, 23–56. Bonn: Bonn University Press, 2013.

———. "Mamluk Literature: misunderstandings and new approaches". *MSR* 9:2 (2005): 105–132.

———. "al-Nawājī" in *Essays in Arabic Literary Biography 1350–1850*, edited by J. Lowry and D. Stewart, 321–31. Wiesbaden: Harrassowitz, 2009.

———. "Raffinement und Frömmigkeit. Säkulare Poesie islamischer Religionsgelehrter der späten Abbasidenzeit". *AS/EA* 50:2: Literatur und Wirklichkeit—Littérature et Réalités (1996): 275–95.

———. "Vom Sinn der Zeit: aus der Geschichte des arabischen Chronogramms". *Arabica* 50:4 (2003): 501–31.

———. "„Was kann aus dem Jungen noch werden!" Das poetische Erstlingswerk des Historikers Ibn Ḥabīb im Spiegel seiner Zeitgenossen" in *Studien zur Semitistik und Arabistik. Festschrift für Hartmut Bobzin zum 60. Geburtstag*, edited by Otto Jastrow, Shabo Talay, and Herta Hafenrichter, 15–56. Wiesbaden: Harrassowitz, 2008.

Bauer, Thomas and Angelika Neuwirth (eds). *Ghazal as world literature. Vol. 1: Transformations of a literary genre*. Ser. Beiruter Texte und Studien, Band 89. Beirut: Ergon Verlag [Würzburg], 2005.

Baumbach, Manuel, Andrej Petrovic, and Ivana Petrovic (eds). *Archaic and Classical Greek Epigram*. Cambridge: Cambridge University Press, 2010.

Bausani, Alessandro. "The development of form in Persian lyrics". *East and West* n.s. 9:3 (September 1958): 145–53.

Beebee, Thomas O. *The Ideology of Genre: a comparative study of generic instability*. University Park, PA: The Pennsylvania State University Press, 1994.

de Beer, Susanna. "The *Pointierung* of Giannantonio Campano's Epigrams: theory and practice" in *The Neo-Latin Epigram. A Learned and Witty Genre*, edited by S. de Beer et al., 137–63. Ser. Supplementa Humanistica Lovaniensia, 25. Leuven: Leuven University Press, 2009.

de Beer, Susanna, Karl A. E. Enenkel, and David Rijser (eds). *The Neo-Latin Epigram. A Learned and Witty Genre*. Ser. Supplementa Humanistica Lovaniensia, 25. Leuven: Leuven University Press, 2009.

Beeston, A. F. L., T. M. Johnstone, R. B. Serjeant, and G. R. Smith (eds). *Arabic Literature to the end of the Umayyad Period*. Ser. Cambridge History of Arabic Literature. Cambridge: Cambridge University Press, 1983.

van Bekkum, Wout Jac. *The Secular Poetry of El'azar ben Ya'aqov ha-Bavli. Baghdad, Thirteenth Century on the basis of manuscript Firkovicz Heb. IIA, 210.1 St. Petersburg.* Leiden: Brill, 2007.

Bencheikh, Jamal Eddine. *Poétique arabe: essai sur les voies d'une création.* Paris: Éditions Anthropos, 1975.

Benedict, Barbara M. *Making the Modern Reader: cultural mediation in early modern literary anthologies*. Princeton, NJ: Princeton University Press, 1996.

Berenbaum, Michael and Fred Skolnik (eds). *Encyclopaedia Judaica.* 2nd ed. Detroit: Macmillan Reference USA, 2007.

Biblioteca de al-Andalus. ed. Jorge Lirola Delgado and José Miguel Puerta Vílchez. 9 vols. Ser. Enciclopedia de la cultura andalusí. Almería : Fundación Ibn Tufayl de Estudios Árabes, 2004-2013.

Bing, Peter. "Between Literature and the Monuments" in *Genre in Hellenistic Poetry*, edited by M. A. Harder, 21–43. Ser. Hellenistica Groningana, 3. Groningen: Egbert Forsten, 1998.

———. *The Scroll and the Marble: studies in reading and reception in Hellenistic poetry*. Ann Arbor, MI: University of Michigan Press, 2009.

———. "The Un-Read Muse? Inscribed Epigram and its Readers in Antiquity" in *Hellenistic Epigrams*, edited by M. A. Harder et al., 39–66. Leuven: Peeters, 2002.

Bing, Peter and Jon Steffen Bruss (eds). *Brill's Companion to Hellenistic Epigram: down to Philip*. Leiden: Brill, 2007.

Blachère, Régis. *Histoire de la Littérature Arabe. Des origines à la fin du XVe siècle de J.-C.* 3 vols. Paris: Librairie d'Amérique et d'Orient, Adrien-Maisonneuve, 1952–66.

———. "Un jardin secret: la poésie arabe". *SI* 9 (1958): 5–12.

Bloch, Alfred. "Qaṣīda". *AS/EA* 2 (1948): 106–32.

Bond, Henry. *Lacan at the Scene*. Cambridge, MA: MIT Press, 2009.

Bonebakker, S[eeger] A[drianus]. "Adab and the concept of belles-lettres" in *'Abbasid Belles-Lettres*, edited by Julia Ashtiany et al., 16–30. Ser. Cambridge History of Arabic Literature. Cambridge: Cambridge University Press, 1990.

———. "Early Arabic Literature and the Term *Adab*." *JSAI* 5 (1984): 389–421.

———. *Materials for the History of Arabic Rhetoric*. Naples: Istituto Orientale, 1975.

———. *Some Early Definitions of the Tawriya and Ṣafadī's* Faḍḍ al-Xitām 'an al-tawriya wa-l-istixdām. The Hague: Mouton, 1966.

Bosworth, C[lifford] E[dmund]. "A Janissary Poet of Sixteenth-Century Damascus: Māmayya al-Rūmī" in *The Islamic World: from classical to modern times. Essays in Honor of Bernard Lewis*, edited by C. E. Bosworth et al., 451–66. Princeton, NJ: The Darwin Press, 1989.

Bowie, Ewen. "From Archaic Elegy to Hellenistic Sympotic Epigram?" in *Brill's Companion to Hellenistic Epigram: down to Philip*, edited by P. Bing and J. S. Bruss, 95–112. Leiden: Brill, 2007.

Bray, Julia Ashtiany. "Third and fourth-century bleeding poetry". *Arabic & Middle Eastern Literatures* 2:1 (1999): 75–92.

Brill's New Pauly. See under *Der Neue Pauly*.

Brockelmann, Carl. *Geschichte der arabischen Litteratur*. 2 vols and 3 supplementary vols. Leiden: E. J. Brill, 1898–1942 [repr. 1943–49].

Brower, Robert H. and Earl Miner. *Japanese Court Poetry*. Stanford, CA: Stanford University Press, 1961.

Browne, E[dward] G[ranville]. *A Literary History of Persia*. 4 vols. Cambridge: Cambridge University Press, 1920–25.

———. *A Supplementary Hand-List of the Muḥammadan Manuscripts in the libraries of the University and Colleges of Cambridge*. Cambridge: Cambridge University Press, 1922.

al-Buḥturī, al-Walīd b. ʿUbayd. *Al-Ḥamāsah*. ed. Muḥammad Ibrāhīm Ḥuwar and Aḥmad Muḥammad ʿUbayd. Abu Dhabi: al-Majmaʿ ath-Thaqāfī, 2007.

———. *The Ḥamâsah of al-Buḥturî (Abû ʿUbâdah al-Walîd Ibn ʿUbaid) A.H. 205-284 : photographic reproduction of the ms. at Leiden in the university library.* Indexes by R. Geyer and D. S. Margoliouth. Ser. Publication of the De Goeje Fund, 1. Leiden: E. J. Brill, 1909.

Bürgel, J. Christoph. *Die ekphrastischen Epigramme des Abū Ṭālib al-Maʾmūnī*. Ser. Nachrichten der Akademie der Wissenschaften in Göttingen. I. Philologisch-Historische Klasse. Nr. 14, 1965. Göttingen: Vandenhoeck and Ruprecht, 1966.

———. Review of S. Sperl, *Mannerism in Arabic Poetry*. JSS 39:2 (Autumn 1994): 367–72.

Cachia, Pierre. *The Arch Rhetorician. Or, The Schemer's Skimmer: a handbook of late Arabic* badīʿ *drawn from ʿAbd al-Ghanī an-Nābulsī's* Nafaḥāt al-azhār ʿalā nasamāt al-asḥār. Wiesbaden: Harrassowitz, 1998.

Cai, Zong-Qi (ed.). *How to Read Chinese Poetry: a guided anthology*. New York, NY: Columbia University Press, 2008.

Cameron, Alan. *Callimachus and his Critics*. Princeton, NJ: Princeton University Press, 1995.

———. *The Greek Anthology: from Meleager to Planudes*. Oxford: Clarendon Press, 1993.

Chamberlain, Basil Hall. "Bashō and the Japanese Poetical Epigram" in B. H. Chamberlain, *Japanese Poetry*, 145–209. London: John Murray, 1911. [This article first appeared in *Transactions of the Asiatic Society of Japan* vol. 30, pt. 2 (1902)].

———. *The Classical Poetry of the Japanese*. London: Trübner & co., 1880 [repr. London: Routledge, 2000].

———. *Japanese Poetry*. London: John Murray, 1911.

Chinn, Christopher. "Statius Silv. 4.6 and the Epigrammatic Origins of Ekphrasis". *The Classical Journal* 100:3 (February–March 2005): 247–63.

Chipman, Leigh. *The World of Pharmacy and Pharmacists in Mamlūk Cairo*. Leiden: Brill, 2010.

Chow, Rey. *The Age of the World Target: self-referentiality in war, theory, and comparative work*. Durham, NC: Duke University Press, 2006.

Cole, Peter. *The Dream of the Poem: Hebrew poetry from Muslim and Christian Spain, 950–1492*. Princeton, NJ: Princeton University Press, 2007.

Colie, Rosalie L. *The Resources of Kind: genre-theory in the Renaissance*. Berkeley and Los Angeles, CA: University of California Press, 1973.

Conermann, Stephan. Review of Jalāl ad-Dīn as-Suyūṭī, *Kawkab ar-rawḍah fī tārīkh an-Nīl wa-jazīrat ar-Rawḍah*, ed. Muḥammad ash-Shishtāwī. *MSR* 11:2 (2007): 206–9.

Conermann, Stephan (ed.). *Ubi Sumus? Quo Vademus? Mamluk Studies—State of the Art.* Bonn: Bonn University Press, 2013.

Conermann, Stephan and Anja Pistor-Hatam (eds). *Die Mamlūken: Studien zu ihrer Geschichte und Kultur: zum Gedenken an Ulrich Haarmann, 1942–1999*. Hamburg, 2003.

Cooperson, Michael. "ʿAlāʾ al-Dīn al-Ghuzūlī" in *Essays in Arabic Literary Biography 1350–1850*, edited by J. Lowry and D. Stewart, 107–17. Wiesbaden: Harrassowitz, 2009.

Damrosch, David. *How to Read World Literature*. Oxford: Wiley-Blackwell, 2009.

Dasgupta, S. N. et al. (eds). *A History of Sanskrit Literature, Classical Period.* Calcutta: University of Calcutta [Press], 1947–.

Davis, Dick. *Borrowed Ware: medieval Persian epigrams*. London: Anvil Press, 1996.

———. *Borrowed Ware: medieval Persian epigrams*. Washington, DC: Mage Publishers, 2004.

Defter-i Fatih Kütüphanesi. Istanbul: Mahmut Bey Matbaası, n. d.

Defter-i Kütüphane-i Nur-i Osmaniye. Istanbul: Mahmut Bey Matbaası, 1303/1886.

Derenbourg, Hartwig. *Les manuscrits arabes de l'Escurial.* Paris, 1884 [repr. Hildesheim: Georg Olms Verlag, 1976].

Der Neue Pauly. Antike (Antiquity): 14 vols. Edited by Hubert Cancik and Helmuth Schneider. English ed. by Christine F. Salazar; Rezeptions- und Wissenschaftsgeschichte (Classical Tradition): 5 vols. Edited by Manfred Landfester. English ed. by Francis G. Gentry. Original ed.: Stuttgart; Weimar: Verlag J. B Metzler, 1996–. *Brill's New Pauly*: Leiden, Brill, 2002–.

Derrida, Jacques. "The Law of Genre". trans. Avital Ronell. *Critical Inquiry* 7:1 (Autumn 1980): 55–81.

Diem, Werner. "The Role of Poetry in Arabic Funerary Inscriptions" in *Poetry and History. The Value of Poetry in Reconstructing Arab History*, edited by Ramzi Baalbaki et al., 121–36. Beirut: American University of Beirut Press, 2011.

Diem, Werner and Marco Schöller. *The Living and the Dead in Islam: studies in Arabic epitaphs*. 3 vols. Wiesbaden: Harrassowitz, 2004.

Dozy, Reinhart. *Supplément aux dictionnaires arabes*. 2 vols. Leiden: Brill, 1881. [repr. Beirut: Librairie du Liban, 1991].

Drory, Rina. *Models and Contacts: Arabic literature and its impact on medieval Jewish culture*. Leiden: Brill, 2000.

Duff, David (ed.). *Modern Genre Theory*. Harlow: Longman, 2000.

EAL: *Encyclopedia of Arabic literature.* Edited by Julie Scott Meisami and Paul Starkey. 2 vols. London: Routledge, 1998.

El-Rouayheb, Khaled. *Before Homosexuality in the Arab-Islamic World, 1500–1800*. Chicago, IL: University of Chicago Press, 2005.

El Shamsy, Ahmed. *The Canonization of Islamic Law: a social and intellectual history*. Cambridge: Cambridge University Press, 2013.

El Tayib, Abdulla. "Pre-Islamic Poetry" in *Arabic Literature to the end of the Umayyad Period*, edited by A. F. L. Beeston et al., 27–113. Cambridge: Cambridge University Press, 1983.

Elwell-Sutton, L. P. "The Omar Khayyam Puzzle". *Journal of the Royal Central Asian Society* 55:2 (June 1968): 167–79.

Encyclopædia Britannica. 11th edition. 1910–11.

Encyclopaedia of Islam. 1st edition. Edited by M. Th. Houtsma, T. W. Arnold, R. Basset, and R. Hartmann. 5 vols. Leiden: Brill, 1913–38.

EI²: *Encyclopaedia of Islam. New Edition.* Edited by P. Bearman , Th. Bianquis , C.E. Bosworth , E. van Donzel and W. P. Heinrichs. 11 vols. Leiden: Brill, 1960-2009.

EI³: *Encyclopaedia of Islam, Three.* Edited by Gudrun Krämer, Denis Matringe, John Nawas, and Everett K. Rowson. Leiden: Brill, 2007–.

EIran: *Encyclopaedia Iranica.* General ed. Ehsan Yarshater. London: Routledge & Kegan Paul, 1982–. Also online at <http://www.iranicaonline.org>.

Enderwitz, Susanne. *Liebe als Beruf. Al-ʿAbbās ibn al-Aḥnaf und das Ġazal.* Beirut [Stuttgart]: Franz Steiner Verlag, 1995.

van Ess, Josef. *Der Ṭailasan des Ibn Ḥarb: 'Mantelgedichte' in arabischer Sprache.* Heidelberg: Winter, 1979.

Fakhreddine, Huda J. "Defining Metapoesis in the ʿAbbāsid Age". JAL (42:2–3) 2011: 205–35.

———. "From Modernists to *Muḥdathūn*: metapoesis in Arabic". Unpublished doctoral thesis. Indiana University, 2011.

Farrell, Joseph. "Classical Genre in Theory and Practice". *New Literary History* 34:3 (Summer 2003): 383–408.

Farrin, Raymond. *Abundance from the Desert: classical Arabic poetry*. Syracuse, NY: Syracuse University Press, 2011.

———. "Reading Beyond the Line: organic unity in classical Arabic poetry". Unpublished doctoral thesis. University of California, Berkeley, 2006.

Ferguson, Charles A. "Arabic Baby Talk" in *Structuralist Studies in Arabic Linguistics. Charles A. Ferguson's Papers, 1954–1994*, edited by R. Kirk Belknap and Niloofar Haeri, 179–87. Leiden: Brill, 1997.

Ferry, Anne. *Tradition and the Individual Poem: an inquiry into anthologies.* Stanford, CA: Stanford University Press, 2001.

Fischer, Wolfdietrich and Helmut Gätje (eds). *Grundriss der arabischen Philologie.* 3 vols. Wiesbaden: Reichert, 1982–92.

Fishelov, David. *Metaphors of Genre: the role of analogies in genre theory*. University Park, PA: Pennsylvania State University Press, 1993.

Fitzgerald, William. *Martial: the world of epigram*. Chicago, IL: University of Chicago Press, 2007.

Flügel, Gustav. *Die arabischen, persischen und türkischen Handschriften der kaiserlich-königlichen Hofbibliothek zu Wien*. 3 vols. Vienna: kaiserliche-königliche Hof- und Staatsdruckerei, 1865.

Fowden, Garth. *Quṣayr ʿAmra: art and the Umayyad elite in late antique Syria.* Berkeley, CA: University of California Press, 2004.

Fowler, Alastair. "The Formation of Genres in the Renaissance and After". *New Literary History* 34:2 (Spring 2003): 185–200.

———. *Kinds of Literature: an introduction to the theory of genres and modes*. Oxford: Oxford University Press, 1982.

Fraistat, Neil. *The Poem and the Book: interpreting collections of Romantic poetry*. Chapel Hill, NC: University of North Carolina Press, 1985.

Fraistat, Neil (ed.). *Poems in their Place: the intertextuality and order of poetic collections*. Chapel Hill, NC: University of North Carolina Press, 1986.

Frankel, Hans H. *The Flowering Plum and the Palace Lady: interpretations of Chinese poetry*. New Haven, CT: Yale University Press, 1976.

Frow, John. *Genre*. Ser. The New Critical Idiom. London and New York, NY: Routledge, 2006.

———. *Marxism and Literary History*. Oxford: Basil Blackwell, 1986.

Frye, Northrop. *Anatomy of Criticism: Four Essays.* Princeton, NJ: Princeton University Press, 1957.

Fück, Johann. *Die arabischen Studien in Europa bis in den Anfang des 20. Jahrhunderts*. Leipzig: Otto Harrassowitz, 1955.

Gabrieli, Francesco. *Storia della Letteratura Araba.* Terza edizione. Milan: Nuova Accademia Editrice, 1962.

GAL: See under Carl Brockelmann. *Geschichte der arabischen Litteratur.*

GAP: See under Wolfdietrich Fischer and Helmut Gätje (eds). *Grundriss der arabischen Philologie.*

Galan, František W. "Literary System and Systemic Change: the Prague School of literary history, 1928–48". *PMLA* 94:2 (March 1979): 275–85.

Gamal, Adel Suleyman. "The Basis of Selection in the 'Ḥamāsa' Collections". *JAL* 7 (1976): 28–44.
———. "The Organizational Principles in Ibn Sallām's *Ṭabaqāt Fuḥūl al-Shuʿarāʾ*: a reconsideration" in *Tradition and Modernity in Arabic Language and Literature*, edited by J. R. Smart, 186–209. Richmond: Curzon, 1996.
van Gelder, Geert Jan. "Against Women and other Pleasantries: the last chapter of Abū Tammām's *Ḥamāsa*". *JAL* 16 (1985): 61–72.
———. "Arabic Poetics and Stylistics according to the Introduction of *al-Durr al-Farīd* by Muḥammad Ibn Aydamir (d. 710/1310)". *ZDMG* 146 (1996): 381–414.
———. *Beyond the Line: classical Arabic literary critics on the coherence and unity of the poem*. Leiden: Brill, 1982.
———. "Brevity: the long and the short of it in classical Arabic literary theory" in *Proceedings of the Ninth Congress of the Union européenne des arabisants et islamisants: Amsterdam, 1st to 7th September 1978*, edited by Rudolph Peters, 78–88. Leiden: Brill, 1981.
———. "The Classical Arabic Canon of Polite (and Impolite) Literature" in *Cultural Repertoires: structure, function and dynamics*, edited by G. J. Dorleijn and H. L. J. Vanstiphout, 45–57. Leuven: Peeters, 2003.
———. *Close Relationships: incest and inbreeding in classical Arabic literature*. London: I. B. Tauris, 2005.
———. "Compleat Men, Women and Books: on medieval Arabic encyclopaedism" in *Pre-Modern Encyclopaedic Texts. Proceedings of the Second COMERS Congress, Groningen, 1–4 July 1996*, edited by P. Binkley, 241–60. Leiden: Brill, 1997.
———. "The Conceit of Pen and Sword: on an Arabic literary debate". *JSS* 32:2 (1987): 329–60.
———. "A Cotton Shirt: an 'unparalleled' poem by Ibn Abī Karīma (early 9th century)" in *Festschrift Ewald Wagner zum 65. Geburtstag, Band 2: Studien zur arabische Dichtung*, edited by W. Heinrichs and G. Schoeler, 283–96. Beirut: Franz Steiner Verlag, 1994.
———. "Dubious Genres: on some poems of Abū Nuwās". *Arabica* 44 (1997): 268–83.
———. "Genres in Collision: *nasīb* and *hijāʾ*". *JAL* 21:1 (1990): 14–25.
———. "Mirror for Princes or Vizor for Viziers: the twelfth-century Arabic popular encyclopedia *Mufīd al-ʿulūm* and its relationship with the anonymous Persian *Baḥr al-fawāʾid*". *BSOAS* 64:3 (2001): 313–38.
———. "Mixtures of Jest and Earnest in classical Arabic literature: Part I". *JAL* 23:2 (1992): 83–108.
———. "Mixtures of Jest and Earnest in classical Arabic literature: Part II". *JAL* 23:3 (1992): 169–90.
———. "A Muslim Encomium on Wine: *The Racecourse of the Bay* (*Ḥalbat al-kumayt*) by al-Nawāǧī (d. 859/1455) as a post-classical Arabic work". *Arabica* 42:2 (June 1995): 222–34.

van Gelder, Geert Jan. "Al-Mutanabbī's Encumbering Trifles". *Arabic & Middle Eastern Literatures* 2:1 (1999): 5–19.

———. "Poetry for Easy Listening: *insijām* and related concepts in Ibn Ḥijjah's *Khizānat al-Adab*". MSR 7:1 (2003): 31–48.

———. "Poetry in Historiography: the case of *al-Fakhrī* by Ibn al-Ṭiqṭaqā" in *Poetry and History. The Value of Poetry in Reconstructing Arab History*, edited by R. Baalbaki et al., 61–94. Beirut: American University of Beirut Press, 2011.

———. "Poetry in Historiography: some observations" in *Problems in Arabic Literature*, edited by M. Maróth, 1–13. Piliscsaba, The Avicenna Institute of Middle Eastern Studies, 2004.

———. "Pointed and Well-Rounded. Arabic Encomiastic and Elegiac Epigrams". *Orientalia Lovaniensia Periodica* 26 (1995): 101–40.

———. "Some Brave Attempts at Generic Classification in Premodern Arabic Literature" in *Aspects of Genre and Type in Pre-modern Literary Cultures*, edited by Bert Roest and Herman Vanstiphout, 15–31. Groningen, Styx, 1999.

———. *Sound and Sense in Classical Arabic Poetry*. Ser. Arabische Studien, 10. Wiesbaden: Harrassowitz, 2012.

———. "The Terrified Traveller. Ibn al-Rūmī's Anti-*Raḥīl*". JAL 27 (1996): 37–48.

———. Review of R. Farrin, *Abundance from the Desert. Speculum* 87:4 (2012): 1190–91.

———. Review of an-Nawājī, *Kitāb ash-Shifāʾ fī badīʿ al-iktifāʾ*, ed. Ḥasan Muḥammad ʿAbd al-Hādī. MSR 11:1 (2007): 233–35.

al-Ghazzī, Najm ad-Dīn. *al-Kawākib as-sāʾirah bi-ʾayʿān al-miʾah al-ʿāshirah*. 3 vols. ed. Khalīl al-Manṣūr. Beirut: Dār al-Kutub al-ʿIlmiyyah, 1418/1997.

Ghersetti, Antonella. "An Unpublished Anthology of the Mamluk Period on Generosity and Generous Men". MSR 13:1 (2009): 107–20.

al-Ghuzūlī, ʿAlāʾ ad-Dīn ʿAlī b. ʿAbd Allāh. *Maṭāliʿ al-budūr fī manāzil as-surūr*. 2 vols. Cairo: Maṭbaʿat Idārat al-Waṭan, 1299–1300/1882–83.

Gibb, E[lias] J[ohn] W[ilkinson]. *A History of Ottoman Poetry*. 6 vols. ed. Edward G. Browne. London: Luzac, 1900–09.

Gibb, H[amilton] A. R. *Arabic Literature: an introduction*. 2nd rev. edition. Oxford: Clarendon Press, 1963.

Gies, Hermann. *Ein Beitrag zur Kenntnis sieben neuerer arabischer Versarten*. Leipzig: W. Drugulin, 1879.

Giese, Alma. *Waṣf bei Kušāǧim: eine Studie zur beschreibenden Dichtkunst der Abbasidenzeit*. Berlin: Klaus Schwarz Verlag, 1981.

Girón Negrón, Luis M. "Fortune ibéro-médiévale d'une epigramme arabe". *Horizons Maghrebins* 61 (2009): 49–62.

de Goeje, M. J. *Catalogus codicum orientalium bibliothecae academiae Lugduno-Batavae, volumen quintum*. Leiden: E. J. Brill, 1873.

de Goeje, M. J. and M. Th. Houtsma. *Catalogus codicum arabicorum bibliothecae academiae Lugduno-Batavae, editio secunda, volumen primum*. Leiden: E. J. Brill, 1888.

Goldziher, Ignaz. "Der Dîwân des Ġarwal b. Aus Al-Ḥuṭej'a". Part I: ZDMG 46 (1892): 1–53; 173–225; 471–527; Part II: ZDMG 47 (1893): 43–85; 163–201.

Gopnik, Alison. "Explanation as orgasm and the drive for causal understanding: the evolution, function and phenomenology of the theory-formation system" in *Explanation and Cognition*, edited by F. Keil and R. Wilson, 299–323. Cambridge, MA: MIT Press, 2000.

Görke, Andreas and Konrad Hirschler (eds). *Manuscript Notes as Documentary Sources*. Ser. Beiruter Texte und Studien, 129. Würzburg, Ergon Verlag, 2011.

Gottschalk, H. L. *Islamic Arabic Manuscripts. Vol. 4 of Catalogue of the Mingana Collection of Manuscripts*. Birmingham: Selly Oak Colleges Library, 1948.

Gramlich, Richard (ed.). *Islamwissenschaftliche Abhandlungen. Fritz Meier zum sechzigsten Geburtstag*. Wiesbaden: Franz Steiner Verlag, 1974.

Greene, Roland et al. (eds). *The Princeton Encyclopedia of Poetry and Poetics*. 4th ed. Princeton, NJ: Princeton University Press, 2012.

Gruendler, Beatrice. "Ibn Abī Ḥajalah" in *Essays in Arabic Literary Biography 1350–1850*, edited by J. Lowry and D. Stewart, 118–26. Wiesbaden: Harrassowitz, 2009.

———. *Medieval Arabic praise poetry: Ibn al-Rūmī and the patron's redemption*. London: RoutledgeCurzon, 2003.

———. "Motif vs. Genre: reflections on the *Dīwān al-Maʿānī* of Abū Hilāl al-ʿAskarī" in *Ghazal as World Literature. Vol. 1: Transformations of a Literary Genre,* edited by Th. Bauer and A. Neuwirth, 57–85. Beirut: Ergon Verlag [Würzburg], 2005.

———. "*Qaṣīda*. Its Reconstruction in Performance" in *Classical Arabic Humanities in their Own Terms: Festschrift for Wolfhart Heinrichs on his 65th birthday presented by his students and colleagues*, edited by B. Gruendler (with M. Cooperson), 325–89. Leiden: Brill, 2008.

———. "*Tawqīʿ* (Apostille): verbal economy in verdicts of tort redress" in *The Weaving of Words: approaches to Classical arabic literature*, edited by L. Behzadi & V. Behmardi, 101–29. Beirut-Wiesbaden: Ergon, 2009.

Gruendler, Beatrice (with Michael Cooperson) (ed.). *Classical Arabic Humanities in their Own Terms: Festschrift for Wolfhart Heinrichs on his 65th Birthday Presented by his Students and Colleagues*. Leiden: Brill, 2008.

von Grunebaum, Gustave E. *Dirāsāt fī l-adab al-ʿArabī*. trans. Iḥsān ʿAbbās et al. Beirut: Dār Maktabat al-Ḥayāh, 1959.

———. "Growth and Structure of Arabic Poetry, A.D. 500–1000" in *The Arab Heritage*, edited by Nabih Amin Faris, 121–41. Princeton, NJ: Princeton University Press, 1944. German translation: "Wesen und Werden der arabischen Poesie von 500 bis 1000 n. Chr." in G. E. von Grunebaum, *Kritik und Dichtkunst. Studien zur arabischen Literaturgeschichte*, 17–27. Wiesbaden: Otto Harrassowitz, 1955.

von Grunebaum, Gustave E. *Kritik und Dichtkunst. Studien zur arabischen Literaturgeschichte*. Wiesbaden: Otto Harrassowitz, 1955.

———. *Medieval Islam*. 2nd ed. Chicago: University of Chicago Press, 1954.

———. "The Response to Nature in Arabic Poetry". *JNES* 4:3 (July 1945): 137–51.

Guillén, Claudio. *Literature as System: essays toward the theory of literary history.* Princeton, NJ: Princeton University Press, 1971.

Guo, Li. *Commerce, Culture, and Community in a Red Sea Port in the thirteenth century: the Arabic documents from Quseir*. Leiden: Brill, 2004.

———. *The Performing Arts in Medieval Islam: shadow play and popular poetry in Ibn Dāniyāl's Mamluk Cairo*. Ser. Islamic History and Civilization: Studies and Texts, 93. Leiden: Brill, 2012.

———. "Reading *Adab* in historical light: factuality and ambiguity in Ibn Dāniyāl's 'occasional verses' on Mamluk society and politics" in *History and Historiography of Post-Mongol Central Asia and the Middle East. Studies in Honor of John E. Woods,* edited by J. Pfeiffer and S. A. Quinn, with E. Tucker, 383–403. Wiesbaden: Harrassowitz Verlag, 2006.

Gutas, Dimitri. *Greek Thought, Arabic Culture: the Graeco-Arabic translation movement in Baghdad and early 'Abbāsid society (2nd–4th/8th–10th centuries)*. London: Routledge, 1998.

Gutzwiller, Kathryn J. "Anyte's Epigram Book". *Syllecta Classica* 4 (1993): 71–89.

———. "Gender and Inscribed Epigram: Herennia Procula and the Thespian Eros". *Transactions of the American Philological Association* 134 (2004): 383–418.

———. "The Literariness of the Milan Papyrus or 'What Difference a Book?'" in *The New Posidippus: a Hellenistic poetry book*, edited by Kathryn J. Gutzwiller, 287–319. Oxford: Oxford University Press, 2005.

———. "The Poetics of Editing in Meleager's *Garland*". *Transactions of the American Philological Association* 127 (1997): 169–200.

———. *Poetic Garlands: Hellenistic epigrams in context.* Berkeley, CA: University of California Press, 1998.

Gutzwiller, Kathryn J. (ed.). *The New Posidippus: a Hellenistic poetry book*. Oxford: Oxford University Press, 2005.

Hafez, Sabry. "The Transformation of the Qasida Form in Modern Arabic Poetry" in *Qasida Poetry in Islamic Asia and Africa*, 2 vols, edited by S. Sperl and C. Shackle, 1:99–120. Leiden: Brill, 1996.

Ḥāfiẓ, Shams ad-Dīn Muḥammad. *Dīvān-i Ḥāfiẓ*. ed. Qāsim Ghanī, Muḥammad Qazvīnī, and Muṣṭafā Khudādādī. Tehran: Kitābkhānah-yi Millī-yi Īrān, 1377/1998.

Ḥājjī Khalīfah. *Kitāb Kashf aẓ-ẓunūn 'an asāmī l-kutub wa-l-funūn*. 2 vols. ed. Şerefettin Yaltkaya and Rifat Bilge. Istanbul: Maarif Matbaası, 1941. (See also under Kâtib Çelebi).

al-Ḥamawī, 'Uways. *Sukkardān al-'ushshāq wa-manārat al-asmā' wa-l-āmāq*. (See in the annotated bibliography: 16th century, 2. a).

Hamilton, Albert Charles (ed.). *The Spenser Encyclopedia.* London: Routledge, 1990.

Hammond, Marlé. *Beyond Elegy: classical Arabic women's poetry in context.* Oxford: Oxford University Press [for the British Academy], 2010.

Hamori, Andras. *The Composition of Mutanabbī's Panegyrics to Sayf al-Dawla.* Leiden: Brill, 1992.

———. *On the Art of Medieval Arabic Literature.* Princeton, NJ: Princeton University Press, 1974.

———. Review of G. J. van Gelder, *Beyond the Line.* JAOS 104:2 (April–June 1984): 385–87.

al-Ḥarīrī, ʿAlāʾ ad-Dīn aṣ-Ṣāliḥī. *ad-Durr al-maṣūn fī niẓām as-sabʿ funūn.* (See in the annotated bibliography: 16th century, 5. a).

Harris, Joseph and Karl Reichl (eds). *Prosimetrum: crosscultural perspectives on narrative in prose and verse.* Cambridge, MA: D. S. Brewer, 1997.

Hartman, Geoffrey H. "Beyond Formalism" in G. H. Hartman, *Beyond Formalism: literary essays, 1958–1970*, 42–57. New Haven, CT: Yale University Press, 1970. [First published in *MLN* 81:5 (December 1966): 542–56].

———. "Toward Literary History" in G. H. Hartman. *Beyond Formalism: literary essays, 1958–1970*, 356–86. New Haven, CT: Yale University Press, 1970. [First published in *Daedalus* 99:2 (Spring 1970): 355–83].

Hartmann, Martin. *Das arabische Strophengedicht. I[:] das Muwaššaḥ.* Weimar: Emil Felber, 1897.

Ḥasan, ʿAzzah. *Fihris Makhṭūṭāt Dār al-Kutub aẓ-Ẓāhiriyyah. ash-Shiʿr.* Damascus: al-Majmaʿ al-ʿIlmī al-ʿArabī, 1384/1964.

Ḥasan Khān, Muḥammad Ṣiddīq. *Nashwat as-sakrān min ṣahbāʾ tadhkār al-ghizlān.* Bhopal: al-Maṭbaʿah ash-Shāh-Jahānī, 1294/1877 [repr. al-Khurunfish, Cairo: al-Maṭbaʿah ar-Raḥmāniyyah, 1338/1920].

al-Ḥātimī, Muḥammad b. al-Ḥasan. *Ḥilyat al-muḥāḍarah.* ed. Hilāl Nājī. Beirut: Dār Maktabat al-Ḥayāh, 1978.

———. *ar-Risālah al-mūḍiḥah.* ed. Muḥammad Yūsuf Najm. Beirut: Dār Ṣādir; Dār Beirut, 1965.

Hava, J.G. *al-Farāʾid al-durriyyah: Arabic-English dictionary.* Beirut: Catholic Press, 1915.

al-Ḥaymī al-Kawkabānī, Shihāb al-Dīn Aḥmad b. Muḥammad. *Ḥadāʾiq al-nammām fī l-kalām ʿalā mā yataʿallaq bi-l-ḥammām.* ed. ʿAbd Allāh Muḥammad al-Ḥibshī. Beirut: Dār at-Tanwīr, 1986.

Heinrichs, Wolfhart. *Arabische Dichtung und griechische Poetik: Ḥāzim al-Qartağannīs Grundlegung der Poetic mit Hilfe aristotelischer Begriffe.* Beirut: [In Kommission bei Franz Steiner Verlag, Wiesbaden], 1969.

———. "Der Teil und das Ganze: die Auto-Anthologie Ṣafī al-Dīn al-Ḥillīs". AS/EA 59:3 (2005): 675–96.

Heinrichs, Wolfhart. "„Manierismus" in der arabischen Literatur" in *Islamwissenschaftliche Abhandlungen. Fritz Meier zum sechzigsten Geburtstag*, edited by R. Gramlich, 118–28. Wiesbaden: Franz Steiner Verlag, 1974.

———. "Literary Theory: the problem of its efficiency" in *Arabic Poetry: Theory and Development*, edited by G. E. von Grunebaum, 19–69. Malibu, CA: Undena, 1973.

———. review of J. C. Bürgel, *Die ekphrastischen Epigramme des Abū Ṭālib al-Maʾmūnī*. *ZDMG* 121 (1971): 166–90.

Heinrichs, Wolfhart (ed.). *Orientalisches Mittelalter*. Wiesbaden: AULA-Verlag, 1990.

Heinrichs, Wolfhart and Gregor Schoeler (eds). *Festschrift Ewald Wagner zum 65. Geburtstag*. 2 vols. Band 2: Studien zur arabischen Dichtung. Beirut: [Stuttgart: Franz Steiner Verlag], 1994.

Henderson, Harold Gould. *The Bamboo Broom: an introduction to Japanese haiku*. London: Kegan Paul, Trench, Trübner, 1934.

Herder, Johann Gottfried. *Zerstreute Blätter*. 2. Ausgabe. Gotha: bei Carl William Ettinfer, 1791–98.

al-Ḥijāzī al-Khazrajī, Shihāb ad-Dīn Aḥmad b. Muḥammad. *Jannat al-wildān fī l-ḥisān min al-ghilmān*. (See in the annotated bibliography: 15th century, 6. b).

———. *al-Kunnas al-jawārī fī l-ḥisān min al-jawārī*. (See in the annotated bibliography: 15th century, 6. c).

———. *al-Lumaʿ ash-Shihābiyyah min al-burūq al-Ḥijāziyyah*. (See in the annotated bibliography: 15th century, 6. d).

———. *Nadīm al-kaʾīb wa-ḥabīb al-ḥabīb*. (See in the annotated bibliography: 15th century, 6. e).

———. *Rawḍ al-ādāb*. (See in the annotated bibliography: 15th century, 6. a).

al-Ḥillī, Ḥaydar b. Sulaymān. *Dīwān ad-Durr al-yatīm wa-l-ʿiqd an-naẓīm*. Bombay: al-Ḥājj Shaykh ʿAlī al-Maḥallātī, 1312/1894.

al-Ḥillī, Ṣafī ad-Dīn ʿAbd al-ʿAzīz b. Sarāyā. *Dīwān*. ed. Muḥammad Ḥuwwar. 3 vols. Beirut: al-Muʾassasah al-ʿArabiyyah li-d-Dirāsāt wa-n-Nashr, 2000.

———. *Dīwān al-Mathālith wa-l-mathānī fī l-maʿālī wa-l-maʿānī*. (See in the annotated bibliography: 14th century, 2. a).

Hillman, Michael Craig. "The Persian Rubāʿī: common sense in analysis". *ZDMG* 119 (1970): 98–101.

Hinds, Martin and El-Said Badawi. *A Dictionary of Egyptian Arabic: Arabic-English*. Beirut: Librairie du Liban, 1986.

Hindūshāh b. Sanjar al-Jayrānī. *Mawārid al-ādāb*. (See in the annotated bibliography: 14th century 1. a).

Hirschler, Konrad. *The Written Word in the Medieval Arabic Lands: a social and cultural history of reading practices*. Edinburgh: Edinburgh University Press, 2012.

Hitti, Philip K. et al. *Descriptive Catalog of the Garrett collection of Arabic manuscripts in the Princeton University Library*. Princeton, NJ: Princeton University Press, 1938.

Horbury, William and David Noy. *Jewish Inscriptions of Graeco-Roman Egypt*. Cambridge: Cambridge University Press, 1992.

Hornblower, Simon, Antony Spawforth, and Esther Eidinow (eds). *The Oxford Classical Dictionary*. 4th ed. Oxford: Oxford University Press, 2012.

Houtsma, M. Th. *Catalogue d'une collection de manuscrits arabes et turcs appartenant à la maison E. J. Brill à Leide*. Leiden: E. J. Brill, 1886.

Howatson, M. C. (ed.). *The Oxford Companion to Classical Literature*. 3rd edition. Oxford: Oxford University Press, 2011.

Huart, Cl[ément]. *Littérature Arabe*. Paris: Librairie Armand Colin, 1902.

Ḥusayn, Ṭāhā. *Ḥāfiẓ wa-Shawqī*. Cairo: Maktabat al-Khānjī wa-Ḥamdān, 1933.

al-Ḥuṣrī, Ibrāhīm b. ʿAlī. *Nūr aṭ-ṭarf wa-nawr aẓ-ẓarf : Kitāb an-nūrayn*. ed. Līnah ʿAbd al-Quddūs Abū Ṣāliḥ. Beirut: Muʾassasat ar-Risālah, 1996.

———. *Zahr al-ādāb wa-thimār al-albāb*. 2 vols. ed. Zakī Mubārāk. (Cairo: al-Maṭbaʿah ar-Raḥmāniyyah, 1925).

Hussein, Ali. "Classical and Modern Approaches in Dividing the Old Arabic Poem". *JAL* 35:3 (2004): 297–328.

Hutton, James. *The Greek Anthology in Italy to the year 1800*. Ithaca, NY: Cornell University Press, 1935.

———. "Ronsard and the Greek Anthology". *Studies in Philology* 40:2 (April 1943): 103–27.

Ibn Abī ʿAwn, Ibrāhīm b. Muḥammad. *The Kitāb al-Tashbīhāt of Ibn Abī ʿAun*. ed. M. ʿAbdul Muʿīd Khān. London: Luzac, 1950.

Ibn Abī Ḥajalah at-Tilimsānī, Aḥmad b. Yaḥyā. *Dīwān*. ed. Aḥmad Ḥilmī Ḥilwah. Cairo: Dār al-Kutub wa-l-Wathāʾiq al-Qawmiyyah, 2014.

———. *Dīwān aṣ-Ṣabābah*. ed. Muḥammad Zaghlūl Sallām. Alexandria: Munshaʾat al-Maʿārif, n.d.

———. *Maghnāṭīs ad-durr an-nafīs*. (See in the annotated bibliography: 14th century, 5. a).

Ibn al-ʿAdīm. *Bughyat aṭ-ṭalab fī tārīkh Ḥalab*. 12 vols. ed. Suhayl Zakkar. Beirut: Dār al-Fikr, 1995–98.

Ibn al-Aḥnaf, ʿAbbās. *Dīwān*. ed. Karam Bustānī. Beirut: Dār Ṣādir, 1385/1965.

Ibn al-Anbārī, Abū l-Barakāt. *Nuzhat al-alibbāʾ fī ṭabaqāt al-udabāʾ*. ed. by Attia Amer. Ser. Stockholm Oriental Studies, 2. Stockholm: Almqvist & Wiksell, 1963.

Ibn al-ʿArabī, Saʿd ad-Dīn Muḥammad b. Muḥammad b. ʿAlī. *Dīwān*. (See in the annotated bibliography: 13th century, 3. a).

Ibn ʿAsākir. *Tārīkh madīnat Dimashq*. 80 vols. ed. ʿUmar b. Gharāmah al-ʿAmrawī et al. Beirut: Dār al-Fikr, 1415/1995.

Ibn Aydamir, Muḥammad. *Kitāb ad-Durr al-farīd wa-bayt al-qaṣīd*. ed. Fuat Sezgin et al. Facsimile ed. 7 vols. Frankfurt: Institut für Geschichte der arabisch-islamischen Wissenschaften, 1988–97.

Ibn Aydamir, Muḥammad. *Muqaddimat Kitāb ad-Durr al-farīd wa-bayt al-qaṣīd*. ed. Walīd Maḥmūd Khāliṣ. Abu Dhabi: al-Majmaʿ ath-Thaqāfī, 2003.

Ibn Ḥabīb al-Ḥalabī, Badr ad-Dīn al-Ḥasan b. ʿUmar. *Nasīm aṣ-ṣabā fī funūn min al-adab al-qadīm wa-l-maqāmāt al-adabiyyah*. ed. Maḥmūd Fākhūrī. Aleppo: Dār al-Qalam al-ʿArabī, 1993.

———. *ash-Shudhūr* (See in the annotated bibliography: 14th century, 6. a).

———. *Tadhkirat an-nabīh fī ayyām al-Manṣūr wa-banīh*. 3 vols. ed. Muḥammad Muḥammad Amīn and Saʿīd ʿAbd al-Fattāḥ ʿĀshūr. Cairo: al-Hayʾah al-Miṣriyyah al-ʿĀmmah li-l-Kitāb, 1976.

Ibn Ḥajar al-ʿAsqalānī. *Inbāʾ al-ghumar bi-anbāʾ al-ʿumar*. ed. Ḥasan Ḥabashī. 3 vols. Cairo: al-Majlis al-Aʿlā li-sh-Shuʾūn al-Islāmiyyah, 1392/1972.

———. *Dīwān*. (See in the annotated bibliography: 15th century, 7. a).

———. *Dīwān*. ed. as-Sayyid Abū al-Faḍl. Hyderabad: J. M. Press, 1381/1962.

———. *Dīwān as-Sabʿ as-sayyārah an-nayyirāt*. ed. Muḥammad Yūsuf Ayyūb. Jeddah: Nādī Abhā al-Adabī, 1992.

———. *ad-Durar al-kāminah fī aʿyān al-miʾah ath-thāminah*. 6 vols. ed. Fritz Krenkow and Sharaf ad-Dīn Aḥmad. Hyderabad: Maṭbaʿat Majlis Dāʾirat al-Maʿārif, 1929–31.

———. *al-Muʿjam al-mufahras aw tajrīd asānīd al-kutub al-mashʾhūrah wa-l-ajzāʾ al-manthūrah*. ed. Muḥammad Shakkūr Amrīr al-Mayādīnī. Beirut: Muʾassasat ar-Risālah, 1418/1998.

———. *Uns al-ḥujar fī abyāt Ibn Ḥajar*. ed. Shihāb ad-Dīn Abū ʿAmr. Beirut: Dār ar-Rayyān li-t-Turāth, 1988.

Ibn Hāniʾ al-Andalusī, Muḥammad. *Dīwān Muḥammad b. Hāniʾ al-Andalusī*. ed. Muḥammad al-Yaʿlāwī. Beirut: Dār al-Gharb al-Islāmī, 1994.

———. *Dīwān Muḥammad b. Hāniʾ al-Andalusī*. ed. ʿUmar aṭ-Ṭabbāʿ. Beirut: Dār al-Arqam, 1998.

Ibn Ḥijjah al-Ḥamawī. *Kitāb Kashf al-lithām ʿan at-tawriyah wa-l-istikhdām*. (See in the annotated bibliography: 15th century, 2. a).

———. *Khizānat al-adab wa-ghāyat al-arab*. 5 vols. ed. Kawkab Diyāb. Beirut: Dār Ṣādir, 2001.

———. *Qahwat al-inshāʾ*. ed. Rudolf Veselý. Beirut [Berlin]: Klaus Schwarz Verlag, 2005.

———. *Thamarāt al-awrāq fī l-muḥāḍarāt*. ed. Muḥammad Abū l-Faḍl Ibrāhīm. Cairo: Maktabat al-Khānjī, 1971.

———. Same Work. Bayerische Staatsbibliothek (Munich), MS cod. arab. 579.

———. *Thamarāt shahiyyah min al-fawākih al-Ḥamawiyyah*. (See in the annotated bibliography: 15th century, 2. b).

Ibn al-ʿImād. *Shadharāt adh-dhahab fī akhbār man dhahab*. 8 vols. Cairo: Maktabat al-Qudsī, 1350–51/1931–32.

Ibn Iyās. *Badāʾiʿ az-zuhūr fī waqāʾiʿ ad-duhūr*. 6 vols. ed. Paul Kahle, Muḥammad Muṣṭafā, and Moritz Sobernheim. Wiesbaden: in Kommission bei Franz Steiner Verlag, 1931–32.

Ibn al-Jiʿān al-Batlūnī, ʿAlam ad-Dīn Shākir b. ʿAbd al-Ghanī. *Masāyil ad-Dumūʿ ʿalā mā tafarraqa min al-majmūʿ*. (See in the annotated bibliography: 15th century, 10. a).

Ibn al-Kattānī, Muḥammad b. al-Ḥasan. *Kitāb at-Tashbīhāt min ashʿār ahl al-Andalus*. ed. Iḥsān ʿAbbās. 2nd ed. Beirut; Cairo: Dār ash-Shurūq, 1981.

Ibn Khaldūn. *The Muqaddimah. An Introduction to History*. 3 vols. trans. Franz Rosenthal. London: Routledge & Kegan Paul, 1958.

Ibn Khallikān. *Wafayāt al-aʿyān wa-anbāʾ abnāʾ az-zamān*. 8 vols. ed. Iḥsān ʿAbbās. Beirut: Dār Ṣādir, 1977.

———. *Ibn Khallikān's Biographical Dictionary*. 4 vols. trans. Baron MacGuckin de Slane. Paris: Oriental Translation Fund of Great Britain and Ireland, 1842–71.

Ibn al-Khaṭīb. *Khaṭrat aṭ-ṭayf: riḥalāt fī l-Maghrib wa-l-Andalus*. ed. Aḥmad Mukhtār al-ʿAbbādī. Beirut: al-Muʾassasah al-ʿArabiyyah li-d-Dirāsāt wa-n-Nashr, 2003.

Ibn Khaṭīb Dāriyā, Jalāl ad-Dīn Muḥammad b. Aḥmad. *Dīwān*. (See in the annotated bibliography: 15th century, 1. a).

Ibn Maʿṣūm. *Sulāfat al-ʿaṣr fī maḥāsin ash-shuʿarāʾ bi-kull Maṣr*. (See in the annotated bibliography: 18th century, 1. a).

———. Same Work. Cairo: Aḥmad Nājī al-Jamālī wa-Muḥammad Amīn al-Khānjī, 1324/1906.

Ibn Maʿtūq al-Mūsawī. *Dīwān*. (See in the annotated bibliography: 17th century, 3. a).

Ibn Manẓūr. *Lisān al-ʿArab*. 20 vols. Būlāq: al-Maṭbaʿah al-Kubrā al-Miṣriyyah, 1300–08/1882–91.

Ibn Maṭrūḥ. *Dīwān*. ed. Jawdah Amīn. Cairo: Dār ath-Thaqāfah al-ʿArabiyyah, 1989.

Ibn al-Muʿtazz, ʿAbd Allāh. *Ṭabaqāt ash-Shuʿarāʾ al-muḥdathīn*. ed. Abbas Eghbal. facsimile edition. Cambridge: E. J. W. Gibb Memorial Trust, 1939.

———. *Ṭabaqāt ash-Shuʿarāʾ*. ed. ʿAbd as-Sattār Aḥmad Farrāj. Cairo: Dār al-Maʿārif, 1956.

Ibn Munīr aṭ-Ṭarābulusī. *Dīwān*. ed. ʿUmar ʿAbd as-Salām Tadmurī. Beirut: Dār al-Jīl, 1986.

Ibn al-Mustawfī. *Tārīkh Irbil al-musammā «Nabāhat al-balad al-khāmil bi-man waradahu min al-amāthil»*. 2 vols. ed. Sāmī b. as-Sayyid Khammās aṣ-Ṣaqqār. Baghdad: Dār ar-Rashīd li-n-Nashr [Wizārat ath-Thaqāfah wa-l-Iʿlām], 1980.

Ibn an-Naqīb. *Shiʿr Ibn an-Naqīb al-Fuqaysī al-Ḥasan b. Shāwir*. ed. ʿAbbās Hānī al-Chirākh. Baghdad: Dār al-Furāt, 2008.

Ibn Nubātah, Jamāl ad-Dīn Muḥammad. *Dīwān*. (See in the annotated bibliography: 14th century, 4. b).

———. Same Work. ed. Muḥammad al-Qalqīlī (Cairo: Maṭbaʿat at-Tamaddun, 1323/1905).

Ibn Nubātah, Jamāl ad-Dīn Muḥammad. *al-Qaṭr an-Nubātī.* (See in the annotated bibliography: 14th century, 4. a).

———. *Sūq ar-raqīq*. (See in the annotated bibliography: 14th century, 4. d).

———. *Zahr al-manthūr.* (See in the annotated bibliography: 14th century, 4. c).

Ibn Qānṣūh [or: Qānṣawh] b. Ṣādiq, Muḥammad. *Marātiʿ al-albāb fī marābiʿ al-ādāb.* (See in the annotated bibliography: 16th century, 1. a).

———. *ar-Rawḍ al-bahīj fī l-ghazal wa-n-nasīj*. (See in the annotated bibliography: 16th century, 1. b).

Ibn al-Qaysarānī. *Dīwān*. (See in the annotated bibliography: 12th century, 1. a).

Ibn Qutaybah, ʿAbd Allāh b. Muslim. *ash-Shiʿr wa-sh-shuʿarāʾ*. 2 vols. ed. Aḥmad Muḥammad Shākir. Cairo: Dār al-Maʿārif, 1966–67.

Ibn Rashīq al-Qayrawānī. *al-ʿUmdah fī maḥāsin ash-shiʿr wa-ādābih wa-naqdih*. 2 vols. ed. Muḥammad Muḥyī ad-Dīn ʿAbd al-Ḥamīd. Cairo: al-Maktabah at-Tijāriyyah al-Kubrā, 1383/1963.

———. Same Work. 3 vols. ed. Tawfīq an-Nayfar, Mukhtār al-ʿUbaydī, and Jamāl Ḥamādah. Carthage: al-Majmaʿ at-Tūnisī li-l-ʿUlūm wa-l-Adāb wa-l-Funūn, 2009.

Ibn ar-Rūmī. *Dīwān Ibn ar-Rūmī.* 6 vols. ed. Ḥusayn Naṣṣār et al. Cairo: Maṭbaʿat Dār al-Kutub, 1973–81.

Ibn Saʿīd al-Andalusī [al-Maghribī]. *al-Ghuṣūn al-yāniʿah fī maḥāsin shuʿarāʾ al-miʾah as-sābiʿah.* ed. Ibrāhīm al-Ibyārī. Cairo: Dār al-Maʿārif, 1977.

———. *al-Muqtaṭaf min azāhir al-ṭuraf.* ed. Sayyid Ḥanafī Ḥasanayn. Cairo: al-Hayʾah al-Miṣriyyah al-ʿĀmmah li-l-Kitāb, 1983.

Ibn Sallām al-Jumaḥī, Muḥammad. *Ṭabaqāt fuḥūl ash-shuʿarāʾ*. 2 vols. ed. Maḥmūd Muḥammad Shākir. Cairo: Maṭbaʿat al-Madanī, 1974.

Ibn ash-Sharīf Daftarkhʷān, *Kitāb Alf ghulām wa-ghulām* (See in the annotated bibliography: 13th century 2. a).

Ibn ash-Sharīf Daftarkhʷān, *Kitāb Alf jāriyah wa-jāriyah* (See in the annotated bibliography: 13th century 2. b).

Ibn Sūdūn al-Bashbughāwī, ʿAlī. *Nuzhat an-nufūs wa-muḍḥik al-ʿabūs.* Edited in Arnoud Vrolijk, *Bringing a Laugh to a Scowling Face: a study and critical edition of the* "Nuzhat al-nufūs wa-muḍḥik al-ʿabūs" *by ʿAlī Ibn Sūdūn al-Bašbuġāwī* (*Cairo 810/1407–Damascus 868/1464*). Leiden: CNWS, 1998.

Ibn Taghrībirdī. *Ḥilyat aṣ-ṣifāt fī l-asmāʾ wa-ṣ-ṣināʿāt* (See in the annotated bibliography: 15th century, 8. a).

———. *al-Manhal aṣ-ṣāfī wa-l-mustawfī baʿd al-Wāfī.* 8 vols. ed. Muḥammad Muḥammad Amīn. Cairo: al-Hayʾah al-Miṣriyyah al-ʿĀmmah li-l-Kitāb, 1984–99.

———. *an-Nujūm az-zāhirah fī mulūk Miṣr wa-l-Qāhirah*. 16 vols. Cairo: al-Muʾassasah al-Miṣriyyah al-ʿĀmmah li-t-Taʾlīf wa-ṭ-Ṭibāʿah wa-n-Nashr, 1963–71.

Ibn ʿUnayn. *Dīwān*. ed. Khalīl Mardam Bek. Damascus: al-Majmaʿ al-ʿIlmī al-ʿArabī, 1946.

Ibn ʿUthmān, Muwaffaq ad-Dīn. *Murshid az-zuwwār ilā qubūr al-abrār*. ed. Muḥammad Fatḥī Abū Bakr. Cairo: ad-Dār al-Miṣriyyah al-Lubnāniyyah, 1415/1995.

Ibrahim, ʿAbdullah. "The Role of the Pre-Modern: the generic characteristics of the *band*" in *Arabic Literature in the Post-Classical Period*, edited by Roger Allen and D. S. Richards, 87–98. Ser. Cambridge History of Arabic Literature, Cambridge: Cambridge University Press, 2006.

al-Ibshīhī, Muḥammad b. Aḥmad. *al-Mustaṭraf fī kull fann mustaẓraf*. 2 vols. ed. Ibrāhīm Ṣāliḥ. Beirut: Dār Ṣādir, 1999.

———. *Al-Mostaṭraf : recueil de morceaux choisis çà et là dans toutes les branches de connaissances réputées attrayantes par Śihâb-ad-Dîn Âḥmad al-Âbśîhî*. trans. Gustave Rat. Paris: E. Leroux, 1899–1902.

Imruʾ al-Qays. *Dīwān*. Ed. Muḥammad Abū l-Faḍl Ibrāhīm. Ser. *Dhakhāʾir al-ʿArab*, 24. Cairo: Dār al-Maʿārif, 1964.

al-ʿInnābī, Aḥmad b. Muḥammad. *Nuzhat al-abṣār fī maḥāsin al-ashʿār*. ed. al-Sayyid Muṣṭafā as-Sanūsī and ʿAbd al-Laṭīf Aḥmad Luṭf Allāh. Kuwait: Dār al-Qalam, 1986.

al-Iṣbahānī, Abū l-Faraj. *Kitāb al-Aghānī*. 16 vols. ed. Muṣṭafā as-Saqqā et al. Cairo: Dār al-Kutub, 1927–61.

al-Iṣbahānī, Abū l-Faraj. (or Pseudo-Iṣbahānī). *Adab al-ghurabāʾ*, ed. Ṣalāḥ ad-Dīn al-Munajjid. Beirut: Dār al-Kitāb al-Jadīd, 1972.

———. *The Book of Strangers: mediaeval Arabic graffiti on the theme of nostalgia*. trans. Patricia Crone and Shmuel Moreh. Princeton, NJ: Markus Weiner, 2000.

al-Iskandarī, Aḥmad, Aḥmad Amīn, ʿAlī al-Jārim, ʿAbd al-ʿAzīz al-Bishrī, and Aḥmad Ḍayf (eds). *al-Mufaṣṣal fī tārīkh al-adab al-ʿArabī*. 2 vols. Cairo: Maṭbaʿat Miṣr, 1934.

İslam Ansiklopedisi. Istanbul: Millî Eğitim Basımevi, 1943–.

Ismāʿīl Pāshā. *Īḍāḥ al-maknūn fī dh-dhayl ʿalā «Kashf aẓ-ẓunūn ʿan asāmī al-kutub wa-l-funūn»*. 2 vols. ed. Şerefettin Yaltkaya and Rifat Bilge. Istanbul: Mıllî Eğitim Basımevi, 1945–47. [Published as Bağdatlı İsmail Paşa. *Keşf-el-zunun zeyli. Īżāḥ al-maknūn fī l-ẕayli ʿalā «Kaşf al-ẕunūn ʿan asāmi al-kutubi va'l funūn»*].

Jacobi, Renate. "The Origins of the Qaṣīda Form" in *Qasida Poetry in Islamic Asia and Africa*, 2 vols, edited by S. Sperl and C. Shackle, 1:21–34. Leiden: Brill, 1996.

———. *Studien zur Poetik der altarabischen Qaṣide*. Wiesbaden: Franz Steiner Verlag, 1971.

al-Jāḥiẓ, Abū ʿUthmān ʿAmr b. Baḥr. *al-Bayān wa-t-tabyīn*. 4 vols. ed. ʿAbd as-Salām Muḥammad Hārūn. Cairo: Lajnat at-Taʾlīf wa-t-Tarjamah wa-n-Nashr, 1948–50.

Jamāl ad-Dīn, Muḥsin. "*Dīwān Saʿd ad-Dīn Ibn ʿArabī al-Andalusī. Shāʿir al-ḥiraf wa-ṣ-ṣināʿāt*". *al-Mawrid* 2:2 (Ḥazīrān [June] 1973): 225–32.

al-Jārim, ʿAlī. *Jārimiyyāt: buḥūth wa-maqālāt ash-shāʿir wa-l-adīb al-lughawī ʿAlī al-Jārim*. ed. Aḥmad ʿAlī al-Jārim. Cairo: Dār ash-Shurūq, 1992 [repr. 2001].

Jauß, Hans Robert. "Literaturgeschichte als Provokation der Literaturwissenschaft" in H. R. Jauß, *Literatur als Provokation*, 144–207. Frankfurt am Main: edition Suhrkamp, 1970. [Originally published in Hans Robert Jauß, *Literaturgeschichte als Provokation der Literaturwissenschaft*, chs 5–12 (Konstanz, 1967)].

———. "Literary History as a Challenge to Literary Theory". trans. Elizabeth Benzinger. *New Literary History* 2:1 (Autumn 1970): 7–37.

———. "Theorie der Gattungen und Literatur des Mittelalters" in *Grundriss der romanischen Literaturen des Mittelalters, Volume I: Généralités*, edited by H. U. Gumbrecht, 107–38. Heidelberg: Carl Winter Universitätsverlag, 1972.

———. "Theory of Genres and Medieval Literature" in Hans Robert Jauß, *Toward an Aesthetic of Reception*, trans. Timothy Bahti, 77–109. (Minneapolis, MN: University of Minnesota Press, 1982).

Javitch, Daniel. "The Poetics of *Variatio* in *Orlando Furioso*". *Modern Language Quarterly* 66:1 (March 2005): 1–19.

Jones, Alan. *Early Arabic Poetry.* 2 vols. *Vol. 1:* Marāthī *and* ṣuʿlūk *poems*. Ser. Oxford Oriental Institute monographs, 14. Reading: Ithaca Press, 1992; *Vol. 2: Select Odes*. Ser. Oxford Oriental Institute monographs, 15. Reading: Ithaca Press, 1996.

Joyce, James. *A Portrait of the Artist as a Young Man*. ed. J. P. Riquelme. New York, NY; London: W. W. Norton & co., 2007.

———. *Ulysses*. [1960 reset ed.]. London: Penguin Classics, 2000.

Karatani, Kojin. *Transcritique: on Kant and Marx*. trans. Sabu Kohso. Cambridge, MA: MIT Press, 2003.

Karatay, Fehmi Edhem. *Topkapı Sarayı Müzesi Kütüphanesi Arapça Yazmalar Kataloğu.* 4 vols. Istanbul: Milli Eğitim Basımevi, 1969.

Kâtib Çelebi. *Keşf el-Zunun*. 2 vols. ed. Şerefettin Yaltkaya and Rifat Bilge. Istanbul: Maarif Matbaası, 1941. (See also under Ḥājjī Khalīfah).

al-Kattānī, Muḥammad Ibrāhīm and Ṣāliḥ at-Tādlī. *Fihris al-makhṭūṭāt al-ʿArabiyyah al-maḥfūẓah fī l-khizānah bi-r-Ribāṭ. Vol. 5.* Casablanca: Maṭbaʿat an-Najāḥ al-Jadīdah [for al-Khizānah al-ʿĀmmah li-l-Kutub wa-l-Wathāʾiq], 1997.

Kawamoto, Kōji. *The Poetics of Japanese Verse: imagery, structure, meter*. trans. Stephen Collington, Kevin Collings, and Gustav Heldt. Tokyo: University of Tokyo Press, 2000.

Kazimirski, Albert de Biberstein. *Dictionnaire arabe-français. Nouvelle edition*. 2 vols. Paris: G.-P. Maisonneuve, 1960.

Keith, A. Berriedale. *A History of Sanskrit Literature*. Oxford: The Clarendon Press, 1928.

Kerr, Malcolm H. (ed.). *Islamic Studies: a tradition and its problems. Proceedings of the 7th Giorgio Levi della Vida Conference, 27–29 April, 1979, Los Angeles*. Malibu, CA: Undena Publications, 1980.

Khairallah, As'ad. "Collective Composition and the Collector's Art. Observations on the Dîwân of Mağnûn Lailâ" in *La Signification du bas moyen âge dans l'histoire et la culture du monde musulman: actes du 8me Congrès de l'Union européenne des arabisants et islamisants,* 117–25. Aix-en-Provence: Edisud, 1978.

Khalidov, A. B. *Arabskie rukopisi instituta vostokovedeniīa : kratkiĭ katalog.* 2 vols. Moscow, 1986.

al-Khaṭīb, ʿAbd al-Bāqī. *ʿIqd al-farāʾid fī-mā nuẓima min al-fawāʾid.* (See in the annotated bibliography: 16th century, 4. a).

Kilito, Abdelfattah. *The Author and His Doubles: essays on classical Arabic culture.* trans. Michael Cooperson. Syracuse, NY: Syracuse University Press, 2001.

Kilpatrick, Hilary. "A genre in classical Arabic literature: the *adab* encyclopedia" in *Proceedings of the 10th Conference of the Union Européenne des Arabisants et Islamisants: Edinburgh, 9–16 September, 1980*, edited by R. Hillenbrand, 34–42. Edinburgh: [UEAI], 1982.

———. *Making the Great Book of Songs: compilation and the author's craft in Abū l-Faraj al-Iṣbahānī's* Kitāb al-Aghānī. Ser. RoutledgeCurzon Studies in Arabic and Middle Eastern Literatures. London: RoutledgeCurzon, 2003.

Kilpatrick, Hilary. Review of R. Allen and D. S. Richards (eds), *Arabic Literature in the Post-Classical Period. MEL* 12:1 (April 2009): 71–80.

Krevans, Nita. "The Arrangement of Epigrams in Collections" in *Brill's Companion to Hellenistic Epigram: down to Philip*, edited by Peter Bing and Jon Steffen Bruss, 131–46. Leiden: Brill, 2007.

Kristeva, Julia. *La Révolution du langage poétique. L'Avant-garde à la fin du XIXe siècle: Lautréamont et Mallarmé.* Paris: Éditions du Seuil, 1974; English translation: *Revolution in Poetic Language.* trans. Margaret Waller. New York, NY: Columbia University Press, 1984.

Kushājim, Maḥmūd b. al-Ḥusayn. *Dīwān Kushājim.* ed. Khayriyyah Muḥammad Maḥfūẓ. Baghdad: Wizārat al-Iʿlām, 1390/1970.

———. Same Work. ed. Majīd Ṭarād. Beirut: Dār Ṣādir, 1997.

al-Kutubī, Muḥammad b. Shākir. *Fawāt al-Wafayāt wa-dh-dhayl ʿalayhā.* 5 vols. ed. Iḥsān ʿAbbās. Beirut: Dār Ṣādir, 1973–74.

Lane, Edward William. *An Arabic-English Lexicon.* 8 vols. supp. Stanley Lane Poole. London: Williams and Norgate, 1863–93.

Larkin, Margaret. "The Dust of the Master: a Mamlūk-era *zajal* by Khalaf al-Ghubārī". *QSA* n. s. 2 (2007): 11–29.

———. "Popular Poetry in the Post-Classical Period, 1150–1850" in *Arabic Literature in the Post-Classical Period*, edited by Roger Allen and D. S. Richards, 189–224. Ser. Cambridge History of Arabic Literature, Cambridge: Cambridge University Press, 2006.

Lāshīn, Muḥammad ʿAbd al-Majīd. *aṣ-Ṣafadī wa-āthāruh fī l-adab wa-n-naqd.* Cairo: Dār al-Āfāq al-ʿArabiyyah, 2004.

Leaf, Walter. *Versions from Hafiz. An essay in Persian metre*. London: Grant Richards, 1898.

Leder, Stefan. "Postklassisch und vormodern: Beobachtungen zum Kulturwandel in der Mamlūkenzeit" in *Die Mamlūken: Studien zu ihrer Geschichte und Kultur: zum Gedenken an Ulrich Haarmann, 1942–1999*, edited by S. Conermann and A. Pistor-Hatam, 289–312. Hamburg, 2003.

Lerer, Seth. "Medieval English Literature and the Idea of the Anthology". *PMLA* 118:5 (October 2003): 1251-1267.

Lessing, Gotthold Ephraim. *Gotthold Ephraim Lessings Sammtliche Schriften, 1. Theil*. Berlin: In der Vossischen Buchhandlung, 1771.

Lewis, Franklin. "Reading, Writing and Recitation. Sanā'ī and the origins of the Persian *ghazal*". Unpublished doctoral thesis. University of Chicago, 1995.

Lewis, Charlton and Charles Short. *A Latin Dictionary*. Oxford: Clarendon Press, 1879 [1958].

Liddell, Henry George and Robert Scott. *A Greek-English Lexicon. A New (9th) Edition*. Revised and augmented by Henry Stuart Jones with Roderick McKenzie. Oxford: Clarendon Press, 1940.

Little, Donald P. "Al-Ṣafadī as Biographer of His Contemporaries" in *Essays on Islamic Civilization Presented to Niyazi Berkes*, edited by D. P. Little, 190–210. Leiden: Brill, 1976.

Longxi, Zhang. "The Complexity of Difference: individual, cultural, and cross-cultural". *Interdisciplinary Science Reviews* 35:3–4 (2010): 341–52.

Lowin, Shari L. *Arabic and Hebrew Love Poems of al-Andalus*. London: Routledge, 2013.

Lowry, Joseph and Devin Stewart (eds). *Essays in Arabic Literary Biography: 1350–1850*. Wiesbaden: Harrassowitz, 2009.

[Pseudo-]al-Maʿārrī. *Sharḥ dīwān Ḥamāsat Abī Tammām al-mansūb li-Abī ʿAlā' al-Maʿarrī*. 2 vols. ed. Ḥusayn Muḥammad Naqshah. Beirut: Dār al-Gharb al-Islāmī. 1991.

al-Maʿrūfī al-Khalwatī al-Ḥamawī, Muḥammad b. Abī l-Wafā'. Untitled poetry collection. (See in the annotated bibliography: 17th century, 1. a).

Mach, Rudolf. *Catalogue of Arabic Manuscripts (Yahuda section) in the Garrett Collection, Princeton University Library*. Princeton, NJ: Princeton University Press, 1977.

Mackay, P. A. "Patronage and Power in 6th/12th century Baghdad. The Life of the Vizier ʿAḍud al-Dīn Ibn al-Muẓaffar". *SI* 34 (1971): 27–56.

al-Makkī, ʿAlī b. Muḥammad. *Nadīm al-mustahām wa-rawḍat ahl al-ʿishq wa-l-gharām*. (See in the annotated bibliography: 17th century, 4. a).

Māmayah ar-Rūmī, Muḥammad b. Aḥmad b. ʿAbd Allāh. *Rawḍat al-mushtāq wa-bahjat al-ʿushshāq*. (See in the annotated bibliography: 16th century, 3. a).

de Man, Paul. "Semiology and Rhetoric". *Diacritics* 3:3 (Autumn 1973): 27–33.

al-Maqqarī, Aḥmad b. Muḥammad. *Nafḥ aṭ-ṭīb min ghuṣn al-Andalus ar-raṭīb*. 8 vols. ed. Iḥsān ʿAbbās. Beirut: Dār Ṣādir, 1988.

al-Marābiṭī, Saʿīd. *Fihris al-makhṭūṭāt al-ʿArabiyyah al-maḥfūẓah fī l-khizānah bi-r-Ribāṭ. Vol. 7: Khizānat al-Awqāf (ḥarf al-qāf)*. Casablanca: Maṭbaʿat an-Najāḥ al-Jadīdah [for al-Khizānah al-ʿĀmmah li-l-Kutub wa-l-Wathāʾiq], 2002.

Marchand, Suzanne L. *Down from Olympus: archaeology and philhellenism in Germany, 1750-1970*. Princeton, NJ: Princeton University Press, 1996

———. *German Orientalism in the Age of Empire: religion, race, and scholarship*. Cambridge: Cambridge University Press, 2009.

Margoliouth, D[avid] S[amuel]. "On Ibn al-Muʿallim, the Poet of Wāsiṭ". *Zeitschrift für Assyriologie und verwandte Gebiete* 26 (1912): 334–44.

Marino, Giambattista. *La galeria del cavalier Marino: distinta in pitture, & sculture*. Milan: Appresso Gio. Battista Bidelli, 1620.

Marzolph, Ulrich. "Medieval Knowledge in Modern Reading: a fifteenth-century Arabic encyclopaedia of *Omni re scibli*" in *Pre-Modern Encyclopaedic Texts. Proceedings of the Second COMERS Congress, Groningen, 1–4 July 1996*, edited by Peter Binkley, 407–19. Leiden: Brill, 1997.

al-Marzūqī, Abū ʿAlī Aḥmad b. Muḥammad. *Sharḥ Dīwān al-Ḥamāsah*. 4 vols. ed. Aḥmad Amīn and ʿAbd as-Salām Hārūn. 2nd ed. Cairo: Lajnat at-Taʾlīf wa-t-Tarjamah wa-n-Nashr, 1387–92/1967–72.

Masʿūd-i Saʿd-i Salmān. *Dīvān-i ashʿār-i Masʿūd-i Saʿd*. ed. Mahdī Nūriyān. Esfahan: Intishārāt-i Kamāl, 1364 [Solar Hijrī]/1985.

McKinney, Robert C. *The Case of Rhyme versus Reason: Ibn al-Rūmī and his poetics in context*. Leiden: Brill, 2004.

———. "Ibn al-Rūmī's Contribution to the 'Nautical *Raḥīl*' Tradition". *JAL* 29:3–4 (1998): 95–135.

Meisami, Julie Scott. "Arabic Poetics Revisited". *JAOS* 112:2 (1992): 254–68.

———. *Structure and Meaning in medieval Arabic and Persian poetry: Orient Pearls*. London: RoutledgeCurzon, 2003.

———. "Unsquaring the Circle: rereading a poem by al-Muʿtamid ibn ʿAbbād". *Arabica* 35:3 (November 1988): 293–310.

———. "The Uses of the *Qaṣīda*: thematic and structural patterns in a poem of Bashshār". *JAL* 16 (1985): 40–60.

Meisami, Julie Scott and Paul Starkey (eds). *Encyclopedia of Arabic literature*. 2 vols. London: Routledge, 1998.

Melas, Natalie. *All the Difference in the World: postcoloniality and the ends of comparison*. Stanford, CA: Stanford University Press, 2007.

Menocal, María Rosa, Raymond P. Scheindlin, and Michael Sells (eds). *The Literature of al-Andalus*. Ser. Cambridge History of Arabic Literature. Cambridge: Cambridge University Press, 2000.

Meyer, Doris. "The Act of Reading and the Act of Writing in Hellenistic Epigram" in *Brill's Companion to Hellenistic Epigram: down to Philip*, ed. Peter Bing and Jon Steffen Bruss, 187–210. Leiden: Brill, 2007.

Mikics, David. *A New Handbook of Literary Terms*. New Haven, CT: Yale University Press, 2007.

Miner, Earl. "On the Genesis and Development of Literary Systems: Part I". *Critical Inquiry* 5:2 (Winter 1978): 339–53.

———. "On the Genesis and Development of Literary Systems: Part II". *Critical Inquiry* 5:3 (Spring 1979): 553–68.

———. *Comparative Poetics: an intercultural essay on theories of literature*. Princeton, NJ: Princeton University Press, 1990.

Mingana, A[lphonse]. *Catalogue of the Arabic Manuscripts in the John Rylands Library, Manchester*. Manchester: The Manchester University Press, 1934.

Badr ad-Dīn Muḥammad al-Minhājī. *Basṭ al-aʿdhār ʿan ḥubb al-ʿidhār*. (See in the annotated bibliography: 15th century, 5. a).

Miyamori, Asatarō (trans.). *Classic Haiku: an anthology of poems by Basho and his followers*. Mineola, NY: Dover Publications, 2002 [first published as A. Miyamori (trans.). *An Anthology of Haiku Ancient and Modern*. Tokyo: Maruzen Company, 1932.]

Monroe, James T. "«Its *Maṭlaʿ* and *Ḫarja* are Twofold in Function»: form and content in Ibn Quzmān's «*Zajal* 59» and «138»". *Boletín de Literatura Oral* 1 (2011): 14–39.

———. *Structural Coherence and Organic Unity in the Poetry of Ibn Quzman*. Leiden: Brill, forthcoming [unseen].

Monroe, James T. and Mark F. Pettigrew. "The Decline of Courtly Patronage and the Appearance of New Genres in Arabic Literature: the case of the *zajal*, the *maqāma*, and the shadow play". *JAL* 34:1–2 (2003): 138–77.

Montgomery, James E. "Dichotomy in *Jāhilī* Poetry". *JAL* 17 (1986): 1–20.

———. "On the Unity and Disunity of the *Qaṣīdah*". *JAL* 24:3 (November 1993): 271–77.

———. *The Vagaries of the Qasidah: the tradition and practice of early Arabic poetry*. Cambridge: Gibb Memorial Trust, 1997.

———. "Of models and amanuenses: the remarks on the *Qaṣīda* in Ibn Qutayba's *Kitāb al-Shiʿr wa-l-shuʿarā*" in *Islamic Reflections, Arabic Musings: studies in honour of Professor Alan Jones*, edited by R. Hoyland and P. Kennedy, 1–47. Cambridge: E. J. W. Gibb Memorial Trust, 2004.

———. "Abū Nuwās, The Justified Sinner?". *Oriens* 39:1 (2011): 75–164.

More, Paul Elmer. *A Century of Indian Epigrams. Chiefly from the Sanskrit of Bhartrihari*. London and New York, NY: Harper and Brothers, 1899.

al-Mufaḍḍal b. Muḥammad b. Yaʿlā aḍ-Ḍabbī. *The Mufaḍḍalīyāt: an anthology of Ancient Arabian Odes compiled by al-Mufaḍḍal son of Muḥammad according to the recension and with the commentary of Abū Muḥammad al-Qāsim Ibn Muḥammad al-Anbārī.* 2 vols. ed. and trans. Charles James Lyall. *Vol. 1: Arabic Text.* Oxford: The Clarendon Press [Beirut: Maṭbaʿat al-Ābāʾ al-Yasūʿiyyīn], 1921. *Vol. 2: Translation and Notes.* Oxford: The Clarendon Press, 1918.

al-Mufaḍḍal b. Muḥammad b. Yaʿlā aḍ-Ḍabbī. *al-Mufaḍḍaliyyāt.* 3rd ed. [1st ed. 1361/1942; 2nd ed. 1371/1952]. Ser. *Dīwān al-ʿArab: majmūʿāt min ʿuyūn ash-shiʿr,* ed. Aḥmad Muḥammad Shākir and ʿAbd as-Salām Muḥammad Hārūn. Cairo: Dār al-Maʿārif, 1383/1963 [repr. 1993].

Mufti, Aamir R. *Forget English! Orientalisms and World Literatures.* Cambridge, MA: Harvard University Press, 2016.

———. "Orientalism and the Institution of World Literatures". *Critical Inquiry* 36 (Spring 2010): 458–93.

Muḥammad, aṭ-Ṭayyib ʿAbd ar-Raḥīm. *al-Makhṭūṭāt al-ʿArabiyyah fī Nijīriyā al-Ittiḥādiyyah.* Edited and abridged by Khālid ʿAbd al-Karīm Jumʿah. Kuwait: Manshūrāt Maʿhad al-Makhṭūṭāt al-ʿArabiyyah, 1406/1985.

Muhanna, Elias. "Encyclopaedism in the Mamluk Period: the composition of Shihāb al-Dīn al-Nuwayrī's (d. 1333) *Nihāyat al-arab fī funūn al-adab*". Unpublished doctoral thesis. Harvard University, 2012.

al-Muḥibbī, Muḥammad Amīn b. Faḍl Allāh. *Khulāṣat al-athar fī aʿyān al-qarn al-ḥādī ʿashar.* 4 vols. Cairo: 1248/1867–8. [repr. Beirut: Dār Ṣādir, n.d.].

———. *Nafḥat ar-rayḥānah wa-rashḥat ṭilāʾ al-ḥānah.* 5 vols. ed. ʿAbd al-Fattāḥ Muḥammad al-Ḥilw. Cairo: Dār Iḥyāʾ 1389/1969.

al-Murādī, Muḥammad Khalīl b. ʿAlī. *Kitāb Silk ad-durar fī aʿyān al-qarn ath-thānī ʿashar.* 4 vols. ed. Muḥammad ʿAbd al-Qādir Shāhīn. Beirut: Dār al-Kutub al-ʿIlmiyyah, 1997.

al-Musawi, Muhsin J. *The Medieval Islamic Republic of Letters. Arabic Knowledge Construction.* South Bend, IN: University of Notre Dame Press, 2015.

Muslim b. al-Walīd. *Dīwān Ṣarīʿ al-Ghawānī.* ed. Sāmī ad-Dahhān. Ser. *Dhakhāʾir al-ʿArab,* 26. Cairo: Dār al-Maʿārif, 1958.

an-Nawājī, Shams ad-Dīn Muḥammad b. Ḥasan. *Ḥalbat al-kumayt.* Būlāq: Maṭbaʿat al-Mīriyyah al-ʿĀmirah, 1276/1859.

———. *Ḥalbat al-Kumayt,* chs 1–16, edited in Fahmy Muḥammad Yousuf Ḥarb, "A Critical Edition of Chapters 1–16 of al-Nawājī's Ḥalbat al-Kumait, with a Critical Introduction". Unpublished doctoral thesis. University of Lancaster, 1976.

———. *al-Ḥujjah fī sariqāt Ibn Ḥijjah* [*al-Ḥamawī* (d. 837/1434)] (See in the annotated bibliography: 15th century, 3. d).

———. *Khalʿ al-ʿidhār fī waṣf al-ʿidhār.* (See in the annotated bibliography: 15th century, 3. b).

———. *Marātiʿ al-ghizlān fī waṣf al-ghilmān al-ḥisān* (See in the annotated bibliography: 15th century, 3. c).

———. *al-Maṭāliʿ ash-shamsiyyah fī l-madāʾiḥ an-nabawiyyah.* ed. Ḥasan Muḥammad ʿAbd al-Hādī. Amman: Dār al-Yanābīʿ, 1999.

an-Nawājī, Shams ad-Dīn Muḥammad b. Ḥasan. *Ṣaḥā'if al-ḥasanāt fī waṣf al-khāl*. ed. Ḥasan Muḥammad ʿAbd al-Hādī. Amman: Dār al-Yanābīʿ, 2000 (See further in the annotated bibliography: 15th century, 3. a).

———. *ash-Shifā' fī badīʿ al-iktifā'*. ed. Ḥasan Muḥammad ʿAbd al-Hādī. Amman: Dār al-Yanābīʿ, 2004.

———. *ʿUqūd al-la'āl fī l-muwashshaḥāt wa-l-azjāl*. ed. ʿAbd al-Laṭīf ash-Shihābī, 1982; and in Samir Haykal, "The Eastern *Muwashshaḥ* and *Zajal*: a first study including edition of the *ʿUqūd al-la'ālī* of al-Nawājī". Unpublished doctoral thesis. University of Oxford, 1983.

Nedzinskaitė, Živilė. "'*Finis epigrammatis est anima eius*': transformations of the content of the Latin Epigram in the epoch of the Baroque". *Interlitteraria* 19:2 (2014): 276–92.

Nemoy, Leon. *Arabic Manuscripts in the Yale University Library*. New Haven, CT: Connecticut Academy of Arts and Sciences, 1956.

Neuwirth, Angelika, Michael Hess, Judith Pfeiffer, and Boerte Sagaster (eds). *Ghazal as World Literature. Vol. 2: From a literary genre to a great tradition: the Ottoman gazel in context*. Beirut: Ergon Verlag [Würzburg], 2006.

Neuwirth, Angelika, Nicolai Sinai, and Michael Marx (eds). *The Qur'ān in Context: historical and literary investigations into the Qur'ānic milieu*. Leiden: Brill, 2007.

Nicoll, Alexander. *Bibliothecae Bodleianae codicum manuscriptorum orientalium catalogi partis secundae volumen primum Arabicos complectens*. Oxford: Clarendon Press, 1821.

Nöldeke, Theodor. *Beiträge zur Kenntnis der Poesie der alten Araber*. Hannover: Carl Rümpler, 1864.

———. "Moʿallaḳát" in *The Encyclopaedia Britannica*. 9th edition. Edinburgh: Adam and Charles Black, 1883. 16:536–39.

an-Nuwayrī, Aḥmad b. ʿAbd al-Wahhāb. *Nihāyat al-arab fī funūn al-adab*. 33 vols. Cairo: al-Mu'assasah al-Miṣriyyah al-ʿĀmmah li-t-Ta'līf wa-t-Tarjamah wa-ṭ-Ṭibāʿah wa-n-Nashr, 1964–98.

O'Kane, Bernard. "Persian Poetry on Ilkhanid Art and Architecture" in *Beyond the Legacy of Genghis Khan*, edited by L. Komaroff, 346–54. Leiden: Brill, 2006.

Oliver, Raymond. *Poems Without Names: the English lyric, 1200–1500*. Berkeley and Los Angeles, CA: University of California Press, 1970.

Olson, Gary M., Robert L. Mack, and Susan A. Duffy. "Cognitive Aspects of Genre". *Poetics* 10 (1981): 283–315.

Orfali, Bilal. *The Anthologist's Art: Abū Manṣūr al-Thaʿālibī and his* Yatīmat al-dahr. Leiden: Brill, 2016.

———. "*Fann al-ikhtiyār fī l-adab al-ʿArabī al-klāsīkī*". *al-Machreq* (2012): 587–99.

———. "*Ghazal* and Grammar: al-Bāʿūnī's *taḍmīn Alfiyyat Ibn Mālik fī l-ghazal*" in *In the Shadow of Arabic: the centrality of language to Arabic culture. Studies presented to Ramzi Baalbaki on the occasion of his sixtieth birthday*, edited by B. Orfali, 445–93. Leiden: Brill, 2011.

Orfali, Bilal. "A Sketch Map of Arabic Poetry Anthologies up to the Fall of Baghdad". *JAL* 43:1 (2012): 29–59.

———. "The Works of Abū Manṣūr al-Thaʿālibī (350–429/961–1039)". *JAL* 40:3 (2009): 273–318.

Ouyang, Wen-Chin. "Genres, Ideologies, Genre Ideologies and Narrative Transformation". *MEL* 7:2 (July 2004): 125–31.

The Oxford Dictionary of the Classical World. Edited by John Willoby Robert. Oxford: Oxford University Press, 2005.

Oxford English Dictionary. 2nd Edition. OED Online. June 2012. Oxford University Press. <http://www.oed.com>.

Özkırımlı, Atilla. *Türk Edebiyati Ansiklopedisi.* Istanbul: Cem Yayınevi, 1982–87.

Papoutsakis, Nefeli. "The *Ayrīyāt* of Abū Ḥukayma (d. 240/854): a preliminary study" in *The Rude, the Bad and the Bawdy. Essays in Honour of Professor Geert Jan van Gelder*, edited by A. Talib, M. Hammond, and A. Schippers, 101–22. Cambridge: Gibb Memorial Trust, 2014.

———. *Desert Travel as Form of Boasting: a study of Ḏu r-Rumma's poetry*. Wiesbaden: Harrassowitz, 2009.

———. "Ibn al-Muʿtazz, the Epigrammatist". *Oriens* 40:1 (2012): 97–132.

Parlett, H. Review of H. G. Henderson, *The Bamboo Broom. JRAS* 2 (1935): 416–17.

Pavel, Thomas. "Literary Genres as Norms and Good Habits". *New Literary History* 34:2: *Theorizing Genres, I* (Spring 2003): 201–10.

Pellat, Ch[arles]. "Variations sur le thème de l'*adab*". *Correspondance d'orient.* Études 5–6, 19–37. Brussels, 1964. [repr. in Ch. Pellat. *Études sur l'histoire socio-culturelle de l'Islam* (VII-XVe s.). London: Variorum Reprints, 1976].

Perho, Irmeli. *Catalogue of Arabic Manuscripts: Codices Arabici and Codices Arabici Additamenta, Book Three*. Copenhagen, 2007.

Pertsch, Wilhelm. *Die orientalischen Handschriften der Herzoglichen Bibliothek zu Gotha. Dritter Theil: die arabischen Handschriften.* Vienna: Kaiserlich-königliche Hof- und Staatsdruckerei, 1859–93.

Petry, Carl. *The Civilian Elite of Cairo in the Later Middle Ages.* Princeton, NJ: Princeton University Press, 1981.

Pollock, Sheldon. "Future Philology? The fate of a soft science in a hard world". *Critical Inquiry* 35 (Summer 2009): 931–61.

Pomerantz, Maurice. "An Epic Hero in the *Maqāmāt*? Popular and elite literature in the 8th/14th century". *Annales Islamologiques* 49 (2015): 99–114.

Preminger, Alex and T[erry] V. F. Brogan (eds). *The New Princeton Encyclopedia of Poetry and Poetics.* Princeton, NJ: Princeton University Press, 1993.

Price, Lawrence Marsden. *English Literature in Germany*. Ser. University of California Publications in Modern Philology, 37. Berkeley and Los Angeles, CA: University of California Press, 1953.

Pritchett, Frances W. "Orient Pearls Unsung: the quest for unity in the Ghazal". *Edebiyât* n. s. 4 (1993): 119–35.

Pryce-Jones, David. *The Closed Circle: an interpretation of the Arabs.* London: Harper & Row, 1989.

al-Qāsimī, Muḥammad Jamāl ad-Dīn b. Muḥammad Saʿīd. *Iṣlāḥ al-masājid min al-bidaʿ wa-l-ʿawāʾid*. 5th ed. ed. Muḥammad Nāṣir ad-Dīn al-Albānī. Damascus; Beirut: al-Maktab al-Islāmī, 1403/1983.

al-Qīrāṭī, Burhān ad-Dīn. *Dīwān* (See in the annotated bibliography: 14th century, 7. a).

———. *Kitāb Maṭlaʿ an-nayyirayn* (See in the annotated bibliography: 14th century, 7. b).

———. *Taḥrīr al-Qīrāṭī* (See in the annotated bibliography: 14th century, 7. c).

al-Qurashī, Abū Zayd Muḥammad b. Abī l-Khaṭṭāb. *Jamharat ashʿār al-ʿArab fī l-jāhiliyyah wa-l-islām*. 2 vols. ed. Muḥammad ʿAlī al-Hāshimī. Damascus: Dār al-Qalam, 1419/1999.

al-Qurṭubī, Abū ʿAlī al-Ḥasan b. ʿAlī b. Khalaf . *Rawḍat al-azhār wa-bahjat an-nufūs wa-nuzhat al-abṣār* (See in the annotated bibliography: 13th century, 1. a).

ar-Rāfiʿī, Muṣṭafā Ṣādiq. *Tārīkh ādāb al-ʿArab*. Cairo: Maṭbaʿat al-Akhbār, 1329–1332/1911–14.

ar-Rāghib al-Iṣfahānī. *Muḥāḍarāt al-udabāʾ*. 2 vols. Būlāq: Jamʿiyyat al-Maʿārif, 1287/1870.

ar-Rāzī, Zayn ad-Dīn Muḥammad b. Abī Bakr. *Maghānī al-maʿānī*. ed. Muḥammad Zaghlūl Sallām. Alexandria: Munshaʾat al-Maʿārif, 1987.

Reinert, Benedikt. "Der Concetto-Stil in den islamischen Literatur" in *Orientalisches Mittelalter*, edited by W. Heinrichs, 366–408. Wiesbaden: AULA-Verlag, 1990.

Rescher, Otto. "Arabische Handschriften des Top Kapú Seraj [Privatbibliothek S. M. des Sultans]". *RSO* 4 (1911–12): 695–733.

Reynolds, Dwight. "Lost Virgins Found: the Arabic songbook genre and an early North African exemplar". *QSA* n.s. 7 (2012): 69–105.

Richardson, Kristina. *Difference and Disability in the Medieval Islamic World: Blighted Bodies*. Edinburgh: Edinburgh University Press, 2012.

Riedel, Dagmar. "The sum of the parts: a pre-Islamic *qaṣīda* by Bišr b. Abī Ḫāzim al-Asadī". *Der Islam* 79 (2002): 274–315.

———. "Searching for the Islamic 'episteme': the status of historical information in Medieval Middle-Eastern anthological writing". Unpublished doctoral thesis. Indiana University, 2004.

Rieu, Charles. *Catalogus codicum manuscriptorum orientalium qui in museo britannico asservantur. Pars secunda, codices Arabicos amplectens*. London: Impensis Curatorum Musei Britannici 1846.

———. *Catalogus codicum manuscriptorum orientalium qui in museo britannico asservantur. Pars secunda, codices Arabicos amplectens. Supplementum*. London: Impensis Curatorum Musei Britannici 1871.

———. *Supplement to the catalogue of the Arabic manuscripts in the British Museum*. London, 1894.

Rikabi, Jawdat. *La Poésie Profane sous les Ayyûbides et ses Principaux Représentants*. Paris: Libraries Orientale et Américaine, G.-P. Maisonneuve et Co. [Beirut: L'Imprimerie Catholique], 1949.

Rizzitano, Umberto. "Il *Dīwān aṣ-ṣabābah* dello scrittore magrebino Ibn Abī Ḥaǵalah". RSO 28 (1953): 35–70.

Rosand, Ellen. *Opera in seventeenth-century Venice. The Creation of a Genre*. Berkeley and Los Angeles, CA: University of California Press, 1991 [repr. 2007].

Rosenthal, Franz. "'Blurbs' (*Taqrīẓ*) from Fourteenth-Century Egypt". *Oriens* 27–28 (1981): 177–96.

———. "Fiction and Reality: sources for the role of sex in medieval Muslim society" in *Society and the Sexes in Medieval Islam*, edited by A. Lutfi al-Sayyid Marsot, 3–22. Proceedings of the sixth Giorgio Levi Della Vida Conference, University of California, Los Angeles, 1977. Malibu, CA: Undena Publications, 1979.

———. *Das Fortleben der Antike im Islam*. Zürich: Artemis Verlag, 1965. English translation: *The Classical Heritage in Islam*. trans. Emile and Jenny Marmorstein. London: Routledge and Kegan Paul, 1975.

———. *The Herb: hashish versus medieval Muslim society*. Leiden: Brill, 1971.

———. "Male and Female: described and compared" in *Homoeroticism in Classical Arabic Literature*, edited by J. W. Wright, Jr. and E. K. Rowson, 24–54. New York: Columbia University Press, 1997.

———. "Poetry and Architecture: the *bādhanj*". JAL 8 (1977): 1–19.

Roth, Norman. "'Deal Gently with the Young Man': love of boys in medieval Hebrew poetry of Spain". *Speculum* 57:1 (January 1982): 20–51.

Rowson, Everett K. "Two Homoerotic Narratives from Mamlūk Literature: al-Ṣafadī's *Law'at al-shākī* and Ibn Dāniyāl's *al-Mutayyam*" in *Homoeroticism in Classical Arabic Literature,* edited by J. W. Wright, Jr. and E. K. Rowson, 158–91. New York: Columbia University Press, 1997.

———. "An Alexandrian Age in Fourteenth-Century Damascus: twin commentaries on two celebrated Arabic epistles". MSR 7:1 (2003): 96–110.

———. "al-Ṣafadī" in *Essays in Arabic Literary Biography 1350–1850*, edited by J. Lowry and D. Stewart, 341–57. Wiesbaden: Harrassowitz, 2009.

Rowson, Everett K. and Seeger A. Bonebakker. *A computerized listing of biographical data from the* Yatīmat al-dahr *by al-Thaʿālibī*. Ser. Onomasticon Arabicum, 3. Paris: Centre national de la recherche scientifique and Los Angeles, CA: University of California, 1980.

———. *Notes on Two Poetic Anthologies: Taʿālibī's* Tatimma *and Bāhārzī's* Dumya. Ser. Onomasticon Arabicum, 7. Malibu, CA: Undena [on behalf of University of California, Los Angeles and Institut de Recherche et d'Histoire des Textes, CNRS], 1984.

Russell, Daniel. "The Genres of Epigram and Emblem" in *The Cambridge History of Literary Criticism. Vol. 3: The Renaissance*, edited by Glyn P. Norton, 278–83. Cambridge: Cambridge University Press, 1999.

Sadan, Joseph. "Maidens' Hair and Starry Skies. Imagery system and *maʿānī* guides; the practical side of Arabic poetics as demonstrated in two manuscripts" in *Studies in Medieval Arabic and Hebrew Poetics*, edited by Sasson Somekh, 57–88. Ser. Israel Oriental Studies, 11, Leiden: Brill, 1991.

aṣ-Ṣafadī, Ṣalāḥ ad-Dīn Khalīl b. Aybak. *Alḥān as-sawājiʿ bayn al-bādī wa-l-murājiʿ*. (See in the annotated bibliography: 14th century, 3. b).

———. Same Work. 2 vols. ed. Ibrāhīm Ṣāliḥ. Damascus: Dār al-Bashāʾir, 2004.

———. Same Work. 2 vols. ed. Muḥammad ʿAbd al-Ḥamīd Sālim. Cairo: al-Hayʾah al-Miṣriyyah al-ʿĀmmah li-l-Kitāb, 2005.

———. *Aʿyān al-ʿaṣr wa-ʾaʿwān an-naṣr*. 3 vols. facsimile edition of Istanbul Süleymaniye MS Atıf Efendi 1809 published by Fuat Sezgin with Mazen Amawi. Frankfurt am Main: Institut für Geschichte der Arabisch-Islamischen Wissenschaften, 1990.

———. *al-Ghayth al-musajjam fī sharḥ Lāmiyyat al-ʿAjam*. 2 vols. ed. Ṣalāḥ ad-Dīn al-Hawwārī. Sidon, Beirut: al-Maktabah al-ʿAṣriyyah, 1430/2009.

———. *al-Hawl al-muʿjib fī l-qawl bi-l-mūjib*. ed. Muḥammad ʿAbd al-Majīd Lāshīn. Cairo: Dār al-Āfāq al-ʿArabiyyah, 2005. This edition is based on unicum Dār al-Kutub (Cairo) MS 435 *balāghah*, autograph, 104 ff.

———. *al-Ḥusn aṣ-ṣarīḥ fī miʾat malīḥ*. ed. Aḥmad Fawzī al-Hayb. Damascus: Dār Saʿd ad-Dīn, 1424/2003. (See further in the annotated bibliography: 14th century, 3. a).

———. *Kitāb Jinān al-jinās fī ʿilm al-badīʿ*. Istanbul: Maṭbaʿat al-Jawāʾib, 1881.

———. *Kashf al-ḥāl fī waṣf al-khāl*. ed. ʿAbd ar-Raḥman b. Muḥammad b. ʿUmar al-ʿUqayl. Beirut: ad-Dār al-ʿArabiyyah li-l-Mawsūʿāt, 1426/2005. (See further in the annotated bibliography: 14th century, 3. c).

———. *al-Kashf wa-t-tanbīh ʿalā l-waṣf wa-t-tashbīh*. ed. Hilāl Nājī. Leeds: Majallat al-Ḥikmah, 1999.

———. *Ladhdhat as-samʿ fī waṣf ad-damʿ*. See *Kitāb Tashnīf as-samʿ bi-nsikāb ad-damʿ*.

aṣ-Ṣafadī, Ṣalāḥ ad-Dīn Khalīl b. Aybak. *Rashf az-zulāl fī waṣf al-hilāl*. ed. Muḥammad ʿĀyish. Damascus: Dār al-Awāʾil, 2009. This edition is based on one MS: Arif Hikmet (Istanbul) MS 810/107, 83 ff., copied in Medina, n.d.

———. *ar-Rawḍ al-bāsim wa-l-ʿarf an-nāsim*. ed. Muḥammad ʿAbd al-Majīd Lāshīn. Cairo: Dār al-Āfāq al-ʿArabiyyah, 2004.

———. *Ṭard as-sabʿ ʿan sard as-sabʿ*. al-Maktabah al-Waṭaniyyah (Rabat) MS D 1646; printed ed. by Muḥammad ʿĀyish Mūsā. Jeddah: Dār al-Minhāj, 1439/2017 [unseen].

———. *Kitāb Tashnīf as-samʿ bi-nsikāb ad-damʿ*. Cairo: Maṭbaʿat al-Mawsūʿāt, 1903.

———. *al-Wāfī bi-l-Wafayāt*. 30 vols. 2nd edition. ed. Helmut Ritter et al. Wiesbaden: Franz Steiner Verlag, 1931–2007.

aṣ-Ṣaftī ash-Sharqāwī, ʿAbd ar-Raḥmān. *Talāqī l-arab fī marāqī l-adab*. (See in the annotated bibliography: 19th century, 2. a).

as-Sakhāwī, Muḥammad b. ʿAbd ar-Raḥmān. *aḍ-Ḍawʾ al-lāmiʿ li-ahl al-qarn at-tāsiʿ*. 12 vols. Cairo: Maktabat al-Qudsī, 1353–55/1934–36.

———. *al-Jawāhir wa-d-durar fī tarjamat Shaykh al-Islām Ibn Ḥajar*. 3 vols. ed. Ibrāhīm Bājis ʿAbd al-Majīd. Beirut: Dār Ibn Ḥazm, 1999.

Saleh, Walid A. "The etymological fallacy and Qurʾānic studies: Muḥammad, paradise, and Late Antiquity" in *The Qurʾān in Context: historical and literary investigations into the Qurʾānic milieu*, edited by A. Neuwirth et al., 649–98. Leiden: Brill, 2007.

———. "A piecemeal Qurʾān: *furqān* and its meaning in classical Islam and modern Qurʾānic studies". JSAI 42 (2015): 31–71.

Sallām, Muḥammad Zaghlūl. *al-Adab fī l-ʿaṣr al-Mamlūkī*. 2 vols. Cairo: Dār al-Maʿārif, 1971.

———. "*al-Balāghah wa-n-naqd fī ʿaṣr al-Mamālīk wa-Kitāb Jawhar al-kanz li-Najm ad-Dīn Aḥmad b. Ismāʿīl b. al-Athīr al-Ḥalabī al-Miṣrī*". *Fuṣūl* 6:1 (October–December 1985): 154–64.

al-Samarrai, Qasim. "Some Biographical Notes on al-Thaʿālibī". *Bibliotheca Orientalis* 32:3/4 (Mei-Juli 1975): 175–86.

as-Sarī ar-Raffāʾ. *Kitāb al-Muḥibb wa-l-maḥbūb wa-l-mashmūm wa-l-mashrūb*. 4 vols. ed. Miṣbāḥ Ghalāwanjī and Mājid Ḥasan adh-Dhahabī. Damascus: Majmaʿ al-Lughah al-ʿArabiyyah, 1986. This edition is based on two MSS: (1) Leiden MS 559 [complete MS], 228 ff., copied in 646/1249 and (2) al-Jamʿiyyah al-Gharrāʾ (Damascus) [taken to Jāmiʿat Muḥammad b. Suʿūd in Riyadh], no number, 67 ff. comprising sections on *al-Maḥbūb* and *al-Muḥibb*, copied in 1034/1624.

Sarkīs, Yūsuf. *Muʿjam al-maṭbūʿāt al-ʿArabiyyah wa-l-muʿarrabah*. Cairo: Maṭbaʿat Sarkīs, 1928.

Sato, Hiroaki (trans.) *Japanese Women Poets: an anthology*. Armonk NY; London: M. E. Sharpe, 2008.

Sayyid, Fuʾād. *Fihrist al-makhṭūṭāt al-muṣawwarah*. Cairo: Dār al-Riyāḍ li-ṭ-Ṭabʿ wa-n-Nashr, 1954.

Scheindlin, Raymond P. *Form and Structure in the poetry of al-Muʿtamid Ibn ʿAbbād*. Leiden: Brill, 1974.

Schimmel, Annemarie. *As Through a Veil: mystical poetry in Islam*. New York, NY: Columbia University Press, 1982.

———. *Mystical Dimensions of Islam.* Chapel Hill, NC: University of North Carolina Press, 1975.

———. *Stern und Blume: die Bilderwelt der persischen Poesie.* Wiesbaden: O. Harrassowitz, 1984.

———. *A Two-Colored Brocade: the imagery of Persian poetry*. Chapel Hill, NC: University of North Carolina Press, 1992.

Schippers, Arie. "Arabic Influence in the Poetry of Todros Abulafia" in *Proceedings of the Eleventh World Congress of Jewish Studies,* 9 vols, 3:17–24. Jerusalem: World Union of Jewish Studies 1994.

———. *Arabic Tradition & Hebrew Innovation: Arabic themes in Hebrew Andalusian poetry.* 2nd rev. ed. Amsterdam: Institute for Modern Near Eastern Studies, 1988.

———. "Short Poems in Andalusian Literature. Reflections on Ibn Ḫafāǧa's Poems about Figs". QSA 5/6: *Gli Arabi nella Storia: Tanti Popoli una Cola Civilità* (1987–88): 708–17.

Schoeler, Gregor. "Alfred Blochs Studie über die Gattungen der altarabischen Dichtung". AS/EA 56 (2002): 737–68.

———. *Arabische Naturdichtung: die Zahrīyāt, Rabīʿīyāt und Rauḍīyāt von ihren Anfängen bis aṣ-Ṣanaubarī: eine gattungs-, motiv- und stilgeschichtliche Untersuchung*. Ser. Beiruter Texte und Studien, bd. 15. Beirut: Orient-Institut der Deutschen Morgenländischen Gesellschaft [Wiesbaden: Franz Steiner], 1974.

———. *Écrire et transmettre dans les débuts de l'Islam.* Paris: Presses universitaires de France, 2002. English Translation: G. Schoeler. *The Genesis of Literature in Islam: from the aural to the read.* trans. Shawkat M. Toorawa. Edinburgh: Edinburgh University Press, 2009.

———. *Einige Grundprobleme der autochthonen und aristotelischen arabischen Literaturtheorie. Ḥāzim al-Qarṭağannīs Kapitel über die Zielsetzungen der Dichtung und der Vorgeschichte der ihm dargelegten Gedanken.* Wiesbaden: Franz Steiner Verlag [in Kommission bei Deutsche Morgenlandische Gesellschaft], 1975.

———. "Die Einteilung der Dichtung bei den Arabern". ZDMG 123 (1973): 9–55.

———. "The Genres of Classical Arabic Poetry. Classifications of Poetic Themes and Poems by Pre-Modern Critics and Redactors of Dīwāns". QSA n.s. 5–6 (2010–11): 1–48.

———. "The Genres of Classical Arabic Poetry. Classifications of Poetic Themes and Poems by Pre-Modern Critics and Redactors of Dīwāns. Addenda". QSA n.s. 7 (2012): 241–46.

———. "Ibn al-Kattānī's *Kitāb at-Tašbīhāt* und das Problem des „Hispanismus" der andalusisch-arabischen Dichtung". ZDMG 129 (1979): 43–97.

Schoeler, Gregor. "On Ibn ar-Rūmī's Reflective Poetry". *JAL* 27:1 (1996): 22–36. Also published in a German version in W. Heinrichs and G. Schoeler (eds). *Festschrift Ewald Wagner zum 65. Geburtstag, Band 2: Studien zur arabische Dichtung,* 318–36. Beirut: Franz Steiner Verlag, 1994.

———. *The Oral and the Written in Early Islam.* trans. Uwe Vagelpohl and ed. James E. Montgomery. Ser. Routledge Studies in Middle Eastern Literatures. Abdingdon and New York, NY: Routledge, 2006.

Schubert, Gudrun and Renate Würsch. *Die Handschriften der Universitätsbibliothek Basel. Arabische Handschriften.* Basel: Schwabe & Co., 2001.

Seidensticker, Tilman. "An Arabic Origin of the Persian *Rubāʿī*". *MEL* 14:2 (2011): 155–69.

Sellheim. Rudolf. *Materialen zur arabischen Literaturgeschichte.* Teil 1. Wiesbaden: Franz Steiner Verlag, 1976. [VOHD 17A:1].

Sells, Michael. "The *Qaṣīda* and the West: self-reflective stereotype and critical encounter". *al-ʿArabiyya* 20:1–2 (1987): 307–57.

Sens, Alexander. "One Thing Leads (Back) to Another: allusion and the invention of tradition in Hellenistic epigrams" in *Brill's Companion to Hellenistic Epigram: down to Philip*, edited by P. Bing and J. S. Bruss, 371–90. Leiden: Brill, 2007.

Serrano, Richard. *Neither a Borrower: forging traditions in French, Chinese and Arabic poetry.* Ser. Studies in Comparative Literature, 7. Oxford: Legenda, 2002.

Seyed-Gohrab, Ali Asghar. *Courtly Riddles: enigmatic embellishments in early Persian poetry.* West Lafayette, IN: Purdue University Press, 2008.

ash-Shanīṭī, ʿIṣām Muḥammad. *al-Makhṭūṭāt al-ʿArabiyyah fī l-Hind. Taqrīr ʿan al-makhṭūṭāt al-ʿArabiyyah fī khams mudun Hindiyyah tammat ziyāratuhā fī shahr Abrīl / Māyū 1984.* Kuwait: Manshūrāt Maʿhad al-Makhṭūṭāt al-ʿArabiyyah, 1405/1985.

ash-Sharīshī, Aḥmad b. ʿAbd al-Muʾmin. *Sharḥ Maqāmāt al-Ḥarīrī.* 5 vols. ed. Muḥammad Abū l-Faḍl Ibrāhīm. Cairo: al-Muʾassasah al-ʿArabiyyah al-Ḥadīthah li-ṭ-Ṭabʿ wa-n-Nashr wa-t-Tawzīʿ, 1970–76.

Sharlet, Jocelyn. *Patronage and Poetry in the Islamic World: social mobility and status in the medieval Middle East and Central Asia.* London: I.B. Tauris, 2010.

———. "The Thought that Counts: gift exchange poetry by Kushājim, al-Ṣanawbarī and al-Sarī al-Raffāʾ". *MEL* 14:3 (December 2011): 235–70.

Sharma, Sunil. *Persian Poetry at the Indian Frontier: Masʿûd Saʿd Salmân of Lahore.* Delhi: Permanent Black, 2000.

Sharon, Moshe. *Corpus Inscriptionum Arabicarum Palaestinae.* 5 vols. Leiden: Brill 1997–.

ash-Shawkānī, Muḥammad b. ʿAlī. *al-Badr aṭ-ṭāliʿ bi-maḥāsin man baʿd al-qarn as-sābiʿ.* ed. Ḥusayn b. ʿAbd Allāh al-ʿAmrī. Damascus: Dār al-Fikr, 1998.

ash-Shayzarī, Amīn ad-Dawlah Abū al-Ghanā'im Muslim b. Maḥmūd. *Assembly of Islam in Prose and Poetry. Jamharat al-islām dhāt al-nathr wa'l-niẓām*. [Facsimile of Leiden MS Or. 287]. 5 vols. Ser. C: Facsimile Editions, 36. Frankfurt am Main: Institut für Geschichte der Arabisch-Islamischen Wissenschaften, 1986.

Shihāb ad-Dīn Muḥammad b. Ismā'īl b. 'Umar. *Safīnat al-mulk wa-nafīsat al-fulk*. Cairo: Maṭba'at al-Jāmi'ah, 1309/1891 [repr. adh-Dhakhā'ir Series, Cairo: al-Hay'ah al-'Āmmah li-Quṣūr ath-Thaqāfah, 2010].

ash-Shirwānī, Aḥmad b. Muḥammad al-Anṣārī al-Yamanī. *Nafḥat al-Yaman fīmā yazūl bi-dhikrih ash-shajan*. Cairo: Maṭba'at at-Taqaddum, 1324/1906.

Sindawi, Khalid. "Visit to the Tomb of Al-Husayn b. 'Alī in Shiite Poetry: first to fifth centuries AH (8th–11th centuries CE)". *JAL* 37:2 (2006): 230–58.

de Slane (William MacGuckin), baron. *Catalogue des manuscrits arabes*. Paris: Imprimerie nationale, 1893–95.

Sobieroj, Florian and Kathrin Müller. *Arabische Handschriften der Bayerischen Staatsbibliothek zu München unter Einschluss einiger türkischer und persischer Handschriften. Band 1*. Stuttgart: Franz Steiner Verlag, 2007. [VOHD 17B:8].

Somekh, Sasson (ed). *Studies in Medieval Arabic and Hebrew Poetics*. Ser. Israel Oriental Studies, 11. Leiden: Brill, 1991.

Sperl, Stefan. *Mannerism in Arabic Poetry: a structural analysis of selected texts (3rd century AH/9th century AD—5th century AH/11th century AD)*. Cambridge: Cambridge University Press, 1989.

Stekel, Wilhelm. "Criminal Impulses" in W. Stekel, *Compulsion and Doubt*. trans. Emil Gutheil. London: Peter Nevill, 1950.

Stetkevych, Jaroslav. "Arabic Poetry and Assorted Poetics" in *Islamic Studies: a tradition and its problems*, edited by M. H. Kerr, 103–23. Malibu, CA: Undena Publications, 1980. [This article has also been reprinted and translated into Arabic in J. Stetkevych. *Arabic Poetry & Orientalism*. ed. Walid Khazendar. Oxford: St. John's College Research Centre, 2004].

———. "The Discreet Pleasures of the Courtly Hunt. Abū Nuwās and the 'Abbāsid *Ṭardiyyah*". *JAL* 39 (2008): 141–83.

———. *The Hunt in Arabic Poetry: from heroic to lyric to metapoetic*. Notre Dame, IN: University of Notre Dame Press, 2016.

———. "The *Ṭardiyyahs* of Ibn al-Mu'tazz: breakthrough into lyricism". *JAL* 41 (2010): 210–44.

Stetkevych, Suzanne Pinckney. "The 'Abbasid Poet Interprets History: three Qaṣīdahs by Abū Tammām." *JAL* 10 (1979): 49–64.

———. *Abū Tammām and the poetics of the 'Abbāsid Age*. Ser. Studies in Arabic Literature, 13. Leiden: E. J. Brill, 1991.

———. *The Mute Immortals Speak: pre-Islamic poetry and the poetics of ritual*. Ithaca, NY: Cornell University Press, 1993.

Stetkevych, Suzanne Pinckney. *The Poetics of Islamic Legitimacy: myth, gender, and ceremony in the classical Arabic ode.* Bloomington, IN: Indiana University Press, 2002.

———. "Structuralist Interpretations of Pre-Islamic Poetry: critique and new directions". *JNES* 42:2 (April 1983): 85–107.

———. Review of G. J. van Gelder, *Beyond the Line*. *JNES* 47:1 (January 1988): 63–4.

Stetkevych, Suzanne Pinckney (ed.). *Early Islamic Poetry and Poetics*, Farnham: Ashgate, 2009.

Stewart, Devin. "Ibn Ḥijjah al-Ḥamawī" in *Essays in Arabic Literary Biography 1350–1850*, edited by J. Lowry and D. Stewart, 137–47. Wiesbaden: Harrassowitz, 2009.

Stoetzer, W. F. G. J. "Sur les quatrains arabes nommés '*dubāyt*'". *QSA* 5–6 (1987–88): 718–25.

———. *Theory and Practice in Arabic Metrics*. Leiden: Het Oosters Instituut, 1989.

Sublet, Jacqueline and Muriel Rouabah. "Une famille de textes autour d'Ibn Ḫallikān entre VIIe/XIIIe et XIe/XVIIe siècle". *BEO* 58 (2009): 69–86.

Subtelny, Maria Eva. "A Taste for the Intricate: the Persian poetry of the late Timurid period". *ZDMG* 136 (1989): 56–79.

Sullivan, J. P. *Martial, the Unexpected Classic: a literary and historical study.* Cambridge: Cambridge University Press, 2005.

Sumi, Akiko Motoyoshi. *Description in classical Arabic poetry: waṣf, ekphrasis, and interarts theory*. Leiden: Brill, 2004.

as-Suyūṭī, Jalāl ad-Dīn. *Kitāb Ḥusn al-muḥāḍarah fī akhbār Miṣr wa-l-Qāhirah*. 2 vols. Cairo: Maṭbaʿat al-Mawsūʿāt, 1321/1903.

———. *Rasf al-laʾāl fī wasf al-hilāl* in *at-Tuḥfah al-badīʿah wa-ṭ-ṭurfah ash-shahiyyah*, 66–78 (Constantinople: Maṭbaʿat al-Jawāʾib 1302/1884).

———. *Naẓm al-ʿiqyān fī aʿyān al-aʿyān*. ed. by Philip Hitti as *as-Suyuti's Who's Who in the fifteenth century*. New York, NY: Syrian-American Press, 1927.

Szombathy, Zoltán. *Mujūn: libertinism in mediaeval Muslim society and literature.* Cambridge: Gibb Memorial Trust, 2013.

Tabbaa, Yasser. *The Transformation of Islamic Art during the Sunni Revival.* Seattle, WA: University of Washington Press, 2001.

Talib, Adam. "Caricature and obscenity in *mujūn* poetry and African-American women's hip hop" in *The Rude, the Bad and the Bawdy. Essays in Honour of Professor Geert Jan van Gelder*, edited by A. Talib, M. Hammond, and A. Schippers, 285–307. Cambridge: Gibb Memorial Trust, 2014.

———. "The Many Lives of Arabic Verse: Ibn Nubātah al-Miṣrī mourns more than once". *JAL* 44:3 (2013): 257–92.

———. "Pseudo-Ṯaʿālibī's *Book of Youths*". *Arabica* 59:6 (2012): 599–649.

———. "Topoi and Topography in the histories of al-Ḥīra" in *History and Identity in the Late Antique Near East*, edited by Philip Wood, 123–47. New York, NY: Oxford University Press, 2013.

Talib, Adam. "Woven Together as Though Randomly Strung: variation in collections of naevi poetry compiled by al-Nuwayrī and al-Sarī al-Raffāʾ". *MSR* 17 (2013): 23–42.

———. Review of three editions of Khalīl b. Aybak al-Ṣafadī, *Kashf al-ḥāl fī waṣf al-khāl* [see also in the annotated bibliography: 14th century, 3. c]. *MSR* 16 (2012): 168–71.

Talib, Adam, Marlé Hammond, and Arie Schippers (eds). *The Rude, the Bad and the Bawdy. Essays in Honour of Professor Geert Jan van Gelder*. Cambridge: Gibb Memorial Trust, 2014.

Tannous, Jack B. V. "Syria Between Byzantium and Islam: making incommensurables speak". 2 vols. Unpublished doctoral thesis. Princeton University, 2010.

Taymūr Bāshā, Aḥmad. *al-Ḥubb wa-l-jamāl ʿind al-ʿArab*. Cairo: ʿĪsā al-Bābī al-Ḥalabī wa-shurakāh, 1391/1971.

ath-Thaʿālibī, Abū Manṣūr ʿAbd al-Malik. *Aḥsan mā samiʿtu*. ed. Muḥammad Ṣādiq ʿAnbar. Cairo: al-Maktabah al-Maḥmūdiyyah, n.d. [1925].

———. *al-Laṭāʾif wa-ẓ-ẓarāʾif*. Būlāq, 1300 [1882].

———. Same Work. Staatsbibliothek zu Berlin MS. Wetzstein II 1786 [= Ahlwardt 8334].

———. *The Book of Curious and Entertaining Information: the* Laṭāʾif al-maʿārif *of Thaʿālibī*. trans. C. E. Bosworth. Edinburgh: Edinburgh University Press, 1968.

———. *Yatīmat ad-dahr fī shuʿarāʾ ahl al-ʿaṣr*. 4 vols. Cairo: Maṭbaʿat aṣ-Ṣāwī, 1934.

Pseudo-Thaʿālibī. "*fī asmāʾ al-ghilmān al-ḥisān*". Edited in Talib, "Pseudo-Ṯaʿālibī's Book of Youths", *Arabica* 59:6 (2012): 599–649. (See also in the annotated bibliography: 17th century, 7. a).

at-Tibrīzī, Abū Zakariyyā Yaḥyā b. ʿAlī b. Muḥammad ash-Shaybānī. *Sharḥ al-Mufaḍḍaliyyāt*. 3 vols. ed. ʿAlī Muḥammad al-Bijāwī. Cairo: Dār Nahdat Miṣr li-ṭ-ṭabʿ wa-n-Nashr, 1977.

———. *Sharḥ al-qaṣāʾid al-ʿashar*. Cairo: al-Maṭbaʿah as-Salafiyyah, 1343/1924.

Tkatsch, Jaroslaus. *Die arabische Übersetzung der Poetik des Aristoteles und die Grundlage der Kritik des griechischen Texts*. 2 vols. Vienna and Leipzig: Akademie der Wissenschaften in Wien [Hölder-Pilcher-Tempsky A. G.], 1928.

Tobi, Yosef. *Between Hebrew and Arabic Poetry: studies in Spanish medieval Hebrew poetry*. Leiden: Brill, 2010.

Tobi, Yosef. *Proximity and Distance: medieval Hebrew and Arabic poetry*. Leiden: Brill, 2004.

Todorov, Tzvetan. *Les genres du discours*. Paris: Éditions du Seuil, 1978. English translation: *Genres in Discourse*. trans. Catherine Porter. Cambridge: Cambridge University Press, 1990.

Türkiye Diyanet Vakfı İslâm Ansiklopedisi. Istanbul, 1988–.

Turner, Bryan S. *Orientalism, Postmodernism and Globalism*. London: Routledge, 1994.

"Twtr. Which tongues work best for microblogs?" *The Economist* (31 March 2012).

Tynyanov, Yury. "The Literary Fact". trans. Ann Shukman in *Modern Genre Theory*, edited by David Duff, 29–49. Harlow: Longman, 2000.

Ullmann, Manfred. *Untersuchungen zur Rağazpoesie. Ein Beitrag zur arabischen Sprach- und Literaturwissenschaft*. Wiesbaden: Otto Harrassowitz, 1966.

Ummī, Muṣṭafā Kamāl. *Dīvān*. Bodleian Library (Oxford) MS Turk. d. 51.

Uri, Joh[annes] *Bibliothecæ Bodleianæ codicum manuscriptorum orientalium catalogi partis secundæ volumen secundum Arabicos*. Oxford: Clarendon Press, 1787.

Utas, Bo. "'Genres' in Persian Literature, 900–1900" in *Literary History: towards a global perspective, Vol. 2: Literary Genres: an intercultural approach*, edited by G. Lindberg-Wada, 199–241. Berlin: de Gruyter, 2006.

ʿUthmān aṭ-Ṭā'ifī ash-Shāfiʿī, *Kitāb Maḥāsin al-laṭā'if wa-raqā'iq aẓ-ẓarā'if*. (See in the annotated bibliography: 17th century, 8. a).

Vagelpohl, Uwe. *Aristotle's* Rhetoric *in the East: the Syriac and Arabic translation and commentary tradition*. Leiden: Brill, 2008.

Valencia, Adriana and Shamma Boyarin. "'*Ke adame filiolo alieno*': three *Muwaššaḥāt* with the same *Kharja*" in *Wine, Women, & Death: medieval Hebrew poems on the good life*, edited by R. P. Scheindlin, 75–86. Philadelphia, PA: Jewish Publication Society, 1986.

Veselý, Rudolf. "Das *Taqrīẓ* in der arabischen Literatur" in *Die Mamlūken: Studien zu ihrer Geschichte und Kultur: zum Gedenken an Ulrich Haarmann, 1942–1999*, edited by S. Conermann and A. Pistor-Hatam, 379–85. Hamburg, 2003.

Villon, François. *The Complete Works of François Villon*, trans. Anthony Bonner, New York, NY: Bantam, 1960.

Voorhoeve, Petrus. *Handlist of Arabic Manuscripts in the library of the University of Leiden and other collections in the Netherlands*. Leiden: University Library, 1957.

Wagner, Ewald. *Grundzüge der klassischen arabischen Dichtung*. 2 vols. Darmstadt: Wissenschaftliche Buchgesellschaft, 1987–88.

———. *Arabische Handschriften*. Reihe B. Teil 1. Wiesbaden: Franz Steiner Verlag, 1976. [VOHD 17B:1].

———. Review of G. J. van Gelder, *Beyond the Line*. ZDMG 135 (1985): 116–17.

Wahba, Magdi. *A Dictionary of Literary Terms* (*English-French-Arabic*). Beirut: Librairie du Liban, 1974.

Waines, David (ed.). *Food Culture and Health in Pre-Modern Muslim Societies*. Leiden: Brill, 2011.

al-Waṭwāṭ al-Kutubī, Jamāl ad-Dīn Muḥammad b. Ibrāhīm. *Manāhij al-fikar wa-mabāhij al-ʿibar*. 2 vols. ed. Fuat Sezgin and Mazin Amawi. Frankfurt: Institut für Geschichte der arabisch-islamischen Wissenschaften, 1990.

Webb, Ruth. "*Ekphrasis* ancient and modern: the invention of a genre". *Word & Image* 15:1 (January–March 1999): 7–18.

Webster's Third New International Dictionary, Unabridged. ed. Philip Babcock Gove et al. Springfield, MA: G. & C. Merriam Co., 1966.

Wehr, Hans. *Dictionary of Modern Written Arabic*. 4th ed. ed. J. Milton Cowan. Wiesbaden: Harrassowitz, 1979.

Weil, Jürgen W. "Girls from Morocco and Spain: selected poems from an *adab* collection of poetry". Archív Orientální 52 (1984): 36–41.

———. *Mädchennamen, verrätselt. Hundert Rätsel-Epigramme aus dem adab-Werk Alf ǧāriya wa-ǧāriya (7./13. Jh.)*. Berlin: Klaus Schwarz Verlag, 1984.

Weipert, Reinhard. *Classical Arabic Philology and Poetry. A Bibliographical Handbook of Important Editions from 1960 to 2000 [Klassisch-Arabische Philologie und Poesie. Ein Bibliographisches Handbuch Wichtiger Editionen von 1960 bis 2000]*. Ser. Handbuch der Orientalistik, 63. Leiden: Brill, 2002.

———. "Der *Durr al-Farīd* des Muḥammad B. Aidamur: ein Thesaurus gnomischer Poesie aus dem 7/13. Jahrhundert" in *Festschrift Ewald Wagner zum 65. Geburtstag, Band 2: Studien zur arabische Dichtung*, edited by W. Heinrichs and G. Schoeler, 447–61. Beirut: Franz Steiner Verlag, 1994.

Whipple, T. K. *Martial and the English Epigram. From Sir Thomas Wyatt to Ben Jonson*. Ser. University of California Publications in Modern Philology, 10:4. Berkeley, CA: University of California Press, 1925.

Wittgenstein, Ludwig. *Philosophische Untersuchungen. Philosophical Investigations*. trans. G. E. M. Anscombe, P. M. S. Hacker, and J. Schulte. rev. 4th ed. by P. M. S. Hacker and J. Schulte. Oxford: Wiley-Blackwell, 2009.

WKAS: Manfred Ullmann (ed.). *Wörterbuch der klassischen arabische Sprache*. 2 vols. Wiesbaden: Harrassowitz, 1970 [i.e. 1957]–2009.

Wright Jr., J. W. and E. K. Rowson (eds). *Homoeroticism in Classical Arabic Literature*. New York, NY: Columbia University Press, 1997.

Wright, O[wen]. "Music and Verse" in *Arabic Literature to the end of the Umayyad Period*, edited by A. F. L. Beeston et al., 433–59. Cambridge: Cambridge University Press, 1983.

Xie, Ming. *Ezra Pound and the Appropriation of Chinese Poetry*. New York, NY: Garland, 1999.

al-Yāfiʿī. *Mirʾāt al-janān wa-ʿabrat al-yaqẓān*. 4 vols. ed. Khalīl al-Manṣūr. Beirut: Dār al-Kutub al-ʿIlmiyyah, 1417/1997.

Zaborski, Andrzej. "Etymology, Etymological Fallacy, and the Pitfalls of Literal Translation of some Arabic and Islamic Terms" in *Words, Texts and Concepts Cruising the Mediterranean Sea. Studies on the sources, contents and influences of Islamic civilization and Arabic philosophy and science. Dedicated to Gerhard Endress on his sixty-fifth birthday*, edited by R. Arnzen and J. Thielmann, 143–47. Leuven: Peeters, 2004.

Zanker, Graham. "New Light on the Literary Category of 'Ekphrastic Epigram' in Antiquity: the new Posidippus (Col. X 7-XI 19 p. Mil. vogl. VIII 309)". *Zeitschrift für Papyrologie und Epigraphik* 143 (2003): 59–62.

Zargar, Cyrus Ali. "The Poetics of *Shuhūd*. Ibn al-'Arabī's 'Intuitive, Enamored Heart' and the Composition of Erotic Poetry". *Journal of the Muhyiddin Ibn 'Arabi Society* 54 (2013): 13–36.

Žižek, Slavoj. *The Parallax View*. Cambridge, MA: MIT Press, 2006.

———. Review of K. Karatani, *Transcritique: on Kant and Marx*, trans. Sabu Kohso. *New Left Review* 25 (January–February 2004): 121–34.

Online repositories and finding aids

al-Maktabah ash-Shāmilah <http://shamela.ws>.

al-Maktabah al-Waqfiyyah <http://waqfeya.com>.

Maktabat al-Muṣṭafā al-Iliktrūniyyah <http://www.al-mostafa.com>.

Markaz Wadūd li-l-Makhṭūṭāt <https://wadod.org>.

Shabakat al-Alūkah <http://www.alukah.net>.

Thesaurus d'Épigraphie Islamique. ed. Ludvik Kalus and Frédérique Soudan. 10th edition. October 2011 <http://www.epigraphie-islamique.org>.

al-Warrāq <http://www.alwaraq.net>.

Wikipedia <https://www.wikipedia.org>.

Staatsbibliothek zu Berlin, Digitalisierte Sammlungen <http://digital.staatsbibliothek-berlin.de>.

Bibliothèque nationale de France, Gallica <http://gallica.bnf.fr>.

Royal Library (Copenhagen), Oriental Digitized Materials <http://www.kb.dk/en/nb/samling/os/osdigit.html>.

Digitale historische Bibliothek Erfurt/Gotha <https://archive.thulb.uni-jena.de/ufb/templates/master/template_ufb2/index.xml>.

Princeton Digital Library of Islamic Manuscripts <http://library.princeton.edu/projects/islamic>.

Index

NB: the index does not include references to the annotated bibliography or list of sources

Abate, Frank 165n
Abbas, Adnan 254n
ʿAbbās, Iḥsān 1, 38n, 160n
ʿAbd al-Hādī, Ḥasan Muḥammad *see* an-Nawājī
Abū l-ʿAtāhiyah 207
Abu Deeb, Kamal 192n
Abū al-Faḍl, as-Sayyid 14n, 16n, 217n, 279
Abū l-Futūḥ ad-Dabbāgh al-Mīqātī 260
Abū Ḥanīfah 129–30
Abulafia, Todros 187n
Abū Nuwās 4, 6, 24–5, 206n, 207, 210n, 225
Abū Tammām 24–5, 71, 80, 198, 207n
Adab al-ghurabāʾ (pseudo-Iṣbahānī) 185n
Aḥāsin al-maḥāsin (ath-Thaʿālibī) 83–4
Ahlwardt, Wilhelm 189n, 200n, 257n, 259n
Aḥsan mā samiʿtu (ath-Thaʿālibī) 81, 83–5
Ajami, Mansour 28n
al-Akhṭal 90–4
Akkach, Samer 260n
ʿAkkāwī, Riḥāb 245n
Alamanni, Luigi 173
Alḥān as-sawājiʿ bayn al-bādī wa-l-murājiʿ (aṣ-Ṣafadī) 42–3, 43n, 77n, 117–28, 227n
Ali, Samer M. 83n, 90n, 193n, 205n, 209n
Allen, Joseph R. 74
Allen, Roger 201n
al-Musawi, Muhsin J. 89n
Altick, Richard D. 71n
Amer, Sahar 67n
al-Ānisī, Aḥmad b. Aḥmad 255
Anṣār (supporters of the Prophet) 90–4
al-Anṭākī, Dāwūd 253, 262n
Antoon, Sinan 129n
Anyte 80n
al-Aqfahsī, Khalīl b. Muḥammad 242, 247
Arazi, Albert 24n, 186n, 206n
Arberry, A[rthur] J. 23n, 184n, 187n, 188n, 189, 191n, 245n
Argentieri, Lorenzo 80, 85
Aristotle 160, 174n
al-Asʿardī, Nūr ad-Dīn 142–43, 146–47
Ashtor, E. 131n
al-ʿAskarī, Abū Hilāl 205
al-Aṣmaʿī 80
al-Aṣmaʿiyyāt (al-Aṣmaʿī) 80
al-ʿAsqalānī *see* Ibn Ḥajar al-ʿAsqalānī
al-ʿAṭṭār, Muḥammad b. ʿUbayd 110–11
al-ʿAṭṭārī, Aḥmad b. ʿAbd ar-Raḥīm 262
Aʿyān al-ʿaṣr wa-aʿwān an-naṣr (aṣ-Ṣafadī) 231n
al-Ayyūbī, Muḥammad Amīn 112–13
al-Ayyūbī, Muḥammad b. Raḥmat Allāh 102–3
al-Azdī, ʿAlī b. Ẓāfir 37, 72–3, 74n, 255n

Badāʾiʿ al-badāʾih (al-Azdī) 37, 255n
Badāʾiʿ az-zuhūr (Ibn Iyās) 85–86
Badawi, El-Said 68n
Badawi, Mustafa M. 46n
al-Badīʿ al-Asṭurlābī 227n, 237–38
al-Badrī, Taqī ad-Dīn 43, 53, 59–61, 77n, 90, 245n, 247
Badry, R[oswitha] 30n
al-Baghdādī, ʿAbd al-Qādir b. ʿUmar 256
al-Bākharzī, Abū l-Ḥasan 226
Baldick, Chris 165n
Barceló, Carmen 185n
Bāshā, ʿUmar Mūsā 41n
Bashō 176–77
Bateson, Mary Catherine 192n
al-Bāʿūnī, Burhān ad-Dīn Ibrāhīm b. Aḥmad 245
Bauer, Thomas 13n, 15n, 17–8, 24–5, 31n, 41n, 43n, 44n, 47n, 48n, 53, 76n, 81n, 89n, 129n, 134n, 138n, 139n, 140n, 153n, 156n, 184, 192n, 205, 207n, 210, 211, 235n, 236n, 237n, 254n
Baumbach, Manuel 166n
Bausani, Alessandro 190
al-Bayān wa-t-tabyīn (al-Jāḥiẓ) 77n
Beebee, Thomas O. 216n
de Beer, Susanna 20n, 176n
van Bekkum, Wout Jac 187n
Bencheikh, Jamal Eddine 206–8

Benedict, Barbara M. 71n
Bhartrihari 177n
Bilāl b. Rabāḥ 78–9
Bing, Peter 71n, 80n, 162n, 166n, 168n, 169–70, 219
Blachère, Régis 186n
Bloch, Alfred 197n, 198n, 199n, 210n
Boileau-Despréaux, Nicolas 177–78
Bonebakker, Seeger A. 35n, 73n
Bowie, Ewen 170n
Boyarin, Shamma 93n
Bray, Julia 206n
Brockelmann, Carl 15n, 90n
Brower, Robert H. 179, 182
Browne, Edward Granville 199n
de Bruijn, J. T. P. 187n
Bruss, Jon Steffen 162n, 169–70, 219
Bughyat aṭ-ṭalab fī tārīkh Ḥalab (Ibn al-ʿAdīm) 37
al-Buḥturī, al-Walīd b. ʿUbayd 207n
Bürgel, J. Christoph 201n, 204n, 206, 211n

Cachia, Pierre 9n, 14n, 29n, 31n, 32n, 33n, 34n, 54n, 55n, 67n, 109n, 139n, 145n, 153n
Cai, Zong-Qi 205n
Cameron, Alan 86, 169
Catullus 170–71, 174
Chamberlain, Basil Hall 176–82, 188
Chinn, Christopher 27n
Chipman, Leigh 97n
Chow, Rey 158n, 159, 160n
Coiro, Ann Baynes 163n
Cole, Peter 187n
Colie, Rosalie L. 173n, 174n, 217
Cowan, J. Milton 13n

Dalton, John 188n
Damaj, Ahmad 37n
ad-Damāmīnī, Badr ad-Dīn 239
ad-Darārī s-sāriyah fī miʾat jāriyah (Ibn al-Wardī) 241
Davis, Dick 169n, 187n
aḍ-Ḍawʿ al-lāmiʿ li-ahl al-qarn at-tāsiʿ (as-Sakhāwī) 61, 247–49
Degani, Enzo 162, 166–67
Derrida, Jacques 221
Diem, Werner 162n, 185n
Dīwān ad-Durr al-yatīm wa-l-ʿiqd an-naẓīm (Ḥaydar al-Ḥillī) 261n, 262
Dīwān al-Ḥamāsah (Abū Tammām) 71, 80, 197–98
Dīwān al-Maʿānī (al-ʿAskarī) 205
Dīwān al-Mathālith wa-l-mathānī fī l-maʿālī wa-l-maʿānī (Ṣafī ad-Dīn al-Ḥillī) 17–8, 36, 47–50, 82, 85, 236
Dīwān aṣ-Ṣabābah (Ibn Abī Ḥajalah) 50, 52, 86–8, 148n, 233n, 234–35, 239–40
Dozy, Reinhart 75n
Duff, David 159n
Duff, J. W. 169n, 170n, 171, 172n
Dumyat al-qaṣr wa-ʿuṣrat ahl al-ʿaṣr (al-Bākharzī) 226
ad-Durar al-fāʾiqah fī l-maqāṭīʿ ar-rāʾiqah (anon.) 261
ad-Durar al-kāminah fī aʿyān al-miʾah ath-thāminah (Ibn Ḥajar al-ʿAsqalānī) 15n, 42n, 52n, 233n, 241
ad-Durr al-maṣūn fī niẓām as-sabʿ funūn (aṣ-Ṣāliḥī al-Ḥarīrī) 254

El-Rouayheb, Khaled 130n
El Shamsy, Ahmed 81n
El Tayib, Abdulla 197
Elwell-Sutton, L. P. 25n
Enderwitz, Susanne 193n
van Ess, Josef 226n

Faḍḍ al-khitām ʿan at-tawriyah wa-l-istikhdām (aṣ-Ṣafadī) 35n, 239
Fakhreddine, Huda J. 185n, 203n
Farrell, Joseph 195n
Farrin, Raymond 192n, 202
al-Fattāl, al-Khalīl b. Muḥammad 108–9
Fawāt al-Wafayāt (Ibn Shākir al-Kutubī) 41, 81n, 144n, 146n, 210n, 232n
"fī asmāʾ al-ghilmān al-ḥisān" (pseudo-Thaʿālibī) 19, 21n, 22n, 43n, 85n, 86–8
Ferguson, Charles A. 68n
Ferry, Anne 71n
Fishelov, David 164n, 216–17, 219
Fityān ash-Shāghūrī 225
Fitzgerald, William 170n
Fowden, Garth 160n
Fowler, Alastair 71n, 174, 199n
Fraistat, Neil 71n, 74
Frankel, Hans H. 28n, 196n
Frow, John 221
Frye, Northrop 205
Fück, Johann W. 37n, 183n

Galan, František W. 210n
van Gelder, Geert Jan 30n, 53n, 77n, 185n, 188n, 194–98, 199n, 200–2, 203n, 204n, 208–12, 242n
Gharā'ib at-tanbīhāt ʿalā ʿajā'ib at-tashbīhāt (al-Azdī) 72–3, 74n
al-Ghayth al-hātin fī l-ʿidhār al-fātin (al-Bāʿūnī) 245
al-Ghayth al-musajjam fī sharḥ Lāmiyyat al-ʿAjam (aṣ-Ṣafadī) 148n
al-Ghazzī, Ibrāhīm 40, 223
al-Ghazzī, Muḥammad Kamāl ad-Dīn 260–61
al-Ghazzī, Najm ad-Dīn 69, 255–56
Ghurrat aṣ-ṣabāḥ fī waṣf al-wujūh aṣ-ṣibāḥ (al-Badrī) 59–61, 77n, 245n, 247
al-Ghuzūlī, ʿAlā' ad-Dīn 67n, 85–6, 124n, 127n, 239
Giese, Alma 205n
Girón Negrón, Luis M. 203n
von Goethe, Johann Wolfgang 189–90
Gopnik, Alison 196n
Görke, Andreas 41n
de la Granja, F. 38n
The Greek Anthology (Planudes) 88–9, 171–72, 175
Griffel, Frank 209n
Gruendler, Beatrice 14n, 28n, 83n, 193n, 205, 230n
von Grunebaum, Gustave 191n, 204, 206
Guillén, Claudio 220n
Guo, Li 13n, 35n, 82n
Gutas, Dimitri 160n
Gutzwiller, Kathryn J. 71n, 80n, 167–70, 215, 216

Ḥadā'iq an-nammām fī l-kalām ʿalā mā yataʿallaq bi-l-ḥammām (al-Ḥaymī al-Kawkabānī) 258
Hafez, Sabry 203n
Ḥāfiẓ (of Shiraz) 35, 188n, 189n
al-Ḥājibī, Shihāb ad-Dīn 144–45
Ḥājjī Khalīfah (Kâtib Çelebi) 50n, 69, 234n, 246n, 256
al-Ḥalabī, Muṣṭafā b. Bīrī *see* Ibn Bīrī, Muṣṭafā
Ḥalbat al-kumayt (an-Nawājī) 52–3, 90, 242–43, 248
al-Ḥamawī, ʿUways 252
Hammond, Marlé 193n
Hamori, Andras 192n, 200n
Ḥarb, Fahmy Muḥammad Yousuf 242n
al-Ḥarīrī, al-Qāsim b. ʿAlī 142–43
Hartman, Geoffrey H. 176n, 220n
Hartmann, Martin 207n
Hārūn ar-Rashīd 166n
Ḥasan Khān, Muḥammad Ṣiddīq 262–63
al-Ḥātimī 72–3
Hava, J. G. 2n
al-Hawl al-muʿjib fī l-qawl bi-l-mūjib (aṣ-Ṣafadī) 228–29
al-Hayb, Aḥmad Fawzī 43n
Haydar, Adnan 192n
al-Ḥaymī al-Kawkabānī, Aḥmad b. Muḥammad 258
al-Ḥaẓīrī, Abū l-Maʿālī 224–25
Heinrichs, Wolfhart 158n, 209, 210n
Henderson, Harold Gould 181
von Herder, Johann Gottfried 176
Highet, G. A. 169n, 170n, 171, 172n
al-Ḥijāzī al-Khazrajī, Shihāb ad-Dīn 30–1, 53, 55–59, 90, 131–56, 244, 245–46
al-Ḥillī, Ḥaydar b. Sulaymān 261n, 262
al-Ḥillī, Ṣafī ad-Dīn 15n, 17–8, 36–7, 40, 43n, 47–50, 81n, 82, 85, 117–18, 210, 230, 236
Hillman, Michael Craig 25n
Ḥilyat al-muḥāḍarah (al-Ḥātimī) 72–3
Ḥilyat aṣ-ṣifāt fī l-asmā' wa-ṣ-ṣināʿāt (Ibn Taghrībirdī) 61–8, 249–50
al-Ḥimṣī, Sālim b. Saʿādah 37
Hinds, Martin 68n
Hirschler, Konrad 41n
Holgado-Cristeto, Belén Tamames 37n
Horbury, William 185n
Howatson, M. C. 166n
al-Ḥujjah fī sariqāt Ibn Ḥijjah (an-Nawājī) 45, 90, 244
al-Ḥusn aṣ-ṣarīḥ fī mi'at malīḥ (aṣ-Ṣafadī) 17, 19, 43, 82, 85, 228
al-Ḥuṣrī, Ibrāhīm b. ʿAlī 77
Hussein, Ali 194n
Hutton, James 170n, 171–75, 176n

Ibn ʿAbbād, al-Muʿtamid 37, 38, 189n, 201n, 233
Ibn ʿAbbād, aṣ-Ṣāḥib 101n
Ibn ʿAbd al-Ḥaqq, Ṣadr ad-Dīn 144–45
Ibn ʿAbd Allāh, Muḥammad (colonel-commandant) 106–9
Ibn ʿAbd Allāh, Badr ad-Dīn Muḥammad b. Aḥmad 229

Ibn ʿAbd al-Qawī, Yaḥyā b. Muḥammad 248
Ibn Abī ʿAṣrūn *see* al-Kanjī, Muḥammad b. Aḥmad
Ibn Abī ʿAwn 72–3, 74n, 80
Ibn Abī Ḥajalah at-Tilimsānī 14n, 36n, 50–2, 86–8, 129–31, 138n, 148n, 194n, 231n, 232–35
Ibn Abī Ṭālib, ʿAlī 146n
Ibn al-ʿAdīm 37
Ibn al-Aḥnaf, ʿAbbās 193n, 207
Ibn al-ʿArabī, Muḥyī ad-Dīn 33, 34n
Ibn al-ʿArabī, Saʿd ad-Dīn 33–36, 40, 230–31
Ibn ʿAsākir 40, 223
Ibn Bīrī, Muṣṭafā 106–7
Ibn Dāniyāl 13n, 148–49
Ibn Dāwūd al-Iṣbahānī 80
Ibn al-Furāt 44–5
Ibn Ḥabīb al-Ḥalabī, Badr ad-Dīn 15n, 17–8, 36, 42, 43n, 47, 74–7, 81, 82, 85, 210, 235, 236, 254n
Ibn Ḥajar al-ʿAsqalānī 13–16, 19–21, 42, 52–3, 57, 61, 69, 90n, 117n, 146–47, 217n, 233n, 241–42, 247–48
Ibn al-Ḥajjāj 136–37
Ibn Ḥamdawayhi al-Ḥamdawī, Ismāʿīl 226–27
Ibn Hāniʾ al-Andalusī 203n
Ibn Ḥarb, Aḥmad 227n
Ibn Ḥijjah al-Ḥamawī 35n, 45, 52, 67n, 77n, 90, 114–15, 127n, 136n, 227n, 239–41, 244
Ibn al-ʿImād 223n
Ibn Iyās 85–6
Ibn al-Jiʿān 69, 251
Ibn al-Khall 225–26
Ibn Khallikān 37–41, 152–53, 223–27
Ibn al-Khaṭīb, Lisān ad-Dīn 232
Ibn Khaṭīb Dāriyā 140–41
Ibn al-Khiyamī, Shihāb ad-Dīn 30–1
Ibn al-Labbānah 38
Ibn Makānis, Fakhr ad-Dīn 146–47
Ibn Mammātī, al-Asʿad 224
Ibn Manṣūr al-ʿUmarī ad-Dimashqī, Abū Bakr 91–4
Ibn Manẓūr 2n, 13n
Ibn Maʿṣūm 257–58
Ibn Maṭrūḥ 229, 257
Ibn Maʿtūq al-Mūsawī 253–54
Ibn Maymūn 256
Ibn al-Milḥ, Abū Bakr 37, 38, 255
Ibn al-Mubārak al-Yazīdī, Yaḥyā 226
Ibn Munqidh, Usāmah 224
Ibn Muṣallī, Ḥusayn 106–07
Ibn al-Mustawfī, Sharaf ad-Dīn 40, 223
Ibn al-Muʿtazz, ʿAbd Allāh 80, 185n, 206n
Ibn Muẓaffar adh-Dhahabī 144–45
Ibn al-Muzawwir, Ṣāliḥ 104–5
Ibn an-Nābulusī 226
Ibn an-Naqīb 232
Ibn Nubātah, Jamāl ad-Dīn 16–8, 36, 37, 40, 41–3, 47–8, 52, 66, 77n, 81n, 82, 85, 90, 117–28, 134–41, 208n, 227–29, 236–37, 241
Ibn Qalāqis 40, 230
Ibn al-Qaysarānī 223
Ibn Qutaybah 91n, 196
Ibn Quzmān 201n, 233–34
Ibn Rashīq al-Qayrawānī 13n, 229
Ibn Rayyān, Sharaf ad-Dīn 15, 138n, 150–51
Ibn ar-Rūmī 28n, 83n, 145n, 204, 211n
Ibn Ṣādiq, Muḥammad b. Qānṣūḥ 251–52
Ibn aṣ-Ṣāḥib, Badr ad-Dīn 241
Ibn aṣ-Ṣāʾigh 227n
Ibn aṣ-Ṣāʾigh, Muḥammad b. ʿAbd ar-Raḥmān 52, 66, 129–31, 142–43, 233, 239–40
Ibn Sallām al-Jumaḥī 91n
Ibn as-Sammān, Saʿīd 259
Ibn Sanāʾ al-Mulk 240, 243, 254
Ibn Shaddād, Bahāʾ ad-Dīn 226–27
Ibn Shākir al-Kutubī, Muḥammad 41, 81n, 144n, 146n, 230n, 232
Ibn ash-Sharīf Daftarkhwān 16–7, 29–30, 40, 43, 61, 231
Ibn Shiḥnah, ʿAbd al-Barr 59, 247
Ibn Shirshīr 225
Ibn Sukkarah 227n
Ibn Ṭabāṭabā 224
Ibn Tamīm, Mujīr ad-Dīn 36, 40, 194n, 230
Ibn Taghrībirdī, Yūsuf 43n, 44–5, 61–8, 227n, 249–50
Ibn ʿUmar, Shihāb ad-Dīn Muḥammad 261–62
Ibn ʿUnayn 39, 226
Ibn Wafā, Abū l-Faḍl 148–49
Ibn al-Walīd, Muslim 138–39
Ibn al-Wardī, Zayn ad-Dīn 43, 61, 66–7, 240–41
Ibn Yaghmūr 132–33
Ibn Yaḥyā al-Kātib, ʿAbd al-Ḥamīd 211n
Ibn Yazīd al-Kātib, Khālid 24n, 206

Ibn Ẓafar 227n
Ibn Ẓāfir *see* al-Azdī, ʿAlī b. Ẓāfir
Ibrahim, ʿAbdullah 254n
Ibrāhīm, Ḥāfiẓ 34–5
Ibrāhīm al-Miʿmār 36n, 40, 52, 90, 132–33, 146–47, 154–55, 194n, 231, 233–34
Ibrāhīm b. Naṣr *see* al-Mawṣilī, Ibrāhīm b. Naṣr b. ʿAskar
al-Ibshīhī, Muḥammad b. Aḥmad 85–6
al-ʿImādī, Ḥāmid 98–9
Imruʾ al-Qays 134–35
Inbāʾ al-ghumar bi-anbāʾ al-ʿumar (Ibn Ḥajar al-ʿAsqalānī) 90n, 117n, 242
al-ʿInnābī, Aḥmad b. Muḥammad 6–10
al-Iṣbahānī, Abū l-Faraj 71n, 91n, 185n
Pseudo-Iṣbahānī 185n
al-Iṣfahānī, Ḥamzah 4n
al-Iṣfahānī, ʿImād ad-Dīn al-Kātib 40, 224, 225, 226
Iṣlāḥ al-masājid min al-bidaʿ wa-l-ʿawāʾid (al-Qāsimī) 45
Isrāfīl (angel) 134–35

Jacobi, Renate 194n, 196n, 198, 208n
al-Jāḥiẓ, ʿAmr b. Baḥr 77n
Jamāl ad-Dīn, Muḥsin 33n
Jamāl ad-Dīn aṣ-Ṣūfī 231
Jannat al-wildān fī l-ḥisān min al-ghilmān (al-Ḥijāzī al-Khazrajī) 55, 245–46
al-Jārim, ʿAlī 16
Jauß, Hans Robert 202, 217–19
Javitch, Daniel 76n
al-Jazzār, Abū l-Ḥasan 144–45
Jones, Alan 197–99
Joyce, James 213, 214
al-Jurjānī, ʿAlī b. ʿAbd al-ʿAzīz 227n

al-Kalām ʿalā miʾat ghulām (Ibn al-Wardī) 241
al-Kanjī, Muḥammad b. Aḥmad 96–9, 102–3, 108–9, 113n, 117, 260–61
Karatani, Kojin 215n
Kashf al-ḥāl fī waṣf al-khāl (aṣ-Ṣafadī) 19, 44, 77–9, 86–8, 228
Kashf aẓ-ẓunūn ʿan asāmī l-kutub wa-l-funūn (Ḥājjī Khalīfah) 50, 69, 234n, 246n, 256
al-Kashf wa-t-tanbīh ʿalā l-waṣf wa-t-tashbīh (aṣ-Ṣafadī) 72–3
Kâtib Çelebi *see* Ḥājjī Khalīfah
al-Kawākib as-sāʾirah bi-ʾaʿyān al-miʾah al-ʿāshirah (Najm ad-Dīn al-Ghazzī) 255–56
Kawamoto, Kōji 182
Kazimirski, Albert de Biberstein 123n
Keith, A. Berriedale 177n
Khadīm aẓ-ẓurafāʾ wa-nadīm al-luṭafāʾ (anon.) 21–9, 254
Khalʿ al-ʿidhār fī waṣf al-ʿidhār (an-Nawājī) 53
Kharīdat al-qaṣr wa-jarīdat al-ʿaṣr (ʿImād ad-Dīn al-Kātib al-Iṣfahānī) 40, 224, 225, 226
al-Kharrāṭ, Ṣādiq b. Muḥammad 102–3
Khaṭrat aṭ-ṭayf fī riḥlat ash-shitāʾ wa-ṣ-ṣayf (Ibn al-Khaṭīb) 232
Khayyām, ʿUmar 25n
Khizānat al-adab wa-ghāyat al-arab (Ibn Ḥijjah al-Ḥamawī) 67n, 77n, 136n, 227n, 240–41
Khizānat al-adab wa-lubb lubāb «Lisān al-ʿArab» (al-Baghdādī) 256
al-Khubzʾarruzī 227n
Khulāṣat al-athar fī aʿyān al-qarn al-ḥādī ʿashar (al-Muḥibbī) 90–4, 203n
al-Khūlī, Amīn 214
Kilito, Abdelfattah 220n
Kilpatrick, Hilary 71n
al-Kinānī, Saʿīd 104–6, 118n
Kitāb al-Aghānī (al-Iṣbahānī) 45, 71n, 91n
Kitāb Alf ghulām wa-ghulām (Ibn ash-Sharīf Daftarkhwān) 16, 29–30, 43
Kitāb Alf jāriyah wa-jāriyah (Ibn ash-Sharīf Daftarkhwān) 13n, 22n, 43
Kitāb al-Ashbāh wa-n-naẓāʾir (al-Khālidiyyān) 80
Kitāb al-Badīʿ (Ibn al-Muʿtazz) 80
Kitāb al-Ghilmān (ath-Thaʿālibī) 43, 61, 86; *see also* pseudo-Thaʿālibī
Kitāb Ḥusn al-muḥāḍarah fī akhbār Miṣr wa-l-Qāhirah (as-Suyūṭī) 55n, 85–6
Kitāb Kashf al-lithām ʿan wajh at-tawriyah wa-l-istikhdām (Ibn Ḥijjah al-Ḥamawī) 239
Kitāb Maḥāsin al-laṭāʾif wa-raqāʾiq aẓ-ẓarāʾif (aṭ-Ṭāʾifī) 257
Kitāb al-Muḥibb wa-l-maḥbūb wa-l-mashmūm wa-l-mashrūb (as-Sarī ar-Raffāʾ) 81
Kitāb Nasīm aṣ-ṣabā (Ibn Ḥabīb al-Ḥalabī) 74–7

Kitāb at-Tashbīhāt (Ibn Abī ʿAwn) 72–3, 74n, 80
Kitāb Tashnīf as-samʿ bi-nsikāb ad-damʿ see *Ladhdhat as-samʿ fī waṣf ad-damʿ* (aṣ-Ṣafadī)
Kitāb az-Zahrah (Ibn Dāwūd al-Iṣbahānī) 80
Krenkow, Fritz 190n
Krevans, Nita 89
Kristeva, Julia 216
Kunnas al-jawārī fī l-ḥisān min al-jawārī (al-Ḥijāzī al-Khazrajī) 55
Kushājim, Maḥmūd b. al-Ḥusayn 46, 205n, 225

al-Labābah fī muʿāraḍat «Dīwān aṣ-Ṣabābah» (Ibn aṣ-Ṣāʾigh, Muḥammad b. ʿAbd ar-Raḥmān) 239–40
Lacan, Jacques 194n, 208n
Ladhdhat as-samʿ fī waṣf ad-damʿ (aṣ-Ṣafadī) 44
Lāmiyyat al-ʿAjam (aṭ-Ṭughrāʾī) 148n, 229
Lane, Edward William 151n
Lascaris, Janus 172
Lāshīn, Muḥammad ʿAbd al-Majīd 203n, 208n
Lausberg, M. 170n, 171n
Leaf, Walter 187–89
Leaman, O[liver] 160n
Lecomte, Gérard 190n
Leo X (Pope) 173
Lerer, Seth 71n
Lessing, Gotthold 174–76
Lévi-Provençal, E[variste] 38n
Longxi, Zhang 183
Lowin, Shari L. 37n
al-Lumaʿ ash-Shihābiyyah min al-burūq al-Ḥijāziyyah (al-Ḥijāzī al-Khazrajī) 55, 57–9, 246
al-Luqaymī, Muṣṭafā b. Asʿad 110–11

Mabāhij al-fikar wa-manāhij al-ʿibar (al-Waṭwāṭ al-Kutubī) 72–3
Maghnāṭīs ad-durr an-nafīs (Ibn Abī Ḥajalah) 50–2, 129–31, 138n, 231n, 232–34
al-Maḥāsinī, Mūsā 104–6
al-Maḥmūdī, Muḥammad 102–3
al-Makkī, ʿAlī b. Muḥammad 257
al-Malik al-Afḍal 48
al-Malik al-Muʾayyad 41
al-Mālikī, Muḥammad Abū l-Fatḥ 255–56
Māmayah ar-Rūmī 31–2, 252–53
al-Maʾmūnī, Abū Ṭālib 206
de Man, Paul 209n
Manāhij al-fikar wa-mabāhij al-ʿibar (al-Waṭwāṭ al-Kutubī) see *Mabāhij al-fikar wa-manāhij al-ʿibar*
al-Manāzī al-Kātib 39
al-Manhal aṣ-ṣāfī wa-l-mustawfī baʿd al-Wāfī (Ibn Taghrībirdī) 44–5, 227n, 250
al-Manīnī, Aḥmad b. ʿAlī 100–1, 109n, 259
al-Maqāmah as-Samarqandiyyah (al-Ḥarīrī) 142–43
Maqāṭiʿ ash-shurb (ad-Damāmīnī) 239
al-Maqqarī 37, 69, 254–55
Marātiʿ al-albāb fī marābiʿ al-ādāb (Ibn Ṣādiq) 251–52
Marātiʿ al-ghizlān fī waṣf al-ḥisān min al-ghilmān (an-Nawājī) 53, 243
Marchand, Suzanne L. 159n, 183n
Mardam Bek, Khalil 39n
Martial 34, 170–71, 174–76, 186, 212
Marino, Giambattista 27n
Marot, Clément 172, 173
Maṣāriʿ al-ʿushshāq (as-Sarrāj) 118n
al-Maṣāyid wa-l-maṭārid (Kushājim) 225
Masāyil ad-dumūʿ ʿalā mā tafarraqa min al-majmūʿ (Ibn al-Jiʿān) 251
Maṭāliʿ al-budūr fī manāzil as-surūr (al-Ghuzūlī) 67n, 85–6, 124n, 127n, 239
al-Mathānī wa-l-mathālith (aṣ-Ṣafadī) 43n, 250
Mawāṣīl al-maqāṭīʿ (Ibn Abī Ḥajalah) 50, 234n
al-Mawṣilī, Ibrāhīm b. Naṣr b. ʿAskar 40, 223
McKinney, Robert C. 83n, 145n, 204n
Meisami, Julie Scott 3n, 5, 187, 190–91, 192n, 196n, 201n
Melas, Natalie 158n
Meleager 80n, 86n, 176n
Meyer, Doris 88–9
al-Mihyār ad-Daylamī 226
Mikics, David 171n
al-Miʿmār *see* Ibrāhīm al-Miʿmār
Miner, Earl 164n, 179, 182, 201n
Mirʾāt al-janān wa-ʿabrat al-yaqẓān (al-Yāfiʿī) 237–38
Miyamori, Asatarō 181–82

Monroe, James T. 5n, 192n, 193n, 201n, 202n
Montgomery, James E. 187n, 192n, 196n, 200n, 201, 220n
More, Paul Elmer 177n
al-Mubarrad 226
al-Mufaḍḍal aḍ-Ḍabbī 71, 80
al-Mufaḍḍaliyyāt (al-Mufaḍḍal aḍ-Ḍabbī) 71, 80
Mufti, Aamir R. 158, 221n
Muḥāḍarāt al-udabāʾ (ar-Rāghib al-Iṣfahānī) 77n
Muḥammad (Prophet) 21–4, 29, 42n, 79n, 84, 90–1, 93n, 153n, 241
Muhanna, Elias 35n, 86n
al-Muḥibbī, Muḥammad Amīn 90–4, 203n
Mujtabā l-udabā see *Maghnāṭīs ad-durr an-nafīs*
Muntahā ṭ-ṭalab min ashʿār al-ʿArab (Ibn Maymūn) 256
Muqaṭṭaʿāt an-Nīl (Ibn Sanāʾ al-Mulk) 240–41, 243, 254
al-Murādī, Ḥusayn 112–13
al-Murādī, Ibrāhīm b. Muḥammad 94, 96–7, 260
al-Murādī, Muḥammad Khalīl 69, 94–117, 118n, 259–60
al-Mustaṭraf fī kull fann mustaẓraf (al-Ibshīhī) 85–6
al-Mutanabbī 13n, 63n, 192n, 198n, 205n, 208n
al-Muwashshā (al-Washshāʾ) 185n

an-Nābulusī, ʿAbd al-Ghanī 9n, 29n, 31n, 32n, 33n, 34n, 54n, 55n, 103n, 107n, 109n, 110–11, 114–15, 139n, 145n, 153n, 260–61
an-Nābulusī, Ismāʿīl 90–4
Nadīm al-kaʾīb wa-ḥabīb al-ḥabīb (al-Ḥijāzī al-Khazrajī) 55, 246
Nadīm al-mustahām wa-rawḍat ahl al-ʿishq wa-l-gharām (al-Makkī) 257
Nafḥat ar-rayḥānah wa-rashḥat ṭilāʾ al-ḥānah (al-Muḥibbī) 90n
Nafḥ aṭ-ṭīb min ghuṣn al-Andalus ar-raṭīb (al-Maqqarī) 37, 83, 254–55
Nafḥat al-Yaman fīmā yazūl bi-dhikrih ash-shajan (ash-Shirwānī) 261
an-Nahshalī, ʿAbd al-Karīm 13n
an-Nāshiʾ al-Akbar *see* Ibn Shirshīr
Nashwat as-sakrān min ṣahbāʾ tadhkār al-ghizlān (Ḥasan Khān) 262–63
an-Nawājī, Shams ad-Dīn 19, 43, 45, 46, 52–5, 61, 90, 242–44, 248
Naẓm al-ʿiqyān fī aʿyān al-aʿyān (as-Suyuṭī) 53–5
Naẓm as-sulūk wa-waʿẓ al-mulūk (Ibn al-Labbānah) 38
Nedzinskaitė, Živilė 174n
Nihāyat al-arab fī funūn al-adab (an-Nuwayrī) 35n, 71n, 85–6
Nile Coves see *Muqaṭṭaʿāt an-Nīl*
Nöldeke, Theodor 189n, 196n
Noy, David 185n
an-Nujūm az-zāhirah fī mulūk Miṣr wa-l-Qāhirah (Ibn Taghrībirdī) 250
Nūr aṭ-ṭarf wa-nawr aẓ-ẓarf (al-Ḥuṣrī) 77n
an-Nuwayrī, Shihāb ad-Dīn 35n, 71n, 85–6
Nuzhat al-abṣār fī maḥāsin al-ashʿār (al-ʿInnābī) 6–10

Ockley, Simon 184n
O'Kane, Bernard 185n
Oliver, Raymond 173
Opitz, Martin 176n
Orfali, Bilal 71n, 83n, 84n
Ouyang, Wen-Chin 215n

Papoutsakis, Nefeli 50n, 129n, 185n, 196n
Pavel, Thomas 217
Pellat, Charles 186n
Pettigrew, Mark 5n
Planudes, Maximus 86n, 88–9, 171–72, 175
Pollock, Sheldon 214n
Pomerantz, Maurice A. 15n
Possevino, Antonio 175
Price, Lawrence Marsden 176n
Pritchett, Frances W. 188n
Pryce-Jones, David 184n

Qahwat al-inshāʾ (Ibn Ḥijjah al-Ḥamawī) 90, 127n, 239n, 239n
al-Qāsimī, Muḥammad Jamāl ad-Dīn 45
al-Qaṭr an-Nubātī (Ibn Nubātah) 17–8, 41–2, 52, 82, 85, 134n, 138n, 140n, 236–37, 241
al-Qīrāṭī, Burhān ad-Dīn 52, 129–31, 132–33, 138–39, 152–53, 232–33, 238
Qurʾan 22–3, 58, 66n, 67, 77, 108–9, 245n, 253
Quraysh (tribe) 91

al-Qurṭubī, al-Ḥasan b. ʿAlī 37

ar-Rāfiʿī, Muṣṭafā Ṣādiq 16n
ar-Rāghib al-Iṣfahānī 77n
Rasf al-laʾāl fī waṣf al-hilāl (as-Suyūṭī) 251
Rashf az-zulāl fī waṣf al-hilāl (aṣ-Ṣafadī) 44
Rawḍ al-ādāb (al-Ḥijāzī al-Khazrajī) 30–1, 55–7, 131–56, 246
ar-Rawḍ al-bahīj fī l-ghazal wa-n-nasīj (Ibn Ṣādiq) 252
ar-Rawḍ al-bāsim wa-l-ʿarf an-nāsim (aṣ-Ṣafadī) 17–8, 43–4, 82, 85, 203n, 208n, 250
Rawḍat al-azhār wa-bahjat an-nufūs wa-nuzhat al-abṣār (al-Qurṭubī) 37
Rawḍat al-mushtāq wa-bahjat al-ʿushshāq (Māmayah ar-Rūmī) 31–2, 252–53
Rawḥ ar-rūḥ (pseudo-Thaʿālibī) 72–3
Reinert, Benedikt 22n
Reitzenstein, Richard 169n
Reynolds, Dwight 45, 261n
Richardson, Kristina 101n
Riḍwān al-maḥbūb wa-mufarriḥ al-qulūb (al-Kanjī) 112–13, 117, 260–61
Riedel, Dagmar 192n
Rippin, Andrew 22n, 209n
ar-Risālah al-mūḍiḥah (al-Ḥātimī) 73n
Rizzitano, Umberto 235n
Rosand, Ellen 81–2
Rosenthal, Franz 13n, 160n, 211n, 247n
Roth, Norman 187n
Rouabah, Muriel 38n
Rowson, Everett K. 42n, 43n, 228n
Rūmī, Jalāl ad-Dīn 33

Sadan, Joseph 205n, 209n, 211n
aṣ-Ṣafadī, Khalīl b. Aybak 14n, 15, 17–9, 35–36, 40–5, 61, 72–3, 77–9, 82, 85–88, 90, 117–28, 134–35, 136n, 148–49, 194n, 203n, 206n, 208n, 211n, 224n, 227–31, 239, 250, 251
Safīnat al-mulk wa-nafīsat al-fulk (Ibn ʿUmar) 261–62
aṣ-Ṣaftī ash-Sharqāwī, ʿAbd ar-Raḥmān 69
Ṣaḥāʾif al-ḥasanāt fī waṣf al-khāl (an-Nawājī) 19, 53, 243–44
Said, Edward 183n
as-Sakhāwī, Muḥammad b. ʿAbd ar-Raḥmān 14n, 53, 61, 247–49
Saleh, Walid A. 196n
aṣ-Ṣāliḥī al-Ḥarīrī, ʿAlāʾ ad-Dīn 252
aṣ-Ṣanawbarī 204n, 205n, 211n
as-Sarī ar-Raffāʾ 71n, 81, 85, 205n
as-Sarrāj, Jaʿfar b. Aḥmad 118n
as-Sarrāj al-Warrāq 136–37
as-Saʿsaʿānī, Saʿīd 100–1
Sato, Hiroaki 176n
Scaliger, Julius Caesar 174–75
Scheindlin, Raymond P. 189n, 191n, 192n
Schimmel, Annemarie 34
Schippers, Arie 185n, 187n, 196n
Schoeler, Gregor 3–6, 15n, 167, 194n, 195n, 197n, 198n, 203n, 204, 205n, 209–11
Schöller, Marco 162n, 185n
Sebillet, Thomas 173–74
Seidensticker, Tilman 15n, 91n
Sells, Michael 188n, 191n, 192
Serrano, Richard 159n
Seyed-Gohrab, Ali Asghar 29n
Shadharāt adh-dhahab fī akhbār man dhahab (Ibn al-ʿImād) 223n
Sharḥ Maqāmāt al-Ḥarīrī (ash-Sharīshī) 142n
ash-Sharīf al-Murtaḍā 81, 227n
ash-Sharīshī, Aḥmad b. ʿAbd al-Muʾmin 142n
Sharlet, Jocelyn 193n, 205
Sharma, Sunil 5n
Sharon, Moshe 185n
ash-Shawkānī 83, 241n
Shawqī, Aḥmad 32–3
Shiʿār an-nudamāʾ (ath-Thaʿālibī) 72–3
Kitāb ash-Shifāʾ fī badīʿ al-iktifāʾ (an-Nawājī) 46, 244
ash-Shihāb fī sh-shayb wa-sh-shabāb (ash-Sharīf al-Murtaḍā) 81
ash-Shiʿr wa-sh-shuʿarāʾ (Ibn Qutaybah) 91n, 196
ash-Shirwānī, Aḥmad b. Muḥammad 261
ash-Shudhūr (Ibn Ḥabīb al-Ḥalabī) 17–8, 47, 74, 81n, 82, 85, 235, 236, 254n
Silk ad-durar fī aʿyān al-qarn ath-thānī ʿashar (Muḥammad Khalīl al-Murādī) 94–117, 118n, 259–60
Sindawi, Khalid 203n
de Slane, Baron 40n
Sperl, Stefan 28n, 201n, 209, 210n
Stekel, Wilhelm 194

Stetkevych, Jaroslav 5n, 9n, 183n, 188n, 189–90, 192, 195, 196n, 199, 200n, 201n, 203n, 204n, 206n
Stetkevych, Suzanne Pinckney 71n, 83n, 191n, 192, 193n, 196n, 201
Stewart, Devin 239n
Stoetzer, W. F. G. J. 15n
Sublet, Jacqueline 38n
Subtelny, Maria Eva 31n
Sukkardān al-ʿushshāq wa-manārat al-asmāʿ wa-l-āmāq (al-Ḥamawī) 252
Sulāfat al-ʿaṣr fī maḥāsin ash-shuʿarāʾ bi-kull maṣr (Ibn Maʿṣūm) 257–58
aṣ-Ṣūlī, Abū Bakr 4, 227n
Sullivan, J. P. 174n, 175–76
Sumi, Akiko Motoyoshi 41n, 193
as-Suʿūdī, Shihāb ad-Dīn 53–5
as-Suyūṭī, Jalāl ad-Dīn 53–5, 69, 85–6, 251
Szombathy, Zoltán 129n

Ṭabaqāt fuḥūl ash-shuʿarāʾ (Ibn Sallām al-Jumaḥī) 91n
Ṭabaqāt ash-shuʿarāʾ (Ibn al-Muʿtazz) 80
Tabbaa, Yasser 185n
Tadhkirat an-nabīh fī ayyām al-Manṣūr wa-banīh (Ibn Ḥabīb al-Ḥalabī) 36, 42n, 47n, 81n, 235–36
Tadhkirat aṣ-Ṣafadī 251
Taḥrīr al-Qīrāṭī (Ibn Ḥijjah al-Ḥamawī) 238–39
aṭ-Ṭāʾī, Ḥātim 142–43
aṭ-Ṭāʾifī, ʿUthmān 257
Talāqī l-arab fī marāqī l-adab (aṣ-Ṣaftī) 69
The Tale of Genji (Murasaki) 164
Tannous, Jack 160n
aṭ-Ṭarābulusī, Sulaymān b. Muḥammad 114–15
Tārīkh Irbil (Ibn al-Mustawfī) 40, 223n
Tārīkh madīnat Dimashq (Ibn ʿAsākir) 40, 223
Taymūr Bāshā, Aḥmad 69, 263
Tazyīn al-aswāq bi-tafṣīl ashwāq al-ʿushshāq (al-Anṭākī) 253, 262n
ath-Thaʿālibī, Abū Manṣūr 43, 50, 61, 71n, 72–3, 80, 81, 83–5, 224, 230
Pseudo-Thaʿālibī 43n, 72–3, 86–8
Thamarāt shahiyyah min al-fawākih al-Ḥamawiyyah (Ibn Ḥijjah al-Ḥamawī) 240
Tkatsch, Jaroslaus 160n
Tobi, Yosef 203n
Todorov, Tzvetan 214
Tritton, A. S. 188
aṭ-Ṭughrāʾī 148n, 224–25, 229
Turner, Bryan S. 183n
Tynyanov, Yury 219

Ullmann, Manfred 197n
al-ʿUmarī, Muṣṭafā 98–9
al-ʿUmarī, Saʿdī 98–9
al-ʿUmarī, Shihāb ad-Dīn Ibn Faḍl Allāh 42, 229–30, 250
al-ʿUqayl, ʿAbd ar-Raḥmān 79n, 228n
al-ʿUrḍī, Zayn ad-Dīn ʿUmar 93–4
al-Usṭuwānī, Ibrāhīm b. Muṣṭafā 108–11
Utas, Bo 209, 210n

Vagelpohl, Uwe 160n
Valencia, Adriana 93n
Villon, François 173

Wafayāt al-aʿyān wa-anbāʾ abnāʾ az-zamān (Ibn Khallikān) 37–41, 223–27
al-Wāfī bi-l-Wafayāt (aṣ-Ṣafadī) 15, 35–6, 40n, 41, 42n, 43n, 118n, 136n, 206n, 224n, 229–31
Wagner, Ewald 201n
Wahba, Magdi 164–65, 169
Waines, David 94n
al-Washshāʾ 185n
Watt, W. Montgomery 93n
al-Waṭwāṭ al-Kutubī 72–3
Webb, Ruth 27n
Wehr, Hans 13n
Weil, Jurgen W. 13n, 22n
Whipple, T. K. 166n, 173n, 176n
Will, Frederic 158, 162n, 163n
Wittgenstein, Ludwig 212
Wright, Owen 46n
Wyatt, Thomas 173n

Xie, Ming 177n

al-Yāfiʿī 237–38
Yatīmat ad-dahr (ath-Thaʿālibī) 50, 71n, 80, 224, 230
Yazīd b. Muʿāwiyah 90–1
Young, Robert V. 173n
Yūnus b. Ḥabīb 77n

az-Zabīdī, Muḥammad b. Ibrāhīm b. Barakah 248
Zaborski, Andrzej 196n
Zahr al-ādāb wa-thimār al-albāb (al-Ḥuṣrī) 77
Zahr al-manthūr (Ibn Nubātah) 42, 237
az-Zamzamī, ʿAlī b. Muḥammad b. Ismāʿīl 248
Zanker, Graham 27n
Zargar, Cyrus Ali 34
Zīnat ad-dahr (al-Ḥaẓīrī) 224–25
Žižek, Slavoj 215–16
Zwettler, Michael 192n